SO-ADX-584

In the Beginning

In the Beginning

A Short History of the Hebrew Language

Joel M. Hoffman

New York University Press

New York and London

New York University Press
New York and London
www.nyupress.org

Library of Congress Cataloging-in-Publication Data
Hoffman, Joel M., 1968-
In the beginning: a short history of the Hebrew language/
Joel M. Hoffman
p. cm.
Includes bibliographical references and index.
ISBN 0-8147-3654-8 (cloth : alk. paper)
I. Title.
PJ4545.H58 2004
492.4'09—dc22   2004040255

New York University Press books are printed on acid-free paper,
and their binding materials are chosen for strength and durability.

Manufactured in the United States of America
10 9 8 7 6 5 4 3 2 1

Contents

IV   Now

V   Appendices

List of Tables

List of Figures

Acknowledgments

It is a great joy for me to acknowledge the many people who have helped, directly and indirectly, in the preparation of this book. This book owes its existence to Rabbi Ruth Gais, director of HUC-JIR's New York Kollel, who invited me to give a lecture about the history of Hebrew, and to Jennifer Hammer of NYU Press, who heard that lecture and convinced me to turn it into a book. I am grateful to them both. Jennifer Hammer and the people she works with, including particuarly Despina Papazoglou Gimbel and Charles Hames, have since provided invaluable support, including detailed comments that have improved these contents immensely. I am likewise indebted to Dr. Robert Fradkin, who read a draft of this book and offered many helpful suggestions and corrections.

The linguistics faculty at Brandeis University, where I spent my undergraduate years, gave me a far better background in linguistics than I appreciated at the time. The linguistics faculty at the University of Maryland at College Park helped me refine my skills as I worked toward my Ph.D., and taught me how to do serious research. I am indebted to both groups of people.

Most of my professional life has been spent at three places of academic and spiritual excellence, where I met people of the highest caliber and gained the skills that would let me write this book.

Kutz Camp in Warwick, N.Y., was the first place I was able to thrive. The wonderful people I have met there and to whom I am greatly indebted are far too numerous to list here, but I must single out Rabbi Allan "Smitty" Smith and Paul Reichenbach, who created that wonderful place, and Rabbis Stuart Geller, Lawrence Hoffman (my father), and again Allan Smith, who taught me how to teach.

My second spiritual and academic home is Hebrew Union College-Jewish Institute of Religion in New York City. I am continually amazed that I have the high privilege of calling the faculty members there my colleagues, and I remain in their debt for all they have taught me and done for me.

Thirdly, for several years I have taught and learned at Stephen Wise Free Synagogue in New York City. My students — also too numerous to list by name — have joined my fellow teachers there in becoming my teachers and friends, and these pages are the richer because of all of them. I am particularly grateful to Rabbis Gary Bretton Granatoor and Manny Gold for their pivotal role in creating an environment so conducive to learning.

I must mention by name my good friend Tal Varon, with whom I have taught and learned for many years. Our numerous conversations specifically about the various contents herein, and about much broader matters, have been a continuing source of great joy and enlightenment, from which this book and its author have benefited enormously.

Finally and mostly, I wish to thank my parents, who believed in me, and to whom I dedicate this book.

Part I
Getting Started

Chapter 1
Introduction

Roughly 3,000 years ago, in and around the area we now call Israel, a group of people who may have called themselves *ivri*, and whom we call variously "Hebrews," "Israelites," or more colloquially but less accurately "Jews," began an experiment in writing that would change the world.

The Hebrews inherited a writing system from the Phoenicians — another group of people living in the same region — who in turn were the recipients of older systems of writing, some of which had hundreds or thousands of symbols. Rather than using these older systems, the Phoenicians developed a more compact set of two dozen or so symbols, with each symbol roughly representing one consonantal sound. But while their consonant-based system offered a vast improvement in simplicity over earlier ones, the Phoenician approach was not widely learned and used by the masses: reading and writing remained primarily the domain of expert scribes, as it had been been since the inception of writing.

The Hebrews took the Phoenician consonantal system and doubled up three of the letters (*h*, *w*, and *y*) for use as vowels, so that, for example, the Hebrew letter *h* represented not only the consonant *h* but also the vowel *a*, thereby making it possible to record some vowel sounds alongside the consonantal sounds. This seemingly minor addition (which followed a long string of innovations) completed the process that had begun thousands of years earlier, making it possible for the first time for non-experts to write. Suddenly, with the Hebrew alphabet, anyone who cared to could record thoughts for posterity.

The Hebrew alphabet proved wildly successful. Perhaps through Aramaic — a language similar to Hebrew, written with the same letters, and spoken in antiquity by the Aramaeans — Hebrew was used as the basis for the Greek and Latin alphabets, which, in turn, along with Hebrew itself, were destined to form the basis for almost all of the world's alphabets.

For example, the "Roman" alphabet that forms the English part of this book is almost identical to the Latin alphabet used by the Romans, as are the alphabets used for most of Western Europe's other languages. To the east, Russian and similar languages are written in an alphabet called Cyrillic, dating from over 1,000 years ago; it is based on Greek, in turn based on Hebrew. The cursive alphabet in which Arabic is usually written comes from Hebrew via the Aramaeans. Most of the languages used on the Indian subcontinent are written in scripts derived from Brahmi, which probably also developed out of Hebrew some 2,500 years ago. And, of course, the Hebrew used in modern Israel is written in an alphabet directly descended from the Hebrew of 3,000 years ago. In this sense, most of the reading and writing that goes on in the world today can be traced back to the Hebrews' experiment with vowels (though Chinese and some other languages are still written in non-alphabetic systems).

In addition to their system of writing, the ancient Hebrews left their actual writings, later to become part of the Bible, the all-time most popular collection of anything ever written. The debate about divine authorship of the Bible is ongoing, and certainly not to be decided here. (For the purposes of this book we will ignore any role God may have had, as discussed on pages 8 and 218.) But even disregarding potential involvement on the part of God, any observer must acknowledge the almost unbelievably wide impact Scripture has made, particularly in light of how little impact was made by other documents from the same and even later time periods. For example, the Ten Commandments are widely known throughout Western civilization (though different groups differ in their enumeration of them), while similar ancient codes are mostly known only to scholars.

Thus the ancient Hebrews left the world not only a popular system of writing, reflected in most of today's alphabets, but an immensely popular set of writings written in their alphabet.

However, owing partly to their religious significance, partly to their antiquity, and ironically partly to their popularity, reliable information about ancient Hebrew writings and about the ancient Hebrew in which they were first written is often difficult to come by. For example, many people who are familiar with Scripture do not know that the oldest extant copy of the Hebrew Bible is but 1,000 — not 3,000! — years old, dating only roughly to the period of the Crusades. The currently popular pronunciations of Hebrew, whether those of modern Israeli spoken Hebrew or of Jewish liturgical Hebrew, reflect even more recent innovations, and probably differ significantly from the Hebrew of 1,000 years ago, let alone the Hebrew of antiquity.

This surprising paucity of direct information presents a challenge to those who would investigate the story of Hebrew. Fortunately, in place of direct evidence we have a wide variety of indirect evidence, including ancient Hebrew inscriptions, some only partially deciphered, dating back perhaps 3,200 years; ancient Hebrew graffiti from roughly 2,800 years ago; at least two sets of translations or transliterations of Hebrew into ancient Greek, one from 2,300 years ago and the other from at least 1,800 years ago; Hebrew writings from roughly 2,000 years ago, found only in the 20th century in caves near Jerusalem; and various Hebrew and Arabic documents from 1,000 years ago.

In addition to the light they shed on ancient Hebrew, these various clues, particularly the Hebrew ones, contribute to a fascinating story of their own, ending with Hebrew's rebirth as a spoken language of daily life after a hiatus of almost two millennia.

So the Hebrews' experiment set the stage for almost every modern alphabet, and made it possible, for the first time, to make a written record available to the masses. Their written record, the Jewish Bible, has remained an integral part of an expanding number of societies almost since the time it was first penned, and their language, Hebrew, has flourished through changes they could not have imagined.

The pages that follow take the reader on a journey through history that reveals the story of that experiment in writing and what has happened in the trimillennial aftermath.

Chapter 2
Rules of the Game

We have a few preliminary matters to attend to before embarking on our journey through history and becoming acquainted with the first stages of Hebrew.

There are at least three ways one might look at history, and at least two ways one might look at language. Because we are concerned here in no small part with looking at the history of a language, we will do well to sort out these matters, along with some matters of notation. But we are anxious to start our actual investigation of Hebrew, so we'll take only a brief look at some of the relevant issues here, with more complete discussions appearing in Appendix A.

Three Theories of the World

There are, in principle, at least three ways one might try to understand the world. We can call these:

1. The Dumb-Luck Theory;
2. The God Theory; and
3. The Science Theory.

Our choice of theories will have important consequences for how we interpret data about the past, so it is important to understand the three before we get started.

The Dumb-Luck Theory explains everything as being coincidence. With this approach, the world is basically orderless, and any order that

7

may seem to present itself is the result of coincidence. For example, if you shuffle a deck of regular playing cards for a while and it turns out that after being shuffled the cards are arranged from ace to king in order of suit, the Dumb-Luck Theory explains that every so often, by pure dumb luck, that particular order will present itself, and no further explanation is necessary. Similarly, the sun may or may not rise tomorrow, but if it does, it is just happenstance. The fact that the sun rose this morning is also happenstance.

By contrast, the God Theory explains everything as being determined by God. If you shuffle a deck of playing cards and the cards nonetheless end up in order, the God Theory explains that this is God's will. The sun will rise tomorrow because God makes the sun rise; or, if the sun does not rise, it is because God does not want it to rise. The sun rose this morning because God made it.

Finally, the Science Theory claims that there is an underlying order to the universe that we humans can understand. If you shuffle a deck of playing cards and they end up arranged by suit in ascending order, there must be some ordering force at work. (For example, maybe you cheated.) Likewise, we fully expect the sun to rise, and we believe we know why. We also know why the sun rose this morning.

Many accounts of Hebrew and antiquity suffer from a confusion among these three theories, so we will be very clear that, for the purposes of this book, we are adopting the Science Theory and ignoring the Dumb-Luck Theory and the God Theory. More details about the three theories, and the ramifications of our decision, appear in Appendix A.

Two Theories of Language

In large part, this book is about language. Accordingly, just as we chose the Science Theory over two others, we must decide what view of language we will adopt. Having already chosen to pursue the Science Theory in this book, we will, naturally, choose a scientific theory of language.

There are two common (and, often, competing) theories of language:

1. prescriptive linguistics
2. descriptive linguistics[1]

Prescriptive linguistics is the approach to language that most people

---

1. It is unfortunate that the names for these two competing theories sound so similar. This is not the only pair of opposites that sound alike. Others include the English (Greek-derived) prefixes *hypo-* ("too little") and *hyper-* ("too much"), and the French *au dessous* ("under") and *au-dessus* ("over").

meet in high-school English class. It teaches that there is a right and wrong way to speak, and that most of us, left to our own devices, speak incorrectly, which is why we have to be taught to speak correctly. For example, most of us tend to end sentences with prepositions ("Who are you talking to?"). But we are taught that ending a sentence with a preposition is wrong. The preposition — as the name "pre-position" suggests — belongs before the word it modifies ("To whom are you talking?").

The prescriptive system uses "rules" to describe what ought to be.

By contrast, descriptive linguistics assumes that there is a phenomenon of human language to be studied, and it is the scientist's goal to study and describe that language. For example, the descriptive approach to English notes that the most natural place for a preposition in many sentences is the end, and then asks why. Most people are considerably less familiar with this approach.

The descriptive system uses "rules" to describe what is.

By comparison, consider two potential theories of how people dress. The first, parallel to the prescriptive theory of linguistics, is the sort of advice that Miss Manners gives: you can't wear white after Labor Day, your belt and shoes have to be the same color, etc. This is a theory of how people ought to dress. Clearly, however, people do wear white after Labor Day, and people do wear shoes and belts of different colors. But this doesn't mean that there are no patterns to be discerned in how people dress. For example, people do not tend to wear T-shirts over ski jackets. So a second approach to dress, parallel to the descriptive theory of linguistics and contrasting with the Miss Manners theory of dress, notes what is: people's shoes are not always the same color as their belts, but when they wear a ski jacket and a T-shirt, the ski jacket goes on the outside.

In the end, the prescriptive approach to language, like the Miss Manners approach to dress, is a social policy, while the descriptive approach to language is a scientific theory.

We will adopt the scientific, descriptive approach to language. (We take a slightly more in-depth look at that approach in Appendix A. The "Further Reading" section lists some sources for even more information.) When we look at Hebrew as it developed over the past three millennia, we will study it as it was, not how it ought to have been or how we wish it were.

Loose Ends

Transliterations

Beyond the major decisions we have just made — namely, to see how far the Science Theory, including, in particular, modern descriptive linguistics, can take us — some details remain.

There is, obviously, a lot of Hebrew to follow. We will also see considerable Greek and even some Russian. Wherever possible, these foreign languages will be presented in at least two forms, with their original (foreign) letters appearing alongside English ones. But unlike many other scientific descriptions of language, we will not limit ourselves to one particular scheme for choosing the English that will represent the foreign words.

Regarding the Hebrew examples, we will try to use whatever English letters best give a sense of why the example is relevant. Sometimes the English will mimic the letters that comprise the example and sometimes the sounds. (Even though this latter approach is technically called a "transcription," we will refer to it using the more common word "transliteration.") Because of this utilitarian approach, the same letters are often transliterated differently, with notes about the details of the transliteration scheme helping the reader who is unfamiliar with the Hebrew alphabet.

The details of the Greek and Russian examples are less important for our purposes but follow the same principles. We will not limit ourselves to just one scheme but, rather, will use whatever seems most convenient for each example. And once again, the original Greek or Russian will be printed right next to the transliterations for those who care to read them.

Other Matters of Notation

We will spend significant time sorting through an amazing three thousand plus years of history. While Western Society has agreed on a single numbering system to represent those years, three conventions regarding that system have become prevalent, according to which this book was published in "2004 C.E.," "A.D. 2004," (sometimes "2004 A.D.") or "+2004." The year 3,000 years earlier is denoted by one of "997 B.C.E.," "997 B.C.," or "–996." Without prejudice, we have chosen the first scheme here. (Sadly, the year 2,004 years before the year 2004 C.E. is not the year 0 C.E. or the year 0 B.C.E., that year having been most inconveniently omitted in the official numbering system. For this reason the negative numbers do not match up exactly with the "B.C.E." numbers that we have chosen to use.)

From time to time we will want to distinguish between a letter and the sound it makes, or, more generally, between spelling and pronunciation. To do this, we will put sounds between slashes. We might thus write that "the letter *c* makes two sounds in English: /k/ and /s/," or that "the word *cat* is pronounced /kat/."

There are a variety of technical schemes used to record the sounds of language, and, as with transliterations above, we will not limit ourselves to one system, preferring convenience over technical accuracy. In this regard, one specific note is in order. Hebrew has had a variety of sounds that are very roughly the same as the *ch* in the German pronunciation of *Bach*. Typical English representations of this sound include /ch/, /kh/, and /x/. We will use all three, as circumstances dictate.

Having attended to these matters, we are ready to embark on our journey through time, looking at the first attempts to write.

Part II
Antiquity

Chapter 3
Writing

*There is nothing better than writings ... the
office of the scribe is greater than any calling.*
— Egyptian Scribe, c. 2000 B.C.E.

A Difficult Task

Approximately 3,000 years ago, the ancient Hebrews discovered what
would be the precursors to almost every modern system of writing. For
those who can read and write, writing is an obvious extension of speech.
But for those who had to develop the first writing systems, it was anything
but obvious; its discovery should astound us in retrospect as it astounded
those who discovered it.

Modern English speakers, for example, "know" that their words are
made up of consonants and vowels, but they don't often appreciate the
complexity of that knowledge. For example, most people know that *cat* is
comprised of three sounds, that *dog* is comprised of three sounds, and that
both *cats* and *dogs* are comprised of four sounds. But most people never
stop to realize that the *s* in *cats* does not sound the same as the *s* in *dogs*.
The final sound of *dogs* is, in fact, the sound usually written with a *z*.

Examples such as this abound in any language, including "phonetic"
languages like Russian or Spanish. Russian and Spanish speakers usually
think their languages are completely phonetic, as English speakers likewise think that *s* is always pronounced the same at the end of a word.
But speakers of a language are in general a very poor source of information about the rules of that language, because they take the rules for
granted. This is no exception. English speakers will readily agree that

dogs and *cats* do not end with the same sound once that fact is pointed out, but most will not realize it for themselves. Likewise, in Spanish, too, the pronunciation of the letter *s* differs from word to word. And in Russian, the pronunciation of the letter *g* (г) differs from word to word (though, admittedly, the Russian *g* is somewhat anomalous, in that most Russian letters show less variation from word to word); the pronunciation of the vowels also varies considerably from word to word. The imperfect match between sounds and letters in these languages reflects the fact that even native speakers often do not understand the sounds of their langauge.

A second impediment to isolating the sounds in language presents itself: most of the sounds cannot be produced in isolation. For example, the sound that *t* represents cannot be pronounced without a vowel before or after it. Of the three sounds in the word *cat*, only one can be pronounced by itself (/a/). Reading teachers often say that *cat* is made up of the three sounds /kuh/, /ah/, and /tuh/, but, of course, the word is not the three-syllable /kuh-ah-tuh/ but the one-syllable /kat/ comprised of two consonants that cannot be pronounced without a vowel and one vowel that makes the pronunciation of the consonants possible. Imagine how difficult it was for the ancients to isolate the sounds /k/ and /t/ when they only appear as parts of words, never by themselves. How did the first person thinking about this communicate it to the second? ("I've discovered that our words are made up of basic building blocks, but I can't tell you what they are.")

So far we have seen two potential impediments to the discovery of the alphabet:[1] speakers of a language do not always know which sounds they are pronouncing, and some of those sounds cannot be pronounced in isolation. But a third, even more difficult, challenge faced ancient would-be alphabet inventors. They had to discover not only which sounds went where, but even before that, they had to determine the basic inventory of sounds. They had to discover what set of sounds would let them write their words.

By comparison, we can ask what basic inventory of sounds will let us write some non-linguistic or marginally linguistic sounds today: the sound made when blowing out a candle ("whoooooooo"), the sound of snapping one's fingers, and the clicking sound of scolding often spelled "tsk tsk." It is immediately clear that the common alphabetic representations of the first and last of these ("whooooooo" and "tsk tsk") bear almost no similarity

---

1. Or the invention of the alphabet. By "discovery" we probably mean noticing the existence of something, and by "invention" the creation of something that was not there before. The reader can contemplate the difficult question of whether the alphabet was there, waiting to be discovered.

to the actual sounds. For example, the sound of blowing out a candle does not rhyme with "zoo" and the clicking sound of scolding does not almost rhyme with "whisk." The sound of snapping is so far from our usual inventory of alphabetic sounds that not even a misleading spelling has become popular.

How long would it take modern English speakers to devise a system of symbols that could be used to represent just the three sounds in the preceding paragraph? How many basic sounds comprise "whoooooo"? Does it start with a consonant? Are there vowels? Etc.

Though these three obstacles would have been plenty, a fourth obstacle stood in the way of the writing: How did people know where their words began and ended? For that matter, how did they know there were words at all? Once again, modern people who know about modern writing "know" that speech is divided into words, but that division, like so many other aspects of language, is not obvious. The word *an* (as in "an orange"), for example, is never used by itself, but only in front of another word. Why is it considered a word and not a prefix? The suffix *-ness* only appears at the end of a word. We therefore call it a suffix and not a word. How is *-ness* different than *an*? Why is one a "word" and the other a suffix? What about *the*? For that matter, *writes* is never spoken in isolation in regular speech, because conjugated verbs in English never appear without either a subject or an object, even in casual speech. Why are *write* and *writes* separate words, when the *-s* at the end of *writes* is not? More generally, what do we gain by calling some sounds prefixes or suffixes, and others words? In fact, to this day, there is confusion in English over when two word parts coalesce to form one word and when they do not. Do we write "database" or "data base"? "Snowman" or "snow man"?

Given all this complexity, it is no wonder that the first writing systems were not alphabetic. In fact, alphabetic writing was the fourth stage in writing. The first stage was pictorial or logographic, the second syllabic, and the third consonantal. It wasn't until the Hebrews that alphabetic writing began.

Before looking at the Hebrews' alphabetic writing, let's take a quick look at the other stages of writing.

Non-alphabetic Writing

Logographs

The most basic and ancient form of writing uses a written symbol for either a word or a thought. (Though, as we just saw, it is not easy to determine

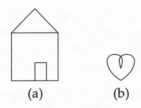

(a)   (b)

Figure 3.1. Some icons.

what a "word" is, and it is more difficult to determine exactly what a "thought" might be.) Drawing a picture of a cat to represent either the thought "cat" or the word "cat" or the cat itself is a pretty straightforward task. The term for this picture is **logograph.**

By definition, of course, the development of writing belongs to prehistory, and drawings have been around for at least 20,000 years, according to most estimates. But there is general agreement that pictorial writing developed not long before 3500 B.C.E. in Uruk, in what is now the southern part of Iraq. (Pictorial writing developed independently halfway around the world in Central America before 600 B.C.E. It never progressed into alphabetic writing, and has nothing to do with the story of Hebrew.)

Clay tablets found in Uruk dating back over 5,000 years contain iconic depictions of animals, plants, people, and a variety of other symbols. Although the exact meaning conveyed by these tablets is unknown today, two facts about them make it almost certain that they were used as writing: the symbols are not arranged in any particularly artistic way, and the symbols are iconic.

This latter notion, iconicity, is an important one, as it represents the first step in moving toward written language. If two people each draw a picture of, say, a plant, the two pictures will likely look quite different. The differences will be more pronounced if the people are not accomplished artists and if they are using crude tools with no erasers. They may not even draw the same kind of plant.

However, at a certain point, before the first writing in Uruk, people with a common culture agreed on a common way of drawing an object. This common way of drawing an object is an "icon," and the drawing is "iconic." Icons need be neither aesthetic nor accurate. Instead, they represent a communal decision on how to draw an object so that it may be recognized.

We have written icons in the United States so ingrained in our culture that most people seldom stop to realize how little the icons look like the objects they are supposed to be drawings of. For example, the common drawings in Figure 3.1 are readily recognized as a house and a heart. But they bear almost no physical resemblance to an actual house or heart. There are no houses that look anything like Figure 3.1(a), and whatever else might be said about hearts, they have four chambers, while Figure 3.1(b) clearly has but two.

Icons — in our culture or ancient cultures — represent common symbolic meaning. That is, the icons do not function only as pictures, but take on the symbolic meaning of things that they, in fact, don't even greatly resemble. It is for this reason that logographic writing, even though it involves pictures, is writing and not necessarily art. (Of course, even though the writing need not be artistic, it can be, just as alphabetic writing can be artistic. Calligraphy is an example.)

Writing involves symbolic representation of language. The tablets from Uruk are the first known to us today to use this symbolic representation.

Logographic writing represented an enormous leap forward. But as ingenious as the system was, it suffered two great drawbacks: it required so many symbols (thousands) that only experts could manage it, and it could not be readily expanded. In terms of expansion, names were particularly problematic, but so too were new words. For example, if a visitor from a foreign culture brought a new type of animal, not only was logographic writing ill equipped to write the visitor's name, but a scribe was faced with the problem of either inventing a new logograph for the new animal or using a combination of existing logographs. Either way, a second scribe would have little way of understanding what the first scribe had written, thereby defeating the purpose of a unified script in the first place.

Syllabic Writing

The next enormous leap forward in writing was to use symbols to represent sounds instead of words. A system that represents sounds has two great advantages over a purely logographic system: far fewer symbols are needed; and far more words, including names, can be conveniently written down.

There are probably many ways of writing down the sounds of our language systematically. In practice, three have been devised and widely used: syllabic writing (a symbol for each possible syllable); consonantal writing (a symbol for each consonant); and vowel-consonantal writing (a symbol for each consonant and vowel).

The earliest attested written sound systems are syllabic and come from an area know either as "Sumer" or, biblically, as "Shinar," located in what is now southern Iraq. Sumerian texts as early as the end of the 4th millennium

B.C.E. evidence some syllabic writing. By and large, the Sumerians took short words and used the symbols for those words to represent not only the meanings of those words but also the sounds of those words. For example, the sign for "strike," pronounced /ra/[2] in Sumerian, came to be used not only to express striking but to express the sound /ra/.

Eventually this Sumerian writing would be written in what we call **cuneiform.** (The word *cuneiform* comes from the Latin for "wedge-shaped," reflecting the triangle-shaped marks from which the symbols are built. While it is common to use "cuneiform" to mean "Sumerian cuneiform," "cuneiform" is actually a writing style, and is used to write other languages as well.) "Sumerian cuneiform" is the oldest attested writing that attempts to capture sounds.

It appears that the change from logographic writing to syllabic writing was gradual, with even early stages of cuneiform demonstrating some syllabic writing, and late stages of cuneiform 2,000 years later still using some logographs.

In the meantime, Akkadian writers picked up Sumerian cuneiform and used it for their writings, too, following the same general transition from logographic to syllabic writing. (Akkadian is an ancient Semitic language, related to Hebrew, once spoken in areas north of Sumer.)

The cuneiform records of both of these languages, Sumerian and Akkadian, are technically logo-syllabic, because they used logographs in addition to pure syllable notation. (Evidence of at least three purely syllabic systems from the region has survived: Linear A, from about 1800 B.C.E.; Linear B from about 1450 B.C.E.; and the Cypriot Syllabary, from perhaps the middle of the 11th century B.C.E. Linear A has yet to be decoded; Linear B and the Cypriot Syllabary represent very early forms of Greek.) Even though Sumerian and Akkadian mixed in logographs with their syllabic writing, they illustrate the first attempt to write down sounds rather than just words or thoughts.

Consonantal Writing

Logo-Consonantal Writing

Logo-syllabic systems are more complex than purely syllabic systems, but even a purely syllabic system requires several dozen symbols. While it is easier to learn the tens or hundreds of symbols required for syllabic systems

---

2. As discussed extensively elsewhere in this volume, current knowledge of the pronunciation of ancient languages is tentative, based on significant hypothesis and conjecture. For now, we don't really care how the sign for "strike" was really pronounced, of course, but let us not imagine we know things we do not.

than it is to learn the thousands required for a purely logographic system, consonantal systems — that is, systems that record only the consonants in a language — generally require fewer than 30 symbols.

The earliest attested consonantal writing system, like the earliest syllabic writing system, is actually a hybrid. It is ancient Egyptian hieroglyphics, dating back to approximately 3,100 B.C.E.

The origins of Egyptian hieroglyphics are mysterious. While logosyllabic Sumerian seems to have come from logographic Sumerian (which, though not discussed here, came from other forms of pictorial writing), ancient Egyptian seems to have popped into place fully formed just after the Sumerians had figured out logo-syllabic cuneiform. (Surprisingly, this is the first of two similar mysteries about fully formed writing apparently coming into being suddenly. The second, concerning Greek, is discussed a bit later on.)

Did Egyptian come from Sumerian? There are two schools of thought.

The first notes the apparent difficulty in creating a writing system. While many useful inventions were invented independently at different places and times around the world (agriculture, spoken and signed languages, clothing, etc.), the only two clearly independently-developed writing systems are Sumerian and Mayan, halfway around the world, in roughly 600 B.C.E. It is unlikely that so difficult a feat was accomplished independently and nearly simultaneously by two near neighbors.

The second school of thought notes first that other difficult inventions, such as differential calculus, have indeed been invented independently and nearly simultaneously by near neighbors, and goes on to note that while the principles underlying Egyptian hieroglyphics and Sumerian cuneiform are similar, the implementation in each case is completely different. The two writing systems do not share any symbols. Furthermore, while Sumerian seems to have been written in a logo-syllabic system, Egyptian seems to have opted for more of a logo-consonantal system. If Egyptian were really copied from Sumerian, wouldn't it use a syllabic system, too, and in fact use the syllabic system the Sumerians did?

To this the first school of thought counters that details of Egyptian and Sumerian may explain why the Egyptians ended up with a consonantal system. Sumerian words, like English words, are mostly indeclinable, that is, they do not change a great deal. For example, the word *toe* in English is pronounced the same way whether it is the subject ("the toe is broken") or object ("he broke his toe") of a verb, or governed by a preposition ("he put a bandage on his toe"). By contrast, an Egyptian word would be pronounced with different vowel endings in each of these situations. That is, Egyptian (like, say, Russian or German) had a case system while Sumerian did not.[3] Therefore, perhaps, the Egyptians tried to use a symbol for their equivalent of "toe," but, because the final vowel kept changing, the symbol ended up just meaning the sound /t/.

In the end, both schools of thought have convincing arguments, though the evidence in favor of Egyptian having come from Sumerian, at least indirectly, seems to outweigh the evidence against this hypothesis. Whatever the case, Egyptian's logo-consonantal system set the stage for purely consonantal systems.

It should be noted that some scholars consider Egyptian a "reduced syllabic" system rather than a true consonantal system. In a "reduced syllabic" system, a symbol would represent any syllable starting with a particular consonant, whereas in a consonantal system, it would just represent the consonant. For example, if we used the symbol "$\mathcal{R}$" to mean the sound /r/, we would have part of a consonantal system. If we used that symbol to mean any syllable starting with the sound /r/, we would have part of a reduced syllabic system. But because most consonants cannot be pronounced in isolation, and because, in any event, so little is known about the actual pronunciation of these ancient languages, these two amount to almost the same theory in practice, only reflecting potential differences in the minds of the people who used them. And at any rate, Egypt's system was in fact either logo-consonantal or logo-reduced syllabic. But true consonantal systems, unlike true syllabic systems, eventually became widespread, as we see immediately below.

True Consonantal Writing

Neither Linear B nor the Cypriot Syllabary ever became widely used in the Near East, but pure consonantal systems formed the foundations for the modern alphabet.

Around 1800 B.C.E., we find examples of what is commonly called "proto-Canaanite." Because the symbols used to write Proto-Canaanite number around thirty, proto-Canaanite must have been written either in true consonantal writing or in true alphabetic writing, but because the writing system has not been fully decoded, we do not know which of these two systems was used.

Proto-Canaanite (like other "proto" languages) is a language whose existence is posited to account for later languages. In this case, the Canaanite languages share certain features, and so scholars assume that these Canaan-

---

3. Once again, our knowledge of the pronunciation of ancient languages is dubious. Perhaps this understanding of Sumerian or Egyptian is flawed.

ite languages all developed out of an earlier language, proto-Canaanite. ("Canaanite" languages are the languages once spoken in and around ancient Canaan, now parts of Israel, Lebanon, and Syria.) Latin could have been called proto-Romance, because the Romance languages (Spanish, French, etc.) share traits that they inherited from Latin. But because so much is known about Latin, it merits a name that defines it beyond the languages that it preceded. By contrast, little is known about proto-Canaanite, and not much more about the earliest proto-Canaanite writings.

What we do know is that during the beginning of the 2nd millennium B.C.E., consonantal writings begin to appear. These writings have been preserved on pottery shards and even on a dagger dating from roughly 3,800 years ago. Though the meanings of these writings have been lost, the writing seems to be consonantal in nature.

By 1000 B.C.E., however, we see Phoenician writings in what is clearly a consonantal script. (The Phoenicians probably lived in what is now Lebanon, and were probably the descendants of the Canaanites.) Part of the Canaanite family of languages, Phoenician bears a great deal of resemblance to ancient Hebrew. It is even possible that Phoenician *was* Hebrew, a fact that could be masked by different writing schemes. At any rate, thousands of inscriptions from Byblos (north of Beirut on the Mediterranean shore) dating from the 11th century B.C.E. attest to a fairly standardized 22-letter Phoenician consonantal alphabet. This Phoenician alphabet would continue to be widely used for over half a century, basically in its original form.

The incredible advantage of a consonantal alphabet such as Phoenician is that only approximately two dozen symbols are required. The major disadvantage is that, because it does not record vowels, it is somewhat difficult to read. This difficulty, the final impediment to a writing system usable by the masses, would be eliminated by the Hebrews, in the first stage of Hebrew writing.

The First Hebrew Alphabetic Writing

Adding Vowels

So as we have seen, by the year 1000 B.C.E., the Phoenicians were writing in a 22-letter consonantal script. Their script represented an enormous improvement over previous syllabic and logographic writing systems, because the 22 letters could be easily learned. However, while it was much easier to write in their script, reading was not so easy, because their system did nothing to indicate the vowels in a word.

The Hebrews, however, solved this problem. They took three letters, *w* (now called *vav* and written ו, though it was written differently back then), *h* (now called *heh* — ה), and *y* (now called *yud* — י), and used them to represent vowels (in addition to their consonantal sounds), as described immediately below. These letters, traditionally called *matres lectiones* ("mothers of reading"), may originally have been intended as mere aids to reading, for differentiating identically spelled words, but they provided the final piece of the puzzle of writing, completing a process begun 2,500 years earlier.

In terms of the time scale, then, the Hebrews' experimentation with vocalic letters falls very roughly halfway between the first logographic writing in Uruk and modern civilization in the 21st century.

The Old Script and the New Script

Before looking at the details of the Hebrews' innovations, a few words on the actual forms of the old Hebrew letters are in order.

The letters in which Modern Hebrew is usually written belong to the "Aramaic script," also called "Square Jewish" or "Square Hebrew," which came into use only several hundred years after Hebrew was first written. The first letterforms belonged to the "paleo-Hebrew" script, also called "Phoenician."

A "script," like a font, is a way of writing letters. For example, English is commonly written in two "scripts." We call one of them "print" or sometimes "block," and tend to use it in printed material; confusingly, we call the other script just "script" or, less confusingly, "cursive."

A whole field of study **(paleography)** deals with ancient letterforms and what can be learned from them, but for our purposes, the actual forms of the ancient letters are pretty much irrelevant. In the same way that an English essay written in cursive says exactly the same thing as the same essay written in print, here we don't much care which script was used for ancient Hebrew, and most of our discussion will ignore the issue. Furthermore, because so many people are familiar with the more modern script, we will use it for examples in our text even when the original writing was in some variety of the older script, just as a book about English postal letters might rewrite cursive letters in print for convenience.

The "Further Reading" section lists some sources for more information about the older script and its variations.

How It Worked

A Natural Connection

The Hebrews started with three of their consonants, *yud*, *heh*, and *vav*. In all likelihood, those were the equivalent of our modern *y*, *h*, and *w*, respectively. (Chapter 6 discusses what we do and do not know about the pronunciation of ancient Hebrew.)

There is a certain natural connection between the consonant sound /y/ (represented in English by the letter *y*) and the vowel sounds represented by *i* and *e*. Likewise, there is a connection between the sound /w/ and the sounds /o/ and /u/; and between /h/ and the sound /a/. This natural connection comes from the way the mouth forms the consonants and related vowels. We see these connections in English spelling: The *y* in *happy* is used for the sound /i/. The *y* in *day* is used for /e/. The *w* in *yellow* is used for the sound /o/. In *dew* it is used for /u/. The *h* in *say* "*ahhh*" is used for /a/.

The reader may at this point object, noting that other combinations in English seem to suggest other connections, such as the *w* in *saw*. But English spelling has a long and convoluted history, with the result that some letters represent long-gone pronunciations, such as the *ght* in *night*, or the *w* in *saw*. Only some English examples demonstrate the wider principle that vowels and consonants are connected.

Fortunately, we have a second way of demonstrating these pairings (*h* with /a/, *y* with /i/ and /e/, *w* with /u/ and /o/). Because the mouth is in a similar configuration for the consonants and vowels, words that contain paired consonants and vowels involve fewer changes to the shape of the mouth as they are pronounced than words that contain unpaired consonants and vowels. For example, the pronunciation of the words *woo* and *woe*, which contain a consonant matched to a similar vowel, involves less variation than the pronunciation of *why* or *wad*. Similarly, *ye* involves less variation than *you*. Most English speakers can feel these differences if they pay attention to their mouths as they speak the words.

Helping Letters

The letters *yud*, *heh*, and *vav* had been used as consonants for at least hundreds of years before their introduction as vowels toward the beginning of the 1st millennium B.C.E. During that pre-vocalic stage of writing, only the consonants of a word would be written down.

The following Hebrew words demonstrate that pre-vocalic stage of writing: "priest," "priests," and "my priest." (Once again, we note that our modern understanding of their pronunciation may be wrong.) The Hebrew for "priest" was /kohen/. Because the Hebrews did not use vowels, they wrote this with three letters: *khn*. The word "priest" was made plural by adding /im/ to it and (perhaps) changing some of the vowels: /kohanim/, written *khnm*. However, the ending "theirs" was /am/. The letters *khnm* could thus also have represented /kohanam/ "their priest." Furthermore, the ending /i/ meant "mine." The letters *khn* could have been /kohani/ "my priest."

The second problem, in which *khn* represented both "priest" and "my priest," was more serious than the first (*khnm* = "their priest" or "priests") because Hebrew verbs matched their adjectives. So, for example, "good priests ..." would have an /m/ sound at the end of the word for "good" to indicate the plural, while "their good priest ..." would not. However, both "my good priest ..." and "a good priest ..." would appear with the same form of the adjective "good." Perhaps to solve this problem, a *yud* was added to the end of the word "my priest": *khny*.

This disambiguation stage was the first stage of vocalic Hebrew writing. But fuller use of vowels quickly followed, in which a *yud* was used not only to disambiguate (for example) "my priest" from "a priest," but also "their priest" from "priests," which were soon written *khnm* and *khnym*, respectively.

Why Did It Take So Long?

It is worth pointing out that, though the timing is well established by historical record, the fact that vowels were the last sounds for which symbols were invented seems counterintuitive. After all, vowels are the easiest sounds in a language to isolate. We saw above that many consonants (*t*, e.g.) cannot even be pronounced without a vowel, but all of the vowels can be pronounced without consonants. In other words, while the inventor of a symbol for /t/ could not pronounce the sound represented by the symbol, the inventor of a symbol for any of the vowels could. Why then were vowel symbols the last to be invented?

Two possibilities come to mind. The first possibility is that the vowels in ancient languages were so complex that the original inventors of the alphabet had difficulty in sorting them out. The second possibility is that vowels were unnecessary until the masses tried to write. So long as writing was solely the purview of experts, symbols for consonants (or syllables, or even words) sufficed.

Regarding the first possibility, English faces a similar problem. There are many more vowel sounds in English than vowel symbols, or even than vowel combinations. (Depending on the dialect, there are roughly fifteen vowel sounds in English.)[4] For example, the nine words *bat, bet, bit, bought, but, boot, bait, beet,* and *boat* each have a different vowel between the *b* and the *t*. If we allow diphthongs, we can add *bite* and *bout* to the list. And we have still not exhausted the vowel sounds in English. (English is further complicated by a related but separate problem: the spelling often doesn't convey the sound. Why don't *put* and *but* rhyme? Why don't *to* and *go* rhyme?" Etc.) Perhaps ancient languages, too, had vowel systems that were so complicated that ancient would-be alphabet inventors could not isolate the vowel sounds.

Regarding the second possibility, if writing began as a code among well-trained scribes, vowel symbols may indeed have been unnecessary. After all, even English can usually be deciphered if the vowels are left out. In the pre-vocalic Phoenician system, any set of letters expressed only a small number of words (depending on the unwritten vowels) and the writers may not have seen the need to narrow this small number down. Again, in English we face a somewhat similar situation. We have words that are written exactly the same even though they are not pronounced the same.[5] Why have we not bothered to rectify this ambiguity? Probably because our system is good enough. Or, at least, the energy society would have to exert to change the system is not worth the improvement the change would yield.

Additionally, ancient writers may have considered vowel symbols not only unnecessary but perhaps undesirable as well. Scribes, after all, were very highly regarded in their role as writing professionals. They may not have wanted to see the masses write.

At any rate, the Hebrews doubled up their consonants to indicate vowels, and it is here that the story of Hebrew begins.

---

4. Actually, there are many, many more vowel sounds in English. But only fifteen are used to differentiate words. For example, the vowels in *tight* and *tide* differ one from the other, but only in the way that the diphthong they share always changes before a /d/ or /t/ sound. See the "Further Reading" section for authors who discuss this more fully.

5. For example, "read" sounds like either "red" or "reed." Other examples, such as "number," are more difficult. While English speakers clearly recognize "number" as being pronounced /number/, they are considerably less likely to recognize it as /numer/, that is, the comparative form of the adjective "numb" (as in numb, number, numbest).

How Do We Know?

The Question

Was it really the Hebrews who invented the alphabet? In a sense, the question is too vague to have a precise answer. The Phoenicians had a perfectly usable alphabet that included no vowels. The Egyptians could have had an alphabet if they'd thought to use it. The Greeks were the first to use separate symbols for vowels, rather than relying on letters also used to represent consonants.

A more precise question is: Who first started using symbols to represent vowels? And who, therefore, paved the way for widespread use of the alphabet? Usual answers to this include: the Aramaeans, the Moabites, the Greeks, and the Hebrews. But to really understand the situation requires looking at the evidence in more detail. So let's take a walk through the historical evidence and see what we find.

The Answers

Ugaritic Cuneiform

Long before the Hebrews and Aramaeans began using vowels, Semitic cuneiform writers tried to differentiate words that began with different vowels. (This cuneiform is neither the original Sumerian cuneiform nor the adapted Akkadian cuneiform, though it appears to be related to the latter.) It is particularly difficult to decode a vowelless representation of a word when the word begins with a vowel. For example, when English speakers are asked what *bt* might be, they usually think of *but, bat*, etc., but not *abate* or *about*; similarly, when asked what *t* might represent, *tea* and *tie* come to mind before *eat*. Perhaps cuneiform Ugaritic writers had trouble reading words that began with vowels, and therefore invented symbols to represent those vowels at the beginning of words.

Tablets found in Ugarit (modern-day Ras Shamra, on the northern coast of Syria), probably from around 1350 B.C.E., include three word-initial symbols, each representing — it would seem — a different vowel. (The usual guess as to which vowels these represent is /a/, /i/, and /u/.) But while those tablets may suggest the beginnings of symbols used for vowels, they do not seem to contain any intra-word vowels. An example comes from how the plural suffix *-im* was written in the word for "priest": *kohen*. (Once again, we must stress that we do not know what vowels were actually used to pronounce the words and suffixes. The /i/ in /im/ is a pretty good guess, based on later Semitic dialects; our guess about the vowels in *kohen* is shakier.)

On two ancient axe-heads from Ras Shamra, the word for "priests" is written *khnm*, without any symbol (a *yud*, e.g.) in the plural suffix. But if it were written with vowels, the word would be not *khnm* but rather *khnym* or even *kohnym*. (On the other hand, even 600 years later, when vocalic letters were in widespread use, the *yud* in the plural was not always written.)

The writers of this Ugaritic Cuneiform do not seem to have taken the crucial step of recognizing that vowels are linguistic entities to themselves divorced from consonants. Their "vowel" symbols seem to be "syllable" symbols, representing specifically the syllables /a/, /o/, and /i/ at the beginning of words. Though it may seem as though the vowel /a/ and the syllable /a/, for example, are the same because they are pronounced the same, conceptually syllables and vowels are very different.

If Ugaritic Cuneiform had true vowel symbols, we would expect to see them combined with consonants in a way that we do not.

But even so, the symbols are used at the beginning of words that begin with vowels. As with Egyptian hieroglyphics, which came tantalizingly close to an alphabet, it looks like Ugaritic had everything in place for the widespread use of vowels, but never took that final step.

The Izbet Sartah Abecedary

An "abecedary" (pronounced "ay-bee-see-dary," like A-B-C-dary) is something upon which the alphabet is written in order. So far, we have ignored the question of how (and why) the letters got put in order. But before the Hebrews even started using symbols for vowels, the order of the Semitic alphabet had been more or less established.

The earliest Hebrew example of this order comes from an ostracon (clay tablet used for writing) from approximately 1200 B.C.E. found in Izbet Sartah (in today's Israel), from what looks like an early Israelite settlement. The tablet contains five lines of Phoenician (ancient Hebrew) letters.

The fifth line is the alphabet, written in order from left to right. (The left-to-right order is unusual for Hebrew, but early writing was known to vary in direction, even being written in boustrophedon, that is, with alternating lines going in alternating directions.)[6] But, curiously, two pairs of letters are reversed in this alphabet. In the usual Hebrew alphabet, *zion*

---

6. The word *boustrophedon* comes from the Greek for "ox turning," and represents the way an ox plowed a field. My teacher and friend Rabbi Manny Gold has used a similar but more modern metaphor in explaining this back-and-forth writing to New York City students: "as you look for a parking place."

(now written ז) comes before *chet* (ח) and *ayin* (ע) comes before *pe* (פ), but not here.

On the one hand, these reversed letters solve a problem. The Biblical book of Lamentations (*aicha* in Hebrew) starts with four acrostic poems, that is, poems in which the first letters of the lines form the alphabet. But while the first such acrostic poem follows the traditional Hebrew alphabetic order (including putting *ayin* before *pe*), the next three place *pe* before *ayin*, in accordance with the alphabet we have from the Izbet Sartah abecedary. Combined with other examples of this *pe-ayin* order known to exist, we have reason to believe that the order of *pe* and *ayin* may not have been fixed, or may have been subject to local variation.

However, while the reversal of *ayin* and *pe* is well attested, this tablet gives us the only example of reversing *zion* and *chet*. The discoverers of the tablet suggest that this second letter reversal may have been an error on the part of the writer, who, they assume, was a student learning to write. This assumption accords well with the observation that in place of *koof-resh* on the Izbet Sartah tablet, we have two *koof*'s (though this is still the matter of some debate).

The first four lines have yet to be deciphered. The discoverers of the tablet, continuing their hypothesis that the tablet was written by a student, propose that the first four lines are nothing more than a writing exercise and contain random letters.

But it seems (based on physical evidence) that the fifth line was written first, and that it was not written by the same person who wrote the first four. Are we really to assume that two independent students wrote on the tablet, both skilled enough to write the letters but neither skilled enough to write any words or even to write the alphabet correctly? It seems implausible.

The writing on the tablet is odd in other ways. The *mem* is missing from the alphabet in the fifth row, and also does not appear in the four lines of "random" letters. But *mem* is a very common letter in all Semitic dialects. Were the two poor students who wrote on this tablet not being taught one of the most common letters? By contrast, the considerably less common letter *ayin* appears eight times in addition to its inclusion in the alphabet. The letter *koof*, also uncommon, appears seven or eight times. But then again, the common letter *aleph* appears eight times as well. These numbers all suggest a substitution code, along the lines of the common cryptoquote puzzles in (modern) daily newspapers. But no successful solution to the code has been found.

It is also telling that academicians assume that this tablet was written by students, because that hypothesis recurs time and again regarding the few samples of ancient writing that have been preserved. For example, we will see that one standard assumption about the Gezer Calendar (described next) is that it was written by a student. Are we really to believe that most of the surviving ancient writing samples were written by students? Again, it seems unlikely.

Perhaps the reason this written-by-a-student theory keeps popping up has to do with the fact that the writing samples tend not to confirm well-known theories about ancient languages. Faced with this discordant data, researchers can either assume that the old samples do not reflect old languages, or that their theories do not reflect old languages. The trend in academia has been toward the former.

The Izbet Sartah abecedary could provide invaluable evidence about the nature of Hebrew, were it only decoded.

The Gezer Calendar

A piece of inscribed limestone found at Tel Gezer, in modern-day Israel, dates from the early 10th century B.C.E. and represents the earliest surviving record of a Hebrew-like dialect that has been even partially deciphered. The stone is commonly referred to as the "Gezer Calendar" because it is commonly assumed to be a calendar.

This Gezer Calendar, the second-oldest surviving example of Hebrew-like writing and the only one to have been even partially decoded, seems not to contain any vowel symbols. If we assume that it does not in fact contain vowel symbols (as is the common assumption), vowel symbols would seem, then, to have been invented after the 10th century B.C.E. The Gezer Calendar thus might establish the 10th century as a likely date before which Hebrew did not use vowel symbols.

But the Gezer Calendar is problematic for several reasons.

First, it contains several instances of the word *yrhw*, in which the final *vav* (*w* — ן) looks like a vowel letter. The root *yrh* is probably "month," while the final *vav* looks like the suffix used in later Hebrew to mean "his." The text reads something like this:

yrhw of harvest
yrhw of sowing
yrhw of pasture
yrh of cutting flax
yrh of reaping crops
etc.

The word *yrhw* has received many explanations, but none of them is free of significant conjecture. Possibilities rampant in the literature include: "two months," although a *vav* used to represent "two" is otherwise unattested; and "months," which suffers from the same problem. The translation "two months" was suggested so that the text would reference all 12 months. (Their months, like ours, numbered 12.) An equally possible (and equally unlikely) translation would be "his month is harvest, his month is sowing, etc.," with the result that the text was used to indicate which months were "his" and which were not.

In addition, the calendar contains *'byh* in the margin, possibly a signature by the author, and this, too, creates as many problems as it solves. The *-yh* ending looks like /yah/, which might serve to establish the text as belonging to a Hebrew (because Hebrew names back then commonly ended in /yah/), but which also might demonstrate vocalic use of *yud, heh,* or both.

Even the content seems problematic. For example, "flax" was probably pulled out of the ground, not cut, a difficulty that, along with others, pops up from time to time in discussions regarding the Gezer Calendar.

These are not the only problems with the text. An additional difficulty is the possibility that it was written by a schoolchild, perhaps still learning to write. (But we saw this guess regarding the Izbet Sartah abecedary as well; it will recur regarding other ancient writing specimens. We must be wary of the conclusion that so many surviving samples of ancient writing were written by students.)

Even if we do not accept the hypothesis that the writer was a student, the nature of the text and its extremely limited vocabulary both make it a dubious source for solid information about the overall state of Hebrew.

Mesha Stone

The next-oldest surviving record, the Mesha Stone, dates from roughly 850 B.C.E. and makes clear use of vowel letters. The content of the inscription makes it clear that it is Moabite: "I am Mesha ... the king of Moab... My father was king over Moab for thirty years, and I was king after my father..." The text goes on to describe how Mesha, the king of Moab, defeated the Israelites. To judge both from this text and from the Old Testament, the Moabites and Israelites were bitter enemies. The recorded written languages of the Israelites and the Moabites are all but indistinguishable, with the exception of the four-letter reference to God, *yhwh*, which we discuss in great detail in Chapter 4 and which seems to have been used exclusively by the Israelites. Because this word appears in the Mesha Stone in reference to Israelite pottery (or vessels), we can be reasonably certain that its author was familiar with Israelite culture.

Based on the incredibly similar nature of Moabite and Hebrew writing, the reference to *yhwh* in Moabite, and the physical and cultural proximity of the Israelites and Moabites, we can reasonably assume that the two languages were all but identical. (Additionally, some scholars have even assumed that this particular inscription was written by an Israelite.)

Because the Mesha Stone makes clear use of vowel letters, we can use it to establish a latest possible date for the adoption of vowel letters in something Hebrew-like: 850 B.C.E. (It is, however, exceedingly unlikely that the Moabites invented vowel letters. Even if we accept the hypothesis that Moabite and Hebrew were different languages, the author of the Mesha text uses *yhwh* to refer to other people, the Israelites, and we will see good evidence that that four-letter name for God came about in connection with the first use of vowel letters.)

The Mesha Stone also demonstrates another important principle in archaeological reconstruction of the past, because it was almost destroyed before it was decoded. In 1868, an Arab guide showed the Mesha Stone to a missionary from Jerusalem, assuring him that the writing on the stone had never been decoded. The missionary notified a local consul, who became mildly interested. At roughly the same time, French and English researchers were also making inquiries about the stone. Before long, so much interest in the stone had been generated that the locals — so goes the story — became convinced that they had something magnificent in their possession. They heated it and then poured cold water over it, breaking it into tiny pieces. One version of the story is that the tiny pieces were for good luck, and that they were scattered among various Bedouin crops to insure their growth. Another version holds that the Bedouins thought they could make more money by selling pieces of the stone than by selling it in its entirety.

Whatever the case, the stone was destroyed. It is only because a man by the name of Charles Clermont-Ganneau had already had squeezes made of the stone[7] that it was recovered at all.

The Mesha Stone, which has played a pivotal role in analyzing antiquity, was almost lost. What else that might further sharpen our understanding of antiquity has in fact been lost?

---

7. A "squeeze" is a copy of an inscribed text made by pressing ("squeezing") damp paper or wax into an inscription.

Siloam Tunnel

An inscription from the Siloam Tunnel, near where the great temples once stood in Jerusalem, is clearly written in classical Hebrew and clearly demonstrates vocalic letters. Archaeological evidence dates the Siloam Tunnel to the end of the 8th century B.C.E. (The inscription itself describes how the tunnel was created, with two sets of workers working toward each other from opposite ends. The sets of workers called out to each other as they drew near, and thus met in the middle.)

Some vocalic letters that we would expect are missing, such as a *yud* to represent the /i/ in the plural suffix /im/. While that suffix would, one hundred years later, be spelled *yud mem*, it appears as just a *mem* in the Siloam inscription. But evidence of vocalic letters is clear and unambiguous. The Mesha inscription establishes 850 B.C.E. as the latest possible date for the introduction of vocalic letters in something Hebrew-like, and the inscription in the Siloam Tunnel establishes 700 B.C.E. as the latest possible date in a language that is certainly Hebrew.

Aramaic

So far, we have seen that Hebrew developed the use of vowel letters by the 8th century B.C.E. The earliest Aramaic inscriptions seem to come from roughly the same period as the earliest Hebrew ones with vowels.

Tel Halaf (Biblical Gozan) has produced some samples that may date from the early 9th century B.C.E. One such sample, an incised inscription on a small altar, is among the earliest known examples of Aramaic, but, unfortunately, it was destroyed during World War II, and only facsimiles remain.

Excavations from Tel Dan (in modern-day northern Israel) have also yielded some well-known material in Aramaic, also probably from the 9th century B.C.E.

All of this material, as with Hebrew from the same time period, demonstrates vowel letters.

Many Aramaic researchers assume that Aramaic had been written essentially the way we see it in the 9th century for at least a few hundred years, but that no examples survive. However, we must be careful not to draw any conclusions about writing during a period of time from which we have no written samples to read and analyze.

Greek

Greek writing from the 8th century on has always had vowels, and (unlike Hebrew, which used consonant symbols to represent vowels) had symbols devoted to vocalic representation.

But Greek presents its own unique puzzle, because the Greek alphabet suddenly appears in the 8th century B.C.E. Where did it come from? The names of the Greek letters are certainly Semitic in origin. They seem to be derived from Aramaic, but could be derived from Hebrew by way of Aramaic, or even directly from Hebrew. (The familiar Greek *alpha, beta* ... parallel the Hebrew *aleph, bet* ...) The order of the alphabet suggests that it was adopted from Phoenician or Hebrew or Aramaic. The forms of the letters also suggest that the alphabet was taken from Phoenician. And the official Greek myth is that the alphabet was borrowed from the Phoenicians.

But whereas the Semitic branch of writing has a long history, the Greek alphabet seems to have popped up fully developed. There are no existing clearly Greek written records from the half-millennial "dark period" between the end of Linear B (roughly 1250 B.C.E.) and the Semitic-based Greek writing of the 8th century.

The only hint of anything Greek comes from the Izbet Sartah abecedary (discussed above), dating from roughly 1200 B.C.E. The forms of the Hebrew letters on that tablet seem closer to Greek than they ought to be. In particular, the letters *aleph, heh,* and *tav* look almost exactly like their Greek equivalents. The unexpected resemblance of these letters, combined with the fact that the abecedary is written left-to-right, may suggest that Greek may have borrowed an early version of Phoenician. However, because we do not know more about the Izbet Sartah tablet, and because its peculiar ordering of the letters *ayin* and *pe* accord poorly with the established Greek order, it is difficult to draw any firm conclusions.

While much more has been written about where Greek may have come from, there is little more to be said. It remains a mystery.

Summary

So who discovered vowel letters?

The physical evidence is equivocal. The earliest existing Hebrew and Aramaic texts with vowel letters both date from the middle of the 9th century, with Aramaic coming ever so slightly before Hebrew; Greek texts, also with vowels, follow shortly thereafter. Based on this, most researchers, with a few notable exceptions, conclude that the Aramaeans invented vowels. But it is highly unlikely that the few remnants of these ancient written languages are actually the earliest examples of the written languages.

We have already seen that the Mesha Stone came very close to being destroyed before it could be analyzed and appreciated. Surely we have lost other important evidence that could have shed light on the timing of writing's development among these various cultures. The problem of Greek and the vast body of missing material, as noted above, is enormous.

Furthermore, the evidence as we have it presents a major problem, for it is hardly credible that in the span of tens of years a system so revolutionary as vowels was discovered by the Aramaeans (in, say, 950 B.C.E.), institutionalized by them, exported to the rest of the world, and then adopted by the Hebrews before 850 B.C.E. Because writing changes tend to be adopted slowly, and because adults do not generally relearn how to spell their words, even under the most favorable of conditions the transition would have taken at least two full generations.

To conclude that the Hebrews learned to use vowels from the Aramaeans we would have to accept the following five hypotheses, each of which is possible but unproven: (1) the Gezer Calendar is representative of the Hebrew in use at the time (say, 950 B.C.E.); (2) the Gezer Calendar does not use any vowel symbols; (3) the Mesha Stone is roughly the earliest use of vowel letters in Hebrew (say, 850 B.C.E.); (4) the surviving Aramaic documents (perhaps as early as 950 B.C.E.) are not the earliest use of vowel letters in Aramaic; (5) the use of vowels in Aramaic was institutionalized by the Aramaeans and spread to the neighboring Hebrews, who integrated them into their language, all in less than a century. With the fall of any of these hypotheses, we come instead to the much more likely conclusion that the extant physical evidence tells only part of the story.

The puzzle about Greek adds to the mystery. Are we to assume that the Aramaeans not only exported their vowel system to the Hebrews, but also spread their idea to the Greeks, who in turn took less than a century to pick up on the Aramaic or Phoenician alphabet, modify the forms of some of the letters, change some of the sounds, and then start writing, when for the previous half millennium they had written nothing in this system? To the contrary, the Greek evidence reinforces the notion that the physical evidence left us tells an incomplete story.

Perhaps several cultures began using vowels at the same time. This is the second time (the first was with Egyptian and Sumerian, as discussed above) that we find what looks like mimicry but where we cannot figure out exactly what happened. In the present case, did these varied cultures all stumble upon the idea of vowels simultaneously? It seems unlikely.

In support of the theory that vowel letters surfaced at the same time in different cultures, we might suppose that, for reasons we have yet to discover, around the 9th century B.C.E. it was suddenly desirable for the masses to read and write, and only vowels could make that possible. That conjecture not only substitutes one unknown for another — we don't know why varied cultures independently decided that the masses had to read and write — but also makes it hard to understand why the masses did *not* write, or, if they did, why so few records remain. That is, because we assume that vowel letters were a Hebrew invention, we have no problem with the fact that we see little widespread evidence of the masses writing in other cultures. By contrast, the assumption that many cultures started using vowel letters simultaneously because the masses needed them is plagued by this lack of evidence.

Amid this mass of confusing and sometimes contradictory theoretical and physical evidence, however, we have one final set of facts. The Hebrews seem to have recognized the incredible power of reading and writing, and they seem to have recognized the power of vowels.

In terms of the former, we find Deuteronomy 6:9, "write them [the instructions mentioned earlier in the text] on the doorposts of your house and on your gates." Without taking a stand on divine authorship for the text, we may note that a command to "write them" almost certainly means that the intended recipients of the command either were able to write or were expected to learn. Unfortunately, it is difficult to date the original text of Deuteronomy, so this piece of evidence, too, is equivocal.

We turn to the second set of facts, the Hebrews' appreciation of the vowels themselves, in the next chapter.

Chapter 4
Magic Letters and the Name of God

When they ask what [God's] name is, what
shall I tell them?
— Exodus 3:13

Magic Letters

Setting the Stage

We saw in the last chapter that the Hebrews took the letters *yud, heh,* and *vav,* which had already been used to represent consonantal sounds, and used them to represent vowel sounds as well. In so doing, they paved the way not only for the preservation of their own writings, but also for the widespread use of alphabets throughout the world. With some notable exceptions, such as the writing systems of East Asia (Chinese, Japanese, etc.), the major civilizations of the modern world all use alphabets descended from the Hebrews' experimentation with vowels.

Latin was written in the "Roman" alphabet, derived from Greek, which in turn based its letters on Hebrew. A slightly modified Roman alphabet is used today for English, Spanish, etc., in the Americas, and a host of languages in Western Europe. The Eastern European languages are written either in the Roman alphabet, with minor variations, or in Cyrillic (commonly called "Russian"), also descended from Greek. In the Middle East, of course, we have Hebrew, and — much more widely used — Arabic writing, which is used for many dialects of Arabic and for Persian. It, too, comes from Hebrew, by way (probably) of Aramaic. Indian scripts, not surprisingly, dominate the subcontinent of India, as well as parts of Asia;

while the exact connection between the precursors of these scripts and Hebrew is unclear, there is general consensus that some 2,200 years ago the Indians took the Hebrew alphabet and modified it for their purposes.

So the short story is that the Hebrews invented vowel letters, and with those vowel letters their alphabet was used as the basis for almost every other major alphabet used today, almost 3,000 years later. Of course, that short story is an oversimplification, ignoring both lack of knowledge on our part and some details that are known. For example, as noted immediately above, the exact connection between the Indian scripts and Hebrew is unclear, and even the connections among Hebrew, Aramaic, and Greek remain a topic of scholarly debate. And, of course, the general agreement in the literature that it was the Phoenician script that set the stage for the other alphabets cannot be ignored, even in light of the arguments in the last chapter that cast doubt on this widespread claim.

Nonetheless, the leap from consonant-based writing to vowel-and-consonant-based writing ranks as one of the most important steps forward in the history of human progress. For the first time, the masses could read and write, and it was the invention of vowel letters that made this possible. The Hebrews seem not only to have made the discovery, but also to have appreciated its importance. They also seem to have ascribed special import to the letters that only they had: the vowel letters.

The Magic H

Genesis 17:1–8 tells of a covenant between God and a man whose name is spelled *abrm* in the text, and commonly called "Abram" today. (The *a* in *abrm* here represents the letter "Aleph." A more scientific representation would be *'brm*, but because *abrm* is so much more convenient, we'll use that for the purposes of this discussion.) Part of the covenant entails changing *abrm*'s name to *abrhm* ("Abraham"), that is, adding a *heh* into *abrm*'s name. This is not the only instance of inserting a *heh* into a name. Also in Genesis, *sry* ("Sarai"), Abram's wife, becomes *srh* ("Sarah").

We are not interested here in the accuracy of the story, or the questions of the existence of a God and a person *abrm* with whom the covenant may have been made. (The first question sits firmly in the realm of the God Theory, which we are ignoring in this book; the second belongs either to the God Theory or historical aspects of the Science Theory that are irrelevant for our purposes.) Nor are we interested in God-Theory answers to the meaning of the *h* in Abram or Sarai's name, such as Rashi, a preeminent biblical commentator from the 11th century C.E., provides. We are interested rather in finding a scientific answer to why inserting a *heh* in the middle of a name marked the name as belonging to the Hebrews, and what that tells us about how the Hebrews used their alphabet and language.

Why was a *heh* used to mark initiation into Hebrew culture?

The most likely answer is that the Hebrews, recognizing the importance of their newly-found vowel letters, and recognizing that no other culture had them, used their vowel letters not only for their original purpose, namely, of marking vowels in existing words, but also for the purpose of marking something as belonging to the very culture that invented the vowels in the first place.

The letter *heh* was thus "magical" to the Hebrews in that it produced twofold wonderful effects. First, they seem to have used it for marking membership, a role that far exceeded its role as a sound-representing symbol. Secondly, it was part of a system (vowels) that offered great power, namely, the power to give the gift of reading and writing to the masses. Of course, we do not claim that the letters really possess magic, though God theories that ascribe supernatural power to the letters abound.

First the Hebrews discovered their vowel letters. The Hebrews then realized how useful they would be, and that no other culture had them. In this sense, the Hebrews were the "vowel-letter" people. Because they were the vowel-letter people, they used these vowel letters magically (in their minds) to mark membership in the tribe of vowel-letter people.

One of the three[1] major names for "God" in the Old Testament provides corroboration for this theory. One of God's names — we'll deal with the others immediately below — is spelled *elhym*. (Here the *e* is an *aleph*, used, as with *a* above, for convenience.) Where does that word come from? Unlike with Abraham and Sarah, above, the text does not answer this question for us, but the source is so clear that we do not need an explanation. The word *elym* (אלים) meant "gods," from the word *el* (אל), "god," and the plural suffix *-ym* (ים-).

Clearly, *elhym* (אלהים), which refers to the Hebrew God, is the word *elym* with a *heh* (*h*) inserted to mark the word as belonging to the Hebrews.[2] (We should note that other etymologies are prevalent in the literature. The most common alternative is that the word is the plural of *eloah* — אלה. Readers who wish to evaluate this other claim for themselves are referred to the "Further Reading" section.)

With the addition of *elhym* to *abrhm* and *srh*, we find that the patriarch, matriarch, and God of the Hebrews all have names derived by adding a "magic" *heh* to a previously known name or word.

---

1. Many people count two names. But that is due to the fact that, of the three names, two (spelled *adny* and *yhwh*) are traditionally pronounced identically.

2. Though this etymology is clear once pointed out, I remained unaware of it until I heard a lecture, quite some time ago, by my teacher and friend Rabbi Bernard Zlotowitz.

Of "God" and "Gods"

One troubling detail, of course, is that the Hebrews, well known for their insistence on "one God," seem to have based the name of their deity on the plural word "gods." Why didn't they take the singular word *el* and add a *heh* to that, instead?

One possibility is that the word may have come from an older Akkadian or Phoenician word *ilum*, which, related to the Hebrew *el*, meant "god," not "gods." If so, *elhym* is the Hebrew *ilum*, that is, the Hebrew God, and there is no puzzle. On the other hand, if in fact *elhym* represents the Hebrew version of the plural word *elim*, "gods," we find not only a puzzle but two possible solutions to it, both supported by considerable evidence.

One theory, widely accepted, is that the word *elhym* goes back to an earlier time in the Hebrews' history, before they adopted monotheism. (This position is usually put forth without mentioning the insertion of the *heh* into the name. Regardless of how the *heh* got there, the word looks plural.) In further support of this theory, it is often noted that the other[3] word for "God," /adonai/, sounds like the word "my lords." So both common words for God seem plural. But this theory is problematic because, from what we have seen, the *heh* could not have been added before the Hebrews starting using vowels in their writings, by which time their writings seem to indicate a monotheistic outlook (though the timing of their adoption of monotheism is also a matter of some debate).

The second possibility is that the Hebrews' one God was seen as the equivalent of other cultures' many gods. In other words, the Hebrews were not (only?) trying to express the concept "God" but also "gods." Every culture had their "gods," and so did the Hebrews. An obvious question, then, was how many gods were in the group "gods." For some cultures, the answer may have been a vague "many," or a particular number. For the Hebrews, the answer was "one." This second theory is buttressed by the well-known passage from Deuteronomy (6:4) usually translated: "Hear, O Israel, the Lord is our God (*elhym*), the Lord is One." This one line has received inordinate attention, owing at least in part to its centrality in Jewish religious practice. The problems with the line are many. The line would make considerably more sense if it read ". . . the Lord alone." And, indeed, this is another common translation. But opponents of that translation are quick to point out that the Hebrew word used for "one" (/exad/) does not mean "alone." (To this, advocates of the theory counter that we could have a scribal error here.)

---

3. Actually, we have two other names for God, both traditionally pronounced identically, but one spelled the way it sounds, and one spelled *yhwh*. This is discussed extensively below.

At the heart of the problem is the seemingly nonsensical (or, at least, tautological, and so superfluous) statement that "Adonai" is "one." Consider a similar statement: "John Smith is one." Of course "John Smith" is "one," because a name always represents one person. Even when lots of people share a name, a particular usage of the name refers to a particular person. Whether "the Lord" is God's name or a reference to God, the phrase "the Lord is one" seems as odd as "John Smith is one" (if "the Lord" is God's name) or as "the president is one" (if "the Lord" is God's title).

But if, based on what we saw above, *elhym* meant not only "God" but also the Hebrew equivalent of other cultures' "set of gods" then the statement makes sense. It claims first that Adonai is "the Hebrew set of gods," and then, recognizing that a set of gods generally contains more than one member, adds that this particular set contains but one member. Of course, this may be a solution in search of a problem, because the word may not be plural at all, as noted above.

Either way, our understanding that the Hebrews used their writing to define their deity accords well with another aspect of Hebrew culture that, apparently, connected writing (and, therefore, vowels) and God, as we see next.

Of God and Writing

It can hardly be coincidence that the central statement about the Hebrews' culture just discussed is the same one that the Hebrews are to make sure they do not forget. According to Deuteronomy, the way they are to make sure they do not forget this statement is both by repeating it (presumably to memorize it) but also, significantly, by writing it down. As noted earlier, the Hebrews were instructed to write things down. A similar instruction in our modern culture would be entirely unremarkable, but the Hebrews were the first people that could instruct their masses to write something down.

A picture thus emerges that ties monotheism to writing. We noted earlier that the vowel letters may have been invented by scribes for the purpose of making it easier for the masses to write. Perhaps what the scribes wanted the masses to write was nothing less than the central creeds of the emerging Judaism. A religious leader, or leaders, may have realized that writing was central to spreading the word of God. And vowels were central to letting people read and write. In one short paragraph we find the name of the one member of the Hebrew god-set as marked by the letter *heh*, and the instruction to write down the creed that the Lord is in fact one.

The next section makes the connection between the Hebrews' God and the Hebrews' vowel letters even more concrete.

The Name of God

Elhym is one of the three common words used to refer to God in Scripture. We just saw that that word almost certainly came about by adding the letter *heh* to the common word for "gods."

But another major word for God is even more amazing in its connection to the vowel letters invented by the Hebrews, for it contains nothing but those letters! The tetragrammaton (from the Greek for "four-lettered"), as it is called, is the four letters *yhwh* (that is, *yud-heh-vav-heh*), and is used in addition to *elhym* to refer to God in Scripture. While many modern names for God have come from trying to pronounce these letters (Jehovah, Yahweh, etc.), traditional Judaism teaches that the original pronunciation of this name for God has been forgotten.

Of course, from a scientific point of view, that theory is preposterous. It is hardly credible that a society focused on worshiping one God would forget that one God's name. Even with the added detail of the traditional religious theory that only the High Priest knew the pronunciation, the theory remains untenable. Surely the secret could not have been so well guarded as tradition teaches. (Surprisingly, the incredibility of the theory has not prevented its introduction into otherwise sound scientific treatises, as discussed in the suggestions for further reading.) So we must seek another explanation for why no traditional pronunciation is associated with those letters.

But before answering the question of why *yhwh* has no pronunciation, let us be clear, for there is in fact a traditional pronunciation associated with that word; but it seems not to come from the letters in the word. In Jewish tradition, *yhwh* is pronounced / adonai /[4] (whose literal meaning is "our Lords," and from which, by way of the Greek Septuagint, the English appellation "the Lord" comes). But clearly, *yhwh* does not spell "adonai." So while tradition provides a pronunciation for the word, that pronunciation seems completely divorced from the letters that comprise it. Whether we assume that *yhwh* spelled / adonai / (making it the only word in Scripture that was not pronounced roughly phonetically) or we assume that *yhwh* had no pronunciation, and so, when one was needed, / adonai / was chosen, we must ask why the four-letter word *yhwh* was chosen to

---

4. The Christian appellation "Yehovah" comes from a literal reading of a Masoretic tradition. (The Masoretes are discussed in Chapter 5.) The vowels from another word for God, / adonai / (spelled אדוני in Hebrew), were added to the letters *yhwh* for religious reasons. That combination of vowels and *yhwh* happens to spell, roughly, Yehovah, which was adopted as a name for God. The name "Jehovah" comes from German, in which the lettter *j* is used to represent the sound /y/. Neither of these pronunciations can be traced back to antiquity.

Figure 4.1. The Tetragrammaton as written in Dead Sea Scroll 11QPs.

represent the Hebrew God.

The obvious answer is that the letters in *yhwh* were chosen not because of the sounds they represent, but because of their symbolic power in that they were the Hebrews' magic vowel letters that no other culture had; *yhwh* has no traditional pronunciation not because the pronunciation was lost but because it never had a pronunciation to begin with. After all, the Hebrews' great invention was the doubling up of *yud* (*y*), *heh* (*h*), and *vav* (*w*) as vowel letters. It is those exact letters that were used for God. We have already seen the letter *heh* used magically, both in the names of the first patriarch and matriarch, and in the name of God. Here we see the other vowel letters used magically. We also see the *heh*, so prominent elsewhere, used twice.

The theory that the letters of the tetragrammaton were chosen for their symbolic value, rather than their pronunciation, is further supported by a curious detail about the Dead Sea Scrolls ("DSS"). We will discuss the DSS extensively in Chapter 7, but for now we note one detail about them.

There were two different scripts (basically, fonts) used to write Hebrew, the older "Phoenician" script and the more modern "Aramaic" or "square" script. Some DSS, such as the widely studied 11QPs (or 11Q5) "Psalms Scroll," are written in the newer script but revert to the older Phoenician script for the tetragrammaton, as depicted in the (digitally enhanced) photograph in Figure 4.1. (Figure 4.2 has a sample of the newer script.) Why would only the tetragrammaton be written in the older Phoenician letters? From all indications, this was (then) a modern text. Its spelling, for example, reflects not the older spelling of Scripture, but the more modern spelling of the period of the DSS, which accords well with the fact that it is mostly written in the then-current script.

We might assume that, out of reverence, "God" was written in the older script, but *elhym*, the other word for "God," was written in the newer script, like the rest of the text, as depicted in the digitally enhanced photograph in Figure 4.2. (However, in some scrolls, the words *el* [God] and *ely* [my God] were also written in the older script.) But the tetragrammaton is the only word that was written solely in the older script in some DSS. We can make sense of this fact if we assume, in keeping with what we saw above, that the

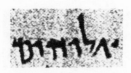

Figure 4.2. The word *elohim* as written in Dead Sea Scroll 11QPs.

point of the tetragrammaton was not its pronunciation (for which modern letters would have been required) but rather the letters themselves. The author of the DSS, knowing that the point of the tetragrammaton was the letters, tried to preserve the old letters in their original form.

The Septuagint — the 3rd-century B.C.E. translation of the Hebrew Bible into Greek — further buttresses this theory. While the tetragrammaton was usually translated as the Greek equivalent of "Lord" ($K\upsilon\rho\iota o\varsigma$, that is, *Kurios*), in some old copies we find instead *Hebrew* letters, written, once again, in the old Hebrew script. The tetragrammaton is the only word in the Septuagint written in the old Hebrew script.

One final bit of evidence suggests that the tetragrammaton was not simply a name for God. God is frequently referred to as "the name of God." For example, Psalms commonly exclaims, "may Adonai's name be blessed," rather than the seemingly more straightforward "may Adonai be blessed." That curious expression is used primarily with *yhwh*, seldom with *elohim*, and never with the name *adonai* spelled out. While there are many reasons why this might be the case, what we clearly see is an asymmetry between the tetragrammaton and other ways of expressing "God." This fact adds to the likelihood that *yhwh* was not simply another name for God.

The solution proposed here, namely, that the letters in *yhwh* were chosen not for their phonetic value but because they were the Hebrews' magic letters, accounts for everything we have seen, and even solves another problem: in addition to a lack of clear pronunciation, *yhwh* seems to defy any clear etymology. That is, even in form — regardless of its pronunciation or lack thereof — the word seems anomalous in Hebrew.

The Bible itself contains one potential etymology, in Exodus 3:13–14. Moses asks what God's name is, and there the reply is the cryptic "I will be that which I will be." The connection to the tetragrammaton is that the word for "I will be" is *aleph-heh-yud-heh*, that is, roughly the letters *yud-heh-vav-heh*. The root "to be" in Hebrew, like the tetragrammaton, consists only of vowel letters. Exodus 3:14 even quotes God as telling Moses to tell the Israelites: "I-will-be [*aleph-heh-yud-heh*] sent me." At first glance, that passage in Exodus seems to derive God's name from the verb "to be."

But etymologies in the Bible tend to be symbolic, not scientific, often taking advantage of coincidences for rhetorical purposes. Van der Toorn, in analyzing this and other potential sources for the name *yhwh*, correctly points out that "[t]he significance of the name Yahweh has been the subject of a staggering amount of publications," including the one from Exodus. He then spends several pages demonstrating that none of the theories presented in those publications is free of significant conjecture and difficulty. The magic-letter theory put forth here accounts for the apparent lack of etymological derivation for *yhwh* by specifically claiming that the word was created by the Hebrews and not borrowed from any more ancient source.

What we see, then, is strong evidence that the Hebrews appreciated the value of their newly-found vowel letters so much that they used them to define membership in their group, as with Abraham, Sarah, and one name for God, and to write the other name of their God.

These vowel letters were destined to play a pivotal role in all of Hebrew's various stages.

Chapter 5
The Masoretes

Why We Care

In the last chapter, we saw a quote from Deuteronomy, and assumed that it was representative of what the Hebrews were writing around the time they started using vowel letters, probably in the 8th or 7th century B.C.E. But, surprisingly, the oldest copy of the Hebrew Bible as we have it now is but 1,000 years old, leaving nearly a 2,000-year gap.

Working perhaps as early as 600 C.E. and certainly by 800 C.E., several groups of people collectively called the **Masoretes** attempted to record and annotate the "authentic" version of the Bible in Hebrew. Some of their efforts were successful, in that to this day the version produced by one of these groups (from Tiberias) is considered authentic in religious circles. Because of its religious endorsement, and because it is published today in traditional Bibles, most people wrongly assume that this Tiberian version is not only completely religiously accurate, but also completely historically accurate. It is not.

Our next task should be to look at the Hebrew that was originally used to write the Bible, that is, "Biblical Hebrew," which, as we shall see, is not the same as the traditional religious version used as "the Bible" today.[1] In Chapter 6 we'll look at the pronunciation of Biblical Hebrew, and in Chapter 8 we'll look at other issues surrounding Biblical Hebrew. But

---

1. Even though the term "Biblical Hebrew" ought to be reserved for the Hebrew originally used to write the Bible, that is, the Hebrew in use around the 7th century B.C.E. onward, many authors, even those working in a scientific framework, use it both for that Hebrew and for the current religious understanding of the Bible. In other words, they use the same term for the religious understanding of what Hebrew was like and the scientific understanding of what Hebrew was like. Here, we will limit the phrase "Biblical Hebrew" to the Hebrew that (we think) was actually used when the Bible was written.

before addressing the question of what, exactly, Biblical Hebrew was like, it will be convenient to jump ahead in time to the Masoretes, because they gave us the currently accepted canonical version of the Hebrew Bible that is familiar to so many people.

We will thus break down the question of what Hebrew was like in the 1st millennium B.C.E. into two questions: what was Masoretic Hebrew like (at the end of the 1st millennium C.E.), and how closely did it match the earlier Hebrew? This approach will also tell us about the origins and scientific accuracy of the Hebrew text in the Hebrew Bible. So we turn now to the Masoretes, who gave us the Hebrew Bible as we know it today.

The Masoretic Groups

Probably sometime before the 8th century B.C.E., various groups of people — now called Masoretes — became dissatisfied with the traditional Hebrew text of the Bible because it was written only with consonants and the helping vowel letters *yud, heh,* and *vav.* (These "helping vowel letters" are commonly referred to by their Latin name: *matres lectiones.*) As we have seen, before the Hebrews started using vowel letters (almost 2,000 years before the Masoretes undertook their work) even speakers of a language could not read the written language without practice. The addition of vowel letters made it possible for speakers of a language to read the written language, but did not address one of the two problems the Masoretes faced: They wanted the Bible to be accessible even to non-Hebrew speakers. (The other problem, which we discuss below, was that the Masoretes wanted to preserve the meaning of the text.)

While a Hebrew speaker could readily read the Bible and pronounce its words, a non-Hebrew speaker, or one who knew Hebrew only as a studied language and not as a spoken language, had great difficulty. (Even native speakers of Hebrew probably had some difficulty, as evidenced by the fact that every time since antiquity that Hebrew has been used as a spoken language it has adopted far more vowel letters than the traditional Bible contains. But non-Hebrew speakers would have had no way of reading the Bible aloud.)

At the time of the Masoretes, Hebrew writing was mostly consonantal, with but hints of vowels, as indicated, as we have seen, by the vowel letters *yud, heh,* and *vav.* Even though the original move to introduce those letters was, in its time, state of the art, the Masoretes lived many hundreds of years later, and had the benefits of knowing about even more successful systems. Latin and Greek, for example, both had systems with two big improvements over Hebrew. Their alphabets (mostly) used *different* letters for vowels than they did for consonants (like English does), and (mostly) used a symbol for every vowel. Hebrew, by contrast, indicated only enough vowels to make reading possible by the masses. Hebrew did not indicate every vowel. To represent those vowels, Hebrew used symbols that were also used for consonants. Either of these problems would have been enough to make Hebrew unreadable by people who did not speak the language.

To solve the problem of pronunciation, the Masoretes started adding diacritic marks to the original Hebrew to indicate sound information that the original Hebrew did not. So, for example, the letters *shin-mem* (שם) in the Bible can represent either "name" (probably pronounced /shem/) or "there" (/sham/), depending on the unwritten vowel between the first and second letters. The various groups of Masoretes invented sets of symbols to mark the vowels. One such set differentiated the words by writing "name" as שֵׁם, that is, with two dots to represent the vowel /e/, and "there" as שָׁם, that is, with a *T*-like symbol to represent the vowel /a/. (Similar considerations led early writers of Romance languages to adopt their various systems of accents: aigu, grave, etc.) Readers familiar with modern Hebrew or with our modern way of writing classical Hebrew will quickly recognize the vowel signs under the first letter of our example. Other systems, as discussed below, were used as well.

Lack of vowel information was not the only obstacle to pronouncing Hebrew correctly. Some letters represented more than one sound (like our English *c*, which can represent /s/ or /k/). The various Masoretic systems also corrected this shortcoming of Hebrew orthography. Continuing the example above, we note that the same letters used for "name" and "there" can also be "put," pronounced /sam/, in which case (again using but one of several systems) the word is written שָׂם, with a dot to the upper left of the *shin*, rather than to its right, indicating that the letter is to be pronounced /s/ and not /sh/.

In addition to the goal of making sure the words were pronounced correctly, the Masoretes also wanted to make sure people understood the text. Toward this end, they devised intricate punctuation systems designed to let a reader know which words should be grouped together. Our modern English punctuation (though actually less detailed than the Masoretes') serves roughly the same purpose. A period between two words tells the reader that the words are not part of the same sentence. A hyphen, by contrast, tells a reader that two words are more closely connected than might otherwise be thought.

Beyond these two additions to Hebrew — pronunciation and punctuation — the Masoretes gave us an intricate musical system for singing the text in liturgical settings. (The issue of why, exactly, the text had to be sung is involved and ultimately irrelevant for our discussion here.)

We can isolate three different groups of people who did this kind of work, according to where they lived. We turn to these groups next.

Tiberias

Two Families

Historically, the most influential Masoretes were the Tiberian Masoretes, and of the Tiberian Masoretes, the most influential family was the ben-Asher family, of which five generations are known to us today. The second most influential family, about which less is known, is the Ben-Naftali family.

These two families seem to have disagreed about many details of the Biblical text, so much so that other authors discussed their differences in great detail. We are fortunate that the other authors did this, because, to our knowledge, none of the manuscripts written or annotated by any member of either family remains in its entirety.

Because the ben-Asher family ultimately achieved prominence, we will look at their system in detail.

The Vowels

Both Tiberian families used a set of diacritic marks to indicate vowels in Hebrew words. Table 5.1 shows those marks and their traditional pronunciation. The table uses the letter *aleph* to demonstrate the vowel marks, because those marks do not appear in isolation.

The "traditional pronunciations" in the table represent the traditional view about how the Masoretes spoke. Almost everyone believes that the *kamatz* and *patach* were pronounced differently; views about how they differed vary. Almost everyone believes that the *kamatz* had two values, representing at times /o/ and at times /a/. Almost everyone believes that the *kibutz* and *shuruq* were pronounced identically. Almost everyone believes that the two *cholam*s were pronounced identically. (Incidentally, when the two *cholam*s must be distinguished by name, the one with a *vav* is called a "full *cholam*," or *cholam maleh*, in contrast to a "missing *cholam*," or *cholam chaseir*.)

Beyond this, disagreement abounds. The *chataf* vowels are traditionally described as "murmured" vowels, though that description offers little actual insight. Traditionally, there are two kids of *shewa*, one that is silent and one that — impossibly! — is pronounced as a vowel that does not

Table 5.1. Vowels used by the Tiberian Masoretes

Mark	Name	Traditional Pronunciation
אַ	Patach	"a" as in "father"
אָ	Kamatz	"a" as in "father" or "aw" as in "paw" or "o" as in "go"
אֶ	Segol	"e" as in "bet"
אֵ	Tzere	"ai" as in "bait"
אִ	Chiriq	"i" as in "bit" or "e" as in "beet"
אְ	Shewa	no sound, or "shewa"*
אֻ	Kibutz	"oo" as in "moon"
אוּ	Shuruq	"oo" as in "moon"
אֹ	Cholam	"o" as in "go"
אוֹ	Cholam	"o" as in "go"
אֲ	Chataf Patach	"a" as in "father"
אֳ	Chataf Kamatz	"o" as in "go"
אֱ	Chataf Segol	"e" as in "bet"
אֱ	Chataf Chiriq	"i" as in "bit"**

* A "shewa" is the almost non-sound represented, for example, by the apostrophe in the colloquial English "Can I have that t'go please?"
** The currently accepted tradition does not use the chataf-chiriq.

create a syllable. (The *shewa* is discussed in detail immediately below.)

Furthermore, numerous articles have been written about the exact pronunciation of the vowel symbols when the Tiberian Masoretes introduced them. For example, the question is often asked whether the *kamatz* represented something closer to the *a* in *father* or the *ou* in *bought*. We will address the issue of the exact pronunciation of the Masoretes below, but the short answer is that — considerable literature notwithstanding — we don't know exactly how the Masoretes spoke.

The Shewa

Much has been written about the Tiberian Masoretic *shewa*. Because the topic is important for understanding Tiberian Masoretic Hebrew and how it relates to Biblical Hebrew, we'll take a look at some of the issues here. The issues are technical, however, and the casual reader may wish to skip to the discussion of the letters *sin* and *shin* on page 56, and return to this section later.

Traditional Hebrew grammars either teach that there are two kinds of *shewa* or that there are three, the third being a hybrid of sorts that attempts to combine features of both of the two main kinds of *shewa*. For our purposes, we can ignore the third kind and focus on the first two.

Everyone agrees that one use of the *shewa* was to mark the complete lack of a vowel. So, for example, the Hebrew *yisrael* ("Israel") is written like this: יִשְׂרָאֵל, with the two dots under the *sin* (שׂ) marking the lack of a vowel sound after the /s/ sound. This first type of *shewa* is commonly called *nach* ("resting") in Hebrew, or "silent" in English. (Some books also use *shewa quiescens*.)

It is commonly argued that another use of the *shewa* was to mark a sound of some sort. Weingreen, for example, in his classic grammar of Hebrew, uses the example שְׁמוֹ, in which he claims that the *shewa* is pronounced as a "quick vowel-like sound." However, he quickly adds that "שְׁמוֹ is regarded as one syllable." But these claims conflict. If the word is one syllable, then the *shewa* must be silent. If the *shewa* is pronounced, we have two syllables. This vocalic-but-not-really-vocalic *shewa* goes by the name of *na* ("moving") or "vocal" in English. (It is also called *shewa mobile* in some books.) Variations on the pronunciation scheme of the vocal *shewa* abound, but, in short, there is no reason to accept the traditional notion that a silent *shewa* is always silent and that a vocal *shewa* is always pronounced.

Indeed, there is little reason to accept the notion that there are two types of *shewa*. Three arguments against there being two types of *shewa* present themselves.

Firstly, the Tiberian Masoretes were concerned with preserving the pronunciation of Hebrew. It is hardly likely that they would choose one symbol to represent at once the lack of sound and presence of sound.

More importantly, the analysis that requires two types of *shewa* is based on a flawed premise. Beyond pronunciation issues, two types of *shewa* are usually posited because of the way *shewa* interacts with certain letters, known as *"beged kefet* letters." After a vowel, the *beged kefet* letters lose their dot — called a *dagesh* — unless the letters are doubled. (See immediately below for more information about *beged kefet* letters and what a *dagesh* is.) However, the *beged kefet* letters only sometimes lose their *dagesh* after a *shewa*.

Because a *shewa* sometimes behaves like a vowel (in that it eliminates the *dagesh* of a following *beged kefet* letter) and sometimes like the lack of a vowel (in that it does not eliminate the *dagesh*), it was assumed that some *shewa*s actually *were* vowels, whereas some were not. But the reasoning is flawed, as we see next.

It is a basic premise of linguistics that the pronunciation of one part of a word (call it the "trigger part") can affect the pronunciation of another part of the word ("affected part"). So it is not surprising, for example, that a vowel in Tiberian Masoretic Hebrew changes the pronunciation of the letter it precedes. The vowel is the trigger, and the letter after it is affected. By way of comparison, consider that in English a *t* between two vowels is usually pronounced /d/. The word *water* (in America) is actually pronounced with a /d/ in the middle: /wader/. The vowels around the letter *t* are the trigger, and the *t* is affected.

However, in addition to that first basic premise of linguistics is another: The trigger itself can be affected! In particular, the trigger can be affected so that it is no longer pronounced. So, Trigger One can affect a letter, and then Trigger Two can affect Trigger One so that Trigger One is no longer part of the word. Again, an example in English is in order. In English, the sound /yoo/ (the trigger) can change a /t/ before it into /ch/. So, for example, the word *fortune* is pronounced /forchin/; the phrase *I'll bet you* ... is pronounced *I'll* /betchoo/, etc. However, unstressed vowels in English are often (under circumstances far too complex to discuss here) not pronounced fully, or sometimes at all. So, even though the word "actual" has three syllables, "actually" does not always have four; it too can have three.

Continuing our English example, we note that the word "actual" is pronounced /akchoo'al/ because the /yoo/ sound changes the /t/ into a /ch/. However, the word "actually" is (often) pronounced /akch'ly/. The /yoo/ sound in "actual" (the first trigger) changes the /t/ sound into a /ch/ sound. But then the /yoo/ sound itself is affected by a second trigger, which eliminates the /oo/ sound from the word. It would be a grave error to assume that "actually" is always pronounced with a /yoo/ sound because the /t/ changes to /ch/. Rather, the second trigger has eliminated the first trigger from the word.

A similar error led people to think that every instance of *shewa* that forced the following *beged kefet* letter to drop its *dagesh* had to be pronounced. It did not. In this case, Trigger One in the word is the vowel. Trigger One affects the *beged kefet* letter, which loses its *dagesh*. But a second trigger eliminates the vowel from the word.

What we end up with, then, is only one purpose for the *shewa*: to indicate the lack of a vowel. However, the "lack of a vowel" could be because the word never had a vowel where the *shewa* appeared, or because the word used to have a vowel but some other part of the word got rid of it.

In addition to the first two reasons for rejecting the two-*shewa* theory, we have a third. Technical details of the theory require that the *shewa* at the beginning of a word must be of the "vocal" (*na*) variety, while the *shewa* before a *dagesh* must be silent (*nach*). However, the common word שְׁתַּיִם ("two") has a *dagesh* in the letter after an initial *shewa*. These two rules therefore conflict. The system doesn't work.

In the end, then, we find no support for two different kinds of *shewa* in Tiberian Masoretic Hebrew, in spite of very widespread claims to the contrary. We also understand the flawed reasoning that led to the flawed conclusion in the first place.

What we do not know, however, is exactly how the *shewa* was pronounced. "Vowel reduction," the process by which unstressed vowels become less pronounced than stressed vowels, is very common throughout the languages of the world. We have already seen that in English unstressed vowels are not always pronounced. Other examples from English include the *o* in *together* (usually pronounced /t'gether/) and the *-er* and *-or* endings in *better* and *bettor* (both of which are pronounced identically). However, the exact conditions under which vowel reduction takes place, as well as the degree of reduction, vary not only from language to language, but within a language depending on the register of speech.

So it looks like a *shewa* was used to indicate both the complete lack of a vowel and a reduced vowel, but we do not know the extent to which vowels reduced in Tiberian Masoretic Hebrew. As a guess, we can assume that the *shewa* was pronounced whenever it had to be, and only then. But it remains a guess.

Consonants with Dots over Them: *Shin* and *Sin*

Beyond the symbols in Table 5.1, the Tiberian Masoretes used dots to distinguish various consonants. The simplest such distinction is shown in Table 5.2. It seems that through historical accident two different sounds came to be written by the same letter: שׁ. The Masoretes used a dot on the left to indicate the sound /s/ and a dot on the right to indicate the sound /sh/.

Table 5.2. *Shin* and *sin* as marked by the Tiberian Masoretes

Symbol	Traditional Pronunciation
שׁ	"sh" as in "show"
שׂ	"s" as in "sow"

Table 5.3. Beged Kefet letters as marked by the Tiberian Masoretes

Symbol	Traditional Pronunciation	
	with dot	without dot
בּ	/b/	/v/
גּ	/g/ as in *go*	/γ/*
דּ	/d/	/th/ as in *this* or /z/
כּ	/k/	/ch/ as in *Bach*
פּ	/p/	/f/
תּ	/t/	/th/ as in *with* or /s/

* See text for discussion of the sound represented by the symbol γ.

Consonants with Dots in Them: *"Beged Kefet"*

The Masoretes also had another set of distinctions. Six letters, *bet, gimel, daled, kaf, pe,* and *taf* — ת, פ, כ, ד, ג, ב — each had two pronunciations. These are traditionally called the **beged kefet** letters, because those two Hebrew words form an acronym for the six letters whose pronunciation changed. (Older books often call these letters *b'gad k'fat.*)

It turns out that the *beged kefet* letters, and their treatment by the Tiberian Masoretes, give us invaluable clues about how accurately the Masoretes captured Biblical Hebrew, so it is important to understand them. (We have already seen that the *beged kefet* letters play an important role in understanding the *shewa.*)

The *beged kefet* symbols and their alternations are listed in Table 5.3.

When these (and, actually, many other) letters have a dot in them, the the dot is called a **dagesh.** As we see in Table 5.3, the *dagesh* changes the pronunciation of the *beged kefet* letters.

Some Tiberian Masoretic manuscripts further indicate a letter without a *dagesh* by writing a horizontal line over it. This line is a called a **rafeh.** Because, in principle, every *beged kefet* letter that doesn't have a *dagesh* ought to have a *rafeh,* modern practice has more or less abandoned the Tiberian *rafeh.* (The same *rafeh* was also placed over the letters *heh* and *aleph* when those letters were used to mark vowels, instead of representing consonantal sounds.) Of all the Tiberian "vowel symbols," the *rafeh* has been least incorporated into Modern Hebrew.

Of the six alternations, three (*bet, kaf,* and *pe*) still change in modern Israeli Hebrew, depending on whether they have a *dagesh* or not, and a fourth (*taf*) changes in the Ashkenazic religious pronunciation of Hebrew. Modern Yemenite Hebrew maintains alternations for all of the six letters but their distinctions are different than the ones listed in Table 5.3.

The alternations fall into a pattern. Each letter with a dot is what linguists call a "stop," while each letter without a dot is a corresponding "fricative."

A "stop" is a sound that you make by completely stopping the flow of air somewhere in the oral tract, that is, somewhere between your larynx deep in your throat and your lips. For example, if you close the air passage at your lips, you get either a /p/ or a /b/. If you close the air passage in your throat, you get either a /k/ or a /g/ (as in "go"). If you close the passage by placing your tongue against the front part of the top of your mouth (or against the back of your teeth), you get a /d/ or a /t/. One consequence of the way stops are created is that a stop is necessarily a short sound. You can say the sound /l/ for as long as you like. But you cannot say /b/ for a long time. (You can say it over and over again quickly, but that is different.)

By contrast, a "fricative" is a sound made when the airflow is significantly restricted but not stopped completely. If you place your tongue as though you are about to say /t/, but release the pressure just a little bit, just enough to let some air through, you get the sound /s/ or /th/, depending on how you make your /t/ sound. Because some air is flowing, fricatives can be short sounds or much longer sounds, unlike stops.

In fact, one useful way to find out which fricative corresponds to a particular stop is to try to say that stop for a long time. If you try to make the sound /t/ last for a long time without repeating lots of little /t/ sounds you'll either get the sound /s/ or the sound /th/. (Again, which one you get depends on how you make your /t/ sound.)

The seemingly arbitrary alternations between the six letters that take dots in the middle to change their sounds thus reflect a very simple notion: The Tiberian Masoretes used a dot in a letter to denote a stop. (Curiously, modern English writing uses a dot — a period — to denote a "full stop" in punctuation. This is almost certainly a coincidence.)

The realization that a pattern underlies the Tiberian Masoretic treatment of *beged kefet* letters offers an answer to the hotly debated question of which modern system of pronouncing Hebrew is more "authentic," the Ashkenazic system or the Sephardic system. In the Sephardic system, adopted by modern Israel and by some groups for religious purposes, the *taf* has but one pronunciation (/t/), regardless of any dot in it. By contrast, the Ashkenazic system, still widely used for religious purposes in America and Europe, pronounces a *taf* without a dot as /s/. If our understanding of the pattern is correct, there can be little doubt that in this regard the Ashkenazic system better reflects the Tiberian Masoretic system.[2]

A second pattern in Table 5.3 presents itself. Sounds can be divided into two types: **voiced** and **unvoiced**. Voiced sounds are made by bringing the vocal chords close enough together to vibrate when the sound is being made. In the production of unvoiced sounds, the vocal chords are too far apart to vibrate. (You can actually feel your own vocal chords vibrating. If you hold your hand on your throat and say "vvvvvvvvvvvvv" and "fffffffffff" in alternation, you will feel your vocal chords vibrating only for the "v.") In English, *k* and *g*, like *f* and *v*, differ in that the latter consonant in each pair is voiced. The mouth and tongue are in the same configuration for both letters, but only for *g* are the vocal chords vibrating.

The sounds represented by the first three *beged kefet* letters — *bet, gimel,* and *daled* — are voiced, while the next three are their unvoiced counterparts. The letters *bet* and *pe* form a voiced/unvoiced pair, as do *gimel/kaf* and *daled/taf*.

We can use this voice/voiceless observation to help figure out how the Tiberian Masoretes pronounced an undotted *gimel*, a sound represented here as γ. According to the patterns we have seen, we know two things. The sound represented by an undotted *gimel* should be the voiced equivalent of the sound represented by an undotted *kaf*, and should be the fricative corresponding to /g/. To make this sound, either try (as you did with /t/ to get /s/) to say /g/ for a long time, or try to say the *ch* in *Bach* with your vocal chords vibrating. English doesn't have this sound, and so it seems very foreign to English speakers, even more foreign than the (German-sounding) *ch* in *Bach*. But if you are successful, you will end up with a sound that is vaguely like a guttural /r/.

To be fair, the reconstruction of the original Tiberian Masoretic sounds is based in part on the two linguistic patterns just discussed, but those patterns are themselves based in part on the reconstruction of the sounds. However, some of the sounds are known to us, and based on those sounds

---

2. Rabbi Bernard Zlotowitz, who has taught me so much else, has been telling people for years that the Ashkenazic system is more authentic.

that are known, a clear pattern emerges. The pattern may seem arbitrary to those unfamiliar with linguistics, but, in fact, the stop/fricative alternations we see here are among the most common in the world's languages. (Even more common is the voiced/unvoiced alternation.) The alternation is so common that we even see it in English pairs, like *father* and *papa,* which demonstrates the same alternation between /p/ and /f/ that we see with the letter *pe.*

We thus have very good reason to believe we are on the right track.

However, we still have only a rough guess at the exact sounds the Masoretes had in mind. If you pay careful attention, you will notice that even though *p* in English is pronounced by bringing both lips together, *f* (the fricative that corresponds to *p* in English) is made by pressing the top teeth against the lower lip. The two are, thus, not exactly equivalent. (You can make a sound that is almost the same as *f* by saying *p* and separating your lips just a little bit.) What we learn from this is that stop/fricative alternations are sometimes approximated in various languages. It is for this reason that a few options are presented in Table 5.3. In particular, the *daled* without a dot may have been /z/ or /th/ (as in *these*). The *taf* without a dot may have been an /s/, but it also may have been a /th/ (as in *with*).

In the end, though, we can be reasonably certain that we have reconstructed the Tiberian Masoretic pronunciation of the *beged kefet* letters with a high degree of accuracy. This is important not only in understanding how those Masoretes spoke, but because the *beged kefet* alternation will be important in determining if the Tiberian Masoretes correctly recorded the pronunciation of Biblical Hebrew.

More Dots

Surprisingly, the Tiberian Masoretes used a *dagesh,* a dot in a letter, not just to differentiate a stop from a fricative, but for a second purpose as well. Traditionally, this second purpose is called "doubling." Rather than write a letter twice in a row, the letter is written once with a *dagesh* or dot in it. If this doubled letter is one of the *beged kefet* consonants, it is pronounced as a stop. So, for example, it is traditionally assumed that a doubled /v/ was pronounced as a doubled /b/. (Refer to Table 5.3.)

However, there is some disagreement as to how a "doubled" letter was supposed to be pronounced. One traditional understanding is this: (It is important to remember that by "traditional" here we mean the traditional understanding of the Masoretic pronunciation.) A doubled letter is pronounced as a **geminate,** that is, a doubly long sound. This "doubly long sound" can be heard in the (standard American) pronunciation of "hot tea" as compared with "hot 'E.' " For most Americans, these phrases are pronounced as one word, but in "hot tea" the /t/ lasts longer. This is a geminate /t/. Some languages — such as Italian or Arabic — have lots of geminates in their words, and others, like English, have few or none. However, the theory that "doubled" letters in Masoretic Hebrew (letters with a *dagesh*, where the *dagesh* indicates that the letter is doubled) were pronounced as geminates is based on little evidence.

Furthermore, a modern linguistic understanding of Tiberian Masoretic Hebrew, while supporting the view that the dot represented a double letter, suggests that the doubled letter was not pronounced any differently than a single letter. (By comparison, consider that English doubled letters are not pronounced any differently than undoubled letters. For example, the double *t* in *attention* is not geminate.)

So while we can accept the theory that the dot has two purposes (doubling a letter and marking a stop versus a fricative) we are left with two questions: How were the doubled letters pronounced? And why did the Tiberian Masoretes use the same symbol for these two seemingly unrelated purposes?

The answer to the first is almost certainly that the doubled letters were not pronounced any differently than non-doubled letters, modern Jewish tradition notwithstanding.

Regarding the second question, we note that modern linguistics attests to a connection between doubling and stops. While the exact connection is complicated and only partially understood, the two phenomena are obviously related, and so the use of a single symbol for them both is not as arbitrary as it might seem. Without knowing the details of how Masoretic Hebrew was pronounced we cannot know for sure, but one likely possibility is that doubled fricatives became stops.

Babylonia

In addition to the Tiberian Masoretic system of vowels, two other, lesser-known systems, have been preserved. The first of these is the Babylonian system.

The Vowels

It turns out that there are actually two Babylonian systems, a "simple" and a "complex." Because the "simple" is the closer parallel to the Tiberian system, we will only look at that one here. The "complex" system, in addition to the distinctions made in the "simple" system, marks aspects

Table 5.4. Vowels used by the Babylonian Masoretes

Mark	Tiberian equivalent
אַ	אַ אָ
אׅ	אָ
אֺ	אֶ
אֵ	אֶ
אֵ	אֵ
אֵ	אֶ

of Hebrew grammar that are not discussed in this book. Table 5.4 lists the basic Babylonian vowel marks and their Tiberian equivalents.

One of the important facts about the Babylonian system is that it employs but one sign for the Tiberian *patach* and *segol*. Let's look at an example.

The Biblical Hebrew word for "king" is spelled *mem, lamed, kaf* (מלך), while the word for "my king" adds a *yud* at the end: *mem, lamed, kaf, yud* (מלכי). The modern pronunciations of those words are /melex/ and /malki/, in accordance with the Tiberian Hebrew representation of those words: מֶלֶךְ and מַלְכִּי. In this pair, as in many other words, the Tiberian system shows a change from /e/ to /a/ for the first vowel when the suffix "-i" is added to indicate possession. (The words that undergo this change are called **segolates,** reflecting the final *segol* vowel in the unsuffixed form.)

The vowel shift from /a/ to /e/ is typically attributed to very ancient Hebrew patterns, going back to the days before Hebrew was written at all. (The change from /x/ to /k/ is based on similarly complicated rules, and involves the *beged kefet* distinctions discussed above.)

By contrast, the Babylonian representations for "king" and "my king," while still using the Biblical Hebrew consonants מלך and מלכי, do not indicate any shift in vowel sound. Both words start with the same sounds /mal-/ according to the Babylonian Masoretes.

Because most people are so much more familiar with the Tiberian system (which is used in modern versions of the Jewish Bible, traditional Jewish prayers, and in the modern state of Israel), we are tempted to ask why the Babylonians got it wrong, or why the Babylonians failed or didn't bother to distinguish between these two important sounds. But we have not seen any scientific reason to suppose that the Tiberians got it right and the Babylonians got it wrong. An equally valid (or invalid) question is why the Tiberians invented a distinction that the Babylonians did not.

Therefore, a more reasonable question is why two traditions of the same Hebrew surfaced, and whether, in fact, one of them is more accurate than the other, that is, whether one of them more accurately reflects Biblical Hebrew as it was pronounced. We will turn to this latter question later. (In particular, the discussion of "segolate nouns" starting on page 111 adds some important data from several hundred years before the Masoretes did their work.)

As to the first question, of course, the Babylonians were living in Babylonia and the Tiberians in Tiberias. We know that they spoke different dialects of Hebrew, based on their other writings. We also know that it is not uncommon for different people in different places to speak different dialects of the same language. The pronunciation of English as spoken in the United States differs greatly from the North to the South, for example. We therefore might assume that the differences in the Babylonian and Tiberian vowel systems reflect the different ways Hebrew was spoken by the Jews in Babylonia and Tiberias. This is probably part of the answer.

The other part of the answer is more complicated. We will see below that the Tiberians were almost certainly doing more than just recording their own speech; they were making decisions about how they believed Hebrew ought to be pronounced. Whether or not the Babylonians were also recording more than their own speech, too, the differences between these two systems might reflect not only differences in how the two groups spoke, but also differences both in how they reconstructed ancient Hebrew and in how they decided Hebrew ought to be pronounced.

The Shewa

Babylonian Masoretic Hebrew has a symbol corresponding to the Tiberian *shewa*. But in the "simple" system it is only used for what is traditionally called the (Tiberian) vocal *shewa*. (Compare the discussion above on page 54.) The equivalent of the "silent" *shewa* is not marked.

In discussing the "silent" and "vocal" *shewa*, we noted that there is little reason to believe that more than one kind of *shewa* actually existed. Here we have what may look like a very good reason to think there were two different kinds of *shewa*s: Of the two, the Babylonian Masoretes only marked one in their simple vocalization system.

One possibility, of course, is that even though it was based on sound evidence, our conclusion that only one *shewa* exists is wrong.

Another possibility, though, is more likely. Of the two purported types of *shewa*, the Babylonian system marks the one that is used in contradistinction to a vowel. Remember that in Tiberian Masoretic Hebrew, a *shewa* is called "vocal" if there is a vowel in a more basic form of the word, that is, where it seems as though a vowel in one form of a word becomes silent in another as the word is changed. It is precisely in this case that someone who knew Hebrew might need to be reminded that the vowel is no longer pronounced.

For example, the word for "he wrote" is /katav/. The feminine past-tense verbal ending in Hebrew is "-a," and so one might expect the word for "she wrote" to be /katava/. However, the form the Masoretes recorded is /kat'va/, where the apostrophe represents a *shewa*. This is the kind of *shewa* that even the Babylonian simple system recorded. We do not need to assume that the vocal *shewa* was pronounced to understand why the Babylonians recorded it. Rather, we can assume that they recorded this type of *shewa* to indicate "you might think there is a vowel here but there is not."

Similarly, when the plural ending "-tem" is added to "katav" to yield /k'tav'tem/ — "you wrote" — the Tiberian Masoretes put a *shewa* where each apostrophe appears. But the Babylonian simple system only records a *shewa* in the first case ("k'tavtem"). The word comes from "katav," and there used to be a vowel where the first apostrophe appears, so one might have thought that the word was "katavtem." A symbol was used to make sure people did not make that mistake. But there was no reason to think a vowel may have appeared after the "v" and before the "t," so the Babylonian simple system saw no need for a "no vowel goes here" symbol.

In this context, it is worth noting that modern Israeli Hebrew, while generally written without vowels, does put a *shewa* in every so often, precisely to indicate "you might think there is a vowel here but there is not."

This view — that the Babylonian system used a *shewa* to indicate "don't make the mistake of putting a vowel here" while the Tiberians used a *shewa* for the broader purpose of indicating "there is no vowel here" — is entirely consistent with everything we know about the Tiberian and Babylonian Masoretic systems. It also suggests that the Babylonian Masoretes, at least, and maybe the Tiberian Masoretes as well, were still speaking some form of Hebrew. How else, one wonders, would they expect people to be familiar enough with Hebrew to know some of the vowels but not all?

Finally, regarding the *shewa*, the complex Babylonian system uses the same symbol for "vocal" and "silent" *shewa*. Even without the other arguments against two types of *shewa*, it is unlikely that two groups working independently (one in Tiberias, one in Babylonia), each using a different set of symbols, and each representing different pronunciations for Hebrew, would both choose to introduce ambiguity into their system by using one symbol to represent both a vowel and the lack of a vowel. We once again come to the conclusion that there is but one kind of *shewa*.

Other Differences

The Babylonian vowel system differs from the Tiberian one in other ways as well. There is no *chataf-kamatz*, for example. The guttural letters are handled differently. Other minor differences that can be understood only in the context of a more detailed treatment of the details of Masoretic Hebrew abound.

Once again, this should not be understood to mean that the Babylonians had a wrong understanding of Hebrew. Rather, it should reinforce the point that the Tiberian understanding of Hebrew — the one we currently use by default — is but one of many interpretations from a millennium ago.

We turn next to a third interpretation, from "the Land of Israel."

The Land of Israel

The third Masoretic system we will look at is called "the Land of Israel" (or, sometimes, "Palestinian"). This appellation refers to a unique vowel system, different from both the Babylonian system and the Tiberian system (even though Tiberias is in the Land of Israel). It gets its name from a reference in an 11th (or perhaps 12th) century prayerbook and manual of custom known as Machzor Vitry, which refers to the pointing of *eretz yis'rael*, that is, "the Land of Israel." (Machzor Vitry gets its name from the city of Vitry — in modern-day France — in which its author, Simcha of Vitry, lived.)

In one regard, this pointing system matches the Tiberian system more closely than the Babylonian system: it has separate symbols for *segol* and *patach*. However, its use of *patach* and *kamatz* does not always match the Tiberian system; nor does its use of *tzere* and *segol*. Many manuscripts use but one sign for each pair. Additionally, some manuscripts pointed in the Land of Israel system contain the same symbol for *tzere* and *shewa*.

While there is good reason — based on physical distance — to assume that different dialects of Hebrew were spoken in Tiberias and Babylonia, it is harder to understand how two radically different dialects could have been spoken in Israel.

Various attempts to reconcile the differences have been proposed, none of them entirely convincing. Some assume that the "Land of Israel" Masoretes were simply careless or ignorant. Some of the attempts fall back to the God Theory, and assume that the Tiberian system is "right," wondering why the Land of Israel system got Hebrew "wrong."

Once again, the most plausible explanation of the various Land of Israel systems is that the Masoretes working in this system were trying to do more than simply record their own Hebrew pronunciation. They were trying to record a more ancient pronunciation of Hebrew. We thus add this to the growing list of evidence that the goal of the Masoretes was to reconstruct history.

It is worth pointing out that two pairs of interchanged signs (*kamatz/patach* and *tzere/segol*) are exactly the ones that are pronounced identically in modern Israeli Hebrew. It is not clear what to make of this fact, but surely it is not coincidence. Regarding the *kamatz/patach* and *tzere/segol* alternations, if we assume that there are seven vowel symbols in Tiberian Hebrew (and ignore the *chataf* variants and the *shewa*), there are 105 ways of choosing two pairs of symbols.[3] It is ridiculous to believe that of those 105 possibilities, the pointing system of the Land of Israel randomly chose the exact same one that surfaced in modern Israel, particularly in light of the fact that the modern Israeli system came about not by conscious design, but was the most natural way for Israelis to speak their language. Why did the Land of Israel system end up with the same pairs that modern Israelis did?

We can use the modern data to conclude that these pairs of vowels are more closely related than other pairs, and therefore conclude that the Land of Israel Masoretes spoke Hebrew, and, in particular, a dialect similar in at least some respects to the Hebrew of the modern state of Israel. We thus conclude that these Masoretes were both recording their spoken language and trying to capture a more ancient dialect of Hebrew.

Most people believe that the Land of Israel system is the earliest system, though, of course, disagreement is not hard to find. And, as we see next, the systems did not evolve in complete isolation.

Other Systems

So far, we have seen three different groups of Masoretes, living in Tiberias, Babylonia, and "the Land of Israel," all of whom created a system of dots and other marks — "diacritics" — to indicate Hebrew pronunciation.

At least three other systems can be identified, in addition to variations within each system.

---

3. The number of pairs among n elements is equal to $(n - 1)n/2$. There are thus $6 \times 7/2 = 42/2 = 21$ pairs of Tiberian vowels. After taking out the first pair, there are $20/2 = 10$ pairs remaining. There are $10 \times 21 = 210$ ways of choosing one pair and then another. Because we don't care which pair comes first, there are 105 total sets of two pairs.

Some manuscripts are pointed with what looks like the Land of Israel system written with Tiberian symbols. This is a fourth tradition. Yemen had its own pointing system, bringing the count to five. And from East Syriac grammarians we have a sixth system.

In terms of variations within each system, we have records of two different Tiberian families (ben-Asher and ben-Naftali) and their differences. Even within the ben-Asher family we see considerable variation.

The Babylonian system had at least two major variants, the simple and the complex. Beyond these two major strands, researchers have identified at least six different Babylonian styles, dating from various periods.

The Palestinian ("Land of Israel") system, likewise, shows evidence of considerable internal variation.

In short, without diminishing the degree to which the Tiberian, Palestinian, and Babylonian Masoretes were separated geographically (and, incidentally, politically and culturally), we must not assume that there were only three, or even only six, distinct Masoretic theories about how to record Hebrew. Rather, we seem to find many groups throughout the Jewish world all working to record an official version of Scripture.

The enormous energy they devoted to this task brings us to our next major question: "What were the Masoretes doing?"

What Were the Masoretes Doing?

The various Masoretic groups invested unbelievable energy in their endeavors. Not only did the different groups each invent a set of symbols to record the sounds (as discussed extensively above) and the grammar of Hebrew, they painstakingly copied and corrected manuscripts, and then compiled lists of how the various manuscripts differed one from the other.

The Hebrew Bible contains roughly half a million words. The energy required to copy a work of this size by hand even once is almost beyond comprehension, all the more so when the complexity of Masoretic Hebrew writing is taken into account. Consider, for example, just the first word of the Bible as written in the Leningrad Codex, a Masoretic manuscript, described on page 76 below. The first word is *b'reshit*, "In the beginning." (A digitally enhanced photograph of the word *b'reshit* from that manuscript appears in Figure 5.1.) In addition to the six letters required to write the word, the Masoretes included three vowel symbols below the letters, to indicate the vowels that accompany the consonants they had written; a dot in the first letter to distinguish the *bet* from a *vet*; a dot above the right stem of the *shin*, to distinguish it from a *sin*; a *rafeh* (horizontal line — see the discussion on page 57) over the *aleph* and *taf*, to indicate that

Figure 5.1. The word *b'reshit* from the Leningrad Codex.

the *aleph* is not pronounced and that the *taf* does not have a *dagesh*; and finally a trope symbol under the *shin* to indicate where the stress falls on the word, how the word is sung, and the syntactic role the word has in the sentence. In other words, to write just the first word fourteen symbols of four different sorts are required. The words were written by hand in permanent ink, in columns, with both right and left justification. Yet the accuracy and consistency of many Masoretic manuscripts competes admirably with the accuracy of today's documents that take full advantage of modern technology.

So there can be no doubt that the Masoretes considered their task hugely important and devoted enormous amounts of energy to it. But two questions still remain: First: What did the Masoretes try to do? And second: Were the Masoretes successful, or did they actually do something else?

We turn to these questions next.

What Did the Masoretes Try to Do?

Two main possible Masoretic goals present themselves:

1. preserving the ancient pronunciation and understanding of the Bible.
2. establishing a standard pronunciation and understanding of the Bible.

We group pronunciation and understanding together not only because the pronunciation of the words affects their meaning sometimes, but because the trope system was used, in part, to show how the words of a sentence came together to form a meaning: the trope marks were an indication of where stress falls in a word, how the word is sung in religious contexts, and the syntactic role the word plays in a sentence.

To the extent that the Masoretes tried to rely on the first goal listed above in achieving the second, the two goals overlap. It is perfectly possible to try to use ancient patterns to establish modern norms. But while we have considerable evidence that both of these goals were important to the Masoretes, we have little information about how they may have balanced the two when they conflicted.

Furthermore, because the Masoretes were working in a religious framework, they may not have had a clear notion of historical accuracy. Also, they may have tried to preserve "traditional" pronunciations and understandings instead of ancient ones, perhaps not realizing that there might be a difference, or perhaps not caring about the latter. Beyond these two main goals, we might consider other, more subtle, possibilities, such as the extent to which the Masoretes were influenced by Arabists working at the same time who were doing for Arab texts what the Masoretes were doing for Jewish texts.

In the end, though, all we really need to know is that the Masoretes were not trying to perpetuate a fraud. The only reason we even consider (and reject) that possibility is the substantial mystery about the documents the Masoretes were presumably working from. While many Masoretic manuscripts have survived to this day, the original (pre-Masoretic) manuscripts have not. What happened to all of the documents that the Masoretes were presumably copying? Two conceivable answers to the lack of any substantial pre-Masoretic documents that the Masoretes may have used are that the Masoretes destroyed them or that they never existed. Either answer would suggest that the Masoretic work is fraudulent.

By comparison, we imagine a photographer proudly publishing a photograph of a very ancient, valuable, and holy manuscript he had just found. If it turned out that in spite of its greatness, the original no longer existed, the photograph would certainly be suspect. Similarly, we have Masoretes annotating versions of what were, presumably, ancient, valuable, and holy manuscripts, but we do not have the original manuscripts. It is cause for concern.

But the excruciating detail we find in Masoretic works and the existence of several Masoretic groups, in particular the existence of various schools of thought within those groups, all combine to make the possibility of actual fraud very low. The mystery of the missing documents from which the Masoretes were working remains unsolved, to be revisited in Chapter 8, but we are on solid ground when we assume that the Masoretes' goals were some combination of preserving the text of antiquity and standardizing the text of their day.

What Did the Masoretes Really Do?

For our purposes, of course, preserving antiquity and creating a new standard text are not at all the same thing. We want to know how much of antiquity is preserved is the Masoretes' work. Because the Tiberian Masoretic tradition has become so well known, preserved in modern religious and scientific versions of "the Bible," we will focus on the question of how much of antiquity was preserved by the Tiberian Masoretes. And for convenience we will use the more general "Masoretes" here to mean "the Tiberian Masoretes," or, even more precisely, "the Tiberian Masoretes whose work ended up being canonized in the Bible as we now know it."

Parts of Chapters 7 and 8 will consider external and internal textual evidence that help us answer that question. Chapter 6 specifically addresses the extent to which the Masoretes accurately captured the ancient sounds of Hebrew.

The aspects of the Masoretic system that do not reflect antiquity might have a variety of sources, ranging from the Masoretes' own pronunciation of Hebrew to changes in Hebrew that occurred long after the Bible was canonized but before the Masoretes undertook their work.

By and large, we suspect that the Masoretes captured their own way of speaking rather than anything particularly ancient. This conclusion, while tentative, is based on the differences we see in the various Masoretic systems as well as on the linguistic fact that untrained people cannot generally reproduce foreign accents especially well. A modern example of this difficulty is reflected in the variations seen in transliterating Hebrew in various Jewish communities. While all of the transliterations share common features, they also tend to reflect the languages spoken by the people who created the transliterations.

However, we will also see one detail of the Masoretic system that the Masoretes almost certainly invented. The fact that we can show that the Masoretes actually invented part of their system, rather than preserving something ancient or even preserving something in their own versions of Hebrew, opens the door to the troubling possibility that they invented much more.

What the Tiberian Masoretes Invented

The Masoretic system includes a complex interaction between the *beged kefet* letters and the trope system. We have already seen that the *beged kefet* rules are complicated. The trope system is much more complicated.

But here we will review some relevant details of the exceedingly complex trope system as well as relevant details of the *beged kefet* system, and show that the interaction of the two could not have represented any spoken language. We thus conclude that at least this tiny aspect of the Tiberian Masoretic system not only was not representative of any ancient dialect of Hebrew, but was also not representative of any language spoken or heard by the Masoretes. The Masoretes invented this aspect of Hebrew.

Even the simplified discussion that follows is somewhat complex, but it is worth working through to understand how we know that the Masoretes invented one aspect of the Hebrew system that they have given us.

Beged Kefet   We have already seen the letters that alternate between stops and fricatives (the *beged kefet* letters) and how the Masoretes used a dot (*dagesh*) in them or a line (*rafeh*) over them to show whether they were to be pronounced as stops or as fricatives. The Masoretic rules for when these letters are stops and when they are fricatives are quite complicated, but one aspect can be simplified: **A *beged kefet* letter is a fricative only when it follows a vowel; otherwise it is a stop.**

The application of this stop / fricative rule is complex because it interacts significantly both with rules about double letters (which are also indicated with a *dagesh*) and with rules about the *shewa*, so the reader should not be surprised to see many *beged kefet* letters pronounced as stops even after vowels, in apparent violation of that rule, as well as many *beged kefet* letters pronounced as fricatives after a *shewa*, also in apparent violation of the rule. But we will focus on applications of this rule that are not so involved.

The first letter of a word cannot come after a vowel, precisely because it is the first letter. It follows that when the first letter of a word is a *beged kefet* letter, it must take a *dagesh* and be pronounced as a stop, not as a fricative. In general this is true in Masoretic Hebrew, and people who study Hebrew even memorize a mnemonic to this effect: *beged kefet b'rosh milah* ("*beged kefet* at the beginning of a word [gets a *dagesh*]").

However, there is one significant class of situations in which the first letter of a word, even though it's a *beged kefet* letter, does not take a *dagesh*. **A word following a word that ends in a vowel may lose its word-initial dagesh.** That is, sometimes the final vowel of one word influences the initial *beged kefet* letter of the next word. For example, the word for "morning" in Hebrew is *boker* בֹּקֶר. It is not *voker* because the *bet* at the beginning of the word must take a *dagesh*. However, in Genesis, for "there was evening, there was morning," the Masoretes give us precisely the word *voker*, in which the *bet* has become a *vet*, because the word for "there was" that precedes "morning" is *vay'hi* וַיְהִי and that word ends in a vowel. (In many Masoretic manuscripts, but only rarely in modern printed versions of Genesis, the *vet* is further marked with a *rafeh* to emphasize that it is a fricative and not a stop.)

We should not be surprised to see that one word can influence the word it follows, for this is a common occurrence in many languages. We already saw, for example, how the *t* and *y* in "I'll bet you" interact, even though they are not part of the same word.

However, we only see this cross-word *beged kefet* / vowel interaction sometimes in Hebrew. It is the distribution of this interaction that is artificial, as we will see presently.

Trope   The trope system is exceedingly complicated, so we will look at a simplification of it here, focusing only on the details that we need to understand how the trope system and *beged kefet* system interact.

In addition to its other purposes, the trope system serves to show which words form syntactic units.

One of the phenomena confirmed by modern linguistics is that words in a phrase naturally form subunits. For example, in the sentence "The book is on the table," we find that the two words "The book" form a unit in a way that "book is" do not. Similarly, the pair "the table" comprises a unit. Furthermore, "on the table" is a unit in a way that neither "is on the" nor "book is on" is. It is sometimes difficult for non-linguists to know which words form units. (For example, should "is" be placed with "The book" to form "The book is" as a unit, or should it be placed with "on the table" so that "is on the table" is a unit?) But there is generally only one right answer, in that the grouping of words seems to reflect very basic and universal qualities in human language. (In our example, "is on the table" forms a unit.)

One issue in discussing these groupings and subgroupings is how to represent the structure that results. One common (modern) way of showing the structure is with square braces. So we might write:

$$\left[\left[\text{the book}\right]\left[\text{is}\left[\text{on}\left[\text{the table}\right]\right]\right]\right]$$

which shows how all of the units and subunits come together. Of course, we needn't use differently sized braces. This:

[[the book][is[on[the table]]]]

shows the same thing. It's just harder to read.

Another common way of showing how different parts of the sentence relate to each other is a "syntactic tree," and it is not hard to conceive of other possible (though probably undesirable) mechanisms for indicating which words go together. For example:

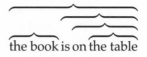

the book is on the table

is almost the same as a tree, and gives us the same basic information. One final example:

$$\text{THE}_1 \ \text{BOOK}_1 \ \text{IS}_{2a} \ \text{ON}_{2b\alpha} \ \text{THE}_{2b\beta} \ \text{TABLE}_{2b\beta}$$

uses subscripts to show what belongs with what. Words with the same subscript elements all go together. So everything with a subscript "1" forms a group ("the book"), everything with a subscript "b" forms a group ("on the table"), everything with a subscript *beta* forms a group ("the table"), etc.

Although this aspect of trope is seldom emphasized, **the trope system is another way of indicating the groupings.** The Masoretes managed to devise a set of symbols that indicates all of the complicated information that we have indicated variously with braces, brackets, or subscripts.

The details of exactly how the trope system manages to convey this complicated information are, of course, exceedingly complicated themselves. But a few details will suffice for our current discussion. The Masoretes broke passages down into successively smaller groups by means of the trope symbols, putting various trope symbols on words to indicate where group divisions took place.

The Masoretes used two different kinds of symbols, one (generally) inside a group that had more than two words, and the other (generally) inside a group that had only two words in it. The symbols that are used inside groups that have more than two words are called either "lords" or "disjunctive tropes" and those used inside two-word groups are called either "servants" or "conjunctive tropes," but the common terms "disjunctive" and "conjunctive" are misleading, in that they wrongly suggest that the purpose of one kind of symbol was to disjoin ("move apart") and the other was to conjoin ("move together"). Rather, they were simply two kinds of trope symbols, just as, in our English example above, numbers, Latin letters, and Greek letters were the devices we employed to show structure.

Had the Masoretes used their system on the English example above ("The book is on the table"), they would have used a disjunctive trope symbol on "on," because it is the first word in a group that has more than two words, but a conjunctive trope symbol on both instances of "the," because both times "the" occurs in a group of only two words.

The final complication is that what counted as a "word" to the Masoretes depended on what was written as a word. Various "words" such as "and," "to," "in," "the," etc., are always written as prefixes in Hebrew, never by themselves, and the object of a verb can be written as a suffix. So, for example, the word *v'ra'ahu* ויראהו, "and he saw him," only counts as one word for the purposes of the Masoretic system, in particular, for the purpose of deciding between a conjunctive and disjunctive trope.

Furthermore, hyphenated words count as only one word. The issue of hyphenation in the Masoretic system is not fully understood, in that it is not clear why some words get a hyphen between them and some do not, but once two words are joined with a hyphen, they count as only one word for the Masoretic purpose of deciding between a conjunctive and disjunctive trope.

Beged Kefet and Trope   Finally, with all of this background, we can turn to the main point: When a word ends with a vowel and is **marked with a conjunctive trope,** it affects the *beged kefet* letter that starts the next word. When a word ends with a vowel and is **marked with a disjunctive trope,** it does *not* affect the *beged kefet* letter that starts the next word. In other words, if two words (say, "Word A" and "Word B") appear in a row, a vowel at the end of the Word A will only affect a *beged kefet* letter at the beginning of Word B only if Word A has a conjunctive trope.

It is this aspect of the interaction between the *beged kefet* system and the trope system that cannot represent a natural language. This interaction must be artificial because it is an interaction not between the pronunciation of the sentence and its structure, but rather an interaction between the pronunciation of the sentence and the way the Masoretes chose to represent the structure. We saw above that the same structure can be respresented in a variety of ways, each way using its own symbols. We do not expect to see linguistic phenomena tied to symbols that represent arbitrary symbolic choices of the system of notation, and not of the language they are trying to capture. It would be as though words marked with a *beta* in one of the examples above received special treatment.

Two examples from Judges demonstrate. The first phrase comes from Judges 1:1 and the second from Judges 1:8. The relevant parts of the verses are listed here, using English words for the Hebrew. Dots in English connect words that are written as one word in Hebrew, and hyphens in English represent hyphens in Hebrew:

וַיִּשְׁאֲלוּ בְּנֵי יִשְׂרָאֵל

1:1 and.inquired children.of Israel ("[It was after the death of Joshua] **and the children of Israel inquired** [of Adonai] ... ")

וַיִּלָּחֲמוּ בְנֵי-יְהוּדָה

1:8 and.fought children.of-Judah ("**And the children of Judah fought** [in Jerusalem] ... ")

Three general grammatical points are in order. First, in Hebrew, the verb usually comes before the subject, so "inquired children of Israel" means "The children of Israel inquired." "Fought children of Judah" means "the children of Judah fought." Second, in the construction "children of ... " the word "of" is implied by the Hebrew form of the word "children." (This construction is explained in more detail, in a different context, starting on page 140.) Third, the word "the" is implied by the "of-" form of the word coming before a name.

The two phrases have exactly the same syntactic structure, namely, a verb followed by a two-word subject. The two words in the subject form a group, which then joins the verb to form a larger group: [inquired [children [of Israel]]] and [fought [children [of Judah]]].

For reasons we do not know, only in the second example is the phrase "children of" followed by a hyphen. Because the two words thus joined by a hyphen count as only one word for the Masoretic purposes of counting the words in a group, the phrase "fought children of Judah" ends up being only two words, while the phrase "fought children of Israel" is three. Therefore, the word for "fought" gets a disjunctive trope in one place and a conjunctive trope in the other. It is important to realize that this choice of disjunctive versus conjunctive trope on the verb has nothing to do with the relationship of the verb to the words in the subject that follow. It is only a reflex of the particular way in which the Masoretes chose to write those words.

However, it just so happens that both of these plural verbs end in a vowel (as is usually the case in Hebrew), and the word for "children" starts with a *beged kefet* letter, namely, *bet*. Therefore, the *bet* in Judges 1:1 keeps its *dagesh*, because it comes after a disjunctive trope; by contrast, the *bet* in Judges 1:8 loses its *dagesh*, because it comes after a conjunctive trope.

What we see, then, is that the word "children" is pronounced differently, once starting with a stop and once starting with a fricative, only because of the way the Masoretes chose to record the structure of the sentences. While the examples in Judges are convenient because they are so close together (which means they were probably written by a single author) and so close in their grammatical structure, the phenomenon they exemplify is very widespread through the Masoretic text.

But this phenomenon cannot reflect any real ancient pronunciation scheme, nor the Masoretes' own dialect of Hebrew. Language does not work that way.

The Masoretes must have invented the interaction between the trope system and the *beged kefet* letters.

Conclusions

While the detailed example above involves only one aspect of the Masoretic system, it is a troubling one. If the Masoretes were really only trying to preserve ancient pronunciation and structure, we would not expect to find any such examples. Even if the Masoretes mistook their own dialect of Hebrew for an older one, we could not account for the pattern we see. We must therefore conclude that the Masoretes had at least two goals: preserving antiquity and establishing a standard.

While some of what the Masoretes gave us may represent older Hebrew, we cannot simply rely on Masoretic Hebrew to give us an indication of what older Hebrew was like.

In the next few chapters, we will try to evaluate the extent to which various aspects of the Masoretic record reflect older Hebrew, and we will try to learn what we can about older Hebrew without relying on the Masoretic record. Before we turn to that, let's look at some of the evidence used in understanding the Masoretes themselves.

How Do We Know?

We have many ways of knowing about the work of the Masoretes, including the work they have left us and descriptions of their work. The two most important original works that have survived are the Leningrad Codex and the Aleppo Codex, as described next, along with some minor manuscripts and external descriptions.

The Leningrad Codex

The Leningrad Codex (also called "Codex Leningradensis" by those who prefer Latin) dates from roughly 1009 C.E.

A prologue dates the manuscript according to five different reckonings: the traditional Jewish year (4770), years since King Johoiakin's exile (1444), years since the reign of the Greeks (1319), years since the Second Temple's destruction (940), and the traditional Muslim Hijrah year (399), that is, years since Mohammad's flight from Mecca in 622 C.E. Alas, the dates do not entirely agree, representing (except for the date since Johoiakin's exile) variously 1008 C.E., 1009 C.E., or 1010 C.E. The careful reader will note that 399 years of Hijrah seems to correspond to 1021, because 622 + 399 = 1021, but because the Hijrah uses a purely lunar calendar, its years progress more rapidly than our solar years or the Jewish lunar-solar years. Johoiakin was exiled in 597 B.C.E., or roughly 1,607 years before the document was probably written, not 1,444 years; the 163-year difference may be the result of an arithmetic error or misunderstanding of history on the part of the original author, or the result of a misunderstanding of the text on our part.

The Leningrad Codex represents the oldest surviving complete copy of the Hebrew Bible. The original codex is housed in the Russian National Library, and facsimile editions are widely available.

In addition to being the oldest extant complete copy of the Hebrew Bible, the Leningrad Codex is important for two reasons.

First, the Leningrad Codex is the basis for the official Jewish version of the Bible: Modern computer and printed versions of the Hebrew Bible try to match the Hebrew in the Leningrad Codex. Because of its religious authority, this is the version most people are familiar with, and this is what many people think of when they think of "the Hebrew Bible." (However, for many years a printed version from 1524/25 C.E., called the "Venice Edition" or "Second Rabbinic Bible," was considered the most authentic. Religious texts preferring the Venice Edition over the Leningrad Codex are still in widespread use.)

Secondly, this is the oldest complete Masoretic manuscript, containing every word of the Hebrew Bible.

Of course, from a scientific point of view, the version in the Leningrad Codex is only one version among many. We will see that much older historical evidence confirms the accuracy of much of the text contained in the Leningrad Codex, but also clearly contradicts some of it.

Surprisingly, the order of the later books in the Leningrad Codex does not match the order listed in the Babylonian Talmud, preferring instead an order based on (the author's understanding of?) the chronological order of the original books: Chronicles, Psalms, Job, Proverbs, Ruth, Song of Songs, Ecclesiastes, Lamentation, Esther, Daniel, Ezra-Nehemiah. This is one aspect of the codex that modern religious publications do not copy. (The Aleppo Codex, as described next, seems to agree with the order set out in the Leningrad Codex.)

The Aleppo Codex

The Aleppo Codex dates from the first third of the 10th century C.E. Like the Leningrad Codex, its prologue may have contained date information, but the prologue has been lost over time. Numerous copies and reports about the prologue have survived, so that it has been possible to reconstruct what the prologue may have been, but opinion is divided as to the authenticity of the prologue based only on copies and reconstructions. Most scholars, however, agree that the prologue is authentic.

The name of the codex derives from the city of Aleppo in Syria, where the document was kept from the Middle Ages until 1948, when riots against the Jews erupted. By the end of the violence, only 294 (of a probable 380) original pages remained. Almost the entire Torah has been lost, along with portions of the Prophets and the end of Writings. Any non-Biblical notes at the beginning or end of the original have also been destroyed.

So far as we can tell, the Aleppo Codex adheres to the same ordering of books as the Leningrad Codex, though, of course, it is possible that the destroyed books were in a different order.

The Aleppo Codex ought to be considered a better representation of the ben-Asher Masoretic school than the Leningrad Codex, but political and practical matters have combined to give the latter preeminence.

The Aleppo Codex contains a few features that were never fully accepted into the Tiberian (and, hence, mainstream Jewish) understanding of Hebrew, among them *chataf-chiriq* vowels (Table 5.1) and other *chataf* vowels where they now cannot appear.

Other Manuscripts

In addition to the Aleppo and Leningrad Codices, a manuscript from roughly 930 C.E. (Codex 17 of the Second Firkowitz collection, kept in the Leningrad Public Library), bears a prologue in which the scribe claims to be Shlomo ha-Levi, son of Buya'a. (Shlomo ben Buy'a — "ben" means "son of" — is also credited with the Aleppo Codex.) His brother, "Ephraim, son of Rabbi Buya'a," takes credit for adding the vowels and other Masoretic notes.

A document called "British Museum Codex Or. 4445," probably also from the beginning of the 10th century C.E., was written by two people, one who seemed to prefer the ben-Asher readings (as in Aleppo and Leningrad), and one who preferred ben-Naftali readings.

An earlier version, dated in a prologue as "year 827 after the destruction of the Second Temple [in 72 C.E.]" (that is, 899 C.E.) and known as the "Cairo Codex," bears even more resemblance to the ben-Naftali system, but contains only the Prophets. (Confusingly, the Leningrad Codex is also sometimes called the "Cairo Codex.")

Descriptions of the Manuscripts

Beyond the manuscripts themselves, a handful of descriptions of Masoretic work have survived.

Probably in the 11th or 12th century, a man named Mishael ben Uzziel wrote an Arabic treatise called *Kitab al-Hulaf* ("Book of Variants," later published in Hebrew as *Sefer ha-Hilufim*) in which he set out to detail the differences between the ben-Asher and ben-Naftali systems. In so doing, he also pointed out instances where both ben-Asher and ben-Naftali agreed against other Masoretes. Most of the differences are minor, relating to such technical matters as how to prefix some prepositions to words that begin with the letter *yud* pointed with a *chiriq*. (Ben-Naftali says the vowel under the prefix should be a *chiriq* and the *yud* should get no vowel, while ben-Asher says the prefix should get a *shewa* while the *yud* should keep its *chiriq*. One result is that "to Israel" in the ben-Naftali system was pronounced something like "lis-ra-el" while in the ben-Asher system it was pronounced "l'-yis-ra-el.") Some 200 trope symbols are listed as differing. A handful of times actual consonantal differences are listed, such as the presence or absence of the word "and" (-ו). And so forth.

Scholars generally agree that the accuracy of the Book of Variants falls short of the accuracy of the manuscripts it describes, but nonetheless the book offers insight into manuscripts that no longer exist. To date, no manuscript that completely adheres to either the ben-Asher or the ben-Naftali school, as listed in the Book of Variants, has been found, but Aleppo comes very close (on the order of 94%) to matching all of the details listed for ben-Asher; Leningrad comes almost as close (92%). Because the 6% or 8% falls within the plausible margin of error for the Book of Variants itself, either manuscript may actually match the ben-Asher school exactly. (Nonetheless, scholars generally assume that the Aleppo Codex comes closer.)

A collection of Masoretic rules called *dik'duke ha-t'amim* ("Grammars of the [cantillation or vowel] Symbols") exists in two modern forms, published in 1879 and 1967. The collection, taken from Masoretic rules that were included in various texts (including the Leningrad Codex), gives rules for adding vowels to words, pronunciation hints, and other insights into the goals of the Tiberian Masoretes.

Another list purports to detail some 250 differences between the "East-erners" and the "Westerners." (This list, too, is contained in the Leningrad Codex.) Because the list only concerns consonants, it is probably older than the other ones.

All of these various documents combine to give us a very good picture of what Masoretic Hebrew was like. Unlike the challenge faced with other dialects of Hebrew, where we must wonder which documents authentically reflect antiquity, we can clearly trace the history of Hebrew back to the Masoretes. This was, of course, the reason we started with the Masoretes in the first place.

We will turn next to the question of how closely Masoretic Hebrew matches older Hebrew.

Chapter 6
Pronunciation

Take care of the sense and the sounds will
take care of themselves.
— Lewis Carroll, 1865

We saw in Chapter 5 that several versions of Hebrew — collectively called "Masoretic" Hebrew — were floating around in the 10th century C.E. As part of the more general question of what Biblical Hebrew sounded like, we turn now to the question of which of those Masoretic versions, if any, reflect the pronunciation of Biblical Hebrew, that is, the Hebrew that was spoken during the 1st millennium B.C.E.

It is common to assume that Biblical Hebrew is best reflected in the Tiberian version of Masoretic Hebrew, for three reasons: That is the version used in religious circles today; that is the version published in "standard" printed versions of the Hebrew Bible; and that is the version upon which Modern Israeli Hebrew is (mostly) based. Yet we will see that from a scientific point of view there is very little reason to think that the Tiberian Masoretes successfully captured the sounds of Biblical Hebrew.

Methods

Unfortunately, clues about ancient pronunciation are limited. In principle, there are only three reliable ways to know how a language is spoken:

1. listen to a native speaker making the sounds;
2. listen to a recording of a native speaker making the sounds;
3. know the position of the tongue and mouth used to make the sounds of the language.

Obviously, we do not have any native speakers or tape recordings from the 1st millennium B.C.E. To date, we also do not have any descriptions of the position of the mouth and tongue. (The idea of ancient people recording the sounds of their language by describing the position of the mouth and tongue is not as preposterous as it might sound. Such descriptions exist for classical Arabic, from roughly 1,000 years ago, and for ancient Sanskrit, from probably 2,500 years ago.)

Because none of the three reliable sorts of information are available to us, we are forced to rely on less accurate methods.

Table 6.1 summarizes the various methods researchers have used to figure out what Biblical Hebrew sounded like.

Comparison with Modern Hebrew

It is tempting to try to understand Biblical Hebrew by comparing it with Modern Hebrew, but it is almost always a mistake to do so. We will see in Chapter 10 that Modern Hebrew is a language built on the remnants of Biblical Hebrew as reflected in the Tiberian Masoretic tradition, but even when Hebrew was reborn roughly 100 years ago, it differed both from Biblical Hebrew and from Tiberian Hebrew in significant ways, and over the past 100 years it has changed even more.

The Modern Hebrew of today does not even tell us exactly what the Modern Hebrew of 50 years ago sounded like. For example, the pronunciation of the word for "book" — סֵפֶר — had two different vowels 50 years ago in Israel, whereas now it has the same vowel repeated twice, a fact hidden by the continued use of two different vowel symbols under the letters. (The older pronunciation with two different vowels is, however, still the one generally taught in Hebrew schools in North America and some parts of Europe.) In light of these changes, and much more drastic ones over longer periods of time, we certainly cannot expect to learn what Biblical Hebrew sounded like thousands of years ago by listening to Modern Hebrew.

In short, there is no reason to look at Modern Hebrew to try to understand what Biblical Hebrew sounded like.

Comparison with Masoretic Hebrew

Regarding Masoretic Hebrew, it is important, once again, to distinguish between the God Theory, the Science Theory, and the Dumb-Luck Theory, because it is common in traditional Jewish circles to point to an "unbroken chain of tradition" that connects the Masoretes to the Rabbis before them

Table 6.1. Methods of understanding ancient pronunciations

Method	Drawbacks	Advantages
Comparison with Modern Hebrew	Modern Hebrew is too far removed from Biblical Hebrew.	Almost no advantages.
Comparison with Masoretic Hebrew	Masoretic Hebrew is too far removed from Biblical Hebrew.	Almost no advantages.
	We don't know what Masoretic Hebrew sounded like.	
Comparison with other Semitic languages	Comparisons between languages are often unreliable.	Almost no advantages.
	We have less information about other Semitic languages than we do about Hebrew.	
Comparison with ancient Latin/Greek	Comparisons between languages are often unreliable.	Large body of evidence.
	We don't know what Latin and Greek sounded like.	
Language games	Very hard to find.	Detailed, specific information.
Spelling errors	Hard to find.	Detailed information.

and to the speakers of Biblical Hebrew before them.

The Science Theory tells us that such a chain of tradition is unlikely to preserve the ancient pronunciations. A few examples are in order.

An unbroken chain of English speakers connects British English from a few hundred years ago to many current dialects of English, including these four: American English as it spoken in the northern United States, American English as it is spoken in the southern United States, "high" British English, and finally Cockney British English.

Almost every vowel of every word is pronounced differently in the two American dialects. To take but one example, the first-person singular pronoun "I" is a clear diphthong (a vowel that changes as it is pronounced) in most northern dialects, but almost a pure vowel in many southern dialects.

Some consonants are pronounced differently in the British dialects and the American dialects. For example, the *t* in the word *water* is almost always pronounced as a /d/ in America, while it is either a /t/ or glottal stop in England. (A glottal stop is the consonant heard between the *uh* and the *oh* of *uh oh*.)

Certainly all four dialects cannot represent older British English. In just 300 years, the pronunciation of English has changed dramatically, in spite of continuous unbroken chains of native speakers. So we see that language pronunciation changes quickly, even when people continuously speak the language.

As mentioned above, Modern Israeli Hebrew has changed even in just the past 50 years, further demonstrating how quickly languages change. In addition to the example above with vowels, many Israelis today do not preserve a distinction among the consonants *heh*, *aleph*, and *ayin*.

More generally, most people cannot reliably reproduce their grandparents' accents from only two generations ago. The Masoretes lived over a millennium — or fifty generations — after the Bible was written.

These examples about preserving a language across generations have involved people who continuously speak the language natively. But Hebrew had ceased to be spoken natively by around the 2nd century C.E. Is it possible that the pronunciation of a language changes more slowly when people only use it religiously, and do not speak it as their native language?

Again, we can look at some examples. The current American and British pronunciations of the classical Greek letters differs. In America, the second letter in the Greek alphabet ("beta") starts with the same sounds as the word "bay," while in England, it starts with the same sounds as the word "be." Certainly they cannot both be the ancient Greek pronunciation, even though they both stem from the same original pronunciation.

As a second example, consider the divergent pronunciations of Hebrew attested in Ashkenazic and Sephardic Hebrew. The former preserves a distinction between a *tav* with and without a *dagesh* (that is, between "תּ" and "ת"), while the latter does not. Yemenite tradition, while siding with Ashkenazic Hebrew in preserving a difference between the two versions of *tav*, has a different understanding of how they differ. Again, it is clear that not all three pronunciations can represent the original pronunciation.

From all of these examples we come to a clear conclusion. Unless God or Dumb Luck has intervened, we must assume that the Masoretes did not know how Biblical Hebrew was pronounced, and we therefore turn to other methods to learn about Biblical Hebrew.

Comparison with Other Semitic Languages

By and large, more is known about Biblical Hebrew than any other Semitic language of the time. In terms of vowel sounds, we know much more about Hebrew than more ancient languages because Hebrew was the first language to introduce vowel symbols. In terms of the consonants, there is no ancient Semitic language that is better understood than Hebrew.

In addition to all of the other problems inherent in trying to figure out the pronunciation patterns of one language based on another (as discussed below), the paucity of hard data about other Semitic languages makes them a poor source of information about Biblical Hebrew, and so, along with comparison to Modern Hebrew or Tiberian Hebrew, we abandon comparison with other ancient Semitic languages as a source of information about Biblical Hebrew as well.

Comparison with Ancient Greek

Of all of the methods of inquiry, comparison with ancient Greek provides the best evidence about how ancient Hebrew was spoken. In this case, however, even the best is not as good as we would like.

What Did Greek Sound Like?

The first enormous problem with learning about Hebrew by comparing it to ancient Greek is knowing how ancient Greek sounded. Modern scholars agree that our understanding of ancient Greek pronunciation is, at best, approximate, largely because the problems that hide the pronunciation of ancient Hebrew also hide the pronunciation of ancient Greek.

It is temping to use modern Greek to understand ancient Greek, but we saw above that using a modern language directly to understand an ancient one does not work. And at any rate, rather than going down the erroneous route of using modern Greek to understand ancient Greek to understand ancient Hebrew, we could equally well take the erroneous but simpler route of comparing modern and ancient Hebrew directly.

Some researchers base their understanding of ancient Greek on ancient Latin, but, of course, we don't know how Latin was pronounced, either. And certainly the erroneous and circuitous route of using a modern Romance language to understand Latin in order to understand Greek in order to understand Biblical Hebrew is to be avoided.

Nonetheless, at least in Greek we have a good sense of where the vowels lie, because Greek made even wider use of vowel symbols than Hebrew did. Greek seems to have marked every vowel. Also — it would seem — Greek did not double up its consonant symbols as vowel symbols. That is, unlike Hebrew (which, for example, used *vav* both as a consonant and a vowel), a Greek symbol represented either a vowel or a consonant, but not both.

For example, the Hebrew spelling of Adam's name in Genesis (אדם) offers little in the way of understanding how that name was pronounced. (Remember that the vowel symbols under the letters did not get added by the Masoretes until much later.) So the ancient Hebrew is something vaguely like *ADM*. By contrast, the ancient Greek equivalent (Αδαμ or "Adam" in English letters) suggests, like the English, a bisyllabic word with two similar vowels.

Transliterations

Most of the evidence we can use to compare ancient Hebrew and ancient Greek comes in the form of transliterations, that is, Hebrew words written in Greek letters.

Before looking at these transliterations, a technical point is in order. As we discussed earlier, when the sounds of one language are written in another language, the process is technically called **transcription**. The word *transliteration* technically refers to the process of writing the *letters* of one language using the letters of another. For example, the modern Israeli Hebrew letters *samech* and *sin* represent the same sound. In a transcription, then, they might both be represented by the letter *s* in English. By contrast, in a transliteration, they would each get a different symbol, because they are different letters.

But in spite of these technical definitions, we will continue to use the more popular term *transliteration* for any process that takes a word in one language and writes it in another. Our use of *transliteration* will match the popular use, which subsumes both transcription and transliteration. But we will still be careful to distinguish between transliteration, which tries to capture the sounds of another language, and **translation,** which tries to capture the meaning of another language.

The Greek translation of the Bible (the Septuagint, or "LXX")[1] contains Greek versions of all of the names and places listed in the Hebrew Bible. Admittedly, the LXX, written not before the 3rd century B.C.E., is several hundred years too late to help us understand early Biblical Hebrew, but it is the closest we have, and was at least written when people were still speaking Hebrew fluently.

In addition to the Septuagint, we have a curious document, Origen's Hexapla, from the 3rd century C.E. Although it was written a full millennium after the earliest Biblical Hebrew that interests us, it contains an actual Greek transliteration of full Hebrew sentences, so, unlike the Septuagint, the information it contains about Hebrew pronunciation is not limited to names and places.

Before looking at those sources in detail, however, we should understand the nature of evidence that comes from transliteration. Specifically, how accurate is data culled from transliterations? To answer this question, we will look at some transliterations in modern languages, where we can easily check the success of a hypothesis based on transliteration data. For example, if we could compare modern Russian and modern English and always come up with the correct pronunciation of English based on Russian (or vice versa) we would have good reason to believe that transliterations are reliable tools for learning about one language based on another. By contrast, if we could not reliably learn anything about English based on Russian, we have reason to suspect transliteration-based information in other languages as well, including ancient languages.

Finally, we should also be clear to distinguish between two different types of transliteration in addition to the technical distinction we made above regarding "transliteration" and "transcription." The more commonly found kind of transliteration is a name (of a person or place) from one language written in another (as in the LXX). The second kind is actual words of one language written in another (as in Origen's Hexapla).

---

1. The word "Septuagint" comes from the Latin *septuāgintā*, meaning "seventy." It is (Christian) tradition that Ptolemy Philadelphus (285–247 B.C.E.) put 72 Palestinian Jews on the island of Pharos, and in 72 days, the group created a Greek translation of the Bible. In reference to the 72 people and 72 days, the book is called "Septuagint." Reflecting a bit of academic cleverness, this Greek translation is commonly denoted "LXX," that is, the Roman-numeral representation of 70.

Table 6.2. Various modern names across languages

English	Foreign Language	Pronunciation of Foreign Language
Paris	Paris (French)	paree
Lincoln	לִנְקוֹלְן (Modern Hebrew)	linkolen
Moscow	Москва (Russian)	moskva
Harvard	Гарвард (Russian)	garvard
Ohio	Огайо (Russian)	ogayo

Names and Places

Table 6.2 looks at some modern names and places as they are written in various modern languages.

In the first example we see that even though the English word for the capital of France is spelled the same as the French word, the two are not pronounced identically. In English, the final *s* is pronounced, whereas in French it is not. It would be a mistake to use the English version of the word to understand how French is pronounced (or vice versa). Furthermore, the Russian for "Paris" ("Париж") is also pronounced with a sound at the end, but that final sound is the same as the *s* in *leisure*. Even though Russian is generally more phonetic than English or French, this information tells us little about how the French pronounce their capital.

The second example is similar. The second *l* is pronounced in the Hebrew version of the common English name *Lincoln* (as in "Abraham Lincoln"), while it is not pronounced in English. Once again, it would be a mistake to use a foreign language's version of the English name to understand how the English version is pronounced. Two possible conclusions based on the Hebrew and English for "Lincoln" are both wrong: The *l* is not pronounced in English, and Hebrew does not have silent *lamed*s.

These first two examples show that the letters that are silent in one language's version of a name may be pronounced in another language's version. We thus cannot use transliterated names to determine which letters are silent and which are not.

The third example shows that sounds can change from language to language. The Russian capital /moskva/ becomes "Moscow" in English. The *v* has vanished, and the vowel sound at the end of the word has changed. We cannot use transliterated names to determine the sounds of letters in a language.

The next two pairs show a curious aspect of Russian. The English *h* is usually pronounced /g/ in Russian. Russian does not have the sound /h/ but does have a sound (similar to the Hebrew *chet* or the German *ch* in *Bach*) that — at least to American ears — sounds closer to /h/ than /g/ does. Nonetheless, the Russians use г (*g*) to represent American *h* (in addition to the American *g*). It would obviously be a mistake to conclude from the Russian evidence that the *h* in English sounds something like a Russian *g*.

What we see, then, is that names in one language are generally unreliable indicators of how those names are pronounced in another language.

But even though transliterations of names and places offer only unreliable evidence, they can be used to help evaluate the likelihood of a pronunciation theory being right. For example, the letter *g* in English is almost always transliterated into Russian as either "Г" ("G") or "Дж" ("DZh"). While the examples above caution us against drawing any firm conclusions, the fact that one letter in English has two possible transliterations suggests (correctly, in this case) that the English *g* is used to represent two different sounds. By contrast, the English *m* is almost always transliterated as a Russian "M," suggesting (again, correctly) that the English *m* has but one common pronunciation.

Names and places are subject to one final source of difficulty: Sometimes two different languages will simply have two different words for the same name or place. For example, the German for "Germany" is "Deutschland." The French for "The Netherlands" is "les Pays-Bas." The Modern Hebrew for "Spain" is סְפָרַד ("s'farad"). Unlike the pairs we saw earlier, which — at least in part — reflect the same pronunciation, each of the pairs here reflects two different sources for the same place. The English "German" does not give any information about how the German "Deutschland" is pronounced; neither do the other pairs.

Sometimes words will have enough in common that we may be tempted to think that they are transliterations, when in fact they are not. For example, the Hebrew *s'farad* ("Spain") and the English *Spain* share *s* as their first letter, and one of the two sounds (/p/ and /f/) represented by the Hebrew letter *peh* as their second. Based on this, one might conclude that they are variations of the same word, and then ask how the sounds /r/ and /d/ relate to the sound /n/. And, in fact, /n/ and /d/ are closely related phonologically. But *s'farad* is an ancient Hebrew word (appearing but once in Scripture, in Obadiah 20) referring to a place whose location, though unknown, was identified in an Aramaic *targum* (translation) as Spain. The English *Spain* comes from a word that goes back at least to ancient Greek: σπανια ("Spania"). The two have different sources. How are we to know, when looking at other pairs, when we have two sources and when we have one?

Real transliteration solves this problem, as discussed next.

Transliterated Words

In addition to names and places, we sometimes find actual transliterated words. Transliterations are usually used to tell a reader of one language how to pronounce a word in another language. It is rather uncommon for readers to need to know how to pronounce words in a language they cannot read, so this kind of transliteration evidence is rare, but still sometimes available.

While transliterated words ought to provide much better evidence than names or places, two factors limit their usefulness.

The first limiting factor is that these transliterations are often done for religious purposes, and so adhere to the God Theory rather than the Science Theory.

The second limiting factor is that, confronted with written and spoken versions of a word, most people are incapable of teasing apart the spelling and the pronunciation. For example, as we have seen, most American speakers (until they are specifically told to think about it) believe that the *s* in *dogs* and the *s* in *cats* are pronounced the same. They are not. Most American speakers believe that *sing* has an /n/ sound followed by a /g/ sound at the end of the word. It does not. (*Sing* actually ends with a single consonant that is a cross between /n/ and /g/. A quick demonstration of the fact that *sing* doesn't have the sound /n/ in it is to say they word *seen* or *sin*, and realize that neither of those can constitute the start of the word *sing*.)

Because of the first difficulty, transliterations often do not make a serious attempt to capture the sounds of the language they are purportedly transliterating. Because of the second difficulty, even when transliterators try to capture the original sounds, they often fail.

The Septuagint and Hebrew

We turn now to what the Septuagint ("LXX") can teach us about Hebrew. The Septuagint, written sometime after 300 B.C.E., is a Greek translation of the Hebrew Bible, and, as such, contains Greek spellings for all of the

Hebrew names and places in the Bible. As we saw above, we cannot use the Greek versions of the Hebrew names and places to conclude anything about Hebrew for sure, but we can use it to help decide if the Masoretes correctly understood Biblical Hebrew. We want to see the degree to which Masoretic pronunciation of Hebrew names matches the Greek pronunciation of the Hebrew names.

Of course, we do not expect to find an exact match, for all of the reasons enumerated above. Indeed, we might even have trouble detecting an exact match, because we do not know exactly what the Masoretes meant for their symbols to convey, and we do not know exactly how ancient Greek was pronounced.

Nonetheless, an interesting pattern emerges: We will see that the Masoretes probably got most of the consonants right, but not the vowels. We will also see that the one area where the Masoretes probably erred was the stop/fricative alternations in the "Beged Kefet" letters (as described above starting on page 57).

A few preliminary examples are in order, to help sort out all of the different bits of information we will be looking at.

Let's start with Adam and Eve, who appear in the Creation story.

A First Example

The Biblical Hebrew version of Adam's name is אדם, that is *'dm*, where the apostrophe represents the letter *aleph*. The Biblical Hebrew version of Eve's name is חוה or *xvh*, where *x* represents the letter *chet*, and, probably, something like the sound at the end of the German *Bach*. It is important to remember that Biblical Hebrew did not include any of the Masoretic marks commonly used to indicate vowels, relying instead on the vowel letters *yud*, *heh*, and *vav*, as discussed extensively above starting on page 23.

The Tiberian Masoretic versions of those names are אָדָם and חַוָּה or *'adam* and *xAva*, where the *x* again represents the letter *chet*. The dotted *v* represents a *vav* with a *dagesh* or dot in it. The lowercase *a* represents a *kamatz* and the uppercase *A* represents a *patach*.

The Greek versions of those two names (which were written after the original Hebrew but long before the Tiberian Masoretic versions), as recorded in the LXX, are Αδαμ (*Adam* in English letters) and Ευα (*Eua*).

Table 6.3 summarizes all of the data we are trying to reconcile.

Many people are so used to thinking that only one understanding of Biblical Hebrew exists that they find it hard to remember that the Masoretic tradition is but one interpretation of the original Biblical record. Still, we ask to what degree does all of this information confirm the work of the

Table 6.3. "Adam" and "Eve" in various traditions

English Name	Biblical Hebrew	Masoretic Hebrew	Greek
"Adam"	אדם 'dm	אָדָם 'adam	Αδαμ Adam
"Eve"	חוה xvh	חַוָּה xAvah	Eυα Eua

Tiberian Masoretes? That is, given the ambiguities of the original Hebrew record, to what degree do the Masoretic and Greek versions agree?

We'll start with the consonants.

Neither the *aleph* in Adam nor the *chet* in Eve have made their way into Greek. If our understanding of the pronunciation of *aleph* is correct, we are not surprised that it is not represented in Greek, because the *aleph* was either silent or the nearly silent "glottal stop," such as, as we have seen, the sound between the *uh* and *oh* in *uh oh*. By contrast, the lack of a representation for *chet* seems less expected, particularly in light of the fact that Greek has a letter *chi* (χ) that may have sounded somewhat like the modern-day *chet*. (The exact pronunciation of the ancient Greek letter χ is, of course, not known.) Based in part on this evidence, there is general consensus that the *chet* was closer to /h/ (which, when it starts a word, also tends not to be included in the Greek versions of Hebrew names) than it is in Modern Israeli Hebrew; it was probably somewhat like the current Yemenite pronunciation of the letter.

The *d* and *m* in *Adam* become the Greek letters for *d* (δ) and *m* (μ), respectively, just as we expect.

By contrast, the *vav* (/v/ or /u/) in Eve's name, presumed by the Masoretes to be a consonantal *v*, is the vocalic *u* (v) in Greek. Even though the "ו" that the Masoretes considered to be consonantal is often represented by *u* (v) in Greek, this is not what we would expect. If the Masoretes were right, we would expect a Greek consonant, not the vowel *u*.

While it is not immediately clear which Greek consonant we would expect in Eve's name, because Greek did not have a letter for *v*, usually the letter *b* (β) was used for *v*. If the Masoretes were right about Eve's name, we would expect the Greek consonant *b* (β) instead of what we have. II Kings gives us an example. (II Kings in the traditional Jewish Bible is called IV Kings in the LXX, because the LXX uses "I Kings" and "II Kings" for what Hebrew tradition calls "I Samuel" and "II Samuel.") There (II Kings 18:34 and 19:13) we find the name עוה — or *'vh*, where

the backward apostrophe represents the Hebrew letter *ayin* — which the
Masoretes assume is עַוָּה or *'ivah.* (Based on this Masoretic tradition, the
English in Jewish circles for this name is usually *Ivvah.*) The LXX gives us
Aβα — or *Aba* — for this name, using, as we expect, the Greek *b* (β) for the
Hebrew *v.* (Based on this Greek tradition, the English in Christian circles
for this name is usually *Aba.*)

In short, the Masoretes assumed that the Hebrew letter *vav* had two
pronunciations, one as a vowel, one as a consonant. The LXX agrees,
sometimes using a vowel (υ) for *vav* and sometimes a consonant (β). However, the Masoretes assumed that the *vav* in Eve's name was consonantal,
while the LXX uses a vowel. Though we must be careful not to draw any
firm conclusions about the pronunciation of Greek or Hebrew based on
this limited evidence, we also must note that the LXX does not confirm the
Masoretic understanding of Eve's name.

More about Vav

As noted immediately above, some other purported consonantal uses of
vav also end up as *u* (υ) in the LXX. For example, there's a month named
"Ziv" (זִו) in I Kings, which becomes "Ziu" (Ζιυ) in Greek. (If you want
to look this up, remember that the LXX uses "III Kings" for the Hebrew
"I Kings.")

Names that begin with the letter *vav* ought to be particularly helpful,
because these *vav*s are almost certainly consonantal. Biblical Hebrew put
an *aleph* before a vowel that started a word — or, at least, that is our
current understanding. Unfortunately, there are only six, possibly seven,
names in the Hebrew Bible that begin with a *vav*: Vaheb (Numbers 21:14),
Vayzata (Esther 9:9), Vanya (Ezra 10:36), Vaspi (Numbers 13:14), Vashni
(I Chronicles 6:13), and — the most famous — Vashti (throughout the book
of Esther); additionally, the word "v'dan" in Ezekiel 27:19 may be a name.

The *Vehab* of Numbers 21:14 appears in the Hebrew sentence, "Therefore the Book of Wars of the Lord: Vehab in Suphah, and . . . " But the LXX
has a different version: "Therefore it is said in a book: A war of the Lord
has set on fire Zoob . . . " We thus learn nothing about the pronunciation of
the *vav* from Numbers 21:14.

Vayzata in Esther 9:9 is the last of the ten sons of Haman. But whereas
the traditional Hebrew understanding is that the initial *vav* is part of a
name, the LXX prefers the (much more sensible) understanding that the
vav is the prefix "and," giving us "and Zabuthaeus," Haman's last son.
This example, too, offers little insight.

Vanya in Ezra 10:36 is *Ououania* (Ουουανια) in the LXX, which would seem to indicate a vocalic interpretation of the *vav*.

Vaspi in Numbers 13:14 appears in the LXX in Numbers 13:15, but there his name is *Sabi* ($\Sigma\alpha\beta\iota$).

Vashni in I Chronicles 6:13 appears in the LXX in I Chronicles 6:28, where his name is *Sani* ($\Sigma\alpha\nu\iota$).

Queen Vashti in the book of Esther is called *Astin* ($A\sigma\tau\iota\nu$) in the LXX.

The usual understanding of Ezekiel 27:19 reads something like "Vedan and Yavan from Uzal traded for your wares," but always with the acknowledgment that the meaning of the Hebrew is unclear to us. The LXX reads, "out of Asel came iron," so "Vedan" might not be a name at all.

If a general trend is to be isolated, it would be that the initial *vav* in Hebrew names does not make its way into Greek, as attested by the pairs Vaspi/Sabi, Vashni/Sani, Vashti/Astin, and maybe Vanya/Ououania. However, the general paucity of names beginning with *vav*, combined with the odd fact (coincidence?) that three of the names have the same general form (Vaspi, Vashni, and Vashti) leave us only with the conclusion that we find no support for the Masoretes' system of pronunciation. We do not have enough information to conclude that they are wrong, but so far we have not seen any confirmation that they are right.

General Patterns

We turn next to a more general look at some Hebrew names as transliterated into Greek. Table 6.4 lists the (Tiberian version of) various Hebrew names, and their Greek equivalents, as recorded in the LXX.

The table uses *a* in English for both Masoretic *kamatz* and *patach*. The Masoretic *shewa* is marked with an apostrophe in English. Hebrew letters with a *dagesh* are marked with a dot under them in English. We will be comparing the English transliterations of the Masoretic Hebrew and of the Greek. The evidence is detailed, but not difficult, and ultimately worth working through to appreciate what scholars understand about the pronunciation of ancient Hebrew.

We looked at *Adam* and *Eve* above, and concluded that the Greek suggested that the Masoretes correctly understood most of the consonants, but perhaps not the vowels. Looking at *Zilpa* and *Milcah* next, we see that the Greek generally supports the basic Masoretic understanding of the words. Both in Hebrew and in Greek, the words are bisyllabic, with /i/ in the first syllable and /a/ in the second.

However, the Greek fails to support the Masoretic distinction between letters with and without a dagesh. According to the Masoretes, the *peh* in *Zilpa* and the *kaf* in *Milcah* both have a *dagesh*, and, therefore, are pro-

Table 6.4. Various names in Hebrew and Greek

English Name	Masoretic Hebrew	Greek
Adam	אָדָם adam	Αδαμ Adam
Eve	חַוָה xavah	Eυa Eua
Zilpah	זִלְפָּה zil'pah	Ζιλφα Zilfa
Milcah	מִלְכָּה mil'kah	Μελχα Melxa
Rebekah	רִבְקָה riv'kah	Ρεβεκκα Rebekka
Joktan	יָקְטָן yak'tan	Ιεκταν Iektan
Balaam	בִּלְעָם Bil'am	Βαλααμ Balaam
Jethro	יִתְרוֹ Yit'ro	Ιοθορ Iothor
Zebulun	זְבֻלוּן z'vulun	Ζαβουλων Zaboulon
Keturah	קְטוּרָה k'turah	Χεττουρα Xettoura
Cain	קַיִן kayin	Καιν Kain
Calneh	כַּלְנֶה Kal'neh	Χαλαννι Xalanni
Admah	אַדְמָה Ad'ma	Αδαμα Adama
Heshbon	חֶשְׁבּוֹן Xesh'bon	Εσεβων Esebon
Hanoch	חֲנוֹךְ xanox	Ενωχ Enox
Damascus	דַּמֶּשֶׂק damesek	Δαμασκος Damaskos
Damascus	דַּרְמֶשֶׂק dar'mesek	Δαμασκος Damaskos
Gamali	גְּמַלִּי G'mali	Γαμαλι Gamali
Gadiel	גַּדִּיאֵל Gadiel	Γουδιηλ Goudiel
Jephunneh	יְפֻנֶּה Y'funeh	Ιεφοννη Iefonne
Manasseh	מְנַשֶּׁה M'nasheh	Μανασση Manasse

(See text for discussion of English transliterations.)

nounced /p/ and /k/ respectively. The Greek suggests that the letters were pronounced /x/ and /f/, that is, as though they had no *dagesh*.

Above we saw that Greeks used their *beta* (β) for both *bet* and *vet* — that is, the Hebrew letter both with and without a *dagesh* — even though the Masoretic tradition assigns different sounds to the two variations. But there we assumed it was because Greek had no way of writing /v/. Here we cannot fall back on deficiencies of Greek to account for the discrepancy between Masoretic Hebrew /k/ and /p/ versus Greek /x/ and /f/.

It is particularly useful to look at the k/x and p/f alternations because, of all the sounds of Masoretic Hebrew, we are most certain about these variations. Our certainty comes from the regular linguistic pattern exhibited by these and the other "beged kefet" letters, as discussed on page 57. (There, we saw that the six stops /b/, /g/, /d/, /k/, /p/, and /t/ alternate with similar fricatives. In particular, the stops we see here, /k/ and /p/, alternate with the fricatives /x/ and /f/.) When our understanding of an ancient scheme of pronunciation corresponds with a common linguistic pattern, we have good reason to believe that we have correctly understood the ancient pattern.

Unfortunately, while we are fairly certain we have correctly understood the Masoretic pronunciations, those pronunciations do not seem to be confirmed by the Greek. Greek could have written *Zilpa* and *Milkah* to better match the Hebrew, but did not. Bearing in mind the caveats from the first part of this chapter, we must not assume that the Masoretes were wrong and the Greeks were right, but we also must not assume the opposite.

The next name, Rebecca, poses an even bigger problem. While the LXX forms of *Zilpah* and *Milcah* at least coincide with the Masoretic forms in terms of general syllable structure, the LXX gives us *rebekka* for the Masoretic *rivkah*. The Masoretes have but two syllables while the LXX gives us three. Furthermore, the *koof* mysteriously appears doubled in the Greek. The Masoretes had a convention for marking doubled letters (the *dagesh*, or dot), but did not employ it here. So other than the values of the three consonants and the value of the last /a/ sound, the Greek and Masoretic Hebrew do not agree on Rebecca's name. This is not good news for the Masoretes.

It turns out that the /k/ sound in Rebecca is part of a group of "emphatic" sounds that includes *koof, tet,* and maybe *tsadi*. It is a reasonable hypothesis that these emphatic sounds could have been written as doubled letters, and that doubled letters change the pattern of a word in Greek. In terms of the double-letter-for-emphatic-sounds hypothesis, we see that in Keturah's name the *tet* is indeed doubled. (However, we also see that the *koof* in the same word is not doubled; the theory would need some modification.)

In other words, we might assume that, for reasons peculiar to Greek, emphatic letters had to be preceded by a vowel. We have already seen other systematic name changes based on properties of Greek: /v/ becomes /b/, for example, and *chet* and *heh* tend to disappear. So we wonder if this is another systematic change based on Greek, and perhaps that change masks the fact that the Masoretes were correct after all.

Unfortunately, Joktan's name (next in Table 6.4) shows us a *koof* and *tet* which are not doubled, and, furthermore, the *tet* in Joktan is in exactly the same place as the *koof* in Rebecca's name. While there is certainly something generally right about connecting doubled letters, emphatic sounds, and additional vowels, the phenomenon is not systematic enough to explain the difference between the Greek and Masoretic Hebrew versions of Rebecca's name. Once again we find that the Greek does not confirm the work of the Masoretes.

The three names Zilpa, Milka, and Rivka demonstrate a common Hebrew word pattern. Many, many Hebrew words start with a consonant, the sound /i/, and then two more consonants. In fact, it is a general pattern of Masoretic Hebrew that when a word would otherwise start with three consonants in a row, the sound /i/ is inserted between the first and second consonants. This process, like the stop/fricative alternation we just discussed, is a very common linguistic pattern. It is called **epenthesis**, and the /i/ is called an **epenthetic** vowel.

However, while those three names — and Bil'am and Yit'ro as well — all demonstrate this epenthetic /i/ in Hebrew, the Greek contains various vowels, /i/ in Zilfa, /e/ in Melxa and Rebecca, /a/ in Balaam, and /o/ in Iothor.

This is certainly not good news for the Masoretes. A regular pattern in one language but no pattern in a transliteration can be most easily explained by assuming that the pattern was invented in the language that has the pattern. In this case, we come to the conclusion that the Masoretes took a whole bunch of words that did not previously sound the same and tried to make them sound the same nonetheless.

The alternative hypothesis is so much more convoluted that we reject it immediately. It is folly to assume that the Greeks took a handful of similar-sounding names and wrote them in vastly different ways.

We turn next to Zebulun's name, which is interesting because it has two Masoretic spellings: זְבֻלוּן and זְבוּלֻן, that is, with the letters *zion, bet, lamed, vav, nun* or *zion, bet, vav, lamed, nun*. (There is some confusion about the spelling of this name. The very widely used Mandelkern concordance lists a third spelling of the name in Judges that does not appear in modern official copies or in the Leningrad Codex upon which they are based.

Some Hebrew print versions of the Bible, however, match Mandelkern's concordance.)

Recall that the Hebrew letter *vav* was used for both /o/ and /u/ (we think), and that the Masoretes additionally used three dots in a diagonal row under a letter for /u/. There are thus two ways to represent /u/ in Masoretic Hebrew. Additionally, Biblical Hebrew tended not to use two vocalic *vav*s in the same word. We are not, therefore, surprised to see that it is sometimes the first /u/ that is marked with a *vav* in Biblical Hebrew and sometimes the second. (We see a similar phenomenon with the word *m'komot* ["places"]. Usually only the first or second vowel is marked with a letter, but sometimes we see both.)

In Zebulun's name, however, we are at a loss to explain why the first /u/ is written differently in Greek than the second one, regardless of how the word is actually spelled in Hebrew. The Greek would suggest that the first *vav* represented /u/ but that the second one represented /o/. In other words, the LXX agrees that the two spellings are pronounced identically, but differs on what that pronunciation is. Once again, the most likely hypothesis is that the Masoretes got it wrong, though here it is almost as likely that the Greek is wrong.

The next name, Keturah, demonstrates another doubling of an emphatic consonant in Greek. The Hebrew *tet* is marked in Greek with a double *tau* (τ). However, the initial *koof* in Hebrew, rather than being transliterated as /k/ in Greek (as it was in Rebecca's name) is not only not doubled but indeed written as /x/ (χ). Once again, we see some confusion between stops and fricatives, but here the confusion involves not the Hebrew letter *kaf* but the Hebrew letter *koof*. According to the Masoretes, one difference between these two letters is that the former alternates with /x/ but the latter does not. The LXX does not confirm this distinction. (And just to be sure that Greek didn't have some pattern prohibiting the use of /k/ at the start of a word, we compare the name Cain, which the LXX does record as Kain: Καιν.) If the *koof* in Cain can stay a /k/ in Greek, why didn't the *koof* in Keturah? We see a new pattern emerging: there is little reason to think that the Masoretic understanding of the stop/fricative alternations (such as /k/ vs. /x/) was correct.

The final pair of names, Calneh and Admah, show once again that the LXX often has more vowels in names than the Masoretic versions. Both of these names are, apparently, bisyllabic in Masoretic Hebrew but trisyllabic in Greek. We have already seen (with Zilpah) that nothing about the Greek language prevents a bisyllabic name, so we once again come to the conclusion that there is little to support the Masoretic understanding of the vowels in Biblical Hebrew.

Doubled Letters

Doubled letters provide a very important clue about how well the Masoretes understood Biblical Hebrew. According to the Masoretes, Biblical Hebrew did not mark doubled letters, so a single Hebrew letter in Biblical Hebrew was ambiguous. It might represent one letter or it might represent two. However, the Tiberian Masoretes used a *dagesh* to mark a doubled letter. (They also used this symbol to mark the difference between stops and fricatives, presumably because fricatives when doubled became stops.)

Greek, by contrast (as we have already seen), does mark doubled letters. The question we therefore ask ourselves is the degree to which the Greek doubled letters match up with the Tiberian use of *dagesh*. If we find that Greek always doubled letters where the Masoretes put in a *dagesh*, we will have good reason to assume that the Masoretes were correctly capturing an ancient aspect of Hebrew. If, by contrast, we find no correspondence between the Greek doubled letters (as marked by actual double letters) and the Masoretic doubled letters (as marked by a *dagesh*) we will — as before — have to assess whether the lack of evidence is neutral regarding the success of the Masoretes, or whether it speaks against their success.

What we find is a partial correspondence between the Greek doubled letters in names and the Masoretic use of *dagesh*.

In Calneh, for example, we see another instance of a letter that is doubled in Greek but not in Hebrew. The n (ν) is doubled but the *nun* is not. Incidentally, the doubling here is further refutation of the theory proposed and rejected above, namely, that only emphatic letters in Hebrew were doubled in Greek. We furthermore must ask why the n was doubled at all. (We cannot assume that ns were always doubled in Greek, because Hanoch's name contains a single n.) And to this question, we can add why we find doubled letters in the Greek versions of Keturah and Rebekah.

We are left with two possibilities: Either Greek doubled consonants at random when writing Hebrew names, or the Greek reflected a doubling that the Masoretic Hebrew did not.

While at first the conclusion that Greek randomly doubled consonants may seem surprising, we do see roughly the same phenomenon in common modern English transliterations of Hebrew words. The Jewish Festival of Lights, for example, enjoys at least three common spellings in English: *Hanukah*, *Hanukkah*, and *Hannukah*. The New Year is commonly written either *Rosh Hashanah* or *Rosh Hashannah*. Neither the doubling in the variations of *Hanukah* nor those of *Rosh Hashanah* reflects anything other than lack of knowledge about Hebrew.

So one possibility is that the doubling of letters in Greek, too, may reflect nothing more than chance.

There is at least one case, however, where we are almost sure that the Masoretes correctly recorded a doubled letter. This is the place *Damascus*, or, in Hebrew *Damesek*. We have very good reason to believe that the middle *m* was doubled, because in addition to *Damesek*, we also find the form *Darmesek*.

In general, one source of doubled letters is the elision of two adjacent letters. We see this, for example, in the double *m* of *immaterial*, which has as its source *in-material*. *Irresponsible* from *in-responsible* is another example. Across the world's languages, we commonly see *ns*, *ms*, *ls* and *rs* involved in this sort of elision. In Masoretic Hebrew, it is very common for an *n* to elide to create a doubled letter that is marked with a *dagesh*. Less frequently in Hebrew we see *ls* eliding, and much less frequently *rs*.

When we see the two forms *Damesek* and *Darmesek* in Masoretic manuscripts, we assume that when the word was written without the *r*, that is, as *Damesek*, the *m* was doubled. While that doubling is (correctly, we assume) marked with a *dagesh* by the Masoretes, we do not find a doubled letter in the Greek. (Curiously, we also only find the spelling *Damascus* in Greek. We do not find *Darmascus*.) It is tempting to use this fact to assume that Greek did not systematically mark doubled letters in Hebrew. While that conclusion would accord well with what we have already seen, we must also keep in mind the possibility that the Greeks knew of a place Damascus, and used their own spelling for it.

The next set of names in Table 6.4 is taken from Numbers 13. (If you want to compare the Hebrew and Greek, keep in mind that the last verse of the Hebrew Chapter 12 is the first verse of the Greek Chapter 13, so the verse numbers do not quite match up.) There we see a genealogical list of tribes, replete with names. According to the Masoretes, some of these names, a sampling of which appear in Table 6.4, have doubled letters. From that table, we see that the letters in Gamali and Gadiel that are doubled in the Masoretic tradition are not doubled in Greek. By contrast, the letters in Jephunneh and Manasseh that are doubled in the Masoretic tradition are also doubled in the Greek.

The examples given in the table are representative of the list, and we see two trends: The first trend is that if a letter is doubled in the LXX it is also doubled in the Masoretic tradition; that is, there are no "randomly" doubled Greek letters here. The second trend is one of inconsistency: if a letter is doubled in the Masoretic tradition it may or may not be doubled in the Greek tradition.

It is important to understand a final nuance. The doubled *n* in *Jephunneh* reflects a very basic element of Hebrew verbal grammar. Hebrew verbs come in (roughly) seven varieties, some of which, by their nature, have doubled letters. At least, that is our Masoretic understanding of them. For example, the common verb *dibber* (דבר) "he spoke" is of the variety that has a doubled middle letter. And, in fact, the Masoretes always put a *dagesh* in the *bet* of that verb: דִּבֶּר. (The *dagesh* in the initial *daled* marks the letter as a stop and not a fricative; it has nothing to do with doubling.)

The name *Jephunneh* is actually a verb, and, furthermore, is one of the verbs that has a doubled letter. The double letter in *Manesseh* likewise has its roots in the verbal system. The fact that the doubled letters in the LXX in each of these names correspond precisely with the Masoretic understanding of the verbal system suggests that the Masoretes may have correctly understood and conveyed the very fundamental element of Hebrew grammar that doubles up letters in certain verbs.

Other instances of double letters in names that come from verbs with inherent double letters tend to follow the same pattern.

This is good news for the Masoretes.

It is, however, difficult to reconcile the regularity we see here (in Jephunneh and Manessah, for example) regarding doubled letters with the irregularly doubled letters in Rebecca and Keturah that we saw above.

Summary

In sum, then, we see that the LXX agrees with the Masoretes about most of the consonants. The Masoretic *mem* (*m*) is almost always the Greek *mu* (μ or *m*), the Masoretic *resh* (*r*) is almost always the Greek *rho* (ρ or *r*), etc. We do not, however, see any confirmation of the Tiberian Masoretic difference between *shin* (שׁ) and *sin* (שׂ).

By contrast, the LXX completely fails to confirm three aspects of the Masoretic system:

1. The LXX does not confirm the Masoretic stop/fricative alternations among the consonants: k/x, p/f, b/v, etc.
2. The LXX does not confirm the Masoretic vowels.
3. The LXX does not confirm the Masoretic distinction between consonantal and vocalic *vav*.

While all three of these unconfirmed aspects were almost certainly a part of Biblical Hebrew, we have no evidence that the Masoretes correctly recorded the details. That is, the Masoretes probably did not correctly record when stops and fricatives were used; the Masoretes did not correctly record the vowels of the ancient Hebrew words; and the Masoretes did not correctly record when a *vav* was consonantal and when it was vocalic.

In light of these three failures, we are surprised to find that the Masoretes probably did correctly understand and record the nature of doubled letters in verbs.

Based on the data from the LXX, then, we are left with but a partial success for the Masoretes. We will see immediately below that Origen's Hexapla paints a similar picture.

Origen's Hexapla and Hebrew

What Is the Hexapla?

Toward the end of his life in the 3rd century C.E., a well-known Christian theologian named Origen compiled a six-column summary of the Hebrew and Greek versions of the Bible. This six-column work, called a **hexapla** (from the Greek for "six-fold"), contained one column of Hebrew in Hebrew letters (the first column), and four columns of various Greek translations of the Bible (the last four columns). It is the second column that interests us now, because that column contained a transliteration of the first column. That is, Origen's Hexapla contained a whole column of transliterated Hebrew.

This "Second Column" (commonly called simply "the Sec.," an abbreviation of the Latin "Secunda Columna") predates the Masoretic work on the pronunciation of Hebrew by several hundred years at least, and serves as a bridge between the LXX, from 300 B.C.E., and the Masoretic work from not earlier than 600 C.E. The LXX is much closer to the original Hebrew, but the Sec. contains much more information.

Origen's death in 254 establishes a latest-possible date for the compilation of his great work. However, scholars remain divided on when the transliteration was written. A significant minority of researchers believe that Origen himself prepared the transliteration, while the majority hold that he used a transliteration that was already in circulation.

Some other attempts to date the Sec. more precisely rely on the pronunciation of Greek during various stages of its history, with arguments along the lines of: the Greek vowel *eta* (η) was pronounced one way during Origen's life and another way in the Sec. But such arguments assume that we not only know exactly how Hebrew was pronounced during various stages of its development, but that we also know which Greek vowels were used for those Hebrew vowels. We have none of this information.

Origen probably knew Hebrew only poorly. If he prepared the transliteration himself, we must wonder how much of it reflects actual Hebrew pronunciation and how much Origen's own lack of knowledge. But, judging from his research and notes in the other four (Greek) columns of his Hexapla as well as from other details about his life, we conclude that Origen was a careful scholar. If he did not use a preexisting transliteration, we can be reasonably certain that he obtained qualified help in preparing his own.

However, all transliterations are fraught with difficulty. It is difficult to convey the sounds of language in writing (as discussed on page 15), and even more difficult to convey those sounds in an alphabet not usually used for the task. So when we see Hebrew written in Greek letters, we face the difficult task of determining which aspects of the Greek reflect the transliteration process into Greek and which the original Hebrew.

In the case of Origen's Hexapla, we also face a much more devastating reality: the only original copy of his work was destroyed in the 7th century. Excerpts from the Hexapla are preserved in various early Christian writings, and, fortunately, in a palimpsest[2] from the 10th century, with additional text added some few hundred years later. Although the palimpsest contains but fragments of Psalms, and although it is missing the first (Hebrew) column, there is little doubt that this 10th-century document captures Origen's 3rd-century work containing the earliest extant transliteration of Hebrew. In spite of the limited text that still remains, the Sec. provides some of the most important clues about pre-Masoretic Hebrew, and so we will examine it in detail.

In the first part of this chapter, we addressed the question of what the LXX could teach us about the ancient pronunciation of Hebrew. In answering that question, we learned that, while the Masoretes correctly conveyed most of the consonants in Biblical Hebrew, and perhaps some of the doubled letters, they did not correctly convey the values of the vowels, nor of the stop/fricative alternations. We were careful not to draw any firm conclusions about Hebrew based on the LXX transliterations of names (for reasons discussed below starting on page 86), so all we know so far is that we have no solid evidence for the correctness of the Masoretes' understanding of Hebrew.

We will see that the Second Column of Origen's Hexapla ("the Sec.") more closely matches the Masoretic tradition, but we will also see that we still do not have an exact match. Furthermore, the additional closeness may reflect changes Hebrew had undergone in the several hundred years that separate the LXX from the *Secunda Columna*.

2. A "palimpsest" is a manuscript that contains text that has been erased and overwritten.

Table 6.5. Some Hebrew as reflected in the Sec.

English	Biblical Hebrew	Masoretic Hebrew	Secunda
God	האל h'l	הָאֵל ha'el	αηλ ael
pure	תמים tmim	תָּמִים tamim	θαμμιν tammin
his way	דרכו drko	דַּרְכּוֹ dar'ko	δερχω derxo

A First Example

Once again, it will be helpful to look at some simple examples, to understand the nature of the data. We start with Table 6.5, which contains the first three words of Psalm 18, Verse 31.

In the first line, we see the Hebrew *ha'el*, literally "the God," used (as is common in Psalms) to refer to God. The Biblical Hebrew gives us only the consonants, and the Masoretes tell us that the vowel under the *heh* (ה) meaning "the" is /a/, and the vowel in God's name (אל) is /e/.

As we expect, the Greek does not record the letter *heh*, though we suspect that this has more to do with Greek than with the Hebrew it is trying to represent. The Greek vowel in God's name is /e/ (η). Of course, we do not know exactly what sound (or sounds) the Greek vowel η represented, but we do see it used fairly consistently where Masoretic Hebrew has the vowel *tzere*. We will assume that both of these represented something like the *ay* in the American pronunciation of *day*. Finally, the Sec. confirms the pronunciation of the *lamed* in Hebrew by using a *lambda* (λ or *l*) in Greek.

Regarding "pure," we find that the *taf* is represented by the Greek letter *theta* (θ). Throughout the Sec., *theta* is used for *taf*, and, although we cannot know for sure, there is good reason to believe that when the Sec. was written, *theta* represented one variety of /t/ sound (technically called aspirated, a topic we return to below) while *tau* (τ) represented another ("unaspirated") variety of /t/ sound. (This may be an indication about how *taf* was pronounced back then, or it may merely represent the particular transliteration scheme employed by the author.)

More surprising is the double *mu* (μ or *m*), because the Hebrew clearly has but one *mem* to represent the /m/ sound. Perhaps this is another case of the arbitrary doubling of consonants we saw above. If so, we should note that it would be a mistake to draw too firm a conclusion based on other instances of doubling. If it is not arbitrary doubling, we must ask ourselves why the Greek transliterator thought the /m/ sound was doubled. Another possibility is that the double letter is simply an error.

Most surprising, however, is that the final consonant of the word is recorded in Hebrew as another *mem*, while it is recorded in Greek as being a *nu* (ν). Some scholars argue that this /n/ in Greek where Hebrew has an /m/ is a scribal error. But the sounds /m/ and /n/ are more closely related than their respective letterforms μ and ν. Our first assumption, then, ought to be that the author of the Greek heard, and wrote down, an /n/ sound. Against this hypothesis we must consider that the same word is spelled a few verses earlier as $\tau \alpha \mu \iota \mu$ (*tamim*), without the double letter or the final consonant mutation. Then again, a few verses later the word is spelled $\tau \alpha \mu \mu \iota \mu$ (*tammim*) again without the consonant mutation but with the double *m* in the middle of the word.

Regarding "his way," we find, once again, general confirmation in the Greek of the Masoretic Hebrew consonants, but also confusion about the stop/fricative distinction. For the Hebrew /k/ we have Greek χ, which was either /x/ or an aspirated /k/. What we do not find is confirmation of the Masoretic /a/ sound in *dar'ko*. Rather than the *alpha* (α) used to represent /a/, we find an *epsilon* (ϵ or *e*).

Some More Background

In order to better understand the Greek examples that follow, a little more background about the Sec. and Greek is in order. Our current purposes are limited to using the Sec. to understand how Hebrew may have been spoken during or before the 3rd century C.E. We want to know the degree to which the currently popular Tiberian Masoretic system agrees with that older pronunciation, and how that older pronunciation agrees with the pronunciation suggested by the LXX several hundred years earlier. Accordingly, we will not digress into a discussion about other interesting but irrelevant aspects of the Sec. and the Greek in which it was written. (But see "Further Reading" for suggestions on where you can find this information.) Nonetheless, one linguistic concept and one aspect of Greek each warrant our attention.

Aspiration

We know that consonants can be divided into two categories: stops and fricatives. This is but one division, however. Another dichotomy calls some consonants "aspirated" and some "unaspirated." The English /p/, for example, comes in both aspirated and unaspirated varieties. When p starts a word, it is aspirated; when a consonant precedes p at the start of a word, the p is unaspirated.

You can actually feel this difference by putting your hand in front of your mouth and saying both *pin* and *spin*. When you say *pin*, you will feel an explosion of air hitting your hand; this explosion of air, which is the aspiration of the letter, is absent in the word *spin*, because the p in that word is unaspirated.

It is commonly assumed that, during the 3rd century, the Greek letter *theta* (θ) represented not the /th/ sound of today but rather an aspirated /t/ sound. Similarly, the Greek letter *chi* (χ) may have represented not the /ch/ of today's *Bach* but rather an aspirated /k/.

These facts will be important below.

The Greek Letters for "E"

Greek has two letters that we commonly transliterate as *e* in English: *eta* (η) and *epsilon* (ϵ). (You may also see the former, η, transliterated as *i*.) The Greek *iota* (ι) is transliterated into English as *i*.

The debate about the exact pronunciation of these (and other) Greek vowels is fierce, but here we acknowledge that any conclusion about the pronunciation of vowels so long ago is supported at best by conjecture. While it is tempting to use three different symbols in English for the three different Greek letters *eta, epsilon,* and *iota,* to do so would exhaust the English vowels that sound most like what we think the Greek vowels represented. Rather than introduce additional symbols, we have chosen to use *e* for both *eta* and *epsilon* here.

General Patterns

We turn now to what the Sec. teaches us about the pronunciation of Hebrew. As before, we will be careful not to draw any firm conclusions, because data based on transliteration is notoriously unreliable. Rather, we will look for confirmation or lack of confirmation of what we already know or suspect.

We will see that the Sec., like the LXX, confirms most of what we know about the pronunciation of the consonants as recorded by the Tiberian Masoretes. And unlike the LXX, the Sec. contains good support for the Masoretic *dagesh*. The Sec. contains mixed evidence about the pronunciation of the vowels.

Finally, the Sec. diverges from the Masoretic tradition in some key areas.

Consonants

By and large, the Sec. confirms most of what we know about the pronunciation of the Hebrew consonants. So, *mem* (*m*) is *mu* (מ or M) in Greek, *resh* (ר or R) is *rho*, etc.

One peculiarity of the transliteration in the Sec. (which is true of names in the LXX, too) is that *shin* (Masoretic שׁ) and *sin* (שׂ) are both recorded as *sigma* (σ). Not surprisingly, *samech* (ס) is also recorded as *sigma*. Furthermore, *tzadi* (צ) is transliterated as *sigma*. However, we have external evidence that *tzadi* was pronounced differently than *samech* and *sin*, in that only *tzadi* tends to alternate with *ayin* in Aramaic. We therefore come to the conclusion that the Greek alphabet was unsuitable for recording the various *s*-like sounds (collectively called **sibilants**).

So while we have no confirmation for the Tiberian Masoretic notion that the symbol שׁ was used for two sounds, we also recognize that had there been a difference we would likely not have seen it reflected in the LXX or the Sec., which offer us only very general information about the pronunciation of the various sibilants in Hebrew.

In addition to *sigma* being used for three Hebrew symbols (which may have represented four sounds) in the Sec., we find that none of *heh* (ה), *aleph* (א), *ayin* (ע), or *chet* (ח) make their way into the Greek transliteration. There are two likely reasons for this.

One possibility is that the letters that were not recorded made no sound. Another possibility is that the letters that were not recorded made a sound that Greek could not capture. Our best guess is that *aleph* and *heh* made no sound, and that *ayin* and *chet* made sounds that did not exist in Greek. However, the Sec. gives us no confirmation of this guess.

It is somewhat surprising that the author of the Sec. was content with so much ambiguity. With three (or four) sibilants expressed by the same letter in Greek, and another four letters not expressed at all, we find not only that words that (probably) sounded very different in Hebrew are recorded identically in Greek, but that often only context tells us which Hebrew word is conveyed by a particular Greek transliteration. (St. Jerome, who compiled a Latin translation of the Hebrew Bible toward the end of the 4th century C.E., made copious notes about what he thought Hebrew sounded like. He specifically mentions this problem.) Starting on page 113 below, we will see that this ambiguity gives us clues about the nature of the transliteration.

Also concerning the consonants, we find that the Hebrew letter *tav* (ת) is almost always *theta* (θ) in Greek and *tet* (ט) is *tau* (τ). We do not see any indication of the Masoretic (and modern Ashkenazi) notion that *tav* represented two sounds, be they the stop /T/ and the fricative /Th/, or the stop /T/ and the fricative /S/.

Similarly, *kaf* (כ) is *chi* (χ) and *koof* (ק) is *kappa* (κ). Again, we see that different letters were transliterated differently, but we see no confirmation of the Masoretic and, in this case, modern Israeli, notion that *kaf* represents two sounds, a stop and a fricative. Indeed, none of the "beged kefet" stop/fricative alterations are confirmed by the Sec.

We turn to doubled letters next.

Doubled Letters

The Sec. usually uses a double letter in Greek to mark what the Masoretes marked with a *dagesh*. The Sec. thus differs from the LXX, which, as we saw above, was inconsistent in this regard. (Let us not assume, of course, that the LXX was wrong.)

To understand the doubled letters in the Sec. we have to know a little bit more about how Hebrew works. By and large, Hebrew words come from a three- or four-letter **root**, and a **paradigm**, or form. We noted above that Hebrew has roughly seven verbal paradigms, and that three of them require one of the root letters to be doubled. Nouns, too, come in paradigms, and some of these paradigms require one of the root letters in the noun to be doubled.

With this in mind, we can look at three different reasons a letter might be doubled, and, therefore, marked with a *dagesh* by the Tiberian Masoretes. (Recall that the Masoretes also used the *dagesh* to mark the difference between stops and fricatives. We have already seen that the Sec. does not contain anything similar.)

First, a letter in a verb might be doubled because the verbal paradigm requires a double letter. We saw some examples of this verbal doubling, such as the double *n* in *Jephunneh*, in our discussion of names based on verbs in the LXX.

Secondly, a letter in a noun might be doubled for one of two reasons: either the noun form requires a double letter, or the word comes from a root with a double letter.

Thirdly, the first letter in a word might be doubled because the word that precedes it causes it to be doubled. For example, according to the Tiberian Masoretes, the words *the* (-הַ) and *from* (-מִ) cause the next letter to be doubled, as does the word *what* (מַה). The Masoretes record this doubling with a *dagesh*. (Furthermore, the words *the* and *from* are written as part of the word they precede, a fact which, though in principle irrelevant for our current discussion, is worth noting because they don't look like separate words; they look like prefixes.)

One final bit of information about doubling in Tiberian Masoretic Hebrew is important: Guttural letters are never doubled, that is, they never receive a *dagesh*; often, instead of the doubling, the vowel before the would-be doubled letter is changed. This change in a vowel before a letter that should be doubled but which cannot be, technically called **compensatory lengthening,** is very common in the languages of the world. The prevalence of this pattern in other languages reinforces our belief that we have correctly understood the nature of the *dagesh*, and that it is used to mark doubling. (Without this evidence, we might be tempted to think that a *dagesh* that follows words such as *the* in Masoretic Hebrew represents not doubling but some third use of the *dagesh*.)

At any rate, this very complex system of Masoretic doubling as marked by a *dagesh* is almost fully reflected in the Sec. The details are a little complex, but give us great insight into the stages of Hebrew's development between the LXX and the Masoretes.

We turn first to the verbs.

Of the three verbal paradigms that require a *dagesh*, that is, that are marked by doubled letters, two (the ones traditionally called *pi'el* and *hit'pa'el*) are fairly consistently marked by doubled letters in the Sec. Roughly 80% of the forms that have a doubled letter in the Masoretic tradition also have a doubled letter in the Sec. Curiously, four verbs have a doubled letter in the wrong place. The second root-letter ought (according to the Masoretes) to be doubled, but instead the first root-letter is doubled. We will return to this point below. In a handful of cases, details of the Greek transliteration scheme mask any potential doubling.

We have only one example of the third letter-doubling verbal paradigm (*pu'al*). While the example we see does not contain a doubled letter, we do not know if the lack of doubling reflects the 20% of all doubled letters in verbs that are not marked in the Sec., or if *pu'al* verbs did not receive doubling at all, for reasons we don't know. In light of the high degree of consistency between Masoretic doubling and doubling in the Sec., we assume that the one *pu'al* verb left us is not indicative of *pu'al* verbs in general. (Remember, most of the Sec. was destroyed.)

We turn next to look at the nouns. We have but a handful of nouns that have intrinsic doubled letters, that is, letters that double but not because of a preceding word. Of these, most forms in the Sec. seem to match the Masoretic version. For example, the word *lev* "heart" (לב) takes a *dagesh* in the second letter to mark its doubling when the the second letter does not appear at the end of the word, that is, when the word has a suffix. (The actual process is probably the other way around. Probably, the word always has a double letter, but double letters in Hebrew almost always become single letters at the end of the word. The effect is that words like *lev* have a doubled letter whenever they have a suffix.) The Sec. contains three instances of the word *lev*, once alone and twice with suffixes. Without a suffix we find one *lambda* representing the *lamed*, and with the suffixes we find two. The word *sak* "sack" or "sackcloth" (שק) behaves similarly. As with the verbs, we find that the nouns in the Sec. comply very highly with the Masoretes' notion of doubling.

Finally, we look at words preceded by words that induce doubling in the following word. Here we find a curious pattern.

On the one hand, when the word *the* is adjoined to a word, the first letter of that word is doubled in twelve out of fourteen times where the Tiberian system suggests that it should be.

On the other hand, when the word *the* is part of another prefix (one of *in, like,* or *to* — -ב, -כ and -ל, respectively), the Sec. generally shows us no doubling in spite of the Tiberian system that mandates (and attests) such doubling. This combined form of the prefix *the* is the only time the Sec. does not systematically adhere to the Tiberian system of doubling letters.

Two final points about doubling prove important. First, with very few exceptions, we see no cases of doubled letters in the Sec. that are not doubled according to the Masoretes. Secondly, while the the Sec. did not mark most of the guttural letters, the guttural letter *resh* (*r*) was always marked by a *rho* (ρ). This *rho* is never doubled in the Sec., a fact which matches the Masoretic prohibition against doubling guttural letters.

The degree to which the doubling in the Sec. matches the Tiberian use of *dagesh* provides very strong evidence that the *dagesh* was, in fact, used to mark a doubled letter, and, furthermore, that this doubling reflects a pattern in Hebrew that goes back at least to the 3rd century.

Vowels

In one sense, the vowels in Sec. correspond well with the Tiberian Masoretic vowels, and in another sense they do not. There seems to be consistency in terms of which vowels are used for a particular purpose, but less consistency throughout the entire transliteration. That is, it looks like the Sec.

adhered to a consistent grammar, but not precisely the grammar that the Tiberian Masoretes gave us.

For example, the Tiberian system uses the vowel *chiriq* for (among others) three purposes: It is the first vowel in a *niph'al*[3] verb, and it is the first vowel in the normal infinitive of a *kal*[4] verb. (We will see a third purpose immediately below.) However, in the Sec. we find that *epsilon* (ϵ or E) is normally the first vowel of a *niph'al* verb, while *alpha* (α or A) is normally the first vowel of an infinitive. Similarly, Tiberian Hebrew has a *shewa* as the first vowel of a *pi'al* infinitive, while the Sec. has once again an *alpha*.

A third purpose for which the Masoretes used a *chiriq* demonstrates a contrary pattern, however: we see the suffix "-i" meaning "my" — always written with a *yud* in Hebrew and annotated by the Tiberian Masoretes as being preceded by a *chiriq* — written inconsistently in the Sec., sometimes with an *iota* (ι), sometimes with an *eta* (η).

By and large, however, the vowels in the Sec. more or less correspond to what the Masoretes thought were there. Though we certainly do not have an exact match, we also do not see the sorts of massive deviance from Masoretic forms that we saw in the LXX, where, for example, the name *Riv'ka*, which the Masoretes recorded as being bisyllabic, was recorded as being trisyllabic. The general syllable structure evidenced in the Sec. tends to be the same as what the Tiberian Masoretes recorded.

Segolate Nouns

It is worth noting two other ways in which the Sec. systematically disagrees with the Tiberian Masoretes before we try to come to a conclusion about what the Sec. tells us about the degree to which the Masoretic pronunciation and grammar correctly reflect more ancient dialects of Hebrew.

The first of these involves a class of nouns called **segolates**. Without straying into complicated and irrelevant details, we can note that the segolates are the nouns that the Masoretes recorded as being accented on the second to last syllable, rather than the usual last syllable. (The name "segolate" comes from the fact that the Masoretes assigned the vowel *segol* to the last syllable of these words.) We have already encountered the segolates briefly (page 61), where we noted that *segol* alternates with *patach* in the Tiberian Masoretic system, but in the Babylonian system no such alternation is seen.

Here we find variation not in the first vowel, as with the Tiberian

---

3. *Niph'al* is one of the seven verbal paradigms.
4. *Kal* is another paradigm.

versus Babylonian Masoretes, but variation in the second vowel. Rather than the typical Masoretic *segol*, the nouns tend not to have any second vowel recorded at all. For example, rather than the (Tiberian) forms *shemesh* "sun," *boker* "morning," and *eretz* "land" — שֶׁמֶשׁ, בֹּקֶר, and אֶרֶץ, respectively — we find the Greek forms *sams* (σαμς), *bekr* (βεκρ), and *ars* (αρς).

It is well known that the segolate nouns in Hebrew are odd for a variety of reasons. In the Masoretic system, they are not only the only nouns that regularly take penultimate rather than ultimate word stress, but when they appear with a suffix they behave as though, indeed, they did not have a second vowel. (The details of this are complicated and not directly relevant to our current point about the Sec.)

In light of the high degree of similarity between the Sec. and Tiberian understanding of most nouns, this systematic difference is surprising.

The Pronominal Suffix "You"

The second systematic difference between the Sec. and the Masoretic understanding of Hebrew involves the pronominal suffix for "you." In Hebrew, the letter *kaf* is suffixed to a verb to indicate a (usually, direct) object "you," or to a noun to indicate "your." For example, from אשכיל (*'skil*) meaning "I will teach" we have the word אשכילך (*'skilk*) meaning "I will teach you." Similarly, from טוב (*tuv*) meaning "goodness" we find טובך (*tuvk*) meaning "your goodness."

When this suffix appears in Masoretic Hebrew, it is usually pronounced with the vowel /a/ after the last consonant: /askil/ becomes /askil'xa/ and /tuv/ becomes /tuv'xa/. (Again, x is roughly the sound at the end of the name *Bach*, and we have an /x/ sound instead of a /k/ sound because of the *beged kefet* rules.) By contrast, the Sec. puts the vowel /a/ *before* the suffix. For example, the Greek transliteration of *askil'xa* and *tuv'xa* is εσχιλεχ (*eskilek*) and τουβαχ (*tubak*).

Once again, we are surprised to see such a systematic difference between the Sec. and the Masoretic forms. It is tempting to conclude that the Masoretes just got this wrong, and, indeed, for many years researchers came to exactly that conclusion, but we will see that the Dead Sea Scrolls (Chapter 7) suggest that this might be one aspect of ancient Hebrew that the Masoretes got right. In this case, therefore, we will ask the reverse question, and wonder why the Sec. got this aspect so wrong.

Table 6.6. Some errors in Origen's Secunda Columna

Hebrew	Erroneous Greek	Correct Greek (?)
תתמם act blamelessly	θεμαμμαμ temammam	θεθαμμαμ tetammam
תתברר act purely	θεθβαραβ tetbarab	θεθβαραρ tetbarar
תושיע you will save	θωει toei	θωσι tosi
ועינים and eyes	ουνναιμ ounnaim	ουηναιμ ouenaim
תשפיל make humble	θεοφιλ teopil	θεσφιλ tespil
תמים pure	θαμμιν tammin	θαμμιμ tammim
אלהינו our God	ελωννου elonnou	ελωηνου eloenou
חיל power	αιδ aid	αιλ ail

Errors

We should consider one final point about the Sec. It is replete with errors. For example, Table 6.6 lists the eight errors in the first ten lines of what remains of Psalm 18 (verses 26 to 33). Eight errors in sixty-six words is astoundingly high; but these verses are typical at least of what remains of the Sec. Furthermore, the errors seem to be of several sorts: letters that sound the same are confused; letters that look the same are confused; letters are erroneously repeated in words.

It is difficult to know, of course, to what degree the errors reflect Origen's original document (destroyed in the 7th century) and to what degree they merely reflect the sloppiness of a later copyist, but the fact that so many errors have crept into the material we are analyzing warns us against drawing any conclusions based on only one or two words.

What Is the Secunda Columna?

Having looked at myriad details of the Sec., we turn now to the general question of what it really was. That it was some sort of transliteration is, obviously, abundantly clear. But beyond that, we have more questions than answers.

The purpose of the Sec. has been and remains a matter of scholarly debate. Why, after all, would Origen need a transliteration of the Hebrew in his quest for better understanding of the Bible?

Some have suggested that the Greek transliteration was designed for people who knew the Hebrew language, but could not read Hebrew letters. The transliteration, it is claimed, would have let these people read and understand the original Hebrew of the Bible. But the transliteration is hardly accurate enough to facilitate understanding. Because (as we saw above) four consonants are not transliterated at all and another three (perhaps four) are denoted with the same symbol, only skilled Hebrew scholars would be able to understand the Hebrew they were reading in Greek. It seems implausible that there were enough Hebrew scholars who could not read Hebrew that a transliteration had to be prepared just for them.

Another theory holds that the Greek was only meant to help people pronounce the Hebrew, perhaps for liturgical purposes. Various attempts have been made to support this theory with ancient material, and various attempts have been made to denounce it.

One aspect of the transliteration, however, cries out for an explanation. This is the careful attention paid to double letters.

We do not know, of course, what the double letters were meant to represent, either in Greek or, presumably, in the Hebrew that the Greek captured, but in the discussion starting on page 108 we saw that the transliteration faithfully recorded several complex aspects of grammatical doubling in Hebrew. If the doubling represented gemination (as reviewed on page 60), we note that gemination is, by and large, a difficult thing to hear in language. The difference (to continue the example from above) between "hot tea" and "hot 'E' " in standard American English is subtle.

We would not expect a transliterator to distinguish geminate from non-geminate forms with anything approaching the consistency we see in the Sec. regarding doubled letters. How, then, did the Sec. come to contain such an accurate description of the geminates? One very likely answer is that the Sec. was not a guide to the pronunciation of Hebrew, but rather to the *grammar* of Hebrew (perhaps in addition to its pronunciation). If the transliteration was designed to take into account the grammar of Hebrew, we immediately understand five otherwise odd aspects of the transliterations.

First, we understand why the transliteration so faithfully copies the doubled letters in Hebrew. Those doubled letters are matters of grammar, regardless of pronunciation. Anyone who knew Hebrew grammar could have known which letters were doubled, without having to listen carefully to spoken Hebrew. In this regard we may note that many modern-day "transliterations" into English strive to double letters where a *dagesh* appears in Hebrew, even though the pronunciation is unchanged. For example, in the common spelling *Hanukkah*, the double *k* represents a *dagesh* in Hebrew. Certainly, in English, *Hanukah* and *Hanukkah* are pronounced identically. The *b* is doubled in the English word *Sabbath* — derived from the Hebrew *shabbat* — for this same reason.

Secondly, we understand why some verbs in the Sec. show doubling on the wrong letter. The author knew that — for grammatical reasons — a letter was doubled somewhere, but the author doubled the wrong letter by accident. Similar confusion gave us "Hannukah" for "Hanukkah" in English. We may also note that modern American students of Hebrew will frequently place a *dagesh* in the wrong letter of a verb by accident. It is a common and easy mistake to make. (However, we also have to allow for the possibility that these wrongly doubled letters are to be counted among the numerous errors to be found in the Sec.)

Thirdly, we understand why a whole class of doubled letters does not appear in the Sec. Recall that, like some other prepositions, *to* (written as a a prefixed *lamed*: -ל) as well as *the* (written as a prefixed *heh*: -ה) are written attached to the words they precede in Hebrew. The word *the* induces doubling in the letter that follows. The word *to* does not. However, when both *to* and *the* are prefixed to a word, rather than write both the *lamed* (for *to*) and the *heh* (for *the*), Hebrew just writes the *lamed*. It is precisely in this case that the Sec. does not mark any doubled letters. As a matter of pronunciation, it is linguistically absurd to think that the word *the* only induced doubling if it were not preceded by a preposition that happened to be written as a prefix. But as a matter of general knowledge, it is reasonable to believe that the author of the Sec. assumed that only when the word *the* was actually written out did it induce doubling.

Fourthly, we understand why the Sec. goes through such great pains to record doubled letters when it makes absolutely no attempt to record four consonants and to distinguish among another three (or four). That is, if the point of the Sec. were to assure proper pronunciation, we would be surprised at the lack of attention paid to matters so important for pronunciation. But if the point is grammar, we understand immediately why the consonants in Greek were unimportant. After all, they were present in the Hebrew for anyone who cared to look.

Finally, we understand why Origen needed the transliteration in the first place. It was a guide to understanding the Hebrew, not (merely?) to pronouncing it.

Based on all of this, we conclude that the Sec. was designed at least in part to convey the grammar of Hebrew at its time, and we remain uncertain about its role in conveying pronunciation.

Summary

Summing up all of the evidence about the Sec., we find that it generally agrees with the Masoretes. Like the LXX, it does not confirm the stop/fricative alternation among consonants, nor does it confirm the distinction between consonantal and vocalic *vav*. However, unlike the LXX, the Sec. by and large confirms the Masoretic grammatical system of doubled letters, as well as the general Masoretic understanding of the structure of words.

Combined with the LXX, this lets us build a tentative timeline for the development of Hebrew, as discussed next.

Conclusions

We have looked at two main sources in our attempt to figure out how well Tiberian Masoretic Hebrew captured Biblical Hebrew. One source dates from around the 3rd century B.C.E., and the other from approximately the 3rd century C.E.

Other, more detailed, evidence is available from the 4th century C.E. onward, but we ignore this as being too far removed from Biblical Hebrew to tell us anything of value. Indeed, the Sec., too, may be too far removed to tell us much.

In Table 6.1, we noted that language games offer detailed, specific information about the pronunciation of a language. One such example from Biblical Hebrew survives. Judges 12 recounts the conflict between the Gileadites and the Ephraimites. In verse 6, we read of a pronunciation test that the Gileadites gave to the Ephraimites, regarding the pronunciation of the letter *shin* (שׁ). We are told that the Ephraimites mistakenly pronounced the *shin* as a *samech* (ס): "(5) ... When any fugitive from Ephraim said, 'let me cross,' the men of Gilead would ask him, 'are you an Ephraimite?' and he would say, 'no.' (6) They would tell him to say the word *shibolet* [שׁבלת] but he would say *sibolet* [סבלת], not being able to pronounce it properly."

From this we learn that the pronunciations of *shin* and *samech* were related, but we still have no verification of our current understanding that *shin* represented two sounds, one of them shared by *samech*. (We can use this pronunciation quiz to learn about Hebrew regardless of our position about the veracity of the actual story.)

Beyond this one language-game example, however, we are forced to rely on the transliteration evidence to put together a complete picture.

Because the LXX fails to support so much of the Masoretes' work (including, even, general syllable structure), and because the Masoretes lived so long after Biblical Hebrew had ceased to be spoken, we conclude that we have no scientific reason to think that the Tiberian Masoretes correctly captured Biblical Hebrew beyond its most basic structure.

By contrast, the Sec. seems to support not only the Tiberian understanding of the words but even the Tiberian system of grammar. It does not, however, accord as well with the Tiberian system of pronunciation. We conclude, therefore, that the Tiberian system of grammar had its antecedents as early as the 1st or 2nd century C.E. And because the names in the LXX that come from verbs show doubled letters in the places that the Tiberian Masoretes predict, we conclude that some aspects of the Tiberian system of grammar reflect Hebrew from as early as the 3rd century B.C.E.

Nowhere have we seen any confirmation of the stop/fricative ("*beged kefet*") alternations we see in Tiberian Hebrew. We have likewise seen only vague confirmation that the vowels the Tiberian Masoretes used were roughly correct.

In the end, then, the Tiberian system seems to reflect some grammar that goes all the way back to early Biblical Hebrew, and some grammar that was invented later on. The Tiberian system seems to capture roughly the proper Biblical pronunciation of the consonants, but, probably, not of the vowels; the system also probably does not capture Biblical syllable structure.

This should not come as a surprise. The Tiberian system correctly captures roughly what can be retrieved from the largely consonantal script that Hebrew used: the consonants. The fact that part of the Tiberian system of grammar seems to have very ancient sources is a surprising success for the Tiberian Masoretes.

So when we look at current copies of the Bible, which follow the Tiberian Masoretic tradition, we see the consonants of perhaps 3,000 years ago and parts of grammar that may go back that far, but general pronunciations that go back only 2,000 years, and sometimes but 1,000 years.

Part III
Moving On

Chapter 7
The Dead Sea Scrolls

Background

When we looked at the Leningrad Codex (page 76) we noted that it dates from the end of 1st millennium C.E., that it is the oldest surviving complete copy of the Bible as we know it, and that modern printed Bibles are usually based on its text. But during the past century, documents twice that old were discovered in the Judean Desert near the Dead Sea. These are the Dead Sea Scrolls (or "DSS").

In addition to offering new information about the state of Judaism around the turn of the era, the DSS have provided invaluable evidence about the state of Hebrew 2,000 years ago. We will see that the DSS confirm some of the Masoretes' work, contradict other parts of their work, and contradict one very important part of Origen's Secunda. Unlike the indirect evidence that we can glean from the LXX (as discussed on page 90) or the Secunda (page 102), or the secondhand information provided in more modern manuscripts, the Hebrew in the DSS that has survived intact from two millennia ago offers direct evidence about the Hebrew of the time.

The DSS contain parts of the Bible as we know it, "para-Biblical" literature that looks like Biblical material but is not included in any current religious version of the Bible, commentaries, prayers, calendars, and a host of other writings.

Before looking at the contents of the DSS, we'll take a lengthy but intriguing detour to learn how they were found. It started with a goat.

How Did We Get Them?

A Lost Goat (Cave 1)

In 1947, three Bedouin shepherds of the Ta'amireh tribe were wandering around the Judean desert northwest of the Dead Sea trying to find a goat they had lost from their herd. While looking, one of them threw a stone into the upper opening of a cave, and, rather than hearing the appropriate "thump" of a stone landing on the desert floor, he heard the "ping" of a stone hitting something hollow. Though the ground-level entrance to the cave was blocked by stones, the Bedouin entered the cave through the top, and found therein ten potted jars. Eight of them were empty and one contained dust, but the final jar contained three scrolls, two of them wrapped in cloth. A few days later, members of the tribe returned to the cave and found four more scrolls.

The Bedouins took the scrolls and jars and kept them in their tent as a curiosity for a while before taking them to Bethlehem and offering them for sale. After some unsuccessful attempts, they eventually found a Syrian Orthodox "dealer in antiquities," Jalil "Kando" Iskandar Shalim, who purchased the scrolls from the Bedouins.

Kando brought the scrolls to a man named Athanasius Samuel, the archimandrite[1] of a Syrian Orthodox monastery in Jerusalem, who bought four of the seven scrolls for 6 liras apiece, or roughly $110 in total. As nearly as we can tell, none of the people involved at this point knew what the scrolls were or that the seven scrolls would be separated across continents for almost a decade before being reunited in Jerusalem.

After purchasing them from Kando, Samuel tried to resell the four scrolls. Thinking that scrolls from the holy city of Jerusalem would be much more valuable than scrolls found in the middle of the desert, Samuel claimed that the scrolls had been found in his monastery, in the Jewish quarter of the Old City.

The three scrolls that Samuel did not purchase were offered to Professor Elizer Sukenik, who was at the Hebrew University in Jerusalem at the time. Sukenik used university money to purchase the three scrolls, and two of the jars in which they had been stored.

At this point, the Bedouins had discovered and sold seven scrolls, four of which had been resold to a Syrian Orthodox cleric who was trying to sell them under false pretenses, and three of which had been sold to the Hebrew University.

Then the war broke out.

---

1. An archimandrite is the equivalent of an abbot.

Samuel took his four scrolls to the American School of Oriental Research (ASOR), where a research student named John Trever examined them and recognized the text of one of them as Isaiah. He photographed three of the scrolls, hoping to publish them on behalf of ASOR. The fourth scroll was in such bad shape that Samuel refused to let Trever open it to photograph. Samuel may also have realized that his four-scroll collection would be more valuable if one of the scrolls remained unphotographed.

Unsure of what would happen in Jerusalem during and after the war, Trever convinced Samuel to smuggle the four scrolls to the United States. There, Samuel tried once again to sell them, and once again he was unsuccessful. Not only was the legal status of the scrolls unclear, but Trever had already published his photographs, and researchers who were busy trying to understand the contents had no need for the originals.

It wasn't until 1954, when Samuel published an advertisement in the *Wall Street Journal*, that he managed to sell his four scrolls. His advertisement read, "Biblical manuscripts dating back to at least 200 B.C. are for sale. This would be an ideal gift to an educational or religious institution by an individual or group."

Professor Sukenik, the one who had bought three scrolls on behalf of the Hebrew University, had a son in the United States who had just retired after serving as chief of staff of the Israel Defense Forces ("IDF"). Sukenik's son, Yigael Yadin, was trying to return to his field of archaeology when he saw Samuel's advertisement. (Yadin doesn't share his father's surname because he took the name "Yadin" while in the pre-Israel military movement called the Haganah.) Yadin raised $250,000 to buy the four scrolls, which he then sent to Jerusalem. There, together with the three scrolls that his father had purchased, the seven original scrolls were united again. The scrolls were deemed so important that the Israel Museum built a special hall to house them, "The Shrine of the Book."

Back in April of 1948, shortly after the Bedouins' original discovery, ASOR and Sukenik both issued press releases about their scrolls. With the possibility that one of the scrolls was a copy of Isaiah 1,000 years older than the previously-known oldest Hebrew copy (the Leningrad Codex, as discussed on page 76), the press releases brought enormous interest in both the scrolls and the caves in which they had been found. What were the scrolls? Were they authentic? How old were they really?

The Bedouins, for obvious reasons, refused to tell the world which of the thousands of caves around the Dead Sea contained the scrolls. And at any rate, the caves were in Jordan. Because of the hostilities surrounding the Israeli War of Independence, excavations for Jewish scrolls in Jordan were difficult. But academic publications in 1948 and 1949 describing and analyzing the scrolls — which at this point had been dubbed the "Jerusalem

Scrolls" — only intensified interest in these finds.

In January of 1949, with the help of the Arab Legion of Jordan, the location of the amazing cave that had yielded these seven scrolls was made public. G. Lankester Harding of the Jordanian Department of Antiquities and Father Roland de Vaux of the French *École Biblique et Archéologique Française* co-led an archaeological excavation to what is now called Cave 1. When the team arrived, the archaeologists found that the cave had already been excavated ("raided," they said) by Bedouins and monks from the Syrian monastery of St. Mark. These previous excavations made it difficult to determine the actual date of the material in the cave, or to verify the authenticity of the original seven scrolls. But the team managed to find pieces of dozens of scrolls, including fragments of the seven original scrolls.

Together with pottery that the team found, the scroll fragments enabled the archaeologists to state with certainty that the seven original scrolls were both authentic and ancient. Because they were actually found in the Qumran area around the Dead Sea (and not in Jerusalem, in spite of what Samuel had claimed), the scrolls were called the Dead Sea Scrolls, and proved to be the most important archaeological find for the modern study of the Bible.

The scrolls turned out to be two copies of the Book of Isaiah, with language in each that varies only slightly from the canonical Book of Isaiah; a commentary on Habakkuk; a document about how the people who wrote the scrolls lived, known now as the "Rule of the Community" or the "Manual of Discipline"; a document about an eventual battle between the sons of light and the sons of darkness ("The War Scroll"); a book of vaguely psalm-like poetry; and a paraphrase of Genesis in Aramaic ("the Genesis Apocryphon").

Another Cave (Cave 2)

In 1952, the Bedouins found more scrolls to sell. Unlike the first set of scrolls, these were mainly from the time of Bar Kokhba's revolt (132–135 C.E.). The scrolls were found south of Cave 1, in an area called the Murabba'at Wadi.[2] Naturally, archaeologists rushed to the Murabba'at Wadi in the wake of the Bedouins, where they set up excavations and found five caves, from which a few hundred documents, mostly from the Bar Kokhba revolt, were retrieved.

While the archaeologists were in Murabba'at, the Bedouins returned to Qumran, embarking on their own archaeological expeditions. Back at Qumran, they found a second cave ("Cave 2") just south of the first. This

---

2. A *wadi* is a dry riverbed.

second cave yielded fragments from over thirty different scrolls, including a small piece from the Book of Ben Sira.

When word of the second cave reached the French archaeologists from the *École Biblique et Archéologique Française,* they, with ASOR and the Palestine Archaeological Museum, set out on a massive exploration of the entire Qumran region. In the process, they were able to discern the location of the Bedouins' Cave 2, which still had a few tiny fragments left in it.

Of Copper and Gold (Cave 3)

During their excavations, the team of archaeologists found what is now called Cave 3, northeast from Cave 1. Delighted to have beaten the Bedouins to this cave, they quickly began exploring its contents, and found the usual scroll fragments, in this case containing parts of over a dozen different works. They also found a scroll unlike any that had been found to date. This one — dubbed the "copper scroll" — was made of copper. It was found rolled midway, as though its previous reader had not rolled it back to the beginning. But because the copper had hardened over two millennia, it was too brittle for the archaeologists to open.

Only four years later were the contents revealed. Technicians in Manchester, England, used a saw of the sort used for brain surgery to cut the scroll into tiny parallel strips, which they then reassembled. The mysterious copper scroll turned out be a verbal treasure map, describing the location of a quarter-million pounds of gold and silver, stashed in various locations throughout Jerusalem and the surrounding region. The scroll begins in Hebrew,[3] "In the ruin in the dark valley [or: in the Valley of Akur], under the steps leading east, forty cubits [?]: a chest of silver and its vessels, weighing 17 talents *KEN.*" (The "KEN" appears in the original, in those Greek letters — *kappa, epsilon, nu* — which happen to look like their English counterparts.)

Unless modern science has radically misunderstood the situation, the amount of treasure described in the Copper Scroll exceeds the total in existence in antiquity. There are, thus, few scholars who think that the scroll describes real hoards. Nonetheless, reports of so much buried treasure brought more than a few private citizens to Israel in search of riches. To date, none of the treasure has been found.

---

3. We know we do not completely understand the Hebrew. Probable areas of confusion are marked by square brackets [like this].

A Wounded Partridge (Cave 4)

South and slightly east of Cave 1 lie the ruins of Khirbet Qumran, which in 1951 appeared to be the remnants of a Roman fortress. In light of the great finds in the caves nearby, archaeological excavations at Khirbet Qumran were undertaken, again under the joint leadership of Harding and de Vaux. The pottery found in Cave 1 is unique, but similar pottery was found at Khirbet Qumran, helping to establish that the ruins were connected in some significant way to the scrolls. The finds at Khirbet Qumran have since given researchers important information about the people who lived at Qumran and who probably left us the scrolls.

The Judean desert in which Qumran is located is a geologically complex place, lying as it does between the heights of Jerusalem and the depths of the Dead Sea. The sedimentary rock upon which Khirbet Qumran was built forms cliffs ("marl terraces"), some of which have deep cavities carved within them. Working on the assumption that these holes had been caused by water — either driven rain or perhaps the water from the wadi, Harding and de Vaux had decided not to search them.

But de Vaux tells the story that one evening an old Ta'amireh Bedouin heard about the scrolls and the money they fetched, and recalled the days of his youth during which he would hunt in the Qumran region. One day a partridge he had wounded managed to flee to one of the holes in the wadi wall. The Bedouin went in search of his prey, only to find that the hole that the partridge had found led to a room full of pottery shards, including a lamp, which he retrieved and kept.

This story prompted a decision to search for additional lucrative scrolls. After hearing a description from the old man, some younger members of the tribe managed the difficult task of finding the hole and then the even more difficult task of entering the cave to which it led. There over 15,000 scroll fragments awaited them, apparently remains from the central Qumran library. This was Cave 4. Not wanting the Bedouins once again to beat them to undiscovered scrolls, and not wanting them once again to destroy archaeological evidence, the archaeologists sent a team of police to the site to protect it from any unauthorized excavations. The police arrived too late.

Although only some 1,000 fragments of the original 15,000 remained for Harding and de Vaux to retrieve, those remaining pieces could be linked with the thousands the Bedouins had removed, so that the authenticity of all of the pieces could be verified.

The pieces were found in 1952, but, because there were so many of them, they were not all sold and collected for six years. The Jordanian government did not have the resources to buy all the fragments, and so turned to major internationally known universities and the Vatican Library for help. These institutions helped purchase the contents of Cave 4, in return for the right to publish the results they yielded.

Even with the help of graduate students, the task of reassembling 15,000 fragments was a daunting one. But the international team that helped purchase the contents of Cave 4 managed the task. The team, working in Jerusalem and directed by de Vaux, reassembled parts of over five hundred different manuscripts.

Although the documents were assembled fairly quickly, their publication for the world to see was not forthcoming, with the first fragments not officially published until 1968. By contrast, the finds from Cave 1, which had, after all, been discovered only four years before Cave 4, had been published in 1955.

The Race Is On

The race between the Bedouins and the archaeologists continued for some time. The archaeologists found Cave 5. The Bedouins found Cave 6. In 1955, de Vaux found some stairs in the area, which, it turned out, led to 3 collapsed caves, numbered 7 to 9. Cave 10 was discovered under a mat of sorts in Cave 4. Though no scrolls were found in the cave, it did contain a decorated lamp and a pottery shard with letters that might spell "Jesus" in Hebrew. In 1956, the Bedouins found Cave 11, the last cave to be found (to date).

Among the scrolls found in Cave 11 was the "Temple Scroll," apparently (it would be learned) a replacement or addition to Deuteronomy, containing summaries both of other known Biblical books and books unknown to us. The book is written in the first person, as though Moses himself wrote it, containing idioms such as "God said to me, 'Tell your brother Aaron ...' "

The Temple Scroll was the best preserved in the cave, and, at roughly 25 feet, was (and is) the longest scroll found in Qumran. Kando — who was still involved as an intermediary, helping the Bedouins sell their finds to the Jordanians — refused to sell this extraordinary scroll to the Jordanian authorities, hoping to find a purchaser with deeper pockets. To keep the scroll safe, Kando buried it in a cache he had dug under the floor of his Bethlehem house.

Kando approached Yigael Yadin, who had purchased scrolls in the past, and, in 1961, tried to sell him the newly found scroll. Depending on who tells the story, either the sale didn't go through or Yadin paid $10,000 for the scroll but never received it.

The Six-Day War in 1967 brought Bethlehem under Israeli control. As chance would have it, Yadin served as a military adviser to Israel's prime minister during the war, and was in a position to have the military search Kando's home for the scroll. Members of the IDF found the scroll under Kando's floor, confiscated it, and brought it to Yadin. To Yadin's great dismay, during the eleven years in Kando's cache the top half of the scroll had rotted away. Nonetheless, the government of Israel eventually paid $100,000 for the confiscated scroll.

Publish or Perish

The political tensions in the area were running high. In 1965, the title under which the Dead Sea Scrolls were published was changed from "Discoveries in the Judaean Desert" to "Discoveries in the Judaean Desert of Jordan." We have already seen that the longest and best preserved scroll suffered incredible damage while it was being hidden. We have also already seen the not-so-friendly competition between the professional archaeologists and the Ta'amireh Bedouins. But these controversies would pale in comparison to the battle over who had the right to see, use, and publish the scrolls.

Many scholars felt that the multi-organizational consortium that had custody over the scrolls was taking too long to publish them. The fact that only Christians were involved with the initial work contributed to claims that the scrolls contained devastating evidence for Christianity, and that their contents were therefore being kept secret. The fact that only thirty scholars worldwide (dubbed "the clique") were allowed access to the scrolls enraged academic institutions.

By 1990, these factors had so aggravated the situation that accounts of the fierce debates between the keepers of the scrolls and those who wanted unfettered access to them made their way into editorials in the American media, which spoke of the "cartel" that prevented anyone from seeing the Dead Sea Scrolls. Additionally, Hershel Shanks, editor of the popular *Biblical Archaeology Review*, took up the cause, calling for intellectual freedom.

A list of words with the context in which they appear (technically called a **concordance**) had been compiled of all the non-Biblical texts found in Cave 4. Under worldwide pressure to grant more access to the scrolls, the consortium released thirty copies of the concordance to be used only by the thirty or so members of the authorized clique of scholars.

Professor Ben Zion Wacholder of HUC-JIR in Cincinnati let a graduate student named Martin Abegg enter the information in the concordance into a computer. It is a fairly simple matter to write a computer program that will generate the text from which a concordance is created, and Abegg did just that. In September of 1991, the *Biblical Archaeology Review* used Wacholder and Abegg's re-creation of the texts to begin publishing the scrolls from Cave 4 that had been kept secret for so many years.

The publication of this material marked the end of the secrecy, and other publications followed quickly.

It took a half century, thousands of hours of tedious work, several clandestine excavations, one smuggled scroll and one buried scroll, an advertisement in the *Wall Street Journal*, a team of soldiers, and an unauthorized computer reconstruction, to say nothing of a lost goat and an injured partridge, but the Dead Sea Scrolls have been found, thoroughly authenticated, and published in original and translated form. Anyone with access to a good library or bookstore can now read them.

Are They Real?

There has been so much (mostly unfounded) controversy surrounding the Dead Sea Scrolls that significant discussion of their authenticity has surfaced in popular and even academic literature. It is therefore worth briefly reviewing the ways scholars know that these documents are genuine, and that they come from roughly 2,000 years ago.

One way of knowing the age of the DSS is carbon dating. Carbon, part of all organic material, occurs naturally in more than one form, and, in particular, in non-radioactive and radioactive forms. In naturally occurring carbon in the air, about one part in a million is radioactive carbon-14, while the rest is mostly carbon-12. Because plants and animals take in this carbon mixture until they die, the carbon in live plants and animals contains about one carbon-14 atom for every million carbon-12 atoms. Once the plant or animal dies, no new carbon is introduced, but the radioactive carbon-14 keeps decaying. By looking at the ratio of carbon-12 to carbon-14, scientists can determine the date at which organic material died.

Using this technique on the cloths that had been used to wrap the documents found in the caves near Qumran, scientists in 1950 came up with a date of production of 33 C.E. While carbon dating techniques in the 1950s had margins of error of perhaps 200 years, the possibility of recent forgeries was thus eliminated. (Academicians still remembered the case of another "dealer in antiquities" in Jerusalem, M. Shapira, who, in 1883, had announced the discovery of an ancient copy of Deuteronomy. His copy proved to be forged.)

In addition to its rather large margin or error, the carbon-dating process in the 1950s also suffered from the drawback that it destroyed a significant amount of the material to be dated. Researchers were, obviously, unwilling to destroy material only to prove that it would have been worth saving.

Other, less accurate and potentially more error-prone methods were also applied to the material in Qumran. The pottery found in the caves was unlikely to have been potted after the 1st century C.E., for example. The content of the Biblical and para-Biblical scrolls was most compatible with those same dates. The archaeologists who unearthed the pottery and scrolls likewise concluded that their material was roughly 2,000 years old. The content of some of the material refers to historical figures who can be precisely placed in history. Some of the documents contain dates. Some coins with dates were found.

The most widespread and (then) controversial supporting evidence for the carbon dating was **paleography**, analysis of the letterforms used to write the scrolls. The forms of the letters suggested dates ranging between the 3rd century B.C.E. and the 1st century C.E., with, according to the paleographers, margins of error of only tens of years. But even as the fledgling field of Hebrew paleography grew, it was difficult to know whether the paleographers were on the right track. So until 1990, the DSS were "probably roughly 2,000 years old." More precise dates were speculative or unconfirmed.

Fortunately, a new technique of dating — Accelerator Mass Spectrometry (AMS) — was discovered in the 1980s. Still based on the ratio of carbon-14 to carbon-12, this technique required very little material, often less than a milligram, to obtain a date. It could therefore be used on the scrolls themselves. In 1990, this new technique was applied to over a dozen scrolls, four of which contain dates. (The documents with dates were included as a check on the AMS method of dating.) This newer scientific method confirmed the paleographically derived dates, giving researchers added confidence in their dating of the scrolls, and further bolstering their confidence in paleographic dating.

There is now no doubt in the scientific community that some of the Dead Sea Scrolls were penned as early as the 3rd century B.C.E., and none later than 68 C.E.

What Are the Dead Sea Scrolls?

Thousands of documents have been retrieved from the caves in Qumran. Martínez (1996) divides the content into nine non-Biblical categories, recognizing that his categories overlap to some degree, and that not all of the documents fit precisely into any category.

The list below gives a sense of the documents found in the caves at Qumran, and of their potential significance for understanding both the Hebrew of 2,000 years ago and for putting the Hebrew that came before and after into context.

Here are Martínez's categories, along with a tenth category ("Biblical material").

1. **Rules.** These are very general documents, typical of Qumran (and later Christian periods, as well) that describe myriad aspects of life in the Qumranic society. Their content includes rules and regulations (hence their technical name), as well as a variety of tangents. The best-known Rule is the "Rule of the Community" (copies of which were found in Caves 1, 4, and 5), describing the Qumranic way of life. Because that Rule describes Qumran itself, and was therefore almost certainly written by the people there, it offers us insight into the Hebrew that was actually in use in Qumran.

2. **Halakhic Texts.** "Halakha" is Jewish law. While many of the DSS, including the Rules and some exegetical material, contain halakhic writing, some documents were devoted primarily to halakha, and even sometimes to the differences between halakha in Qumran and elsewhere. Like the Rules, these offer us information about the Hebrew of Qumran in addition to their valuable content.

3. **Eschatological Literature.** "Eschatology," from the Greek $\epsilon\sigma\chi\alpha\tau o\varsigma$ (*esxatos*) meaning "last," is the department of theology that deals with what happens when things end: death, the end of the world, final judgment, and so forth. To judge from the documents we have retrieved, the Qumranic Sect was obsessed with the imminent end of days, and much of their literature has eschatological themes. But some documents focus exclusively on such matters, including the War Scroll, one of the first scrolls found in Cave 1. These documents, too, were probably written at Qumran, and offer evidence both about the state of Hebrew at the time and the people who wrote them.

4. **Exegetical Literature.** "Exegesis" is the process of interpreting (usually religious) text. The exegetical DSS are documents that deal with interpreting the traditional Bible as we know it today, and offering commentary on it. Some of these texts are in Aramaic, putting them in a category with other translations and interpretations into Aramaic known as *targums*. Others are in Hebrew, offering *midrash*-like interpretations of the Bible. Because these do not deal directly with Qumran, it is more difficult to know whether these were composed by members of the sect, copied from memory by those members but composed earlier, or, even, imported from elsewhere.

5. **Para-Biblical Literature.** In terms of content, this is some of the most

interesting material. The corpus of DSS contains considerable material that looks Biblical, but which does not appear in the traditional collection of "the Bible."

Of particular interest are the "non-canonical" psalms. The Bible as we know it contains exactly 150 psalms (which, because they are canonized, are known as "the Psalms"), but a Psalter (book of psalms) found in Qumran contains additional psalms mixed in with some of the 150 "canonical" psalms. While we call the extra psalms "non-canonical," we once again see a potential collision between the God Theory and the Science Theory. The God Theory, in its current Jewish and Christian instantiation, insists that the Bible as we have it now contains the correct and authentic version of Psalms. The Science Theory, by contrast, notes that Jews living 2,000 years ago, long before our oldest remaining copy of the Bible, had more than 150 psalms. The Science Theory must also take into account the round number 150. One way the nice round number 150 could have come about is for there to have been many more Psalms once, with the 150 in the traditional Bible representing one editor's choice of the 150 best psalms. Perhaps the Qumranic Sect had a different set of best psalms. Perhaps they even had an original set. We will not analyze the situation further here, but we do note that calling this material "para-Biblical" represents our modern-day religious point of view. We will retain the term because it is so convenient, but we must be careful to remember that our "non-canonical," or "para-Biblical," material may have been what the Qumranic Sect considered "Biblical." (Surprisingly, the non-canonical psalms are not listed as para-Biblical material in Martínez (1996); he puts them in the next category, Poetic Texts.)

In the end, a fine line divides this category from the previous one, in that one could consider as commentary or interpretation any material that seems to be like the Bible but which is not technically Biblical. And like the exegetical material, it is difficult to know where this material was composed and where it was written.

6. **Poetic Texts.** As with the other categories, the poetic texts comprise an assortment of documents, including some that might equally be considered para-Biblical. In addition to the non-canonical psalms, which we discussed above, this category includes various metrical material that we presume may have been sung. While some of the poetic texts are almost certainly Qumranic in origin, others may represent material from the wider community.

One reason the poetic texts are so similar to the para-Biblical texts is that the Bible seems to haved formed the basis for poetry back then (as it does, to a lesser degree, in some modern Israeli poetry). The division between para-Biblical texts, poetic texts, and liturgical texts (as discussed next) is not only vague, but hampered by our lack of knowledge about how each specific text was used.

7. **Liturgical Texts.** Some of the texts found in the Qumran caves contain hints or even specific instructions about their liturgical use. For example, some texts tell us that they are a "song for the fourth Shabbat." Again, it is difficult to know, given our limited understanding of Qumran, which texts were originally Qumranic and which may have been imported from elsewhere.

8. **Astronomical Texts, Calendars, and Horoscopes.** This category subsumes a variety of texts that describe the calendar as it interacts with the life of the members of Qumran, including the location and movements of various heavenly bodies, priestly rosters, and horoscopes. One of these documents, "Astronomical Enoch," seems to be summarized (poorly) in chapters 72 to 82 of Ethiopic Enoch, a 1st- or 2nd-century B.C.E. apocryphal book originally written probably in Aramaic. (Even before the discoveries in Qumran, this Book of Enoch was known both from references to it in early Jewish and Christian literature and from an Ethiopic translation of the book from perhaps the 4th century C.E.) If these chapters in Ethiopic Enoch are really a summary of the DSS document, Astronomical Enoch may represent a mainstream document more widely known in the Jewish world that, by chance, was preserved only in Qumran.

9. **The Copper Scroll.** The Copper Scroll, truly *sui generis*, gets its own category, for it is unlike anything else found in Qumran. Its fanciful contents and unique character suggest that the scroll may not be from Qumran at all. For all we know, a member of the Qumran Sect may have found it while returning from Jerusalem. Because it is so extraordinary, it is difficult to draw any conclusions about Hebrew from it.

10. **Biblical Material.** In addition to all the non-Biblical material found at Qumran, significant Biblical material has been preserved, including parts of all five books of the Torah and many other books of the Bible. These Qumranic versions of parts of the Bible help us establish the state of the Bible 2,000 years ago.

Who Wrote the Dead Sea Scrolls?

The general question of who wrote the Dead Sea Scrolls has a very short answer, almost too ridiculous to bother considering, and a long answer, too complex to fit into this volume.

The short answer is, almost tautologically, that the DSS were written by the people who lived in the caves around the Dead Sea, that is, the members of the Qumran Sect. The list above indicates which DSS texts were probably created by the members of the Qumran Sect, and which may have been composed elsewhere, but of all the scrolls, only the Copper Scroll stands any significant chance of having been simply brought from elsewhere. People living in caves around the Dead Sea copied almost all of the Dead Sea Scrolls, and composed some of them.

The longer answer, of course, tries to offer more insight into the nature of the people who lived at Qumran. The great 1st-century C.E. historian Flavius Josephus tells of three groups of Jews — the Sadduccees, the Pharisees, and the Essenes — the last of which were a separatist group that seceded from mainstream Judaism when the Maccabees took over the office of the high priest in the middle of the 2nd century B.C.E. What is known about the Essenes — from Josephus's work and from other sources — corresponds well with what is known about the Qumran Sect, and so most scholars conclude that the authors of the DSS were Essenes.

However, not only do some scholars disagree, but enormous questions remain about the Qumran Sect.

One of the biggest questions concerns the apocalyptic nature of the group. By and large, apocalyptic groups, that is, groups who believe that the end of the world is nigh, generally do not last long. After a generation or two of preaching the end of the world, the members of the group tend to realize the inaccuracies of their belief, and either change it ("the end of the world is coming, but it's far off") or abandon it. It remains a mystery how the Qumran Sect managed to maintain its message of the imminent demise of the world during their three-century occupation of Qumran. This is the sort of glaring paradox that tends to suggest that modern scholars have misunderstood something fundamental.

Other mysteries confound our understanding of the authors of the DSS. Why were the scrolls in jars? Why were some jars empty? What about the Copper Scroll? How connected to mainstream Judaism was the sect? Why were the members of the Qumran Sect living in the desert?

We should also be careful about the terms "separatist" and "mainstream." Historical accident (or, by some, divine planning) has cast the Essenes to the side. But a more balanced scientific view suggests several groups of Jews from the end of the 1st millennium B.C.E., some who would eventually become mainstream and some who would not.

In spite of these issues, and some dissenting scholarly opinions, we can be fairly sure that the DSS represent the writings from members of an early form of Judaism who lived in the desert.

What Do We Learn
from the Dead Sea Scrolls?

Having taken an extensive look at the various sorts of Dead Sea Scrolls (DSS) and how we got them, we turn now to what we can learn about Hebrew from the DSS, and, in particular, three different kinds of information.

First, because the DSS comprise the oldest significant surviving body of Hebrew, they offer the best information about the ancient Hebrew in which the Bible was written. While the Septuagint (LXX) is older than the DSS by perhaps 200 years, that Greek translation offers little evidence compared to the actual Hebrew documents found in Qumran. And the DSS are certainly closer in time to the Hebrew of the Bible than is the Hebrew of the Masoretes, who lived roughly a millennium later. By historical accident, the Masoretic version of the Bible is commonly regarded as "the Bible," but from a scientific point of view, we must regard the DSS as more authentic, or, at least, closer to the original, so we will use the DSS to judge the accuracy of the Masoretic versions of the Bible. (We do this in keeping with the scientific approach we have adopted. Some religious approaches, of course, use the Masoretic version to judge the accuracy of the DSS.) We will see that the DSS support much of the work of the Masoretes but also contradict some of it.

Secondly, the DSS provide information specifically about the Hebrew of their time. By comparing the scrolls that were composed at Qumran (such as the Rules, as listed above) with the Biblical material that was probably written earlier, we can discern patterns in the development of Hebrew. As we will see, these patterns are interesting not only in their own right, but they also give us information about general trends in Hebrew, which are important for understanding all stages of Hebrew.

Thirdly, the DSS provide direct evidence about the state of the Hebrew Bible from roughly 2,000 years ago.

With these three issues in mind, we start looking at the DSS in more detail.

The Hebrew of the DSS

The DSS represent some 300 years of manuscripts, and documents from one time period may represent more than one period of Hebrew, just as even today we publish material in English with different dialects of English. Nonetheless, about a fifth of the material found at Qumran seems to represent a single dialect and even a single writing style, in that both the Hebrew and the penmanship adhere to similar principles. It is this Hebrew that we will look at, calling it either (more conveniently but less accurately) "Dead Sea Scroll Hebrew" or (more accurately but less conveniently) "Qumran-style Dead Sea Scroll Hebrew."

Vowel Letters

We saw above (starting on page 23) that the early Hebrews used the letters *yud, heh,* and *vav* as vowels, in addition to their consonantal uses. But they did not do so consistently.

For example, Rebecca's Hebrew name רבקה (*resh, bet, koof, heh*), whether it was a trisyllabic word (in the LXX: *rebekka*) or a bisyllabic word (as the Masoretes recorded: *riv'kah*) has too many letters to be monosyllabic, yet the original orthography only indicates one vowel: the final /a/. Similarly, as we saw in Table 6.4, the name "Zebulun" in Hebrew was usually written with a *vav* for either the second vowel or the third vowel, but seldom for both. (The first vowel was never written.) As it is usually spelled in the Bible, David's name, too, is ambiguous. Spelled *daled, vav, daled* (דוד), it could either be a monosyllabic name (say, /dod/) in which the middle *vav* functions as a vowel, or a bisyllabic name (say, /davad/ or /david/) in which the middle *vav* functions as a consonant. (The LXX suggests the latter.)

While still not indicating every vowel, the Hebrew of the DSS supplies more vowels than the older Hebrew we find in the Bible. In particular, we seem to find *heh* for /a/ at the end of a word, *vav* for /o/ and /u/, and *yud* for /i/ and /e/. Of course, as before, the exact sounds those letters represented have been lost, but there are good reasons to think that we have a good approximate understanding of the ancient sounds.

For example, "David" in the DSS is almost always spelled with an extra *yud*: *daled, vav, yud, daled* (דויד). While the Hebrew is still ambiguous — a reader might not know if the *vav* is the vowel (say, /doyad/) or if the *yud* is the vowel (e.g., /david/), or what the first vowel sound is — this spelling offers more information than the original Hebrew. (We also see

Table 7.1. Some words in the Masoretic and DSS traditions, with probable pronunciations

Word	Masoretic Version	DSS Version
all	כֹּל *kol*	כול *kol**
not	לֹא *lo*	לוא *lo*
head	רֹאשׁ *rosh*	רואש *rosh*
very / strength	מְאֹד *m'od*	מאוד *m'od*
God	אֱלֹהִים *elohim*	אלוהים *elohim*
your name	שְׁמֶךָ *shim'xa*	שמכה *shVm'xa***
examination	חֵקֶר *xeker*	חיקר *xekVr*
hundreds	מֵאוֹת *me'ot*	מיאות *me'ot*
Sodom	סְדֹם *s'dom*	סודום *sodom*
captivity	שְׁבִי *sh'vi*	שובי *shovi*
embroidery	רִקְמָה *rikma*	רוקמה *rokma*

* The /o/ sounds may also be /u/. We don't know.
** A capital "V" represents a vowel whose value we do not know.

this spelling sometimes in the Bible.) The technical term for Hebrew that contains extra vowels is "full" (מלה — *maleh* — in Hebrew).

What we see, then, is that the Hebrew of the DSS is fuller than the Hebrew of the Bible. Other examples of the fuller nature of DSS Hebrew compared with the Hebrew of the Bible (listed at the beginning of Table 7.1) include the word "all," which is spelled just *kaf, lamed* (כל) in the Bible but *kaf, vav, lamed* (כול) in the DSS. Similarly, "no" or "not," which is (almost always) spelled just *lamed, aleph* (לא) in the Bible, appears (almost always) as *lamed, vav, aleph* (לוא) in the DSS.

God's name — *elohim* according to the Masoretic tradition — is always written without a *vav* for the middle vowel (probably /o/) in the Bible: *aleph, lamed, heh, yud, mem* (אלהים). By contrast, in the DSS it appears as *aleph, lamed, vav, heh, yud, mem* (אלוהים).

Furthermore, a vowel corresponding to a particular grammatical feature appears consistently in some DSS texts, and almost never in the Bible, as follows.

Hebrew, it would seem, had two forms of the suffix meaning "you" or "your(s)," a masculine version and a feminine version. In the Bible both are spelled simply with a *kaf* "ך" (and, in particular, a "final" *kaf*, because the Hebrew script used by the Masoretes has special forms of five letters, including the *kaf*, that are used only when the letter is the last letter of the word). In spite of the two forms being spelled identically, the Masoretes recorded the masculine version as being pronounced *-xa* and the feminine version as being pronounced *-ax*. For example, the word for "to" is the prefix *l-* (-ל). According to the Masoretes, the word for "to you" is *l'xa* (לְךָ) when the "you" is masculine, and *lax* (לָךְ) when the "you" is feminine. (Additionally, *lax* is used for the masculine form when the form comes at the end of a phrase, in what Hebrew grammarians call the "pausal form." We can ignore this nuance.)

Similarly, from the word *yad* (יד) meaning "hand" we get two words for "your hand": *yadex* when the "your" refers to a woman, and *yad'xa* when the "your" refers to a man. In the Bible, both of the forms are (almost always) spelled the same: *yud, daled, kaf* (ידך). Unlike the Hebrew of the Bible, the DSS Hebrew indicates the final vowel /a/ in this common suffix meaning "you" or "your" with the letter *heh*. So the masculine form of "to you" was written *lamed, kaf, heh* (לכה) rather than the Biblical *lamed, kaf* (לך). The word "your hand," when the "your" referred to a man, was written *yud, daled, kaf, heh* (ידכה) rather than the Biblical *yud, daled, kaf* (ידך). (Surprisingly, Exodus 13:16 also spells "your hand" with a final *heh*, just as it would appear in the DSS. It is not clear what to make of this: It looks like a late addition, particularly in light of the fact that it seems to be a rewritten version of a passage that means almost the same thing and that appears just a few lines earlier in Exodus 13:9.)

These examples of a *heh* at the end of a word in the DSS are important because, even though the Masoretes were working with a text that did not have a letter to indicate any final vowels in these cases, they marked the sound /a/ with a vowel mark, namely, the *patach*. (The vowels are listed in Table 5.1.) This might lend credence to the Masoretes' work, because the vowel sound they recorded, even though not indicated in the written text from which they were working, seems to have been recorded independently by the authors of the DSS.

But in addition to the extra *heh* that matches the Masoretic tradition, there seems to be a *heh* that appears on other pronouns in DSS Hebrew, where we otherwise have no hint that it ought to. So, in addition to *lamed, kaf, heh* (לכה) for "to you," we also find *aleph, taf, mem, heh* (אתמה) for the plural form of "you" ("y'all" in some American dialects), where the Masoretes give us only *aleph, taf, mem* (אתם).

The extra *heh* in these pronouns is not the only example of full Hebrew that does not match the Masoretes' work. Some further mismatches appear toward the end of Table 7.1. For example, the word for the city Sodom as recorded by the Masoretes is *s'dom*, while the DSS give us "sodom." Curiously, the DSS version matches the LXX, which also records "Sodom" (Σοδομ). Likewise, the extra *vav* in the DSS version of the word for "embroidery" is hard to understand if we assume that the word was pronounced as the Masoretes thought. These examples and others work against the evidence brought by the first words in the table, and diminish the credibility of the Masoretes' work.

Though we are primarily focusing on the Qumran-style Hebrew DSS, it is worth pointing out that some other scrolls actually contain *fewer* vowel letters than the Masoretic version we use today. Cave 11 yielded a copy of Leviticus written in the older ("paleo-Hebrew") script. This scroll, 11Q1 or "PaleoLev," accords well with the traditional version of Leviticus, but also deviates from it in some minor ways. For example, the word for "seventh" (*sh'vi'i*) in Leviticus 23:24 is spelled with two *yud*s (שביעי) in our Masoretic version of the Bible, but with only one (שבעי) in the DSS version. While that shorter spelling does appear a handful of times in the Masoretic text, this is not one of those times. By contrast, in Leviticus 13:4 the word "its [her] appearance" (*mar'eha*) is spelled with a *yud* in the DSS but not in the Masoretic text.

Numerous other minor differences between 11Q1 and the Masoretic text of Leviticus, both in spelling and wording, are evident.

God's Name

We noted in the discussion on page 44 that the tetragrammaton — that is, the four-letter name of God — consisted of four magic Hebrew letters, and we suggested that it was never meant to be pronounced. The DSS add credence to that conclusion.

As we saw on page 24, two different scripts ("fonts") were used to write Hebrew, an older one, sometimes called Paleo-Hebrew, and a more modern one, called "Square" Hebrew. The latter, Square Hebrew, is basically the one used to this day to print Hebrew, and is the letterset with which most people are familiar.   Qumran-style DSS Hebrew is written in the more modern Square Hebrew, even though some DSS (such as 11Q1, the "Paleo-Leviticus" scroll) are written in the older script, presumably for reasons having to do with their older content. However, the tetragrammaton is commonly written in the older script even in scrolls that otherwise use only the newer script. For example, while the Hebrew in the 11QPs^a scroll that we have been using to compare the DSS and the Masoretic versions of the text is written in the more modern script, the four-letter name of God there is written in the older script, as depicted in Figure 4.1.

Grammar

Like the unique DSS spelling, a unique DSS grammar presents itself. However, a full discussion of the differences in grammar would necessitate two complete books, one on the grammar of the Bible and one on the grammar of the DSS. But for our purposes we can make do with one observation about compound words.

Hebrew has a unique way of expressing compounds, such as "school principal" (the principal of the school), "car door" (the door of the car), "bathing suit" (a suit for bathing), etc. Unlike English, where the main word comes second (so a school principal is a kind of principal, not a kind of school, and a car door is a kind of door, not a kind of car), in Hebrew the main word comes first. A common example is the phrase for "house of prayer," *bet t'filah*, literally, "house-prayer," which is what in English we would call a "prayer-house." Similarly, the (Modern) Hebrew for "car door" is *delet m'xonit* (דלת מכונית), literally "door car."

Hebrew changes the form of the main (first) word to be what is called the **construct case.** In terms of form, the principle behind the construct case is that the main word doesn't get accented, and so some of its vowels change, but the details are complicated and for our purposes irrelevant. In terms of meaning, the construct case expresses pretty much the same relationship that is expressed in some other languages (such as Latin) by the **genitive case,** except that the genitive is used for the secondary word in a compound, while the construct is used for the main word.

The construct case, like compounds in English, is used to represent some relationship between the main word and the secondary word. The relationship may be ownership, association, etc. Again, experts have investigated the complicated conditions that allow or prohibit a compound, but these details, too, are irrelevant here.

Different languages have different rules about plurals in compounds. In English, by and large, the second word gets pluralized when the compound becomes plural. So houses for dogs are called "dog-houses" (usually written "doghouses"), not "dogs-house" or "dogs-houses." Similarly, in Biblical Hebrew, to make a compound plural usually only the main (first) word gets a plural marking. The compound "man-capability" (*ish-xayil* — איש חיל) is used to mean either "reliable person" or "brave person." The plural is "men-capability" (*anshei-xayil* — אנשי חיל), not "men-capabilities." (There are a few surprising exceptions to this general pattern.)

By contrast, in the DSS, we commonly find "double-plural" compounds. For example, the plural of "war tool," which of course in Hebrew is "tool war" (*kli mil'xama* — כלי מלחמה), in DSS Hebrew is both "tools war" (*kle mil'xama* — כלי מלחמה), as we would expect to find in Biblical Hebrew, and also "tools wars" (*kle mil'xamot* — כלי מלחמות). (The word "tool" is one of the few words that looks the same in the singular and the plural, but we don't care about that word. Our focus is on the second word of the compound.)

We will see that some dialects of Hebrew spoken before the DSS use double-plural compounds, and some dialects spoken after the DSS use them, too, with an increase in their use over time.

No future dialect of Hebrew seems to be based on DSS Hebrew. We make this presumption based on the linguistic fact that no other dialect has adopted the unique DSS Hebrew spelling system, as well as the sociological facts that the speakers of DSS Hebrew never became part of any mainstream group and their written documents remained buried in caves for almost 2,000 years.

Because later dialects of Hebrew adopted many of the changes we see in DSS Hebrew even though they were not based on DSS Hebrew, we conclude that the changes were natural ones based on the nature of the language. This gives us further evidence that DSS Hebrew was a spoken dialect, because, by and large, only spoken dialects follow the rules of natural languages.

The Content of the DSS

The same people who copied over seemingly familiar passages of Hebrew with slightly different spellings also gave us versions that differ from the Masoretic Bible. These differences range from minor word variations that do not affect the meaning to entire new passages.

Minor Differences

For example, Psalm 136 appears in the DSS 11QPs^a (also known as 11Q5), with some minor variations. The opening two verses match the Masoretic version (with some extra *vavs*, following the same spelling principles described above), but in line three, the DSS author writes, "Give thanks to the lord [*adon*] of lords," rather than "Give thanks to the Lord [*adonei*][4] of lords." That is, the author uses the word that refers to any lord rather than the word for "the Lord." Both versions make sense, and the difference is but a single *yud* in Hebrew. In the next verse, the DSS reads, "... to the one who alone creates wonders," rather than the Masoretic "... to the one who alone creates great wonders." In Verse 7, the DSS has *m'orot* (מאורות) instead of the Masoretic *orim* (אורים); both words mean "lights." Translations of the two versions appear in Table 7.2.

Because the Masoretic version is so much better known, it is tempting to ask, "Why did the DSS authors get the text wrong?" But, of course, we could equally ask, "Why did the Masoretes get the text wrong?" In this case, the Masoretic version, which has the "sun as [one] dominion" and not "as [several] dominions" makes more sense, and even suggests an error on the part of the DSS copyist.

But in other cases, the DSS version makes more sense.

For example, the canonical version of Psalm 145:4 reads "generation to generation will praise your deeds ...," but the verb for "will praise" is singular. Most translations thus assume that the subject of the verb is "generation," and the meaning is "one generation will praise your deeds to the next generation." But "generation to generation" — דור לדור — is a common idiom in Hebrew, usually meaning something like "from generation to generation" or "in every generation." The line would make more sense if the verb were plural, because plural verbs without a subject are commonly used in Hebrew to refer to what linguists call "arbitrary subjects," that is, an unspecified group of one or more people. (Although many other languages use a plural verb without a subject for an arbitrary subject, English commonly uses "they," as in: "They say it's going to rain," "In Judaism they pray to one God," etc. In more formal dialects, "one" or the passive voice is commonly used: "One prays only to one God in Judaism" or "Only one God is worshiped in Judaism.")

In fact, the second half of Psalm 145:4 contains a plural verb: "... [they] will declare your mighty acts." The common translation, "... and will declare your mighty acts," leaves the reader under the mistaken impression that the subject of "will declare" might be the same as the subject of "will

---

4. The word is *adonei* rather than *adonai* because it means "Lord of."

Table 7.2. Differences between the Masoretic and DSS versions of Psalm 136

Masoretic Version	11QPs^a (DSS)
Praise Adonai, for He is good	Praise Adonai, for He is good
— His love is eternal!	— His love is eternal!
Render praise to the God of gods	Render praise to the God of gods
— His love is eternal!	— His love is eternal!
Render praise to the Lord of lords	Render praise to the lord of lords
— His love is eternal!	— His love is eternal!
... to the one who alone creates great wonders	... to the one who alone creates wonders
— His love is eternal!	— His love is eternal!
... to the one who creates the sky in wisdom	... to the one who creates the sky in wisdom
— His love is eternal!	— His love is eternal!
... to the one who spreads the earth over the water	... to the one who spreads the earth over the water
— His love is eternal!	— His love is eternal!
... to the one who creates great lights	... to the one who creates great lights
— His love is eternal!	— His love is eternal!
	... the sun and moon
	— His love is eternal!
... the sun as dominion by day	... the sun as dominions of day
— His love is eternal!	— His love is eternal!
... the moon and stars as dominions by night	... moon and stars as dominion by night
— His love is eternal!	— His love is eternal!

143

praise" in the first part. But the first verb is singular while the second one is plural. By contrast, in the DSS, we find two plural verbs, thus giving the much more sensible reading, "in every generation they will praise your deeds and declare your mighty acts."

The two versions of Psalm 145, in which the DSS rendition makes more sense than the canonical one, thus differ from the two versions of Psalm 136 which display the opposite pattern, with, as we saw, the canonical version seeming to make more sense. If we were to think in terms of "right" and "wrong," we might come to the conclusion that in Psalm 145 the DSS got it right, while in Psalm 136 the Masoretic version got it right. But this is probably an answer to the wrong question. We should not, generally, ask which version is "right." Rather, the right question is, "Why did the Masoretes and the Qumran Sect have different versions?"

Major Differences

We just saw that sometimes the DSS and the Masoretic Bible differ in their wording. At other times, as we will see now, they differ considerably in terms of content.

For example, the DSS version of Samuel 11 as recorded in 4QSam^a has a prologue that's absent in the Masoretic text. Table 7.3 shows the two versions, with the longer DSS text, including the prologue, next to the canonical Masoretic version.

In this case, the Septuagint (LXX) agrees with the Masoretic version, in that the prologue is absent. But in one detail the LXX agrees with the DSS over the Masoretic text. Both the Septuagint and the DSS have the line, "And it was after roughly a month . . . ," a phrase lacking in the Masoretic version. But that short phrase probably corresponds to the last line of the preceding story in Samuel, which, in the Masoretic version, ends with "And he was like a silent one." Though "it was after roughly a month" and "he was like a silent one" seem to have nothing in common in English, the Hebrew is quite similar. In Hebrew, "he was" is the same as "it was," and "like" is the same as "roughly." Furthermore, the letters in "like a silent one" and "roughly a month" are almost the same: the differences are where the words begin and end, and a *resh* (ר) in one versus a *daled* (ד) in the other, letters which look almost identical in Hebrew. (A similar though slightly more complex example in English would be if the phrase "William bought" were mistakenly copied as "Will lamb ought," because the letter *el* and the letter *eye* look similar.)

So we have the DSS version with a long introduction that's missing in the LXX and the canonical Masoretic version. The DSS and LXX share a

Table 7.3. Differences between the Masoretic and DSS versions of Samuel 11

Masoretic Version	4QSam^a (DSS)
[And he was like a silent one.] Nahash the Ammonite alighted and besieged Jabesh-Gilead. All the men of Jabesh said to Nahash, "Make a pact with us and we will serve you." But Nahash the Ammonite said, "This is how I will make a pact with you, by gouging out your every right eye, that I will use the eye to humiliate all of Israel."	And Nahash, king of the children of Ammon, was the one who severely oppressed the children of Gad and the children of Reuben, and gouged out their every right eye and visited terror and dread on Israel; not one man among the children of Israel was left beyond the Jordan whose right eye was not gouged out by Nahash, king of the children of Ammon. Only 7,000 men left the children of Ammon and came to Jabesh-Gilead. And it was after roughly a month that Nahash the Ammonite alighted and besieged Jabesh-Gilead. All the men of Jabesh said to Nahash the Ammonite, "Make a pact with us and we will serve you." But Nahash the Ammonite said, "This is how . . . "

short introductory line that looks almost like the last line of the preceding story in the canonical version. What are we to make of this situation?

There are good reasons to believe that the Masoretic version is corrupt and that the DSS version represents the original story, so that the DSS here actually helps us recover an original story that was hidden through mistakes in our canonical version of the Bible. Among the reasons for preferring the DSS over the Masoretic text are these: The DSS version is more convincing, putting the eye gouging in the story into a context, whereas the Masoretic version cries out for some explanation of such harsh treatment. The phrase "after about a month" in the DSS matches the LXX's introduction, and makes considerably more sense than the Masoretic "he was like a silent one." Finally, much of the Masoretic text for Samuel is corrupt — or, at least, currently unintelligible — so one more corrupt section is not surprising.

Unfortunately, there are also some reasons to think that the Masoretic text is original, among them the fact that the LXX, presumably predating the DSS version, matches the Masoretic text. If the Masoretic text is indeed corrupt, we would have to assume that the matching LXX text is corrupt, which argues for a corruption of the text before the LXX was written, that is, before the 3rd century B.C.E. But if the "wrong" version of the text goes back that far, it's not clear how the authors of the DSS, writing after the 3rd century B.C.E., ever got the "right" text.

The spelling in the text is confusing, too. Both the DSS and the Masoretic texts spell "Jabesh" inconsistently, first without a *yud* and then with a *yud*. "Jabesh" is spelled both ways elsewhere in the Masoretic version of the Bible, but only the latter is consistent with the "full" spellings (as discussed on page 136 above) of Qumranic Hebrew. The rest of the DSS passage is spelled "full," while the Masoretic text is not. (For example, the word for "all" has a *vav*, as listed in Table 7.1.)

We can account for the fuller spellings in the DSS by assuming that it was written at Qumran, in accordance with their spelling system. But if so, we cannot understand why "Jabesh" is spelled two different ways. If we assume that the scribes at Qumran were simply copying older documents, perhaps culled from a variety of sources, we can understand why "Jabesh" might have been spelled in two different ways, but then we are at a loss to understand why the longer passage does not appear in the LXX.

In the end, most scholars believe that the DSS version is the original, and that the Masoretic version known to us is the result of a copying oversight that inadvertently omitted a passage. The minority dissenting opinion is that the Qumran Sect added the passage as commentary.

This type of puzzle gives a flavor for how the LXX, DSS, and Masoretic texts are compared and contrasted.

The Big Picture

As an overall trend, then, the DSS confirm that the Masoretes' text goes back at least as far as the end of the 1st millennium B.C.E. While we had no real reason to doubt this, it was somewhat troubling that the oldest actual copy of the Bible was but 1,000 years old. The DSS, too, are too recent to provide direct evidence about the original Bible as it may have been written, but they are much closer in time.

The DSS also have the benefit of having been left undiscovered in caves. We can thus be reasonably sure that the Masoretes did not copy them. Indeed, the Masoretes were probably unaware of them.

Because the Masoretes did not copy the DSS but their work nonetheless is generally the same as (some of) the DSS, we reasonably conclude from the DSS that the Masoretes roughly captured not only the Bible as it was known by the end of the 1st millennium C.E., but the Bible as it was known by the end of the 1st millennium B.C.E. The DSS have moved us 1,000 years closer to the source.

While the lack of substantial documents from the 1,000-year period between the DSS and the Masoretic material remains a substantial mystery, particularly in light of the holy status that the Masoretes presumably ascribed to the documents they were presumably working with, and even in light of the results of our discussion on page 70 where we saw that the Masoretes must have invented one aspect of the grammar they claimed to preserve, we do not have to worry that the Masoretes invented the written Bible. We have clear evidence that it existed, more or less in the form we now know it, considerably earlier.

Recall the example above in which two spellings for the word "Jabesh" appeared in the same places in the DSS and in the Masoretic version of the Bible. It is hard to imagine how this might have come about if the Masoretes did not have a manuscript with two different spellings to work from. It seems likely that that manuscript was a reliable copy of a manuscript going back to the days before Qumran, or the DSS version could not have incorporated the two different spellings.

The other possibility is that both the Masoretic text and the DSS text had random spelling variations, and, as a matter of chance, spelling variations will sometimes match.

In favor of the random variation theory, and against the theory that the Masoretes and the Qumran Sect had identical texts, recall that the Leviticus Scroll found in Qumran does not confirm the spelling of the word "seventh" as it appears in the Masoretic text.

Once again, we have contradictory evidence.

We also find surprising support for some of the Masoretic vowels. We find that the unwritten /o/ vowels in *kol* ("all"), *rosh* ("head"), etc., are actually written out in the DSS. So are some of the /e/ vowels (*xeker* "examination," or *me'ot* "hundreds," for example). With regard to the /a/ vowels, we find evidence that the Masoretic tradition of using *-xa* as a masculine ending and *-ax* as a feminine ending is likewise evidenced in the DSS. This last bit of information is particularly surprising in light of the fact that Origen's Secunda does not reflect this pattern (as discussed starting on page 112). We must wonder if perhaps the Masoretes knew something about the pronunciation of ancient Hebrew that Origen, who lived long before them, did not.

But based on the forms for "you (plural)" that end in /a/ we must also consider the possibility that the DSS reflect an odd dialect of Hebrew that just happens to match the Masoretic form sometimes. Of course, we should also consider the possibility, for which we have no counterevidence, that the DSS forms that do not match the Masoretic forms (e.g., "you (plural)") are right, and that the Masoretes got this part wrong.

What we do not find is support for all of the Masoretic vowels. In fact, precisely those vowels that were suspect based on the evidence in Chapter 6 are still suspect. The DSS augment the evidence, suggesting that the initial ("epenthetic") /i/ vowel seen in many words may have been an invention of the Masoretes.

In terms of the Hebrew of the DSS, we find a trend toward fuller spelling, that is, spelling that includes more vowel letters. As we will see, almost every time Hebrew has been in use as a spoken language, the writing has tended toward fuller spellings.

Furthermore, the changes in compound formation that we saw above will also continue into later dialects of Hebrew, and be seen in modified form in Modern Hebrew.

So while we see a mixed picture, both in terms of not fully having understood everything about the DSS and of finding conflicting degrees of agreement between what we think we understand about the DSS and what we think we understand from other sources, by and large, information gleaned from the DSS matches other stages of Hebrew and other stages of history.

Chapter 8
Dialects in the Bible

So far we have been talking about "Biblical Hebrew" as though all of the Hebrew in the Bible were the same. But it is not. It turns out that more than one stage of Hebrew is evidenced in the Masoretic version of the Bible as we know it today. Of course, it should come as no surprise that a compilation of material that was composed over the course of several hundred years and then copied, edited, and (inadvertently and by design) changed for several hundred more should contain more than one dialect of the language in which it was written.

Scholars have worked to identify the various authors of the Bible based on content and style. They notice that different sections of the Bible tend to place more or less emphasis on the priests, for example, or on the prophetic traditions. They notice wording variations and different ways of referring to God. They find repeated passages within a story, and try to tease apart different original versions of the story that may have been combined at one point.

But we will not review those efforts here. Rather, we will focus on the more limited domain of major linguistic trends, the most important of which is the set of changes that took place after the exile in 586 B.C.E. to create what is known as "Late Biblical Hebrew," a term that is somewhat confusing, because "Biblical Hebrew" generally refers to all of the Hebrew used to write the Bible, and therefore includes "Late Biblical Hebrew." There ought to be a corresponding term, "Early Biblical Hebrew," but it is seldom used. So when we talk about all of the Hebrew of the Bible, we call it simply "Biblical Hebrew," but when we talk about "Late Biblical Hebrew," we contrast it with "Biblical Hebrew," by which we mean earlier Biblical Hebrew.

After looking at Late Biblical Hebrew, we will look at the ramifications of seeing more than one dialect reflected in the Masoretic text of the Bible.

Late Biblical Hebrew

Overview

We saw three aspects of the Dead Sea Scrolls (DSS) in the last chapter. The Hebrew spelling in the DSS is generally fuller — that is, written with more vowel letters — than the spelling in the Bible; the wording of the DSS differs from the Masoretic understanding of some passages; and sometimes the content of the DSS differs from parallel passages in the Masoretic tradition. Occasionally these three patterns of divergence are evident not only when comparing the DSS and the canonical (Masoretic) Biblical text, but within the canonized Bible as well.

For example, we can compare Chronicles, which seems to have been written relatively late, with Samuel or Kings. The Hebrew spelling of David's name in Chronicles matches the fuller spelling we saw in the Hebrew of the DSS, in that it has a *yud* to represent the vowel /i/: *daled, vav, yud, daled* (דויד). By contrast, it is usually spelled without the *yud* in Samuel and Kings.

Sometimes we are lucky enough to find entire passages from Samuel or Kings repeated verbatim or nearly verbatim in Chronicles. When the passages differ in minor ways, we can use the differences to help discern trends in the development of Hebrew. For example, the text in 1 Kings 8:12–16 is repeated in 2 Chronicles 6:1–5, but in Chronicles, David's name has the *yud*, a fact that belongs in a larger context.

Vowel Letters

Table 8.1 shows a passage that appears twice in the Masoretic version of the Bible, once in 1 Kings and once in 2 Chronicles, and Table 8.2 compares some of the Hebrew words as they are spelled in the two passages. Clearly the texts have the same source, so it seems fair to ask why they differ in minor wording details, spelling, and grammar.

One possibility, of course, is that the differences are a matter of chance. For example, the JPS[1] English translation of these two passages differs slightly. The translation of Kings reads, "... **with** the whole congregation of Israel **standing** ... " while the translation of the same Hebrew in Chronicles reads, "... **as** the whole congregation of Israel **stood** ... " (We have put the words that differ in boldface.) In spite of the fact that a footnote tells the

---

1. "Jewish Publication Society." The widely-used JPS translation is listed in the Bibliography under its editor, David Stein.

Table 8.1. A parallel passage in Kings and Chronicles

1 Kings 8:12–15	2 Chronicles 6:1–4
Then Solomon said:	Then Solomon said:
Adonai has said	Adonai has said
to dwell in a thick cloud.	to dwell in a thick cloud
I built You	I built You
an exalted house	an exalted house
a place where you may dwell	And a place where you may dwell
forever.	forever.
The king turned his face and blessed	The king turned his face and blessed
the entire congregation of Israel	the entire congregation of Israel
while the entire congregation of	while the entire congregation of
Israel was standing.	Israel was standing.
He said: "Praised be Adonai the	He said: "Praised be Adonai the
God of Israel who spoke with his	God of Israel who spoke with his
mouth to David my father and with	mouth to David my father and with
his hand fulfilled [the following]."	his hands fulfilled [the following]."

Table 8.2. Different spellings in 1 Kings and 2 Chronicles

Word	1 Kings	2 Chronicles
to dwell	לִשְׁכֹּן	לִשְׁכּוֹן
	LiSH'KoN	LiSH'KON
standing	עֹמֵד	עוֹמֵד
	oMeD	OMeD
David	דָּוִד	דָּוִיד
	DaViD	DaVID

Capital letters in English represent letters in the text. Lowercase letters represent Masoretic vowels.

reader that the two passages are identical in Hebrew, the English has two different wordings. Surely this difference is a matter of chance choices on the part of the translators or editors.

Recall also the discussion of Zebulon's name, as presented in Table 6.4, where we noted that even modern print Bibles differ in the spelling of some words. These modern variations certainly do not reflect anything about ancient Hebrew, and are probably also the result of mere chance. Similarly, the missing "and" in 1 Kings (or, equivalently, the extra "and" in 2 Chronicles) and the difference between "hand" and "hands" in the Masoretic text is likely a matter of chance.

Another possible source for differences in texts is copying errors. Later on in the parallel passages, we see a segment of the text from 2 Chronicles that does not appear in 1 Kings. In the longer text, the phrase "for my name" (שם שמי להיות — literally, "that my name be there") appears twice, while in the shorter version, the scribe seems to have confused the two, writing it only once, and in so doing, jumbling the rest of the text. (The technical name for this sort of error is "parablepsis," from the Greek for "to see wrongly," or "oversight.")[2] So the different content in the two versions merely reflects a copying error, one that we can even identify. In further support of this parablepsis theory, we note that the Septuagint contains the full content both times. (Surprisingly, however, the Greek wording, unlike the Hebrew, is not identical in each case.)

The spelling of the words (Table 8.2), however, not only follows a regular pattern, but follows more or less the pattern that we saw with the DSS. Those two facts (the regular pattern and the consistency of the pattern with more general patterns) lead us to believe that the differences reflect something basic about ancient Hebrew, and not chance or copying errors. Table 8.2 uses capital letters for the Hebrew letters in the text — mostly consonants, but some vowel letters as well — and lowercase letters for the vowels supplied by the Masoretes. We see that the Hebrew in 2 Chronicles is written with more vowel letters than the earlier Hebrew, just as the DSS were written with more vowel letters than their corresponding Biblical texts.

From this and other examples, a pattern about Late Biblical Hebrew emerges. Many of the vowel letters in the Bible are subject to seemingly

---

2. The subspecialty that studies and analyzes scribal copying errors has conveniently assigned long Greek names to other phenomena as well. For example, homoioteleuton ("same ending") is the sort of parablepsis that occurs when a scribe sees the same phrase at the end of two passages, and omits one, whereas homoioarcton ("same beginning") is when a scribe sees the same phrase at the beginning of two passages and omits one. Inadvertently writing a word or letter twice is called dittography ("twice-writing"), and when a word or letter that ought to be written twice is not, it is called haplography ("once-writing"). These sorts of errors are surprisingly common.

random variation (for example, "Zebulun," from Table 6.4, or the common word *m'zuzot* — "doorposts"— variously spelled in the Leningrad Codex מזוזות *mem, zion, vav, zion, vav, taf* or מזוזת *mem, zion, vav, zion, taf*, with a third option not found in the Leningrad Codex creeping into some modern printed editions: מזזות *mem, zion, zion, vav, taf*). But we find a clear tendency toward fuller spellings, that is, more vowel letters, in Late Biblical Hebrew.

While DSS Hebrew and Late Biblical Hebrew both exhibit tendencies toward fuller spellings, the details of the spellings are not the same. The final *heh* used to spell the second-person masculine singular suffix "you" (*-xa*) is found almost exclusively in DSS Hebrew, despite literally thousands of places where it could have appeared in the Bible. Similarly, the common DSS spelling *kaf, vav, lamed* (כול) for "all" appears only once in the Bible out of, again, thousands of uses of the word. The full spelling of "no" (לוא — *lamed, vav, aleph*) appears in less than one-tenth of one percent of the times that word is written.

By contrast, all of the features we see in Late Biblical Hebrew appear in DSS Hebrew. We thus have good reason to believe that Late Biblical Hebrew represents an intermediate step between earlier Hebrew and the DSS, at least in terms of spelling.

Grammar

In addition to spelling changes, the repeated sections in Chronicles evidence some interesting grammatical changes.

For example, Biblical Hebrew sometimes writes a verb twice in a row, once unconjugated and once conjugated. (A vaguely similar example in English would be if it were common practice to say, "I write wrote a book" or "He write writes a book," using the unconjugated verb "write" followed by the conjugated form "wrote" or "writes.") In Hebrew, the unconjugated verb is called the "infinitive absolute" and the doubled form, with the infinitive absolute and the conjugated form, is traditionally called "emphatic." Often, translations into English add "surely" when translating these doubled verbs, as in "you will surely die" for *mot tamut* (מות תמות) — literally, "die you-will-die" — to reflect the emphatic nature of the double-verb construction. But while there is some evidence to suggest that the doubling had emphatic force, we will do well to admit that we do not know its exact meaning.

Even without knowing the nuances of its meaning, however, a doubled verb is, of course, easy to spot in the text. Furthermore, we see a trend away from these doubled verbs in Late Biblical Hebrew. Returning to the example above, the passage in 1 Kings has a doubled verb for "I built" (*bano baniti* — בנה בניתי). The first word means "build" and the second one "I built." (Like in Spanish and many other languages, the pronoun "I" is optional in Hebrew, and generally only included for emphasis.) By contrast, the 2 Chronicles passage has *ani baniti* (אני בניתי), literally "I built." In other words, Chronicles has the pronoun "I" where Kings has an unconjugated verb. The meaning and meter of the two phrases are the same. It looks as though a later author simply modernized the text a little bit, omitting the infinitive absolute that creates a doubled verb and adding the pronoun "I."

We saw above that the spelling changes in Late Biblical Hebrew were precursors to more changes of the same nature in DSS Hebrew. If we are right that Late Biblical Hebrew was a form of Hebrew lying between older Biblical Hebrew and DSS Hebrew, we expect the doubled verb construction that seemed to be disappearing in Late Biblical Hebrew to be rare in DSS Hebrew, as well. It is.

Furthermore, we see a few cases of the double-plural compounds that are so typical of the DSS. (These are described in the discussion on page 140.) For example, 1 Chronicles twice contains the phrase "names men" (*an'she shemot* — אנשי שמות), probably meaning "men of repute." Earlier versions of Hebrew would prefer "name men" (*an'she shem* — אנשי שם), which appears once in Numbers 16:2.

Both times in Chronicles, however, the phrase appears next to "capability men" (*gibore xayil* — גבורי חיל), rather than the expected "capabilities men" (*gibore xayalim* — גבורי חילים). One wonders why the same sentence would have the older style compound ("capability men") right next to the newer one ("names men"). Nonetheless, the appearance of double-plural compounds in the late books of the Bible accords well with the patterns we have seen.

Caveats

So far we have seen a clear picture. Kings, presumably written before the exile, shows one pattern of Hebrew, while Chronicles shows another. We call the pattern we see in Chronicles "Late Biblical Hebrew," noting that it shares features of DSS Hebrew. We thus see a nice progression of Hebrew — from Early Biblical Hebrew to Late Biblical Hebrew to DSS Hebrew — over the course of perhaps 1,000 years.

However, most of the solid data about "Late Biblical Hebrew" comes only from Chronicles, but Chronicles is not the only book that duplicates material from Kings or Samuel. Furthermore, many scholars hold that the

Table 8.3. Different spellings in 2 Samuel and Psalm 18

Word	2 Samuel	Psalm 18
[they] encompassed me	אֲפָפוּנִי	אֲפָפֻנִי
	AFaFUNI	AFaFuNI
[they] terrified me	יְבַעֲתוּנִי	יְבַעֲתֻנִי
	Y'VaATUNI	Y'VaATuNI
[they] encircled me	סְבָבוּנִי	סַבֻּנִי
	S'VaVUNI	SaBuNI
coils [of]	מֹקְשֵׁי	מוֹקְשֵׁי
	MoK'SHE	MOK'SHE

Capital letters in English represent letters in the text. Lowercase letters represent Masoretic vowels.

books of Ezra and Nehemiah should be grouped with Chronicles, in that all four books (Chronicles is two books) seem to have the same origin. But Chronicles has linguistic features that are not shared by Ezra or Nehemiah. So in addition to the clear evidence we saw immediately above, we also see non-late books with repeated and updated passages from Kings or Samuel, as well as late books that do not share the features of Chronicles.

Psalm 18:1–10 is a repetition of 2 Samuel 22:1–10. (Or Samuel is a repetition of Psalm 18, or they are both copies of something else. It doesn't matter.) In addition to minor variations in content, such as "hand" for "palm," we find the spelling differences listed in Table 8.3, where, once again, lowercase letters indicate vowels supplied by the Masoretes and uppercase letters indicate actual letters in the Hebrew.

What we see looks a lot like the differences between 1 Kings and 2 Chronicles (Table 8.2). The "full," presumably more modern, spellings in Psalm 18, with the /u/ and /o/ sounds written out with a *vav*, match the spelling patterns in 2 Chronicles, and are absent in the Samuel rendition. However, Psalm 18 writes David's name without a *yud*, that is, using the old spelling. In fact, though David's name appears dozens of times in Psalms, it never appears with a *yud*. By contrast, that "newer" spelling does appear three times in Kings. (We also see a grammatical change in Table 8.3. The form *s'vavuni* appears instead of *sabuni*. A full discussion of the possible causes of these changes would lead us too far astray into the minutiae of Hebrew grammar.)

There are other problems.

The word "all" is spelled with a *vav* only once in the Masoretic tradition, but not in Chronicles, rather, in Jeremiah. That same book sees two spellings for "not," one with a *vav* and one without, whereas Chronicles only sees the older version, without the *vav*. To make matters worse, the full spelling, with the *vav*, actually appears in Kings and Samuel, the very books that we just used to represent the older dialect of Hebrew.

Even Genesis has one example of the later spelling of "not" (*lamed, vav, aleph* — לוא), and Exodus has an example of the almost exclusively DSS style ending for "your." In Exodus 13:16 we find the surprising form *yud, daled, kaf, heh* (ידכה) for "your hand," rather than the expected *yud, daled, kaf* (ידך).

We also saw examples in Chronicles of older grammar right next to newer grammar. That is particularly hard to explain. If our understanding is correct, that the author of Chronicles rewrote older passages of Hebrew in (then-modern) Late Biblical Hebrew to bring them up to date, why did that same author put (then-archaic) older Biblical Hebrew next to Late Biblical Hebrew? It hardly makes sense.

Another peculiarity of Chronicles is its spelling in Hebrew of the word "Damascus." While everywhere else in the Bible it is spelled with the consonants *d-m-s-k* (דמשק), in Chronicles it appears as *d-r-m-s-k* (דרמשק). While these may have been variant forms of the same word, in that the *resh* may have dropped out at some point, it is difficult to imagine how the *resh* could have been added after the word was already established as not having an /r/ sound. That is, it is a common historical pattern for letters to drop out of words, particularly when nasal sounds such as /n/ or /m/ are involved. So when we see two forms, one with an *r* before an *m* and one without the *r*, the natural assumption is that the form with the *r* is the older one. The fact that the Greek translation has no hint of this *r* may even suggest that the pronunciation we see in Chronicles was the result of an idiosyncrasy of the author of those books. If so, we have to wonder if other aspects of Chronicles that we ascribe to a Late Biblical Hebrew dialect are merely the idiosyncrasies of one author. (We discuss the ramifications of the Greek below.)

In the end, then, the innovations attributed to Late Biblical Hebrew seem plausible compared with what looks like older Hebrew and with the DSS, in that Late Biblical Hebrew seems to form a bridge between the two, but we do not find the clear divisions that we would like. As with so many other aspects of understanding antiquity, we are left with the feeling that we have only partially understood the situation.

The Nature of the Evidence

If we use the books of the Bible to determine what is early Hebrew and what is late Hebrew, we run into a potential chicken-and-egg problem, because in large part we use the Hebrew in the books to determine their date.

We also face a potentially much more devastating problem: we do not have the original copies of the books. We run the very real risk of attributing something to the original version of a book of the Bible when in fact what we see is instead the writing patterns of a scribe who copied the book perhaps many hundreds of years later.

The book of Psalms is a perfect example. Table 8.3 compares the Hebrew in Psalm 18 with a parallel passage in Samuel, noting the spelling patterns, and, in particular, noting that David's name in Hebrew was spelled without a *yud*, as it always is in Psalms. But when we say "in Psalms," what we really mean is "in the Leningrad Codex version of Psalms." If we look at the DSS version of Psalms, we see just the opposite, namely, that David's name is in fact spelled with a *yud*. The DSS manuscripts are about 1,000 years older than the Leningrad Codex, so we need a good scientific reason to favor the content of the Leningrad version over the DSS version. (For our purposes, we cannot rely on the religious decision that the official religious text — Leningrad — is the right one.)

We do have some reasons to believe that the DSS Psalms were rewritten at Qumran, including the fact that they often contain additional lines that seem to be liturgical responses (such as, "Blessed be Adonai!"). Because the Greek Septuagint does not contain these lines, we conclude that the DSS versions were rewritten at Qumran, and therefore do not represent the original Psalms. But the same reasoning might apply to our current version of Psalms. The fact that exactly 150 have been preserved argues in favor of an editor choosing the 150 best Psalms and including them in a Psalm "hit list." (Remember that the DSS have more than 150 Psalms.)

Similarly, while the Septuagint calls into question the content of some of the DSS Psalms, it also calls into question the content of some of the Leningrad Codex. One particularly clear example is Deuteronomy 31:1, as shown in Table 8.4. There we see that the DSS and the Septuagint agree on a perfectly sensible reading ("When Moses finished speaking all these words ... ") whereas the Masoretic text contains a curious idiom, "Moses

Table 8.4. Deuteronomy 31:1 in various traditions

Masoretic Text	DSS (1Q5)	LXX
Moses went and spoke these words to the Children of Israel:	When Moses finished speaking all*...	When Moses finished speaking all these words to all the Children of Israel.

* The text in the DSS fragment presumably continued, but this is all the text that has been preserved.

went and spoke." But the context makes it clear that Moses is staying right where he is. In all likelihood, the Masoretic text results from a transposition of letters ("metathesis"). The word for "went" is *yud, lamed, chaf* (ילך) while the word for "finished" is *yud, chaf, lamed* (יכל).

In addition, we have already seen one instance where the Septuagint contains what appears to be a complete text, while the Masoretic version contains a parablepsis-induced omission.

Leaving aside for the moment the question of which texts are "right" and "wrong," we face the undeniable reality that all of the texts are the result of repeated copying. We must, therefore, face the possibility that the texts were not only copied but emended, and, therefore, that in analyzing the Hebrew of the texts we are in fact analyzing the Hebrew of later copyists or editors. It is, therefore, worth taking a look at some external evidence about various stages of Hebrew before returning to the evidence from the Masoretic text of the Bible.

External Evidence

The most reliable way of understanding the various stages of Hebrew is to ignore any Hebrew that may have been copied, and therefore altered, and focus instead on Hebrew that has been preserved in its original state.

Pre-Exilic Hebrew

We saw above (starting on page 28) that precious few examples of really ancient Hebrew have survived. Among the very little evidence left us are the Izbet Sartah abecedary, which, though dating from probably 1200 B.C.E., has so far not been decoded (the theory that someone wrote random letters above the alphabet notwithstanding); and the Gezer Calendar, which is problematic because it is so short and so poorly understood. We have nothing more than a vague sense of what Hebrew was like before the 9th century.

The Mesha Stone, however, from 850 B.C.E., contains a significant body of text and has been almost fully understood. However, the text is Moabite, not Hebrew. While we believe that the two languages were almost identical, it is difficult to know for sure.

The inscription in the Siloam Tunnel, dating from the end of the 8th century, is certainly Hebrew, and gives us some evidence about early Hebrew.

Beyond this early material, several textual fragments from before the exile in 586 B.C.E. have been preserved. They include numerous seals and stamps, with generally very little text. While the wide distribution of this material attests to the prevalence of writing in Israelite pre-exilic society, they do little to advance our knowledge of the Hebrew they used.

Much more helpful is a set of 18 ostraca (clay tablets) found in burned ruins of the Biblical city of Lachish; these date from the 6th century B.C.E. The Hebrew, some of which describes the final onslaught by the Babylonians, accords well with what we know about Biblical Hebrew, and most resembles Deuteronomy in style. In terms of spelling, the writing lacks the vowel letters that typify the full Hebrew of Late Biblical Hebrew (and the DSS). This is good news, because the material was buried — and therefore written — before the exile, that is, before Late Biblical Hebrew arose. Similar ostraca from Arad offer similar evidence.

Because we do not have any direct Biblical quotations from any of these ostraca, direct comparison with the Masoretic tradition (or the LXX or the DSS) is impossible. But the Hebrew from these samples does record the tetragrammaton. Because the tetragrammaton seems to have originated with the Hebrews and their writing, we can be fairly sure that the writing comes from Hebrew culture.

Perhaps the most important surviving piece of text is found on one of two minute silver rolls found in a burial repository in Ketef Hinnom (Jerusalem) and dating from the 7th or 6th century B.C.E. The text seems to be from Numbers 6:24–26, the well-known priestly benediction. The Kefet Hinnom formulation reads, ". . . May Adonai bless you and keep you. May he shine his face upon you and grant you peace." This is remarkably similar to the Masoretic formulation in Numbers 6:24–26: "May Adonai bless you and keep you. May he shine his face upon you and be kind to you. May he lift his face to you and grant you peace."

We do not know, of course, if the silver rolls are quotations from Numbers, which would demonstrate that the book of Numbers existed in the 6th or 7th century, or if Numbers simply quotes a well-known blessing, which would demonstrate that both the rolls and Numbers stem from a similar culture. Either way, the existence of these rolls potentially extends the corpus of Biblical material several hundred years beyond the next-earliest surviving examples, the DSS. On the other hand, the fact that the details of the text do not agree with any known tradition increases the likelihood that, while our current Masoretic tradition preserves the general sense of the ancient material, the material itself may have been lost.

In short, the few surviving specimens of pre-exilic Hebrew do not contradict anything we think we know about pre-exilic Hebrew, but they do not do much to confirm it, either. We have a general sense that vowel letters are used more than they were 500 years earlier and less than they will be 500 years later, but beyond that the information is hard to assess.

Post-Exilic Hebrew

The most significant post-exilic documents, of course, are the DSS themselves, dating from the 3rd or 2nd century B.C.E. and later. But this still leaves a period of perhaps 300 years unaccounted for, including all of the Persian period (from the first exile in 586 B.C.E. to the invasion by the Greeks toward the end of the 4th century) and the beginning of the Hellenistic period (after the Greek invasion).

While significant Aramaic material has been recovered from this period, little Hebrew evidence remains. (For this reason, some researchers have suggested that the post-exilic books of the Bible were in fact written in Aramaic and then back-translated into Hebrew, perhaps to give them a flavor of authenticity.)

Some coins from perhaps the 4th century bear the inscription *yud, heh, daled* (יהד), presumably *y'hudah* ("Judah"), but we are surprised to find no indication of a final vowel. Similarly, inscriptions with what seem to be an official seal read *yud, resh, shin, lamed, mem* (ירשלם), presumably *y'rushalayim* ("Jerusalem"), but, again, we are surprised to find no vowel letters.

The Hebrew for "Jerusalem" is problematic in its own right, in that the *yud* that ought to be part of the end of the name to indicate the /i/ sound is only written five times in the Bible (out of several hundred), but is always written in the Masoretic tradition with a *chiriq*; but because the *chiriq* has no *yud* to support it, it is written under the final *mem* of the word, where is does not belong: יְרוּשָׁלָם. (It is spelled both ways in the DSS, though, obviously, without the Masoretic vowel marks.)

Still, nowhere in the Bible or the DSS do we find "Jerusalem" spelled without a *vav* representing the second vowel of the word. Why, then, does the official seal spell it this way? One possibility is that the seal purposely preserved an archaic flavor, perhaps in honor of the destroyed First Temple, or perhaps simply because official seals tend to be conservative in their language. (In this regard we may note that American paper currency is still adorned with Latin phrases such as *e pluribus unum* and *novus ordo seclorum*.)

Other examples of Hebrew from this period do demonstrate the fuller spellings that we expect.

In the end, however, we have to extrapolate from Aramaic writings or from the DSS (and other examples of Hebrew from about the same time period) to understand anything about post-exilic Hebrew from actual surviving material. While the coins and seals that do not attest vowel letters are perhaps troubling, they stand by themselves against significant other material, including the trend seen earlier toward vowel letters, and certainly the trend seen a few hundred years later. We do have to allow for the possibility that the exile brought on a temporary regression in writing, but equally likely is that formal writing simply preserved the more ancient writing style.

Like our conclusions about pre-exilic Hebrew, we have little evidence to contradict our assumptions, but also little to support them.

Ramifications

So far we have seen three facts:

1. At least two different spelling patterns are in evidence in the Masoretic text.
2. Some passages appear twice in the Masoretic text.
3. When passages appear twice — to judge by their spelling and grammar — they sometimes look like they were written in different dialects with different spelling conventions.

Our working hypothesis is that the fuller spellings — spellings with more vowel letters — along with some grammatical changes, represent a later stage in the development of Hebrew, but in spite of its obvious appeal, we have had significant trouble substantiating that theory.

If we could discern the nature of pre-exilic and post-exilic Hebrew on independent grounds, we could compare the Hebrew we see to what we already know about the progression of Hebrew, and see which dialects are reflected in various texts. Or if we had access to the original copies of the texts we want to analyze, we would know their date, and we could use the texts themselves to learn about the progression of Hebrew. But we have

neither enough extra-Biblical material nor ancient enough original Biblical
material to learn about the changes Hebrew may have undergone.

Still, we can draw at least one and perhaps two major conclusions.

Ancient Texts

First, the appearance of more than one system of spelling in the Masoretic
texts strongly suggests that the Masoretes were actually copying texts, not
making them up or trying to recall them from an oral tradition. The other
possibility, of course, is that the Masoretes purposely introduced variability
in the spelling in order to create that appearance, but nothing we have seen
suggests that the Masoretes were purposefully deceitful (though we have
seen that they certainly invented some of the diacritic marks).

This conclusion supports our previous tentative conclusion that the
Masoretes sometimes had the same text as the Qumran Sect, because seemingly arbitrary details such as minor spelling matters in the Masoretic text
match the DSS exactly. But we also allowed for the possibility that the
spelling variations were haphazard and only match by chance. Here we
see further evidence in favor of actual documents.

The Masoretes knew the text of the Bible extraordinarily well. In a
time when people's minds were not cluttered with details such as phone
numbers, addresses, and license plate numbers, it was considerably easier
to memorize large quantities of text. Even today, there are people who
know almost every verse of the Bible. There is good reason to think that the
Masoretes did, too. With their extensive knowledge, they would certainly
have known about identical or nearly identical passages. If they were not
copying more ancient manuscripts, they would have had no reason to spell
the words differently in each case.

Having concluded that the Masoretes were, indeed, working from older
manuscripts (and still, of course, keeping in mind the unanswered question
of why none of the manuscripts have survived), we can inquire about the
nature of the manuscripts and move toward our second possible major
conclusion.

Ancient Texts from Different Sources

The Masoretic text contains an enormous amount of seemingly random
spelling variation. We already saw, in the context of the DSS, that the name
"Jabesh" occurs twice in 1 Samuel 11, but it is spelled differently each
time. Local variation in spelling is not common, but neither is the example
from 1 Samuel unique. The spelling variation itself is evidence of our first

conclusion, namely, that the Masoretes were copying manuscripts.

The local variation suggests one of three possibilities.

The first possibility is that we have missed some pattern behind the spelling variations. Because we have no evidence to support this theory we reject it out of hand.

A second possibility is that the manuscripts were the result of writing or editing by people with different spelling habits. When we take into account the two ways of making plural compounds, and the fact that both ways sometimes occur side by side, we expand this possibility beyond the realm of spelling, and consider that the manuscripts were written or edited by people who used different dialects of Hebrew.

The final possibility is that scribal copying practices tended to (accidentally or by design) change spellings and some grammatical features. It is not hard to imagine how a scribe copying an ancient manuscript might spell a word not the way it was written in the manuscript but the way it was written in the dialect of the scribe. It would be as though a modern typist were typing an old document. We would not be surprised to find the typist purposely or accidentally substituting newer spellings for the older ones.

Either the second or third possibility — multiple authors or revisions over the course of time — will account for the random variations we see.

However, we also saw significant patterns in the variations. If the spelling variations were really random, we would expect, when we find duplicate passages, that each copy would have its share of words spelled more fully. That is precisely what we do not find. Rather, we find that one passage is spelled more fully than the other. Although the degree of fullness varies from passage to passage (as with the full passages above, only some of which spelled David's name fully), we do not find random variation.

From this we conclude that the Masoretic tradition contains different copies of manuscripts from either different places or different times (or both).

More importantly, to the extent that the older texts contain older spellings and the later texts contain later spellings, we conclude that the Masoretes had authentic copies that fairly resembled the originals they represented. We assume, in other words, that a correspondence between the age of a text and the spelling it represents as preserved by the Masoretes is most likely to be a result of the Masoretes having had access to copies of the original documents. There are other possibilities, of course, such as willful deceit on the part of the Masoretes, but no other explanation seems worth considering seriously.

Unfortunately, we can go no further. As we saw above, we do not have entirely convincing evidence that only the later books of the Bible have been preserved with Late Biblical Hebrew spelling and grammar. We have good reason to think so, such as the distinctive style of Chronicles, but we have not been able to explain the problems discussed under "Caveats" above. As a best guess, however, it's more likely than not that the Masoretes' record contains significant remnants of the older documents, perhaps going back a few hundred years before the exile.

Our reasoning thus proceeds from the likelihood that the spelling of the various books represents the time in which they were written, to the probable intermediate conclusion that the Masoretes were working from documents that correctly captured those spellings, to the probable final conclusion that the Masoretes were working with documents that correctly captured the content of the original documents.

Unlike the Masoretic vowels, then, we are on fairly solid ground when we assume that the Masoretic consonants represent much older material, though we also recognize that significant errors and emendations crept into the text over almost two millennia.

But we do not know for sure.

Chapter 9
Post-Biblical Hebrew

Background

In the last chapter we saw suggestions that Hebrew changed during the Persian period (following the first exile in 586 B.C.E.) and the Hellenistic period (in the 4th century B.C.E. following the Greek empire's expansion under Alexander the Great to include all of the Near East) into a dialect we called Late Biblical Hebrew. We now turn our attention to what happened to Hebrew in the centuries that followed.

The official written language of the Persian empire was Aramaic — another Semitic language, also usually written in what we call "Hebrew" characters. (A historically more accurate naming scheme might call the characters "Aramaic," and note that Hebrew writers borrowed the script from Aramaic writers.) The official language of the Greek empire was, not surprisingly, Greek, though Aramaic remained important. After the first exile, the Hebrew-speaking Jewish population quickly learned and spoke Aramaic. And shortly after the arrival of the Greeks, they learned Greek as well.

It is clear that Hebrew (probably in the form of Late Biblical Hebrew) remained a literary and religious language during all of this, lasting at least into the 2nd century C.E. But beyond that, we have more questions than answers. Some scholars steadfastly maintain that Hebrew ceased to be spoken shortly after the exile, while others claim that it was a commonly spoken language until the 2nd century C.E.

The controversy probably stems from asking the wrong question, namely, "Which language did the Jews speak?" A better question reflects the widespread practice throughout most of the world and throughout most of history of speaking more than one language. We thus ask, "Which *languages* did the Jews speak?" We answer that during the Persian pe-riod they spoke Hebrew and Aramaic; during the Hellenistic period they spoke Hebrew, Aramaic, and Greek. With this broader understanding, we need not see a conflict between the claim that the Jews learned and spoke Aramaic and the claim that they spoke Hebrew. They could well have spoken both.

Because the role of Aramaic is so important to the development of Hebrew, we should take some time to understand some of the issues sur-rounding the interaction between Aramaic, Hebrew, and the Jews.

Aramaic

The issue of the exact relationship between Aramaic and Hebrew is a hotly debated one. Aramaic as a language can be clearly traced back to the 10th or 9th century B.C.E., thanks to an inscription (now available only in facsimile, the original having been destroyed during World War II). Numerous examples of Aramaic dating from the 9th or 8th centuries B.C.E. onward attest to the increasingly widespread use of Aramaic.

Aramaic in the Bible

A handful of references to Aramaic in the Bible may also suggest its widespread use. For example, in a passage appearing twice, once in 2 Kings 18:26 and once in Isaiah 36:11, Eliakim (also known as Johoiakim) tells a messenger to "speak to your servants in Aramaic." (The Septuagint calls Aramaic "the Syrian language," reflecting a general trend in the later books of the Septuagint to equate "Aram" with "Syria.") Ezra 4:7 makes reference to a letter "written in Aramaic" and "translated in Aramaic." Daniel 2:4 tells of people speaking to the king "in Aramaic," followed by a lengthy passage actually in Aramaic.

But three reasons make it hard to use the Bible to understand history.

First, the Bible was written before history as a science had been es-tablished. The Bible contains what clearly seem to be historical accounts, but they are freely mixed with such non-historical aspects as theology and myth. While it is great fun to look at Biblical accounts and then use them to understand history, most serious historians use the Bible for the more limited task of confirming what they already know.

Secondly, we do not know when the books were actually written, edited, and so forth. While we'd like to believe, for example, that the book of Ezra was written around the time that the person Ezra lived (the 5th century B.C.E.) we do not know for sure, and we certainly don't know the extent to which later authors may have altered the original text.

Thirdly, we do not always fully understand the language of the Biblical accounts. Returning again to Ezra, the claim that a letter was "written in Aramaic" and also "translated in[to] Aramaic" suggests that the author was not using "Aramaic" only to refer to the language. The way we use the word today, anything "translated into Aramaic" would necessarily be written in Aramaic as well. The Septuagint, perhaps recognizing this problem, renders the passage, "... written in Aramaic and translated." While slightly less problematic, the phrase would make much more sense if it were simply "translated into Aramaic." Similarly problematic would be a *New York Times* story about a letter "written in Russian and translated into Russian" or "written in Russian and translated."

Regarding in particular this third problem, we find significant confusion in Hebrew sources over several hundred years, starting with the excerpts above and continuing perhaps until the year 200 C.E., between two important sets of concepts.

The first concepts that are confused are the concepts of a written script and the language written in that script. Modern English demonstrates the same confusion, using, for example, the word "Greek" to mean both "Greek letters" (the script: α, β, γ, etc.) and the "Greek language" (the language spoken in Greece and written in the Greek script). Thus one can claim (correctly and non-redundantly) that "Greek is written in Greek." Similarly, we use "Hebrew" to mean "Hebrew letters" as well as the "Hebrew language," so we claim (again correctly) that "Hebrew is written in Hebrew" and (also correctly) "Yiddish is written in Hebrew." At one point in history, "Hebrew was written in Arabic," by which we mean that the Hebrew language was written in the Arabic script. The use of "Hebrew" in these sentences fluctuates between the language and the letters.

In addition to the confusion between scripts and languages, the concepts of "translated," "Aramaic," and "translated into Aramaic" are not clearly distinguished in many ancient sources. The Hebrew root *t.r.g.m* (ת.ר.ג.מ)[1] means, variously, "to translate," "to interpret," and, surprisingly, "Aramaic."

(Though we know better than to use etymology to understand a word, the etymology of the root *t.r.g.m* is interesting: It seems to come from a very old Semitic root *r.g.m*, meaning "word." The *t* at the beginning came from an old causative construction, so that *t.r.g.m* derived from the notion of "causing to be a word" or "turning into a word." Surprisingly, the same *r.g.m* root in Hebrew means "stone." Though it usually appears in verbal

---

1. It is common to put periods between the letters of a root to distinguish a root (*t.r.g.m* or ת.ר.ג.מ in this case) from a word (*trgm* or תרגם, for example).

form with the meaning "to stone [to death]," one wonders if the connection between words and writing in stone might be preserved in this root.)

In the example above from Ezra, we see the phrase "translated into [*t.r.g.m*] Aramaic," where the root clearly refers only to the act of translation or interpretation. By contrast, the Aramaic translations of the Bible are called *targums*, from the same root.

Aramaic in the Talmud

Further evidence comes from the Babylonian Talmud. Though a look at this evidence will require a digression, the digression itself is interesting, and ultimately relevant.

The Babylonian Talmud consists of two parts. The older part, written probably by the year 200 C.E., is mostly in Hebrew, and is called the **Mishnah.** The second part, the **Gemara,** is written largely in Aramaic, and comprises a commentary on, and expansion of, the first part. The Gemara was probably completed by the 6th or 7th century C.E. (There is another version of the Talmud, written not in Babylonia but in Jerusalem, called the "Jerusalem Talmud." It resembles the Babylonian Talmud, but is smaller, and was probably finished 150 years before its Babylonian counterpart.)

While the Talmud contains six books, references to parts of the Talmud generally refer to parts of each book called "tractates," of which a dozen or fewer comprise a book. References to the tractates consist of a page number and a letter ("a" or "b") which refer to either the front or back of the page as it was printed in a now-classic compilation called the "Vilna edition." For example, "Megillah 8b," which we will look at immediately below, refers to page 8, side b, of the tractate Megillah, as it was printed in the Vilna edition. Modern editions of the Talmud indicate the classic Vilna page numbers for convenience.

We now take a look at some thoughts recorded in the Talmud about languages and writing systems.

Megillah 8b describes some laws about writing Hebrew documents, and in so doing gives us some insight into the terms we will need to understand Hebrew and Aramaic. The Mishnah (the older part, written in Hebrew) claims that books of the Bible "may be written in any language, but *tefillin* and *m'zuzot* may only be written in 'Ashurit.' " Presumably Ashurit refers to the modern Hebrew script. But we see here a confusion between script and language, in that the Ashurit script is compared not to scripts but to languages. The text also tells us that the writing must not be "Ivri" script. While we do not know exactly what this script is, we will see the word "Ivri" used below for a language, too. Table 9.1 summarizes

Table 9.1. Some linguistic terms from tractate Megillah

Word	Location	Possible Meaning(s)
ashurit	Megillah 8b	Hebrew language
	Megillah 8b	"Ashurit" script
	Megillah 17a	Hebrew language
	Megillah 17a	Hebrew script
targum	Megillah 8b	Aramaic
	Megillah 8b	Translation
	Megillah 9a	Aramaic
	Megillah 17a	Translation
ivri	Megillah 8b	"Ivri" script
	Megillah 18a	"Ivri" language
	Megillah 18a	Speakers of the Ivri language
mikra	Megillah 8b	Hebrew language
	Megillah 8b	Hebrew font?
	Megillah 9a	Hebrew language

some of the various words we are trying to understand. (We ignore others, such as *la'az*, variously "foreign language" and "language.")

The Gemara expands on this phrase, noting (in Aramaic) that a document is not sacred until it is written "in Ashurit script and with [a certain kind of] ink." The added word "script" here and the juxtaposition of the concern about "Ashurit" with the concern about the right kind of ink both reinforce the notion that "Ashurit" refers to a way of writing. However, Megillah 17a (again in Hebrew) refers to "a foreigner who heard [the Megillah] in Ashurit." Here it looks like Ashurit refers to the Hebrew language, particularly in light of the point of the passage, which is that the foreigner who hears the Megillah in Ashurit has fulfilled his holy obligation to hear the Megillah, having heard it in a holy language. But to make matters more confusing, this same passage also refers to "writing in Ashurit." What does it mean to hear something in Ashurit? What does it mean to write in Ashurit?

Going back to 8b, we find an expansion on "written in any language" concerning "*mikra* written in *targum* and *targum* written in *mikra*." We are particularly interested in understanding what "*targum*" means, because we want to know if it refers simply to "translation" or specifically to "Aramaic." Based on this passage from the Gemara, it may represent "Aramaic," in that it comes in the context of various languages; if so, "*mikra*" would mean "Hebrew." In support of the theory that "*targum*" means "Aramaic" here, the continuation of the discussion in 9a deals with what possibility there could be of writing *"targum* in *mikra"* in *tefillin* and *m'zuzot,* which was (and is) a reasonable question because the traditional text for both of these contains only Hebrew, not Aramaic. There would, therefore, presumably be no chance of writing either *tefillin* or *m'zuzot* in *targum,* that is, Aramaic.

However, now 17a is a problem, because, again concerning the proper way of reading the Megillah, the claim is made that one who reads it *"targum* into any language" has not fulfilled his obligation to read it. Here, "targum" clearly means "translated." (Some English translations here mistakenly assume that "targum" must be a particular Aramaic version of the Megillah, and so wrongly translate the passage, ". . . in Targum, or indeed in any other language." There is nothing in the text to support this translation.) Looking at the context of this line gives us more information: One may not "read the Megillah out of sequence . . . or by heart . . . or translated into any language. But one may read it in a foreign language for foreigners."

What we see so far is confusion between writing systems and languages on the part of the authors of the Talmud, or perhaps misunderstanding on our part.

The Gemara expounding Megillah 17a is found in part in Megillah 18a. There we are told that one who has a Megillah "written in Ashurit and reads it in Greek" is like one who "reads it by heart." (Remember, reading by heart is not good enough.) Once again, it looks like Ashurit refers to "Hebrew," and that the issue is translation. Translating on the spot is not okay.

However, after a brief digression, the Gemara worries about "Coptic, *Ivrit,* Eilamean [Ilamite?], Medean [and] Greek," finally deciding that the Megillah may be read "in Coptic to Copts, in *Ivrit* to *Ivris* in Eilamean to Eilameans, [and] in Greek to Greeks." (Again, we do not know exactly what *Ivrit* represents, though in Modern Hebrew the word means "Hebrew.")

Finally, we come to the main point. Why don't the authors of the Mishna or the Gemara care about Aramaic here?

If the Gemara itself was written in Aramaic, why doesn't the discussion of languages include the case of Aramaic? How could the authors have been more concerned about Greek, Coptic (spoken in Egypt), and Eilamean than about the very language they were speaking?

Three possibilities present themselves.

The first possibility is that we have misunderstood the text. Based on our considerable confusion surrounding other elements of this text, we do not want to ignore the possibility that we have missed something important. For example, maybe "Ivrit" above actually means "Hebrew" and "Ashurit" means "Aramaic." It's not likely (for one thing, the text about "Ivrit" refers to the "Ivris," as though they represent a nationality, parallel to "Greek" and "Greeks"), but surely we have missed something, and until we know what, we ought to be careful about ruling anything out.

Assuming, though, that we have at least understood the basic situation, in that the text is concerned with the legitimacy of reading in a variety of foreign languages but not in Aramaic, we seem to be faced with the not uncommon problem of ancient texts omitting obvious information. Of course, modern texts omit obvious information, too, precisely because the omitted information is so obvious. But because we live in modernity we generally have little trouble filling in the missing details in these modern texts. For example, a modern article in the United States about the law might discuss the advantages and drawbacks of letting people fill out tax forms in Spanish, but never mention the possibility of filling out those forms in English. It's too obvious a fact to bother stating that tax forms can be filled out in English.

Similarly, when we see the obvious omission of Aramaic in the list of languages in which the Megillah can be read, we can assume that the answer to the question of whether the Megillah could be read in Aramaic was so obvious it never occurred to anyone to ask. However, the fact that the answer was obvious to them does not mean that the answer was obviously "yes." This brings us to our second and third possible answers to why the authors of the Talmud didn't include Aramaic in their discussion of foreign languages: Either it was obvious that the Megillah could be read in Aramaic, or it was obvious that it could not.

We can guess why it may have been obvious that the Megillah could be read in Aramaic: Aramaic was, after all, the language they were all speaking. Similarly, we can guess why reading the Megillah in Aramaic might have been so obviously disallowed: the Aramaic-speaking population found something non-religious in Aramaic so that, unlike Greek or Coptic, it could not be used even by people who spoke it. Aramaic could have been "slang."

It is difficult to decide between these two interpretations of the evidence. But either way, ironically, the failure of the ancient authors to include Aramaic specifically in their list attests to the central role that that language played in their lives.

We see, then, that the issue of Aramaic and Hebrew is complicated and still only partially understood.

Greek

Like Aramaic, Greek played a pivotal role in the lives of the Jews after the exile, specifically after the Greek invasion. Megillah 8b, in the same discussion (in Hebrew) we looked at above, notes that "they" (unidentified Jewish Rabbis) "did not permit books [of the Bible?] to be written in anything other than Greek." Presumably, the point is that the books could not be written in foreign languages other than Greek.

The ensuing discussion (in Aramaic) in 9a refines the permitted use of Greek to the Torah, quoting Rabbi Yehudah as saying, "even when our Rabbis permitted Greek, they permitted it only for a Torah scroll." (The discussion then takes a curious turn, referring to a whole series of segments from the Torah that were purposely changed to appease King Ptolemy [Philadelphus], who lived from 285 to 247 B.C.E. and who — at least according to legend — commissioned the Septuagint. The changes include minor word-order matters, such as changing "in the beginning God created ... " to "God created in the beginning ... " and changing the word for "rabbit" (arnevet in Hebrew) to "short-legged [creature]" in the list of non-Kosher animals, because King Ptolemy's wife's name was "Arnevet," and the Jews didn't want Ptolemy to think they were mocking him by inserting his wife's name among the list of forbidden animals. Though interesting, it is not clear what these changes have to do with writing the Torah in Greek, since the changes only make sense in the original Hebrew.)

Historical evidence, such as a Greek scroll of the minor prophets found in the Qumran Desert, attests to the Jewish practice of writing at least parts of the Bible in Greek. Above, we saw clear but oblique evidence that Aramaic was a strong linguistic component of the Jews' lives. Because we have no problem identifying the words for "Greek" and "Greece," the indirect evidence that Greek was important is augmented by direct evidence.

We will see next that Hebrew changed to incorporate aspects of both Aramaic and Greek during the Persian period, and even more during and after the Hellenistic period, before ceasing to be used as a spoken language sometime between 200 C.E. and 600 C.E.

Rabbinic Hebrew

We use the term "Rabbinic Hebrew" to refer to Hebrew as it existed after it was Late Biblical Hebrew (Chapter 8). We thus have four stages of Hebrew (so far):

1. Pre-Biblical Hebrew, as evidenced in very early inscriptions.
2. Biblical Hebrew, presumably used before the first exile.
3. Late Biblical Hebrew, presumably used after the first exile.
4. Rabbinic Hebrew.

The "Rabbis," who lived from roughly the 2nd century B.C.E. to the 6th century C.E. and from whom "Rabbinic Hebrew" gets its name, comprise the post-Biblical religious authorities who helped form what would become today's normative Judaism. They were so important in deciding the direction Judaism should take that today's Judaism is often called "Rabbinic Judaism."

The traditional names for the various stages of Hebrew, which we have used here, demonstrate the centrality of the Bible regarding Hebrew. Three of the dialects are named for their relation to the Bible, and the fourth is named after the people who studied and interpreted the Bible.

It should come as no surprise, then, that Biblical Hebrew and Late Biblical Hebrew have traditionally been considered the "best" Hebrew, with other dialects taking a back seat. (Of course, our scientific approach to language does not allow for one dialect to be better or worse than another, but we can still use the judgments of the people who spoke and knew the languages to learn about the people.) Nonetheless, Rabbinic Hebrew was used for three very important bodies of Hebrew: the prayers, the Mishnah, and early *midrashim,* as described next.

Where Do We See Rabbinic Hebrew?

The Prayers

The prayers that form today's Jewish liturgy derive from a wide variety of sources. Some parts are Biblical, such as the quotation from Deuteronomy 6, "Hear, O Israel ... " (discussed briefly on page 42). Other parts are medieval additions, written in "Medieval Hebrew," which we discuss below. Still other parts are modern, written after the modern founding of the state of Israel. Some of the prayers are late modifications of earlier texts. But the majority of prayers were composed by the Rabbis in Rabbinic Hebrew, often incorporating significant quotations from the Bible.

For example, one common prayer begins with the words *aleinu l'sha'be'ax* (עלינו לשבח), literally, "it is on us to praise," where "it is on us" means "its is our obligation" or "we must." This usage of "on," although it does appear once in the very late book of Ezra, is primarily a Rabbinic invention.

Similarly, the formulaic language of blessings is Rabbinic. Jewish bless-

ings start in the second person, addressing God with *barux ata adonai* ...
(variously "praised are You ..." or "blessed are You ...") but then finish
in the third person, for example, ... *ohev amo yisra'el* ("... who loves His
people Israel").

These both represent typical Rabbinic Hebrew.

The Mishnah

The second major body of Rabbinic Hebrew comes from the Mishnah (described above). Many of the prayers that made their way into Jewish liturgy
also appear in the Mishnah, and even when the content is different, the
Hebrew found in the Mishnah and the prayers forms a class. Nonetheless,
differences between Liturgical Rabbinic Hebrew and Mishnaic Rabbinic
Hebrew are evident.

These differences should not surprise us, because liturgy always tends
to have its own, generally formal, sometimes archaic, flavor. We see this
in English liturgy composed today, which certainly sounds different than,
say, a newspaper article, and which tends to have a formal and slightly
archaic tone to it.

Furthermore, the Mishnah contains various sorts of content, ranging
from liturgical content to discussion of law to stories. The various kinds of
content each display their own linguistic nuances.

Midrash

The word "midrash" is a technical Hebrew term for "explanation," generally of a Biblical story. (The common English translation, "exegetical
material," is only mildly helpful.) Midrash has played an important role
in Judaism since at least the days of the Qumran Sect.

While the most important collection of midrash, "The Midrash"
(*Midrash Raba*, or "The Great Midrash"), was not compiled until perhaps
as late as the 13th century C.E., parts of that collection go back much earlier.
The content of the Midrash covers a wide range of writing styles, including
legalistic, literary, and even fanciful stories. While not all of the Midrash
is Rabbinic, and while there is some difficulty in dating all of the material,
it is clear that some parts are Rabbinic and written in Rabbinic Hebrew.

Other Sources

Although the Mishnah, Midrash, and the prayers are the largest and most-
studied corpus of Rabbinic Hebrew, other examples have survived, such

as letters (of correspondence), in particular from Bar-Kochva's revolt (2nd century C.E.); a host of inscriptions, in particular synagogue dedications; stamps and seals; and coins. Not surprisingly, these various other sources of Rabbinic Hebrew are not written in precisely the same dialect as either the Mishnah or the Jewish liturgy, but they have enough in common with Rabbinic Hebrew to warrant the conclusion that all of these sources represent a common stage in the development of Hebrew.

On Variety

The wide variety of dialects and writing styles exhibited by the various texts written in Rabbinic Hebrew deserves comment.

Different writing styles can be identified within the Bible (even beyond the major division between Biblical Hebrew and Late Biblical Hebrew). For example, different narrative, legal, and poetic styles are clear, just to name a few. We have already seen the extent of spelling variation in the Bible. But the internal variation seen in Biblical Hebrew pales in comparison to the variety found in Rabbinic Hebrew. It is temping but probably wrong to attribute this difference in variability to the nature of the languages, and to wonder why Biblical Hebrew was so much more uniform than later dialects.

Much more likely is the possibility that Biblical Hebrew and Rabbinic Hebrew alike contained lots of variation, but in the case of Biblical Hebrew, records of most of the variation were lost over the years. After all, for the most part only copies of any significant material from before the exile remain, and scarcely more original material from the Persian and Hellenistic periods remains, with the exception of the DSS. We thus have but a tiny bit of evidence from which to analyze several hundred years of Hebrew.

Furthermore, "Biblical Hebrew" is often specifically defined to include only the Hebrew of the Bible, with other sources being given other designations. For example, the differences between the language in the Mesha Stone (page 32) and some of the Hebrew in the Bible are tiny compared even with the internal variation within the Bible, yet, for political reasons, the contents of the Mesha Stone are not generally called "Hebrew" but rather "Moabite." So the perceived uniformity of Biblical Hebrew stems from a decision to exclude non-uniform material as well as from the paucity of evidence.

We should not, therefore, assume that Hebrew had changed into a more varied language with Rabbinic Hebrew. Rather, we just understand the variety better.

The Nature of Rabbinic Hebrew

Vowel Letters

Because they are so important in understanding earlier dialects of Hebrew (as we have seen) and later dialects of Hebrew (Chapter 10), we will look at the Rabbinic use of vowel letters.

As with evidence about earlier Hebrew, we must be careful to make decisions based on what the original authors wrote, rather than later revisions of the earlier material, because later copyists may have changed the spelling of some of the words. This risk is particularly high in the case of some Rabbinic Hebrew writings, for two reasons. Not only may they not have been assigned the importance that earlier writings were, and so been given less care in copying, but often the spellings were specifically "corrected" so as to mimic Biblical Hebrew.

Fortunately, the extensive evidence left us makes the task easier for Rabbinic Hebrew than it was for Biblical Hebrew. What we find is a continuation of the pattern we saw in Late Biblical Hebrew toward fuller writing (that is, writing with more vowel letters), but only some of the patterns we saw in the DSS resurface.

An internal /o/ or /u/ sound was almost always spelled with a *vav*. (Once again, we must remember that our understanding of the ancient sounds is only approximate. We do not know the precise sounds any of these letters represented.) The somewhat rare Biblical possibility of using just a *taf* (*t*) for the plural ending *-ot* has vanished, being replaced by the fuller spelling *vav-taf*. Similarly, /i/ is almost always written with a *yud*. We saw the beginning of both of these trends in Late Biblical Hebrew and in the DSS; except for the one feature noted immediately below, Rabinnic Hebrew has expanded on these trends.

What we do not find in Rabbinic Hebrew are the unique DSS spellings that use a final *heh* for the sound /a/ in the second-person singular masculine suffix. We similarly do not find pronouns of the *"atema"* variety, with a final /a/ where Masoretic tradition indicates there ought not to be one.

Additionally, we find some innovations not seen in Late Biblical Hebrew or in the DSS. Sometimes the letter *aleph* is used inside a word for the sound /a/.

Another trend is much more significant. Perhaps in response to the increasingly widespread use of vowel letters as vowels at the time, Rabbinic Hebrew sometimes doubles up a potential vowel letter to indicate that it is used as a consonant. So the sound /v/ was often indicated by not one *vav* (ו) but two. (In Yiddish, these two *vav*s are considered a single letter, called, literally, "two *vav*s." Though this "two-*vav*" letter is unique to Yiddish, and not shared in Hebrew nomenclature, we do note a related phenomenon in the Roman alphabet, used for English, French, etc., where two *v*s — *vv* — became a single letter — *w* — called "double-*U*" in English but "double-*V*" in other languages.) Similarly, consonantal *y* was sometimes indicated by two *yud*s. We will see both of these patterns again in Modern Hebrew.

The nearly seamless progression from Biblical Hebrew to Late Biblical Hebrew to Rabbinic Hebrew, and the fact that DSS innovations that do not appear in Late Biblical Hebrew also do not appear in Rabbinic Hebrew, both suggest that Rabbinic Hebrew is the continuation of Late Biblical Hebrew but not of DSS Hebrew. This observation accords well with what we know about the history of the people who spoke these dialects.

Final *Nun*

One of the most striking features of Rabbinic Hebrew is the use of a *nun* instead of a *mem* in the plural ending. Whereas Biblical Hebrew has *-im* (ם‏-) to make (some) nouns and verbs plural, Rabbinic Hebrew often has *-in* (ן‏-) instead. This final /n/ looks like Aramaic, which also uses /n/ instead of /m/ for the plural; indeed, the *-in* endings are found frequently in the books of the Bible (Ezra and Daniel) that contain Aramaic. This final /n/ is further evidence of the close contact between Aramaic and Hebrew.

Other Letters

Rabbinic Hebrew shows a few spelling alternations that give us insight into how some of the letters may have been pronounced.

Bet/Vav and Bet/Pe   The letters *vav* and *bet* are often interchanged. So, for example, the place "Yavneh" is spelled both *yud, vav, vav, nun, heh* (יוונה) and *yud, bet, nun, heh* (יבנה). The letter *bet* also alternates with *pe*. From this we tentatively conclude that the *bet* already had two pronunciations, as eventually it would in the days of the Masoretes, and that those pronunciations were similar (though not necessarily identical) to the sounds made by *vav* and by *pe*.

In Modern Hebrew, the letter *bet* does have two sounds, and one of them is the same as one of the sounds made by the *vav*, so it is tempting to conclude that the sounds of Rabbinic Hebrew were identical in this regard to the sounds of Modern Hebrew. But that is too great a leap. While the sounds may have been the same, there are other ways that these letters could have been pronounced. For example, the *bet* and *vav* could have represented a sound often transcribed by linguists with a *beta* (β), pronounced like an English *v* but with the teeth never touching the lips. Because this sound is actually a closer fricative representation of the stop /b/ than is our *v*, as discussed on page 57, it would make sense if Rabbinic Hebrew had this sound. But, as with so many other aspects of ancient pronunciation, we cannot know for sure.

As for the second alternation we see, *bet* versus *pe*, we note that /b/ is the voiced equivalent of /p/, and alternations between voiced and unvoiced consonants are very common throughout the world's languages. (Again, see page 57.)

Like *bet* and *vet*, two other pairs are commonly interchanged in Rabbinic Hebrew: *sin* and *samech*, and *chet* and *chaf*.

Sin/Samech The issue of the letters *sin/samech* (ס/שׂ) is complicated, as we noted briefly under "Conclusions" on page 116, where we saw some ancient hints that the letter *shin* was related to the letter *samech* in Biblical Hebrew. Rabbinic Hebrew gives us slightly more direct evidence, because some Biblical words with a *sin* are spelled with a *samech* in Rabbinic Hebrew. (We also rarely see the reverse pattern.) So while we once again see evidence that the letters *samech* and *sin* are related, we also once again do not know exactly how. However, we may guess that they both represented the sound /s/, because no other candidate for pronunciation seems plausible.

Chet/Chaf The final alternation we commonly see in Rabbinic Hebrew is *chet* versus *chaf* (ח/כ). In many dialects of Modern Hebrew, these letters also have identical pronunciations. It is, therefore, tempting (as it was with *samech* and *sin* or *vav* and *vet*) to assume that the modern pronunciations mimic the ancient ones. But while only one other pronunciation seemed likely in the case of *vav/vet*, and no others seemed likely with *samech/sin*, the letters *chet* and *chaf* belong to a class of letters — the "gutturals" — that are more complicated. Once again, in the end we are left with guesses.

Vocabulary

Greek influence on Rabbinic Hebrew can be clearly seen in the hundreds of loan words the latter has incorporated. Many of these Greek words were brought into Rabbinic Hebrew as technical terms, to express concepts that didn't exist in the Bible. Examples include the words for both "prosecutor" and "defense (lawyer)": *katigor* (קטיגור) from the Greek *katigoros* (κατηγωρος) and *paraklit* (פרקליט) from the Greek *parakletos* (παρακλητος), and the word for "air," *avir* (אוויר), from the Greek *aer* (αηρ).

Though we do occasionally find, as with Greek, Latin technical words that made their way into Rabbinic Hebrew, they are few in number compared with the Greek words. This probably reflects the more general tendency of the Rabbis to accept the Greeks while shunning the Romans. (That approach was mutual, of course. The Romans did not treat the Jews nearly so well as the Greeks did.)

Other vocabulary innovations may have come from within Hebrew, in the form of new words based on old words. We frequently find plural forms in Rabbinic Hebrew for words that exist only in the singular in Biblical Hebrew, and vice versa. We also find new feminine forms. But we have no way of knowing if these "new" forms represent real innovation, or if they were Biblical Hebrew words that just happened not to be used in the Bible.

Grammar

By and large, the grammar of Rabbinic Hebrew follows the trends we saw with Late Biblical Hebrew and DSS Hebrew. We saw that the double-verb construction of Biblical Hebrew may have been archaic in Late Biblical Hebrew (page 153) and in DSS Hebrew (page 140). Similarly, we do not find that construction in Rabbinic Hebrew.

Likewise, the trend toward double plurals in compounds that we saw in the DSS continues into Rabbinic Hebrew, with such plurals as *batei-k'nesiyot* (בתי כנסיות), literally, "houses of assemblies," from the singular *bet-k'neset* (בית כנסת), "house of assembly."

Rabbinic Hebrew saw many innovations in the verbal system. One of these involved a combination of two previous ways of making a verb passive. Older dialects of Hebrew either prefixed a *nun* (נ) or a *taf* (ת) to indicate (some) passives. (When the *taf* was prefixed, it was generally then preceded by a *heh* ה, but the *heh* came about only to support the *taf*.) With Rabbinic Hebrew came the common practice of prefixing both a *nun* and then a *taf*.

We also see grammatical changes that are further evidence of Greek's influence on Rabbinic Hebrew, but to discuss these matters fully would take us too far astray into the details of Greek grammar.

Conclusions

Rabbinic Hebrew, then, was a vibrant, changing language based on Biblical Hebrew. The changes we see confirm two facts about Rabbinic Hebrew.

First, because many of the changes, particularly the spelling changes, are unlikely to have taken place without people speaking the language, Rabbinic Hebrew must have been a spoken as well as a literary language.

Secondly, because the changes we see are natural continuations of the trends we saw with Late Biblical Hebrew and DSS Hebrew, we not only have added confirmation that our understanding of these older dialects is correct, but we also see that Rabbinic Hebrew was almost certainly a direct continuation of the Hebrew of the Bible.

Non-Spoken Hebrew

Sometime between 200 C.E. and 600 C.E. probably much closer to the former date than the latter, Hebrew ceased being widely spoken, bringing to a close an era that had lasted over a millennium. For over 1,000 years, Hebrew had been a spoken and written language of the Jews, but Rabbinic Hebrew would not even last to the end of the Rabbinic period (which can be said to end with the final compilation of the Talmud), much less into the years that would follow.

It is traditional to use the term "Medieval Hebrew" for the stage of Hebrew that followed Rabbinic Hebrew, but the period of the Middle Ages to which the term "Medieval" refers — from the fall of the Western Roman Empire in 476 C.E. to the Renaissance in Italy in the 15th century — does not represent any particular variety of Hebrew. While 476 C.E. probably corresponds roughly with the end of Rabbinic Hebrew as a commonly spoken language, the Renaissance does not mark any important milestone in Hebrew's development.

Rather, what we see is a number of literary dialects of Hebrew used throughout and beyond the Middle Ages. There can be little doubt, for example, that Jewish scholars continued to read and understand Biblical Hebrew during and after the Rabbinic period, or that Jewish scholars read and understood the Rabbinic Hebrew in the Mishnah for many hundreds of years. We will also see that Hebrew, with various changes and innovations, continued to be used as a literary language. However, these trends neither began nor ended with the Middle Ages.

It is tempting to use "Literary Hebrew" to describe these periods of Hebrew, because the Hebrew was certainly literary, in that it was used for literature, but almost all dialects of Hebrew have been used as literature.

In the end, our choice of terms is arbitrary, and we should not make the mistake of thinking that our term must be literally accurate. After all, we have already accepted the terms "Biblical Hebrew" and "Late Biblical Hebrew," recognizing that a literal interpretation of the former would mean that it necessarily includes the latter. Nonetheless, because "Medieval Hebrew" is so clearly not what we have in mind, we will use the more general term "Non-Spoken Hebrew" to encompass the various non-spoken dialects of Hebrew that followed Rabbinic Hebrew and preceded Modern Hebrew.

But even though we will not let ourselves become slaves to our own terminology, a word of explanation about the term "non-spoken" is in order. Linguists recognize two ways a person might speak a language. The first is the way almost everyone speaks their native language, that is, what is commonly called "fluently" and what might more accurately be called "with native proficiency." The second way is "as a second language."

It turns out that some aspects of language are only mastered by native speakers. For example, English exhibits something called "dative shift," in which the indirect object of a verb can be expressed either after the direct object with the preposition "to," or before the direct object without any preposition. "I gave the Red Cross money" and "I gave money to the Red Cross," which express (almost) the same thing, illustrate dative shift. The indirect object "the Red Cross" can appear either before the direct object ("money") without a preposition, or with the preposition "to" after the direct object.

But while the verb "give" allows this dative shift, the nearly synonymous verb "donate" does not: "I donated money to the Red Cross" is a perfectly good English sentence, but, surprisingly, "I donated the Red Cross money" is not.

It turns out — for reasons no one has successfully explained — that only native speakers of English intuitively know which verbs allow dative shift and which do not. Experiments have shown that, while people who learn English as a second language can memorize lists of verbs that allow dative shift, they never acquire the intuition that lets native speakers classify their verbs without any conscious thought.

This is but one example of the difference between knowing a language natively and any other way of knowing a language.

In general, all languages as spoken natively follow the same linguistic rules, whereas non-natively spoken languages are subject to considerably greater variation.

When we say that the Hebrew following Rabbinic Hebrew and preceding Modern Hebrew was non-spoken, what we mean is that no one (or, at least, very few people) spoke the Hebrew natively. We do not mean that no one spoke it at all. We also mean that it may not have followed the linguistic patterns of natural languages, precisely because it was not spoken natively.

The situation is thus similar to the way many American Jewish professionals know some dialect of Hebrew: they can speak it, but it is a second language for them. With this in mind, we can identify five different times and places non-spoken Hebrew was used:

1. **The Hebrew of the *Piyutim*,** used to write poetry called *piyutim*. A piyut — "Piyut" is the singular form of the Hebrew plural "Piyutim" — is a specific kind of liturgical poem developed perhaps as early as the 4th century B.C.E., typically containing elements of strict rhyme, meter, and complex allusions to the Bible.
2. **The Hebrew of the Masoretes.** The Masoretes (Chapter 5) certainly spoke Arabic, but they also used Hebrew for much of their writing.
3. **The Hebrew of Muslim Spain.** Muslim Spain, from the middle of the 10th century C.E. until the expulsion in 1492, offered freedom and acceptance — and the accompanying opportunities — that Jews would not enjoy again until modernity. Jewish culture thus thrived, and with the increase in culture came a Hebrew revival of sorts. The Jews certainly spoke (Middle) Arabic, but they also used Hebrew to write poetry and prose.
4. **Hasidic Hebrew.** The *hasidim* of the 18th century in Europe used their own form of Hebrew for their writings.
5. **Modern Non-Spoken Hebrew.** Even today, after the rebirth of Hebrew in Israel, various non-spoken dialects of Hebrew continue to be used. In America and Europe, significant portions of the professional Jewish leadership are able to use Hebrew, but the Hebrew they use is not the Modern Hebrew spoken in Israel. Similarly, Jews in the now-defunct Soviet Union taught themselves Hebrew, and ended up learning a modern-but-not-Israeli version of Hebrew.

Of course, the decision to include or not include various populations in this list is somewhat arbitrary.

We could certainly expand on the category "Modern Non-Spoken Hebrew," and list the Hebrew in America, Europe, and Russia separately, or even include the tiny populations of Africa that have taught themselves Hebrew. We could include various modern academic versions of Hebrew.

Similarly, the Hebrew poetry and prose of Muslim Spain are different enough to deserve separate mention. The differences between Muslim Spanish Hebrew prose of the 11th century and Masoretic Hebrew are minor compared to differences among the other dialects.

We could single out various poets, from Saadiah Gaon to Kalir.

All of these various versions of Hebrew — as well as others not listed here — differ in their details but exhibit the same basic patterns:

1. They are all based primarily on Biblical Hebrew.
2. They all incorporate some elements of Rabbinic Hebrew.
3. The people who use these versions incorporate elements of their native language.
4. The people who use these versions consciously invent new words.
5. These are artificial, not natural, dialects of Hebrew.

Beyond these patterns, however, the various dialects of Hebrew vary significantly in their content and style, having taken advantage of their non-spoken nature to expand the language in sometimes arbitrary ways.

The religious and sometimes cultural significance of what was written in these various forms of Hebrew is great, but, because they were not spoken languages, they are tangents to our main story except inasmuch as they form the bridge between antiquity and modernity, as we will see next.

Part IV
Now

Chapter 10
Modern Hebrew

We will be able to create a new language
which is completely old.
— Eliezer Ben-Yehuda, 1886

The Fire of Love for Hebrew

We now jump ahead in time to January 7, 1858, when a man was born in Lithuania in whom "the fire of love for the Hebrew language burned," as he would later write.

The man, Eliezer Ben-Yehuda, was born Eliezer Yitzhak Perelman in a Lithuanian village called Luzhky under circumstances not much different than most of his peers. Most Jewish boys in Luzhky started studying Hebrew and Torah at three years of age, Mishnah (also in Hebrew) a few years later, and by age nine or ten moved to the study of the Talmud (in Aramaic). Young Eliezer was seen as a gifted Hebrew scholar, and so, like other potential scholars, he was sent to a religious *yeshiva* after his *bar mitzvah* to continue his studies. Eliezer thus made his way to neighboring Polotzk.

Though he had been sent to Polotzk to learn religious matters, Ben-Yehuda was exposed there to two related aspects of modernity: the secular thinking of the Enlightenment and the notion that Hebrew could be used to express those secular thoughts. He learned that the Hebrew which he so loved could be used not only to study religious texts, but to express the modern secular thoughts of the 19th century that he was just learning to appreciate.

Ben-Yehuda thus joined the ranks of those 19th-century Jews who struggled with the juxtaposition of antiquity and modernity, and who accepted the latter into their lives. He was not alone in accepting modernity, but he turned out to be too modern for Polotzk. So he left, and made his way to a city called Glubokia. There, a woman named Devora Yonas (who turned out to be his future wife) helped Ben-Yehuda add French, German, and Russian to the Lithuanian, Yiddish, Hebrew, and Aramaic that he had already studied. He would later learn Arabic, too, in Algiers.

In addition to his linguistic interests, Ben-Yehuda was caught up in the nationalism that pervaded 19th-century Europe. The competing goals of nationless inclusion in an empire and national unity were played out most dramatically in Ben-Yehuda's life at the age of twenty, in the form of the Russo-Turkish war, which let the Bulgarians leave the Ottoman empire. Ben-Yehuda saw in this the signs of the ultimate downfall of the Ottoman empire itself, an eventuality that only augmented the need for Jewish nationality.

A year later, Ben-Yehuda published his first article, "A Weighty Question" (שאלה נכבדה, also sometimes translated as "An Important Question"), in the Hebrew periodical "The Dawn" (Ha-shaxar השחר). There he traced European nationalism, and arrived at his own definition of the term. He then asked his "weighty question": What qualities must a nation-state have? His answer included a requirement for a common language. More particularly, his answer for the Jews was that they must not only have a land but a language. Palestine was to be that land and Hebrew was to be that language.

The notion of a people retaking control of a land they had once owned took no one by surprise. After all, earlier in the century the Greeks and Italians had retaken control of their ancient lands. But the Greeks did not return to speaking ancient Greek[1] and the Italians did not return to Latin.

Ben-Yehuda's first attempt at publishing the article, in "The Speaker" (Ha-Maggid המגיד), had been unsuccessful, his ideas having been rejected as nothing more than "visions and exaggerations." Even years later, Ben-Yehuda would face similar criticism, for example, when the editor of a leading Palestinian newspaper called his ideas mere "pious dreams."

His ideas were indeed dreams and visions, representing what seemed to be a wholly unrealistic and unachievable goal. While Hebrew had never been fully abandoned as a spoken language, it is doubtful if anyone spoke

---

1. Modern Greek is so different than ancient Greek that high school students in 21st-century Greece spend four years studying ancient Greek, and yet can only read Aristotle with difficulty. Nonetheless, the great national importance the Greeks place on a "continuously spoken Greek language" prevents many inhabitants of the country today from recognizing the vast differences in the languages. Similarly, many Greeks of the time may have believed they were literally speaking the language of their ancestors. But if so, they also believed that that language had been spoken continuously. No one thought that they had returned to an ancient language.

it fluently in the 19th century. Certainly Ben-Yehuda did not. He, like the other speakers of the language, could read ancient Hebrew and speak some version of Hebrew merely as a second language. (We discussed the issue of knowing a language fluently or as a second language in the section on "Non-Spoken Hebrew" starting on page 180.) The situation was thus similar to speakers of Attic Greek or Latin: while they could converse, they lacked both the fluency and breadth of vocabulary of their native languages. Although classical languages sufficed for articles about philosophy or literature, they were ill-suited to daily discussions about the weather, jokes, child rearing, and myriad other aspects of the human interactions of day-to-day life.

Furthermore, the Jewish inhabitants of then Palestine already spoke a variety of languages, primarily an assortment of dialects of Yiddish, Ladino, and Arabic. Why would these people abandon their native languages in favor of Hebrew?

But neither the public mockery nor the drastic steps Ben-Yehuda felt he would have to take swayed him from his dream of bringing back Hebrew as the common spoken language of the Jews in their homeland.

In 1881, Ben-Yehuda and his wife would move to Palestine, but even before that, he had made perhaps the most dramatic and personal decision of his life: only Hebrew would be spoken in his home. While Ben-Yehuda's knowledge of Hebrew was exemplary, it still did not approach native proficiency, and his wife barely spoke the language. Yet Hebrew was to be the language of his home, the only language he used to speak to his wife, and the only language he and his wife would use with any children they might have.

Ben-Yehuda quickly learned that even he did not know enough Hebrew to communicate easily at home, but he did not give up, even — according to people who knew him — resorting to pantomime rather than speaking in anything other than Hebrew. Along with the pantomime, Ben-Yehuda invented words he needed for day-to-day conversation, hoping his wife might somehow understand them.

It was into this home of broken Hebrew and gesture that Ben-Zion ("Son of Zion") Ben-Yehuda — later called Ittamar Ben-Avi — was born in 1882. As a result of the linguistically confused environment of his childhood, Ittamar did not utter his first words until the age of four. But when he opened his mouth and spoke in Hebrew, Ittamar probably became the first native Hebrew speaker in nearly two millennia. Ben-Yehuda's dream saw its first major success. In a perhaps apocryphal but still endearing and moving account, Ittamar's first words — the first words spoken in Modern Hebrew — are reported to have been "don't fight" (*lo l'hit'lachem* לא להתלחם), in response to an argument between his parents.

Ben-Yehuda's success with his child led to further successes.

On the personal front, other families followed Ben-Yehuda's example. Even families that did not limit their family lives to Hebrew used Hebrew with Ben-Yehuda. Through his writings, Ben-Yehuda convinced Jews living outside of Palestine to adopt Hebrew. Ben-Yehuda founded a society for the "Revival of Israel," devoted in part to reviving Hebrew. At Ben-Yehuda's urging, Hebrew was adopted in some schools.

On the academic front, Ben-Yehuda compiled a magnificent dictionary, including in it not only ancient Hebrew, but the Hebrew he invented as Modern Hebrew. (In a curious bit of circularity, it is reported that Ben-Yehuda also had to invent a Hebrew word for "dictionary.") He also founded a language council to oversee the development of Hebrew. After experimenting with two other names, the committee took the name *va'ad halashon* (ועד הלשון), "The Language Council" or "The Language Committee."

Thus the ancient language of Hebrew was reborn on personal, public, and academic fronts after a nearly 2,000-year hiatus.

Periods of Modern Hebrew

Once again, we do not want to obsess over matters of terminology, but still a few words are in order about the phrase "Modern Hebrew," for, indeed, "Modern Hebrew" ought to refer to any Hebrew of modernity.

We will use the term in its more limited sense of "Modern Hebrew as spoken in the area that is now Israel," recognizing that though the definition is vague there is little doubt about the Hebrew to which we refer. Some prefer the term "Israeli Hebrew" for this, for the dual reasons that its most straightforward abbreviation (IH) does not conflict with the abbreviation "MH," variously used for "Medieval Hebrew" or "Mishnaic Hebrew," and that it distinguishes between the Hebrew of Israel and other modern (non-spoken) dialects used elsewhere in the world, as we discussed above.

But, having abandoned the term "Medieval Hebrew" as a dialect of Hebrew, and recognizing that the Hebrew to which we refer began nearly 70 years before the modern state of Israel, and bearing in mind that in the end we can use terms however we like, we will stick with "Modern Hebrew."

We turn next to distinguishing three periods of "Modern Hebrew": Ben-Yehuda's Hebrew, early Israeli Hebrew, and current Israeli Hebrew.

Ben-Yehuda's Hebrew

The first period of Modern Hebrew is marked by the fact that its native speakers were far outnumbered by its non-native speakers, and ranges from about the time that Ben-Yehuda began bringing Hebrew back to life (when there were no native speakers), to the time that enough native speakers, such as his son, existed to have more influence on the language than those who did not speak Hebrew fluently. However, the constant influx of immigrants into Palestine created an ever-new source of people who did not speak Hebrew natively, so the linguistic boundaries do not match up directly with generational lines, as otherwise they might. Even when Ittamar Ben-Avi was speaking native Hebrew, new immigrants were learning the Hebrew of his father.

As it turns out, of course, Ben-Yehuda's Hebrew was not truly a spoken language in the sense we noted in the last chapter. We could therefore have put this discussion of his Hebrew there, along with other non-spoken dialects of Hebrew. But, just as we will not let our terms dictate our thinking, neither will we give our definitions this privilege. The "non-spoken" Hebrew of Ben-Yehuda's time was so commonly spoken and so clearly the precursor to modern spoken Hebrew that its discussion belongs here.

Early Israeli Hebrew

In 1914, the Technikum (now called the Technion) in Haifa, a major center of high school and higher education, decided to use Hebrew as its official language. Originally, the largely German-speaking board had decided that German should be the official language of the school, but strikes and public demonstrations demanding that Hebrew be the official language ultimately convinced the Americans involved with the school and then, finally, the entire board, to support Hebrew as the Technikum's official language. The Technikum controversy received wide media and popular attention, which, in turn, brought the debate over Hebrew as an official language more generally to the fore. (In the end, the strike at the Technikum prolonged the start of classes long enough for the war and its aftermath to prevent the start of classes until 1924.)

It is difficult for the modern reader, who already knows that Hebrew is the spoken language of Israel and the Jews, to appreciate how radical the decision to use Hebrew was. Until Ben-Yehuda, Hebrew was neither widely spoken nor commonly used for academia. German, by contrast, was spoken by the entire academic community worldwide, and used for instruction even where well-established local languages were spoken by the students. The suggestion to use Hebrew in the Technikum was even more bold than a suggestion today would be to establish a major American university in Puerto Rico and use only a Taino (native) language for instruction.

Jack Fellman, in his detailed account of the revival of Hebrew, uses this 1914 date to mark Ben-Yehuda's victory, and in a political sense it may have been. But the sociological victory came much earlier, as we saw, and it would take another two decades or so for the linguistic victory. In 1914, there were still too few native speakers to call Hebrew a spoken language in its technical sense. While the language was commonly spoken, it was still spoken as a second language.

Another date that might be conveniently noted is the inception of the British administration in Palestine in 1919. The British Mandate gave Hebrew the status of an official language, along with Arabic and English. (Because of the aftermath of the war, the British Mandate did not take legal effect until 1922, at which point it was applied retroactively to 1919. Lawyers and philosophers can bicker over the exact status of Hebrew during that three-year period.) Most of the Hebrew speakers of that time, too, spoke Hebrew only as a second language.

In the period from the end of the First World War to the founding of the state of Israel in 1948, the number of Hebrew speakers grew perhaps sevenfold, from very approximately 50,000 to 350,000. Population estimates from those times vary drastically, but are along the lines of up to 100,000 just after the war to perhaps half a million in 1948. It is exceedingly difficult to know the extent to which these people were conversant in Hebrew, but 50,000 in 1919 to 350,000 in 1948 represents a guess that is, at least, probably not worse than others.

Even without exact numbers, we can see that the number of people who came to Israel and spoke Hebrew only as a second language continued to exceed the number of people who spoke Hebrew natively. Against this statistic we must bear in mind that the arriving immigrants probably had less effect on the language per person than did the established power structure already living there. At any rate, we should take a quick look at what happens to a language under pressure from a power structure to change.

It is well known in linguistic circles that most attempts to control the course of a language by fiat fail, because native speakers generally do not speak the way other people want them to, sometimes for political or social reasons, but more often for reasons having to do with how the brain processes and uses language: they are simply unable to follow artificial rules.

English offers many good examples. One of them involves the decision made quite some time ago that, because Latin does not allow prepositions (such as "to," "for," "in," etc.) at the end of a sentence, neither should English. But the enormous energy spent on official pronouncements to that effect, and spent by schoolteachers teaching schoolchildren, has not affected the vast majority of English speakers, who still find "I want to know who you went to talk to" much more intuitive than the (artificial) "I want to know to whom you went to talk."

Similar considerations of naturalness of language began to influence the direction Hebrew would take once there were sufficient native speakers. This trend, of course, was gradual, starting with one person way back in 1896 (when Ittamar, who spoke naturally, uttered his first words), growing slowly in the years and decades that followed. By the 1930s or 1940s, a well-established Modern Hebrew dialect was in widespread use throughout Israel, alongside numerous other dialects of Hebrew spoken as a second language. Both because the shift was gradual and because we have no widespread studies of the spoken language of the time, exact dates are hard to come by, but 1940 represents a convenient date to mark the start of early Israeli Modern Hebrew. This dialect of Modern Hebrew lasted though the founding of the modern state of Israel and into the 1960s or 1970s.

Current Israeli Hebrew

The course of Hebrew since the state of Israel was founded in 1948 has been influenced by several remarkable factors. Among them are the mass immigration the country saw, which raised its Hebrew-speaking population approximately twelve-fold in half a century. Fewer than half a million Hebrew speakers in 1948 would become (just under) six million Hebrew speakers fifty years later. Even in 2000, somewhere between one-fifth and one-seventh of the population of Israel spoke Hebrew only as a second language.

Nonetheless, the Hebrew spoken in Israel today is remarkably uniform. Furthermore, it differs from the uniform dialect spoken when Israel was founded, with differences in pronunciation, vocabulary, and even grammar. As with the shift from Ben-Yehuda's Hebrew to early Israeli Hebrew, this shift, too, was gradual, and native Hebrew speakers in Israel today still use both dialects, with the more modern one vastly preferred by younger speakers and the older one preferred by older speakers. But for convenience, we can use 1965 as a cutoff date between the two dialects.

With these dates in mind, and remembering that they represent only approximations, we can take a look at the three dialects that have made up Modern Hebrew.

Ben-Yehuda's Hebrew

As we have seen, Ben-Yehuda himself did not speak Hebrew fluently. Ben-Yehuda thus did not affect Hebrew much through his own speech. And while his son Ittamar was the first native Hebrew speaker of modernity, even he did not have a significant direct impact on how Hebrew would be spoken. But Ben-Yehuda's indirect impact was enormous, in that he set the direction for Hebrew's revival through his personal leadership, through the numerous articles he published, and through his dictionary.

By and large, Ben-Yehuda chose the Masoretic tradition of Biblical Hebrew over Rabbinic Hebrew, and in particular he chose the Masoretic version of Late Biblical Hebrew, though it is not clear if he consciously recognized the existence of two Biblical dialects. (It is commonly claimed that Ben-Yehuda used Biblical Hebrew as the base for his Modern Hebrew, but, like us, he had no way of knowing how Biblical Hebrew was pronounced. The persistent theme of this book regarding the degree to which the Masoretes correctly recorded Biblical Hebrew thus returns in our discussion of the foundations of Modern Hebrew.)

Ben-Yehuda also borrowed heavily from spoken and classical Arabic, because of its similarity to Hebrew; from Russian, because he spoke it so well; and from a variety of other languages as the need arose.

Ben-Yehuda, primarily through his *va'ad* (council or committee) on language, made a few key decisions that have greatly affected Modern Hebrew. We will look at the nature of Modern Hebrew below, but for now, we note the following.

Pronunciation

The most pressing issue facing Hebrew speakers at the turn of the century was pronunciation. After all, if Hebrew were to become a spoken language, there would have to be some agreement about how to speak it. In this regard, there were two dominant dialects, commonly known as "Ashkenazic" and "Sephardic." Both of these terms, in fact, refer to collections of dialects, but their main differences involved two sets of consonants (the guttural letters and the *beged kefet* letters) and two pairs of vowels (*kamatz/patach* and *segol/tzere*).

The Sephardic system maintained only three of the *beged kefet* alternations: *bet* ב (*b/v*), *peh* פ (*p/f*), and *kaf* כ (*k/x*), while the Ashkenazic system had retained a fourth: *taf* ת (*t/s*). Also, the Sephardic system, under Arabic influence and somewhat reflecting Masoretic Hebrew, preserved pronunciation distinctions between four pairs of letters where the Ashkenazic system did not. In the Ashkenazic system, the letters *tet, chet, ayin,* and *koof* (ט, ח, ע, and ק) sounded, respectively, like *taf, chaf, aleph,* and *kaf* (ת, כ, א, and כ), while in the Sephardic system the first set was "guttural," or, more technically, either velar or pharyngeal. (Velar sounds are made roughly at the same point in the throat as the letter *g* — as in *go* — while pharyngeal sounds are made by pulling the epiglottis back toward the back wall of the pharynx. Most English speakers have great difficulty pronouncing these sounds. The suggested reading list contains suggestions for readers who want more technical information about what we are calling informally "guttural" sounds.)

Yemenite pronunciation, technically subsumed under the category "Sephardic" but differing considerably in its pronunciation from the Hebrew commonly thought of as "Sephardic," offered distinctions between the two remaining *beged kefet* letters, *gimel* and *daled* (ג and ד), and a unique pronunciation of the letter *chet.*

In terms of vowels, Sephardic tradition did not differentiate between the vowels *patach* (אַ — shown here with the letter *aleph* because vowels never appear without a consonant in Hebrew) and *kamatz* (אָ), pronouncing them both as /a/, and some dialects did not distinguish between *segol* (אֶ) and *tzere* (אֵ). By contrast, the Ashkenazic tradition had a whole host of ways in which the pairs were pronounced differently. Various other differences in the vowels were evident, too, in addition to numerous minor variations.

Finally, Sephardic Hebrew, by and large in keeping with Masoretic Hebrew, tended to accentuate most words on the last syllable, or (in certain grammatical situations that are too complex to warrant discussing here) on the second to last syllable. Ashkenazic Hebrew offered more variation in where a word was accentuated.

The non-Yemenite Sephardic system was already in use in Palestine at the time, and the Ashkenazic system sounded like the Yiddish Ben-Yehuda and his colleagues were trying to abandon, so the *va'ad* — Ben-Yehuda's language committee — chose the Sephardic system over the Ashkenazic one. In practice, though, the people actually invented their own dialect, combining the *beged kefet* pronunciation of the Sephardic system with, by and large, the non-guttural pronunciation of the Ashkenazic one.

But some populations in Palestine continued to use their own pronunciations, with guttural consonants remaining in significant Israeli minorities, and aspects of the Yemenite system still being heard to this day among Jews of Yemenite origin.

Vocabulary

Without doubt, Ben-Yehuda's most lasting contribution to Modern Hebrew (with the exception, obviously, of the crucial role he played in actually bringing it into existence) is in the realm of vocabulary. Though many of the terms and the basic words he coined are no longer in use in Israel, the patterns he set up for creating new words have survived.

The vocabulary of Modern Hebrew is based primarily on Biblical and Rabbinic Hebrew, with (by design) Biblical taking precedence over Rabbinic. Beyond that, Hebrew has gone the usual route of borrowing words from foreign languages, and has also added vocabulary through a fairly unique method of its own, as described next.

Hebrew nouns and verbs come in **paradigms,** called *binyanim* (for verbs) or *mishkalot* (for nouns) in Hebrew. The paradigms are a general correlation between the way a word is built and what kind of word it is. Additionally, roots consisting of (usually) three letters exist independent of any particular paradigm. (Remember that we put periods between the letters of a root to indicate that it is a root and not a word, as in "*g.d.l,*" the three-letter root *gimel-daled-lamed.*) A root and a paradigm combine to form a word.

As an example of a verbal paradigm, we note that a basic past-tense, masculine, singular, third-person verb generally consists of three consonants (the root) separated by two /a/ vowels. This particular way of combining the consonants and the /a/ vowels is the paradigm. Another paradigm adds an /n/ at the beginning of the word, generally contributing a passive meaning to the verb. Yet another paradigm, sometimes adding an emphatic flavor to the verb, separates the root consonants by the vowels /i/ and /a/. The popular description that the root gives the basic meaning and the paradigm adds (for example) the past-tense-ness to the verb is overly simplistic, but still along the right lines.

A concrete example may help. From the three-letter root *g.d.l,* with the general meaning of "grow," and the past tense paradigm of *CaCaC* (where each "C" represents a consonant) we get the word *gadal,* meaning "he grew." Similarly, from the root *sh.m.r,* with the general meaning of "keep," we get the word *shamar,* "he kept." From the passive past-tense paradigm *niCCaC,* we get *nishmar,* meaning "he was kept." (The "Further Reading" list contains suggestions for sources with more detailed information. The approximation given here will work for our current purposes, but it is actually fundamentally wrong.)

Similarly, one common noun paradigm can be described (again, wrongly, but still conveniently) as consisting of the prefix /mi/ and the vowel /a/ between the second and third root letters, that is, *miCCaC*. So from the same roots we get *migdal*, "tower," and *mishmar*, "watch duty."

The reader will quickly realize that the root/paradigm combination does not completely dictate the meaning of the word. In our example, the relationship between "he grew" and "tower" is not the same as between "he kept" and "watch duty."

This system of paradigms was a prime source of new words in Modern Hebrew, as it was in previous dialects of Hebrew. For example, in the case of Modern Hebrew, a paradigm for "diseases" (*CaCeCet*, where again each "C" represents a root letter) was identified, and then used to give names to diseases for which Hebrew had no word.

From the root for "red" (*a.d.m* — א.ד.מ) came the word *ademet* (אדמת), "rubella." From the word "dog" (*kelev* כלב) came the word *kalevet* (כלבת), "rabies." Other pairs along the same pattern include "yellow"/"jaundice," "sugar"/"diabetes," "drip"/"cold," and so forth. (This pattern would later be used to form one of the author's favorite Hebrew words. From the word for "paper" — *niyar* ניר — would come the "disease" *nayeret* נירת: "paperwork.")

Because of the flexibility in connecting meanings with paradigms, the paradigm system was perfect for adding new words to Hebrew. The paradigm *maCCeC* is used for "tools" in the most general sense of the word, as in the ancient words *masrek* (מסרק) "[a] comb" from the root *s.r.k*, meaning "to comb"; or *maxtev* "stylus" from the root *k.t.v*, meaning "to write." (The /k/ becomes a /x/ in accordance with the *beged kefet* rules.) Building on this pattern, Ben-Yehuda took the root for "to clean/to press" (*g.h.tz* ג.ה.צ) and created a word for "[an] iron": *maghetz* (מגהץ). From the root for "cold" (*k.r.r* ק.ר.ר) came the word *makrer*, "refrigerator" (originally, "ice-box").

While some of the new words formed in this manner never caught on, the system remains in use to this day.

Grammar

The issue of Ben-Yehuda's grammar is considerably more complicated than the issue of pronunciation or vocabulary. Ben-Yehuda himself spoke only broken Hebrew, and so his grammar, while reflecting Late Biblical Hebrew, also exhibited significant aspects of Yiddish, Russian, Lithuanian, and sometimes even German and French; in some cases Ben Yehuda may not have been aware that he was mixing grammars, much the way people who speak second languages today often unknowingly make mistakes based on their native grammars.

Until Ittamar, who actually spoke Hebrew natively, other Hebrew speakers suffered from the same sorts of problems, though, obviously, with their own unique quirks. (Of the foreign languages that eventually influenced Hebrew's grammar, Russian, German, and French would play important roles early on, and Russian and English important roles later.) Still, even with this confused grammatical situation, a few clear patterns emerge.

Some of the features that Late Biblical Hebrew abandoned were also rejected by Modern Hebrew. For example, Modern Hebrew never had the Biblical double-verb construction described on page 153.

Other features of Biblical Hebrew were similarly never adopted, such as the often misunderstood Biblical Hebrew *vav* (ו), which in addition to meaning "and," was used, apparently, to reverse the tense of a verb, so that, for example the word "*vav* will go" (*vayelex* וילך) meant either "and he will go" or "he went." (The phenomenon is actually more complicated and, ironically, less mysterious than a powerful tense-changing letter, but the details are unimportant here.) This construction, so typical of Biblical Hebrew, was abandoned in Rabbinic Hebrew, and likewise never made its way into Modern Hebrew.

Two other grammatical points are worth mentioning.

Biblical Hebrew word order was basically verb-subject-object ("VSO"), in that, unless there was good reason to deviate from the norm, the verb was the first element in a sentence, followed by the subject, followed by other stuff, including the object or objects. (In linguistics terminology, "object" here means the things that are not the verb or the subject.) So "God spoke to Moses" in Biblical Hebrew is "spoke [the verb] God [the subject] to-Moses [the object]." Russian word order is loosely SVO (subject-verb-object), but allows considerably more freedom than Biblical Hebrew. German is more complicated, in that it is basically SOV, except that (1) it allows variations in the parts before the verb; and more importantly, (2) simple sentences are XVSO, where the "X" represents anything other than the verb. All of these various grammars were borrowed by Hebrew, creating, as the reader may imagine, more than a little confusion. Ben-Yehuda's Hebrew was basically SVO, but, unlike English, allowed for considerable variation.

The second point involves grammatical subjects and word order. Some languages, such as English, seem always to require a subject, even when the subject doesn't refer to anything. So the "it" in "it's raining" or in "It seems to me that ..." cannot be omitted in English, even though the word, unlike most pronouns, doesn't refer to anything. By contrast, the Spanish equivalents of these sentences do not require an "it." Therefore, Spanish (and languages like it) are called "null-subject languages," reflecting the "null subject" where English (and languages like it) require an actual word. Linguists have noticed that null-subject languages tend to allow more word-order variation than non-null-subject languages. In our present example, we may note that in English "arrives the train at noon" is ungrammatical, but the Spanish equivalent is just fine. This is one demonstration of the connection between Spanish being a null-subject language and its allowing more word-order variation than the non-null-subject language English. French and German pattern with English, Italian with Spanish.

Ben-Yehuda's Hebrew (like the Russian he knew so well) was a null-subject language. The Hebrew equivalents of "seems to me that ..." (‏נדמה לי ש‎-. . .) and "arrives the train" (. . . ‏מגיעה הרקבת‎) were both grammatical for Ben-Yehuda. Below, we will trace a change in Hebrew from null-subject to non-null-subject.

Spelling

The issue of spelling, and in particular of spelling vowels, has been a central theme of Hebrew since it was first written toward the beginning of the 1st millennium B.C.E. Ben-Yedudah's Hebrew tried to adopt the spelling of Late Biblical Hebrew, which is to say, the vowel letters were used sparingly, by and large only where ambiguity might result, but also systematically in a few instances. The word for "all," *kol*, was spelled *kaf, lamed* (‏כל‎), never with a *vav* to indicate the vowel. But the plural endings *-im* and *-ot* required a vowel letter, and were written ‏ים‎- and ‏ות‎-, even in those cases where absolutely no ambiguity might result from leaving out the vowel letters.

But not everyone followed the official guidelines. Some people started doubling up vowel letters to indicate their use as a consonant, similar to the Rabbinic Hebrew practice. Some people used an *aleph* inside words to indicate the vowel /a/.

In general, the issue of spelling caused enormous concern and resulted in almost unbelievable debate. Spelling is usually considered by linguists to be a trivial aspect of language, certainly compared with the much weightier elements such as grammar, but the debates over spelling were often much fiercer than over any other aspect of the language, a sentiment that has remained with those involved with Hebrew. Even Angel Sáenz-Badillos, in his highly academic and scholarly book, *A History of the Hebrew Language,* uncharacteristically introduces value judgments and reports that people strayed from the *va'ad*'s spelling system because it "presupposed too good a knowledge of grammar and was too complicated for new immigrants." In point of fact, the system that was ultimately adopted relies heavily on grammar, and is no less complicated than the official one it replaced. We will see below that spelling remains a problematic area of Modern Hebrew.

Early Israeli Hebrew

By the time the state of Israel was founded, Hebrew was well established as a spoken language. We can look at the Hebrew of that time to see which elements of Ben-Yehuda's Hebrew actually made their way into the spoken language.

Pronunciation

In terms of pronunciation, a combination of the Sephardic and Ashkenazic systems had taken hold. Only the three non-Yemenite Sephardic *beged kefet* alternations (b/v, p/f, and k/x) remained. The Ashkenazic t/s alternation was considered a serious affectation, and the Yemenite alternations were limited to Yemenite speakers, who spoke a combination of Yemenite Hebrew and Arabic.

The guttural alternations listed above were no longer a part of the mainstream language. Unlike the t/s alternation, however, the use of guttural consonants was accepted as "dialectal" rather than "wrong," and in some segments of the population, this dialectal pronunciation was considered better than the more common accent.

As for the vowels, no distinction remained between *patach* (א) and *kamatz* (א), as in the Sephardic dialects, but *segol* (א) and *tsere* (א) were still sometimes differentiated.

The Hebrew of the time also largely, but not completely, adopted the word-final word accentuation pattern of Sephardic (and Masoretic) Hebrew noted above, with some clear exceptions in the realm of some of the verbal forms.

The pronunciation of the Hebrew of the state of Israel thus represented a fitting, though probably accidental, compromise among the various spoken traditions that preceded it.

Vocabulary

Words continued to stream into Hebrew from official and unofficial sources, that is, from people who undertook the job of making up new words for others, and from people using the language who found they needed new words for themselves.

Ben-Yehuda's *va'ad* continued to use the root/paradigm system to invent new words, and to try to ensure what they thought of as the purity of the Hebrew language by excluding any words of foreign origin, with bitter battles being fought between proponents of a pure Hebrew and speakers who didn't really care where their words came from. An example of the intensity with which *va'ad*-oriented thinkers viewed (and continue to view) the new directions Hebrew was taking can be seen in an article by Edward Ullendorff, a professor of Semitic languages, who laments a minor change in a verb form:

> Modern oddities like the grammatically impossible *mekir* instead of the *makkir* and similar monstrosities had not arisen in [Ben-Yehuda's] Hebrew, and I am glad that it is left to those who nowadays watch over the health of contemporary Hebrew either to come to terms with such horrors or to endeavour to discard them.

Similar extreme sentiments pervaded the *va'ad*'s approach to all matters Hebrew.

Foreign words such as *telefon* (טלפון) for "telephone" were officially rejected in favor of "purer" words with purely Semitic roots. In this case, the official suggestion for a Hebrew word for "telephone" attempted to translate "tele-" ("long distance") and "phone" ("sound") literally: the coarse-sounding *saxr'xok* (שׂחרחוק) was coined from the word *sixa* (שׂחה) meaning "conversation" or "speech" and the word *raxok* (רחוק) meaning "far."

But Hebrew, like any other living language, had taken on a life of its own, and was not subject to the whims of language pundits. The Hebrew-based word *saxr'xok* for "telephone" never caught on and is currently listed in dictionaries as "obsolete." "Never used" is more accurate.

But while *saxr'xok* never made it, other words from the *va'ad* eventually became mainstream.

At the same time, ordinary Hebrew speakers were inventing their own words. For example, the common Russian suffix *-nik* was added to the Hebrew *kibutz* (קיבוץ) to form *kibutznik* (קיבוצניק), that is, one who lives on a kibbutz. Later, the English "job" would be combined with that same Russian ending to form the Hebrew word *jobnik* (ג'ובניק), with the meaning of "someone who holds a position in the army that resembles an ordinary job, and not a fighter."

Surprisingly, the *va'ad*, so concerned with not using "foreign" words in Hebrew, adopted a new name in 1953: "The Academy of the Hebrew Language," or, in Hebrew, the *akademiya* (אקדמיה). The body had taken on a "foreign" name.

Grammar

The grammar of early Israeli Hebrew began to diversify. The spoken language continued more or less along the lines of Ben-Yehuda's Hebrew: it never reincorporated the Biblical aspects that Ben-Yehuda had not adopted; its word order remained basically SVO (that is, subject-verb-object); it remained a null-subject language, with its increased word-order variation possibilities. We will take up the issue of grammar more fully in our discussion of current Israeli Modern Hebrew below.

Spelling

Spelling continued to be a tricky subject. The spelling rules from Ben-Yehuda's time were published in 1948, and then adopted in almost unchanged form in 1969. But the divide between popular usage and prescribed spelling continued to widen, as we will see below.

Current Israeli Hebrew

After a brief look at Ben-Yehuda's Hebrew and an even briefer look at early Israeli Hebrew, we turn, finally, to Hebrew as it is used in Israel in the 21st century.

The question of whether Hebrew will be used in Israel, of course, has been unequivocally answered affirmatively. Hebrew is an official language of Israel (along with Arabic and English), and is used in day-to-day conversations, in the public media, in all levels of education, in the military, in the government, and so forth. Daily newspapers in Modern Hebrew are widely read throughout Israel, and distributed around the world. Because of Israel's central role in Judaism around the world, Modern Hebrew is studied and used widely outside of Israel as well, largely replacing Yiddish as the international Jewish language. Ben-Yehuda's vision of the future has come to pass, at least in terms of the overall picture.

It is doubtful, however, if Ben-Yehuda would be able to understand today's spoken Modern Hebrew, or even the written language, though he would do better with the latter than with the former.

Pronunciation

Ashkenazic or Sephardic?

Standard Israeli pronunciation today is similar to the pronunciation of early Israeli Hebrew, in that it mixes the non-Yemenite Sephardic approach to the *beged kefet* letters and vowels with the Ashkenazic approach to the guttural letters. Additionally, Modern Hebrew has no /h/ sound, a fact that is often particularly surprising to American students of Hebrew, who have been taught to pronounce the letter *heh* (ה) like an American *h*; Israelis by and large do not pronounce it at all. Thus the three letters *aleph* (א), *ayin* (ע), and *heh* (ה) are pronounced identically in mainstream spoken Israeli Hebrew.

Alongside this standard pronunciation an "Eastern" dialect — *mizraxi* מזרחי in Hebrew — referring to people from the "Eastern" Arabic countries such as Syria, Yemen, etc., remains popular. This dialect preserves distinctions, to varying degrees, among the guttural and non-guttural letters.

And alongside these two pronunciations we find a third: official Hebrew. Official Hebrew is generally only used by trained experts for public newscasts, on radio or on television. This official Hebrew, like the Eastern dialects, preserves some guttural sounds, as well as the /h/ sound for *heh* (ה).

Accentuation

Word accentuation is in flux, with most words of foreign origin not being subject to the Masoretic rule that words get accented on the final syllable, and with many but not all words of Biblical or Rabbinic origin still showing evidence of the rule.

For example, the Hebrew word *telefon* is generally accented on the first syllable: *TE-le-fon*, and the plural on the third syllable: *te-le-FON-im*. But official Hebrew insists that the words are to be pronounced *te-le-FON* and *te-le-fon-IM*.

In contrast to Masoretic Hebrew, which allowed the main word accent to lie only on the last or second to last syllable, the accent in Modern Hebrew can fall anywhere. Shoes from the Israeli city K'far Sava (*k'var SA-ba*, in spoken Hebrew) are *na'a'LA'yim* [shoes] *k'far SA-ba-i-ot*. The accent is on the fourth to last syllable.

Although the accent can fall anywhere in a word, the accent is not a matter of chance. Rather, like most aspects of spoken languages, it follows rules of which the speakers are not generally aware. In the case of Modern Hebrew, the rules are almost identical with the accentuation rules of Russian, but a full discussion of these rules would take us too far astray into technical details of linguistics. This is but one way in which the grammar of Hebrew has adopted Russian patterns. Based on this and other facts, some linguists have suggested, only half-jokingly, that Modern Hebrew ought to be considered a Slavic language.

Beged Kefet

The reader may also have noticed that the Israeli city K'far Sava is pronounced with a /b/ instead of a /v/ in Modern Hebrew. This reflectives another major shift, this time away from the Masoretic *beged kefet* rules.

According to the Masoretes, the non-doubled *beged kefet* letters were pronounced as fricatives after a vowel. Everywhere else they were pronounced as stops. While Modern Israelis learn this rule in high school, they do not apply it to their speech. By and large, every word with one of the *beged kefet* letters has a base form, with either a stop or a fricative, and the letter does not change.

When the Masoretes recorded the original *beged kefet* rule, it probably applied to all (non-nasal) stops, and so would have been a natural rule for speakers to learn. With the disappearance of three of the *beged kefet* alternations in Ben-Yehuda's Hebrew, the rule became more complex. It was no longer true that all stops became fricatives. Only some did. With the further change that *chet* (ח) was pronounced exactly like a *chaf* (כ), and a *vav* (ו) exactly like a *vet* (ב), it was no longer true that all fricatives were related to stops. The rule was no longer a natural linguistic rule, and, as is so often the case with non-natural rules, native speakers did not learn it intuitively.

An example of a stop that does not become a fricative comes from the common Hebrew word *cos* (כוס), "cup." The word for "in" in Hebrew is the prefix *b-* (-ב), and according to the Masoretic rules changes the stop it precedes into a fricative. Accordingly, the word for "in a cup" ought to be *b'xos*. But it is not. Speakers greatly prefer *b'kos*.

An example of a fricative that does not become a stop comes from the word for "to telephone." From the noun *telefon* Hebrew gets the verb *til'fen*. But the /f/ does not follow a vowel, and so ought to be a /p/. While *til'pen* for "he called" is recognizable, it sounds a little silly to Modern Hebrew speakers.

One result of the Masoretic *beged kefet* rule is that a fricative such as /f/ cannot start a word. Yet the most popular fast food in Israel is called *falafel*, a fact which further indicates the complete loss of systematic *beged kefet*-related alternations in Modern Hebrew.

However, the official broadcast-style speech used by professional announcers still steadfastly maintains the *beged kefet* rules, and Israelis have no trouble understanding this somewhat artificial speech.

Epenthesis

Masoretic Hebrew had another attribute that has been lost in Modern Hebrew. When a word would otherwise start with three consonants in a row, an /i/ was inserted between the first two. (The reader may recall from our discussion on page 94 that this was one aspect of Masoretic Hebrew that could not be confirmed by any ancient evidence, raising the possibility that it was invented by the Masoretes.)

The Masoretes' rules often called for the insertion of this epenthetic /i/ after the consonantal prefixes. The prefix "in," which we just saw, consists of the single consonant *b*. When it was added to a word beginning with two consonants, a word with three consonants would result, and the Masoretes would insert the vowel /i/. So from the word *g'dulato* ("his greatness") we have not the Masoretically impossible *b'g'dulato* but rather *big'dulato* ("in his greatness").

While, once again, high-school students learn this rule, native speakers do not generally use it when they speak, prefering exactly the form that the Masoretes sought to avoid: *b'g'dulato*.

However, the same professional announcers that follow the other Masoretic rules also follow this one. When most Israelis want to say "in K'var Sava," they say *b'k'far SAba*, but the official Hebrew phrase is *bix'FAR saVA*. The official form varies from the spoken form in two of six consonants, in one of four vowels, and in the accentuation of both words; these combine to create a situation in which none of the syllables in the spoken form matches its counterpart in the official form.

Vocabulary

In terms of vocabulary, the trends we saw in early Israeli Hebrew have continued, in that the *akademiya* continues to create words, some of which are incorporated into the spoken language, while Hebrew speakers continue to make up their own words. The foreign influence of Russian has not abated, but in terms of sources of vocabulary it has been surpassed by English.

It is not uncommon to find that two words for the same general concept exist, one from English and one from a Hebrew root. By and large, when this happens the English one takes on an emphatic meaning. For example, the Hebrew word *m'suyam* (מסוים), which is the passive of a more ancient word meaning "to designate" or "to specify," means "specific" in Modern Hebrew. Alongside of that word we find *spetzifi* (ספציפי), which also means "specific," and clearly comes from the English "specific." (The transition from "c" in English to "tz" in Hebrew is common.) But while both words mean "specific," the English-related one represents a bolder, more dramatic, or more emphatic concept, as though, on a continuum from "non-specific" to "specific" to "even more specific," the word from the Hebrew root represents "specific" and the word from the English root represents "even more specific."

In addition to borrowing words and to creating words by combining roots and paradigms (as we saw above), Modern Hebrew has another unique strategy for creating words: acronyms.

An acronym is a word consisting of the initial letter or letters of each word in a phrase. English has a few acronyms that are pronounced, such as "RADAR" (from **RA**dio **D**etection **A**nd **R**anging), but most tend to be pronounced either as letters (e.g., "U.S.A." — "you-ess-ay") or not at all.

But because Hebrew words are generally written without all the vowels, any combination of consonants can represent a pronounceable word, making acronyms a popular source not only of abbreviations but also of new words.

Unlike in English, where we use periods after the letters of an acronym, Hebrew usually uses a double quotation mark before the last letter to mark an acronym. (If we followed this convention in English, instead of *F.B.I.* we would write *FB"I*.)

For example, the Bible is made up of three parts: Torah (*torah* תורה in Hebrew), Prophets (*n'vi'im* נביאים), and Writings or Hagiographa (*k'tuvim* כתובים). From this Hebrew gets the acronym *tanax* (תנ"ך), containing the first letter of each section of the Bible, and vowels inserted as necessary to make the word pronounceable. (The /k/ of *k'tuvim* becomes a /x/ in accordance with *beged kefet* rules.) This acronym-based word is as much a word in Hebrew as any other. For example, it can combine with the adjectival suffix *-i* (י-) to yield the word *tanaxi* ("Biblical").

This process is extremely widespread in Israel. With some common exceptions — such as *byh"s* (ביה"ס) for *bet hasefer* (בית הספר), literally "house book," that is, "school" — which for some reason are never pronounced as the word spelled by the initials, the general pattern is to pronounce the letters of the acronym. These acronymic words then become words in their own right.

One other example will illustrate. The phrase for "member of Parlia-ment" in Hebrew is *xaver k'neset* (חבר כנסת). The acronym for this phrase is *xak* (ח"כ). The plural of the phrase — that is, "members of Parliament" — is *xav're k'neset* (חברי כנסת), with the first word marked for plural with a final *yud* in accord with the rules for making a compound plural. But alongside that plural we find simply the plural of the acronym: *xakim* (ח"כים). The plural ending *-im* gets added to the "acronym," which is really a word.

Grammar

Amazingly, Modern Hebrew has changed from a null-subject language to a non-null-subject language. For example, previous generations would use "was important that . . . ," while the current generation prefers "it was important that . . . " Along with this trend away from null-subjects, Hebrew has also tended to adhere more closely to its SVO word order.

This is mildly interesting in its own right, in that over the course of two generations Hebrew's sentential grammar seems to have changed so dramatically, but it is even more interesting to linguists, who have long suspected a deep-rooted connection between null-subjects and freer word order. The fact that the move away from null-subjects was accompanied by a move away from free word order is dramatic confirmation of the connection between the two phenomena.

Another aspect of grammar warrants our attention.

Late Biblical Hebrew saw a change in the way compounds were made plural (described in "Grammar" starting on page 153), a change that lasted into Rabbinic Hebrew. The original scheme (in early Biblical Hebrew) marked the plural only on the first word of the phrase, while the modified scheme marked the plural on both. Modern Hebrew follows the original Biblical scheme, in that it generally marks the plural only on the first word.

However, in terms of a closely related phenomenon, Modern Hebrew seems more like Rabbinic Hebrew. The definite article "the" (*ha-* -ה) was attached only to the last word of a compound. So "The King's House" was expressed in Biblical Hebrew as "house the-king" (*bet hamelex* בית המלך). An example from Modern Hebrew involves the word for school, literally, "house book" (*bet sefer* בית ספר), as we just saw. But while older Israeli Hebrew maintained the Biblical practice of putting the word "the" on the second word (*bet hasefer* בית הספר — "house the-book"), many mod-ern speakers prefer putting the word "the" on the first word: *habet sefer* (הבית ספר — "the-house book"). Once again, students in high school are taught not to do this, and once again they do it anyway, though educated speakers tend to preserve the older style more in the case of compounds than they do with the issues of pronunciation we saw above.

What we see, then, is that the compound system that seemed unstable, and hence subject to change, in post-exilic Hebrew, is also unstable in modern times.

This is not the only instance where we see the same progressions twice, once from Biblical Hebrew to Rabbinic Hebrew and again from Ben-Yehuda's Hebrew to 21st-century Modern Hebrew. We already saw that both Rabbinic and Modern Hebrew abandoned the double-verb construction, as well as the *vav* that seemed to change tenses. We will see that similar spelling changes took place during both eras, as described below.

The similarity between the Rabbis' innovations and those of Modern Hebrew suggests that both were driven by the same universal linguistic tendencies, which in turn suggests that they were both spoken languages. We know this is true for the latter, of course, and we concluded tentatively above that this was true for the former. Now we see further evidence in support of our conclusion.

The similarity among spelling changes is even more striking.

Spelling

Israel is going through a spelling crisis. The official spelling rules are so out of touch with how people actually spell their words that even very common words are commonly spelled one way in the dictionary and another way, or sometimes several other ways, in printed books. Literate, educated people don't know (and can't understand) the official rules, which rely on arcane details of our current understanding of the Masoretic system, and then, left to their own devices, these same educated speakers of Hebrew still can't agree on how to spell their words.

The problem is the vowel letters.

While the complex Masoretic system of diacritic dots and lines listed in Table 5.1 is used in Modern Hebrew for poetry, children's books, and to differentiate words that otherwise might not be clear, it is not used for most ordinary prose. Indeed, most Israelis are incapable of filling in those diacritic marks, and resort to dictionaries or experts on those rare occasions when they must use them (in what is then called "pointed" Hebrew). Though it is difficult for Israelis to write in pointed Hebrew, there is little debate about how to do it: consult an expert.

By contrast, there is little consensus on how to write "ordinary," that is, unpointed, Hebrew, the sort that is used in newspapers, books, homework assignments, personal letters, e-mail, and so forth.

A few examples of the official rules for spelling will give the reader a sense of why the public has been unable to adopt them. The following is a loose translation and elucidation of the guide given at the end of Evan Shoshan's *hamilon ha'ivri he'xadash,* the most authoritative Hebrew dictionary in Israel:

1. The sound /o/ is to be written with a *vav* in any word whose /o/ sound would be written by the Masoretes with a *vav,* or with a *cholam chaser* or with a *kamatz* that through grammatical derivation comes from a *cholam chaser.* The /o/ sound in those handful of words that the Masoretes chose to write with a *kamatz* in all of their forms shall not be written with a *vav.* But there are many newspaper reporters and authors who write even some of these words with a *vav.*

2. The sound /i/ is to be written with a *yud* when it derives from an open syllable in the uninflected form of the word, except that some words even then don't get a *yud.* If the singular of the word gets a *yud,* then so does the plural. The sound /i/ is not written with a *yud* after the prefix letters; in some short words, among them *milah* meaning "word," to distinguish it from the identically sounding word *milah* meaning "circumcision," which is written with a *yud;* after the *heh* used as part of verbal paradigms; in words with a suffix whose unsuffixed form does not have a *yud,* including *imi* "my mother," even though that word in its unsuffixed form actually does have a *yud . . .*

3. The sound /v/ is to be written with two *vavs* in the middle of a word but with one *vav* at the beginning or end of a word, except that under no circumstances are three *vavs* ever to be written in a row. For example, the word "committee" *va'ad* is spelled with one *vav,* but with two in the combinations "in a committee," "the committee," etc. Sometimes a *yud* will be inserted before a final *vav . . .*

The rules offer little help to those who are not masters of the Masoretic system of pointing. (To be fair, the rules make more sense to the few people who have mastered Masoretic grammar than the examples might indicate. But mastering Masoretic grammar is much like becoming an expert in Medieval English. The system can thus be compared to a spelling system in English that makes sense only to experts in ancient English.)

Furthermore, these Hebrew rules are commonly ignored. A simple example is the word "letter" (as in "correspondence"): *mixtav.* The word appears in the dictionary fully pointed as מִכְתָּב, that is, with the consonants *mxtv,* and with the Masoretic diacritic marks to indicate the vowels. The official rules of spelling dictate that the word be spelled without a *yud* for the /i/ sound even when the vowels are not printed: מכתב, that is, *mxtv.* However, both that form and the form with a *yud* (*mixtv* מיכתב) are commonly found in newspapers, books, etc. Israelis can't agree on how to spell "letter."

This is not just a case of the linguistic elite being out of touch with the masses. In Israel, the educated masses themselves cannot agree on a standard spelling. Nor is the problem in Israel parallel to recent developments in the English-speaking world, where an "alternative," informal, often e-mail-based spelling system has arisen ("thru," for "through" or even "l8er" for "later" etc.). While Israelis also have some cutesie spellings, they often cannot agree on standard spellings.

There is general consensus among Israelis who don't use the official rules (which is to say, almost all of them) that the letter *yud* should be used for /i/ and /e/ and *vav* for /o/ and /u/ except where it really doesn't look good to do so. There is, however, little agreement on "where it doesn't look good to do so." There is also general consensus that the sounds /v/ and /y/ should often be written with a double letter, but, again, little consensus on exactly when. There is widespread agreement that putting three *yud*s or *vav*s in a row doesn't look all that good.

In addition to ordinary words, it is not uncommon to find different spellings of the names of public institutions or companies, which find themselves in the position of having their names printed and publicly displayed with a variety of spellings.

This spelling crisis has brought us full circle. Roughly 3,000 years ago, people began experimenting with Hebrew "vowel letters," which they would use to represent vowel sounds in words that had hitherto had only their consonants recorded in writing. These vowel letters made writing by the masses possible, and paved the way, as we saw, for almost every other alphabet in use around the world.

While our Science Theory prevents us from even considering such a preposterous proposition, we cannot help but marvel at the symmetry, and wonder if perhaps the Hebrew vowel letters, so proud of their pivotal role in the history of writing, simply refuse to be marginalized, insisting instead on preserving their centrality in the Hebrew of today.

Chapter 11
Keep Your Voice from Weeping

In 2001, a new, modern, central bus station was opened in Jerusalem, bearing on its walls a quotation from Psalm 122: *sha'alu shlom Yerusha-layim* — "Ask for peace in Jerusalem." In a tribute to the history of the place, "Jerusalem" there is written in keeping with the idiosyncratic Bibli-cal spelling ירושלם (*YRShLM*), rather than according to the more modern spelling norms that insert another *yud*: ירושלים (*YRShLYM*).

With all we have seen in the previous pages, we can trace how those words came to be inscribed in the bus station in 21st-century Jerusalem.

Roughly 3,000 years ago, a group of people made what seemed like a minor modification to a writing process that had already been in develop-ment for over a thousand years. They took three symbols that represented consonants, and used them to represent vowels as well. With the added convenience those vowel letters offered, the masses started reading and writing. In the centuries that followed, the poem we now call "Psalm 122" was written in Phoenician letters, using a few of those vowel letters as needed.

We know about the poem from the Dead Sea Scroll 11QPs[a], dating from about 2,000 years ago but discovered only last century; from the Masoretic tradition of the Bible, as recorded in the Leningrad Codex over 1,000 years ago; and from various translations of the Bible, most importantly a trans-lation into Greek some 2,300 years ago. While our Science Theory tells us that the Masoretic understanding of the sounds of the letters is prob-ably imperfect, we have good reason to believe that the consonants they recorded, and hence the words, are mostly authentic.

Just over 100 years ago, a man named Eliezer Ben-Yehuda decided that the Jews should speak the language they once did, and so embarked on an experiment in reviving a language. His experiment, like the one with vowel letters nearly 3,000 years earlier, was successful, paving the way for a rebirth of Hebrew as a modern language.

As a result of Ben-Yehuda's experiment, when the time came to build a new bus station in Jerusalem, the people in charge of the building spoke a language close enough to the one in which the poem had originally been written that they could fully understand it. They then took a more modern, though still essentially 2,500-year-old script, and used it to reproduce an ancient poem probably with the same letters in which it was originally penned, thus bridging over 2,000 years of history while completing the mundane task of building a bus station. We do not know exactly how much history they bridged, because we do not know exactly when Psalm 122 was composed.

Other ancient Hebrew material is easier to date, based on its content. The Biblical prophet Jeremiah, for example, lived through the Jewish exile in 586 B.C.E., a fact that helps us pin down his writings almost to the decade. Of course, in keeping with our scientific approach, we do not address the question of any divine intervention Jeremiah may have enjoyed, and we can even remain neutral on whether a man named Jeremiah actually lived, though it will be convenient to use "Jeremiah" rather than the more awkward "whoever wrote the book of Jeremiah." As with Psalm 122, we trace the history of the text of Jeremiah, concluding that it dates from about 586 B.C.E., and that we have preserved the meaning of the text through the letters, though we may have lost the ancient sounds.

Two aspects of the content of the text make it particularly relevant for our story. First, Jeremiah witnessed the exile of the society that gave writing to the masses by inventing vowel letters. And second, Jeremiah seems to have appreciated the great value of that very writing.

In verses 30:2–3, Jeremiah reports that he was to "write down in a scroll all the words ... because the day will come when" Israel and Judah shall be returned. With this, Jeremiah demonstrates his appreciation for the value of writing.

In other parts of what he wrote down, Jeremiah turned his attention to the dramatic events of the exile, personifying Jerusalem as Rachel, who has lost her children:

> Rachel is weeping for her children.
> She refuses to be comforted for her children
> Because they are gone.

Jeremiah could not have known that he was right in writing down his thoughts to ensure their preservation. Along with Psalm 122 and the rest of the Jewish canon, they would later be translated into Greek, buried in caves in Qumran, translated into Latin, analyzed by medieval grammarians who sought (and failed) to preserve their ancient sounds, and preserved for the future in a codex kept in Leningrad, eventually to be used as the foundation for a modern spoken language of Hebrew.

Though there is barely a spot on earth that has not been affected in some way by Jeremiah's words and the rest of the canon, that modern language of Hebrew would be reborn within walking distance from where the experiment that made their preservation possible first started.

Jeremiah thus couldn't have been more correct in consoling Rachel, that is, Jerusalem, 125 generations ago, when he wrote:

> Keep your voice from weeping . . .
>
> There is hope for your future . . .
>
> Your children shall return.

Part V
Appendices

Appendix A
More about the Rules of the Game

I like your game
but we have to change the rules.

In this appendix, we supplement some of the material from Chapter 2, in particular, the "three theories of the world" and the "two theories of language." The theories of the world are crucial for putting our approach to history into a larger context, especially in a field such as Hebrew where the competing theories are so often confused. The theories of language are equally important for putting our analyses of Hebrew into a larger context.

Three Theories of the World

The Dumb-Luck Theory

The Dumb-Luck Theory is at once the simplest and the most comprehensive theory of the past. It is completely consistent with everything that has ever happened, has no exceptions, and can be stated completely in one short sentence. In terms of accuracy and simplicity, the Dumb-Luck Theory describes the past better than any other theory. It thus seems to be the ideal theory.

But one problem with the Dumb-Luck Theory is that it makes no predictions regarding the future. (We will discuss this potential drawback in more detail below when we talk about the Science Theory and "falsifiability.") For example, the Dumb-Luck Theory is neutral on the question of whether the sun will rise tomorrow. If we want to believe that the future and the past are governed by the same rules (as we generally do) and if we want to believe that we have some idea what will happen in the future (again, as we generally do), then the Dumb-Luck Theory must be seen as incomplete.

But this rejection of the Dumb-Luck Theory is based on the claim that the past is generally like the future, while our daily experience, of course, is exactly the opposite. The past is completely unlike the future. The past has already happened, but the future has not; we remember the past but we do not remember the future; we can affect things that will happen, but not things that have already happened; etc.

Furthermore, even if the past were like the future, why would we give up a perfect theory of the past for an imperfect theory of the future, particularly in a history book? We would not.

It turns out that we have no principled reason for rejecting the Dumb-Luck Theory of the past. We will ignore it and focus our energies elsewhere, but in the end the only reason we have for ignoring the Dumb-Luck Theory is that other theories make for more interesting discussion.

The God Theory

Like the Dumb-Luck Theory, the God Theory seems to work very well. And unlike the Dumb-Luck Theory, it even applies to the future as well as the past. Not only does the God Theory completely and perfectly describe the past, it describes the future as well. And it is never wrong. We may be wrong in our understanding of God — those of us who try to understand God — but the fact remains, according to the God Theory, that everything that has happened and everything that will happen (and everything that is happening now) does so only for the reason that God makes it happen.

But while the God Theory makes predictions for the future, the failure of those predictions to materialize does not negate the God Theory. For example, we fully expect that the sun will rise tomorrow, but if it doesn't, it doesn't mean that the God Theory is wrong. It just means that God usually, but not always, makes the sun rise in the morning.

Like the Dumb-Luck Theory, the God Theory cannot be rejected because it is inadequate. When we ignore it, as we have done here, our motivation is once again a search for interesting discussion.

Let us also be very clear that the God Theory is not the only theory compatible with the existence of God. We can certainly imagine a god that creates scientific laws (and therefore advocates the Science Theory) and a god that creates chaos (and therefore advocates the Dumb-Luck Theory). All three of the theories we are considering here are compatible with the existence of God, so ignoring the God Theory means that we will not use that theory for explaining historical events, but it lets us remain neutral about the existence of God.

The Science Theory

In many regards, the Science Theory is the most radical of the three theories, because it is based on assumptions that seem inconsistent with our daily experience.

The Science Theory is based on the assumptions that our universe has underlying rules by which it operates and that we humans can understand those rules. (It is that first assumption the makes the Science Theory incompatible with the Dumb-Luck Theory, and that second assumption that makes it incompatible with the God Theory.)

However, these assumptions seem to be contradicted frequently. If you flip a coin, even the best scientists in the world cannot tell you whether it will land on "heads" or "tails." Yet the Science Theory insists that the coin's behavior is subject to strict rules that, in principle, we humans might understand.

The Science Theory also has the poorest track record of the three theories. The other two theories offer an unfailing account of the past, and in addition the God Theory offers an unfailing account of the future. By contrast, the Science Theory offers but limited success at both. For example, popular questions for the Science Theory are typified by "Why did the dinosaurs disappear?" or "Will it rain tomorrow?" And the Science Theory, at least so far, can answer neither. (The Dumb-Luck Theory answers the first question with "it was just chance that the dinosaurs disappeared" and the second with "it might rain tomorrow." The God Theory answers them with "God made the dinosaurs disappear" and "only God knows if it will rain tomorrow.")

In addition to its reliance on seemingly wrong assumptions and its widespread lack of accuracy, the Science Theory has a third crucial aspect. The Science Theory admits only explanations that are in principle "falsifiable." That is, only explanations that might be wrong but, in fact, happen to be right, are good Science Theory explanations.

The current understanding of gravity, for example, is falsifiable. If you drop an object and it falls the wrong way, that is, in a way that is inconsistent with the current laws of gravity, it proves that the theory of gravity is wrong. Because neither the God Theory nor the Dumb-Luck Theory is falsifiable, in other words, precisely because both theories cannot ever be shown to be wrong, neither one is a scientific theory.

Ironically, unlike the Dumb-Luck Theory or the God Theory, which are always accurate, the Science Theory can certainly be rejected on grounds of inadequacy. It is often inaccurate. Yet in spite of often being wrong, we have adopted it for the purposes of this book, as we saw in Chapter 2 and we explore further below.

Before moving on, we must note that the Science Theory allows partial use of happenstance. Rex Stout's famous (fictional) detective Nero Wolfe claims that "in a world that operates largely at random, coincidences are to be expected, but any one of them must always be mistrusted." This is, more or less, our version of the Science Theory. While modern science does not exactly assume that the world operates "largely at random," it does assume that some events are so complicated that they may as well operate randomly. This is particularly true of unrelated events. When we see coincidences among unrelated events, we must allow for the possibility of chance, because we know that the Science Theory actually predicts coincidence, but equally we must suspect whatever particular coincidence we are considering.

For example, imagine flipping a coin ten times. Even though each flip is as likely to produce "heads" as it is "tails," according to the Science Theory, in roughly one time out of 500, even a balanced coin will fall on the same side ten flips in a row. Therefore, if we flip a coin ten times and see that it lands, say, on heads each time, the Science Theory allows for the possibility that — because each flip is unrelated to the next — the streak of ten heads was a matter of chance. Our approach in general will be to recognize this possibility, but also to be wary of using it.

Consider a second example. It turns out that the English word for "eye" is also the name of a letter (i) and so is the Hebrew word for "eye": *ayin* (ע "*ayin*"). Of course, the Dumb-Luck Theory immediately relegates this to chance, and the God Theory dictates that God wanted it this way. But what can the Science Theory offer by way of explanation?

The answer is that the Science Theory, too, can call this "chance." But this use of "chance" is different than the dumb-luck use of "chance." The Science Theory uses "chance" to describe a situation in which the causes are unrelated, while the Dumb-Luck Theory uses "chance" to describe a lack of cause to begin with.

Philosophers such as Bertrand Russell have spent considerable time trying to understand the nature of causality that connects two events and lets us understand one in terms of the other. We will not rehash those philosophical concerns here, as we do not need to understand the exact nature of causality for our more limited purposes. We only need to recognize that we will use the same word, "chance," for two different purposes.

Choosing the Science Theory

Each of the three theories — the Dumb-Luck Theory, the God Theory, and the Science Theory — is based on assumptions that cannot be shown to be true.

The Dumb-Luck Theory assumes that there is no driving force behind the order we perceive, yet cannot prove that no such force exists. In particular, the Dumb-Luck Theory cannot prove that God is not controlling events and cannot prove that scientific laws are not controlling events.

The God Theory assumes that God is the driving force behind the order we perceive, yet cannot prove that God exists. The God Theory also cannot prove that events are not merely random, and cannot prove that scientific laws are not controlling events.

The Science Theory assumes that scientific laws control events, but cannot show that these are not simply happenstance and cannot show that these are not the will of God.

In the end, then, the choice of theory is a matter of personal preference. Throughout this book we rely on the Science Theory, but only because it makes for a more interesting book. We do not claim that it is in any way more right, or wrong, than the other theories.

Consequences of the Science Theory

For our purposes, it is particularly important to keep these three theories straight, because numerous other accounts of some of the material in this book exist, and these accounts not only use all three theories, but often combine them freely.

For example, the current Jewish Bible can only be directly traced back to manuscripts about 1,000 years old (the Leningrad Codex and the Aleppo Codex, discussed extensively starting on page 76). However, the Dead Sea Scrolls, or "DSS" (also discussed extensively, in Chapter 7), date to roughly 2,000 years ago. All three of these — the Leningrad Codex, the Aleppo Codex, and the various DSS — are written remnants of much earlier material. Which extant version (Leningrad, Aleppo, or DSS) should be considered the most authoritative in trying to determine what the original might have looked like?

The Science Theory tells us that the DSS should be more authoritative than either the Leningrad Codex or the Aleppo Codex, because it is 1,000 years closer to the original. That is, the currently widespread version of the Bible should, according to the Science Theory, be considered a "variation," and the DSS should be considered "right." Or, at least, when the two differ, the DSS should be given greater weight. But because Jewish tradition was formed around the more modern codices, and not the older material, the God Theory tells us that the currently widespread Bible is "right" and the DSS are the "variation."

More specifically, Jewish tradition teaches that "the Rabbis" — that is, the rabbis who wrote the Talmud and Mishnah in the first several hundred years of the Common Era — were inspired by God. Because they were inspired by God, the choices they made in determining which text would be passed down to us was a God-inspired one, and therefore the right one. The Masoretes (Chapter 5) who created the Leningrad and Aleppo Codices were also inspired by God. When the DSS contradict the Leningrad or Aleppo Codices, then, according to one version of the God Theory, it is because God inspired their authors in order to preserve the right text.

Finally, the Dumb-Luck Theory is compatible with either hypothesis. Perhaps the DSS are closer to the original, or perhaps, through sheer dumb luck, the codices are closer.

Many people who live their lives according to the Science Theory are surprised to learn that much of their "knowledge" about the Bible comes through the God Theory. Continuing this example, there are clear cases — according to the Science Theory — where the standard version of the Bible as we know it does not reflect what was written thousands of years ago, but, rather, obvious copying errors. The God Theory assumes that any such copying "errors" were the will of God. The Science Theory asks us to go back and discover the original.

Another example concerns the pronunciation of the Hebrew in the Bible. Most of our "knowledge" about the pronunciation of the Bible comes from a system devised not long before the Leningrad Codex was written, and, indeed, one of the reasons the Leningrad Codex is so important is that it is the earliest complete document to contain not only the Hebrew letters but hints about how they are to be pronounced in words.

However, as we have seen, we have two more clues about the pronunciation of the Hebrew, namely, the Greek Septuagint, or "LXX," and Origen's Hexapla. As we have seen (Chapter 6), the LXX and Origen's Hexapla confirm almost none of the pronunciation of the Bible as reflected in the Leningrad Codex, and, because they were working about a millennium earlier than the authors of the Leningrad Codex, the Science Theory assumes that the LXX authors had, if not a perfect understanding of the pronunciation of Hebrew, at least a better one. The Science Theory, then, rejects almost all of the currently accepted pronunciation clues in the Bible.

Once again, by contrast, the God Theory assumes either that the God-inspired people who wrote the LXX knew the correct pronunciation — this is the Christian understanding — or that the God-inspired people who wrote the Leningrad Codex knew the correct pronunciation (the Jewish understanding). Either way, the 1,000 years separating the two is of no consequence. After all, God knows how the Hebrew was supposed to be pronounced.

And, as before, the Dumb-Luck Theory is compatible with any version we choose to accept. Who's to say the authors of the Leningrad Codex didn't stumble upon the perfect pronunciation in spite of the almost (but not quite) insurmountable odds against such a feat?

These are but two examples of information that "everyone knows," which, it turns out, is based at least in part on the God Theory and not the Science Theory.

It is worth repeating that we are not refuting the God Theory. We are exploring where the Science Theory can take us. And in order to do that, we have to be clear about what is science and what is religion.

Two Theories of Language

Prescriptive Linguistics

Prescriptive linguistics is a set of rules that dictates "proper" language use. Modern respected versions of this approach to language in English are the *New York Times Style Guide*, the *Chicago Manual of Style*, and others; an older but equally respected version is Fowler's *A Dictionary of Modern English Usage*. (In spite of the name of Fowler's book, which might suggest that it describes usage, by and large Fowler tries to dictate usage.) William Safire's *New York Times* column on words, while describing current language usage, likewise notes which current language usage is proper and improper.

All of these variations rely on rules that have three sources:

1. Rules come from "wish lists" about the language.
2. Rules come from archaic versions of the language.
3. Rules come from observations about the language.

So the rules about "proper" speech that you learned in high school generally come from one of these sources.

For example, English and its predecessors going back at least to Chaucer have always had prepositions at the ends of sentences. Indeed Churchill's "Putting a preposition at the end of a sentence is something up with which I shall not put"[1] demonstrates how difficult and awkward it can be to try to

---

1. According to modern linguistics, the "with" in "put up with" is actually a "particle" and not a "preposition." Most versions of prescriptive linguistics, including the one that Churchill apparently learned, do not distinguish the two.

move some prepositions from the end of the sentence (where they naturally fall in English) to some other spot. However, somewhere along the line a decision was made that English should be more like Latin. Latin does not permit prepositions anywhere other than before a noun or pronoun, and therefore English ought not to permit them either. The rule that a preposition in English cannot come at the end of a sentence is nothing more than a wish someone once had.

As an example of a rule that reflects an archaic version of the language, consider the rule that the plural of "mother-in-law" is "mothers-in-law." While this may once have been a natural way of speaking, it is no longer, having been mostly replaced by "mother-in-laws." (Curiously, some early writers seem to have used "mothers-in-laws.")

Finally, many prescriptive rules come from trying to describe the language. For example, pronouns in English come in two varieties: nominative ("I," "he," "she," etc.) and accusative ("me," "him," "her," etc.). Nominative pronouns are generally used as subjects of verbs ("I am happy," but certainly not "Me am happy") while accusative pronouns are generally used as objects of verbs and prepositions: "The news surprised me" but certainly not "The news surprised I," and "The story was about me" but certainly not "The story was about I."

Based on this observation, a seemingly reasonable prescriptive rule was made that required the use of nominative pronouns as subjects. For this reason, in the prescriptive theory, "Me and my friend are happy" is wrong, in spite of the hundreds of millions of English speakers who think it sounds just fine. (Following the same reasoning, the answer to "Who wants ice cream?" ought to be an emphatic "**I!**" rather than the universal "**Me!**")

The reasoning here is important, because it is fundamental to the prescriptive approach to language. When the speakers of the language do not follow the rules — even when those rules were supposed to be descriptive — the rules are right and the speakers are wrong.

In the world of science, if the description of a phenomenon does not match the phenomenon, the description is wrong. For this reason we mostly ignore the prescriptive approach to language in this book. We are interested in language as it is, not as it should be, as it used to be, or as it is not.

As before, we are not rejecting prescriptive linguistics. In understanding language, we need not take a position on the question of whether some language use is better or worse than other language use, any more than in pursuing the Science Theory we need take a position on the existence of God.

Descriptive Linguistics

Many people are surprised to learn that descriptive linguistics is really a field of inquiry. Having been taught prescriptive rules in high school, and having learned that their natural instinct is often not to follow those rules, they are surprised to learn of rules that describe how they actually speak.

But 20th-century advances in linguistics have discovered rules that underlie all human speech. These rules — unlike the rules in the prescriptive approach to linguistics — describe human language, rather than dictate how it ought to be.

Before looking at the general rules, it will be helpful to look at some specific examples in English.

Language-Specific Linguistics

Most speakers of English think that "I am" and "I'm" can always be used interchangeably, with at most the effect that "I'm" is more colloquial than "I am": "I'm going to the movies" or "I am going to the movies," "I am happy" or "I'm happy," etc.

However, while "He's taller than I am" is a perfectly good English sentence, "He's taller than I'm" is not. Thus, a descriptive-linguistics rule of English might be along the lines of "An English sentence cannot end with a contracted form of 'to be.' " (As it turns out, this is not the rule, but rather a consequence of a more general rule whose complexity prevents its introduction here.) For our purposes, it is important to understand the differences between this kind of rule and a prescriptive rule.

Most importantly, the rule exists and works. That is, it describes what is purports to describe, without exception. Simple though it may be, it is completely accurate regarding every English sentence recognized by every English speaker as English. With hundreds of millions of English speakers, that's quite a feat. When descriptive linguistics formulates a successful rule, it does not have exceptions. In this regard, descriptive linguistics is like any other science. Just as modern scientific physics, for example, is the search for rules that describe the nature of physical things, modern scientific linguistics is the search for rules that describe the nature of language.

Let us look at two more rules of English.

The second rule is that an English word cannot start with the two sounds /SR/. While there is one word in English that begins with the letters *sr* — *Sri [Lanka]* — it is pronounced with /ShR/ (also written /šr/) at the beginning, that is, with the same sounds that begin the word "shriek." Once again, this very simple rule about what can and cannot begin an English word covers the entirety of the English language without exception.

The third rule is that most people think that the opposite of "cat" is "dog." (This is a "rule" in the same sense as the first two rules, in that it describes a fact about English.) But if we take "opposite" to mean "completely unlike" or even "most unlike" it is difficult to imagine how "cat" and "dog" are opposites. After all, they both refer to small domesticated mammals commonly kept as house pets. The opposite of "cat" ought to be something like "theology," which, certainly, is more unlike a cat than a dog is. We will return to this conflict between what a word seems to mean and what it really means in a moment.

First we note that from the second rule we learn that rules about a particular language can be idiosyncratic to that language, and need not follow from basic notions such as "easier" or "harder." This is extremely important. English speakers tend to think that English words don't start with /sr/ because it's "too hard to say." But while no word starts with the two sounds /sr/, there are lots of words that start with the three sounds /str/, /skr/ (written, usually, *scr*, as in "scratch"), /spr/, etc., and there are words that start with the two sounds /ShR/ (/šr/). Additionally, words in other languages commonly start /sr/.

So the prohibition against words in English that start /SR/ is a fact about English that can be deduced only from looking at English. But even though it is only a fact about English, and is unique to English, it is part of a larger system that, it would seem, applies to all languages, as we will see below.

The third rule, about opposites, demonstrates the fact that asking people for the rules of their language is, in general, a very poor way to learn about a language. Most people agree with the dictionary definition that opposites are "entirely different" from each other, but still want "cat" and "dog" to be opposites. Similar to asking people for the rules of their language, reading non-expert descriptions of a language generally provides unreliable evidence about the nature of the language.

It may seem at this point that descriptive linguistics has fallen into the same trap as prescriptive linguistics. How can people be wrong about the rule? But being wrong about the rule is different than being wrong about the data to which the rule applies. While English speakers can be wrong about what they think the rules of their language are, they are not wrong about what their language is. In spite of dictionary definitions and common belief to the contrary, "opposite" means something like "the most different within the same category." This is (more or less) how people use "opposite": Most people will tell you that the opposite of "yes" is "no," the opposite of "dog" is "cat," the opposite of "light" is "dark," but "yellow," "nose," and "theology" have no opposites. Speakers of English know these facts, even if they cannot articulate them.

Similarly, when confronted with the fact that "I'm" cannot end a sentence in English, many people formulate the wrong rule that a sentence cannot end with a contraction. But even though "I'm" cannot end a sentence, "don't" most certainly can: "If you're tempted to ignore obvious facts, don't."

So it is important to distinguish between the actual phenomenon that is being studied (the language as people speak it) and the descriptions of the phenomenon. Just like any other phenomenon that science studies, language is neither "right" nor "wrong" according to descriptive linguistics. And just like any other description in science, a linguistic description, even by the speaker of the language it is describing, is only right inasmuch as it describes what it purports to.

So where do we stand? So far, we have seen that English, at least, can be described by rules which have no exceptions, which are unique to English, and of which English speakers may not be consciously aware. This is true of other languages as well.

Universal Linguistics

A second advance in linguistics has been the realization that all languages share the same basic building blocks and have the same kinds of rules, even though the details of languages differ.

Again, an example is in order.

In most conversations, there are two kinds of information: information that the speaker assumes the hearer does not know, and information that the speaker presumes to have in common with the hearer. For convenience, we can call the first kind of information "private information" and the second "shared" information. (These are also called "new" and "old" information.)

A remarkable rule governs how these two kinds of information are used in every language:

> **Every language, to the extent possible, puts shared information before private information in a sentence.**

An example from English will demonstrate. We'll use a simple scenario, in which Sam gives Chris a beach ball. Two questions about this scenario are possible:

1. What did Sam give Chris?

2. Who did Sam gave the beach ball to?

If these questions are answered in full sentences — the reader may want to try this as an experiment — the answers are almost always:

1. (What did Sam give Chris?) Sam gave Chris the beach ball.
2. (Who did Sam give the beach ball to?) Sam gave the beach ball to Chris.

In the first case, the nature of the question ("What did Sam give Chris?") indicates that both people in the conversation know that Sam gave something to Chris. Therefore, the shared information includes everything except the beach ball. The beach ball is part of the private information. For this reason, "the beach ball" in the answer falls at the end of the sentence.

By contrast, in the second case, the nature of the question indicates that both people in the conversation know that Sam gave the beach ball to someone, making that shared information. But the recipient of the beach ball is private information. Therefore, "to Sam" falls at the end of the sentence.

We have looked at English here, but (Modern) Hebrew, Spanish, French, German, Russian, Chinese, American Sign Language, etc., all follow the same patterns. The details about how the private information gets put at the end differs from language to language, but the principle is the same.

The fact that all languages work by the same principles is extraordinarily important in our study of dead languages, such as ancient Hebrew, because it lets us extrapolate from living languages to dead languages. We gain insight into dead languages that would not be possible without the observation that dead and living languages follow the same patterns. In this case, when we see different word orders attested in the Bible, we have some insight into the nature of the word-order variation.

More generally, we can use observed facts about modern languages to deduce facts about ancient languages. Furthermore, we can use the degree to which our knowledge of ancient languages adheres to modern linguistics to evaluate that knowledge.

Appendix B
Further Reading

The number of things I know nothing about
is increasing at an alarming rate.

The purpose of this "Further Reading" section is twofold: to substantiate some of the material presented in this book and to direct readers to sources of more information on what they have found here.

In terms of the former goal, this section serves the same general purpose as academic footnotes. Readers who want more details than space permits in this book will find references here to the original work on which much of this book is based, as well as references to divergent opinions. I present these with only minor commentary, in the hope that curious readers will investigate the various discussions in the literature and then draw their own conclusions.

In terms of the second goal, I have tried to give the reader an indication of what I have found valuable. Those who have enjoyed this book will probably enjoy my recommendations, and those who have not will at least have a list here of other material to be avoided.

The first section ("General") lists some books that broadly complement or expand upon the overall theme of this book, and fulfill one or both of the goals of this reading list. More detailed lists corresponding to each chapter of this book follow, where the reader will find material in support of (and sometimes in opposition to) the information in each chapter, as well as suggestions for where to look for material that expands on the content I've presented.

Happy reading.

General

As a jumping-off point for further research, the serious student of Hebrew will without doubt want to read Sáenz-Badillos' academically rigorous *A History of the Hebrew Language* (1993). Its nearly seventy-page bibliography in eight-point type is a testimony to the enormous amount of scholarship summarized by the author. The text, while academic and not meant to entertain, clearly and succinctly summarizes the state of scholarship about Hebrew in its various incarnations. The book falls short (by the author's own admission) in the area of Modern Hebrew, and also (in my opinion) in not taking the modern study of linguistics seriously enough. It also rarely provides the author's evaluation of conflicting reports in the literature, which can prove frustrating to the casual reader who does not have the means, for example, to decide between an opinion written in German and a conflicting point of view in Italian. In spite of these shortcomings, it is a superb work.

Saggs' *Civilization before Greece and Rome* (1989) is one of the best books I have ever read. While only one chapter (Chapter 4: "Writing") is directly relevant to the material I've presented, the book is a wonderful window into the ancient world. Unlike Sáenz-Badillos, Saggs writes to inform and to entertain, and succeeds admirably at both. His book, which describes the places, people, and events relevant to the early history of Hebrew, is a delightful, informative, insightful and fun tour through material that, while largely well known in academia, is less commonly made available to wider audiences. He also includes new analyses and summaries of old information, making the book a gem for scholars and lay readers alike.

The best introduction to the modern study of linguistics that I have found is Pinker's *The Language Instinct* (2000). Anyone interested in language will want to read this book, which is written to be both informative and enjoyable; it does well on both counts. The modern study of linguistics has revolutionized the study of language and languages, both old and new, and Pinker does a superb job in bringing the underlying principles of this still-evolving field to life.

The nearly fifty plates at the end of Würthwein's *The Text of the Old Testament* (1995) bring over three millennia of Hebrew to life in a way that mere prose cannot. Even without the text of the book, the plates would make his book worthwhile for anyone interested in how Hebrew has progressed and how scholars know about its various stages. The book itself covers the more limited domain of how the text of the Old Testament has reached us, and does so superbly. It is a reference book with succinct and informative summaries of most of the information about the history and study of the text of the Old Testament. It is thus similar in scope to Tov's *Textual Criticism of the Hebrew Bible* (2001), which includes more analysis but fewer and less informative plates. (However, Tov does contain some plates that Würthwein does not, in particular, reproductions and transcriptions of the silver rolls from Ketef Hinnom, which we discuss on page 159.)

Mazar's *Archaeology of the Land of the Bible* (1992) and Orlinsky's *Understanding the Bible through History and Archaeology* (1972) both tie together the history and the archaeology of the period during which Hebrew writing began and first flourished. The former covers more material, walking the reader through the years 10,000 B.C.E. to the exile in 586 B.C.E. and presenting the archaeological evidence that bears on each period. Orlinsky's book is more closely tied to the Bible, using, in addition to archaeological evidence, extensive Biblical quotations in both Hebrew and English translation to support his understanding of historical events from about 5500 B.C.E. to 200 B.C.E. Nearly every page of text in his book contains a graph, chart, or photograph that helps bring the text alive. I recommend both books, Mazar's for its completeness and Orlinsky's for the fun and immediacy it offers. Of the two, Mazar's is easier to find because it is still in print.

Other valuable reference books include the following: Klein's *Etymological Dictionary of the Hebrew Language* (1987) is a source of fascinating information about the etymology of most Hebrew words. Because it systematically distinguishes between various stages of Hebrew, it also serves as a fine Hebrew / English dictionary. (Note that the entry for *p'raklit*, on his page 533, corresponding directly to our discussion on page 178, contains a small typographic error. The Greek verb "to call" from which the word ultimately derives is *parakalein*, not *parakatein*.) Shoshan's Hebrew dictionary *hamilon ha'ivri he'xadash* is the standard authoritative Hebrew / Hebrew dictionary. Serious students of Modern Hebrew will want to own this. *Milon Sapir*, by Avenyon, is another, less authoritative but sometimes easier to use dictionary. Comparing the two also offers interesting insight into the state of Modern Hebrew.

Rules

The division of historical approaches into the Dumb-Luck, God, and Science Theories is largely my own, though of course the basic underlying premises are well known.

The Nero Wolfe qutotation on page 220 is from Rex Stout's *Champagne for One*, and appears on page 71 of the edition cited in the Bibliography. Stout is one of those rare authors who manages to add well-thought-out commentary about the workings of the world to his easy to read entertainment.

As with much of the linguistics I discuss, Pinker's *The Language Instinct* (2000) is an excellent introduction to the two theories of language, and, in particular, to the descriptive theory of language we use here. It is the place to start for those who want more insight into the modern science of linguistics.

Although I ultimately reject the premise of prescriptive linguistics, I continue to enjoy it. The "Fowler" that I mention in regard to the prescriptive theory of language has been reprinted as *A Dictionary of Modern English Usage* (1994), and in addition to being a delight to browse through, gives a good sense of the nature of prescriptive linguistics. (The "modern" usage the title alludes to, however, refers to modernity when the book was written, nearly a century ago.) I have likewise found William Safire's books, such as his *On Langauge* (1980), enjoyable.

Chapter 6 of my *Syntactic and Paratactic Word Order Effects* (1995) contains a detailed analysis of information theory and its syntactic effects, of which the sentences on page 227 are an example. While the bulk of that work is technical, Chapter 6 is more accessible to non-linguists than much of the material that precedes it.

Writing

The overall story of how the ancients discovered writing is well documented.

Saggs' *Civilization before Greece and Rome* (1989) — one of my favorite books — contains a particularly readable and informative account in Chapter 4. Saggs achieves a wonderful compromise between scholarly research and popular accessibility throughout his book, and Chapter 4 is no exception. (The quotation that starts our chapter on writing is also quoted in Saggs' book.)

Another popular account of early writing is Robinson's *The Story of Writing* (1999). Though some of the material in that book is overly simplistic and some is barely relevant, it does go beyond the ancient Near East to include other areas of the world, and includes many photographs and charts that make it worthwhile.

A more scholarly and complete account can be found in Daniels and Bright's *The World's Writing Systems* (1996). (On their page 8 and again on pages 26–27, Daniels argues against our classification of writing systems as logographic, syllabic, consonantal, and alphabetic, and against our conclusion that the move from pictograph to alphabet represented progress in any objective sense. I agree with him that our classification, while useful, may not extend clearly to all scripts, but I disagree with him on the second point.)

Chapter 12 of Diamond's popular *Guns, Germs, and Steel* (1999) has some interesting speculation about how writing systems may have been copied and adapted.

The specific and technical question of "what is a word," raised on page 17, is addressed in detail in DiSciullo and Williams' *On the Definition of a Word* (1987). The more difficult question of words versus thoughts is addressed in a wide body of literature by such philosophers as W. V. Quine, Hilary Putnam, John Searle, and others. Quine's *Quiddities* (1987) is a light, sometimes fanciful, always enjoyable introduction to a range of topics; his entries on "ideas" and on "things" are somewhat relevant. Putnam's *Representation and Reality* (1988) contains a more thorough introduction to many of the philosohpical issues involved, as does Searle's *The Rediscovery of the Mind* (1995).

Sampson's *Writing Systems* (1985), though it suffers from a confusion between Biblical and Masoretic Hebrew in Chapter 5, contains a scholarly introduction to early writing in Chapters 3–5.

Diringer's two-volume *The Alphabet* (1968) is a wonderful source of data that includes and expands upon the introduction given here. Volume 2 is fully devoted to plates, containing numerous photographs of ancient writing specimens, extensive charts, and samples of the writing that has been and is used throughout the world.

Driver's *Semitic Writing from Pictograph to Alphabet* (1976) contains a detailed account of the development of the Semitic alphabet, as well as a wonderful set of plates depicting many early writing specimens.

Pages 117–18 of Gibson's *Textbook of Syrian Semitic Inscriptions* (1971) contains a detailed chart of the various forms of the Hebrew letters in over two dozen ancient specimens. The next page (119) has a map of where those specimens were found.

Zevit's *Matres Lectionis in Ancient Hebrew Epigraphs* (1980) is a detailed analysis of *matres lectionis* in ancient Hebrew.

The issue of who invented the alphabet is still hotly debated, with different answers owing not only to different understandings of the question but also to serious scholarly debate.

The common view that Aramaic was the first to introduce *matres lectionis* can be found, for example, on page 67 of Sáenz-Badillos' *A History of the Hebrew Language* (1993) and the surrounding discussion.

By contrast, on page 1 in his *The History of Hebrew* Plene *Spelling* (1985), Weinberg argues for an earlier date for the introduction of *matres lectionis* in Hebrew, and, hence, a different sequence of events.

Readers who wish to investigate the evidence for themselves may find the following helpful:

In *The Proto-Sinaitic Inscriptions and Their Decipherment* (1966), Albright discusses the original proto-Sinaitic inscriptions; certainly nothing earlier than those inscriptions is relevant to our story of writing. Saggs (*Civilization before Greece and Rome*, page 82), however, laments that Albright's translations are "weak on lucidity and strong on hypothesis," suffering from significant conjecture. But Saggs also admits that nothing more convincing has been proposed. I agree with him on both points.

Regarding early Hebrew (and Moabite), Sáenz-Badillos (*A History of the Hebrew Language*, pages 62–68) summarizes the evidence from various inscriptions, with the author's usual thoroughness. More specific information about the early inscriptions is available as follows:

Kochavi's 1977 article, "An Ostracon of the Period of the Judges from 'Izbet Ṣarṭah" in the *Journal of the Tel Aviv University Institute of Archaeology*, discusses the finds from Izbet Sartah. (Demsky's "A Proto-Canaanite Abecedary Dating from the Period of the Judges and Its Implications for the History of the Alphabet," in the same issue, is interesting reading as well.)

Albright's "The Gezer Calendar" in the 1943 edition of the *Bulletin of the American Schools of Oriental Research* discusses the Gezer Calendar.

Jackson's chapters in Dearman's *Studies in the Mesha Inscription and Moab* (1989) present the Mesha inscription; Jackson also agrees with the specific point raised in the main text here that Hebrew and Moabite were practically the same language. The story of the Mesha Stone, including its discovery, destruction, and reconstruction, can be found in Graham's article "The Discovery and Reconstruction of the Mesha' Inscription" and, more briefly, on pages 127–129 of Pearlman's *Digging Up the Bible* (1980). (Pearlman's account differs somewhat from Graham's, a fact that Graham acknowledges.)

Most of the original information on the Siloam Tunnel is in German, e.g., Donner and Röllig (1971–1976); Gibson's *Textbook of Syrian Semitic Inscriptions: Hebrew and Moabite Inscriptions* (1971) is an English introduction.

Evidence about early Aramaic inscriptions can be found in Friedrich (1967), and about the language itself in Degan (1969), both, unfortunately, in German. In English, pages 119–123 of Driver's *Semitic Writing from Pictograph to Alphabet* (1976) have a nice summary. Beyer's *The Aramaic Language* (1986) contains the confusing claim that "Ancient Aramaic in written form appeared in the 11th cent. B.C.[E.] as the official language of the first Aramaean states," but "the oldest witnesses to it are inscriptions from northern Syria of the 10th–8th" centuries B.C.E. Among the most interesting Aramaic fragments connected with our story (though not discussed in any detail here) is a find from Tel Dan, as discussed in two articles by Avraham

Biran and Joseph Naveh in the *Israel Exploration Journal* (Volumes 43 and 45).

A reasonably accurate summary of the evidence about Greek can be found on page 167 of Robinson's *The Story of Writing* (1999). A much more detailed account can be found in Woodard's *Greek Writing from Knossos to Homer* (1997). Though I do not agree with many of Woodard's conclusions, particularly regarding the pronunciation of ancient Greek, he provides a wealth of detailed information about ancient Greek writing systems.

The curious reader may also want to take a more detailed look at Kochavi's 1977 article or even just page 230 in Würthwein's *The Text of the Old Testament*, both of which describe the Izbet Sartah abecedary. Beyond its limited evidence as part of the Hebrew-Aramaic-Greek puzzle, the abecedary is intriguing because it has not, in my opinion, been successfully decoded yet.

Magic Letters and the Name of God

Much of the material in Chapter 4 is presented here for the first time. In particular, I have not read any public claim that the tetragrammaton was purposely composed of the Hebrews' magic letters, nor have I seen the derivation of *elohim* from *elim* in print.

In terms of the latter, I must credit my friend and teacher Rabbi Bernard Zlotowitz, who first gave me this insight some twenty years ago, and who is preparing his material for publication as I write. It will, I hope, be available in the very near future. The inclusion of *elohim* with the names (Avram/Avraham and Sarai/Sarah) that get a *heh* added seems so obvious to me that I am surprised that the idea has not been more widely circulated. Still, with the volume of quality scholarship outpacing even the careful researcher's ability to read, I have a nagging feeling that these insights cannot be truly new. (By contrast, basic information about the "magic" *heh* as it is used in Avram/Avraham and Sarai/Sarah comes directly from Genesis (17:1–8), and is exceedingly well known.)

Information about all of the names of God can be found in the *Dictionary of Deities and Demons in the Bible* (1999) — commonly called *"DDD"* — an exceptional book that tries to detail what the Science Theory can teach about the names and qualities ascribed to the various gods (including, depending on one's point of view, to God) in the ancient Near East. In spite of its name, the book is more of an encyclopedia than a dictionary.

Karel van der Toorn's article *Elohim* in *DDD* disagrees with Zlotowitz and me, arguing that the word, rather than coming from *elim*, is the plural of *eloah*. However, Pardee's article on *eloah* in *DDD*, though making the same claim, also makes it clear that the origin of *eloah* is unknown, thus reducing one unknown to another.

In his *DDD* article on "Yahweh," van der Toorn summarizes current theories about the tetragrammaton, but temporarily (and unwittingly) abandons the Science Theory in favor of the God Theory in arguing without reasonable support or justification that "the correct pronunciation of the tetragrammaton was gradually lost." In spite of this major shortcoming, his article does a fine job analyzing and rejecting other sources for the tetragrammaton. The crucial aspects we need for our analysis in this book are: (1) The name *yahweh* is unattested before the Hebrews, and (2) the name seems not to have any reasonable etymology. Both of these support the explanation put forth in our Chapter 4.

Modern scholarship has focused more on the nature of ancient gods and less on their actual names. Smith has two books (*The Origins of Biblical Monotheism*, 2001, and *The Early History of God*, 2002) that contain extensive information about the early history of various deities in ancient Israel, including the names *el* and *yahweh*. Of the two books, the latter is the more readable. Both make for fascinating reading and offer insights into the religious life of the people who probably created the name *yhwh*. Surprisingly, however, Smith seems to assume that *yhwh* was pronounced something like *yahweh*. (To be fair, Smith is in very good company, with, for example, the authors in *DDD*, as already discussed, as well as most of the references therein.) But in light of all of the points brought to light in Chapter 4, I find this highly implausible.

Regarding other aspects of *yhwh*, pages 446–450 of Mazar's *Archaeology of the Land of the Bible* (1992) describe the earliest known reference to the tetragrammaton. The name also appears on the Mesha Stone, as described in passing in Jackson's chapters in Dearman's *Studies in the Mesha Stone* (1989).

Masoretes

Chapter 4 of Sáenz-Badillos' *A History of the Hebrew Language* (1993) describes the Masoretes, including, as usual, extensive references to scholarly positions. However, the title of his chapter, "Biblical Hebrew in Its Various Traditions," wrongly suggests that Masoretic Hebrew is Biblical Hebrew. Surprisingly, Sáenz-Badillos does not fully distinguish Masoretic Hebrew from a "Biblical Hebrew tradition," even though, clearly, the Science Theory admits no "traditions of languages" except as they pertain to sociology. Languages are languages, and traditions are traditions. The material in his Chapter 4 also (following one scholarly school of thought) suggests that we know more about the ancient pronunciations than I believe we do. (See the reading list for "Pronunciation.")

Yeivin's *Introduction to the Tiberian Masorah* (1980) is an excellent technical introduction to the Tiberian Masorah.

Yeivin's 1985 book and Ofer's 2001 book (both in Hebrew) are extended discussions and analyses of the Babylonian pointing system.

A beautiful facsimile edition of the Leningrad Codex is available as Freedman (1998).

The plates in Würthwein's *The Text of the Old Testament* (1995) depict sample pages from all of the codices discussed under "How Do We Know?" starting on page 76.

Some parts of the Masoretic verbal system are analyzed in a modern linguistic framework in my IATL paper, *The Behavior of Strong and Weak Verbs in Modern and Tiberian Hebrew* (1998). (The references there refer to some previous analyses, and indicate why I do not think they are adequate.) However, that article is technical, and presumes a familiarity with modern Optimality Theory, as described, e.g., in Prince and Smolensky (1993).

Many books about the trope system do a disservice to science and propagate the myth that the difference between the conjunctive and disjunctive symbols is that the former conjoin and the latter disjoin. By contrast, Chapter 2 of Jacobson's *Chanting the Hebrew Bible* (2002) does an admirable job of presenting the real syntactic details of the Masoretic trope system, though in my opinion it suffers from two drawbacks. The approach taken there of presenting and discussing each trope symbol takes up enormous space, and does not let a reader learn the architecture of the system without also learning its details. Secondly, the supporting linguistics is a haphazard combination of Jewish thought and linguistic thought. Nonetheless, the book is a wonderful compendium of information, both scientific and religious, about the trope system.

Pronunciation

Reliable information about the ancient pronunciation of Hebrew is hard to come by. A great mass of literature fails to distinguish between Masoretic Hebrew and Biblical Hebrew. Other authors work from within a purely religious framework, or freely combine the God Theory and the Science Theory.

Because the general methods of determining the sound patterns of an ancient language are the same regardless of the language, Loprieno's *Ancient Egyptian* (1995) and Sturtevant's *The Pronunciation of Greek and Latin* (1968), even though they deal with ancient Egyptian and Greek/Latin, repectively, may prove interesting. Both of these authors agree with our results in principle, claiming that the sound patterns of ancient languages have been lost.

Loprieno concludes (page 28) that "the traditional pronunciation and transliteration of many Egyptian phonemes" — that is, the sound patterns as understood by Egyptologists — "rest upon hardly anything more than scholarly conventions." His comment is particularly telling because he has been careful to take into account the modern study of linguistics.

Regarding Greek and Latin, Sturtevant similarly laments that "the available evidence does not permit us to do more than determine the approximate pronunciation of Greek and Latin" (page 29). His extended description from page 21 leading up to that conclusion gives a good sense of what types of evidence are available for Greek and Latin. However, while Sturtevant has a good sense about Greek and Latin, he wrote before the advent of modern linguistics, the results from which, therefore, are lacking in his treatment.

An accessible account of the study of phonology in general, that is, the sounds of language, can be found in Chapter 6 of Pinker's *The Language Instinct* (2000). Beyond that, phonology has seen a paradigm shift in recent years. The old paradigm is described extensively in Kenstowicz and Kisseberth's *Generative Phonology* (1979), which, though difficult reading, will give the student a solid understanding of the field of phonology. (But be careful of their discussion of Modern Hebrew on pages 310–311 where the data are overly simplified.) The newer paradigm, which began with Prince and Smolensky's 1993 paper, "Optimality Theory," represents a more modern way of understanding roughly the same data, though all but the most serious students of phonology can make do without it for almost all of the data in this book. However, the theory ("Optimality") they present is so interesting that I recommend it beyond its use in understanding Hebrew.

General books about the Septuagint are plentiful, but, once again, range greatly in their approach, from scientific to religious. For a general scientific introduction, try Jobes and Silva's *Invitation to the Septuagint* (2000). The introduction in Brenton's *The Septuagint* (1851, reprinted 2001) offers a nice brief overview, with the added benefit that it comes with the complete Greek text and translation of the Septuagint. Though the translation (from the 19th century) is somewhat outdated, it is the best English translation available. A discussion of the (un)availability of critical editions can be found on page 71 of Jobes and Silva's book.

Regarding evidence about Hebrew from the Septuagint and Origen's Secunda, Sperber's "Hebrew Based Upon Transliteration" in the 1937–1938 issue of the *Hebrew Union College Annual* contains a wealth of information, including a wonderful word list of the available data and a systematic though, in my opinion, flawed account of the data. Unfortunately, Sperber does not systematically distinguish between the LXX and other material, even though the LXX predates the other material by perhaps half a millennium.

Page 80 of Sáenz-Badillos' *A History of the Hebrew Language* (1993) contains an excellent list and brief evaluation of the scholarly opinions about what Greek (and Latin) can tell us about Biblical Hebrew.

Sperber's article also addresses Origen's Secunda (and, as it happens, St. Jerome's 4th-century translation of the Bible into Latin), and his material on the Secunda is similar in quality to his work on the LXX.

Janssens' *Studies in Hebrew Historical Linguistics Based on Origen's Secunda* (1982) is, as the title of his work suggests, an attempt to learn about Biblical Hebrew specifically from the Secunda. His Chapter II contains an excellent review of other literature on the subject, and explains why he thinks it is not fully adequate. In my opinion, his own work places too much emphasis on Tiberian Hebrew, wrongly emending the data at times rather than emending the analysis of the Masoretes. For example, his discussion of the lack of gemination (double letters) after some prepositions (which we discuss starting on page 108) claims without evidence that even the consonant after a preposition "was also geminated, but this gemination is usually not written." He also spends time analyzing the various Tiberian Masoretic *shewa*s, though I can see no reason to use Tiberian Hebrew as a framework in which to understand the Sec.

Pages 200–201 of Würthwein's *The Text of the Old Testament* (1995) have a photograph from (Mercati 1959) of a Hexaplar fragment, with a transcription, in addition to general discussion of the Hexapla (his page 57).

The specific issue of how Hebrew words are spelled in English is addressed in Weinberg's *How Do You Spell Chanukah?* (1976). Although I do not agree with many of Weinberg's conclusions, including his treatment of the *sh'va*, and although his book is primarily a prescriptive one, the discussion starting on page 14 may prove interesting.

The Dead Sea Scrolls

General books about the DSS are plentiful, but, unfortunately, of widely varying quality.

The introduction on pages xxxii–lxvii in Martínez's *The Dead Sea Scrolls Translated* (1996) is a very good place to start, especially because anyone interested in the DSS will want to own that book anyway.

Another short but superb introduction can be found in a wonderful article by Hanan Eshel in Volume 19 (December 1996/January 1997) of

Teva Ha-d'varim ("The Nature of Things," an Israeli *National Geographic*-like periodical). For Hebrew readers unfamiliar with the Dead Sea Scrolls, I recommend this as the best place to start.

The popularly available *Scrolls from the Dead Sea* (1993) by Sussman and Peled, while much more limited in scope, also contains full-color photographs of some scrolls. It is particularly exciting to look at these photographs, as anyone with even a basic reading level in Hebrew can make out the Hebrew words.

The Israel Museum has a small booklet, *The Dead Sea Scrolls in the Shrine of the Book*, prepared by Pearlman and published in 1988, that contains a wealth of introductory information and some wonderful photographs. (Sadly, Pearlman died shortly after writing the text for the book and did not live to see its publication.)

For more serious study, Martínez and Tigchelaar's "Study Edition" of the Dead Sea Scrolls (*The Dead Sea Scrolls Study Edition*, 2000), available in a two-volume paperback edition, is a must. It contains the most complete summary of transcriptions and translations of the non-Biblical DSS, and offers the original Hebrew (or Aramaic) text alongside a fairly good English translation. Notes to each text direct the reader to more detailed scholarly research.

Readers who do not need the Hebrew transcriptions or scholarly references and only want the English translations may prefer the one-volume edition — Martínez (1996) — cited above, whose excellent introduction makes it worthwhile even in addition to Martínez (1996).

Since 1955, Oxford University Press has periodically published a series in French and English called *Discoveries in the Judaean Desert* (some called *Discoveries in the Judaean Desert of Jordan*). These books are the primary source for scholarly presentation and analysis of the DSS, including translations (into English or French), transcriptions, and photographs of the individual fragments found in the caves. These volumes are quite expensive, and roughly half of them are available only in French. (Because the team working in Qumran was jointly headed by an English speaker and a French speaker, the volumes were published in those two languages.)

Accounts specifically of the discovery of the DSS are likewise widely available. Three nice, accessible summaries are Martínez (1996:xxxvi–xliv), Pearlman's (1980) Chapter 7, and (in Hebrew) Eshel (1996). My account is culled largely from these three (which, sadly, do not agree in all their details). Pearlman's book covers material beyond just the DSS, and makes for fascinating reading.

Martínez (1996:xlv–xlviii) and Eshel (1996), also contain accounts of the task of dating and authenticating the scrolls. Bonani *et al.* (1991), "Radiocarbon Dating of the Dead Sea Scrolls," is an authoritative description of the AMS dating of the scrolls.

Pages 100–117 of Tov's *Textual Criticism of the Hebrew Bible* (2001) contain a concise account of what the DSS have added to our knowledge of the Bible.

For background information on "Astronomical Enoch," see page 102 of Würthwein's *The Text of the Old Testament* (1995), which contains a brief one-paragraph summary of the Ethiopic translation of the Bible, and Charles' *The Book of Enoch* (1999), an easily obtainable translation of the Book of Enoch. His pages 95-111 contain the chapters relevant for comparison with the DSS.

Pages 130–146 of Sáenz-Badillos' *A History of the Hebrew Language* (1993) offer a summary of the academic literature on the Hebrew of the DSS, including (as usual) an exceptionally detailed bibliography.

Qimron's *The Hebrew of the Dead Sea Scrolls* (1986) addresses the Hebrew of the DSS. ("Qimron" is the author. It is, presumably, a coincidence that a major contributor to the understanding of the texts from Qumran is a man named Qimron.)

Tov's *Textual Criticism of the Hebrew Bible* (2001) contains a brief description of how the DSS have contributed to our knowledge of the state of the Bible roughly 2,000 years ago. In particular, page 117 summarizes the evidence the DSS offer and directs the reader to other sections of his book that augment the list there.

The Hebrew for Table 7.2 can be found in photographic form on page 55 of Sussmann and Peled's *Scrolls from the Dead Sea* (1993). It is not transcribed but is fairly easy to read. The Hebrew of the Paleo-Leviticus scroll can be found on page 51 of that book. While the original is difficult for the non-expert to read, the section relevant for the discussion on our page 139 is transcribed. A fuller discussion of that DSS document can be found in Freedman's *The Paleo-Hebrew Leviticus Scroll* (1985), which contains photographs, transcriptions, and detailed analyses.

General information about what linguists know about compounds can be found on pages 140–141 of Pinker's *The Language Instinct* (2000). The brief discussion on pages 74–75 of Qimron's book (1986) contains a list of double-plural compounds in the DSS, though only some of his examples are relevant, because he does not distinguish between double-plural compounds that are used where the second part is semantically singular and double-plural compounds where the second part is semantically plural.

Dialects in the Bible

As for other periods of Hebrew, Sáenz-Badillos provides an excellent overview of various scholarly opinions about Late Biblical Hebrew in his *A History of the Hebrew Language* (1993). His Chapter 5 begins with a discussion of "post-exilic Biblical Hebrew," which, as we saw, is by and large "Late Biblical Hebrew."

Abba Bendavid has published, through Carta in Jerusalem, a series of books called *Makbilot Bamikra*, or "Parallels in the Bible," with side-by-side columns detailing the differences in various parallel passages in the Bible. His compilations are a wonderful and unique resource for identifying parallel passages, differences in which are printed in red, making them very easy to identify. He has four books that deal with different sections of the Bible, but, as nearly as I can tell, none of the books has an ISBN number, and all of them have the same title. My copies were published between 1965 and 1969. I have seen references to a 1972 copy, also with the same title.

Post-Biblical Hebrew

Regarding various opinions about when Hebrew was spoken, Würthwein claims on page 79 of his *The Text of the Old Testament* (1995) that "[i]t is well known that in postexilic Judaism Hebrew ceased to be spoken as the common language and was replaced by Aramaic." Sáenz-Badillos claims on page 166 of his *A History of the Hebrew Language* (1993) that a different "dialect" of Hebrew was spoken after the exile, adding that "for several centuries [this dialect] remained an exclusively spoken language." Orlinsky notes on page 232 of his *Understanding the Bible* (1972) that "unlike the native Egyptians," the Jews in Egypt a half century after the exile "employed Aramaic as their official language." These claims are contradictory only if we assume (wrongly, in my opinion) that the Jews spoke only one language.

Saggs has a succinct summary of the Aramaeans on pages 17–18 of his *Civilization before Greece and Rome* (1989).

The most accessible modern version of the Talmud is the edition published by Mesorah Publications, because it contains all of the Hebrew and Aramaic, fully pointed, for those who wish to read it, along with the most readable translations I have found, replete with phrases and sometimes whole paragraphs intended to help the reader understand the often opaque language of the Talmud; it also contains copious notes. Furthermore, the

English text admirably differentiates between translation and elucidation. Using their *Tractate Megillah*, published as Goldwurm (1991), even the non-Hebrew reader will be able to follow the Talmudic discussion referred to on our page 168. The one drawback of the Mesorah volumes is their tendency to translate religiously, following Rashi, rather than scientifically. But there is hardly any better translation available.

Hoffman's extraordinary book, *The Canonization of the Synagogue Service* (1986), contains the most complete history of the Jewish prayer service, including where the various prayers come from, and how they made their way into the official Jewish liturgy.

Horbury's *Hebrew Study from Ezra to Ben-Yehuda* (1999) is a collection of essays by various authors that traces the study of Hebrew from the Persian period through many of its non-spoken versions. It will help fill in myriad details concerning non-spoken Hebrew that I have omitted in my telling of the story.

Modern Hebrew

For information about Eliezer Ben-Yehuda's life (including the quotation at the start of Chapter 10), an excellent place to start is his autobiography (in Hebrew), published posthumously in 1978, and more readily available in translation as *A Dream Come True* (1993). Much of the introduction to our Chapter 10 is taken from Fellman's *Revival of a Classical Tongue* (1973), a scholarly yet readable account of how Hebrew was revived, including information about the life of Ben-Yehuda. Weeding out accurate information from legends about the founder of Modern Hebrew is a difficult task, and Fellman's success is admirable.

Harshav's 1993 collection of related essays in *Language in Time of Revolution* connects the rebirth of Hebrew with the sociological factors that gave rise to the modern state of Israel.

Regarding both word order and null-subject languages, Pinker's *The Language Instinct* (2000) is the best introduction for the layperson not familiar with the technical details of modern linguistics. Kompeer (1992), in Russian, describes the Russian word-order effects that I claim have made their way into Modern Hebrew.

Ladefoged's *A Course in Phonetics* (1982) is an introduction to the various sounds of the world's languages, and, while technical at times, is fascinating. His pages 148–149 discuss the velar and pharyngeal sounds mentioned on our page 195.

A more extensive discussion of word order in Hebrew, Russian, and other languages can be found in my *Syntactic and Paratactic Word Order*

Effects (1995). While the bulk of the text is highly technical and not particularly entertaining (though, I hope, informative), it contains an appendix, "For the Non-Linguist," that summarizes the key points of the work in a way that does not require any background in linguistics. Chapter 4 of Comrie's *Language Universals and Linguistic Typology* (1981) is a good introduction to the general phenomenon of word order in various languages. This book, though technical, can be understood surprisingly easily by non-linguists.

Jaeggli and Safir's *The Null Subject Parameter* (1989) is a collection of technical essays investigating the nature of null subjects. The first article in that book is particularly relevant to our discussion.

The quotation on page 187 is from Ullendorff (1999:304).

The rules of unpointed grammar are taken from the appendix in Even Shoshan's excellent Hebrew/Hebrew dictionary, generally used as the standard reference dictionary in Israel. Another excellent dictionary, *Milon Sapir*, organizes nouns according to their *maleh* spelling and verbs according to their present tense.

Good descriptions of Modern Hebrew are hard to come by, because most mix in Masoretic Hebrew, either by design or by accident. I have found Glinert's *Modern Hebrew* (1996) to be a pleasing exception, and recommend it highly for those who want a description of the current state of spoken Hebrew. (Glinert agrees with our assessment of spelling, noting, "For students writing Hebrew or using any kind of dictionary, the habits of Israeli spelling are a severe headache.")

And as with so much else, Sáenz-Badillos' *A History of the Hebrew Language* (1993) contains superb references to other sources of information on the subject.

Bibliography

Albright, W. F. 1943. The Gezer calendar. *Bulletin of the American Schools of Oriental Research* 92.16–26.

———. 1966. *The Proto-Sinaitic Inscriptions and Their Decipherment.* Number XXII in Harvard Theological Studies. Cambridge, MA, and Cambridge, England: Harvard University Press and Oxford University Press.

Avneyon, Eitan (ed.). 1997. מילון ספיר. Jerusalem: הד ארצי.

Ben-Yehuda, Eliezer. 1978. החלום ושברו. R. Sivan, ed.

———. 1993. *A Dream Come True.* Modern Hebrew classics. Boulder, CO: Westview Press (trans. T. Muraoka).

Bendavid, Abba. 1969–1985, and 1972. *Parallels in the Bible* (Makbilot Bamikra). Jerusalem: Carta.

Beyer, Klaus. 1986. *The Aramaic Language: Its Distribution and Subdivisons.* Groningen: Vandenhoeck and Ruprecht (trans. John F. Healey).

Biran, Avraham, and Joseph Naveh. 1993. An Aramaic stele fragment from Tel Dan. *Israel Exploration Journal* 43.81–98.

———, and ———. 1995. The Tel Dan insciption: A new fragment. *Israel Exploration Journal* 45.1–18.

Bonani, G., M. Broshi, I. Carmi, S. Ivy, J. Strugnell, and W. Wölfi. 1991. Radiocarbon dating of the Dead Sea Scrolls. *Atiqot* 20.27–32.

Brenton, Sir Lancelot C. L. 2001. *The Septuagint with Apocrypha: Greek and English.* Peabody, MA: Hendrickson Publishers. Originally published by Samuel Bagster and Sons, 1851.

Charles, R. H. 1999. *The Book of Enoch.* Escondido, CA: The Book Tree.

Comrie, Bernard. 1981. *Language Universals and Linguistic Typology.* Chicago: University of Chicago Press.

Daniels, Peter T., and William Bright (eds.). 1996. *The World's Writing Systems.* New York: Oxford University Press.

Dearman, J. Andrew (ed.). 1989. *Studies in the Mesha Inscription and Moab.* Atlanta, GA: Scholars Press.

Degan, Rainer. 1969. *Altaramäische Grammatik: Der Inschriften des 10.-8. Jh. v. Chr..* Berlin: Deutsche Morgenländische Gesellschaft.

Demsky, Aaron. 1977. A proto-Canaanite abecedary dating from the period of the Judges and its implications for the history of the alphabet. *Journal of the Tel Aviv University Institute of Archaeology* 4.14–27.

Diamond, Jared. 1999. *Guns, Germs, and Steel*. New York and London: W. W. Norton and Company.

Diringer, David. 1968. *The Alphabet: A Key to the History of Mankind*. New York: Funk and Wagnalls, third edition. Revised with the assistance of Reinhold Regensburger. 2 volumes.

DiSciullo, Anna Maria, and Edwin Williams. 1987. *On the Definition of Word*. Number 14 in Lingusitic Inquiry Monographs. Cambridge, MA: MIT Press.

Donner, Herbert, and W. Röllig. 1971–1976. *Kanaanäische und aramäische Inschriften*. Wiesbaden: Harrassowitz, second edition. 3 volumes.

Driver, G. R. 1976. *Semitic Writing from Pictograph to Alphabet*. London: Oxford University Press, third edition.

Eshel, Hanan. 1996. מגילות קומראן. טבע הדברים 19.86–107.

Fellman, Jack. 1973. *Revival of a Classical Tongue: Eliezer Ben Yehuda and the Modern Hebrew Language*. Number 6 in Contributions to the Sociology of Language. The Hague and Paris: Walter de Gruyter, Inc.

Fowler, H. W. 1994. *A Dictionary of Modern English Usage*. Hertfordshire, England: Wordsworth Editions Ltd.

Freedman, D. N., and K. A. Mathews. 1985. *The Paleo-Hebrew Leviticus Scroll (11QpaleoLev)*. Winona Lake, IN: American Schools of Oriental Research.

Freedman, David Noel (ed.). 1998. *The Leningrad Codex: A Facsimile Edition*. Grand Rapids, MI; Cambridge, England; Leiden, the Netherlands; New York; Köln: Brill Academic Publishers and Wm. B. Eerdmans Publishing Company.

Friedrich, Johannes. 1967. *Die Inschriften vom Tell Halaf*. Number 6 in Archiv für Orientforschung. Osnabrück: Biblio-Verlag.

Gibson, John C. L. 1971. *Textbook of Syrian Semitic Inscriptions: Hebrew and Moabite Inscriptions*, volume 1. Oxford: Clarendon.

Glinert, Lewis. 1994. *Modern Hebrew: An Essential Grammar*. London and New York: Routledge.

Goldwurm, Hersh (ed.). 1991. *Talmud Bavli: Tractate Megillah*. The Schottenstein Edition. Brooklyn, NY: Mesorah Publications, Ltd.

Graham, M. Patrick. 1989. The discovery and reconstruction of the Mesha' inscription. In *Studies in the Mesha Inscription and Moab*, Chapter 2. Atlanta, GA: Scholars Press.

Harshav, Benjamin. 1993. *Language in Time of Revolution*. Stanford, CA: Stanford University Press.

Hoffman, Joel M., 1995. *Syntactic and Paratactic Word Order Effects*. College Park, MD: University of Maryland dissertation.

——. 1998. The behavior of strong and weak verbs in Modern and Tiberian Hebrew: An OT account. In *IATL 5: The Proceedings of the Thirteenth Annual Conference*, 123–146. The Israel Association for Theoretical Linguistics.

Hoffman, Lawrence A. 1986. *The Canonization of the Synagogue Service*. Notre Dame and London: University of Notre Dame Press.

Horbury, William (ed.). 1999. *Hebrew Study from Ezra to Ben-Yehuda*. Edinburgh, Scotland: T&T Clark.

Jacobson, Joshua R. 2002. *Chanting the Hebrew Bible*. Philadelphia: Jewish Publication Society.

Jaeggli, Osvaldo, and Kenneth J. Safir (eds.). 1989. *The Null Subject Parameter*, volume 15 of *Studies in Natural Language and Linguistic Theory*. Dordrecht, Boston, and London: Kluwer Academic Publishers.

Janssens, Gerard. 1982. *Studies in Hebrew Historical Linguistcs Based on Origen's Secunda*. Number IX in Orientalia Gandensi. Leuven, Belgium: Uitgeverij Peeters.

Jobes, Karen H., and Moisés Silva. 2000. *Invitation to the Septuagint*. Grand Rapids, MI: Baker Academic.

Kenstowicz, Michael, and Charles Kisseberth. 1979. *Generative Phonology*. San Diego: Academic Press.

Klein, Ernest. 1987. *A Comprehensive Etymological Dictionary of the Hebrew Language for Readers of English*. New York: Macmillan Publishing Company.

Kochavi, Moshe. 1977. An ostracon of the period of the Judges from 'Izbet Ṣarṭah. *Journal of the Tel Aviv University Institute of Archaeology* 4.1–13.

Kompeer, K. 1992. A note on word order and its meaning: спит бабушка versus бабушка спит. In *Studies in Russian Linguistics*, ed. by B. M. Groen A. A. Barentsen and R. Sprenger. Amsterdam: Rodopi.

Ladefoged, Peter. 1982. *A Course in Phonetics*. New York: Harcourt Brace Jovanovich, second edition.

Loprieno, Antonio. 1995. *Ancient Egyptian: A Linguistic Introduction*. New York: Cambridge University Press.

Martínez, Florentino García. 1996. *The Dead Sea Scrolls Translated: The Qumran Texts in English*. Leiden, the Netherlands, and Grand Rapids, MI: E. J. Brill and Wm. B. Eerdmans Publishing Company, second edition.

——, and Eibert J. C. Tigchelaar. 2000. *The Dead Sea Scrolls: Study Edition*. Leiden, the Netherlands and Grand Rapids, MI: E. J. Brill and Wm. B. Eerdmans Publishing Company.

Mazar, Amihai. 1992. *Archaeology of the Land of the Bible: 10,000–586 B.C.E.* New York: Doubleday.

Mercati, Giovanni. 1959. *Psalterii Hexapli reliquia*. Number 8 in Codices ex ecclesiasticis Italiae bybliothecis delecti phototypice expressi. Rome: Bibliotheca Vaticana.

Ofer, Yosef. 2001. המסורה הבבלית לתורה, עקרונותיה ודרכיה. Jerusalem: האקדמיה ללשון העברית.

Orlinsky, Harry M. 1972. *Understanding the Bible through History and Archaeology*. New York: Ktav Publishing House.

Pardee, D. 1999. Eloah. In *Dictionary of Deities and Demons in the Bible*, ed. by Karel van der Toorn, Bob Becking, and Pieter W. van der Horst, 285–288. Leiden, the Netherlands, and Grand Rapids, MI: Brill Academic Publishers and Wm. B. Eerdmans Publishing Company, second edition.

Pearlman, Moshe. 1980. *Digging Up the Bible*. New York: William Morrow.

——. 1988. *The Dead Sea Scrolls in the Shrine of the Book*. Jerusalem: Israel Museum Products, Ltd.

Pinker, Steven. 2000. *The Language Instinct*. New York: Perennial.

Prince, A., and P. Smolensky, 1993. Optimality Theory: Constraint interaction in generative grammar. MS. Rutgers University and University of Colorado.

Putnam, Hilary. 1988. *Representation and Reality*. Cambridge, MA, and London: MIT Press.

Qimron, E. 1986. *The Hebrew of the Dead Sea Scrolls*, volume 29 of *Harvard Semitic Studies*. Cambridge, MA: Harvard University Press.

Quine, W. V. 1987. *Quiddities: An Intermittently Philosophical Dictionary*. Cambridge, MA: The Belknap Press of Harvard University Press.

Robinson, Andrew. 1999. *The Story of Writing*. New York: Thames and Hudson.

Sáenz-Badillos, Angel. 1993. *A History of the Hebrew Language*. Cambridge, England: Cambridge University Press (trans. John Elwolde).

Safire, William. 1980. *On Language*. New York: Avon Books.

Saggs, H. W. F. 1989. *Civilization before Greece and Rome*. New Haven and London: Yale University Press.

Sampson, Geoffrey. 1985. *Writing Systems*. Stanford, CA: Stanford University Press.

Searle, John. 1995. *The Rediscovery of the Mind*. Cambridge, MA, and London: MIT Press.

Shoshan, Even (ed.). 1993. ‏המלון העברי המרכז‎. Jerusalem: ‏קרית-ספר‎.

Smith, Mark. 2001. *The Origins of Biblical Monotheism*. New York: Oxford University Press.

———. 2002. *The Early History of God*. Grand Rapids, MI, and Cambridge, England: Wm. B. Eerdmans Publishing Company.

Sperber, Alexander. 1937–1938. Hebrew based upon transliteration. *Hebrew Union College Annual* XII–XIII.103–274.

Stein, David E. Sulomm (ed.). 2000. *JPS Hebrew-English Tanakh*. Philadelphia: Jewish Publication Society.

Stout, Rex. 1996. *Champagne for One*. New York: Bantam Books.

Sturtevant, Edgar H. 1968. *The Pronunciation of Greek and Latin*. Groningen: Bouma's Boekhuis N.V. Publishers.

Sussmann, Ayala, and Ruth Peled (eds.). 1993. *Scrolls from the Dead Sea*. New York: George Braziller, Inc.

Tov, Emanuel. 2001. *Textual Criticism of the Hebrew Bible*. Minneapolis, MN, and Assen, the Netherlands: Fortress Press and Koninklijke Van Gorcum bv, second revised edition.

Ullendorff, Edward. 1999. Hebrew in Mandatary Palestine. In *Hebrew Study from Ezra to Ben-Yehuda*, ed. by William Horbury, 300–306. Edinburgh, Scotland: T&T Clark.

van der Toorn, Karel. 1999a. Elohim. In *Dictionary of Deities and Demons in the Bible*, ed. by Karel van der Toorn, Bob Becking, and Pieter W. van der Horst, 352–365. Leiden, the Netherlands, and Grand Rapids, MI: Brill Academic Publishers and Wm. B. Eerdmans Publishing Company, second edition.

——. 1999b. Yahweh. In *Dictionary of Deities and Demons in the Bible*, ed. by Karel van der Toorn, Bob Becking, , and Pieter W. van der Horst, 910–919. Leiden, the Netherlands, and Grand Rapids, MI: Brill Academic Publishers and Wm. B. Eerdmans Publishing Company, second edition.

——, Bob Becking, and Pieter W. van der Horst (eds.). 1999. *Dictionary of Deities and Demons in the Bible*. Leiden, the Netherlands, and Grand Rapids, MI: Brill Academic Publishers and Wm. B. Eerdmans Publishing Company, second edition.

Weinberg, Werner. 1976. *How Do You Spell Chanukah?* Cincinnati: Hebrew Union College Press.

——. 1985. *The History of Hebrew* Plene *Spelling*. Cincinnati: Hebrew Union College Press.

Weingreen, J. 1939. *A Practical Grammar for Classical Hebrew*. Oxford: Oxford University Press.

Woodard, Roger D. 1997. *Greek Writing from Knossos to Homer*. New York: Oxford University Press.

Würthwein, Ernst. 1995. *The Text of the Old Testament*. Grand Rapids, MI: William B. Eerdmans Publishing Company, second edition (trans. Erroll F. Rhodes).

Yeivin, Israel. 1980. *Introduction to the Tiberian Masorah*. Number 5 in Masoretic Studies. Missoula, MT: Scholars Press (trans. E. J. Revell).

——. 1985. מסורת הלשון העברית המשתקפת בניקוד הבבלי. Jerusalem: האקדמיה ללשון העברית.

Zevit, Ziony. 1980. Matres Lectionis *in Ancient Hebrew Epigraphs*. Number 2 in American Schools of Oriental Research Monograph Series. Cambridge, MA: American Schools of Oriental Research.

Index

Page numbers in parentheses refer the reader to sources of further information. Page numbers ending with an *n* refer to a footnote.

About the Author

JOEL M. HOFFMAN is an independent scholar and lecturer who teaches advanced classes on Hebrew, the history of Hebrew, and translation theory at the New York campus of Hebrew Union College-Jewish Institute of Religion (the seminary for the Reform movement of Judaism) as well as for Kollel (their adult education branch). He has also served on the faculty of Brandeis University, his alma mater. He holds a Ph.D. in theoretical linguistics, and serves as head translator for Jewish Lights Publishing's eight-volume prayerbook and commentary series, *My People's Prayerbook*. He lectures widely, from adult education and congregational settings to invited talks at universities and scholarly conferences in the United States, Europe, and Israel.

THE AGE

OF

CONSTANTINE THE GREAT

THE AGE

OF

CONSTANTINE

THE GREAT

JACOB BURCKHARDT

TRANSLATED BY
MOSES HADAS

Pantheon Books, New York
A DIVISION OF RANDOM HOUSE

First published in 1949
Reprinted in 1964
by Pantheon Books Inc
A division of Random House
501 Madison Avenue
New York

Printed in Great Britain

CONTENTS

TRANSLATOR'S FOREWORD

NO EPOCH *of remote history can be so relevant to modern inter-ests as the period of transition between the ancient and the medieval world, when a familiar order of things visibly died and was supplanted by a new. Other transitions become appar-ent only in retrospect; that of the age of Constantine, like our own, was patent to contemporaries. Old institutions, in the sphere of culture as of government, had grown senile; economic balances were altered; peoples hitherto on the peripheries of civilization demanded attention, and a new and revolutionary social doctrine with an enormous emotional appeal was spread abroad by men with a religious zeal for a new and authoritarian cosmopolitanism and with a religious certainty that their end justified their means. For us, contemporary developments have made the analogy inescapable, but Jacob Burckhardt's insight led him to a singularly clear apprehension of the meaning of the transition almost a century ago, and the analogy implicit in his book is the more impressive as it was unpremeditated.*

That is not to imply that Burckhardt conceived history's util-ity as providing a blueprint for future conduct. "We study his-tory not to be clever for another time," he wrote, in obvious echo of Thucydides, "but to be wise for always." Burckhardt was indeed a pioneer in the humanist reaction against the microscopic but unimaginative history of the "scientific" his-torians, though his wide and deep erudition, aside from his imagination and taste, entitle him to a distinguished place even among the scientific historians. He would have subscribed heartily to the dictum of George Macaulay Trevelyan, the fore-most modern exponent of humanist historiography: "Let the science and research of the historian find the fact, and let his imagination and art make clear its significance." Fifty years ago, when Burckhardt's great work on Greek civilization ap-peared posthumously, professional scholars expressed regret that the work had been published, on the ground that its material was already obsolete. It is true that many aspects of Burckhardt's subjects have received new illumination by detailed researches into administration, economics, and religion that have been carried out in the interval, but it is also true not only that Burckhardt has survived his critics of half a century ago but that his insight and his skill may still afford the lay reader a truer and more meaningful picture than can the production of contemporary professional historians. Surely Constantine communicates not only a more intelligible but also a more valid picture of events, their nexus, and their relevance than does the parallel twelfth volume of the sober Cambridge Ancient History (1939), *which represents the latest technical knowledge, presented by a panel of the world's best specialists.*

Burckhardt's own prefaces disclaim any intention to present a complete and systematic history of the period. For that kind of treatment such works as the Cambridge Ancient History *and the* Cambridge Mediaeval History *with their excellent bibliographies are available, and will surely be consulted by the student who requires fuller information.*

To print Burckhardt's notes without extensive modernization and discussion seemed inadvisable; scholars will recognize the sources for Burckhardt's statements and know where to find full documentation, and an elaborate apparatus would distort the book unduly, both physically and by making it appear a dull, systematic history rather than a penetrating and informed essay.

Concerning two general criticisms of Burckhardt's use of sources the reader must be apprised. The chief literary source for the Emperors from Hadrian to Numerianus (omitting those from 245 to 253) is the collection of biographies, ostensibly by six authors, known as the Historia Augusta. *Burckhardt accepts the book's own statements that it was written under Diocletian and Constantine; most (but not all) scholars now hold that the book was written in the second half of the fourth century, under Julian and Theodosius. If that is the case, incidents told of various Emperors and the occasional anti-Christian bias may be fictive retrojections. The other point concerns*

Burckhardt's attitude toward the Church writers Lactantius and especially Eusebius, whose good faith he impugns and whose portrait of Constantine as a Christian hero he rejects. Scholars jealous for the fair name of Church figures have criticized Burckhardt severely on this point. All that may be said is that Burckhardt knew his authors thoroughly (he was a student of Protestant theology before he became a historian and art critic) and also knew men and affairs; it is tolerably certain that none of the objections which were subsequently adduced to his views would have persuaded him to alter them essentially.

Columbia University   MOSES HADAS
December, 1948

PREFACE TO THE FIRST EDITION (1852)

IN THE PRESENT work it has been the author's design to describe the remarkable half century from the accession of Diocletian to the death of Constantine in its quality as a period of transition. What was intended was not a history of the life and reign of Constantine, nor yet an encyclopedia of all worth-while information pertaining to his period. Rather were the significant and essential characteristics of the contemporary world to be outlined and shaped into a perspicuous sketch of the whole.

This goal the book has achieved in only a limited sense, and the reader may well deny it any title other than "Studies in the Age of Constantine." Those aspects of the life of the age which cannot be adequately recovered and hence could not be woven as a living element into the texture of the whole have been omitted; this applies to questions of property and wealth, industry and trade, state finance, and much else of the sort. The writer has not wished to carry scholarly controversies a single step further by adducing new details, only to leave the controversies essentially unresolved. In general he has addressed himself primarily not to scholars but to thoughtful readers of all classes, who are apt to follow an account only as it is able to present a definite and well-rounded picture. But if the new conclusions which he believes he has reached in the area here treated meet with the approval of specialists, he will value such approval highly. Apart from the choice of materials, which is not wholly free, the principles of arrangement and exposition here followed doubtless leave much to be desired, and the author is not convinced that he has hit upon either the best or the only correct principles. In works of general history there is room for differences of opinion on fundamental premises and aims, so that the same fact may seem essential and important to one writer, for example, and to another mere rubbish utterly without interest. Hence the writer is well aware that his treatment may be impugned as being subjective. It would have been safer, for example, to compose a new history of Constantine by means of subjecting existing accounts to critical examination and providing the whole with an appropriate quantity of citations of sources; but for the writer such an enterprise could not have exerted the inward attraction which is alone capable of repaying every effort. This is not to imply any adverse judgment whatever on the various methods by which the material has hitherto been treated; it will be enough for us if our offering is allowed its little place in the sun.

In the matter of citations the writer has set himself a definite limit. Readers acquainted with the subject will easily recognize how much he owes to Gibbon, Manso, Schlosser, Tzschirner, Clinton, and other predecessors, but also how much he was compelled throughout to resort to his own study of the sources. From the excellent work of Tzschirner, it may be noted in passing, he feels constrained to differ completely in one respect. The influence of Christianity on declining paganism seems to him to be rated much too high in that work, and he has preferred to explain the relevant phenomena as due to an internal development in paganism itself; the reasons for this preference cannot be elaborated here.

The sections of our book devoted to this subject (Chapters 5 and 6), it will be seen, lack virtually any reduction to system. The author was convinced that it was better to venture too little than too much. In general observations on spiritual matters, and especially in the field of the history of religion, he would liefer be reproached for hesitancy than for boldness.

PREFACE TO THE SECOND EDITION (1880)

WHEN the material for this book was assembled, nearly three decades ago, and its writing was taken in hand, the objective in the mind of the author was not so much a complete historical account as an integrated description, from the viewpoint of cultural history, of the important transition period named in the title. He was conscious that such a design involved highly subjective selection among the component elements which comprise the complete picture of the period, but the welcome which the book has received leads him to believe that his method has met the wishes of many readers. Since the book was written the epoch has been the object of much specialized research; in particular the political aspects and those involving Church history have received fresh literary treatment. This second edition will show evidence of great indebtedness for new and important matter to such scholars as Vogel, Hunziker, von Görres, and many others, and in particular to Preuss's excellent work on Diocletian. It has not been necessary, however, to increase the size of the book greatly, nor to change or abandon the scale of emphasis on cultural history by enlarging on political and biographical detail; it has been deemed sufficient to correct numerous errors of fact and to clarify the most essential historical connections where these have been more accurately determined. This is the best recommendation for the work in its new dress that can be offered to a predominantly new generation of readers.

THE AGE

OF

CONSTANTINE THE GREAT

THE GENEALOGY OF CONSTANTINE

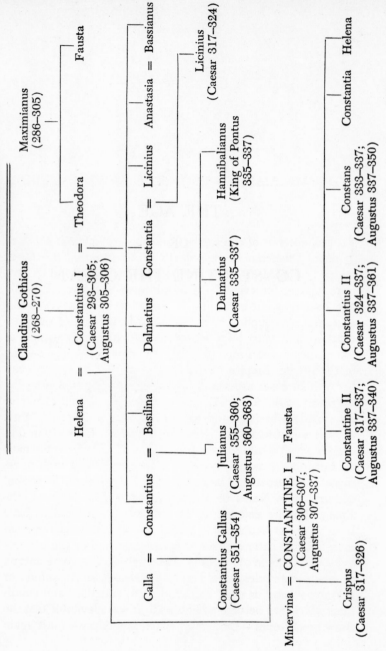

I

THE IMPERIAL POWER IN THE THIRD CENTURY

IN THE account of the period from the accession of the Emperor Diocletian to the death of Constantine the Great which lies before us, each section might well demand its own introduction, for events will be narrated not chronologically and by reigns but according to prevailing movements. But if a general introduction to the entire work be wanted, its principal content must be a history of the changing concepts of the character and function of the Emperor during the decline of the Roman Empire in the third century A.D. And this not because all other aspects of history may be derived from the character of the imperial office; but changes in that character do provide a basis for judging a multitude of events, external as well as spiritual, in the period following. Every form and degree which a rule based on force may assume, from the most frightful to the most beneficent, is here to be met with in remarkable alternation. Under the good Emperors of the second century, from Nerva to Marcus Aurelius (96–180 A.D.), the Roman Empire enjoyed an era of peace, which might have been an era of happiness as well if the profound malaise common to aging nations could have been reached by the benevolence and wisdom of even the best of rulers. The great stature, as men and as rulers, of a Trajan, a Hadrian, an Antoninus, or a Marcus Aurelius must not blind us to situations and conditions which had become patent to all. It was inevitable that the three great forces — Emperor, Senate, and Army — must again

eventually confound one another and lose the harmony which
had been painstakingly preserved. In the sequel the confusion
seemed wholly irremediable when barbarian incursions, stirrings in the provinces, and natural catastrophes combined to
contribute to it.

A prelude is offered by the reign of Marcus Aurelius himself. To speak of that Emperor's personality is superfluous;
among the imperishable ideal figures of antiquity the Stoic
philosopher seated upon the throne of the world is not the
fairest or most youthful, but surely one of the most admirable.
And yet he was not spared the menacing sound of harbingers
of doom, pounding at the gates of the Empire. First, with regard to the imperial office itself, it became clearly apparent
that, despite the system of adoptions which had linked the
four great Emperors to one another, that office might be
usurped by a coup. Avidius Cassius, the most important general of the realm, ventured such a coup, though unsuccess-
fully, after the Empire had enjoyed almost three generations
of excellent or at least benevolent rule. As regards the army,
Marcus Aurelius was reputed "never to have flattered the
soldiers in speech and never to have done aught out of fear of
them"; nevertheless Marcus acquiesced in the traditional abuse
of bestowing a huge donative upon the army at his accession,
and to such a degree that each soldier (at least those of the
Guard) acquired a fortune, and that the soldiers thereafter regarded that amount as a norm. Of external misfortunes there
must be reckoned the first violent incursion of a Germanic-
Sarmatian tribal federation into the Empire, and a fearful
pestilence. The Emperor's last years were filled with perilous
war and deep anxiety. But even in his tent on the Danube he
sought to raise himself above the cares and threats of the
moment by the quiet cultivation of virtue and of the divine in
the life of man.

For his son Commodus (180–192) Marcus is said to have
instituted a kind of regency, "the best of the Senate"; at least
during his first weeks the young ruler accepted the guidance
of his father's friends. But very quickly he developed that repulsive imperial madness to which men had grown unaccus-

tomed since the days of Domitian. Consciousness of dominion over the world and fear of all who might covet his rule begot an urge to quick enjoyment of what was his and to drown anxiety that gave no respite. In a character wanting native firmness such pressures soon evoked a combination of blood-thirstiness and voluptuousness. Occasion was provided by an attempt upon his life, of which his own family was not inno-cent but which was blamed upon the Senate. It was small wonder that the Prefect of the Guard soon became the first personage in the state and responsible for the life of the Em-peror, as had been the case under Tiberius and Claudius, and that the few thousands which he commanded shared his feel-ing of being masters of the realm. One of these prefects in-deed, the energetic Perennis, Commodus made a victim to a deputation of the disaffected Britannic army which, fifteen hundred strong, had made their way to Rome without hin-drance. His successor, the Prefect Cleander, Commodus yielded to a hunger riot of the Roman populace; not, to be sure, with-out cause, for Cleander in his prodigious greed had not only antagonized the upper classes by confiscations and sale of public offices but had incurred the anger of the poor by a monopoly of grain.

When the cowardly and cruel ruler, dressed as a god, ap-peared in the amphitheater to be admired by the Senate which lived in constant peril of death, one might well ask whether this "Commodian Senate" deserved the old title, even though it still participated to some degree in provincial administra-tion and the nomination of officials, and still possessed its own treasury and its external distinctions. Indeed it could hardly longer be called Roman, in the stricter sense, for the majority of its members were perhaps not even Italians, but provincials in whose families the dignity had sometimes become heredi-tary. From an ideal point of view it is easy to condemn this degenerate assembly in the severest terms, particularly since it is difficult to conceive clearly the effect of the deadly peril which hovered constantly over families and groups. Contem-poraries judged more leniently. When Clodius Albinus refused to accept the dignity of Caesar at the bloody hands of Com-

B

modus he still regarded the Senate as sufficiently vital to favor the restoration of a republican constitution in a public harangue to his troops. Whether he was sincere is not to the point; it is enough that the Senate (as we shall see) still contained many of the noblest characters of the period and in times of stress displayed energy and decision in administration. Even the illusions under which we shall see it labor are not altogether to its discredit. Despite the intrusion of unworthy individuals, then, it is easy to understand that the Senate continued to be looked upon as the representative if not of the Empire at least of Roman society, and that it regarded itself as the natural sponsor of the so-called Senates or Curias of the provincial cities. It was still impossible to conceive of Rome without the Senate, even if its effectiveness seemed to be destroyed over long periods by violence from without.

After Commodus had further pillaged the senators in order to assuage the murmuring populace of the capital by monstrous gifts, he succumbed to an ordinary palace conspiracy.

The alarming aspect of imperial succession at Rome was the fact that no one knew precisely where the responsibility for raising a new Emperor lay. No dynasty could be established because the imperial madness — the fate of all the incumbents who were not especially gifted — compelled periodic revolution. Even aside from revolution, the childlessness of the dissolute Emperors and even of some among the better ones made a regular succession impossible. The practice of adoption went back to the house of Augustus, but adoptions could hope for recognition only if the adoptive father as well as the new son possessed the qualities requisite to make them effective.

Historically, the right to nominate the new Emperor obviously resided in the Senate, which had decreed one title of power after another to the divine Augustus. But when the Emperors came to hate the Senate and to rely exclusively upon the Guard, the latter assumed the right of election; and it was not long before the armies in the provinces competed with the barracks of the Praetorian camp at Rome. Soon the advantage of short reigns came to be appreciated, because the

donative to the camp became more frequent. Another element
was the shady intrigue of determined men whose interest
might at times induce them to support a pretender whose early
fall they both foresaw and desired.

Thus the murderers of Commodus put forward Helvius Pertinax, a sound man, as if to justify their deed; and Pertinax was
acknowledged first by the soldiers and then by the Senate
(193). By a show of favor to a certain Triarius Maternus the
Guards extorted an enormous donative from Pertinax, to meet
which Commodus' valuables had to be disposed of. The natural consequence was a second attempt, in favor of the Consul Falco. The third time the Guards began straightway with
the murder of the Emperor. And now there ensued in the
camp that unexampled auction of the imperial dignity. There
was found a rich fool, Didius Julianus, who, for a sum in
excess of one thousand dollars paid to each soldier, purchased
for himself a few weeks of debauchery and terror. But this
was the last and highest pinnacle of Praetorian presumption.
Simultaneously three provincial armies gave themselves the
pleasure of proclaiming their leaders Emperor, and among
them was the gloomy African, Septimius Severus. Feckless
Julian's first recourse was to dispatch assassins; there was an
officer named Aquilius who had often been employed for murder in high places and who enjoyed a reputation like Locusta's
in Nero's day. Then, because he had paid good money for the
realm, Julian tried to negotiate a business deal with Severus.
When Severus drew nearer Julianus declared him co-regent;
but he was deserted and scorned and at the instance of the
Senate executed while Severus was still several days' march
from Rome.

Septimius Severus (193–211) is the first representative of
thorough military rule. There is something un-Roman, something modern, in the pride of military profession and rank
which he displayed even as a legate. The slight appreciation
and esteem he would show the ancient majesty of the Senate
might be apprehended by the deputation of a hundred senators which went to greet him at Terni, and whom he caused
to be searched straightway to see whether they carried dag-

gers. But his clearest manifestation of military logic was his disarming and disgracing of the Praetorians and his banishing them from Rome. His system had no room for a privileged and corrupted Guard with political pretensions. His own army, which he had brought with him, he gave only a fifth of the requested donative. Severus was equally consistent in his campaign against his rivals, Pescennius Niger and Clodius Albinus, and extirpated all their following. It was inconceivable to him that a number of senators could have been in correspondence with them and even that the Senate as a whole could have been neutral. "It was I who gave the city grain, I who waged many wars for the state, I who gave oil to the people of Rome," he wrote to the Senate; "a fine requital truly you have made me, a fine expression of thanks!" The Senate, he continued, had greatly degenerated since the time of Trajan and Marcus Aurelius.

Despite its importance and its indispensable military significance as a stronghold against the barbarians of Pontus, Byzantium, where Pescennius' followers had defended themselves for a year, was razed to the ground, and its garrison, along with many of its inhabitants, was put to death. The world must be given an example of the fate of cities and factions which could not immediately choose among a number of rival usurpers that one who deserved enduring obedience.

Albinus' followers fared no better. Severus had come into possession of their correspondence; he might have burned the letters unread, as Caesar had burned the letters of the Pompeians. That would have been a generous gesture, but altogether unsuitable to the times; the question was no longer one of divergent principles and their amalgamation through reconciliation and persuasion, but simply of subjection. A crowd of senators and other notables in and out of Rome were executed; the Emperor delivered eulogies of Commodus before the Senate, people, and army, surely not out of conviction but in mockery of the Senate. In Rome itself, during this struggle for dominion, a spontaneous lamenting and wailing once broke out at the Circus games; an eyewitness could find no explanation for the phenomenon other than divine inspiration. "O

Rome, Queen, Immortal," the multitudes shouted with a single voice, "how long shall we suffer these things, how long will war be waged over us?" Ignorance of their future was the happier lot.

When peace was restored at home it became apparent that the military rule, with its necessary corollary of foreign war, had become an end in itself. The center of this rule was Severus, with his family, of whom he wished to form a dynasty, distributed over the highest offices; only his brother, who would very willingly have shared the rule, did Severus carefully keep at a distance. The first step for asserting power was the organization of a new Guard, which was more than four times the strength of the old. With such a personal force constantly available, quite a different posture could be assumed toward the provincial armies. With such a force, as events proved, one might travel about in the Empire and murder and pillage everywhere. The former Guard had consisted of Italians, and preferably of men from the region of Rome; now Severus filled Rome with the faces of rude and frightening barbarians. If his donative was meager, Severus raised the regular pay of the soldier higher than any other Emperor had done; instead of flinging away several millions at once, now there was a constant drain on the Empire for the benefit of the soldiers. The fatherly advice which Severus is said to have offered his sons seems to be rather a contemporary comment on Severus' administration than an actual utterance of the Emperor, but it is significant nevertheless: "Be united, enrich the soldiers, despise all others."

One might expect that a professional soldiery so highly esteemed and kept constantly on the alert by an active general would be a credit to the glorious military past of Rome. But this was not the case. Severus himself complained loudly concerning the deterioration of discipline, and in his great Asiatic campaign there were cases of insubordination which he was able to meet only by leniency and additional gifts. Could Severus have blinded himself to the fact that his innovations secured only himself and his own reign, and that they must inevitably bring destruction upon a weak and evil successor

who was not (as Severus was) his own Prefect of the Guard?
Or was he indifferent regarding the person of his successor if
only the military rule as such was maintained?

Here and during the last centuries of paganism in general
one must not forget that even the mightiest figures had no
complete freedom of action, because they yielded to astrology
and portents. There is no other way to explain, to cite one
example, why Severus, who loved strict justice, should so stubbornly have retained in the prefecture of the Guard and in
the closest association with his own house so frivolous a
wastrel as Plautianus. Numerous superstitions encompassed
the life of Severus, from his childhood to the grave. Since the
imperial throne had come to be the first prize in a lottery,
there were parents in all classes of society who scrupulously
observed the daily life of their more gifted children for signs
of future dominion. The fact was noticed if a boy recited odd
verses, if turtles or eaglets or even a purple pigeon's egg was
brought into the house, if snakes moved into the house or a
laurel sprouted, or similar events took place. But if a child
was born with a welt forming a crown on his head, or if a bit
of purple cloth was inadvertently used to cover a newborn
infant, then his future as an Emperor was regarded as fixed.
Many an Emperor was attended by such delusions throughout
his reign, and these delusions affected his acts in a manner to
us incalculable. Compassion is our only reaction when the
aged Severus grows restless and irascible after his last victories
in Britain because a Moor bearing a cypress wreath had encountered him, or because he was taken to the wrong temple
for sacrifice, or because he was given dark-colored victims to
offer up, which then followed him to his quarters.

But there was no need for omens at the imperial headquarters at York; Severus' own son Caracalla desired his life,
persistently and almost openly. Severus had consciously raised
pitilessness to a principle, in order to suppress any thought of
usurpation; but high treason on the part of the heir apparent
had not entered his calculations, nor the possibility that his
Guard would so brazenly support the treachery. When he
whispered to his dehumanized son, "Do not let them see you

kill me!" the cry sounds like an agonized assertion of a principle of rule. Another remark he seems to have repeated several times: "I have been everything, and to no avail."

And now the repulsive monster called Caracalla ascended the imperial throne (211–217). From early youth he displayed an evil arrogance. He boasted that Alexander the Great was his model, and he praised Tiberius and Sulla. Later, perhaps after the murder of his brother Geta, came that authentic imperial madness, which employed the resources and the power of the entire Empire for its own sure destruction. His sole measure for security, which he regarded as adequate, was his camaraderie with the soldiery, whose exertions at least on occasion he shared. His similar easy familiarity with prize fighters and racing jockeys endeared him to the Roman mob. There was no need to please the respectable and the educated. After his fratricide, which the soldiers at first regarded with disapproval, Caracalla devoted himself entirely to such flattery of the mob. His requirements for his soldiers necessitated vast confiscations, and he put twenty thousand persons to death as adherents of Geta, among them a son of Pertinax; one of the more humane aspects of usurpations at Rome was that the relatives of fallen Emperors were generally spared. For his soldiers' sake also Caracalla embarked on a campaign in his own perfectly peaceful realm; the attacks of neighboring peoples he met with payments of money. The mass murders in Alexandria illustrate the attitude which despotism thought proper to meet the sophisticated mockery of the Alexandrians. The real penalty for such misdeeds (aside from the qualms of conscience of which our authors speak) was the tyrant's growing distrust of the privileged soldiery itself; at the end he came to rely entirely, as regards his immediate surroundings, upon a quite barbaric bodyguard composed of Celts and Sarmatians who could have no opinion on Roman matters, and he wore their own costume in order to retain their favor. To embassies from such peoples he used to say that if he should be murdered it would be well for them to invade Italy, for Rome would be easy to take. And yet he was struck down, in the very midst of these Guards, upon the instigation of men who were constrained to dispose of him in order that they might not themselves fall at his hands.

The nomination of his successors fell perforce into the hands of the all-powerful army. The army first named Macrinus, one of the two Prefects of the Guard, without being aware that Macrinus had contrived the death of their beloved Caracalla. Macrinus assumed Caracalla's name and gave him a splendid funeral in order to distract suspicion from himself. With dissembled impudence he greeted the Senate for his confirmation, and received the several titles of imperial power with seemly hesitancy. Nevertheless his first severe measure toward bridling an army which had grown unaccustomed to restraint hastened his destruction. Two young Syrians, collateral relations of the Antonines and Severus, suddenly rose to be heads of the Empire. These were the dissimilar cousins Elagabalus and Alexander Severus, together with their mothers Soaemias and Mammaea and their common grandmother Julia Maesa.

With all its loathsomeness and madness the reign of Elagabalus (218–222) is not without interest for the history of Roman rule. The incredible voluptuousness, the Asiatic pomp of idolatry, the thoughtless surrender to the pleasures of the moment, constituted in fact a reaction against the regime of Septimius Severus, which was by intention a soldier's regime. Elagabalus' war upon all Roman usages, his induction of his mother and grandmother into the Senate, his appointment of dancers, professional athletes, and barbers to high positions in the state, and his sale of public offices — these need not have caused his overthrow. Even his negligence in provisioning the capital might long have been condoned. His destruction arose from an awakened sense of shame in the soldiers, which was abetted by a conspiracy in favor of Alexander among the Emperor's own kindred. The soldiers knew that Alexander's life was in peril, and forced the trembling Emperor to purge his court. Elagabalus took his revenge by expelling the Senate from the city, a measure much to the credit of the Senate, as it proves that that body was not composed wholly of "slaves dressed in togas," as Elagabalus had thought. Finally the

Guards murdered Elagabalus and raised Alexander Severus to the throne.

Of the many Emperors, none so evokes the sympathy of posterity as this man, a true St. Louis of antiquity, a man quite incomprehensible when considered in relation to his environment. His fall was the result of his efforts to turn from the debased abuses of military despotism into a path of justice and moderation. This need not imply any diminution of the reputation of his excellent mother, Mammaea; but his merit is still the greater, because, the course once set, he persevered in it with independent spirit and, motivated purely by virtue, was able to resist the many temptations of despotism. Above all we find a high regard for the Senate, such as had not been known since the time of Marcus Aurelius, and even the equestrian order, long fallen into oblivion politically, was spoken of as "nursery of the Senate." A commission of senators and an inner council of sixteen participated in government, and no effort was spared to train good and conscientious men for administration and to exercise diligent supervision. Unjust or venal officials alone could disrupt Alexander's even temper. With regard to the soldiers, he made no secret of the fact that the fate of the state rested upon them; he equipped them magnificently and treated them well. Yet just as he could boast that he reduced taxes, so he ventured to dismiss a mutinous legion. But things are reported of Alexander which are hard to reconcile with the brighter aspects of the picture. In the army we sense a continuous ferment. The Prefects of the Guard were changed under the most violent circumstances, and when Ulpian, the most eminent of their number, was murdered in the course of serious disturbances, the Emperor could only let the crime go unpunished. On this occasion we learn that the populace and the Guards engaged in bloody battle for three days in the streets of Rome and that the Guard reduced the citizenry to peace only by setting fire to their houses. The most absurd characters ventured to rise as usurpers against their excellent prince. One of them, Ovinius by name, he is said actually to have accepted as co-regent with ironic leniency; but Ovinius was wearied of his throne by being made to share in the hardships of a campaign. Another, whom the soldiers raised, simply decamped. A third, the slave Uranius, the Emperor seems to have been constrained to punish. Furthermore, since Alexander was fated, as his model Marcus Aurelius had been, to suffer special visitations of misfortune, a new and warlike Persian kingdom, that of the Sassanids, arose on the Eastern borders. Alexander's war against them met with only equivocal success. On the Rhine border there were threatening movements among the Germans. The temper of the youthful ruler is said to have grown melancholy; it is reported that he showed a tendency to miserliness, but this need only mean that some of his entourage could no longer control their greed for the war chest. On the campaign at the Rhine, not far from Mainz, the soldiers murdered him and his mother. It is futile to examine the motives of this deed as they are alleged. If the successor of a Severus, a Caracalla, and an Elagabalus wished to dismiss all brutal officials, to show austerity to the soldiers, and yet to practice leniency at dangerous junctures, he was predestined to a violent end. Conspiracy was a disease of the age; it was in the very air. Alexander strove in vain for respect in a century which recognized only fear.

Maximinus, who is conjectured to have been Alexander's murderer, mounted the throne (235–238). He was a Thracian shepherd, son of a Goth and an Alan woman, hence a thorough barbarian by descent and, moreover, by education. But the army was indifferent to such considerations; it consisted of utter barbarians from the Eastern marches to whom it was of no consequence whether or not their candidate was descended from the Antonines, had been trained in high office, or had served as Senator. Instead, Maximinus was over eight feet tall and of gigantic strength, a subaltern perhaps without peer in the entire Roman army.

In principle if not in actuality his rule was more frightful than that of any Emperor. The ancient world with its monuments filled with beauty and its life filled with culture incited a venomous rage in this barbarian, who was ashamed of his origin. Indeed, a gentle soul could not have maintained the usurpation. He required confiscations for the sake of his soldiers, and so a Roman Emperor proceeds to the systematic destruction of the very essence of Rome. He himself refused to be seen in the hated capital; at first he intended to have his son reside there, but ended by keeping him in his encampments on the Rhine and the Danube, whence he ruled the Empire. Terror-stricken Rome was apprehensive that a border army of barbarians might become the headquarters of world empire, an army that was thought of somewhat like that of Spartacus or of Athenion in the slave war. Maximinus' rage was directed against everything that was distinguished or rich or cultivated, and especially against the Senate, which he believed despised him. He caused large pictures of his German victories to be set up before the Senate House. But even the populace of the capital, which might have remained tranquil even if the entire Senate were executed, was embittered to the extreme by the reduction of supplies and the confiscation of funds for public spectacles. The provincial cities fared no better; their municipal resources, like those of their wealthy citizens, were pillaged to enrich the army. So bare and unadulterated a military rule has never reappeared in the West.

There followed a time of indescribable confusion. Of greatest interest is the vigorous and determined attitude of the much misunderstood Senate. Despair drove peasants and soldiers in Africa to revolt, and two respectable Romans, the Gordians, father and son, were forcibly put at the head of the insurrection. Upon report of this insurrection, the Senate declared against Maximinus. It was to be expected that unworthy members of that body would betray the secret resolution to the tyrant. Equally bold were the written invitations to defection which the Senate sent to the provinces. The possibility that others besides the Gordians would be proclaimed Emperor in other provinces and by other armies had to be reckoned with. Danger became critical when a commander in Africa named Capelianus (who secretly desired the Empire for himself) defeated the younger Gordian in the name of Maximinus; Gordian perished and his father hanged himself. Now the Senate named a commission of twenty members who had experience of war, and of its own right proclaimed two Emperors, Pupienus and Balbinus (238). The situation was tense, pregnant with danger and terror. The people, which first had assisted in the proclamation of the Emperors, now again took sides with the Guards, who, irate at the independent choice of the Senate, demanded and forced the choice of a third Emperor or Crown Prince, the youngest Gordian to wit, a near relative of the first two. Our sources are confused and fragmentary; a battle to the death, for example, between Guards, gladiators, and recruits in Rome itself is dismissed with a word. It is hence impossible to pronounce a definitive judgment concerning this crisis; nevertheless, the Senate seems to have displayed singular resolution and fortitude, for it was able to uphold its two Emperors by the side of the Guards' protégé, and at the same time it bore the entire burden of defense against the oncoming Maximinus, and its commissioners directed warlike preparations throughout the provinces. At least they were assisted by the bitterness of the provincials against the cruel tyrant, so that he found Carinthia bare of people and provisions and his march through deserted Haemona (Ljubljana) was accompanied by hundreds of wolves. This experience had disheartened his Mauretanians and Celts when he arrived before Aquileia. And when that city, under the leadership of two senators, offered a long and desperate defense, his starving army struck him down in order to make its peace with the new Emperors.

Whether it was prudent to lead all or most of these troops to Rome we can no longer decide; they would have constituted a peril even in the provinces. But in Rome serious friction was to be expected, because of *esprit de corps*, between the predominantly Germanic army of the Senate's Emperors and Maximinus' troops. In any case the latter, as is the way of vanquished armies and defeated parties, sought an outlet for its ill humor. The victims were the two senatorial Emperors, and after they were dispatched soldiers and populace alike in wild tumult hailed the youthful Gordian (238–244) as Augustus. The Senate was overpowered but apparently by no means crushed; soldiers who forced their way into its session (held, at that time, on the Capitoline) were cut down by senators at the altar of Victory.

The next reign was a regime of eunuchs and cabals which surrounded the inexperienced youth. After a time a great and earnest man, the orator Misitheus, found his way to him and aroused his nobler nature. He became, we know not how, guardian, regent, even father-in-law to Gordian, and Gordian bestowed upon him both prefectures, that of the Guards and that of the capital. Misitheus' position, even the title "Father of the Prince" which the Senate bestowed upon him, recalls the Atabegs of the Seljuk Sultans in the twelfth century. Whether he established an understanding with the Senate cannot be determined; in any case this excellent reign did not long endure. On a campaign against the Persians which was otherwise successful the guardian succumbed to the poison of Philip called the Arab. Then Philip rendered the soldiers unruly by a contrived famine, thrust himself into the position of co-regent to the helpless Gordian through suborned officers, and gradually deprived Gordian of all authority and finally of his life.

Upon the report of Gordian's death the Senate intervened quickly, but the philosopher Marcus whom it named Emperor soon died, as did also a certain Severus Hostilianus who somehow next got possession of the throne. Philip, who had meanwhile arrived in Rome and had won over the most important of the senators by supple talk, was now acknowledged Emperor (244–249). To call Philip an Arab sheik is to do him too much honor; he derived from the disreputable tribe of southern Syrians east of the Jordan.

If the attraction of imperial power were not so utterly blinding it would be hard to conceive how this man could expect, with his negligible military capacity, to master the Roman Empire, which he had obtained by fraud, by distributing its principal offices to relatives and friends. While he was celebrating the Secular Games, which marked the city's thousandth anniversary, in Rome, barbarians were crashing into the Empire from several directions, and at least two armies were setting up new Emperors. In Syria there arose against Philip's brother Priscus the adventurer Jotapian, who claimed descent from Alexander the Great, a name which still received almost superstitious reverence. In Moesia Marinus arose against Philip's son-in-law Severian, while near by the Goths were marching into the Empire.

The Empire's great and obvious peril once more aroused the genius of Rome. The second half of the third century is an era which would surely gain in esteem if we had fuller knowledge of its personalities and the motivation of their measures than our sources afford. Although the leading figures are not for the most part Roman in the strict sense, but rather Illyrian, that is to say, from the regions between the Adriatic and the Black Seas, nevertheless it was Roman culture and tradition, specifically in matters of war, that enabled them to become the new saviors of the ancient world. To be a Roman Emperor was no longer a pleasure but a fateful obligation. Men unworthy of it assumed the purple only under constraint; better men no longer pressed forward to the office but recognized in it duty or destiny. There is an unmistakable atmosphere of moral exaltation.

The great dangers soon put an end to Philip's reign. He turned to the Senate in terror and offered his abdication. There was silence, until the gallant Decius offered his services to subdue Marinus. He was successful, but asked to be recalled, for he saw that because of the general contempt for Philip the army would wish to make him Emperor. Philip refused his request, and the inevitable came to pass. In or after a battle against Decius, Philip was put to death by soldiers at Verona. The fact that Philip's brother Priscus could subsequently be governor of Macedonia proves that Decius need have no shame for what had transpired. In the sequel Priscus repaid him with treason.

Decius (249–251) was primarily an idealist, with the idealist's illusions. To employ his very great military capacity in the service of a refined senatorial regime, to restore ancient Roman virtue and religion and hence the power of the Roman name, and to establish it forever — these were doubtless his designs. It was in keeping with this design that he persecuted the Christians; sixty years later he might have employed similar zeal to guide the Christian spirit of self-sacrifice to the salvation of the Empire.

But he was not fated to attain his life's goal. Besides incursions of barbarians on all sides, famine and pestilence raged abroad; these must have induced permanent alterations in all of Roman life, for an aging people cannot abide the blows a youthful people may disdain. Decius' reward was a glorious death in battle against the Goths.

Again the Senate asserted its right. Besides Gallus, whom the soldiers raised, it named (251) its own Emperor, Hostilian, who soon died of an illness. While Gallus was buying the Goths off with tribute, there was a general with the troops on the Danube, the Mauretanian Aemilian, who spoke to his men of "Roman honor," and in the event of victory promised them the tribute which was being paid to the Goths. The victory was won, and the soldiers made Aemilian Emperor (253). But Decius' ideas were so far effective that Aemilian wished only to be called the Senate's general and to leave the government of the Empire to the Senate itself.

A perceptible lacuna in the *Historia Augusta* prevents valid conclusions concerning the events following. Aemilian marched toward Italy; Gallus, who marched against him, was murdered, together with his sons, by his own troops. But Valerian, one of Gallus' generals, marching down from the Alps, succeeded in some mysterious fashion in winning over the victorious army of Aemilian, which murdered its Emperor "because he was a soldier but no ruler, because Valerian was better suited to be Emperor, or because the Romans must be spared another civil war." The truth glimmers through this justification. Clearly these are not the doings of mutinous bands of soldiers. What is involved is undoubtedly an understanding among the higher officers of the three armies. Only an understanding of such a nature can explain the rise of Valerian (253), who was perhaps the most outstanding of all Romans, in civil offices as in war; left to themselves, the soldiers would either have insisted on their Aemilian or have raised to the throne some tall, handsome figure with the talents of a petty officer.

Henceforward imperial elections generally assume a new form. In the barbarian wars which had persisted since the time of Alexander Severus there must have developed an excellent corps of generals, among whom competence was properly assessed and esteemed. Valerian, at least as Emperor, seems to be the very soul of this corps. His military correspondence, part of which was deliberately preserved in the *Historia Augusta*, demonstrates precise knowledge of men and their capacities and gives us a high opinion of the man who could recognize and promote Posthumus, Claudius Gothicus, Aurelian, and Probus. If there had been peace on the frontiers, perhaps the Senate would have had a regular share in government, as Decius and Aemilian designed. But since simultaneous barbaric incursions from all directions threatened to overwhelm the Empire entirely and since the true Rome had long abandoned the seven hills by the Tiber and was now to be found in the brave camps of Roman military leaders, it was only natural that the power of the state should also gravitate into the hands of the generals. These now constituted a kind of Senate in arms, which was scattered over all the border provinces. For short periods, to be sure, the Empire was quite out of joint, and here and there thoughtless caprice of the soldiers or despair in the provinces clothed the first available man with the purple; but when the initial shock was over, the generals occupied the throne with one of their own number. We can only surmise how prudence and calculation were reconciled with ambition and violence in individual cases, and the nature of the secret oaths that bound the group firmly together. No hostility was shown to the Senate; indeed, it was generally treated with respect, and there was one occasion when the Senate could delude itself into believing that it had once more become the master of the Empire.

This remarkable transition merits examination in detail. Even under Valerian the defection of individual regions had begun, and when Valerian himself was treacherously made captive by the Sassanid King Shapur (260), contrary to all international law, while his son Gallienus was occupied with the war against the Germans, utter confusion set in. While Rome itself was threatened with invasion by nameless hordes and the Senate was constrained to organize a hasty civil guard, the Eastern countries one after the other renounced their allegiance. First the worthless parricide Cyriades allowed himself to be put forward by Shapur as pretender to the Roman throne, until Macrianus with his sons and his brave Prefect Balista rose to be savior of the Roman East (260). Shapur was forced to flee, and his harem was taken captive. The magnificent defense of Caesarea in Cappadocia must at least be mentioned. But the disintegration of the Empire proceeded. Generals and higher officials were constantly constrained to proclaim themselves Emperors only to protect themselves against other usurpers, and perished notwithstanding. So it befell Valens, surnamed Thessalonicus, in Greece, and so it befell Piso, whom Macrianus sent against Valens. So presently it befell Macrianus himself (261) when he marched against Aureolus, who was Gallienus' general on the Danube; and when he proved victorious Aureolus too may have turned against Gallienus. In the East Macrianus and his house were supplanted by Odenathus (262), a rich provincial. Several such usurped the imperial title at this time, but none possessed the talent and enjoyed the success of this Palmyrene patrician, who, with his heroic wife Zenobia, was able to establish a great Oriental kingdom. Descended from the Egyptian Ptolemies, including the famous Cleopatra, Zenobia with her colorful court of Asiatic generals later (267–273) ruled, on her sons' behalf, a realm extending to Galatia and into Egypt. It was in this territory that Gallienus' generals had successfully disposed of lesser usurpers—in southeast Asia Minor the pirate Trebellian, whom the incorrigible Isaurians had raised to be their lord; in Egypt Aemilianus, the former commandant of Alexandria, who, when a rioting mob threatened him with death, had assumed the imperial title (262–265) in order to evade rendering an account to Gallienus.

For a time Gallienus was forced to recognize Aureolus, who was mentioned above, as ruler of the Danube region. But long before (258), the troops on the Danube had raised the Governor Ingenuus, the better to protect the country against in-

c

cursions. Gallienus had suppressed Ingenuus, and had visited fearful punishments on the region. The provincials thirsted for vengeance, and named as Emperor the heroic Dacian Regillianus (260), who claimed descent from the Dacian King Decebalus, Trajan's famous enemy; but they soon gave him up, out of fear of new punishment at the hands of Gallienus, whom events had made merciless. Bithynia had a usurper, but not even his name is known; Sicily too was ruled by nameless robbers (*latrones*).

The most remarkable series of usurpers appears in the West, specifically Gaul, to which Spain and Britain occasionally submitted. Here, because of indescribable distress caused by the barbarians, there arose (after 259) first against Valerian and then against Gallienus' son and generals a series of mighty protectors—Posthumus, Lollianus (or Laelianus), and Victorinus. These were not merely soldier Emperors, but governed with the enthusiastic and almost regular participation of the provincials. A true transalpine realm was in the making, and its notables formed a Senate for the Emperor, who generally resided at Treves. Far from raising the standard of half-forgotten Gallic, Britannic, or Iberian nationality, these countries wished only to be a Western Roman Empire and to protect Roman culture and institutions from barbarian incursions. As much cannot be said of Zenobia's realm. Remarkably enough, however, in the West, too, it was a woman, Victoria, the mother of Victorinus, who instituted adoptions and successions among the Emperors, was called "Mother of the Camps," and like some superhuman being held sway over the armies. Her son and grandson were cut down before her eyes by angry soldiers, but contrition was so great that the nomination of a new Emperor was left to her will. Her first choice, for the soldiers' sake, was a strong armorer, Marius (267); and after Marius was murdered she ventured to name her relative Tetricus, who was unknown to the army but whose unmilitary regime (after 267) the soldiers accepted, at least until Victoria's death.

The last place in this series of usurpations clearly belongs to Celsus in Africa, because his was least justified and least suc-

cessful. Without the ground or pretext of barbarian attack, the
Africans (apparently only the Carthaginians), upon the instigation of the proconsul and a general, proclaimed the Tribune
Celsus Emperor. The deficiency in divine right was supplied
by the cloak of the Heavenly Goddess, which was fetched
from the famous oracular temple at Carthage for investing
the pretender. Here, too, a woman played the leading role. An
aunt of Gallienus caused Celsus to be murdered after seven
days and his corpse to be torn by dogs; the inhabitants of
Sicca insisted on this treatment out of loyalty to the Emperor.
Then in addition Celsus was crucified in effigy.

In these unexampled and for the most part unmerited situations Gallienus' own conduct seems not to have been as indifferent or cowardly as the *Historia Augusta* would have us
believe. Upon some of the so-called Thirty Tyrants, it is true,
he bestowed the title of Caesar or Augustus; but others he
fought with great energy. The indolence for which he was notorious must have seized him by spells, but have left him as
suddenly. It was probably expected of him that he should
march to Persia to liberate his father, but under the circumstances such an enterprise was quite unthinkable. His relation
to the provincial Emperors whom he recognized is comparable
to that of the Caliphs to the dynasties which declared their
independence, except that he received no honorary gifts and
no mention in public prayer. On the other hand, he asserted
his own sway over Italy with great energy; and several of his
father's more important generals remained loyal to him. He
purposely kept the Senate from service in his army, indeed
from visiting it, because even in this unparliamentary age he
was haunted by fear of a senatorial military regime. When
Aureolus carried his attacks into Italy, Gallienus, moving vigorously, compelled him to concentrate his forces in Milan,
and there besieged him. Aureolus' situation had grown desperate when Gallienus was murdered (268). The perpetrator
was a colonel of Dalmatian cavalry, the immediate instigators
a Prefect of the Guard and a general of the Danube troops.
But the prime movers were Aurelian (subsequently Emperor),
who had joined the beleaguerers with cavalry, and the Illyrian

Claudius, a favorite of the Senate and at the same time one of the greatest generals of the day. Claudius had made no secret of it whenever he was displeased with Gallienus' laxity, and it was probably for this reason that he was stationed apart in Pavia. These generals are said to have held a formal council on the life and death of Gallienus, and it was at this council that the decision concerning Claudius' succession must have been reached.

All things considered, such a complot may be partially exculpated in view of the extraordinary circumstances. The men who pronounced judgment were not irresponsible. If the Empire was to regain its unity, Gallienus had to be eliminated as a factor; and this could not be achieved with Gallienus' consent, for he was unable to live without his imperial pleasures. Claudius may also have foreseen the looming Gothic invasion, which was the most frightful of the century, and this was a necessity that knew no law. Apart from this imminent invasion, even while Gallienus was encamped before Milan, the Alemanni were already in Italy, and it was Claudius' most pressing business, after he had quickly disposed of Aureolus in the battle at Pontirolo, to deal decisively with the Alemanni. In his grave inscription Claudius declares that he would have suffered Aureolus to live if consideration for his excellent army had permitted such leniency. We have no grounds to doubt the sincerity of these words.

Claudius (268–270) could only begin the gigantic task of restoring the Empire, and his first measures involved leaving his party in Gaul in the lurch. But his victory over the Goths at Nissa gave the ancient world reprieve. His other talents for government could hardly benefit the Empire, for he survived but a year; nevertheless it is unjust to doubt that these talents were real, simply because Claudius had the misfortune of falling into the hands of panegyrists. His true eulogy is the pride which the Illyrian cavalry took in being his compatriots and the spirited confidence with which his victory inspired individual weak cities and provincial populations to defend themselves against the barbarians. Spain deserted Tetricus to fall into Claudius' arms.

Claudius had an excellent brother, Quintillus, whom the Senate named Emperor out of respect for Claudius. But on his deathbed Claudius himself, in the presence of the assembled generals, had designated Aurelian as his successor, and the army immediately recognized the election. It was only consonant with the times that Quintillus should forthwith open his veins.

Aurelian, who was a native of the Belgrade region, seems a degree more barbarian than his predecessor, but in essentials hardly less worthy of the throne. In a brilliant campaign (272) he subjugated Zenobia and the East, and this immediately enhanced his reputation for invincibility to a wonderful degree. Marcellinus, governor of Mesopotamia, who was instigated by part of his army to usurp the imperial title, himself laid information of the matter before Aurelian. Antiochus, whom the foolish Palmyrenes raised to the office, Aurelian let go, after he had punished the Palmyrenes. But the rich Firmus, a pretender in Egypt, Aurelian ordered crucified as a robber, apparently only to use the opportunity of making a display of the profound and traditional Roman contempt of Egyptian character. To Tetricus, who was under intolerable constraint as a result of his false position with regard to the soldiers and who betrayed his own army in the battle at Châlons (272), Aurelian gave a remunerative office. If we add to these campaigns for restoring the Empire the persistent and victorious wars against the barbarians, we may conceive what an incomparable school of war the reign of Aurelian provided. The most important of his successors on the throne were trained by him and Probus.

Aurelian's relation to the Senate appears in a far less favorable light, and is pictured for us in the same colors as that of Septimius Severus. The Emperor made the Senate responsible for conspiracies and unrest of all sorts in the capital, and a number of its members were even executed. The miserable records of the time, study them as we will, nowhere suffice for definitive conclusions. We cannot say whether Aurelian sought to extend the iron discipline of the camps to civil life, or whether the Senate was blind to the times and wished to

compete with the reconqueror of the Empire for its government. That Aurelian was not personally cruel and that he was
eager to avoid bloodshed is demonstrated by decisive passages
in his life. Nor was he called the "murderer" but only "the
pedagogue of the Senate." But a situation like Aurelian's required a strong spirit indeed not to suffer contempt of mankind to depress him into gloom, or cowardice and convenience
into bloodthirstiness. It is not easy to imagine the position of
an Emperor of the period; it is quite impossible to say how
even the most equable temper might endure it over a long
period. Of Aurelian's sun-worship, which was the prevalent
religion among soldiers at the end of paganism, we shall speak
in the sequel.

Aurelian was murdered by conspirators among his immediate entourage on an expedition against the Persians, not far
from Byzantium. It may be assumed that not more than one of
the more respected generals, Mucapor, was involved in the
deed; the others were men of the Guard, whom a confidential
secretary — himself implicated and expecting punishment —
was able to alarm by a forged signature.

The generals then jointly dispatched the following communication to the Senate: "The courageous and successful armies
to the Senate and people of Rome: Our Emperor Aurelian has
been murdered by the craft of one man and the delusion of
good and bad men. Honorable and sovereign Fathers! Raise
him to the gods and send us an Emperor out of your midst,
one whom you deem worthy to be Emperor; for we will not
suffer it that one of those who has done evil, out of error or
malice, should rule over us." This letter does honor to all concerned — to Aurelian, who is so handsomely justified; to the
Senate; and to the armies, in whose name it is clear that the
generals entered upon the negotiations. On the part of men
who had helped Aurelian subdue the world, this action cannot have been merely an emotional *beau geste*.

But the Senate, whose ancient and august authority was
here so splendidly and unexpectedly recognized, rejected the
honor. After soldier regimes, such as those immediately preceding must have been, the nomination of an Emperor by the

Senate would have been a grievous error. In Rome, furthermore, the possibility that, during the two months which must
elapse while communications were going to and fro, the mood
of the Eastern armies might have altered, either of itself or
through intrigues, must have entered into calculations. But the
army did abide by its resolution. There were three exchanges
of letters, until the Senate finally resolved to make the choice.
During the half year that elapsed all higher officials remained
at their posts; no other army ventured to anticipate the action
of the Eastern army; fear or respect maintained a remarkable
balance among the existing forces.

If after a millennium and a half, in view of exceedingly
fragmentary knowledge of the records, an expression of opinion were allowed us, we should have approved the Senate's
final decision to name an Emperor but should have thought
that the candidate must be one of the better-known generals
who had not participated in the murder — Probus, for example.
Instead it raised Tacitus, an elderly and respected senator who
possessed knowledge of military affairs, and let loose jubilant
rejoicing over this masterpiece of constitutionalism. Exultant
letters went out to all the provinces: the Senate again possessed its ancient right of imperial nomination, and in future
would issue laws, receive the homage of barbarian princes,
decide on war and peace. The senators sacrificed white victims, went about in white togas, and in their palace halls
opened wide the cabinets which held the *imagines* of their
forebears. Tacitus, however, regarded himself as a doomed
man, bestowed his enormous wealth on the state, and went to
join the army. Out of a purely legalistic vagary the Senate in-
considerately refused Tacitus permission to name his brother
Florian consul. This mark of renewed constitutional awareness
is said to have pleased the Emperor; comment is idle.

In the East Tacitus waged a successful war against the
Goths and Alans. But a faction of officers, reinforced by the
threatened murderers of Aurelian, first murdered Maximin,
the strict commandant of Syria and a relative of the Emperor,
and then, out of fear of punishment, the Emperor himself, in
the Pontus region. His brother Florian in Tarsus committed the

imprudence of assuming the posture of successor, without consulting Senate or army, as if the imperial office were hereditary; even if it were, Tacitus' sons would take natural precedence over Florian. After a few weeks he, too, was killed by the soldiers.

In the meanwhile a purely military election had raised the mighty Probus to the throne. Probus was a compatriot of Aurelian, and Aurelian had designated him, at least by inference, as his successor. The Senate recognized him without demur, and Probus was tactful enough to reconcile the somewhat constrained mood of the Senate by bestowing certain honorary privileges upon it. The murderers of Aurelian and Tacitus he had brought before him, manifested his abhorrence and contempt of them, and caused them to be executed. Immediately upon his election he had told the soldiers that they would not find him indulgent, and he kept his word. His discipline was severe, but he led his men to those stunning victories which rid Gaul of Germans and cost the lives of four hundred thousand barbarians. If these victories did no more than preserve the *status quo*, if the subjugation of all Germany which was prerequisite to Rome's continued security, as Probus clearly appreciated, was not achieved, the fault was surely not his.

From the Rhine and the Neckar he moved to the East, and his generals were victorious in the distant Southeast. Usurpers did indeed rise against him — Saturninus, Proculus, Bonosus — but this was not due to the soldiers' ill will because of his severity, but rather to the desperate petulance of the Egyptians, fear of the Lyonnaise and their party of the Emperor's punishment, and a drunkard's terror because of a serious dereliction in border duty. In each case the usurper's sway was very brief. The great ruler, who is regarded as a soldier Emperor exclusively, cherished an ideal of a quite different character. He wished to bring it about — and he made no secret of his designs — that the complete defeat or weakening of the barbarian peoples should make soldiers unnecessary for the Roman state, and that an era of peace and recovery might be introduced. The *Historia Augusta* presents his wistful delineation of a Saturnian utopia. Such talk penetrated to the soldiers, who were already irked that their Emperor employed them, aside from the needs of war, on vineyards, canals, and roads. At a drainage project in Sirmium in his home country the soldiers killed him, apparently without premeditation, and immediately rued the deed. His family, like those of several of the fallen Emperors, left Rome and settled in upper Italy.

This time the army took no thought of the Senate. That the higher officers themselves elected or guided the election is a natural inference from the fact that an old martinet, the Illyrian Carus, was invested with the purple. With his younger and better son Numerianus he marched immediately to the completion of the Sarmatian and the resumption of the Persian wars. The wastrel Carinus he made co-regent, and gave him the supreme command against the Germans. He appears to have regretted this appointment and to have intended to replace his disappointing son by the energetic and noble Constantius Chlorus, father of Constantine; this would constitute a remarkable emancipation from dynastic ideas if the fact could be established.

In the East Carus and shortly thereafter Numerianus died (284) under mysterious circumstances. Numerianus' death was caused by Aper, Prefect of the Guard. Aper was not counted among the generals of the inner group, and apparently boldness was his only asset for making his usurpation successful. But when the death of the Caesar became known, Aper appears to have lost his composure, suffered himself to be overcome, and was bound for trial at court-martial before the entire army. Here, "by the election of the generals and officers," Diocletian, a distinguished commander, was proclaimed Emperor; Diocletian at once sprang upon Aper, who was still awaiting trial at the foot of the tribunal, and pierced him through. It is probably unjust to deduce that Diocletian was privy to Aper's crime; the simple explanation of the startling occurrence is that a Druid priestess in Gaul had once foretold that Diocletian would become Emperor if he dispatched a boar (*aper*). Ever since, whenever Diocletian went hunting, he looked for boars; now he was carried away by impatience when he saw the right boar before him.

It remained for Diocletian to dispute the rule of the world with Carinus. Carinus was not without military talent; he appears to have worsted the usurper Julianus en route in upper Italy (285) without difficulty. His war with Diocletian lasted for half a year, and even in the battle at Margus (not far from Semendria), which is usually regarded as the decisive engagement, it is possible that Carinus was the victor. But personal enmities which he had aroused by his excesses cost Carinus his life. Diocletian was immediately acknowledged by both armies. This and the fact that he dismissed no officers, made no confiscations, and even retained the Prefect of the Guard Aristobulus in his post, might suggest that a preliminary understanding had been reached with the army of Carinus; but we would rather agree with the elder Aurelius Victor in attributing this course to the singular leniency and deep insight of the new Emperor and his retinue. According to his own protestations he desired the death of Carinus not out of ambition but out of concern for the common weal. This may well be credited to a man who showed such unexampled forbearance in other cases.

II

DIOCLETIAN : HIS SYSTEM OF ADOPTIONS
AND HIS REIGN

OMENS WERE FULFILLED and oracles justified when the son
of Dalmatian slaves who had belonged to the Roman
Senator Anulinus, being then some thirty-nine years of age,
ascended the throne of the world. Mother and son received
their name from their native place, tiny Dioclea near Cattaro;
now for the Romans' sake Diocles, "famed of Zeus," added a
proper Latin ending and made his name Diocletianus. The
allusion to the ruler of the gods in *Dio-* he retained; his Latin
cognomen Jovius is a reminiscence of it.

Of his military achievements, his regime, and his character
(which is a much disputed subject) we shall have to speak in
the sequel. What concerns us now is his peculiar concept of
the Emperor's authority, and the methods by which he sought
to secure, to share, and to bequeath that authority.

Of the preceding Emperors, some had been prevented by
violent death from making any dispositions concerning the
crown; others had consciously delegated the decision to their
generals. The fact that Carus had summarily set his sons up as
his successors was perhaps the prime cause of their fall. Diocletian's wife Prisca apparently bore him only a daughter, Valeria, and he was hence constrained to seek another answer to
the problem of succession. If conditions in the Empire were
peaceful, he might have postponed decision; but violent
storms were brewing without, and within there were, after

Carus, crowds of usurpers — Diocletian's own rule was in fact essentially a usurpation, even if it received the recognition of the Senate. What remedy offered?

What Diocletian did reveals nobility and insight in one aspect; in another it seems curious and enigmatic.

Experience of recent decades had shown that even the most energetic of rulers, the saviors of the Empire, must succumb to treachery and the aroused passions of the soldiery. The great generals who surrounded the Emperor could not prevent it; some would not, for ambition pointed, however timorously, to the throne. Eventually a situation like that under Gallienus and the Thirty Tyrants must inevitably recur, and in 285 all indications pointed to its being at hand; the Empire would again have disintegrated, perhaps forever.

Diocletian applied the correct antidote: he surrounded himself with successors and colleagues. Ambition's target was thus made more remote for the usurper, and probability of successful barracks insurrections diminished. For if only one of the Emperors or Caesars should fall, if a conspiracy could not succeed in removing and murdering two or four rulers in a single day, perhaps in Nicomedia, Alexandria, Milan, and Treves, then inexorable avengers would await the individual deed of violence. All good men knew at once what party they must follow; they need no longer throw themselves in unthinking terror into the arms of the soldiers' first chance choice. Another very great advantage of Diocletian's measure was the distribution of the tasks of government. Now these could be confronted calmly and thoughtfully and in accordance with a determined common plan and be carried out brilliantly.

But the artificial system of Diocletian's adoptions presents an enigma. The simplest and obvious solution, superficially considered, would have been for Diocletian to adopt a gifted family of several brothers and to distribute them in the provinces and in other governmental assignments. What the house of Carus had failed to achieve, partly by Carinus' fault, might now have succeeded; a discontinuous Caesarism might have been transformed into a hereditary dynasty, to which of necessity any monarchical government must eventually tend.

Was it that Diocletian feared that a family thus exalted might supplant him? So imposing a personage as Diocletian could not easily have been brushed aside. Was it that he lacked confidence in the moral effectiveness of blood relationship in his degenerate age? He himself subsequently made the Caesars sons-in-law to the Emperors. Did he find it necessary to satisfy as many ambitions as possible by adoption or the hope of adoption? He knew better than anyone that it is precisely the most dangerous men who are never satisfied; nor was it in his nature to trouble about giving universal satisfaction or winning universal approval. If we examine the individual cases and their demonstrable or probable motives more closely, we may find the right path, though gaps in our tradition must leave many questions unanswered.

As early as 285, in view of the peasant war in Gaul, Diocletian raised his companion-in-arms Maximian to be Caesar, and in the year following to Augustus. The adoptive relationship was expressed in Maximian's cognomen Herculius, borrowed from the son of Zeus. After both had waged six years of unceasing war against barbarians, rebellious provinces, and usurpers in all parts of the Empire, without formally dividing the Empire among themselves, they raised (292) to the position of Caesars the Generals Galerius and Constantius Chlorus. On this occasion Diocletian expressly stated that "there shall hereafter be two greater in the state as rulers and two lesser as helpers." Maximian's son Maxentius was unceremoniously passed over; instead, an artificial bond of filial piety was contrived, by making the Caesars marry daughters of the Emperors. Galerius married Valeria, and Constantius Theodora; Theodora was strictly speaking Maximian's stepdaughter. The Caesars had been trained in the school of Aurelian and Probus. Constantius was of noble birth, on his mother's side a great-nephew of Claudius Gothicus. Galerius was a burly shepherd's son, and therefore fond of saying that his mother had conceived him by a divine being in the form of a serpent or, like Rhea Silvia, by Mars himself. Now there were four courts, administrations, and armies. Constantius ruled Gaul and Britain; Galerius the Danube country and Greece; Maximian Italy, Spain, and Africa; and for Diocletian himself, the source of all their authority, Thrace, Asia, and Egypt were reserved. For over twelve years there obtained among men so diverse and in part so crude a most remarkable harmony, a harmony which becomes completely inexplicable when we observe one of the rulers sharing in the government of another's province and commanding armies there, or when we see how little Diocletian's tongue spared the passionate Galerius in the presence of whole armies. All that came from Diocletian -- the most difficult plans of battle, the most questionable orders — was invariably carried out with filial obedience; there was never a doubt that he was the guiding spirit of the whole. "They looked up to him," says Aurelius Victor, "as to a father or a supreme god; what this signifies will become clear if we think of all the parricides committed from Romulus to our own day."

The crucial test of obedience was withstood by the associate Emperor Maximian when after twenty years of dual rule Diocletian required him (in 305) to join in the common abdication they had long before agreed upon. Maximian yielded, but with great reluctance. He patiently accepted the fact that when two new Caesars were named (Galerius and Constantius were promoted to be Emperors) his own son Maxentius was again passed over and that he himself, the veteran conqueror of the Bagaudae, the Germans, and the Moors, had no voice in the selection of Caesars. This privilege Diocletian had reserved exclusively for his adoptive son Galerius; Galerius appointed a loyal officer, Severus, to be Caesar of the West, and his nephew, Maximinus Daia, to be Caesar of the East. Constantius Chlorus received treatment similar to Maximian's; although he was advanced to the dignity of Emperor he must needs be content to accept Severus, instead of one of his own sons, as future Caesar. Christian authors praise his discreet moderation, quite needlessly.

In Lactantius' *De Mortibus Persecutorum*, composed not long after these events, a colorful and dramatic account is given of personal motivations for these statesmanlike measures. Gibbon realized that this report was not factual but the account of an embittered enemy; specifically, it is wrong in representing the retiring veteran Emperors as having been terrorized by Galerius. But one very remarkable detail probably has a basis in fact: Galerius is credited with the intention of retiring, like Diocletian, after twenty years of rule if the future succession should have been provided for. The author regards this as a voluntary decision, and his ardent hatred of Galerius apparently makes him loath to report it. But unless we are wholly deceived we have here a prescribed and essential principle of the Diocletianic system, which contemporaries could only partially divine. The establishment of a twenty-year period for the incumbency of the imperial office constitutes the capstone and safety control of the whole. The limitation was intended to stamp adoptions and successions with the seal of necessity and inevitability. But in the following year (306) the whole system was irremediably shattered by the usurpation of the Emperors' sons who felt they had been passed over. Constantine (the Great), with the help of his soldiers, claimed the inheritance of his father's rule, Maxentius wrested Italy for his own, and even the old Maximian forsook his unwelcome retirement in order to support his son's efforts. This disruption of his plans for the succession shattered Diocletian's solemn arrangements, and with them, he believed, the Empire itself was doomed. Deep sorrow surely filled his last years, which he spent, sick and weary of life, at home in the halls of his palace at Salonae, which was designed like a Roman camp.

In fact his ideal of government for the Empire was a curious and remarkable thing. And in view of the possible consequences of government by generals, as all the Emperors of the time were, we must be prepared for the curious; we cannot now be certain what experiences Europe of our own late day holds in store for our descendants. A dual twenty-year tenure with mandatory retirement; nomination of Caesars; the exclusive prerogative of the elder Emperors; the individual rulers (even if they should be heroes of abnegation) continuously irked and injured by the exclusion of their sons — all this to build an artificial dynasty. Granted that for the sake of im-

perial defense a division of power was essential, and that
usurpation from without was infinitely more difficult against
four rulers than against one — but how could usurpation be
prevented in the imperial houses themselves? These are but a
few of the puzzles for which Diocletian provides us no answers.

Political and psychological motives alone are not sufficient
for a solution. The missing element is provided by the assumption of a religious superstition which pervaded and controlled
all of these arrangements.

The importance of omens and soothsaying in the life of
Diocletian has been mentioned above. He is spoken of as "an
investigator of things to come," "always devoted to holy
usages." We find him, surrounded by priests, zealously ex-
amining the entrails of sacrificial victims, filled with anxiety
because of ominous lightning bolts. He was attentive to omens
even in the matter of proper names. Galerius must take the
name of Maximianus in order to effect a magic bond with the
proven loyalty of the elder Maximian; for a similar reason
the youthful Daia subsequently received the kindred name of
Maximinus. Apparently the Emperor sought to attain a special
relationship with the deity whose name he bore; Jupiter occurs
very frequently on the obverse of his coins. It was under a
pillar bearing the statue of Zeus in an open field near Nicomedia that his act of abdication took place, and the octagonal
temple of Jupiter is still a striking feature in the palace at
Salonae. His public proclamations also reveal a noticeable religious tendency; the preamble to the marriage law of 295
reads like a sermon, and the law against the Manichees of 296
breathes a personal fervor.

His colleagues in the Empire are almost equally devoted to
superstition, without which, indeed, their long obedience is
hardly explicable. They must have known that even their
elevation was due to superstitious considerations. What strange
anxieties, to us quite unintelligible, preceded Diocletian's
adoptions! A figure appeared to him in a dream, for example,
and peremptorily commanded that he choose as successor a
certain man whose name was specified. He believed that

magic was being employed against him and at length summoned the person named and said to him: "Receive the rule which you demand from me each night, and do not begrudge your Emperor his rest!" We do not know to whom this palace anecdote refers, nor indeed whether it is correctly reported; it is surely significant nevertheless.

Maximian was a great, at least a capable, general, and Diocletian might have shown him consideration as an early confidant of his exalted plans; but it may well have been that the decisive factor in Maximian's elevation was the fact that he was born on the same day of the month as Diocletian. Of Constantius we can assume with some certainty that it was essentially because of the prophecy of Druid priestesses that Diocletian named him Caesar.

Constantius, as has been said, was a Dalmatian; Maximian a peasant's son from Sirmium (Mitrovica on the Sava), the home of the bravest Emperors of the third century; Galerius was a shepherd, either from Dacia or from Sardica (modern Sofia, in Bulgaria); Maximinus Daia was apparently from the same region; Constantius Chlorus was living in Nissa in Serbia when his son Constantine was born; Licinius, who later appeared as the friend of Galerius, was a peasant from the lower Danube; the home of Severus is unknown. There is a possibility (but no external evidence) that some local religion or superstition was a special bond among these rulers. Of Maximian's abdication we know only the formula which he pronounced in the temple of the Capitoline God (apparently in Milan): "Take back, O Jupiter, what thou has granted." Oaths, sacrifices, and dedications may have been Diocletian's substitute for what his political arrangements lacked in strength and permanence.

The reader who is unwilling to accept our explanation may assume that at his elevation of Maximian Diocletian could not forgo Maximian's co-operation and military talents, but that he passed over Maximian's son Maxentius because Galerius had long been his enemy. But it is questionable whether such a course of action can be reconciled with the character of Diocletian and his indisputable stature as a ruler. There is a

D

deep seriousness in his regulations, particularly in his reduction of the imperial office to a fixed term. If others regarded this office as a matter of pleasure, that was not Diocletian's fault; he regarded it as an awesome and responsible obligation which children and graybeards must be spared for their own and the Empire's happiness. At the same time the just ambition of the current Caesars was taken into the reckoning; they could now calculate the day and the hour by which at latest (if nothing transpired in the interval) they would ascend the throne. It was with the feeling of a man who knew the day of his death that the Emperor celebrated at five-year intervals the quinquennalia, and then the decennalia, and then the quindecennalia; inexorably there approached the vicennalia, upon which he must divest himself of the purple. Such was the will of the "All-powerful Goddesses of Fate" who are celebrated on a coin of the year of abdication. That successors could not remain forever bound, Diocletian knew well enough; but he wished, it would seem, to provide an example. Furthermore, only the stipulation of a twenty-year term could guarantee the exclusion of the Emperors' sons, which would not have been the case if the term were for life. It may be asked whether it was wise to provide hostile and subversive elements in the state with a fixed term upon which insurrection might be successful; but means of resistance could also be made ready. During the illness which preceded Diocletian's abdication, for a month and a half, the people were uncertain whether he was still alive; nevertheless not a hand was raised in the well-ordered state.

Remarkably enough, the same questions and the same events were afoot in the kingdom of the Sassanids, the Empire's hostile neighbor on the east. Of Bahram III, who ruled for only a few months in 293, our authorities tell us for the first time that the King of Persia had made a certain son or brother, whom he designated as his successor, provisionally prince of a province, with the title Shah; Bahram himself, as long as his father Bahram II was alive, was called merely Shah of Segan or Sistan. After his short reign, which was apparently attended by violent disturbances, his younger brother Narsi succeeded;

and Narsi himself then crowned his son Hormuz as his successor, and in 301 withdrew into the quiet of private life, "under the shadow of the goodness of God." According to Mirk-
hond he was moved to this step by thoughts of death, "whose
season is recorded in eternal decrees and may not be evaded."
Possibly the Magi foretold the precise hour of his death, and
thus banished his joy in life. But it is also suggested that Narsi
wished to avoid the vicissitudes of a royal destiny, of which
his wars with the Romans had given him abundant experience.
"The way is long," he says, "often one must ascend, and often
descend again." It is not impossible that Narsi's example may
have had its effect upon the mind of Diocletian.

Closely related to the solemn pomp and circumstance arising
from superstitious considerations which surrounded Diocletian's
life is the sudden and striking growth of elaborate court ceremonial. The elder Aurelius Victor would explain this development
by the fact that Diocletian was an upstart, and as such naturally
insatiable of outward show. But in that case it is strange that
none of the great soldier Emperors of the third century, virtually
all of whom rose to the throne from humble origins, preceded
him in this affectation. For example, we see the mighty Aurelian
associating quite simply with his old friends, whose wants, indeed, he supplied so that they could no longer be called needy.
Silken clothes were too dear for him, and he wished to eliminate
the use of gold for ornamenting buildings and garments. He was
willing enough to permit others costly baubles, which might
be melted down again, but he denied them to himself. His
servants he dressed no more magnificently than he had done
before he became Emperor. He was not at ease in the splendid
palace on the Palatine whose colored marble walls were
stained with the blood of so many Emperors; like Vespasian
before him, he preferred the Gardens of Sallust, and in its
spacious courts he might be seen daily exercising himself and
putting his horses through their paces. All of this was now
changed. Diocletian had friends from his early days, but confidence was vanished, perhaps on either side; Diocletian had
cause to fear that intimacy with third parties might disrupt
the artfully contrived harmony with his colleagues. Instead of

the simple purple with which almost all his predecessors (ex-
cepting only the mad Emperors) had been content, Diocletian wore, after 293, silk and gold-embroidered garments, and
even his shoes were decorated with precious stones and pearls;
upon his head he wore a diadem, a white band set with pearls.
Naturally, these were the official vestments in which he appeared only on ceremonial occasions. On his flying journeys
and campaigns he and his colleague Maximian adopted a different style, as did also the Caesars, who were quick to follow their every hint; Constantius in particular was devoted to
simplicity. But in Nicomedia Diocletian insisted upon pomp.
Access to his sacred person was daily rendered more difficult
by elaborations of ceremonial. In the halls and forecourts of
the palace, officers, court officials, and guards were posted; in
the inner chambers influential eunuchs held sway. If a man's
business or rank made access to the Emperor possible, he must
follow Oriental usage and prostrate himself to make his address. Even upon the occasion of the meeting of Diocletian
with Maximian in Milan (291) the panegyrist Mamertinus
designates the ceremonial "a reverence enshrined in the sanctuary's innermost chamber, which might delight and astonish
only such natures whose rank and degree granted access to
your person."

Nor was the change confined to mute forms: the critical
word too was pronounced. The Emperor no longer called
himself by the titles of republican Rome, now grown empty,
such as the consulship, the tribunician power, and the like;
he was now called *Dominus,* Lord. Roman feeling had stubbornly resisted the title *Rex* because of the word's disagreeable associations. The Greeks had always been used to the
royal title in Sparta and the semi-civilized neighboring countries and had themselves employed it for centuries for the successors of Alexander; from the very beginning they called the
Roman Emperors Βασιλεῖς, "Kings," because the maintenance
of the republican fiction was to them meaningless. But now
the royal title was not enough; another was introduced to express the relationship between full domination and servitude.
Now a true apotheosis need occasion no surprise. The Senate

had long exercised the right of canonization of deceased Emperors; in point of fact the same honor was shown living Emperors in sacrifices and oaths before their statues, upon which occasion the ambiguous and hence untranslatable expression *numen imperatoris* might be used. Maximian, indeed, had himself represented on coins in the lion-skin of his divine patron, a weakness which he shared with Commodus and similar predecessors in the imperial office.

A man of Diocletian's importance and experience does not assume the burden of so exalted a representation without a sufficient cause. We know, moreover, that he frequently complained of the disadvantages of seclusion. He was aware of the great advantages which might accrue to a ruler from personal contact with his subjects, from higher officials to the humblest petitioner. "Four or five band together," he says, "to deceive the Emperor; they set a decision before him; shut up in his chambers, he cannot know the true situation; he can only know what they tell him. He nominates officials who had better not been appointed, and removes officials who had better remained at their post; thus even the best and cleverest Emperor is taken in."

One reason may be suggested which may have moved him to these restrictive measures despite his clear insight into their disadvantages. After the wars of Aurelian and Probus the court and especially the General Staff may have been filled with a large number of barbarian officers who because of their diverse origin and un-Roman education could not enter into the easy atmosphere of camaraderie which had formerly prevailed in the imperial court. Until the period of the great persecution there was also a great number of Christians at the various courts; and the solemn usages of court ceremonial prevented disagreeable incidents with pagans. To be sure, there was a certain fondness for the grandiloquent, revealed even in edicts; but how little the Emperor was moved by mere vanity and love of pomp is shown by the fact that he postponed to the end of his reign (303) his one triumph after so mighty a succession of victories, and that the celebration of that triumph was on a modest scale.

Diocletian's break with Roman tradition was patent in more than one respect. At the beginning of his reign, for one thing, he showed no special interest in the city of Rome itself. As late as the third century the Emperors had as a rule lived on the Palatine, perhaps less out of piety for its hallowed memories and the sanctuaries of the world capital than because its central situation, and its magnificence, and the wealth of pleasure it offered made it especially suitable for the imperial residence, and because, besides its ancient claims, it still retained a vestige of actual power. For Rome was the seat of the Senate, which had but recently deposed and nominated and recognized Emperors. Only Elagabalus ventured to banish the Senate from the city, but no other Emperor before or after him. Others trod upon its dignity and sought to demoralize it; cleverer Emperors established a *rapprochement* with it. Apprehension of the restless populace and the remnants of the Praetorian cohorts was only a minor motive in the consideration shown the Senate, at least on the part of the more capable rulers; for a weak prince there was fully as much danger within Rome as outside it.

But when requirements of border defense necessitated the division of imperial authority, it was impossible that Rome should remain the residence of one of the two or four rulers. Preservation of the Empire's boundaries took precedence over cordial relations with the Senate, which could in any case be maintained by a prince with true Roman sentiments. Maximian made his residence in Milan, which the pressure of the Alemanni, resumed after the death of Probus, had well-nigh made a border post. It was as well calculated to secure Gaul as any position south of the Alps could be, and at the same time it enabled its occupant to observe Italy or intervene in Africa. The Caesar Constantius, who waged continual war, is most frequently encountered in Treves, and later in York. Diocletian settled in Bithynia at Nicomedia, at the head of a deep gulf in the Sea of Marmora. Thence he could keep under surveillance the movements of the Goths and of other Pontic tribes which threatened the lower Danube, and at the same time be within reach of the plains of the upper Euphrates, where the struggles against the Persians were waged. In the early years of his reign, indeed, no fixed residence was possible; both Augusti hastened from battlefield to battlefield, and the Caesars soon did likewise. This did not affect Diocletian's somewhat morbid passion for building. He transformed a quarter of Nicomedia into a large and regular palace, whose design, like that of the palace he later constructed at Salona, perhaps followed the lines of a military encampment. It included basilicas, a circus, a mint, an arsenal, and separate residences for his wife and his daughter. Naturally the city grew, as is the way of royal residences. At the beginning of the fourth century Nicomedia is said to have resembled a quarter (*regio*) of Rome. In Milan most of the buildings which the fourth-century poet Ausonius found to admire were perhaps built by Maximian.

Rome must have been highly sensitive to the changed position, even if it suffered no outward loss. A hostile source (Lactantius) reports that Maximian attacked wealthy senators who were falsely accused of aspiring to rule, so that the lights of the Senate were continually being extinguished and its eyes pierced. Attempts to blame or exculpate, on this side or on that, are futile. In the history of Zosimus, who alone approaches truth and completeness in describing and appraising the character of Diocletian, there is a gap of twenty years. Perhaps the account of the last great persecution seemed too favorable to the persecutor in the sight of zealous Christians, and they found it easier to maim the work than to refute it, just as contemporary pagans mutilated Cicero's books *On the Nature of the Gods*, to prevent Christians from finding in them weapons for their polemic against polytheism.

Tension between Senate and Emperors arose from the fact that Diocletian had become Emperor, and had nominated his colleagues, without the Senate's co-operation. All that was left for the Senate was to recognize them and for form's sake bestow the consulship upon them from time to time. That distinction Diocletian esteemed so lightly that on one occasion he left Rome only a few days before he was to make his ceremonial entry into the office. On the occasion of the Emperors' meeting in Milan in 291 a deputation from the Senate was in attendance, apparently as a gesture of loyalty. The panegyrist Mamertinus declared in the presence of Maximian: "The Senate has bestowed a similitude of its own majesty upon Milan, so that the city might possess dignity as the seat of empire when both Emperors are there met together." The expression seems unfriendly, and we do not know how it was received; yet it does imply that in the year in question relations between Emperors and Senate were not yet openly hostile. When and how they deteriorated remains a puzzle. Maximian was by nature cruel and deceitful, and Diocletian may not have been beyond transgressing when transgression was expedient. Both found the Romans' "free if not bold manner of speech" highly distasteful. Particularly objectionable to the new rulers were the prearranged slogans, shouted in rhythm and with many repetitions, with which the senators in their precincts and the populace in the Circus offered homage or admonition to the Emperors. Surely without sufficient grounds they would not have sacrificed the heads of the Senate, if indeed things went so far and our author has not expanded some insignificant detail, as is his wont, into a monstrous crime.

But toward the population of Rome (to avoid using the desecrated term "people of Rome") Diocletian and his colleague later showed marked favor. As if Rome wanted for pleasure resorts, they built the most colossal of all Roman baths upon the Viminal (299). Among the ten or so baths erected by earlier Emperors and private philanthropists, those of Caracalla with their gigantic halls were most impressive. The building art was grown too exhausted to vie with the astonishing spans of Caracalla's arches, but Diocletian's baths surpassed Caracalla's in area. Their compass was twelve hundred paces, and they contained three thousand rooms. The astonishing central structure, whose granite columns are fifteen feet in circumference, is now the core of the Church of the Carthusians; other remains of the baths are to be found in cloisters, vineyards, and lonely avenues scattered about in a wide circle. In the same year Maximian started construction

of baths at Carthage, perhaps with a similar view to concili-
ating the populace. In the past Carthagé had been the chief
stage for the debut of usurpers. Other constructions undertaken at Rome during this reign are mentioned by name: the
Senate House, which had been burned in the reign of Carinus, the Forum of Caesar, the Basilica Julia, and the Theater
of Pompey were restored. New buildings included, beside the
baths, two porticoes called Jovia and Herculea, three nymphaea,
temples of Isis and Serapis, and a triumphal arch. Perhaps the
striking mass of splendid buildings with which Diocletian furnished the carping and dangerous Antiochenes was intended as
a distraction from political preoccupations. Among the buildings in Antioch which are recorded by name are temples
of Olympian Zeus, Hecate, Nemesis, and Apollo, a palace in
the city and one in the suburb called Daphne, several baths
and granaries, and a stadium; most of these were new buildings, some were restorations.

In Rome the public distributions and the games were not
interrupted; it was only after the abdication of 305 that Galerius ventured to abolish all special consideration for the
ancient mistress of the world. But Diocletian had offended
Rome in another respect, as has already been indicated. Behind his baths, surrounded on three sides by the Wall of
Aurelian, there is a large vineyard, later the property of the
Jesuits, with dilapidated arched cells built against the wall.
This had once been the Praetorian camp, the denizens of
which had so often caused the imperial purple to flutter in the
breeze upon their swords' points. Many previous attempts had
been made to disband and supplant them; but in the third
century the original practice seems to have been restored,
namely, that a few thousand men were enlisted in the vicinity
of Rome and in adjacent parts of Italy; these are to be regarded not as an Imperial Guard but rather as a garrison for
the capital. Now Diocletian reduced their numbers considerably, surely not merely out of fear of the restless and demanding Italians in their midst, but also for reasons of economy and
because the course of events had supplied a new corps in their
place. The Empire had been saved by a great series of Illyrian

Emperors beginning with Decius; small wonder that thirty years of war had surrounded them with a faithful band of compatriots who were closer to the Emperors than the Latins and Sabines of the Praetorians. These Illyrians were further recommended by their effective use of their national weapon. They comprised two legions, each of six thousand men, now honored by being called Jovians and Herculians, after the supplementary names (*agnomina*) of the Emperors; previously they had been called Martiobarbuli, after the leaden balls of which each man carried five (or five pair) fastened to his shield and which they could sling with the speed and force of an arrow. They now received official preferment above all other legions, but this does not necessarily imply that they were permanently quartered near the Emperor's person. Though the sentiments which the Praetorians had provoked in Rome were chiefly fear and hatred of themselves, their dissolution was now looked upon as an assault upon the majesty of the capital. Common antipathy fashioned a bond, and the few Praetorians who remained in the camp at Rome later participated in the insurrection against Galerius, having reached an understanding with Senate and people.

The Romans might bewail and abhor this turn of events, but in point of fact no injury had been done them. Eventually the great delusion that the Emperor still continued as the magistrate and representative of the local Roman or even Italian life and people and that he ruled the world in their name must have been dissipated. If Diocletian had not given outward confirmation of the extinction of Roman primacy by removal of the imperial residence, introduction of Oriental court ceremonial, depreciation of the Senate, and diminution of the Praetorians, Christianity must soon have performed the same office in its own manner, for of necessity Christianity created new centers of gravity for its power. Presently we shall have to recount under what mighty and fearful circumstances Diocletian's innovations were given effect — while he and his colleagues were forced to defend the Empire upon all its frontiers and wrest it from usurpers' hands bit by bit; these things should not be forgotten in shaping our judgment of Diocletian.

As regards the higher pitch of court procedure and the new ceremonial, there were doubtless people enough to welcome it with enthusiasm. In periods of transition, such as Diocletian's was, the Emperor still felt the need of receiving public praise; a thorough military despotism may dispense with this species of recognition, despise it, or even resent it. But men had only just emerged from the ancient world, with the common and open participation or interest in public affairs which was the breath of its life. Education was still rhetorical and public discourses occupied a position of such importance in the lives of men as the modern world is incapable of imagining. Among these discourses were the panegyrics delivered at annual festivals or other solemn occasions by some distinguished rhetor of the city or vicinity in the presence of the Emperor or some high official. We have preserved the Younger Pliny's well-known *Panegyric* on Trajan; then, after a long gap, as it happens, a heap of eulogies of Diocletian's colleagues together with a few on later Emperors. As historical sources these speeches must naturally be used with caution; but they tell us much that is valuable, and they are by no means negligible as literature. Their flattery is doubtless a continuation of the style which characterized the lost panegyrics of the third century. With realism bordering on impertinence the rhetor identifies himself with the Emperor present in person, whom he conceives in the most exalted terms. One after the other he divines the Emperor's thoughts, plans, and sentiments; here the subtle courtier exercises' restraint, because even idealizing fiction, let alone truth, may be indiscreet. But this is overweighed by a penetrating bouquet of direct and ecstatic praise calculated to delight the senses of a Maximian — though Maximian scarcely possessed sufficient learning to understand the flattering allusions and associations. Much play is made with Maximian's cognomen Herculius, and his history is constantly intertwined with and made parallel to that of Hercules; but even Hercules' prowess falls short, for his victory over Geryon was a petty thing compared to Maximian's over the Bagaudae.

Comparison with Jupiter, usually reserved only for the elder Emperor, carries the panegyrist somewhat further; Jupiter's childhood, like that of Maximian, who grew up on the banks of the Danube, was filled with the alarums of war. Tirelessly the speaker heaps image upon image to celebrate the concord of the Emperors: their reign is common as is the light of day to a pair of eyes; forasmuch as they were born on the same day (see page 49), theirs is a twin rule like that of the Heraclids in Sparta; Rome is now happier than under Romulus and Remus, of whom the one slew the other; Rome may now style herself both Herculea and Jovia. Just as the history of Hercules was employed to glorify Maximian, so was the myth of Zeus applied to Diocletian, particularly with respect to Zeus' omnipresence, which the Emperor's rapid journeys seemed to emulate. But through the measured cadences of these periods there echoes a bold and shameless preference of Maximian, which that Emperor perhaps was pleased to hear, with a straight face. "By accepting co-regency you have given Diocletian more than you have received from him. . . . You emulate Scipio Africanus; Diocletian emulates you." Mamertinus ventured to declaim such sentences as these before the whole court at the palace in Treves. Interspersed among such sentences, to be sure, there was an opulent flow of flowery adulation for both Emperors alike. "Just as the Rhine may confidently dry its stream after Maximian's victories beyond its banks, so the Euphrates need no longer protect Syria now that Diocletian has passed over it. . . . You both postpone your triumphs for the sake of ever new victories; always you hasten to greater things." Much lesser achievements were also boldly inflated. On the occasion of the meeting of 291, when Diocletian hurried to Milan from the East and Maximian crossed the Alps thither in midwinter, Mamertinus declaimed: "One who did not travel with you might well believe that Sun and Moon lent you their diurnal and nocturnal chariots. The might of your majesty shielded you from bitter frost. Gentle spring zephyrs and sunshine followed you where all else froze. Beshrew thee, Hannibal, with thy crossing of the Alps!" It is quite in keeping with this conceit that the reign of these

Emperors marked a sudden increase in the earth's fertility. A
few years earlier the poet Calpurnius Siculus had employed a
similar and more pronounced bucolic tone (in his eighth or
fourth Eclogue) to hymn the Caesar Numerian: in his presence forests fell silent for reverence, lambs frolicked gaily,
fleeces and milk grew abundant, fields and orchards luxuriant,
for within his mortal frame there lurked a god, perhaps supreme Jupiter himself.

The orator Eumenius' approach to the educated Caesar,
Constantius Chlorus, was somewhat more delicate. For example, he speaks of escorting the youth of Gaul to the large
map of the world which was painted upon the wall in the hall
at Autun, between the temple of Apollo and the Capitol with
its sanctuary of Minerva. "There let us see how Diocletian's
clemency pacifies the wild insurrection of Egypt; how Maximian shatters the Moors; how under your hands, Lord Constantius, Batavians and Britons again raise their sorrowful
countenances from their jungles and floods; or how you,
Caesar Galerius, tread Persian bows and quivers down to
earth. For now it is become a joy to behold the painted earth,
for we can see upon it naught that is not ours." His spirited
description of the new Golden Age wins our forgiveness for
the playful symbolism which the orator contrives for the fourfold rule. He sees the number four as the fundamental principle in the cosmic order, expressed in the four elements, the
four seasons, even the four continents. It is not for naught that
a lustrum follows upon the passing of four years; in the heavens
a four-horse team flies before the chariot of the sun; and the
two great luminaries of heaven, sun and moon, are attended
by two lesser lights, the morning star and the evening star. It
would not be surprising if somewhere in Gaul a mosaic should
be excavated in which these notions were worked into an artistic composition. Plastic art and rhetoric must frequently
have resorted to similar means for tasks of this sort. Eumenius,
by the way, is distinguished from the other panegyrists not
only by his tact and his talent; we shall see in him a quite
honest patriot who employed flattery not for personal advantage. Here as in a thousand other cases historical judgment

must be careful to discern what the age and the environment impose upon the individual and what he does by virtue of his own resolution.

Whether language had grown several degrees more servile in Diocletian's court and had been infected by phrases of adulation we do not know. In any case ceremonial requirements, as far as they related to the person of the Emperor, were still quite simple and innocent. Certainly they are not to be compared with those of the later Byzantine court, where in the tenth century the Emperor Constantine Porphyrogenitus was himself constrained to act the court chamberlain and compose a systematic treatise to introduce contemporaries and posterity to the labyrinth of sacred usages, to whose bondage the Autocratores, all-holy and beloved of God, were gradually forced to submit after Church and court ceremonial had interpenetrated and augmented one another.

If from the throne downward a hierarchy of title and rank gradually overwhelmed Roman society, the fault is not necessarily Diocletian's. The ossification which now overtook ancient life made some such development inevitable. For a long while the regime had been almost purely military. Such a regime must always fashion the state mechanism after its own image; subordination is its very soul, and organization must be by ranks and grades, with strict and visible marks of gradation. Many institutions of this character, which tend to be attributed to Diocletian, may well have been introduced by his predecessors. The complete transformation of the state took place only under Constantine.

Diocletian did considerably increase the number of officials. It was surely not so much the four courts as the four administrations that multiplied the burdens. According to Lactantius, Diocletian's reign is liable to the following fearful indictments: "Each of the four rulers kept for himself more soldiers than previous Emperors had had altogether. There was an unexampled rise in taxation. The number of those who received so far exceeded the number of those who paid that the exhausted peasants forsook their farms, and cultivated land reverted to forest. To make terror universal, the provinces were cut up into sections, and every region, every city, was overburdened with crowds of officials, with tax collectors, vice-gerents of prefects, and the like. In consequence little was done for the common interest; nay, there were only condemnations, proscriptions, extortions without number or end, accompanied by intolerable violence." Diocletian is further charged with accumulating infinite treasure.

We now listen to a Christian who is in other respects no less partisan than Lactantius. This is what Eusebius says: "What words are adequate to describe the abundance and the blessed times before the persecution, when the Emperors showed us peace and friendship, when their vicennalia were celebrated in profound peace with festivals, spectacles, and banquets." Can any part of Lactantius' indictment be justified?

Diocletian's increase of the army was absolutely essential, for, as we shall see, he must needs wrest half the Empire from the hands of usurpers and barbarians who had taken possession of it. What strength was necessary for this purpose, none could judge better than he. Concerning the proportions of his increase we have no details; anyone who wishes may believe the fiction writer who says that Diocletian's army was more than four times the size of Aurelian's or Probus'.

Next we glance at the charge of hoarding wealth, a charge which no prince can escape. Many rulers have in fact accumulated great treasures of precious metal, taking a false view of its absolute worth, and have been unable to bring themselves to spend it usefully at the suitable moment. Oriental despotism generally is afflicted with this fault, and its subjects follow their despot's example and bury every piece of silver in the ground. But miserliness can hardly be the explanation in the case of Diocletian. Expenditures for regaining and reconstituting the shattered Empire must have been too enormous for any disproportionately large surplus to have remained in the treasury. The requirements of border security alone, the fortresses which stretched from the Netherlands to the Red Sea, together with their garrisons, would make any surplus impossible even in the later and more peaceful period of his reign.

It was necessary for the Empire to strain every effort, and when objectives are as great and as successfully achieved as Diocletian's generally were, the ruler must at least be absolved of the vulgar charge that he afflicted people only to devour their gold and silver himself. His numerous buildings, indeed, might raise a suspicion of extravagance, but far the greater number appear to have been political gifts to specific cities, by means of which the need for garrisons was reduced. Compared to the extravagant building of Constantine, Diocletian's expenditures are inconsiderable. The palace at Salonae covered a large area, it is true, but its individual rooms were distinguished neither in height nor in size and were not to be compared with the colossal halls of the baths in Rome. In the reconstruction of Nicomedia some expropriations may have been made, as had been done in the city foundations of the Hellenistic kings and was to be done in the refounding of Byzantium; but to believe that Diocletian leveled capital charges against the owner of any fair estate and any handsome dwelling that he saw is possible only to the credulous. It is sad enough that many prosperous people were ruined because of the pressing need for money; but this was doubtless the work of cruel officials, with whom the administration had been cursed long before Diocletian's day.

The new division of the Empire into one hundred and one provinces and twelve dioceses was certainly not introduced by a regime like Diocletian's without good and sufficient grounds; nor was the number of officials increased without need. Diocletian himself was the most industrious official of his Empire. Besides his military campaigns, he was constantly traveling hither and yon on hurried journeys, always governing and making decisions. His itinerary for 293 and 294, for example, can be established almost week by week and day by day by the dating of his rescripts. The lawbooks contain more than twelve hundred of his rescripts on matters of private law. If we are to name a specific ground for the new division of the Empire into smaller provinces and for the increase in the number of officials, it would be that the existing machinery seemed inadequate to the Emperor and that he regarded stricter supervision and better execution of orders as essential. He could only work with the material that he found ready to hand, and none could know better than he how unsatisfactory that material was. In any case, distinctions between the provinces were now finally abolished in favor of a uniform administration. What Diocletian began Constantine completed and perfected.

All are agreed that the Roman system of finance was on the whole bad and oppressive, and there is no ground for assuming that Diocletian had a superior insight for improving the national economy; the most efficient of the Emperors had none. Modern conditions in the great European nations demonstrate how great the interval can be between thorough understanding of these matters and actual abolition of what is bad. But what the elder Aurelius Victor, one of Diocletian's fairest critics, makes as a special charge against him can easily be interpreted to his credit. In a passage unfortunately corrupt and ambiguous the charge is made that "a portion of Italy" was drawn upon for certain general taxes and duties (*pensiones*); "under the restrictions then obtaining" this situation was tolerable, but in the course of the fourth century its effect was to ruin the country. Of whatever nature these taxes may have been, it was in any case just that Italy should help carry the Empire's burdens, since it was no longer able to save the Empire and to rule it.

For criticism of the Roman financial system in general, reference must be made to specialist researches in that subject; but one particular point must be touched upon here. For the year 302, various annals record that "the Emperors at that time commanded that there should be cheapness" — that is, Diocletian established maximum prices for foodstuffs. According to views prevalent today, no measure is to be more severely condemned than the establishment of ceiling prices; their maintenance premises the ceaseless rhythm of the guillotine, as the instructive example of the French National Convention demonstrates. The measure presumes either the most extreme

E

and desperate need, or a total disregard of the true concepts of value and price. The inevitable consequences ensued. Goods were hidden, despite the prohibition they grew dearer than ever, and countless sellers were made liable to the death penalty, until the law was rescinded.

An exact record of this measure is preserved in the famous inscription of Stratonicea, which reproduces the entire edict along with several hundred prescribed prices (in part illegible and difficult to interpret). In the preamble the Emperors express themselves somewhat as follows: "The price of things bought in the markets or brought daily into the cities has so far exceeded all bounds that measureless avarice is restrained neither by rich harvests nor by abundance of goods. . . . Unprincipled greed appears wherever our armies, following the commands of the public weal, march, not only in villages and cities but also upon all highways, with the result that prices of foodstuffs mount not only fourfold and eightfold, but transcend all measure. Frequently a single purchase robs the soldier of his pay and our gifts. . . . Our law shall fix a measure and a limit to this greed." There follow threats of severe penalties for such as transgress the law.

The considerations which led to this measure are as enigmatic as the provisions of the measure itself. The readiest explanation is that some cabal of speculators in the East had caused a rapid rise in prices of indispensable foodstuffs, that everyone suffered from the rise, and that the suffering of the army threatened far the greatest and most immediate danger. The preponderant portion of the Empire's income was in kind, but it may not have been possible to make sufficient stocks available to individual garrisons at the moment of need. When the resolution was taken to correct the situation, perhaps in haste or under emotional stress, the measure was extended to cover all classes of people and all kinds of goods and to afford particular assistance to urban populations.

The tables of the inscription constitute a document of the first importance, for they provide an official indication of the contemporary value of goods and services in relation to one another. The reduction of individual values to terms of modern currency is much more difficult.° Scholars are not yet agreed on the value of the unit which is indicated in the edict merely by an asterisk; some understand it to be the silver denarius, others the copper denarius. If the coin is silver, the prices seem monstrous; if copper, they are not very different from our own. Hence copper has the greater probability, provided that our assumptions regarding weights and measures are correct. On the basis of a copper denarius the chief results are as follows: Fixed wages seem somewhat lower than the average which obtained in France three decades ago (1820), calculated at 1.25 francs. Farm laborers received 65 centimes daily; masons, carpenters, blacksmiths, bakers, lime-burners, 1.25 francs; muleteers, shepherds, water-carriers, sewer-cleaners, and the like, board and 50 to 65 centimes. Among teachers the *paedagogus* (in the strict sense) received 1.25 francs for each ward monthly, as did also the teacher of reading and the teacher of writing; the arithmetic teacher, on the other hand, and the stenography teacher received 1.90 francs; the teacher of Greek language and literature 5 francs, and the teachers of Latin and of geometry the same. The prices of shoes were as follows: for peasants and drivers, 3 francs; for soldiers, 2.50 francs; for patricians, 3.75; for women, 1.50. Naturally, there were variations in quality and workmanship. Prices of meat, in Roman pounds of 12 ounces, were: beef and mutton, about 28 centimes; lamb and pork, about 35 centimes, not to mention the various sausages described and listed in detail, and the special delicacies. Ordinary wine, reckoning the *sextarius* at half a liter, was somewhat cheaper than at present, namely, 20 centimes. Aged and better quality wine was 60 centimes; the noble Italian wines, including Sabine and Falernian, were

° A text, translation, and interpretation of Diocletian's edict on prices may be found in an appendix to Volume 5 of Tenney Frank's *Economic Survey of Ancient Rome* (Baltimore, 1940). The real value of the prices listed is impossible to determine, for we have no fixed gauge like the price of wheat, which is elsewhere used to determine values. It has therefore been thought best to let Burckhardt's estimates in terms of French francs of his own day stand; these give the correct relationship of the prices of commodities to one another, which is essentially all that the edict can tell us. — Translator.

75 centimes. Beer (*cervesia cami?*) was 10 centimes, and a cheaper variety (*zythum*) 5 centimes. These figures, adopted from the calculations of Dureau de la Malle, are doubtless too low, but they serve to demonstrate proportional relationships in values. Unfortunately, no price is given for wheat, which is a reliable index. In the edict itself the prices are doubtless set at a high level, for to set low prices would have been futile from the start; we must not be deceived by the statement of the Idatian chronicles that "the Emperors . . . commanded that there should be cheapness."

Of all Diocletian's measures, his introduction of maximum prices can perhaps be most sharply criticized. For once the absolute state in its reliance upon its means of enforcement was guilty of a miscalculation; nevertheless we must not overlook the Emperor's good intentions. These are apparent in the new tax registers which he caused to be made throughout the Empire in the last year of his reign (305). Our source tells us, indeed, that "he caused the land to be measured and burdened it with levies"; but the intention was clearly not merely to raise the tax but to apportion it more justly.

Considered all in all, Diocletian's reign may be regarded as one of the best and most beneficent which the Empire had ever enjoyed. If we are not prejudiced by the dreadful pictures of the Christian persecutions and by the distortions and exaggerations of Lactantius, the traits of the great ruler assume a quite different aspect. A contemporary who dedicated a work to him may not be rated a competent witness; nevertheless it may be mentioned that according to the biographer of Marcus Aurelius in the *Historia Augusta* (19), Marcus was Diocletian's model for morality, for social behavior, and for clemency, and occupied a principal place in Diocletian's household cult. A later author also merits citation. The elder Aurelius Victor, who was by no means blind to the darker side of Diocletian and is even hostile in questions of the Italian policy, says of him: "He suffered himself to be called Lord, but behaved like a father; doubtless he wished to show, in his wisdom, that not evil names but evil deeds are what matter." And a little further, after enumerating Diocletian's wars: "The institutions of peace also were strengthened by just laws. . . . Diligent zeal was shown for provisioning, for the city of Rome, for the welfare of the officials; and incentives to improvement were given by promoting the efficient and penalizing malefactors." And finally, in connection with the abdication, Victor concludes: "In the conflict of opinions perception of the true situation has been obscured. In our judgment it wanted a lofty character to despise all pomp and to step down to ordinary life."

Furthermore this absolute ruler, who was forced to win his realm back from usurpers step by step, was large-spirited enough to do away with political espionage. Apparently he found that his authority was so fully secured by its division that he no longer required such service. In any case political intelligence had fallen into the hands of a corporation which might have constituted a danger to the regime itself. Originally, the *frumentarii* were supply officers who were sent ahead of the armies; later they were ordnance officers; and finally they came to be used for transmitting and carrying out various questionable orders. They degenerated into a clique which employed false charges and the dread of false charges, especially in remote provinces, for blackmailing respectable citizens. Not much more is known of them, but we may imagine that their abuses were frightful. They were a band of wicked men, enjoying high protection, conniving with and supporting one another, eavesdropping upon and exploiting every suspicious mood of the Emperors; and they used their position to terrify old and respected families in Gaul, Spain, or Syria and to force them to sacrifice their all for fear of being denounced as participants in an imaginary conspiracy. With Constantine, though he generally showed his hatred of informers, the thing came up again, but under another name. Again it was the managers of the Emperor's transport who undertook the despicable role, under the title of *agentes in rebus* or *veredarii*.

In other respects the despotism of the Roman Emperors did not show so much concern with the painstaking supervision of trifles, with regulations for each and every detail of

life, specifically with the dictation and control of cultural
tendencies, as is likely to infect the modern state. The rule of
the Emperors, which has won such ill repute for attending so
little to the life of the individual, for exacting such oppressive
taxes, for providing for public security so badly, was content
to confine itself to its most essential purposes and to make no
restrictions on the local life of the provinces which had once
been subdued with streams of blood. On the other hand, the
government failed to intervene when it might well have done
so. Thus it suffered not only local but also class distinctions
to persist and to develop. An aristocracy of freedom from
taxation was formed, for example, of senatorial families, of
teachers and physicians appointed by the state, and of several
other categories, among which Christian priests were eventually included. There could no longer be any thought of a
new and vital organization of the state; the most that even a
ruler like Diocletian could hope to attain was the preservation
of the extent of the Empire and a moderate improvement of
corruptions within it.

III

INDIVIDUAL PROVINCES
AND NEIGHBORING COUNTRIES : THE WEST

No secret was made, in the preceding chapter, of the inadequacy of generalizations concerning many of the most important issues in the later Roman Empire. What is lacking is the essential basis — knowledge of conditions in the individual provinces. Scattered notices in the historians, the mass of inscriptions which have been collected, and monumental remains yield many certain and valuable facts, some directly and some by inference; but the large intervening gaps which cannot be supplied are all the more distressing. Here we can only assemble, in the manner of a digression, the essential facts concerning those provinces which, as the gaping wounds in the ailing body politic, would in any case claim careful attention. First we shall glance at contemporary Gaul, with whose fate that of Britain was closely bound.

The great tyrants of Gaul had once vigorously defended the West against the invading Germans. But the violence of their successions, their continual warfare against foreign enemies, and finally civil strife between the party of Tetricus and that of the Italian Emperors, which was ended by Aurelian's campaign in Gaul and his battle at Châlons-sur-Marne — all resulted in an intolerable increase of general misery and the dissolution of all political and moral restraints. Now the campaign against the Franks and the Alemanni was renewed; the latter were defeated at Windisch by the General Constantius

Chlorus under Aurelian (274), and indeed on the same day that his son Constantine was born. But victories seemed only to summon new hosts of these inexhaustible and youthful peoples across the Rhine. It no longer availed for capacious colonels to drink their envoys under the table and then draw their secrets out. They were no longer impressed when the Emperor received their deputations with calculated pomp before his crescent-shaped lines, himself clad in purple upon a lofty pulpit, before him the golden eagles of the legions, the imperial images, and the banners of the armies inscribed in gold and borne upon silver lances. Under Probus the war again assumed huge proportions, and without that great Emperor's skill and courage Gaul would definitely have been lost. Even so there arose a new party, chiefly in Lyons and its vicinity, which openly strove for a continuation of a Gallic empire after the model of Posthumus and Victorina. When Diocletian subsequently divided the imperial authority, he may have had to take these circumstances into consideration. But before that happened Probus' conquests in southern Germany were again lost, and unhappy Gaul was again traversed by German hordes. Carinus did defeat them, and left an army in Gaul; this army, however, he had to recall for his war against the usurper Julian and against the approaching Diocletian. Thereupon the entire social structure of Gaul went awry.

Now, and repeatedly thereafter in the great crises in ancient France, it was the peasants who suddenly rose with terrifying power. At the time they lived in forms of slavery which had been handed down from ancient days, though the relationship was not always called by that name. A number of peasants were actual farm slaves; others were serfs, bound to the soil; still others were called *coloni*, that is, tenants who yielded half their produce to their lords. There were also better situated lessees, who paid their rent in money; and finally there was a mass of so-called free workers and wage earners. But all were now united by a common misfortune. The landlords, drained by confiscatory levies for the requirements of the divided state, wished to recoup their losses from the peasants, just as the French nobility did after the Battle of Poitiers, when they required ransom money for the knights who had been taken captive with John the Good. The result in the first instance is styled the Bagauda, in the second the Jacquerie (1358). Peasants and shepherds left their huts in crowds, and wandered about as beggars. Turned away on all sides and driven out by the city garrisons, they gathered into *bagaudae*, which is to say, "bands." They slaughtered their cattle and devoured their flesh; they armed themselves with their farm tools, mounted their farm horses, and rode through the plain country, not only to satisfy their hunger but to devastate it in their unreasoning despair. Then they threatened the cities, where an impoverished proletariat eager for plunder would frequently open the city gates to them. General despair and the native Gallic craving for adventure shortly so increased their army that they could venture to raise two of their number, Aelianus and Amandus, to be Emperors, and so to renew the claim for a Gallic imperium. The court of these rustic Emperors must have been motley and peculiar; the third century had set many stout peasants and sons of slaves upon the throne of the world, but generally such as had served an apprenticeship to royal authority in the armies and then in the imperial General Staff. Aelianus and Amandus could make no such claim, but perhaps they could make another which outweighed their other shortcomings. Christian tradition, documented from the seventh century, made Christians of them and thus justified their stand against the idolatrous Emperors. It can certainly be assumed that there were numbers of Christians among the poor and wretched folk who joined the Bagaudae, and also persecuted men of every sort, even criminals.

It appears that southern and western Gaul was less affected by the movement than the north and east, where pressure must have been much greater because of the barbarians. An hour beyond Vincennes the strong current of the Marne, shortly before it flows into the Seine, forms a peninsula, upon whose ridge the Benedictine abbey of Saint-Maur-des-Fossés was later built. The ancient Celts had shown special preferences for such points in choosing their fortresses (*oppida*), and certainly the peninsula already had rampart, moat, and walls when Aelianus and Amandus made it the Bagaudae Fortress; it bore this name for centuries, though very little can have been built upon it in the year 285–286. From this impregnable point, which could be approached by no ford or shoal, they carried their raids near and far, and to this fortress they brought their booty. In time they grew bold enough not only to impose their confiscations upon weaker cities without more ado, but also to beleaguer stronger cities. They succeeded in taking the ancient and spacious city of Augustodunum (Autun), and they showed no mercy either to its temples or to its basilicas or baths; everything was plundered and destroyed, and the inhabitants were driven into exile.

The Bagaudae had to be got rid of before they should similarly destroy one city after another and with them every stronghold against the barbarians. This was the task of the then Caesar, Maximianus Herculius, and his success earned him the title of Augustus. We learn only that he accomplished the task quickly and easily, crushing some of the bands by direct attack and forcing others to surrender by starvation, assisted by a plague. Whether any direct relief of the oppressive burdens which had provoked the uprising ensued is more than doubtful, for complaints of excessive taxes rather increased than otherwise. But indirectly the situation of the country in general improved, for the Germans remained humbled for some decades and usurpations ceased. But in the fifth century and perhaps even in the fourth similar causes produced similar effects. Bagauda again raised its head, and we may almost surmise that it had never wholly ceased.

But we return to the period of Diocletian. Many regions of Gaul continued prostrate. The landlords of Autun, for example, who were deep in debt, had not so far recovered by the time of Constantine that they could set their old irrigation and reclamation works in progress. Their soil degenerated to marshes and briers; the Burgundy vines withered, and the wooded hills became the haunts of wild beasts. "Once the plain as far as the Saône was happy and rich, as long as the waters were kept under control; now the lowlands have become riverbed or sloughs. The mighty vines are run to wood, and new ones cannot be planted. . . . From the point where the road turns toward Belgian Gaul [that is, from Autun] all is desolate, mute, and gloomy wilderness. Even the military road is rough and uneven, and makes the transportation of produce as well as courier service difficult." Once more during the Middle Ages, about the time of the Maid of Orléans, things had so far degenerated that it could be said that from Picardy to Lorraine no peasant's hut stood erect. But in twenty years a vital nation may recover from what would be a death-blow to a declining people.

What price Maximian's and Constantius' strenuous and constant exertions? The protection of the Rhine, to which they devoted the highest skill and courage, afforded the possibility of recovery for the interior, but not recovery itself. Nevertheless the efforts of the two princes produced substantial results, and the Germans felt their blows over a long period. Several times Maximian forced his way across the Rhine, like Probus, and subdued (287–288) Burgundians, Alemanni, Heruli, and Franks. Constantius liberated the country of the Batavii from the Franks (294) and defeated the Alemanni, who had again broken in, in the frightful battle at Langres (298; according to some, 300) where sixty thousand of their number perished. The Romans, indeed, were aided by an internal crisis among the Germans, of which we unfortunately know little. "The East Goths," we are told, "destroyed the Burgundians, but the Alemanni took up arms for the vanquished. The West Goths, with a host of Taifales, campaigned against the Vandals and the Gepidi. . . . The Burgundians seized the territory of the Alemanni, but paid for it with heavy losses, and now the Alemanni wish to regain what they lost." Here, obviously, is the explanation of the singular truce, broken only for short periods, between Romans and Germans under Constantine the Great. The profoundly significant changes which he was to introduce could be carried out without too great interruption from abroad. Simultaneously, in the far East the peace of 297 and the minority of the Sassanid Shapur II must have served the same end.

Meanwhile Maximian and Constantius had completed the

fortification of the Rhine as a boundary. It was to these "fortresses with troops of cavalry and cohorts" near the river that the reputed restoration of "cities sunk in the forest-night and haunted by wild beasts" must have been limited, although the panegyrist to whom we owe these words makes them the text for a general eulogy of the returning Golden Age. Where there had been cities, the fourth century knew only fortresses, and even so there were significant gaps.

Perhaps only Treves, the imperial residence of the North, was restored with any magnificence. From the ruins which the visit of the Franks, perhaps also of the Bagaudae, left behind, there arose a great circus, several basilicas, a new forum, a huge palace, and several other luxurious structures. Unhappy Autun found a warm advocate in Eumenius, who here shows his better side. He was secretary (*magister sacrae memoriae*) to Constantius and received a pension, probably in reward for important services, of more than twenty-six thousand francs along with a sinecure as president of the schools of Autun, where his grandfather, a native of Athens, had occupied a professorship. Now he made it his ambition to devote his entire income, though he had a family, to the benefit of these schools, and moreover to direct the gracious attention first of Constantius and then of Constantine to these badly disrupted institutions and to the ruined city. It is such local patriotism after the ancient manner that reconciles us to and engages our sympathy for so many of the Greek and Asiatic Sophists of the first and second centuries of the Christian era who appear in the *Lives* of Philostratus. We must learn to understand the singular mixture of nobleness and flattery which that period produced. "With humble adoration I receive this reward," says Eumenius, "for the honor it confers upon me, but I wish to grant it as a gift. . . . For who can now be of so lowly a spirit, and so disinclined toward striving for glory, that he would not wish to create a memorial and to leave behind him a goodly reputation?" The restored schools would teach men how to praise their princes worthily; eloquence could be put to no fairer use. Old Maximian himself is made to stand, quite undeservedly, as parallel to Hercules Musagetes, the leader of the Muses; for nominating a scholarch for Autun was to him as important a matter as dealing with a troop of cavalry or a Praetorian cohort. But the restoration of the city as a whole had to wait a long while; only Constantine, with a significant exemption from taxation and with direct subsidies, was able to give it appreciable help. Eumenius' description of Constantine's entry (311) is almost moving: "For you we have decorated the streets that lead to the Palatium as our poor resources afford. Nevertheless we bear at least the symbols of all our guilds and corporations, and the images of all our gods. Our few musical instruments you have met several times because by byways we hastened to overtake you time and again. You have probably noticed the well-intentioned vanity of poverty."

In the desolate northern and eastern regions of Gaul the system introduced under Claudius and Probus could only be continued for better or worse: German war captives were settled as farm slaves, some even as free peasants, and some, indeed, as border guards. The panegyrists find it a matter for praise that all market halls were filled with captives who sat awaiting their fate; that the Chamavian and the Friesian, once such nimble thieves, were now cultivating the fields in the sweat of their brow and bringing cattle and corn to market; that these erstwhile barbarians were now subjected to Roman conscription and military discipline; that Constantius had brought the Franks from the remotest barbarian shores to educate them to agriculture and military service in the wildernesses of Gaul; and so on. In point of fact these were experiments under constraint of necessity, and indeed pregnant with danger; northern Gaul was already half Germanized. As soon as the kindred of these captives should again invade Gaul they would find faithful allies in the settlers, unless a considerable period should intervene.

Constantine's good fortune, talent, and cruelty succeeded in preventing this eventuality. In the first year after his father's death (306) it fell to his lot to defeat an alliance of several Frankish peoples who belonged to the later so-called Ripuarian Franks (apparently the Chatti and Ampsivarii, along with the

Bructerii). During his father's lifetime they had crossed the Rhine; now he crushed them and took their princes Ascarich and Regais (or Merogais) captive. Both were thrown to the beasts in the amphitheater at Treves, whose impressive ruins may yet be visited in the vineyards. The same fate befell crowds of captive Bructerii "who were too unreliable to serve as soldiers, too willful to serve as slaves"; "the wild beasts were wearied because of the large number of their victims."

Twice again, in 313 and about 319, short campaigns against the Franks are briefly mentioned by the historians; their importance must therefore have been slight. Constantine even regained possession of a section of the right bank of the Rhine, and at Cologne he built a great stone bridge, which stood until the middle of the tenth century, but in so dilapidated and dangerous a condition that Archbishop Bruno, brother of Otto the Great, had it pulled down. The bridgehead was Castra Divitensia, modern Deutz. These successes were commemorated by a periodic festival, the Frankish Games (*ludi Francici*). At the triumphal celebration of 313 the Franks devoted to death rushed to meet the wild animals with impatient longing.

Attempts to construct a complete picture of ancient Gaul as it may have been under Diocletian and Constantine are futile, for our more abundant sources begin only with Valentinian I. What has been said above yields an approximate notion of the lot of the rural population. But the Gaul felt his poverty more keenly than many other peoples of the Empire. Of a superior physique, tall and strong, he was careful of his person, loved cleanliness, and disliked going about in rags. He was a great guzzler, especially of wine and other intoxicating beverages, but he had the temperament of the born soldier who knew no fear and shunned no hardship until advanced old age. It was thought that this was attributable to his copious supply of strong blood, and he was compared to the lean and emaciated southerner, who could indeed still hunger with an onion a day, but in battle was parsimonious of his blood, of which he had so little to spare. Neither did the Gallic women, fair and robust as they were, shun battle; they were terrible when they raised their white arms and distributed blows and kicks "like catapult-shots." Such a peasantry cannot be pushed too far, and a certain degree of misery will inevitably provoke an outbreak — as indeed then came to pass.

But in the cities, too, poverty and need prevailed. The most important possession of the city dweller in this almost exclusively agricultural country was land let to tenants or cultivated by slaves; hence the urban dweller shared the misery of the rustics to the full. Furthermore here, as in the Empire as a whole, the state oppressed the rich by the institution of decurions, inasmuch as it made the owners of more than twenty-five acres of land responsible for the assessed, and often capriciously increased, taxes of the district. Individuals occasionally sought to evade this responsibility by desperate measures, later even by flight to the barbarians. If we nevertheless find examples of extraordinarily wealthy people and great luxury, the readiest explanation is the persistence of so-called senatorial families whose status was hereditary and who, besides their title of *clarissimi* and other distinctions of honor, also enjoyed exemption from the decurionate which was the ruin of other city dwellers. Another explanation is implied in a remarkable trait of the ancient Gallic national character: they were partial to factions of all sorts, and these tended, especially in times of need, to a client relationship, the protection of the weak by the strong. This relationship had assumed a hypertrophied form by the time of Julius Caesar, who found the masses in bondage to the nobility. Half a millennium later the same plaint recurs practically unaltered. Salvian laments the lot of the smallholder who, reduced to despair by oppressive officials and unjust judges, delivered himself and his property to the great of the land. "Then their plots of land become highways, and they the *coloni* of the rich. The son inherits nothing because the father once required protection." In this way it became possible for an individual grandee, the single lessee of public lands and the like, to join endless *latifundia* together and then, after the ancient manner, display generosity to his city or province, for example by erecting splendid public buildings, while all about him languished or lived at his mercy. If this cannot be demonstrated for Gaul in individual cases, it is still the only explanation for the contrast between the outward magnificence of the cities (in so far as this was not the result of imperial munificence) and the notorious poverty. In temples, amphitheaters, theaters, triumphal arches, fountains, baths, monumental gates, the cities of southern Gaul especially can compare with most of those of Italy, as their ruins testify. Even today they are the ornaments of their localities, just as once when they were yet intact they delighted the poet Ausonius. Aside from gifts, the decurions doubtless often helped defray the necessary expenditures from their own or the city's resources.

Of Gaul's educational institutions we shall speak presently; they secured the country its significant position with reference to the Roman culture of which it was so proud. There was no longer any desire to return to the old Celtic ways; every effort was directed toward becoming Roman. The people must have made special efforts, for example, to forget their own language; Roman colonization and administration alone would never have suppressed it so thoroughly. Perhaps the language situation in Alsace may offer a certain analogy to that in ancient Gaul; the old language continues in daily life, but in all matters of higher education or official procedure the new assumes its place and everyone prides himself on it, however faulty his command of the new language may be. The ancient religion of the Gauls also had to adapt itself to Roman dress and the gods not only submitted (where such a thing was feasible) to the Roman style in names, but also in plastic representation; that style seemed not a little provincial and rank once it ventured out of the ancient cities of the South which understood art. But in one case at least the classical sculptor was required to represent a purely Celtic ideal, to wit, that of the mysterious Matrons, who were customarily enthroned in triads, with marvelous headdress and with bowls of fruit in their laps. A whole crowd of local divinities, whose names could for that reason not be translated into Latin, are represented only by dedicatory inscriptions without images.

But what of the Druids, that once so mighty priesthood

which administered the Gallic religion? Of old, together with the nobility, they had constituted the ruling class. The nobles controlled government and war, the Druids the judiciary and the care of occult sciences and powerful superstitions, whereby they enveloped the entire life of the people as with a great web. Their ban was a fearful punishment; a man excluded from sacrifice was accounted unclean and outside the law. Being dedicated to the deity, the Druids were free of imposts and military service. Perhaps their sanctuaries (or temples, if they may be so called) possessed broad domains; certainly they had treasures of precious metals, so abundant that they became proverbial.

From this lofty estate the Druids had long been reduced, but we cannot say when or how. The enormous extortions of Julius Caesar had certainly affected the temple treasures and hence the power of the Druids. That power was reduced, moreover, by the intermingling of Roman worship with their own and by the introduction of Roman priesthoods. Tremors of discontent became evident under Augustus and Tiberius; the latter, at least, is said to have found himself constrained "to abolish the Gallic Druids and similar soothsayers and physicians." But they persisted even after Claudius, according to Suetonius, "completely abolished their fearfully cruel religion, whose practice Augustus had already forbidden to Roman citizens." The reference is to human sacrifice; Claudius also took exception to the dangerous amulets of which the Druids made use — for example, the eggs of certain serpents, which were believed to guarantee victory in disputes and access to princes. The class as such must now have lost its cohesion; the Druid convocations between Dreux and Chartres gradually diminished, and the migration of Druid disciples to Britain, which had been recognized from time immemorial as the highest school of Druid wisdom but had now also become Roman, ceased. But Druids continued to function even in Christian times, doubtless because the people in their daily life could not forgo the superstitious rites which the Druids practiced. Their situation in the third century can easily be imagined. The educated class had long since adopted Roman ways and

F

had given up any connection with the old national priesthood. In consequence the priests lost their higher spiritual significance and became conjurers, quacks, and soothsayers — a transformation analogous to that of the priests in Egypt. The Druid priestesses in particular strike us as the gypsies of the declining ancient world. Aurelian inquired of a number of them — perhaps a corporation of priestesses — concerning the succession in the Empire, and surely not in jest, for in such a matter jesting was dangerous. Sometimes they uttered their prophecies unsolicited. One bold woman, indifferent to consequences, called to Alexander Severus in the Gallic tongue: "Depart, hope for no victory, do not trust your soldiers!" A Druid landlady in the country of the Tungrii (near Liége) with whom the subaltern Diocles, later Diocletian, was reckoning his daily board, said to him: "You are too greedy, too stingy." "I will be generous if I ever become Emperor," he replied. "Do not mock," the hostess answered, "you will become Emperor when you have slain a boar."

The Druid religion must have maintained itself longest in the regions which still retain traces of Celtic character and language, that is in Brittany and the western part of Normandy. We know of one Druid family of the fourth century who derived from this region and whose members were among the most learned rhetors of the school of Bordeaux. They enjoyed a certain prestige by reason of the fact that the priesthood of the Celtic sun-god Belenus was hereditary in their house. But, significantly enough, they found it advantageous to Grecize this connection and to call themselves Phoebicius and Delphidius.

Where they continued to exist, the Druids presumably kept the cult as active as they could, until late in the Christian centuries the common people dedicated this worship to the huge and shapeless stone monuments characteristic of the ancient Celts, those pillars, flagstones, columns, benches, fairy-walks and the like, where lights and sacrifices burned bright by night and revels were celebrated. But deep darkness covers the decline of Celtic paganism. In later times, magnified by distance, the Druids live on as giants, the Druid priestesses as fairies, and over the stone monuments, which were deemed uncanny, the Church pronounced its exorcism in vain.

While Maximian was bringing Gaul to obedience, there was defection in Britain. This was a postlude to the conserving usurpation of the Thirty Tyrants under Gallienus on the one hand, and on the other the prelude to the final loss of Britain, which took place some hundred and forty years later.

Since the time of Probus the waters of the island, as of the coast of Gaul, swarmed with pirates, who are called now Franks (later Salii), now Saxons. To cope with them there was need of a fleet, which was in fact equipped at Boulogne (Gessoriacum). The command of this fleet Maximian entrusted to Carausius, a brave soldier familiar with the sea, who had proved his mettle in the Bagaudae war. Carausius was a Menapian (Brabant) of mysterious, possibly un-Roman origin. He soon began to use his position to play a remarkable game: he allowed the pirates to go on their raids uninterrupted, and then intercepted them on their return, in order to retain their booty for himself. His wealth aroused attention, and Maximian, who had discovered all, issued orders for his death; but Carausius was able to circumvent him. He bound his soldiers, as well as the Franks and Saxons, to himself by rich gifts, so that he could put himself forward as Emperor while still in Gaul (286), but with no intention of remaining there. He moved his entire fleet to Britain, where the Roman soldiers at once declared for him, so that the entire country came into his power; Maximian lacked the most essential means to pursue him. He ruled the island, rich at the time, for seven years, and defended the northern border against its hereditary enemies, the Caledonians. Boulogne and its surroundings he retained as a bridgehead for shelter and for freebooting — a role taken by Calais at the end of the Middle Ages. As ruler of Britain, Carausius sought to retain Roman education and art, but for the sake of his alliance with the Franks in the Low Countries he and his Romans assumed their dress, and he accepted their young men into his army and navy, where they could learn all the Roman art of war. If England had continued isolated under Carausius and similar successors for a longer period, there is no question but that it would have been barbarized before it could have adopted and assimilated itself to the Roman-Christian education which was the most important legacy of the ancient world. On the other hand, the island's sudden realization of its future role as ruler of the seas makes an impressive spectacle; based upon it, a bold upstart rules the mouth of Seine and Rhine and spreads his terror over the entire seacoast. But the only basis of his popularity was that the pirates, now in his service, should no more trouble the coasts, and that he should defend the northern frontier.

Maximian was forced to equip a new fleet (289), but his efforts appear to have been unsuccessful; all the experienced seamen were in the usurper's service. Anxious lest Carausius extend his rule farther, the Emperors decided to come to terms with him (290). He received the island and the title of Augustus; he could in any case not have been prevented from continuing to use that title. But the Emperors were determined not to allow him to keep his gains for long. As soon as the two Caesars were adopted, some pretext, perhaps the situation at Boulogne, was used to effect a breach (293). Constantius Chlorus besieged the city. Carausius' naval station patiently allowed the harbor where it was situated to be blocked by a mole and fell into the hands of the besieger. Perhaps these events affected sentiment in England and gave Allectus, a trusted comrade of the usurper, courage to murder him; people and soldiery at once acknowledged Allectus. Now Constantius took time to provide a broad and reliable base for the future conquest of Britain, and above all to secure his right flank by subjugating those Franks who occupied Batavia. He defeated them (294) and transplanted a large part of them in Roman territory, near Treves and Luxembourg. At the same time a new fleet was equipped, and two years later (296) all was in readiness for the main attack. Allectus posted a fleet at the Isle of Wight to observe enemy movements, but the imperial Admiral Asclepiodotus, who was under sail at the mouth of the Seine, was able to elude it under cover of a thick mist and to land somewhere on the west coat. Here he burned his boats, apparently because his forces were too slight to

admit of division into an attacking arm and a garrison for the
fleet. Allectus, who had expected Constantius' principal attack
with the Boulogne fleet near London, lost his bearing and had
to hasten westward with no preparation. He met Asclepiodotus
en route. It was probably a quite insignificant engagement between a few thousand men, in which Allectus himself fell, that
decided the fate of England. When Constantius landed in
Kent he found the island subdued. The panegyrist takes comfort for the blood spent in this war from the thought that it
was the blood of hireling barbarians.

It was necessary for Constantius to bestow upon the island
the same advantages it had enjoyed under Carausius, particularly in the matter of guarding the frontiers and of residing in
the country for considerable periods. With the Franks now
humbled, the first of these requirements was not difficult; as
for the second, in times of peace he divided his time between
Treves and York, which was the scene of his death (306).

And so was saved the considerable Roman culture which
made a distinction, perceptible to this day, between England
and Scotland, beyond Hadrian's wall, and Ireland, across the
strait. The doom of the fifth century came too late to destroy
its mighty traces entirely.

Our chief task should now be to describe the contemporary
situation of the Germans, not only on the frontiers of the
Empire, but as far to the north and east as they can be traced.
As future heirs of the Empire, they merit the closest attention,
even though, as it happened, the age of Constantine was for
them a period of recession and internal disruption. Even the
most fleeting notices and suggestions must be treasured in
order to restore, as far as possible, the tattered and evanescent
likeness of that great roll of peoples.

But the writer's spirit sinks before the task, in view of the
scientific discussion which has been devoted to the principal
questions of ancient German history for many years — discussion to which he is in no way competent to contribute. The
conclusions of Jakob Grimm's *History of the German Language* would not only alter hitherto prevalent assumptions
concerning the western Germans in many respects, but would

also assign to the Germans in closer or remoter degree the ancient peoples of the Danube and Pontus, in particular the Dacians and Getae and even the Scythians, and would identify the Getae with the later Goths. This would completely alter views hitherto held concerning the power and extent of the Germans, and to no less degree transform the ancient history of the Slavs, who, as the Sarmatae of antiquity, would be thought of as living between and among the above-named Germanic peoples.

But even if we could demonstrate with precision the situations, migrations, and mixtures at least of the frontier peoples, from the Netherlands to the Black Sea, during the half-century from Diocletian to the death of Constantine, their internal conditions would still present a great riddle. Where shall we find information concerning the ferment and transformation of Germanic character from the time of Tacitus, concerning the causes of the great tribal alliances, concerning the sudden drive of Pontic Goths to conquest in the third century, concerning their no less striking repose in the first half of the fourth? Where shall we find a gauge to measure the degree of penetration of Roman ways into the Germanic frontier regions? Little is known even of the customs and condition of the Germans who were accepted in the Roman Empire, soldiers as well as *coloni*. We must therefore be content with brief mention of the remaining wars at the northern hem of the Empire, as we were with those on the Rhine. Those northern wars cannot have been very significant, to judge from the laconic remarks recorded concerning them; virtually all attendant circumstances, even of place and position, are passed over in silence.

"The Marcomanni were defeated thoroughly" — that is our only notice (299) during a long stretch of time concerning the people which constituted the center of a great alliance under Marcus Aurelius and threatened the very existence of the Empire.

The Bastarnae and Carpi, apparently Gothic peoples of the lower Danube, were defeated by Diocletian and Galerius (294–295) and the entire folk of the Carpi were settled upon

Roman soil, after one hundred thousand Bastarnae had experienced the same fate under Probus.

The Sarmatae, apparently a Slavic Danube people, caused recurrent anxiety. Diocletian campaigned against them, first alone (289), then with Galerius (294), and also transplanted many of them in the Empire. Later incursions were punished by Constantine in an expedition (319) which cost their King Rausimod his life. But toward the end of his life (334) Constantine is said to have accepted into the Empire no fewer than three hundred thousand Sarmatae after they had been ejected from their homeland by an insurrection of their slaves (obviously a people they had previously subjugated). Unfortunately, virtually all explanatory circumstances that would afford ground for judging such mass acceptance of whole peoples are wanting; we cannot distinguish the boundary between coercion and voluntary migration, nor can we surmise the military or economic calculations which led the Roman rulers to such measures. A single treaty, if it were preserved, would throw greater light upon these conditions than all our conjectures, to which we must resort for reconstructing the course of events through analogy.

A Gothic incursion is also mentioned (323), apparently of different character than earlier and later invasions, perhaps the work of a single tribe which secret Roman connivance enticed across the badly guarded borders. Constantine is said to have terrified the enemy by his approach and then to have defeated and forced them to restore the captives they had carried off. An equivocal light is thrown over this whole war by its connection with the attack against Licinius (which will be treated below). Some years later (332) Constantine and his son and namesake marched, upon the petition of the harassed Sarmatae, into the country of the Goths, approximately Moldavia and Wallachia. It is said that one hundred thousand men (apparently of both parties) perished of hunger and cold. The son of King Ariaric was received among the hostages. There followed the intervention into the affairs of the Sarmatae, which has been mentioned above, and their transplanting.

The question always arises, What Goths and what Sarmatae are intended? These names embrace entire series of tribes, originally one but long since separated, whose level of education perhaps represented all degrees and shades between a virtually Roman urban culture and the life of savage hunters. The existence and the character of the Gothic Bible of Ulfilas (shortly after Constantine) justify *a posteriori* a very high estimate of the education of the tribes concerned even in the age of Constantine. But other remains betray barbaric crudeness. To work available individual traits into a single picture transcends the writer's purpose as it does his powers.

Nor can adequate attention be given the pendant of the Gothic picture, the Roman or sometime Roman Danube countries of Dacia (Transylvania, Lower Hungary, Moldavia, and Wallachia), Pannonia (Upper Hungary, including the neighboring regions to the west and south), and Moesia (Serbia and Bulgaria), because the writer does not possess control of the considerable new discoveries in these regions. In the period with which we are here dealing these regions were a military frontier, as they are in a measure today, except that the defense was then against the north instead of against the south. After Philip the Arab the alarums of war were never silent in this region, and Aurelian was forced practically to yield Dacia, Trajan's dangerous conquest, to the Goths. But previously, and in the less threatened areas also subsequently, a very significant Roman culture must have obtained; even in a soil rooted up by repeated migrations the effects of this culture were not to be totally effaced, and still persist recognizably, for example in the Romance language of the Wallachs. Cities like Vindobona (Vienna), Carnuntum (St. Petronell), Mursa (Osijek), Taurunum (Semlin), and above all Sirmium (Mitrovica), and then southward Naissus (Nissa), Sardica (Sofia), Nicopolis on the Haemus, and the whole rich itinerary of the Danube imply conditions which possibly considerably surpassed the Rhine border in wealth and importance. If modern hands might sometime remove the Slavic and Turkish debris from the old cities of the Danube, the Roman life of those regions would again come to the light of day.

World history might have taken another direction if in these countries a Germanic people capable of culture had succeeded, by intermixture with the vigorous inhabitants of northern Illyria, in establishing a powerful and enduring realm.

On the Black Sea, finally, the Germans along with other barbarians encountered Greek, mostly Milesian, colonies which, as the northernmost outposts of Hellenism for more than eight hundred years, had made the Pontus a "Hospitable Sea" (*Euxeinos*). Part of them had long since amalgamated with certain barbaric tribes to form the so-called Bosporan Kingdom, which embraced more than half of Crimea and the lower slopes of the Caucasus beyond the Strait of Kerch, and so controlled the entrance to the Sea of Azov and perhaps considerable stretches of its coast also. Coins and inscriptions testify a royal succession without interruption until Alexander Severus; then there follow at intervals the names Ininthimeuos, Teiranes, Thothorses, Phareanzes, and under Constantine, from 317 to 320, a King Rhadamsadis is attested.

When Rome made one after the other of the small kingdoms on its eastern boundary into a province, only Armenia and Bosporus remained, and these detached themselves more and more from Rome and were doubtless barbarized. Under Diocletian the Bosporans in alliance with the Sarmatae waged an unsuccessful war against their neighbors along the entire east side of the Pontus. Constantius Chlorus, who took the field against them in northern Asia Minor, called upon the Chersonesites to invade the Bosporan country from the west, and his maneuver was very successful. The Bosporans were forced to come to terms, whereby they lost almost all of Crimea as far as the region of Kerch (Panticapaeum, the ancient capital of Mithridates the Great) to the Chersonesites. The Greek colony had luckily recognized its obligation as vassal of the Roman Empire, whereas the Prince of Bosporus thought the general crisis of the Empire absolved him from every duty. In relation to the Greek cities of the coast these kings continued to be styled only archons, which was the title of the principal city magistrates in Hellas; in relation with non-Greeks, however, they did not hesitate to assume the style "King of Kings," as the rulers of Persia had once done.

But we turn from this small kingdom back to the West. In the rich garland of ancient Greek colonies whose finds are beginning to fill the museums of southern Russia, two arouse our special sympathy by their zealous efforts to preserve Greek life pure and complete despite their environment. Victorious Chersonesus, modern Sevastopol, was a colony of Heraclea on the Pontus, and thus indirectly of Megara. The near-by promontory of Parthenium bore sacred memories; here there still stood the temple of the importunate Artemis of the Taurians, who until Iphigenia's priesthood required to be conciliated by human sacrifice. The coins of the city bore the figure of the goddess. Under Roman rule Chersonesus again flourished, and under Diocletian, as has been mentioned, it even extended its territory; internally it retained all its Greek institutions and for its victory obtained complete exemption from taxation. The citizens still formed a *demos;* among the archons who were at the head of the council was one for whom the year was named, as at Athens. There followed officials of every kind, strategoi, agoranomoi, gymnasiarchs — usually honorary appointees for services to the state which must often have cost the incumbents dear. An inscription from the end of the pagan period, for example, celebrates Democrates, son of Aristogenes, not only for his legislative proposals, orations, and his two terms as archon, but also because, at his own expense, he journeyed several times as ambassador to the Emperors (Diocletian and Constantius?), because he defrayed the costs of festivals and public services of all sorts out of his own means, and conscientiously administered all matters. The inscription ends, "to the preserver, the incomparable, the friend of his country, from the noble council, the august people." His reward was this inscribed stone and the annual ceremonial reading of a special honorary decree. Like the free cities of the Empire in the later Middle Ages, Chersonesus possessed excellent artillery. In the war with the Bosporans its war chariots bearing catapults were at once put in action; its artillerymen were famous.

Ancient and once powerful Olbia (near modern Ochakov), a Milesian foundation, was no less concerned to preserve its Greek character. The Olbians proclaimed their Ionian descent in language and customs. They knew the *Iliad* by heart, and neglected non-Ionian poets; a number of respectable later Greek authors were natives of Olbia. Internal institutions and offices were not inferior to those of Chersonesus. The city was able to keep quite free of the barbarians who dwelt around it, but at times paid them tribute. Antoninus Pius sent it help against the Tauro-Scythians; we have yet to discover how it fared later when the great Gothic power which surrounded it began to stir.

As if in defiance of the continuous menace of their situation, the Greeks, as far as their settlements reached to the north of Pontus, paid special reverence to Achilles, the ancient embodiment of the heroic ideal of their people. He is the true ruler of the Pontus, the Ποντάρχης, as he is styled in many inscriptions. In Olbia, as in all the cities of the coast, he had splendid temples. Sacrifices were offered to him "for peace, for fertility, and for gallantry in the city." Festive contests in music of the double-flute and in throwing the discus were celebrated in his honor; especially famous was the foot race of boys on a near-by dune which was called the "course of Achilles," because the hero himself was believed to have once held a foot race on the spot. If barbarians of Asiatic origin (the small race of Sinds) inhabited the dune, the island of Leuke in the Pontus, not far from the mouth of the Danube, belonged entirely to the shade of Achilles. A white cliff (so the descriptions have it °) towered from the sea, partly surrounded by overhanging crags. There was no dwelling, no human sound, either on the shore or in the secluded vales; only coveys of white birds hovered over the cliffs. Reverent awe inspired

---

° If ancient descriptions are to be taken literally, Leuke would be as difficult to locate today as the Isles of the Blessed or the Isles of the Hesperides. But if it is merely a matter of a general locality with which the myth and its imaginative imagery can be associated, any of the small islands at the mouth of the Danube, or perhaps a point on its present sand dunes, would do. An author like Ammianus, who insists upon Leuke, must surely have had some definite information.

those who sailed by. None who stepped upon the island ventured to spend the night there; after they had visited the temple and grave of Achilles and inspected the votive offerings deposited by earlier callers from ancient times, voyagers embarked again at evening. This was the place which Poseidon had once promised divine Thetis for her son, not only for his burial but for his continued existence in blessedness. But Achilles was not the sole occupant; gradually legend gave him as comrades other heroes and blessed spirits who had led a blameless life on earth and whom Zeus was unwilling to leave in the gloom of Orcus. Those white birds, which resembled halcyons in appearance, were regarded with devotion. Perhaps they were the visible manifestations of those happy souls for whose lot latest paganism most yearned.

IV

INDIVIDUAL PROVINCES
AND NEIGHBORING COUNTRIES : THE EAST

WE TURN to the Eastern frontiers; here too the Empire struggled for its very existence. Diocletian inherited insurrections and bloody wars; at the cost of endless toil he and his co-rulers had to defend and in part reconquer the East.

The enemy which was destined to prove worst was, indeed, still slumbering. The Arabs who would one day spread over the East with sword and Koran still lived back of Syria and Palestine, divided into hundreds of tribes, devoted to their astrology and idolatry, their soothsaying and sacrifices. Some had gone over to Judaism, and in the following century there were even a few Christian tribes. The nation's central point was the Kaaba at Mecca, which had been founded by Ishmael. Near by, at Ocadh, an annual twenty-day fair was held, where in addition to trade and worship there took place poetic contests, whose remains — seven poems, the *Mu'allaqāt* — have come down to our time. Occasional contacts with Rome were friendly. Arab horsemen served in the Roman army, and not infrequently Arabs visited ancient holy sites in Palestine which were at the same time markets, as for example the oak of Abraham at Mamre; but for the most part they were dangerous neighbors to that country. We are told that Diocletian took defeated Saracens captive, but with no specific details. In the struggles of the Emperors for Mesopotamia and Egypt they are first mentioned only at the end of the fourth century; their hour was not yet struck.

Greater by far and nearer was the danger which, from the time of Alexander Severus, threatened from the Kingdom of the Sassanids. If one considers that Kingdom's moderate extent and the probable sparsity of its population, every advantage seems clearly to be on the side of the Romans. Could not the Empire easily withstand the peoples from the upper Euphrates to the Caspian Sea and the Persian Gulf, eastward as far as the Strait of Hormuz? In point of fact the attacks of the Sassanids were rather in the nature of predatory incursions than wars of conquest; but the danger was and remained great and troublesome because the Emperors were always simultaneously threatened by the Germans and frequently by defection and usurpation in addition, and so could employ only limited resources against the East. Because it was the persistent enemy of the Roman Empire, and for the sake of its own remarkable internal situation, the Sassanid kingdom merits a short treatment at this point.

In the first place that kingdom was an artificial creation claiming to be the restoration of a condition long vanished. The ancient Kingdom of the Persians, conquered by Alexander, fell for the most part into the hands of the Seleucids; the defection of Mesopotamia and the eastern hill country gave rise to the Parthian Kingdom of the Arsacids, which was quickly barbarized. As heirs to Asia Minor, the Romans were compelled to wage strenuous wars against the Arsacids, difficult not so much because of any special internal strength of the loosely confederated state whose supreme king was hampered by the willfulness of the greater vassals, as because of the nature of the country, which was altogether unfavorable for an attacking army. After the last king, Artabanus, had forced Caracalla's successor Macrinus to an ignominious peace and withdrawal, he fell by the usurpation of Ardeshir Babecan (Artaxerxes Sassan), who claimed descent from the old rulers of Persia and at once gathered the Persians of Farsistan about himself in order, after the Oriental fashion, to replace the ruling Parthians by a new ruling people. He not only intended to restore the state of the ancient Achaemenids, of Darius and Xerxes, with its institutions, but the ancient teaching of Zoroaster was to displace Parthian astrology and idolatry. The Magi, many thousands in number, assembled at a council; by a miracle the pure fire-worship, said to have been forgotten, was restored; the King became the first of the Magi; and the counsel and soothtelling of the Magi assumed equal authority with the King. In return the Magi granted him the title of a god, and indeed of a *yazata*, the servant of Ormuzd; he was of equal birth with the stars, and could call himself brother to sun and moon. Christians recognized no claim of this sort, and consequently fared worse than in the Roman Empire; there was no such dogmatic fanaticism as prevailed here in the Roman requirement to offer sacrifice to the Emperors. It appears that many Christians had fled to these regions during the Parthian period and that the Arsacids had tolerated them, perhaps on political grounds; these all now fell into the hands of the Magi. Later, under Shapur II (310–382), the Jews, who were very influential in Persia and had the support of the Queen, are said to have participated in the great persecution in which no fewer than twenty-two bishops, among others, succumbed.

Upon a sheer cliff not far from Persepolis the graves of the ancient Kings of Persia are to be seen, chiseled in the austere style of ancient Persia and on a colossal scale. The Sassanids were unwilling to give up this hallowed site; a series of reliefs added below represents scenes of war, ceremonial, and the chase, in all of which the King appears as the principal personage. The hostile Roman Empire seems to have provided the artists (perhaps captives of war) for this work; at least the sculptures, like the little surviving architecture generally, show the influence of senescent Roman art. The principal remains are some entrances to mountain grottoes vaulted with round arches, and the palaces of Firuz-Abad and Sarbistan, designed in the style of Roman baths with great niche-like openings and vaulted chambers, but much barbarized in execution. There were no temples, properly speaking; the central hearth of the cult was the pyreum or fire-altar, and it is on the steps of this altar that we regularly find the King, surrounded by Magi.

Orthodoxy had become an essential principle of the state. It was in vain that the reformer Mani, who wished to construct a new and loftier whole out of elements of Christian, Parsee, and Buddhist religions, appeared in Persia with his tablet of painted symbols. Bahram I had his doctors defeat him in disputation and then flay him; his skin was stretched over the gate of Djondishapur as a general warning. On one occasion, however, we find that a King sought to liberate his race from the oppressive rule of the Magi. Yezdegerd I Alathim (400–421) had his son Bahram-gur brought up far from his court by an idolatrous Arab chieftain, Noman of Hira, later a convert to Christianity. But in the end the prince was not recognized, "because he had adopted Arab ways," and had literally to fight for his crown with a rival King, Kesra or Khosru, who had been set up by the nobles. Not far from the royal residence at Madain the tiara of the Sassanids was laid down between two hungry lions, to see which of the two suitors for the throne would reach for it first. Kesra willingly allowed Bahram-gur to make the first approach, and Bahram-gur slew the two lions and at once set the crown upon his head. But orthodoxy continued in its full splendor. When King Cobad later (491–498) followed the heretical teacher Mazdak, who preached communism and community of wives, there was a general uprising against him, and he was forced to spend some time in the "castle of oblivion." It is only in the last days of the kingdom that large-scale religious exhaustion can be sensed.

In political matters the picture is the usual one of Asiatic despotism. The people could only offer adoration. When a new King had delivered his first allocution, all prostrated themselves with their faces to the ground and remained in this posture until the King issued his order to arise. It was long before humility developed so far even in the Eastern Roman Empire; under Diocletian prostration still was limited to the interior of the palace. The Oriental's joy in striking acts of mercy or justice, which offer the consolation of equality before despotism, is also involved. Yet the King was surrounded by an aristocracy of uncertain origin, perhaps the families of the grandees whom Ardeshir brought from Farsistan. This nobility seems to have shared influence at court with the Magi, and to have attempted more than one revolution upon its own account. It was this aristocracy which forced Bahram II (296–301), in conjunction with the Great Magus (the Mobed of Mobeds), to submission, which raised the unwilling Bahram III to the throne (301), and which cut through the ropes of Shapur III's tent, so that he was suffocated when the tent collapsed. But in many questions of the succession the nobility exercised its decisive power in so prudent a manner that the Roman Empire might well envy the Persians this element of their political life. It was natural for the nobility to be concerned for the continuance of the dynasty, because its own position depended on hereditary right. What a contrast with the kaleidoscopic change of Emperors when, after the death of Hormuz II (310), the Persian grandees placed the tiara upon the pregnant body of one of his wives! She insisted that she knew the child would be a boy, and Hormuz himself had long before received a response from the astrologers that a great and victorious King would be born to him. The boy was born; the grandees named him Shapur II, and administered the realm until he attained his majority. He received ceremonial attendance in the palace ten times daily. Fortunately, he was a powerful man, who developed and grew independent very early; his life and reign lasted for seventy-two years, his reign being exactly the length of Louis XIV's. Another incidental similarity to Louis is the fact that he compelled the nobility to leave their country castles and settle in his sight in the capital Madain (ancient Ctesiphon and Seleucia).

But the succession, as has been remarked, was not without violence, although the Kings sought to avert it by crowning a prince during their lifetimes (see page 50). The grandees and perhaps the Magi also frequently favored individual princes within the house of the Sassanids; even acknowledged Kings feared usurpation on the part of their kin. To remove such suspicions from his father Shapur I, Hormuz I sent him (with characteristic Oriental transfer of the symbolic to the real) his right

G

hand, which he had amputated; but the father refused to accept this noble declaration of incapacity to rule.

Internally the regime obviously proceeded with higher means toward higher ends than the Parthians, who had always remained crude, had done. Of several Sassanid Kings such benefactions are reported as have always been the ideal of an Oriental prince: protection of agriculture, irrigation works, the prosecution of justice, codification of laws, buildings useful and ornamental (at least on the great royal roads), new city foundations, patronage of scholars and artists from far and near. Of all the Kings, not only their outward appearance but also their manner of thought have been transmitted, after the Asiatic manner, in significant proverbial verses.

The saying of the founder, Ardeshir I, sounds like a motto for the fate of his kingdom in general: "There is no kingdom without soldiers, no soldiers without money, no money without population, no population without justice." It was by such a circuitous route that the King had to achieve insight into the moral end of the state. In any event, military security was the prime task. For this kingdom, which caused the Romans so much anxiety, itself suffered from the same external dangers as did the Empire. From the south the Arabs began to press forward; the Magi are said to have known even then that they would one day conquer Persia. Shapur II, during whose minority they had wrested large stretches from the Persian realm, undertook a terrible campaign of vengeance against the Arabs in his sixteenth year (326). He built a fleet on the Persian Gulf and sailed across to Arabia. After a general massacre on Bahrein Island and among the tribes of Temin, Bekr-ben-Waiel, Abdolkais, and others, he had the shoulders of the survivors bored and ropes passed through by which to drive them; Constantine only threw his German captives to the wild beasts in the arena at Treves.

Another dangerous enemy threatened from the north, from the region of the Caspian Sea—the Ephthalites or White Huns, as they are wrongly named, one of those Turkish tribes which seem to have been born specifically to bring doom to the Near East in the various centuries. The victorious war which Bahram-gur (420–438) waged against them belongs to the adventures, told in many forms, of which the romance of his life is composed; but his driving of the nomads back over the Oxus is probably fact. Nevertheless, not long thereafter they found opportunity to intervene in the war of succession (456) of the two sons of Yezdegerd II; Firuz, the elder of the sons, who had been deposed and had taken refuge with them, they supported with a large army and restored to the Persian throne. Thenceforward their influence, even their intervention, was no longer to be evaded, and the Sassanids often paid them annual tribute.

The later vicissitudes of the realm and its final period of splendor under Koshru Nushirwan do not require to be dealt with here. We turn to special events which fall in the epoch of Diocletian and Constantine.

At the time of Gallienus and the Thirty Tyrants the Kingdom of Palmyra was Rome's champion against the Persians. Odenathus defeated Shapur I, the proud victor over Valerian, and pursued him to Ctesiphon. But when Aurelian later attacked the Palmyrenes, Sassanid policy turned to their support, in order to preserve a weaker neighbor. Bahram I sent an army to help Zenobia, and this army, like the Queen's own, was defeated by the Roman Emperor. Aurelian and then Probus had to be conciliated with gifts. Probus nevertheless prepared for a Persian war, which was actually undertaken by his successor Carus. Brilliant successes again took the Roman army beyond the Tigris, but lost their value by the sudden death of Carus and the return of his son Numerian to Rome (283). As was to be expected, Bahram II, after some hesitation, eagerly exploited the great confusion in the entire Roman Empire at the accession of Diocletian, in order to secure himself and expand to the west. For a time the Emperors could only allow him his way, for nearer troubles occupied their attention. Their struggle was taken over for them by Armenia.

This country, under a collateral branch of the fallen Parthian royal houses of the Arsacids, had formerly enjoyed Roman protection. But when the Roman Empire began to disintegrate under Valerian and Gallienus, Shapur I subdued Armenia with the help of native factions. Tiridates, son of the murdered King

Chosroes, was saved only by the loyalty of the royal servants, and was brought up under the protection of the Roman Emperors. Endowed with prodigious strength and high spirit, honored even for victories at the Olympian Games, he seemed peculiarly suited to step forth as a claimant of the lost kingdom of his fathers. As Nero had once invested his like-named ancestor with Armenia, so Diocletian is now said to have invested Tiridates (286). Tiridates found his country suffering from systematic oppression, even religious. The intolerant Parseeism of the foreign rule had broken the statues of the deified Kings of Armenia and the sacred images of sun and moon, and instead had erected a pyreum to Sacred Fire on Mount Bagavan. Quickly nobles and commoners rallied about the prince; the Persians were ejected, and rescued treasures, even a rescued princess, were brought to light. Mamgo, an allegedly Scythian but probably Turkoman chieftain who had been banished to Armenia by Shapur, went over to the new ruler with his followers. But Narses I mustered his forces, conquered Armenia anew, and forced Tiridates again to seek the protection of the Romans.

Meanwhile Diocletian and his colleagues had mastered most of their enemies and were now able to turn their attention to the East. While the senior Emperor marched to subdue Egypt, which had been rebellious for some time, he entrusted the campaign against Narses to his Caesar, Galerius; their joint headquarters was Antioch. But two indecisive battles and a third which Galerius lost through excessive boldness again drenched with Roman blood the desolate plain between Carrhae and the Euphrates where Crassus had once led ten legions to their death. Diocletian, who had meanwhile subjugated Egypt, while Maximian's Caesar, Constantius Chlorus, was simultaneously returning rebellious Britain to the Empire, was doubly incensed that on the Euphrates alone Roman arms should prove inferior. On his return the defeated Caesar met him in Syria; Diocletian suffered him, dressed in his purple cloak as he was, to run beside his chariot for a mile, in full view of the soldiers and the court. More clearly than anything else, this incident indicates the true tone of Diocletian's rule. Galerius' devotion was not

in the least diminished; his only request was permission to erase
the disgrace by victory. Now instead of the less able Asiatics
the irresistible Illyrians marched out, together with an auxiliary
army of mercenary Goths; all together they were only twenty-
five thousand, but first-class fighting men. This time (297) Galerius moved beyond the Euphrates to the hill country of Armenia,
where he found the people favorable to the Roman cause and
where the Persian army, consisting chiefly of cavalry, would be
less terrifying than in a battle on the plains. (Among the Persians, according to Ammianus, the infantry was regarded only
as camp-followers.) Galerius himself, with only two men accompanying him, spied out the careless Persian camp, and then
suddenly attacked it. His success was complete. After a general
carnage King Narses fled wounded to Media; his and his grandees' tents, filled with rich booty, fell into the hands of the vic-
tors, and his wives and a number of his kinsmen were taken
captive. Galerius understood the value of such pledges, and
treated his captives with kindness and care.

If surviving accounts of the war are brief and scant, those of
the peace negotiations which followed go into minute details.
In the first overtures, which Apharban, a confidant of Narses,
made to Galerius alone, the high-flown Asiatic flattery is quite
amusing. Rome and Persia are for him the two lamps, the two
eyes of the world, and must not irritate one another. It was
only by so great a prince as Galerius that Narses could have
been conquered; even so human affairs are changeable. How
critical the situation of Persia must have been is indicated by
the fact that the King left all political terms to the discretion
of the Romans' "philanthropy" and asked only for the return of
his family. Galerius first spoke to the envoy harshly and reminded him of the Emperor Valerian, whom the Persians had
tortured to death, but then addressed a few kinder words to
him. Then the Emperor and the Caesar met at Nisibis on the
Euphrates. This time as victor Galerius was received with the
highest honor, but again he manifested selfless submission to
Diocletian's superior judgment and declined the easy and cer-
border districts were to be incorporated. A secretary, Sicorius
tain conquest of Hither Persia, of which only the more valuable

Probus, was sent to Narses, who had withdrawn to Media to gain time and gather troops in order to impress the weary Roman envoy. Probus received an audience on the river Asprudus and concluded a treaty by which Narses ceded five provinces, including the land of the Kurds and the entire region of the upper Tigris as far as Lake Van. This secured their earlier possession, the upper Euphrates, to the Romans, and at the same time erected a wall for their protectorate Armenia, of material, to be sure, which had belonged to the Armenians before the Parthian conquest. Still, a considerable stretch of land was ceded to them in the southeast, and Tiridates was again installed as King. The King of Iberia was also henceforward to be vassal of the Romans; this was an important development, for this rough hill country north of Armenia (corresponding more or less to modern Georgia) with its warlike inhabitants could serve as an outpost against the barbarians from beyond the Caucasus. Upon the conclusion of these terms Narses' family, which had been kept at Antioch, was restored to him.

The entire frontier was now provided with fortresses and garrisons. The period of peace which now ensued for Hither Asia lasted for almost forty years, to the end of Constantine's life. The victorious Emperors could hardly have realized that their great successes substantially paved the way for the peaceful spread of the Christianity they hated. The contrary influence which Persia exerted upon the Roman Empire through its Manichaeism and its manifold superstitions will be touched upon later.

Despite later admixtures, even of Shiite Mohammedanism and the culture it involved, the Persian people and their customs are still partly to be recognized from the descriptions which Ammianus gave of them in the fourth century and Agathias in the sixth. They have retained the ambiguous glance, under arched eyebrows which run together over the nose, and the carefully tended beard. Certain rules of etiquette obtain now as then. Of their ancient reputation for moderation there is still a remnant. The singular mixture of effeminate luxury and high personal courage is still characteristic, as is bold braggadocio and self-seeking cunning. Their sweeping and colorful dress and tinsel ornaments were noticed by the Romans as they are by us. Usages dependent upon religion, as for example exposing corpses to dogs and carrion birds, could naturally survive only where Parseeism has persisted. Many of their superstitions Mohammedanism extirpated or transformed into fairy stories. To the Persian of the Sassanid period all his daily life, every step and turn, was filled with threatening or alluring magic, and the holy fire of the pyres issued oracles continuously. The great Shapur II was not content with these; among the Magi proper there were necromancers who had to conjure shades for him at critical junctures — even that of Pompey.

It has often been remarked how closely Sassanid usages correspond to those of the Middle Ages in the West, at least in certain aspects. For one thing there is the monastic abstinence of the Magi and their position as a sort of clergy alongside the nobility. It is to be regretted that we have no details of this matter and are even ignorant of the manner in which they perpetuated themselves as a class. The nobility itself, with its bluff chivalry, is quite Western. Its formal relationship to the King appears to have been feudal; its principal obligation was assistance in war. As represented in monuments, these Persian warriors in mail and plumed helmets, with lance and sword, and with the magnificent accouterments of their steeds, are quite like the knights of our own Middle Ages. As with the knights, the soul of their activity was adventure, whether in war or love. Legend early transformed a figure like Bahram-gur into a splendid pattern of this character, and heroes of the mythical period, a Rustem or a Feridun, were already held in high honor. Such romanticism, as indeed anything impractical, offers a stark contrast to Roman ways.

Let us glance back to Armenia. Hitherto this country with its brave and educatable people had always heeded influences and impressions from abroad; it had achieved only a relatively rudimentary culture, and was soon to be subject to new and lasting poverty and servitude. But the period of Tiridates, which was at the same time the period of its conversion to Christianity, constitutes a bright interval. Christianity, in the form of the Armenian Church, would one day be the chief support for Armenian nationality.

This is the account of Moses of Chorene (*fl.* 440), the chronicler of the Armenians: Gregory the Illuminator, deriving from a collateral branch of the royal house of the Arsacids, was brought as a child to Roman Cappadocia by a peculiar concatenation of circumstances, and there was raised by a Christian family, and later married to a Christian woman, Maria. After three years of marriage they separated, in order to serve God in voluntary abstinence. Of their two sons the younger became an anchorite, and the elder continued the family. Gregory then returned to Armenia with Tiridates, who was still a pagan, and began, with great danger, to convert the people.

From other sources we learn that a saintly woman, Ripsime, labored along with him and even suffered a martyr's death, but that the conversion proceeded with speed. Before the Diocletianic persecution of 302 Gregory baptized Tiridates himself and a large part of the people. He survived the period of the Nicene Council, which he was unwilling to attend because of humility, and spent his old age from 332 onwards as a recluse in the hills which are called Mania Caves. He himself installed his son Aristaces as his successor in the episcopacy or high-priesthood. He died unknown, and shepherds buried him; long afterwards his body was discovered and solemnly interred in Thordan.

Tiridates survived Constantine, and was poisoned by the nobility in 342. Soon civil war and intervention from abroad brought the Arsacid kingship as well as the Arsacid priesthood, which was also hereditary, into great distress and confusion. But the impression of the conversion persisted through all the foreign regimes which followed. Christianity, though petrified in its Monophysite form, still unites the Armenians, who are dispersed as far as Austria, with the exception of the (Roman Catholic) Uniates, who at present include some of the best and most highly cultured elements of their people.

Such was the condition of Rome's friendly and hostile neighbors to the east. The Asiatic provinces of the Empire itself

enjoyed peace in the time of Diocletian and Constantine, interrupted only for short periods by the great imperial wars. A portrait of Syria and Asia Minor at this period would require a
special and considerable investigation. We shall limit ourselves
to pointing to a sore spot which brought shame to the body of
the Empire for centuries, the robber country of the Isaurians,
which is a standard item in all histories of the Roman Empire.

The earlier piracy and slave trade of the Cilicians, which
grew active when the successor kingdoms [of Alexander the
Great] were in their decline, is much better known because it
was suppressed in the memorable last years of the Republic by
Pompey the Great after Cilicia had long furnished base and refuge to piracy of the entire Mediterranean. Even then hoary
Isaura was cited as one of the robbers' nests of the interior, and
after Isaura, all of the region back of Cilicia proper came to be
called Isauria. It is a rough hill country of volcanic formation,
with high peaks, and its cities were rather in the nature of
fortresses. Whether a remnant of the robber character survived
in this back country from the pirate war, or whether the populace newly adopted this manner of life in the Empire because
of total lack of supervision, the Isaurians of the third century
were the plague of southern Asia Minor. At the time of the
Thirty Tyrants they found it expedient to raise one of their
leaders, Trebellian, to Emperor, and he held court at Isaura,
struck coins, and maintained himself in his wild hills for a considerable period. We do not know how Causisoleus, one of Gallienus' generals, succeeded in getting hold of his person; in any
event his death did not mean the conquest of the country, for
the Isaurians held together so much the more firmly out of fear
of the further vengeance of the Roman Emperor. Under Claudius Gothicus a new attack was undertaken against them, and
was so far successful that the Emperor could now form a plan
to transfer the Isaurians down to Cilicia and settle them there
while a loyal follower would receive their empty country for
his own; rebellion thus would have been rendered impossible.
But the early death of Claudius seems to have prevented the
execution of this project, and soon the Isaurians were as bold
and active as before. Under Probus one of their robber chiefs,

Lydius, made Lycia and Pamphilia unsafe. He not only made himself secure against all attacks in inaccessible Cremna (in Pisidia) but also assured himself against starvation by sowing and reaping. The unhappy inhabitants whom he had ejected and whom the Roman commandant wished to send back to him perforce, he hurled down from the city walls into the gorges. An underground passage from Cremna passed under the Roman camp to a distant secret spot in the open; this passage Lydius' men used to bring cattle and provisions into the city from time to time, until the enemy discovered it. Then Lydius felt compelled to reduce his company to the indispensable minimum by murder; a few women were left alive, and were held in common. At length his best artilleryman, with whom he had quarreled, went over to the Romans and from their camp hurled his projectiles at an opening in the walls which Lydius used as lookout. The robber chieftain was fatally wounded, but exacted an oath from his men not to surrender the fortress; this did not prevent them from breaking their pledge as soon as he had given up the ghost. But the best that this victory achieved was to secure Pisidia for some time; Isauria, adjacent on the east, continued in the hands of the robbers as before. This is stated as clearly as possible in a notice from the time of Diocletian: "From the time of Trebellian the Isaurians are regarded as barbarians, and since their land is situated in the midst of Roman territory, they are hedged in with a new species of border guards like an enemy frontier. Their locale alone protects them, for they are themselves neither impressive in stature nor dangerous by reason of courage, nor remarkable by reason of weapons, nor particularly clever; their only strength is the inaccessibility of their domicile in the hills."

That new species of border guards and the manner of their warfare against the robber folk we become acquainted with in several instances in the course of the fourth century. The Empire employed no fewer than three legions, later at least two, for this single purpose. Staff headquarters were apparently at Tarsus in Cilicia and at Side in Pamphilia, supply dumps in Peleas, while the troops were either posted in the villages and fortresses of the interior or moved about in mobile columns.

Nevertheless they did not venture far into the hills after experience taught them that the sheer ascents made any Roman tactic useless, as soon as boulders were rolled down upon them. The Isaurians had to be awaited in the plains, when they came to raid Cilicia, Pamphilia, Pisidia, and Lycaonia; here they were easily mastered, and either dispatched or delivered to the beast hunts in the amphitheaters of large pleasure-loving cities like Iconium. But even the Cilician shore could not always be protected; the old pirate nature of the hill folk occasionally broke out so violently that for long periods (for example, around 355) they held stretches of coastland in their possession and obliged navigation to hug the shores of Cyprus, which lay opposite. The siege of the important Seleucia Tracheotis, Cilicia's second city, did not seem to them too bold an enterprise; only a large Roman relieving army moved them to raise the siege. Then they were again successfully contained in their hill country for several years by a system of redoubts and ramparts until they broke out in large bands in 359 and terrified the country by their robberies. Effective threats rather than punishment are said to have once more restored them to quiet. A new raid into Pamphilia and Cilicia, in which they murdered all who fell into their hands, is reported for the year 368. A company of light Roman troops with one of the highest imperial officials, the Neoplatonist Musonius, at their head, were attacked in a narrow gorge and annihilated. Thereupon the Isaurians were pressed and pursued from place to place until they sued for peace and obtained it upon surrender of hostages. One of their most important localities, Germanicopolis, which was their customary mouthpiece, represented them in these negotiations also; there is no mention of any specially powerful chieftain or prince. Eight years later, under Valens, the Isaurians come into view again; about 400 the General Tacitus was compelled to purge Cilicia of robbers; in 404 the general Arbazacius defeated the Isaurians, but was then bribed by them, and they continued in their ways for years on end. So it went until late in the Byzantine period, with attack, defense, and apparent submission. The people, whose number was small, must have been thoroughly barbarized. The Romans approached them only as enemies, and it is understandable but no less regrettable that we have no description of political, moral, and religious conditions as they developed among the Isaurians. In many respects their relation to Rome was like that of the Circassians to Russia, but in principle it was different. Isauria had been Hellenized at least superficially, and was later gradually barbarized. That such a process could take place unhindered is significant of the internal condition of the Roman Empire in more than one respect.

We now turn to the southern shore of the Mediterranean. Among the unhappiest lands of the Roman Empire we again find Egypt, where Diocletian was to make a sorry name for himself by the cruel suppression of one of those insurrections in which Egyptian history, after the conquest by the son of Cyrus, is so rich.

The attitude of the Roman to Egypt was a curious mixture: profound contempt and strict control of the natives (Egyptians as well as colonized Greeks and Jews) go hand in hand with traditional reverence for the records and monuments of the millennia-old Pharaonic period and its living remains — I refer to that occult priestly religion whose Isis cult, symbols, incantations, and magic arts the late Roman world could least do without. The same Roman prefect or *epistrategos* who held sway with robbery and cruelty would make a pilgrimage to hundred-gated Thebes and Philae, and have his name chiseled on the calf of the statue of Memnon, together with the statement that he heard its famous reverberation at dawn. The secular curiosity of the student of antiquity and the tourist, and the romantic longing of the educated were also directed largely to Egypt and its age-old civilization. Egypt was the scene of the romances of Xenophon of Ephesus and of Heliodorus; in the colorful stories of their lovers, Anthia and Habrocomes, Theagenes and Chariclea, Egyptian robber bands occupy the same role as modern novelists customarily assign to Italian banditti — to say nothing of the symbolic romance of Synesius which clothed events of the age of Arcadius in an ancient Egyptian dress. "Everything that is told of Egypt," says Heliodorus, "interests the Hellenic hearer exceedingly." In plastic art also Egyptian modes became fashionable, especially under Hadrian, and much later there was a fondness for Egyptian landscapes trimmed with marvelous animals, feluccas, the arbors and the shore casinos of the life-giving Nile, somewhat as our fashion has occasionally adopted Chinese motifs. The famous mosaic of Palestrina is of this character.

But the actual conditions were grim and terrible. Ancient civilizations, which after a brilliant past fall into the hands of alien and relatively barbaric conquerors and through long centuries are passed unconsulted from hand to hand, easily assume a character which strikes the foreign ruler as a sullen fractiousness, even though it only partially deserves such a name. The Persian conquest marked the beginning of this attitude; it embittered the Egyptians, and permanently, not only by subjugation and oppression itself, but also by flagrant contempt of their ancient religion. The simple light-worship of the Persians conflicted with the massive half-animal pantheon of their new subjects; to the one, precisely those things which the other regarded as sacred were unclean. Hence arose those endless insurrections which streams of blood could never quench.

The Greek rulers who succeeded the Persian brought no such cleavage with them; in the polytheism of the Near East and Egypt their Hellenic faith sought not the differences but, and very eagerly, kinships with itself. For Alexander the Great Ammon was equivalent to Zeus, whom he regarded as his own progenitor. Even before Alexander, the Greek had no doubt that his Apollo was the same as the Egyptian Horus, Dionysus as Osiris, Demeter as Isis; and now he found counterparts for half his Olympus on the Nile. Ptolemy son of Lagus, who had secured Egypt for himself when Alexander's great legacy was divided among his generals, was especially concerned, as were his immediate successors who organized the new kingdom, to conciliate the Egyptians in certain matters. It was not to their interest to follow the brutal Persian manner of needlessly treading every national characteristic underfoot and thus provoking desperate insurrection. Their interest was rather in the direction of a well-organized and self-contained military and official hierarchy, exercising only so much pressure as was necessary to bring the financial resources of the country into the royal treasury, where, despite one hundred and fifty thousand soldiers and four thousand ships, incredible sums were stored up. Egypt's ancient and original agrarian division into *nomes* was left undisturbed. Even the caste system held no danger, since there was no longer a native warrior caste. The priests and their rule of the temples were encouraged and their worship promoted by solemn royal participation, although at the same time considerable taxes were exacted from them. Ptolemy Euergetes built the magnificent temple of Esne in a style which is not noticeably different from the ancient Egyptian. The Kings of his line continued to have themselves embalmed and were worshiped as "savior gods" along with and even above Isis and Osiris. This was the most manifest symbol of an amalgamation which was more and more fully realized in the fact that the Greeks were no longer secluded in foreign settlements, but were scattered over the country and lived among the Egyptians. The new cosmopolis of Alexandria, however, continued predominantly Greek. Here the Greek character, which had become cosmopolitan and communicable in the form we call Hellenistic, shed its most brilliant light. For a time there was no city in the world which could compare with Alexandria in splendor and in material as well as spiritual activity; but neither was there anywhere so concentrated a measure of corruption as at Alexandria, where three peoples (counting the Jews) had all gone astray from their pristine national character and required policing rather than government.

When, after the victory of Actium, Augustus took over the country, which had declined somewhat in the interval, its only excuse for existence was suddenly reduced to the service of Rome, as source of profit and as granary. No province was watched as closely as this, both because of the dangerous spirit of the people and ominous prophecies, and because of its singular importance. Without imperial permission no Roman senator or knight might visit the country; the position of Prefect of Egypt was one of high importance and trust because nowhere else was such care necessary to prevent defection and usurpation. Naturally, the prefect had to be given broad plenipoten-

tiary powers; his outward bearing was calculated to incarnate
their old kingship to the Egyptians, and the impressive official
journeys of the prefect, at least, did recall ancient Egyptian
royalty. He could be seen with a large retinue, including priests,
sailing up and down the Nile on one of those gilded floating
confections which the luxury of the Ptolemies had introduced.
The system of graded officials subordinate to the prefect was
maintained virtually as it had been taken over from the Ptolemies. Least account was taken of the people; we do not know
whether it could choose even its lowliest functionaries, or
whether it might assemble for any other purpose than to signify
homage to the Emperor. The occupation troops, which were to
guard the country from enemies from within and without, were
few, even for the sparing Roman system. Soon after Augustus
there were at most twenty thousand troops, for eight million
inhabitants (among them a million Jews). The region of Memphis, where the Nile begins to divide, was recognized by the
Romans, as it was later by the Arabs, as one of the most important strategic points; a legion was therefore permanently posted
at Babylon, modern Old Cairo. In times of peace the soldiers
were required to dig Nile canals, drain swamps, and the like.
Probus used them even for constructing temples and other monumental buildings. The outlay could not be too large if the
country was to yield the expected profit. To realize this profit
Rome made enormous demands. A fifth of the entire production
of grain (as had been the requirement under the Pharaohs) or
its partial equivalent in money as a ground tax, or perhaps
even double tithe plus ground rent, had to be delivered to the
state. Temple property was not free of this contribution. In
addition to the more than million and a half hundredweight of
grain annually thus realized, there were head taxes and high
import and export duties. These yielded more than they had
done under the Ptolemies because the entire Roman world had
gradually grown accustomed to certain Indian wares which
came chiefly through Egypt. Custom stations are mentioned
from the mouths of the Nile to Upper Egypt and the Red Sea;
the collectors were Egyptian, apparently because no others were
suitable for the hateful business. Of the mines, perhaps only a

small portion was directly useful to the state. Egypt's valuable minerals, the emeralds of Coptos, the red granite of Syene, the porphyry of the Claudian mountain, served luxury in dress and building. In addition to the Arabs, who were especially skillful in discovering deposits, thousands of condemned persons worked in the mines.

As regards the employment and the economic condition of the people, we can assume that Upper and Middle Egypt, as far as it is irrigated by the Nile, was entirely devoted to agriculture, and that the lively manufacture of textiles of all sorts, together with glassware and pottery, was limited to Lower Egypt, where the Delta and adjacent regions also offered great facilities for agriculture. In the upper country we may imagine that the great ancient cities were practically deserted and reduced to their indestructible temples and palaces; at least the later foundation of Ptolemais (near Girga) had surpassed them all and had come to equal Memphis — which need not mean a great deal. The population of the lower country, it may be conjectured with certainty, was composed predominantly of proletarian wage earners who possessed nothing and required little. Their industry, at least in Alexandria, had aroused the admiration of Hadrian: "Here no one is idle. Some make glass, others paper, still others are weavers; everyone belongs to a trade and makes it his vocation. Even rheumatics and the blind have their employment, and even those whose hands are lame are not idle." Whether this implies an extreme fragmentation of landed property, or, on the contrary, its centralization in a few hands, cannot be determined, for we do not know, for example, how large temple holdings and imperial domains may have been in Lower Egypt. But even freeholds were not in fact free, by reason of the enormous levies.

We have mention, incidentally, of a district called Bucolia, in the neighborhood of modern Damietta, where an ancient people, perhaps neglected for many centuries, developed into a kind of robber polity. In Italy itself the Empire at times permitted robber bands to grow out of hand. Under the very eyes of the mighty Septimius Severus and his victorious army the very capable Bulla Felix with a band of six hundred men was able to lay the entire Via Appia under contribution for two years. A few decades later there is incidental mention of a distinguished and wealthy robber family on the Genoese Riviera near Albenga which could employ two thousand armed slaves in its own affairs. We have already spoken of Isauria and the conditions which were tolerated there. But against the Egyptian Bucoles even Marcus Aurelius was constrained to wage war. "They rose up," says Dio Cassius, "and moved the other Egyptians also to revolt; a priest [and] Isidorus led them. First they trapped a Roman captain; they approached him, dressed as women, as if they would offer him money for the release of their men. Then they murdered him and his companion, swore a covenant over the entrails of the companion, and ate them. . . . They defeated the Romans in open battle, and would almost have taken Alexandria also had not Avidius Cassius, who marched against them from Syria, been able to subdue them by disrupting their unanimity and separating them, for battle could not be ventured against that mad mass."

The Bucoles proper numbered hardly a few thousand, and if number were the significant factor they might well be passed over in a history of the Roman Empire. We should find similar examples of ancient and oppressed peoples reduced to new barbarization elsewhere in the Empire if the history of the provinces were not so mute. The name Bucoles, "Cowherds," suggests a remnant of the old caste of that name; but these men apparently had nothing to do with cows, except perhaps those they stole. The flood of one of the middle arms of the Nile supplied a large lake near the sea, and the reedy marshes about the lake were the dwelling place or at least the hide-out of these pariahs; this was perhaps the most unsanitary spot in Egypt, and hence no one was likely to dispute its possession. Here the Bucoles lived partly on barges, partly in huts on small islands; young children were fastened by straps which were just long enough to prevent them from falling into the water. Passages for their peculiar canoes, where none but they could find the way, were cut through the sedge. We find mention of robber villages, but these are probably the same settlements by the lake. The Bucoles were joined by everyone who was at odds with ordinary

H

organized society; the character which they developed is indicated by the uprising under Marcus Aurelius. Even the appearance of these people, with hair down to the eyes in front and
hanging long behind, was terrifying. The contrasts offered by
localities a few days' walk apart are very striking: rich, industrial Alexandria; the robber state in the marshes; westward on
the Lake Mareotis the last Jewish hermits; in the near-by Nitric
Desert the first Christian recluses. The Bucoles themselves
proved unwilling to have anything to do with Christianity;
even at the end of the fourth century there was no single
Christian among these "wild barbarians."

But it is time to consider the character and special destiny
of the Egyptians in the later Roman period. "The Egyptian is
ashamed," says Ammianus, "if he cannot show his brown and
lean body marked with welts upon welts received for refusal to
pay his taxes. No physical torture has yet been discovered severe
enough to make a hardened Egyptian robber acknowledge his
name." This was the attitude of the lower classes toward their
officials. In any general misfortune, whether war or crop failure, the first complaint was against the government. The permanent temper of the masses was insurrectionary, and would
have been so even against better rulers. In ordinary times this
was revealed by a venomous mockery, which knew no bounds
when it emerged from servile flattery. A respectable Roman
matron who was forced to live in Egypt as the wife of the prefect never appeared in public for thirteen years and allowed no
Egyptian into her house, so that she might at least be ignored.
Those who could not thus protect themselves were exposed to
the most ribald comments and songs, "things which might seem
to the Alexandrians very agreeable, but to the victim annoying."
In the case of Caracalla, as we know, they found the wrong
man; he paid them out with a massacre of many thousands,
which had been contemplated for years. Augustus and Nero
managed more cleverly; they paid no attention to the Alexandrians' mockery, and found amusement in their talent for flattery and applause.

The Egyptians showed an appetite for quarrel and strife and
unparalleled deceit and litigiousness not only to their superiors

but also among themselves. These otherwise gloomy people could then be seen aflame with fiery anger and wild insults, perhaps only because a greeting had not been returned, or place had not been yielded in the baths, or because their insane vanity had otherwise been injured. Since the slightest disturbance might serve embittered thousands as a signal for the eruption of their inner ferment, there was always general danger in such incidents; and the official responsible for order and obedience in Egypt could thus justify inhuman repression, at least to the Emperor. It was known that peace could be restored only after blood had flowed. It is characteristic of Alexandria that in that city earlier than elsewhere in the Empire, perhaps even in Ptolemaic times, ardent partisanship for the charioteers of the Hippodrome regularly led to violence and murder.

One thing in particular can inflame such ancient, misunderstood, and abused people to insane effort, and that is their religion, which, though degenerated and bereft of all moral vitality, still takes the place of the lost national bond. So for the Egyptians first their paganism and then even their Christianity served as the channel for an amorphous and suppressed fury. The need for fanatic outbreaks was present; time and destiny determined its object. Pagan Rome was careful not to give offense in these matters. The Emperors, when they visited the country, participated in ritual and sacrifice; in the monuments they always appear as ancient Egyptian kings, with inscriptions reading, "the Ever-living, the Beloved of Isis, the Beloved of Phtha"; temples were built or completed by them or as votive offerings for them. But within Egypt itself there was always occasion for religious animosities because of jealousies between temple and temple, expressed in divergent partisanship for the sacred animals. Juvenal and Plutarch have left us genre-pictures of the subject, which might be read with unmixed pleasure if the shadowy outline of the oldest civilization on earth did not possess something of the venerable which we do not willingly see wholly trodden in the dust. Orthodoxy in one city took no exception to eating animals which were worshiped in another. "In my day," writes Plutarch (*Isis and Osiris*, 72), "the people of Oxyrhynchus ("Piketown") caught a dog and sacrificed it and ate it as if it had been sacrificial meat, because the people of Cynopolis ("Dogtown") were eating the fish known as the oxyrhynchus, or pike. As a result of this they became involved in war and inflicted much harm upon each other; and later they were both brought to order by chastisement of the Romans." Juvenal (15, 33 ff.) tells of the shameful attack of the Tentyrites against the people of Ombi, who were carefree and drunk at a festival they were celebrating; not only were mutilations and murder involved, but the devouring of a dismembered corpse, as was the case in the story of the Bucoles related above. It was easy for a legend to arise that an ancient King had once prudently prescribed various animal cults for various localities, because without the continuous rivalry thus engendered it would have been impossible to control the numerous and restless people of Egypt. In our summary view of paganism we shall have to return to this mighty religion, with its priests, its magicians, and its proud attitude to Greco-Roman paganism.

The Egyptian language, which survived and which persisted later in the so-called Coptic, was no longer the main vehicle of this religion. Men from all parts of the Empire were eager to submit to the fashionable superstition. Alexandria, which was predominantly Greek, had in its factories and harbors a mob as fanatic as any other on the Nile, as the Christians found to their distress. Here the persecution of Decius was anticipated by a full year (251) when a soothsayer aroused the people with his wild improvisations. Here too there appeared refinements in the executioner's art, as is natural among oppressed people. Those persecuted had their faces and eyes pierced by pointed reeds, were dragged on the pavements, had their teeth knocked out, had their limbs broken separately, and the like, to say nothing of the regular judicial tortures.

Socially, the entire character of this people was repulsive to the Romans. Where traveling Egyptians were to be dealt with anywhere in the wide Roman Empire, some coarse gaucherie was to be expected, "for that is the way they have been brought up." Their shouts and screams in the presence of official personages, be it the Emperor himself, were intolerable. Hence there were few qualms when the time came to bring Egypt to its senses by chastisement. Beyond the general calamities in the shape of war and pestilence which afflicted the Empire after the middle of the third century and depopulated the earth, Egypt was visited by its own special misfortunes.

Under Gallienus (254–268) it came to pass that the slave of an Alexandrian official received a military scourging because he had said, with some Egyptian mockery, that his sandals were better than those of the soldiers. The crowd showed its sympathy and mobs congregated before the residence of the Prefect Aemilianus, though it was not at first known who was to be object of the agitation. Soon stones were thrown, swords drawn, noise and fury mounted; the Prefect must either have fallen victim to the mob, or, if his exertions should succeed in mastering the mob, he could only expect dismissal and punishment. In this crisis he raised himself to Emperor, apparently on the demand of the troops, who hated the indolent Gallienus and required a leadership free of petty responsibilities against the barbarians who were harassing the country. He marched through Egypt, thrust the invading peoples back, and retained the grain in the country; some such deliverance might have been expected as the West found at this period through Posthumus and his successors. But when Aemilianus was preparing for an expedition across the Red Sea, Egypt surrendered him to Theodotus, whom Gallienus had sent as general, and Theodotus sent him as prisoner to Gallienus. Perhaps he was strangled at the same spot in the Tullian prison at Rome where Jugurtha had once starved to death.

Whether Gallienus' vengeance visited any additional special punishment upon the country is not known. In any case it can have done him little good, for Egypt was soon again lost to him (261), for a short time, it is true, but under horrible circumstances, though they can only be surmised. We do not know what battles raged in Alexandria and between whom, during the year in which Macrianus was master of the East; but at the end of that period Bishop Dionysius describes the city as having become unrecognizable by reason of the cruelties; the main thoroughfare, perhaps the famous street of thirty stades, as desolate as the wilderness of Sinai; the waters of the deserted harbor dyed red with blood, and the near-by canals of the Nile floating with corpses.

Gallienus regained mastery of Egypt, but under his successors Claudius Gothicus and Aurelian, the great Queen of Palmyra, granddaughter of the Ptolemies, caused Egypt, or at least Alexandria, to be twice conquered in her name. This was a manifestation (like similar movements in several provinces) of the last national stirring of considerable scale in an otherwise unwarlike and senile people; there was strong partisanship both for and against Zenobia, and native armies, as it appears, reinforced the troops on either side. The Palmyrenes were victorious, but not long thereafter their own kingdom fell through the great campaign of Aurelian (273). The Palmyrene party among the Egyptians which had been hostile to Rome could expect nothing but the severest chastisement; probably out of their desperation a rich Seleucid settled in Egypt, Firmus by name, arose as Emperor. Our only source for this incident assures us that he will not confuse the three persons called Firmus who figured in the contemporary history of Africa; but his description of the usurper of Egypt who is here involved presents such extraordinary contradictions that it can hardly refer to a single individual. His Firmus rides upon ostriches and is also able to digest an entire ostrich and the flesh of hippopotamuses, to say nothing of his familiarity with crocodiles; he has an anvil placed upon his body and beaten upon with sledge hammers. The same man is the friend and companion of Zenobia and one of the greatest merchants and industrialists of Egypt. He boasted that he could maintain an army with the income of his paper factories alone; he had large contracts to supply the Arabs and the Blemmyes, who controlled the trade with the Red Sea and the interior of Africa; his vessels frequently sailed to India. Whereas elsewhere they were officers, provincial nobility, and adventurers who assumed the royal purple, it is significant of Egypt that here a great merchant ventures the attempt after incessant war had in any case threatened him with ruin.

Aurelian wished to dispose of the "throne thief" quickly; he defeated him in battle and then besieged him in Alexandria. Here Firmus and his party appear to have maintained them-

selves for some time in the area of the old royal fortress, Bru-
chion; at least, after Aurelian laid hands upon Firmus and
slew him he thought it appropriate to raze that entire stately
quarter of the city. Thus was reduced to ashes the palace of
the Ptolemies, their magnificent tombs, the Museum to which
was linked all spiritual associations of later Hellenism, and the
gigantic columns of the propylaea upon which a lofty dome
had been raised — to say nothing of the devastated theaters,
basilicas, gardens, and the like. Was it vindictiveness, or did
the victor follow only strategic considerations? We must not
forget that certain areas of the Empire would be reduced to
starvation if rebellious Egypt, as in fact happened under Firmus, restricted its exports. But it is a melancholy sign for
rulers and ruled alike that such sacrifices had to be offered to
render a city incapable of insurrection and defense.

To the Egyptians this destruction served only as an added
goad. Under Probus (276–282), or perhaps earlier, one of the
most energetic of the generals, the Gaul Saturninus, came to
Egypt, and the bold Alexandrians immediately hailed him
Emperor. Terrified at the notion, Saturninus fled to Palestine.
Since he did not know the magnanimous character of Probus,
he concluded upon further reflection that he was lost, and
tearfully wrapped himself in the purple peplum of a statue of
Aphrodite, while those of his party paid him homage. His
solace was that he would at least not perish alone. Probus was
compelled to send an army, and the unhappy captive usurper
was strangled against Probus' will. Later Probus was again
forced to wage war in Egypt, because the Nubian race of the
Blemmyes, which had long been dangerous, had taken possession of a portion of Upper Egypt, specifically Ptolemais on
the Nile, of which we have already spoken. The irreconcilably
rebellious inhabitants had connived with the Blemmyes. These
Blemmyes, a lean, brown, elusive desert folk, had got control
of transportation between the harbor cities of the Red Sea and
the Nile; to subjugate or destroy them would have been
equally impractical, and so from time to time it was necessary
at least to curb them. This time, too, the Roman generals obtained the upper hand, and surely imposed severe penalties.

But under Diocletian all of Egypt again rebelled, and indeed for a period of years, for from Gaul, which had scarcely been subdued, the Emperors had been compelled to reconquer Britain, overthrow a usurper at Carthage, repel invasions of Moorish tribes, and wage war almost along the entire frontier. While the Blemmyes were again in control of Upper Egypt, at Alexandria a man quite unknown otherwise, L. Elpidius Achilleus, proclaimed himself Augustus (286). It was only after ten years (296) that Diocletian was in a position to intervene. He marched to Egypt through Palestine accompanied by the twenty-two-year-old Constantine, whose large and majestic figure outshone the Emperor. Again there was a long siege of Alexandria which lasted for eight months, during which the aqueducts were destroyed; and after Achilleus was killed there was another frightful chastisement. The capital was turned over for plunder to the army, which was presumably extremely embittered, the followers of the usurper were proscribed, and large numbers were executed. When Diocletian rode into the city, legend tells, he ordered his army to murder until blood should reach his horse's knee; but not far from the gate the animal slipped upon a corpse and stained its knee in blood, whereupon the order to murder was straightway rescinded. The spot was long marked by a brazen horse.

In Middle Egypt the city Busiris was entirely destroyed. Upper Egypt fared no better; here the rich market Coptos, where the Blemmyes would naturally take their position, suffered the same fate as Busiris. Upon this occasion Diocletian (according to Eutropius; the Christian Orosius, who uses Eutropius, says nothing of the matter) issued many prudent regulations which continued in force. He abolished, doubtless on good grounds, the old regional divisions and the organization of the country which was instituted by Augustus, and divided the country into three provinces corresponding to the organization of the other parts of the Empire. The security of trade communications was provided by setting up as competitors to the Blemmyes another African tribe from the Great Oasis, the Nobates. The Nobates were retained permanently in the pay of the Empire, and an unproductive strip of Roman territory above Syene was ceded to them, where they were henceforward to live and guard the frontier.

It was not Diocletian's fault that exhaustion of army and treasury made such makeshifts necessary, and that a kind of tribute had to be paid to the Nobates and Blemmyes alike. But quite Diocletianic is the manner by which these people were pledged to their obligations. Upon the frontier island of Philae, which incidentally received new and strong fortification, temples and altars were newly built or extant ones newly dedicated for the common *sacra* of the Nobates and the Romans and provided with a common priesthood. Both desert peoples were of the Egyptian faith, the Blemmyes with special inclination to human sacrifice; they now received or retained the right to carry the image of Isis from Philae to their country at certain holy seasons and to keep it there for a fixed period. An extant inscription depicts the solemn progress of the sacred barge carrying the image of the goddess upon the Nile.

Meanwhile a new city had arisen in Upper Egypt near Coptos, which had been destroyed; this the Emperor named Maximianopolis in honor of his eldest colleague. This was perhaps only a garrison, or perhaps it was the old Apollinopolis rechristened.

Some comfort at least was given to Alexandria itself in its sorrow and depression; Diocletian again assigned the city definite distributions of grain, a favor which many cities outside Italy had come to enjoy. In return the Alexandrians now counted their years according to Diocletian's reign, and the Prefect Pompeius in 302 erected in his honor the pillar which has wrongly been called Pompey's. The pillar still bears the inscription: "To the all-holy Autocrator, the genius of the city of Alexandria, the unconquered Diocletian." The gigantic monolith, taken from an earlier public building or intended for one which was never completed, towers high above the scarcely recognizable remains of the Serapeum.

Finally we have a late and somewhat enigmatic notice to the effect that Diocletian at that time caused all of the writings of the ancient Egyptians concerning the production of gold and silver to be collected and burned so that the Egyptians should no longer draw wealth from such sources and in their consequent pride rise up against Rome. It has been shrewdly remarked that Diocletian would certainly have retained the books for his own and the Empire's use if he had believed in the possibility of alchemy. But it is hardly likely that Diocletian's measure proceeded, as Gibbon assumes, purely out of benevolent enlightenment. Perhaps transmutation into gold was linked with other revolting superstitions in Egypt which the ruler, who was a pious man in his own fashion, wished to discourage.

With Diocletian insurrections in Egypt ceased, and for a considerable period. Had he been able in his wisdom actually to help the country substantially, to improve the character of its inhabitants, or at least to keep them intimidated over a long period? Did the new general imperial regulations suffice to make insurrection unattractive or impossible? The most probable explanation has already been suggested. In the first place the division of imperial authority prevented the rise of native and local usurpers in the provinces. Furthermore, after Constantine Egyptian passions found an outlet in ecclesiastical disputes, which were more appropriate to the sinking energies of that unhappy nation than desperate rebellions against Roman officials and armies. The long series of theological disturbances was initiated by the Meletian and Arian quarrel as soon as Christianity was proclaimed. But in Egypt, as nowhere else in the Empire, the pagans also were zealous for their religion and defended it with bloody uprisings.

From one point of view Egypt, like all Africa, was the securest possession of the Roman Empire; aside from a number of half-savage tribes whose incursions could easily be repelled with moderate effort, the frontiers were only desert. While the frontiers on the Rhine, the Danube, and the Euphrates were menaced by strong and hostile peoples, here relatively slight garrisons, suitably distributed, were sufficient. For at that time none could dream that a religious and conquering fanaticism would one day arise in Arabia and irresistibly roll victorious over the entire southern and eastern portions of the Roman

Empire and assimilate them to itself. In the third century the northern coast of Africa was certainly incomparably more populous than it has ever been since. The monuments of Algeria, the large number of bishoprics later recorded, the considerable cultural activity and its place in later Roman literature, imply conditions which cannot be fairly judged by the relative poverty of external events. Above all Carthage, which had been restored by Caesar, had by reason of its position become one of the first cities of the Empire, and also one of the most dangerous. The city's moral corruption, which later demoralized the brave Vandals as Capua's luxury had demoralized Hannibal's soldiers, was not the worst; the temple which Dido had founded to the celestial deity Astroarche was fatal to the Empire, less on account of its complaisant prostitutes than by reason of the subversive oracles which it issued and the support which it gave to more than one usurper. The purple robe, which hung from the image enthroned upon lions and wielding lightning and scepter, covered the shoulders of more than one anti-Emperor. Now too upon the accession of Diocletian a certain Julian rose in opposition to him. Of his origin and subsequent fate we know nothing; he must have been at the head of the so-called Quinquegentiani or Five Peoples against whom Maximian was forced to campaign and of whom we know little more. They were doubtless Mauretanians, that is, from the western half of North Africa, where the Atlas range must have sheltered, as it does today, a number of small peoples inaccessible to direct attack. No serious occupation on the part of these peoples was to be feared if the Roman officials did not willfully neglect their duty. Maximian undertook this war only after several years of relaxation (297), whence we may infer that the danger was not pressing and that corn shipments to Italy were not interrupted. With the defection of Egypt, which had lasted until the year preceding, the Empire could less than ever have forgone the grain from Africa.

V

PAGANISM : INTERMINGLING OF GODS

MARTYRDOM and the streams of Christian blood shed in the great persecutions have given a frightful reputation to the last period of the reign of Diocletian and Maximian. Efforts to determine the scope of the persecutions and the number of their victims, even approximately, have been in vain. There are no trustworthy data on the number of Christians in the Roman Empire at the time, and without such data calculation is impossible. According to Stäudlin, Christians comprised half the entire population; according to Matter, a fifth; according to Gibbon, only a twentieth; according to La Bastie, a twelfth, which is perhaps nearest the truth. More precisely, we may conjecture that for the West the proportion was a fifteenth, and for the East a tenth.

But let us ignore the numerical relationship for the moment and consider the contemporary internal conditions of the two great rival organizations, Christianity and paganism.

Christianity was brought to the world by high historical necessity, as a period to antiquity, as a break with it, and yet in part to preserve it and transmit it to new peoples who as pagans might well have utterly barbarized and destroyed a purely pagan Roman Empire. The time was come for men to enter into a new relationship with things of the senses and things beyond the senses, for love of God and neighbor and separation from things earthly to take the place of older views of the gods and the world.

Three centuries had stabilized the life and doctrine of the Christians into fixed forms. Constant threats and frequent persecutions had kept the community from early disintegration and enabled it to overcome serious internal cleavage. It had succeeded in separating out of its body ascetic fanatics (Montanist and others) as well as speculative enthusiasts (the Gnostics) who sought to make of Christianity a framework for Platonic and Oriental ideologies. With Manichaeism, the newest and strongest attempt of this character, the struggle had just begun. Forerunners of Arianism, in the shape of disputes concerning the Second Person of the Trinity, seemed effectively disposed of. Numerous quarrels concerning individual points of Church discipline did indeed appear, but in this period of persecution these differences did not prove as dangerous as they later did in the centuries of the Church triumphant when such matters became occasion for permanent cleavages.

Within Christianity itself many things were freely countenanced which were later found irreconcilable. In the fourth and fifth centuries people rightly wondered how it had been possible for the Church to tolerate the speculation and the symbolic interpretation of Scripture of an Origen. Many others who were esteemed as Fathers in the burgeoning and struggling Church were later recognized as half heretic. The catechumens of the old Church derived from too many origins, had received too diverse educations, and had joined the Church out of reasons too various, for complete uniformity of life and doctrine to be possible. As in all earthly concerns, those rare souls filled with spiritual profundity and practical devotion were surely a small minority; the great mass felt attracted by the forgiveness of sins which was made prominent, by the immortality of the soul which was promised, and by the mystery which surrounded the sacraments and which for many was surely only a parallel to the pagan mysteries. The slave was attracted by Christian freedom and brotherly love, and many an unworthy convert by the very considerable alms which were bestowed with true impartiality, particularly by the community in Rome.

The large number of heroic martyrs who from time to time quickened the relaxed tension of the community and implanted contempt of death anew does not testify so much to the internal perfection of the Church as to the future victory which was inevitable to a cause cherished with such devotion. Firm belief in an immediate entry to heaven surely inspired many persons who were internally confused and even debased to voluntary immolation; in any case, the value set upon life in that age of suffering and despotism was slighter than in the centuries of Germano-Roman domination. At times there was a veritable epidemic of self-sacrifice; the Christians thrust forward to death and had to be admonished by their teachers to spare themselves. Soon the martyrs became shining ideals of all life; a literal cult became attached to their burial places, and their intercessions before God became one of the highest hopes of the Christian. Their superiority to other saints is easy to understand: no other religion has so glorified its individual blood witnesses as has Christianity, and none has so preserved its own struggles in memory. Scenes of martyrdom became classic ground, and the persecutions of the earlier Emperors, especially those of Decius, had provided that such ground should be found underfoot everywhere. In view of the usages of the martyr cult which had become traditional, the Diocletianic persecutions would seem to have been ill-advised from the outset.

About this time the organization of the Church already showed the beginnings of a regular hierarchy. To be sure, the choice of spiritual leaders or at least their confirmation remained in the hands of the communities, but these came more and more definitely to be distinguished from the *laity* as *clergy*. Distinctions arose among the bishops according to the position of their cities and with particular consideration for the apostolic foundation of certain congregations. The synods, which were convened for many various reasons, served to unite the bishops as a higher rank. Among the bishops themselves serious degeneration becomes apparent as early as the third century. We find many of them sunk in worldly pomp, as Roman officials, as merchants, even as usurers; the egregious example of Paul of Samosata is rightly thought to be by no means unique. Naturally, by the side of the worldlings we find their extreme opposites, men who retired from temporal concerns, state, and society into solitude. We shall have to discuss the origin of the eremite movement along with other points here touched upon.

A large and widespread literature, which includes several of the best products of modern historiography, deals in detail with the matters mentioned above, each according to the point of view which the author adopts and his reader demands. No one can begrudge the present work because its viewpoint is not that of edification, which a scholar like Neander, for example, may properly adopt.

If we seek to realize in brief the true strength of the Christian community at the beginning of the last persecution we shall find that it lay neither in numbers, nor in a consistent superiority in its members' morality, nor in the excellence of its internal constitution, but in the firm belief in immortality of the soul which permeated each individual Christian. We shall show presently that later paganism directed all its efforts to the same goal, but by gloomy and labyrinthine bypaths and without Christianity's triumphant conviction; it could not maintain competition with Christianity in the long run because Christianity had so utterly simplified this problem. To the political needs of the ancient world, furthermore, which the Roman rule of force had brought to despair of politics, Christianity offered a new state, a new democracy, even a new civic society, if it could have been kept pure. Many an ancient ambition, finding itself without position in the Roman state, threatened and reduced to silence, was able to make its way to an episcopal see in the congregations and thus find some scope at least for self-assertion. On the other hand, the best and most humble must have found the congregations a sacred refuge from the pressure of Roman corruption, now grown rank.

Confronting these great advantages we find paganism in full process of dissolution, so that it can hardly be thought of as likely to endure even without the appearance of Christi-

anity. If we imagine, for the sake of illustration, that Mohammed had straightway introduced his fanatic monotheism
without any preparation on the part of Christianity, Mediterranean paganism would certainly have succumbed to his first
attack as surely as did the paganisms of the Near East. Paganism had been mortally weakened by internal disintegration
and willful intermixture from without.

The state religion of the Empire, which must form our point of
departure, was in any case the Greco-Roman polytheism shaped
by the prehistoric relationship of the two cults and their later
amalgamation. Out of nature divinities and tutelary deities
for every possible situation in life, a remarkable circle of superhuman figures had arisen, in whose myths, however, ancient man everywhere recognized his own likeness. The connection of morality with this religion was quite loose, and
depended largely on the feeling of the individual. The gods
indeed were believed to reward good and chastise evil, but
they were thought of as givers and preservers of life and
property rather than as superior moral forces. His various
mysteries provided the Greek, in addition to popular beliefs,
not a purer religion, even less a sage enlightenment in sacred
matters, but only a secret rite of worship which would render
the gods especially favorable to the initiate. A beneficial effect
was involved, at least incidentally, in the specific requirement
of purity and also in the quickening of national sentiment
which was characteristic of the mysteries as well as of the
festive games of the Greeks.

In opposition to this religion, philosophy, as soon as it was
lifted above questions of cosmogony, proclaimed the unity of
the divine being more or less clearly. Thus a way was opened
to highest religiosity and to the fairest moral ideals, but also
to pantheism and even to atheism, which could claim similar
freedom with respect to popular beliefs. Those who did not
deny the existence of gods explained them pantheistically as
the basic forces of the universe, or, like the Epicureans, left
them idle and indifferent to the world. "Enlightenment" too
had its part in the mélange; Euhemerus and his followers had
long ago made the gods out to be ancient rulers, warriors, or

the like, and had explained miracles rationally as deception or misunderstanding. They were on the wrong trail, and later the Church Fathers and apologetes were constantly being misguided by them in their evaluation of paganism.

All of this ferment the Romans had taken over along with Greek culture, and preoccupation with these problems became to the educated a matter of principle as well as of fashion. Along with superstition, disbelief grew among the higher classes of society, though genuine atheists may have been few. With the third century, however, as a result of the great dangers of the Empire, disbelief waned visibly, and a kind of faith came to the fore, though to the advantage of the foreign cults rather than of the old state religion. But in Rome the ancient native cult was so closely bound up with the state, and the relevant superstition so firmly rooted, that the unbeliever as well as the believer in foreign cults had to show official Roman piety in questions relating to the sacred fire of Vesta, to the secret pledges of rule, to the state auspices, for Rome's eternity depended on these sanctities. Not only were the Emperors themselves *Pontifices maximi*, with specific ritual obligations, but their title of Augustus signified a supernatural consecration, justification, and immunity. It was no mere flattery when superstition finally accorded them the status of *daimones* after Christianity put an end to the ·apotheoses, temples, altars, and priesthoods which had been their prerogative for three hundred years.

There can be no doubt that even in the latest period of paganism's dominance the genuine Greek and Roman religion had not been supplanted in the hearts of many individuals by alien deities, not replaced by magic and incantation, not dispersed by philosophic abstractions. This cannot be demonstrated directly because worship of the old gods did not exclude worship of the new, and because in the interchange of deities, which will be noticed below, a new god might be worshiped under the name of an old, and vice versa. But the probability cannot be denied when we see the old and naïve relationship of the sound ancient man to gods and fate break out here and there with compelling force. "Thee I worship," Avienus ad-

I

dresses Nortia, the Etruscan equivalent to Fortuna, "I whom
Vulsinii bore, who dwell at Rome, who was twice honored by
the proconsulship, who am dedicated to poesy, innocent and
without reproach, happy in my wife Placida and in my healthy
and lively children. As for the rest, may it transpire according
to the decree of destiny."

In other cases the old religion and its view of life asserts itself emphatically even though innovations have been added.
Diocletian's own faith must have been of this character. At
least he was faithful to the Etruscan haruspices, which were
not yet at war, as later in Julian's court, with Neoplatonist
conjurers; his tutelary deity continued to be Jupiter; and the
oracle which he consulted in matters of greatest moment was
that of the Milesian Apollo. His morality and religiosity, as
expressed, for example, in his legislation, has closest affinity
with that of Decius; in his cult of the good Emperors, especially of Marcus Aurelius, who was worshiped as a *daimon,*
he also follows Alexander Severus. On the other hand, it may
be assumed that many portions and implications of the old
religion had long died and been forgotten. The crowd of petty
Roman tutelary deities had perhaps come to be regarded as
antiquarian trifles, though Christian writers inveigh against
them as something still persisting. Men scarcely longer thought
of the god Lateranus in connection with the hearth, of Unxia
in connection with anointing, of Cinxia in connection with
girdling, of Puta in connection with pruning, of Nodutis in
connection with grain stalks, of Mellonia in connection with
bee-keeping, of Limentinus in connection with the threshold,
and the like. A quite different and generalized view of *genii*
and *daimones* had long come to prevail in the minds of men.
Much of the earlier belief was and remained quite local in
character.

Greece especially retained in imperial times its affectionate
esteem of local cults and mystery worship. Pausanias, who
wrote a description of Greece in the second century, provides
ample evidence for the special worship of gods and heroes in
every city and locality and for the various priesthoods in
charge of this worship. His silence concerning the mysteries

was a pious duty; posterity would have been grateful to him for transgressing it.

Just as the Roman state required certain *sacra* for its continued existence — with the result, for example, that the sacred fire was tended by Vestal Virgins far into Christian times — so the private life of the individual, from the cradle to the grave, was shot through with religious usages. At home, feasting and sacrifice were inseparable. On the city streets one encountered processions and spectacles, sometimes dignified and handsome, sometimes bacchanalian and orgiastic, which filled the Greek like the Roman calendar of feasts. In the country there were sacrifices without end at chapels, grottoes, crossroads, and under venerable trees. The newly converted Arnobius tells of the devotion he had felt as a pagan when he passed tree trunks decked with gay ribbons or boulders bearing traces of the oil which had been poured upon them. It is difficult to extract the moral content from a cult which seems so superficial and frequently altogether frivolous, and many will deny that such a content is to be found. Does not virtually the same question arise, after fifteen hundred years, concerning the festivals of the Mediterranean Catholic? The sound of thoroughly sensual music surrounds the High Mass and, interrupted by salvos of cannon, accompanies the sacrament; a lively market, abundant food, gaiety of all sorts, and the inevitable fireworks in the evening, constitute the second part of the festival. One who takes exception to all this cannot be prevented from so doing; but we must not forget that this outward conduct is not the whole religion and that in different people the highest feelings are aroused by different means. If we leave aside Christian feelings of sinfulness and humility, of which the ancient world was not capable, we shall be able to judge their worship more justly.

Details of mythology, which were never a matter of faith, were wholly abandoned long before Lucian made a delightful burlesque of them. Christian apologetes were somewhat disingenuous when they sought out a collection of disgraceful items from the most diverse myths and by misunderstanding and mixing elements of disparate character heaped ridicule upon the ancient beliefs. They must have known that attacks of this sort, which they drew from the ancient poets and mythographers, possessed only slight relevance to their own century. Protestantism, for example, might as justly be held responsible for the absurdities in many legends. The religious consciousness of the masses was little concerned with myth; it was satisfied with the existence of individual divinities as rulers and protectors of nature and of human life. How completely contemporary philosophy disposed of the myths we shall see in the sequel. But the pagans continued to put weapons into the hands of Christian polemicists by their dramatic representations of individual myths, and often of the most objectionable.

For in one province mythology reigned supreme until the latest period, the province of art and poetry. Homer, Phidias, and the tragedians had once helped create the gods and heroes, and now what had vanished from faith was preserved in stone, color, masks, writings, and terra cotta. But their life was more apparent than real. Of the fate of the plastic arts and the causes of their decline we shall deal presently; here we must observe that their ability to support the old mythology was nullified by the fact that they entered the service of mythicizing philosophy and even of the foreign cults. Drama was largely and perhaps completely supplanted by the local mime and by the silent pantomime with music and dance. All religious aspects, such as had once made Attic drama a form of worship, disappeared. The description of the elegant Corinthian ballet *Paris on Ida* in the tenth book of Apuleius shows that the theater in Greece itself during the age of the Antonines served only as an eye-filling spectacle. Here at least we may assume a refined and stylized work of art, whereas in the Latin parts of the Empire, especially in regions only half Romanized and only through military colonies, the exhibitions must have been crude indeed, if the theaters presented any dramatic performances at all and were not wholly given to gladiatorial games, wild beast hunts, and the like. The scurrilous aspects of mythology were intentionally made prominent. All the adulteries of Jupiter, even those which involved his transformation into an animal, all the scandals of Venus, were presented to ribald laughter. Similar epiphanies found place even in the mimes. An Aristophanic audience could tolerate such things without prejudice to faith, but in a sick age they were the *coup de grâce* for the old religion as a whole.

If we move from the sphere in which ballet master and stage mechanic were supreme to the realm of poetry, so far as we can follow it in the few survivals from the end of the third century, we still find scattered evidence of great talent for mythologic treatment, most brilliantly represented by Claudian a full century later; but the last trace of inner conviction had long been extinguished. The poem of a certain Reposianus, for example, who may have flourished about 300, depicts the dallying of Mars and Venus with the same purpose as we may assume in the pantomimes: sensually attractive images skirting the obscene. Venus while awaiting the god of war passes the time in dancing, and the poet describes her various postures with a well-developed sense for the coquetry of his time; then when Mars appears he calls upon Cupid, the Graces, and the maidens of Byblos to disrobe him. But what a Mars is this! He is intentionally represented as uncouth as the goddess is seductive. He falls into the bower of roses like a lump of lead, and in the description of his slumber the reader is not spared his lusty snores. When Rubens, for example, tackles ancient myth in his own manner, he may be absolved by the impression of mighty if errant energy he conveys; but here we are at the lowest rung of degradation of ancient saga without other recompense than pretty verses. A satirical Christian could not have effected his purpose better, and we might be prepared to accept some such explanation for this poem if the pretty picture of Cupid did not prevent it. Cupid curiously inspects the weapons which Mars has laid aside, decorates them with flowers, and then, when jealous Vulcan makes his rowdy entrance, creeps under the helmet to hide.

There were some poets who had grown wholly surfeited with mythology as a path trodden to shreds. "Who has not sung," cries Nemesianus, "the sorrows of Niobe bereft, of Semele, and . . . [here follow thirty hexameters of titles of myths]. All of this has been exhausted by a crowd of great poets; the saga of the ancient world is used up." The poet therefore turns to green forests and meadows, not, however, to compose landscape poetry, but to introduce his own theme, the breeding of hunting dogs. Then when he is done with this theme, he remembers to celebrate the deeds of his patrons, the Caesars Carinus and Numerianus.

A similar feeling had long given didactic poetry, especially among the Romans, marked preference over epic; but the preference had never been expressed so bluntly. One charming poem of mythologic content, the *Bacchus* of Calpurnius Siculus (*Eclogue* 3), may be cited here for its remarkable dependence upon works of plastic art; it recalls Philostratus' descriptions of pictures but surpasses them in style. We even find the hoary Silenus, who rocks the infant Bacchus in his arms as a nurse, makes him laugh, amuses him with castanets, and good-naturedly allows him to pluck at his ears, chin, and the hair of his chest. Then the growing god teaches the satyrs the first vintage, until they grow drunk with the new beverage, smear themselves with wine lees, and abduct nymphs. This bacchanal, in which the god even gives his panthers drink out of the mixing-bowl, is one of the last ancient works of living beauty.

All this goes to prove that mythology was rather a burden than a support for sinking classical religion. Of attempts to maintain and justify myths by philosophic interpretation we shall speak in the sequel.

But this classical religion was also disturbed and breached by another factor, namely, admixture of the cults of subjugated provinces and foreign countries. We are now in a period of a consummated theocrasy (intermingling of gods).

This came about not because of the mingling of peoples in the Empire or because of caprice and fashion alone, but because of the age-old urge of polytheistic religions to approach one another, to seek out similarities, and to transform them into identities. In all ages parallels of this sort have suggested the intriguing idea of a common primitive religion, which each man pictures according to his own bent, the polytheist differently from the monotheist. And so worshipers of similar deities sought and found themselves, some unwittingly and some with philosophic intent, before the same altars. Hellenic Aphrodite was willingly recognized in the Astarte of the Near East, in the Hathor of the Egyptians, in the Celestial Goddess of the Carthaginians; and other divinities were similarly identified. This must be especially noticed, even for the later Roman period: the mixture of gods is at the same time a substitution of gods; the alien gods were not only propagated by the side of the native, but were substituted for the native according to their inward kinship.

A second cause of theocrasy is to be seen in the recognition, as it were, political, which the Greek and Roman and the polytheist generally paid to the gods of other peoples. He acknowledged them as gods, even if they were not his own. There was no strict dogmatic system to guard the frontiers of native belief. Rigidly as ancestral superstitions were preserved, there was rather friendliness than hate for the superstitions of others. Certain solemn transfers of divinities from one country to another were enjoined by oracles and other supernatural admonitions. Thus Serapis of Sinope was moved to Alexandria under the first Ptolemy, and the Great Mother of Pessinus to Rome during the Second Punic War. Among the Romans it became virtually a conscious principle, half political and half religious, not to offend the gods of the many subjugated peoples, but rather to show them reverence and even to accept them among their own gods. The attitude of the provinces was very diverse. Asia Minor willingly met the Roman halfway. Egypt was unyielding; it translated what it received from the Ptolemies and the Romans into its own ritual and art forms, whereas the Romans sought to please the Egyptians by worshiping the Egyptian gods in something approximating the Egyptian forms. The Jew, finally, would have nothing to do with Roman religion, whereas Romans of good taste observed his Sabbath and Emperors came to worship in the temple on Moriah. There took place, as we shall directly see, a partly active and partly passive mingling of gods.

A third cause for accepting foreign cults lay in the fear and anxiety which oppressed the pagan who had grown to disbelieve in his old gods. It is no longer a matter of "gods everywhere" in the pleasing sense of earlier centuries. Rather, the thoughtful man sought for new symbols daily, and the thoughtless for new fetishes, which were the more welcome the more distant and mysterious their origin seemed. A special factor multiplied confusion. The polytheism of ancient civilizations survived in all the stages of its development simultaneously. As fetishism it continued to worship aeroliths and amulets, as Sabaism stars and elements, as anthropomorphism partly nature gods and partly tutelary gods — while the educated had long since inwardly discarded these husks and wavered between pantheism and monotheism. And now all these stages of various paganisms interacted upon Greco-Roman paganism, and vice versa. We have reports of remarkable instances, and sometimes they make melancholy reading. Nero was brought up in the Roman religion, but he soon despised it, and adhered only to the Syrian goddess. Presently he deserted her, played knavish tricks with her image, and placed his sole faith in an amulet which a man of the people had given him and to which he now offered sacrifice thrice daily.

This example, one of many that might be cited, provides a hint of the nature of the cults of foreign gods in general. They were not approached in the same spirit as were the old Olympians; wrenched out of their natural environment and alien to Roman life, government, and climate, they could impress the Romans only as weird and daimonic powers which could be prevailed upon only by mysteries and magic rites, perhaps also by great material expenditures. It is not for nothing that Lucian assigns to foreign gods the superior rank when, in *Jupiter Tragoedus* (Ch. 8), he establishes a hierarchy of the gods based on the material they were made of; anxious superstition preferred to have its gods made of the most precious metal. "You see the peculiarity of the Greek contingent: they have grace and beauty and artistic workmanship, but they are all marble or bronze—the most costly of them only ivory with just an occasional gleam of gold, the merest surface plating;

and even those are wood inside, harboring whole colonies of
mice. Whereas Bendis here, Anubis there, Attis next door, and
Mithras and Men, are all of solid gold, heavy and intrinsically
precious." * But this sort of cult demoralized the attitude to
the ancient national gods.

Let us now look at the active (from the Roman point of
view) mixture of gods, in which the Romans were rather the
givers than the receivers.

Such a relationship obtained, it is obvious, chiefly for those
peoples which Rome took over in a semi-civilized state and in
which it could give currency to its superior culture as well as
to its religion; these were the peoples of Gaul, Spain, and
Britain. Unfortunately, it is only in Gaul that we know something of the religious conditions, and that chiefly through
dedicatory inscriptions and sculptures.

The later Romans in their truly universal superstition participated in the local cult in Gaul, as they did elsewhere, as
long as it retained any vitality. They not only consulted the
Druids concerning the future, as we have seen, but they took
part in actual ritual. So the later Emperor Pescennius Niger
solemnly participated in an occult rite in Gaul to which only
continent people could be invited. But no Gallic deity was
transferred to Italy, Africa, or Greece. (If we find the Celtic
sun-god Belenus in Aquileia, other Celtic divinities in Salz-
burg and Styria, Apollo Grannus at Lauingen in Swabia, and
the like, these are not to be understood as importations from
the period of theocrasy but as the latest evidence of the presence of the aboriginal Celtic population of these regions before Germans, Slavs, and Avars penetrated the Alps.) In Gaul
itself every effort was made to clothe the popular religion in a
Roman dress. The gods assumed not only Roman names but
also the art forms of classical anthropomorphism. Taran had to
be called Jupiter, and was depicted as such; Teutates as Mercury; Hesus or Camulus as Mars. Other deities at least retained their names, either alone or along with a Roman name.
Thus we have Belenus or Apollo Belenus, and frequently,

* H. W. and F. G. Fowler, *The Works of Lucian of Samosata,* III, 84.
Oxford 1905. — Translator.

Apollo Grannus, Mars Camulus, Minerva Belisana, and the like. Then the Romanized gods received special cognomens in addition; some we can derive from localities, or explain by conjecture; some are frankly baffling. Thus we have Diana Abnoba (the designation of the Black Forest); Diana Ardoinna (perhaps Ardennes); Mars Vincius (Vence, in southern France); Hercules Magusanus and Saxanus (especially in the Netherlands); Mars Lacavus (at Nîmes); Apollo Toutiorix (at Wiesbaden). Or the Romanized god was associated with a non-Romanized, perhaps kindred, deity; so Veriogodumnus was associated with Apollo in Amiens; and Sirona, who is conceived somewhat as Diana or Minerva (as is Belisana), in Bordeaux and southern Germany. But Romanization went no further. A host of deities retained their Celtic names, mostly with the prefix Deus (or Dea) Sanctus (or Sancta), or even Augustus (or Augusta), which was here employed without reference to the title of the Emperors. At first glance one is tempted to regard all these deities as local, and many in fact are, as for example Vosegus in Bergzabern, Nemausus in Nîmes, Aventia in Aventicum, Vesontius in Besançon, Luxovius in Luxeuil, Celeia in Cilli; but others have no such signification, as for example Abellio in Convennes, Acionna in Orléans, Agho in Bagnères, Bemilucius in Paris, Hariasa in Cologne, Intarabus in Treves. Moreover, many appear in widely disparate localities: Taranucus in Heilbronn and in Dalmatia; the water-goddess Nehalennia in France and in the Netherlands. The eagerness with which the gods were Romanized wherever possible is also indicated by the Roman class names for the numerous minor collective deities: Matres, Matrones, Campestres (field spirits), Silvani (forest spirits), Bivia, Trivia, and Quadrivia (divinities of the crossroads), Proxumi and Vicani (geniuses of neighborhood), and the like. The Sulevi and the Comedovi, which belonged to the same category, must have defied translation. Such expressions as "Genius of the Place" and "Genius of the Region," strictly speaking, imply only Roman ritual practices, but it is probable that they here represent Celtic usages. In any case, until late in the fourth century the mightiest god continued to be Teutates-Mercury, who still offered vigorous resistance to St. Martin of Tours; Jupiter the saint regarded as stupid and dull, *brutus atque hebes.*

The reaction of these Occidental religions upon Rome itself was singularly slight, as we have remarked, or nonexistent.

The situation with reference to the ancient civilizations of the East, Persia, Egypt, Asia Minor, and the Semites, was very different. To the latter the far-flung geographical distribution of their settlements was a great advantage, for the Romans did not first learn their idolatry in Syria; Semitic religion had for many centuries been spread abroad by Phoenicia and Carthage over the entire Mediterranean and even beyond the Pillars of Hercules. As Rome gradually incorporated Spain, Africa, and the islands, it took over broad stretches of Punic territory and Punic cult. The Roman hated Carthage but not its gods. Persian dualism, on the other hand, especially in its later orthodox renewal by the Sassanids, resisted any mixture and compromise with the Greco-Roman circle of gods as vigorously as did Jewish monotheism. But Persia offered an older metamorphosis of Parseeism, which had degenerated in the direction of superstition, and from this Rome borrowed Mithras.

The peoples of the Near East from the Euphrates to the Mediterranean, the Archipelago, and the Pontus, with which it is proper to begin, were by no means derived from the same racial strain, but their religions had so affected one another from high antiquity that for such a late epoch as we are here dealing with we may regard them as one. Determination of origins is not relevant in this place and would lead us far astray. Furthermore, long before the Roman victories over Antiochus the Great another mixture of gods had taken place involving the gods of the Near East and those of Greece, from the period of the Hellenization of Asia Minor and with accelerated speed under Alexander's successors. This mixture was parallel to the mingling of Greek and Oriental language and culture. The magnificent Greek cities, which sprang out of the earth everywhere in the lands of the successors in incredible number, retained, along with their Greek language, civic polity, and mores, their Greek gods. But in the country, particularly at a distance from the sea, the old language maintained itself more or less stubbornly, and at a later period, with the inward exhaustion of the formative force of Greece, its strength actually increased. In Palestine, under the protection of a rigidly exclusive religion and way of life, Aramaic survived despite terrible upheavals. In Syria, so soon as it was a question of popular effectiveness and no longer of classical elegance, writers reverted to the native language, as is shown in the second century in the Gnostic Bardesanes, in the fourth in St. Ephraem, and clearly enough by the Syriac versions of the Bible. We have no detailed information of the language situation in Asia Minor, but as long as the popular language was maintained, the popular gods were also.

The general basis for the religions in question is worship of the stars, but confused to the point of being unrecognizable by an idolatry which was partly an addition from without, partly a necessary internal development. An elaborate sacrificial service sought to conciliate the gods by offerings, chiefly of animal life, but also by regular and occasional human sacrifice. These persisted with singular stubbornness, particularly in regions of Phoenician culture; they survived long after the fall and reconstruction of Carthage, so that Tiberius was compelled to proceed against them with drastic penalties. The highest pair of deities, Baal and Astarte (sun and moon, morning star and evening star), survived in Roman times under the most diverse names and personifications and in numerous temples as Lord and Lady of all life. From the Old Testament we know Baalzebub, Baalpeor, Baalberith, and the like, whose names may have been long forgotten. In Palmyra Baal seems to have been divided into two divinities for sun and moon, as Aglibol and Malachbel, who are represented on a very late Palmyrene relief in the Capitoline Museum bearing the Greco-Roman name of the donor, Lucius Aurelius Heliodorus, son of Antiochus Hadrianus. In the magnificent and exceedingly large and lofty temple at Emesa lay the Black Stone, an aerolith, which was regarded as an image of the sun-god Elagabalus and was worshiped as such far and wide. Elagabalus' priests wore long purple tunics embroidered with gold and diadems of precious stones. In the temple at Hierapolis, beside the famous Syrian goddess (who will be mentioned below), there stood a golden image of Baal, represented as Zeus, seated on a chariot drawn by bulls. At Heliopolis (Baalbek) Baal was worshiped in a quite late half-Roman personification; his golden image bore not only the scourge of the Roman sun-god, but also the lightning of Jupiter. Antoninus Pius built a new temple on the huge foundations of the old; the ruins of this temple still justify its being accounted at the time one of the wonders of the world. After what has been said above, the name of Zeus, to whom Antoninus dedicated the sanctuary, should not mislead us, seeing that the ancient place name referred to Baal and the Greek to Helios. This temple, like that at Emesa, enjoyed a wide reputation for its oracle, which might be consulted by letter — an arrangement not unusual in Asiatic oracles. More dubious and less significant traces of Baal-worship under the Emperors may be passed over; suffice it that this cult, more or less transformed, continued to be the principal worship of the Near East, to which some of the most important temples were dedicated, and hence probably many others also, of which we have no information. Perhaps the god Carmel, who possessed an altar on the mountain of the same name and dispensed oracles, was also a transformation of Baal. As an outpost of this cult to the south was Marnas, the god of Gaza, if Marnas really was a form of the great god. It was Marnas who was the despair of the Christian teachers and settlers of that region throughout the fourth century, and who made the region about Gaza a virtually inexpugnable refuge of paganism. We shall meet him presently as the personal enemy of St. Hilarion.

This major Semite god now forced his way into Roman religion in more than one form. Romans who lived or had lived in the East probably worshiped him as Zeus or Jupiter. But the worship of the sun-god which became so prominent in the later period must have been shared principally by Baal and Mithras; less attention was paid to the ancient Sol-Helios. Elagabalus eventually received, at least for a number of years, a large and distinguished position in the Roman pantheon through the mad youth who had been and continued to be his priest and took the god's name when he sat upon the throne of the world. When this Antoninus Bassianus brought the Black Stone of Emesa to Rome (between 218 and 222) one could say that theocrasy had well-nigh reached its consummation. The new god received a great temple and colossal sacrifices, and soon a wife also. The Emperor fetched the image and treasures of the Celestial Goddess from Carthage and married her to Elagabalus; mythologically no exception could be taken to the match. Rome and Italy were required to celebrate the marriage in a festive manner. The palladium, the fire of Vesta, and other ancient Roman *sacra* were brought to the temple of the new god. After the murder of the imperial priest the stone is said to have been escorted back to Syria, apparently because of the loathsome memories connected with it.

But much more powerful than the worship of Baal in the Roman Empire was that represented by the Great Goddess of many names. In relation to the sun-god she is the moon; in a broader sense she is Nature, mother of all living things. From high antiquity onwards the Near East celebrated her with wild bacchanalian tumult, as was appropriate to a divinity devoid of all moral attributes. Joyous shouts and mourning wails, orgiastic dances and lugubrious flute music, prostitution of women and self-castration of men had always accompanied this cult of the sensual life of nature. A myth not very widely dispersed but varying in its forms according to place and time was woven about these celebrations and provided the Romans of a quite late period occasion for strange mysteries.

For the moment we shall disregard Egyptian Isis, who is a kindred collateral form of the Great Goddess, and follow the latter in the forms which are still recognizable in the third century.

The Old Testament knew and abhorred her as Ashtaroth, and there were still temples of Astarte in Phoenicia; Lucian knew one in Sidon. He mentions it in passing in his famous piece *On the Syrian Goddess;* this essay is our source for facts, but is of no less interest as illustrating the attitude of this frivolous, Greek-educated Syrian to his pagan cult. Nowhere has Lucian pushed his mockery so far; he assumes naïveté and imitates the style and Ionic dialect of respectable old Herodotus in order to make the ridiculous aspects of that particular idolatry more uproarious. But we also learn what scenes must have surrounded and influenced the mocker's youth before he broke with all cults and all religions. No Athenian could have written Lucian's books.

From Phoenicia this worship, under the title of the Celestial Goddess, spread far over the Mediterranean and mingled with the classical cult. The Greeks recognized the goddess as Aphrodite Urania, the Romans as Venus Coelestis, and these names later obtained currency even in Semitic countries. This Aphrodite was not thought of as the goddess of love and charm, but as a fertility goddess. The island of Cyprus, where Greek and Semitic culture met, was chiefly dedicated to this goddess; its cities of Paphos and Amathus were proverbial for her service. The island of Cythera and the sanctuary of Mount Eryx in Sicily also belonged to Urania. In Carthage, at least in her later transformation, she was the most important deity, and the name of the city Gades, Gadeira (Cadiz), perhaps signifies the location of a temple of Urania. These sanctuaries were designed quite differently from the temples of the Greek gods. The idol stood in the open, in a high and roofless niche, and frequently consisted only of a conic stone; railings, halls, and courts, in which doves were kept, surrounded the sanctuary. Free-standing pillars also occur in these precincts, and recall the pillars Jachin and Boaz before the temple in Jerusalem.

A transformation of the name Astarte is Atargatis, the goddess with human shape above and fish shape below. She doubtless still possessed her once famous temples at Askalon, near that of the Philistine fish-god Dagon, and also elsewhere. In a very late Hellenized form, she was enthroned in the famous temple of Hierapolis in northern Syria which Lucian describes and which may have survived intact until the fourth century. In a raised choir behind, to which only the priests had access, beside the Baal-Zeus which has been mentioned, there was the golden image of the goddess on a chariot harnessed with lions. Her attributes were borrowed from various Greek goddesses: in her hands were scepter and spindle, about her body the girdle of Urania, on her head the rays of the mural crown, and a stone which illuminated the entire temple area at night. In addition, space was found in the precinct for various other Greek or Grecized gods. There was a bearded and robed Apollo who stirred when an oracle was requested; on such occasions the priests lifted him and carried him about, as he directed. A forward motion signified an affirmative, a backward motion a negative reply; and the god is said to have sweated profusely the while. There were also an Atlas, a Hermes, and an Eileithyia in the interior, and outside, near or on the great altar which stood in the open air in front of the principal entrance to the temple, there was a large number of brazen figures representing kings and priests from highest antiquity until the Seleucid period; there was also a number of figures from the Homeric cycle of legends. But the most remarkable thing was not the statues but the cult, whose vastness and confusion can only here be apprehended. In the great court sacred bulls, horses, and tame lions and bears moved about freely; near by was a pool full of sacred fish, and at its center an altar, to which devotees swam daily, to crown it in accordance with vows. Around the temple lived a crowd of flautists, emasculated priests (*galli*), and raving women; these spent their time in noisy and spectacular processions, in sacrifices, and in every possible indecency. The spring festival, for which there was an enormous pilgrimage from all Syria to Hierapolis, appears to have been entirely devoted to madness. Not only was half a forest burned at this festival with sacrifices of all kinds (animals, clothing, valuable objects), but it was an occasion for recruiting the *galli;* many an unhappy man was carried away by the orgies, to the point of emasculating himself in honor of the goddess. And this temple was one of the most revered of the Near East; Cappadocia as well as Assyria, Cilicia as well as Phoenicia contributed to its treasures. Its Ionic colonnades resting upon masonry terraces with huge propylaea, upon a hill which towered over the city, made a brilliant and conspicuous spectacle. It is remarkable that this temple precinct, with its wild scenes, also supplied a model for the later stylites; from the propylaea there towered two enormous stone pillars representing phalluses, such as were found in Asia Minor wherever similar cults obtained, and upon these annually a man would climb, to pray for seven days and sleepless nights; those who wished his intercession brought an appropriate gift to the foot of the pillar. Could such an obscene cult better be atoned for in the Christian period than by a saintly penitent ascending the pillar to serve God after his own manner, not for weeks, but for decades on end?

An especially revolting service of this goddess, finally, who is here again designated as Aphrodite, was associated with the solitary temple in the grove of Aphaka in the Lebanon. Harlotry and the obscenities of the eunuchs laid all shame aside; nevertheless year after year worshipers came to throw precious gifts into the lake near the temple and to wait for the miracle, a ball of fire which appeared on the mountain height and then sank into the lake. It was believed that this was Urania herself.

Beside this great and many-formed Mother of Life there appears, also in diverse forms, the personification of that which she brings forth, which sprouts in spring and dies in winter. Sometimes this is her son or her daughter, sometimes her husband or, especially, her lover. After the wild joy of the spring festival there follows the mourning and wailing for the departed, celebrating the sorrow of the Great Goddess. As Isis mourned for slain Osiris in Egypt, so in Phoenicia the heavenly Aphrodite mourned for Adonis, the "Lord" who becomes completely acclimated in Cyprus and penetrates deep into Greek cult, so that Rome could receive him as a Greek divinity. But the most magnificent celebration of this service was in Alexandria, where it survived the introduction of Christianity by a century, though hardly with the exuberance which Theocritus shows (in *Idyll* 15) it possessed under the first Ptolemies. The festival closed with a procession of women to the seacoast,

K

where an image of Adonis was sunk in the waves. In Antioch too the festival of Adonis showed a stubborn vitality.

If this god can be regarded as Greco-Roman because of his immemorial position in the circle of classic deities, such was not the case with a special form which he assumed in Asia Minor. In Phrygia and neighboring countries we meet the Great Goddess as Cybele, Magna Mater, Acdestis, Dindymene, Berecynthia, Pessinuntis, and otherwise, and with her as her lover Atys or Attis, whose emasculation and death are mourned. The ancient temple of Pessinus, with its priests who ruled like princes, and its great revenues, had long bestowed its image and its cult on Rome, and even earlier the Greeks had adopted the goddess under various names, so that her image with its mural crown and lion team was familiar everywhere, and even the emasculated Phrygian priests were accepted in Rome. But Rome insisted, at least in the beginning, that the swarm of eunuchs, flautists, trumpeters, tambourine girls, and the rest must not recruit from the Roman population. When their license of mendicancy was later not withdrawn, this was perhaps calculated to separate the cult the more clearly from Roman life. It had been received at the bidding of the Sibylline Books and the Delphian Oracle; but republican Rome and for a long period imperial Rome was not inclined to propagate it in the provinces. Juvenal finds the drunken eunuch, his tambourine at his side, sleeping in a corner tavern among sailors, thieves, runaway slaves, and cutthroats. But by their mendicancy the priests of the Goddess Mother with their Phrygian caps gained access to the homes of wealthy Rome; they exploited the superstitions of women, and in return for gifts of eggs and worn clothing gave good advice against the threatening fevers of late summer. From attendance at the toilette of great ladies it was no great step to their being accepted into the household and to conversation. In that age superstitions prospered in the degree of their absurdity. Soon we find inscriptions of priests of the Great Mother, *archigalli* and arch-priestesses, bearing Roman names, and sanctuaries of the cult begin to spread over all Italy and Gaul. Itinerant priesthoods were formed which — the veritable scum of so-

ciety — traveled from place to place and engaged in the most
shameless beggary in the name of the small images which they
carried about on the back of an ass. Dressed and bedizened
in feminine fashion, they sang and danced to tambourine and
flute, whipped and mutilated themselves till the blood flowed,
only to compensate themselves by thefts and nameless excesses. So are the mendicant priests painted in Lucian and
Apuleius in the age of the Antonines. Later, at least in Rome,
the cult of the Great Mother must have shown a more respectable side and, specifically, have given up castration;
otherwise the participation of distinguished citizens, openly
acknowledged in monuments, would be inexplicable. Of the
mysteries proper, which were connected with this worship at
least by the third century, we shall speak presently.

The symbolic acts at the great annual festival in April, whose
meanings had long since become unintelligible, gave Church
writers special offense. The festival began at the vernal equi-
nox. A pine — the tree under which Atys had mutilated himself
— was felled in the forest and carried in procession to the temple
of the goddess, in Rome on the Palatine hill. A special rank of
Tree Bearers (*dendrophori*) is several times mentioned in later
inscriptions. On this occasion the *galli* appeared with disheveled
hair and smote themselves upon the breast as if in great anguish. On the second day there was a search for strayed Atys,
accompanied by trumpet blasts. The third day was called the
Day of Blood, because to honor Atys' memory the *galli* wounded
themselves in the shade of a pine decorated with violet wreaths
and an image of the unfortunate youth. These were days of
gloomy and unrestrained mourning — even of a kind of peniten-
tial fast. On the fourth day, the so-called Hilaria, joy was unrestrained, and all Rome joined in, probably because an earlier
spring festival had become amalgamated with this; otherwise
the celebration signified the assumption of Atys among the im-
mortals. The fifth day marked a pause. On the sixth the image
of the goddess — a head of black stone set into a silver figure —
along with sacred vessels was taken to the water (at Rome to
the Almo brook), rinsed, and then brought back to the temple
in a barefoot, disorderly procession.

If the Westerner was incapable of appreciating this festival in its original mythologic sense, he abandoned himself fully to it as a habit and a welcome occasion for release. The ceremony proved to be one of those the pagans were most loath to give up, and despite the change of date, the erection of Maypoles before churches, in Italy *piantar il Maggio,* may have been a final echo of the festival of the Great Mother. Another consequence of this cult may be surmised in the retinues of eunuchs which became common in noble Roman houses. In the fourth century the presence of eunuchs among the domestics of even pious Christian families was accepted as natural; as a purely Oriental fashion the custom could not have gained headway in Rome if the swarms attending the goddess of Pessinus had not accustomed people to the unedifying sight of an unsexed crowd.

Another figure of the Great Goddess may be mentioned here, though very briefly — Anaïtis (Enyo) of Eastern Asia Minor, whose cult was no less dissolute. Hers was the powerful temple rule of Comana in Cappadocia, with its numerous sacred prostitutes of both sexes. Some think she is to be recognized in the ancient Roman war goddess Bellona, whose priests annually cut their arms in a wild revel. Later, in the third century, there were even mysteries of that name, in which the blood of the priest of Bellona was caught up on a shield and distributed to those seeking initiation.

Besides these two great divinities of the Semites, there is a third which must not be passed over, though its intermingling with Greco-Roman religion dates not from the Empire but from remote antiquity. This is Melcart of the Phoenicians, of whom the Greek Heracles is only one aspect. His cult, though now under a Roman name, extended from remote ages as far as Phoenicians and Carthaginians settled; one of his most famous temples was that at Gades (Cadiz). In Italy and Greece the classical concept of the son of Zeus and Alcmene was sufficient; but later theocrasy specifically received the so-called Tyrian Hercules also into its great pantheon. A southern Italian inscription of the time of Gallienus is dedicated to him, somewhat as in modern times names and copies of widely dispersed miraculous images are repeated on many altars.

With all that has been said, we are still not in a position to sketch a true and lifelike picture of religious conditions in Asia Minor and Syria in the late Empire. In any case the mixture was extremely diverse, according as Greek life in general penetrated or was restricted. A melancholy spectacle is afforded by those magnificent temples of the Greco-Roman style erected to some amorphous Asiatic idol. The noblest and fairest was put to the service of the most repulsive, because some temple administration had accumulated enough lands, moneys, and contributions to undertake a monumental and luxurious building. Waxing superstition, indeed, impelled more and more Greeks and Romans of Asia Minor to these altars of Oriental gods, even to gods newly sprung up, if their interpreters and priests possessed sufficient effrontery. From Lucian we know that charlatan Alexander of the second century, who first gulled the simple Paphlagonians of Abonoteichos with his little snake-god, and then all Asia Minor, including the most distinguished Roman officials.

Adequate reports concerning the later history of the temple administrations generally, of which Strabo knew no inconsiderable number in the time of Augustus, are unfortunately wanting. Even at Palmyra the relationship in which the warrior and commercial aristocracy stood to the great Temple of the Sun and its treasures is not clear. How many ruins of the Near East of the Roman period stand mute! To begin with, there are the majestic Petra in Arabia and the pillar city of Gerasa, east of the Jordan, both places which would hardly have been known by name from the writers of the Empire, if their solitary splendor had not been discovered by astonished modern travelers.

Acceptance of Near-Eastern divinities involved only new superstition and an extension of worship; no new cultural element came to Rome with these cults. The impressive entry of Egypt's gods into the great mixture was quite different. They were accompanied by the ancient reverence of the Greek for the priestly wisdom of the Egyptian, in which it was expected that theology, astronomy, natural history, medicine, and prophecy would be found in equal perfection. Here it was not an affair of raving eunuchs but of a priestly caste which had once ruled the Pharaohs and their people, and had bequeathed mighty monuments.

This caste appears to have suffered significant degradation at the time of the Ptolemies, and temple holdings were made to contribute to the burdens of the state, without resistance. The old esteem for their occult wisdom disappeared after Alexander's city rose on the sands of the Delta and became the laboratory for Greek scholars and Greek-educated Egyptians who formed the greatest center for the newly discovered modes of scientific collecting and research. The Macedonian King, his officials, and his soldiers were no longer guided from the temples, and hence it was no longer worth the effort to maintain the old system of priestly knowledge intact. Upon the occasion of his visit to Heliopolis in Lower Egypt Strabo reports: "We also saw great houses in which the priests resided, who were once philosophers and astronomers; but now the sense of corporate obligation and tradition are vanished. At least we saw no representative of this sort, but only officials for sacrifice and custodians who explained objects of interest to foreigners." Among other points of attraction, the place was shown where Plato was said to have lived for thirteen years without being able to obtain the essence of their secrets from the priests. Now anyone who treated these matters seriously was laughed at among educated people. But in the realm of superstition Egypt soon regained the influence which it had lost in the realm of knowledge.

In the first place the old religion was strongly entrenched in the country itself (see p. 108). This was due partly to the native stubbornness of the Egyptian, who found no better way to preserve his national consciousness against foreign rulers, and partly to the traditional organization. No people of the ancient world made its entire life so completely dependent upon sacred doctrines and prescriptions as the Egyptian. For millennia the best energies of the nation were directed toward glorifying their relationship to the supernatural by symbols. Temple buildings, festivals, sacrifices, and burials occupied a position in comparison with which ordinary civic life, agriculture, and commerce could only claim subordinate importance. Such a situation, never completely abolished or supplanted by anything essentially different, must have continued to exert a very strong effect. Most of the temples still stood intact; a passionate repugnance kept the memory of the destruction perpetrated by Cambyses and the Persians fresh even in the Roman period. The priests who still possessed palaces near and at the temples doubtless did everything possible to preserve the oracles and sacrifices in all their brilliance and dignity and to celebrate the processions through the broad halls and courts and through the corridors of sphinxes and rams with all magnificence. If we may assume that the entire hierarchy persisted in the proportions it demonstrably had under the Ptolemies, it would comprise a whole army of consecrated priests. To be sure, the head was broken off this dangerous spear; the Ptolemies identified the chief priest of their own deified persons with the chief priest of all Egypt and assigned him a seat in Alexandria. The Romans too understood how to provide for the danger; at least under Hadrian the position of "chief priest of Alexandria and all Egypt" was occupied by a Roman, L. J. Vestinus, who was at the same time head of the Museum at Alexandria. But the mass of priests doubtless continued to be Egyptians. There were the *prophetes,* who issued oracles or carried out certain especially sacred sacrificial usages; the *hierostoli,* who cared for the wardrobe of the idols; the *pterophori,* who wore wings upon their heads; the *hierogrammateis,* who had once administered all sacred wisdom but were now probably degraded to be interpreters of dreams; the *horoscopi* or casters of nativities; the *pastophori,* who carried the receptacles with the images of the gods in the processions; the singers; the stampers of sacrificial animals; the keepers of sacred animals; the various grades of embalmers and funerary attendants; and finally numerous temple slaves who lived partly as monks in voluntary seclusion, and partly as itinerant mendicants. Around the temples of Serapis, especially that near Memphis, there were to be found since the second century B.C. the cells of those "immured ones" who hoped to become pure by lifelong incarceration in the vicinity of the god — obviously a close and undeniable pattern for Christian recluses; they received their food only through small windows, and died in their holes. This entire great host, whether it was maintained at full strength or not, had only one interest: to preserve Egyptian superstition by every means and to impress the Romans as much as possible.

In addition to a great number of more or less local divinities, the general Egyptian deities Isis, Osiris, and Anubis had their temples everywhere. In Alexandria and several other cities there was added the god Serapis, who had been brought from Sinope and was thought to be connected with Osiris as god of the dead. Serapis' temple was regarded as one of the marvels of ancient architecture and was surrounded by structures which, after the destruction of the Museum under Aurelian, contained the still highly important scientific institutions, among others one of the two great libraries. It is worth while to hear Rufinus' remarks concerning this remarkable structure, fabulous and vague as they are, because we can apprehend here more clearly than elsewhere how much Hellenism was able to accommodate itself to national character in this home of all superstition. The Serapeum, towering above the city upon a foundation a hundred steps high, appears to have been a gigantic domed structure surrounded upon all four sides by chambers, stairs, and secret corridors, and above even by quarters for the priests and cells for penitents. A fourfold portico ran either about the building itself or surrounded an open court. The most precious materials, including gold and ivory, were not spared anywhere in the structure. In the great central hall stood the image of the god, in proportions so colossal that its outstretched hands touched either wall; it was fashioned, after the manner of chryselephantine statues, of various materials over a wooden core; the uncovered portions were probably of some sort of sacred wood. The walls were plated with bronze, and Alexandrian fantasy imagined a second inner plating of silver, and an innermost plating of gold. The entire great chamber was dark, and intended to be illuminated artificially. Only on the festive day, when the image of the sun-god was brought to visit Serapis, was a small aperture to the east opened at a specific moment, when brilliant sunlight struck the lips of the image of Serapis; this was called the sun kiss. Other optical or mechanical devices, for which the temple must have been equipped like a theater, are not described in detail, or seem quite fanciful, like the story of the magnet in the ceiling which held the sun image, made of thin sheet iron, hovering in the air; the same story was later told of Mohammed's coffin. Like all temples of Serapis, this temple was also famous for so-called incubation. Sick persons slept there or sent others to sleep there in order to learn remedies through divinely sent dreams. The Greeks employed a similar method in their temples of Asclepius, and this was made the ground for identifying the two gods with one another.

Moreover, every wall and every doorpost throughout the city was marked with a symbol of the great god, and there were countless temples, chapels, and images of the other divinities in every street. It was believed that equipment for deceptive phantasmagoria was to be found or assumed in other temples also. Thus in the temple of a god who is designated Saturn in the Latin account, the great image was placed against the wall and its interior left hollow so that a priest might enter and speak through its open mouth; the temple candelabra were arranged so that they might be extinguished suddenly. But some devices of this character were perhaps not intentional deception, but machinery known and approved by everyone to enhance the great symbolic celebrations in which Egypt had been rich immemorially; if simple fanaticism caused anyone to regard them as miracles, the priests would naturally not disabuse him. We shall find the priests occupied also with theurgy and exorcism; but they themselves share in the delusion or at least do not stand completely outside it as deceivers. For superstition had here become the actual breath of life; at a quite late date the Egyptian divine family produced new shoots, as for example Serapis himself and the odious Canopus, who was worshiped in the shape of a pitcher with human head and extremities in the city of the Delta bearing his name. In Strabo's time the city of Canopus with its taverns was a favorite resort of the Alexandrians. Excursions were made on the Nile canal, which was alive day and night with barges filled with men and women who danced to the tune of flutes and indulged in all manner of excess. At that time a temple of Serapis, which was resorted to for curative dreams, was still the principal building in the city; later the sanctuary of Canopus himself occupied the foreground, and in the fourth century became an advanced school for all manner of magic.

Of the persistence and rivalry of animal cults we have spoken in the preceding section. Each nome or district worshiped its peculiar animal—sheep, wolf, baboon, eagle, lion, goat, shrew, and the like. The principal object of universal worship were the two famous bulls: Mnevis, who was kept in a chapel near the Temple of Heliopolis as late as Strabo's time, and Apis, who was thought to incarnate the soul of Osiris, at Memphis. A black bull with a white mark upon its forehead and a crescent upon its flank was not always to be found; in the fourth century, upon one occasion, long search was necessary. When the bull was discovered he was conducted to Memphis in reverent procession together with the cow which had given him birth; a hundred priests welcomed him and escorted him to the temple which was to serve as his stall. There and in the court before the temple visitors inspected him and discovered omens in his every move. Once the bull refused to eat out of Germanicus' hand, and this was taken as ominous. At Arsinoë there were still priests who knew how to tame, or at least to feed, the crocodiles which were there worshiped. Among these countless natural beings which received worship mention must be made of the mightiest of all, to whom all Egypt owed its existence. The Nile possessed its own college of eunuch priests who "served and entertained" him with sacrifices so that he might vouchsafe his benison to the land. According to Eusebius, Constantine was to have abolished this priesthood, but his intention cannot have been carried out, for the priesthood long survived Constantine's day. All that he was able to do, perhaps, was to transfer the Nile gauge from the Serapeum to a Christian church.

Of the other Egyptian priests, as they existed at the time of Trajan, Plutarch provides a somewhat excessively reverent description of the priests of Isis and wherever he can do so interprets their usages and ceremonies as symbols. Their distinguishing mark was their white linen dress and shorn head. They practiced a kind of abstinence and avoided many foods, both to prevent obesity and for a variety of symbolic reasons. They also avoided the sea and salt. With all its repetitious lamentations, their cult possessed no spiritual dignity; its place was taken by orgiastic ululations and bacchanalian gesticulations. Here an ass was flung down a cliff, there a gilded ox was led about covered with a black robe. A peculiar noise-making instrument, the sistrum, was supposed to restrain the wicked Typhon (the destroying principle) by its din. Many aspects of this cult bear the stamp of later meaningless contrivance or borrowing. The Isis image was clothed in various colors, some dark and some light, to represent day and night, fire and water, life and death. Incense varied according to the time of day: resin in the morning in order to banish the mists of night, myrrh at noon, and at night *kyphi,* which was compounded of sixteen ingredients to the accompaniment of constant prayer. *Kyphi* was also prepared in potable form; it was a specific whose constituents lent themselves to symbolic interpretation, but its effect must have been narcotic.

Plutarch deals with his subject with complete seriousness; nevertheless he indicates that among the Egyptians there were also people who found superstition and particularly the animal cult distasteful. "While the weak and the simple fall into unqualified superstition," he says, "bolder and prouder spirits necessarily succumb to unruly and atheist thoughts."

We must now determine how much of this religion was adopted by Rome in its bloom and later in its decline, and in what spirit.

Aside from purely artistic borrowing which brought a large number of Egyptian figures and ornamental motifs to Rome, especially in the age of Hadrian, it is almost exclusively the circle of Isis which for centuries had found a welcome in Greek and Roman religions.

Isis, the earth and indeed blessed Egypt itself, and Osiris, the fertilizing stream of the Nile, were both conceived of by the Egyptians themselves as general symbols of all life, and thus were made ready to enter into the divine cult of other peoples. A collateral significance, which the divine pair may have received from a Semitic source, to wit as moon and sun, had virtually receded into the background by the time of Herodotus.

The Greeks unanimously regarded Isis as Demeter and Osiris as
Dionysus, but did not therefore completely disregard Isis' function as moon-goddess. Indeed she shared, one after the other, in
the affairs of widely different deities; she was goddess of the
underworld, of dreams, of childbirth, even ruler of the sea. When
as a result of the conquest of Egypt by Alexander that country
was received into the great complex of Greco-Oriental life, the
worship of Isis spread everywhere in the Greek world and eventually reached Rome in the time of Sulla, though for a hundred
years thereafter it encountered vigorous public opposition.
Among the Romans Isis was accompanied sometimes by her
husband Osiris, but much more frequently by Serapis as the
Osiris of the underworld; by the dog-headed Anubis (a bastard
of Osiris who, as a messenger between the gods and the underworld, was identified with Hermes); and finally by Horus, Grecized as Harpocrates, to whom Isis gave birth after the death
of Osiris.

The original mythological significance of these beings, even
if we knew it for certain, does not suffice for an understanding
of the meanings associated with them by the Romans. Besides
his function as a god of healing, Serapis was also a sun-god; a
number of foreign gods and even some native ones came to
have that aspect. But this concept did not detract from his rule
over souls in life and in death. Similarly, Isis and the other deities were transformed into gods of salvation in a broad, and of
healing in a specific, sense, without thereby losing their connection with the underworld. At this stage it is difficult to distinguish
Isis from Hecate, the three-formed goddess of the underworld
who rules in heaven as Luna, on earth as Diana, and in the underworld as Proserpina. To the elegiac poets, on the other hand,
she is the awesome and frequently conciliated mistress in the
realm of love. As the number of aspects of life subject to her
dominion increased, it became less possible to define her nature,
as the Romans conceived it, in a common formula. She is found
in widely disparate metamorphoses, even as Fortuna and Tyche,
to say nothing of the purely philosophic interpretation which
subsequently discovered in her the great universal deity. The
goddess had long Romanized her figure and laid aside the famil-

iar Egyptian headdress. The costume of the priestess seems to
have supplanted that of the old goddess. The permanent insignia
of the goddess in pictures and statuary are now the fringed man-
tle fastened to the tunic under the breasts with a peculiar knot,
and the sistrum in the hand.

Roman arms spread the worship of Isis to the frontiers of the
Empire, in the Netherlands as in Switzerland and South Germany. It penetrated private life more thoroughly and earlier
than the cult of the great Semitic goddess. It enjoyed imperial
favor only after Vespasian, who had expressly shown Serapis
reverence at Alexandria. His son Domitian then built an Iseum
and Serapeum in Rome; previously the two deities had to content themselves with unobtrusive chapels, at least within the city
walls. Later there were several considerable sanctuaries of the
goddess in Rome. At the temple discovered at Pompeii, which
had been restored sixteen years before the final catastrophe,
there is a secret stairway and an empty depression behind the
pedestal which bore the images and beside it a small accessory
structure with underground chamber. This arrangement gives
ground for conjecture, but there is neither room nor equipment
for large and spectacular phantasmagoria such as the fancy of
archaeologists and poets has associated with these slight structures.

The priests of Isis united into numerous colleges (as *pastophori* and the like) in the larger cities had a consistently bad
reputation as late as the first century. Among other things they
were said to arrange assignations, for which Isis in her temple,
as has been remarked above, must have afforded protection.
Juvenal shows profound contempt for the shorn swarm dressed
in linen, which thrust its way with priestly cries of lamentation
into the chambers of respectable Roman ladies, from which the
eunuchs of the great Syrian goddess had just departed. The
latter only begged; but the leader of the priests of Isis, who
appeared in the costume of Anubis, could also utter threats and
prescribe penances for certain agreeable sins. Even if the prescription involved a plunge in the Tiber in midwinter, it would
be obeyed, for the lady's faith was firm and she believed that
she heard Isis' own voice in her sleep.

From the second century onward the worship of Isis, like that of the Great Mother, was given a more elevated tone and probably greater dignity also by the participation of the Emperor and the higher classes. The difference as compared with earlier practice was so great that it gave rise to the theory that Commodus or Caracalla had first brought the cult to Rome. At the great processions there were henceforward *pausae,* that is, halting places, perhaps fitted with special structures. One such festive procession Commodus had represented in mosaic in a hall of his gardens. On these occasions he himself, shorn like a priest, would carry the image of Anubis, and with its snout strike the heads of the priests of Isis who walked beside him. But far the most circumstantial description of an Isis procession, which may serve as a general gauge for such processions at this time, is supplied by Apuleius in the last book of his *Metamorphoses.* The scene is laid in dissolute Corinth. The procession begins in the gayest carnival style with colorful masks of soldiers, hunters, gladiators, elegantly coiffured women, magistrates, philosophers (with robe, staff, slippers, and goatee), fowlers, and fishermen. There followed a tame bear on a sedan chair dressed as an old lady, an ape dressed as Ganymede with cap and orange-colored suit and with golden cup in hand, and even an ass with wings attached as a travesty on Pegasus, and running beside him a lame dwarf representing Bellerophon. Now the procession proper began. Garlanded women dressed in white, the attendants of Isis' toilette, strewed flowers and perfumes and gesticulated with mirrors and combs. A crowd of both sexes followed with lamps, torches, and tapers as if to do homage to the astral divinities. There followed harpists, pipers, and a choir of singers dressed in white; then the flautists of Serapis blowing a ritual temple melody, and heralds to clear the way. Then came devotees of all classes and ages dressed in white linen, the women with anointed hair and transparent veils, the men with hair cropped short; the sistrums which they swung noisily were made of silver or even of gold according to their means. Now the priests themselves appeared with the secret symbols of the goddess: lamps, miniature altars, palm branches, serpent staves, an open hand, and several vessels of peculiar form. Others carried the gods themselves, the image of Anubis with its dog's head half black and half gold, a cow standing erect, a mystic chest. Finally there came the chief priest pressing to his bosom the golden urn with serpent hooks which represented the goddess herself. In this order the procession moved out of the city of Corinth — where the novelist had laid his scene — down to the sea. Here the colorful "Isis boat" decorated with hieroglyphs was filled with incense and votive offerings amid much ceremony, and in sight of sanctuaries set up on shore the ship was launched on the waves. The inscription upon the sail, "For a happy voyage in the new year," and the date, known from other sources of the widely celebrated Roman *navigium Isidis,* which was March 5, supply an explanation for the entire festival, which was to celebrate the opening of the sea which had been closed during the winter. For it was precisely in her latest, non-Egyptian character as ruler of the sea that Isis received specific worship in the Mediterranean, and the Corinthians, with a gulf on their either side, must have been especially devoted to her. The procession returned to the temple, and a priest standing upon a high pulpit before the gate pronounced a blessing for the Emperor, the Senate, the knights, the Roman people, seafaring, and the entire Empire; he closed with the formula λαοτς ἄφεσις, which has the same significance as the *Ite, missa est* of Christian worship. At this entire celebration there was a distinction between the gay crowd of worshipers and the initiates of the mysteries, concerning whom we shall have to speak in the following section.

What we are told of sacred script, partly hieroglyphic, partly of other secret character, in connection with this and other occasions, may well be factually correct; but the Roman, Greek, or Gallic priest of Isis who preserved these writings and could perhaps copy and recite them certainly knew nothing of their meaning. Indeed, far from drawing any profound science from priestly Egypt (whose strong point in any case was no longer doctrine), Rome adopted the many-named gods with no regard for theological consistency in willfully altered interpretations. This has already been noticed in the case of Isis. Another eloquent example is the figure of Harpocrates, whose gesture —

index finger pointing toward mouth — is meant to indicate that
he has been nursed by Isis; in the excellent Capitoline sculpture
of the Hadrianic period instead of the Egyptian idol we find a
young Cupid bidding silence with his fingers on his lips as a
deus silentii. Anubis, on the other hand, although he is regarded
as identical with Hermes, was required to retain his dog's head;
its combination with a human body in Roman drapery is peculiarly objectionable.

A notion of the symbols of this entire cycle is supplied by the
brazen hands found here and there which have been recognized
as *ex votos* dedicated by women in childbirth to Isis as helper
in travail. The fingers are arranged in the posture of an oath,
and the inner as well as the outer surface of the hand is completely covered with attributes — mystery-vessels, small busts of
the divinities Isis, Serapis, Osiris, and Anubis, the latter represented as Dionysus and Hermes. This is not the place to enumerate the symbols; perhaps their number corresponds to petitions
made in time of need.

The subject of the mixture of cults is far from exhausted by
the alien divinities thus far named; many who fit into the category will more appropriately receive cursory treatment in the
section following. Heretofore we have spoken only of officially
recognized and generally propagated *sacra peregrina;* there was
nothing to prevent the individual worshiper from surrounding
himself with masses of images and symbols of all countries and
religions. How different in this respect, and incidentally how
significant, is the attitude of the two dissimilar cousins, Elagabalus and Alexander Severus! Elagabalus brought his Semitic idols,
the palladia of Rome, and the stones of Orestes from the Temple
of Diana at Laodicea together haphazardly in a single heap.
Just as the Black Stone of Emesa was married to the image of
Urania of Carthage, so the Emperor-priest himself married the
chief Vestal; he is even said to have expressed an intention to
make his central sanctuary a point of union for the worship of
Samaritans, Jews, and Christians. All gods were to be ministers
of his great god, and all mysteries concentrated in that god's
priesthood. Alexander Severus, on the other hand, celebrated the

founders of all religions as ideals of humanity, and set their likenesses up in his domestic chapel, where Abraham and Christ were placed near Orpheus, as supposed founder of the Hellenic mysteries, and Apollonius of Tyana, as neo-philosophic wonder-worker. The best of the earlier Emperors were also given place in his chapel, just as colossal statues of them were set up in the Forum of Nerva. A second chapel contained statues of Vergil, Cicero, Achilles, and other great men; the noble and unhappy prince sought to form a new Olympus out of the best that he knew. But what was done in the imperial palace at Rome on a large scale was certainly repeated manifold on a small scale. Many of the nobler spirits would gladly have turned to Christianity in such aspects as they could apprehend; even more eagerly would common superstition have looked up to the Christian mysteries, which must have had a peculiar fascination because they communicated to their devotees so remarkable an attitude in life and in death. It is difficult to imagine the feeling of many a pagan, compounded of revulsion and desire, and we can scarcely be said to have any direct account of the subject, if we are unwilling to reckon the story of the Samaritan magician Simon as such. Of the philosophic *rapprochement* of the two religions we shall speak in the sequel.

Once the revulsion against alien divinities had completely vanished, once the overwhelming lure of the mysterious, especially in the Oriental cult, had made itself felt, there was no foretelling where this appropriation of alien elements would stop. The Roman world had already been invaded, in the train of Neoplatonic philosophy and Manichaeism, not only by Persian but even by Indian principles of religion. Anything that could present a mysterious aspect and produce a claim to affinity with Roman notions of deity was sure of a welcome.

It is precisely from this later period of Roman history that we find numerous inscriptions dedicated to "all the gods and goddesses," "all the heavenly ones," "the assembly of the gods," and the like. Doubtless the inscribers included the alien gods in their intentions, so that none might feel offended. Frequently the attributes of a number of native and alien divinities were be-

L.

stowed upon a single figure, which was then designated *Deus Pantheus*, or All-godly God. So *Silvanus Pantheus* and *Liber Pantheus* occur; on images of Fortuna there are to be seen, beside the oar and cornucopia which are appropriate to her, the breastplate of Minerva, the lotus of Isis, the thunderbolt of Jupiter, the fawn-skin of Bacchus, the cock of Aesculapius, and the like. This is perhaps no more than a compendious expression for the whole host of gods, and so to be differentiated from philosophic menotheism, which (as we shall see below) recognized the actual identity of all the gods in a supreme being.

There is a well-known statement of the philosopher Themistius, of a considerably later period, when Emperor Valens as an Arian was bitterly persecuting orthodox Christians. "Difference in belief among Christians," says the philosopher, "is no cause for astonishment; it is quite inconsiderable in comparison with the mass and confusion of varying pagan religious views. Here there are more than three hundred sects, forasmuch as the Deity desires to be glorified in diverse modes and is the more respected, the less anyone knows about them." Themistius' figure may well be too high; furthermore, these pagan sects and dogmas were not mutually exclusive, as were the Christian, so that an individual might belong to several simultaneously. Nevertheless, three hundred various manners of worship, even if they are not mutually contradictory, indicate a fragmentation of paganism which could not have been produced merely by the introduction of the foreign gods. We shall now have to show how infinite variety was introduced into the declining religion of paganism both through tangible objects of the cult and, to a greater degree, through its inward principles, and how at the same time powerful tendencies toward simplification were operative.

VI

IMMORTALITY AND ITS MYSTERIES
THE DAIMONIZATION OF PAGANISM

ALONG WITH the ancient worship and the cults brought in from abroad, a temper of disbelief had long pervaded the educated classes, as has been noticed above, and in the most favorable cases this disbelief took on a philosophic coloring. But with the third century, under the influence of the great calamities which had befallen the Empire, a change of heart is perceptible among the upper classes. On the one hand they were attracted to the miraculous and superstitious interests of the common people; on the other, they were provided for by a new spiritual dispensation which contrived to link philosophy with the most extreme superstition, to wit, Neoplatonism so-called.

These two tendencies were not disparate in contemporary life, and cannot be wholly separated in our account of it. It is quite impossible to say where popular belief ceases and where philosophic superstition begins; the latter regularly recognizes the former, in order to make place for it in its system, specifically in its doctrine of daimons.

Every page of the history of the third century gives evidence of these individual phenomena, increasing credulity in the matter of miracles and pagan fanaticism, mysticism and the asceticism of enthusiasts. But the total impression is that attitudes to the supernatural as a whole had substantially altered. The change becomes evident when we consider the new views concerning the ultimate fate of man himself.

Enemies of Christianity make it their constant charge that Christianity is an other-worldly religion which regards life on earth only as a period of preparation, grim and rich in trials, for eternal life in the world to come. Paganism, on the contrary, is praised as a joyous doctrine which taught ancient man to give untrammeled expression, and in his own particular manner, to his potentialities, his inclinations, and his individual destiny. It might be objected at once that even the world view of the Greek at its most powerful was far from being as joyous as is customarily believed. But in any case we must realize that the paganism of the third century can certainly make no unqualified claim to this praise, if one wishes to style it such, and that it had also become a religion of the beyond. Christian dogma places its doctrine of death and immortality at the end of its doctrine of man; in the present case we must begin with death and immortality, because comprehension of late pagan religions depends entirely upon this point.

The lamentable condition of the state and society certainly contributed greatly to the development of this other-worldliness, but it cannot explain it fully. New tendencies such as these draw their essential strength from unplumbed depths; they cannot be merely deduced as consequences of antecedent conditions. The earlier pagan view granted man a persistence after death, to be sure, but as a mere shadowy form, as a nerveless dream life. Those who pretended to fuller wisdom spoke of a transmigration of souls, after the Egyptian or Asiatic manner. Only a few friends of the gods were destined to sojourn in Elysium or on the Isles of the Blessed. When paganism reached its crisis the circle of these favored ones was suddenly enlarged and soon everyone made claim to eternal blessedness. On numberless sarcophagi we find trains of Tritons and Nereids, quite tastefully executed for this late period; these signify the journey to the Isles of the Blessed. The tomb inscriptions leave no doubt of the matter. "Ye unhappy survivors," we find, "bewail this death; but ye gods and goddesses, rejoice over your new fellow citizen!"

In other cases there is formal profession that true life begins only in the world beyond. "Only now dost thou live thy happy life, far from all earthly doom; high in the heaven thou dost enjoy nectar and ambrosia with the gods." Such happy immortality is expected even for children, for eight-year-old girls. "Ye exalted souls of the pious, lead innocent Magnilla through the Elysian fields and meadows to your dwelling-places!" A ten-month-old infant is represented as speaking: "My heavenly divine soul will not go to the shades; the universe and the stars take me in; earth has received only my body, this stone my name." A widower professes to know the constellation where his wife abides; it is the Lock of Berenice near Andromeda. More modest is the prayer of a son: "Ye gods of the underworld, open for my father the groves where eternal day shines purple." There is also expression of a specific hope to see the deceased again, but only upon a late pagan stone of the fourth century. We find another logical consequence of belief in immortality, and that is a belief in intercession for survivors. A high official speaks: "Just as I have cared for your welfare on earth, so am I concerned for it now among the gods." A Christian origin has been claimed for many of these inscriptions, but wrongly; specific mythological additions clearly refute the possibility of Christian origin.

That such ideas of immortality were widespread in the age of Diocletian is proven by the admonition which Arnobius addresses to the pagans: "Do not flatter yourselves with vain hope when inflated sages declare they were born of God and are not subject to the laws of fate, and that, if their lives were on the whole virtuous, God's court stands open to them and after their death they may ascend thither without hindrance as to their home." The best result of all of this was that henceforward at least the deeply rooted belief in an earthly predestination no longer stood in such stark opposition to an ethical order of the universe, since man's destiny in the beyond was acknowledged.

These pious-sounding beliefs seem in fact to have involved, from the pagan point of view, nothing more than an enlightened monotheism and a rigid ethic, as was maintained among the Stoics in principle and partly also in practice. But for contemporary men the problem could not be so simply stated. Between themselves and the highest problems of their existence there intervened in layers numberless gods and systems of gods, and account had to be taken of these daimonic powers. Even where the pagan of this period achieved so-called monotheism we find him remarkably attached to the idea of subordinate divine beings who had to be worshiped and conciliated each in its own manner. Far from being able to satisfy the yearning for immortality by trustfully throwing oneself upon the bosom of the Eternal by an immediate moral and religious act, the individual felt constrained to undertake a long and circuitous route. Now ancient worship had always had associated with itself certain secret rites which brought the initiate nearer to his god and at the same time involved more or less specific relations to a fairer immortality than that of the usual shadowy Hades. In the Hellenic mysteries of Demeter as of Dionysus this hope is associated with the celebration of the death and resurrection of nature, especially of grain, without its becoming prominent as the essential element of the cult. These mysteries continued to be celebrated; whenever the Emperor or other distinguished visitors came to Greece they were eager to be initiated. The famous address of the Christian Firmicus to the sons of Constantine still denounces the initiations of Eleusis, the Cretan mysteries of Dionysus, and the *sacra* of the Corybantes as things still existing. Perhaps we may go so far as to assume that the mass of mysteries, with which Greece teemed in the second century at the time of Pausanias, persisted in whole or in part, if in shrunken form, until the age of Theodosius.

But remarkable as the proceedings of the mysteries may be in themselves, their details need not detain us here, because they rather point backward to earlier Hellenism and more particularly because they were local in character, even depending upon citizen rights, and thus were incapable of further expansion. For the same reason we must pass over the Roman mysteries of Bona Dea and the like. But the situation is quite different with reference to the universal mysteries of the period of the Empire, which spread over all Roman regions and were usually devoted to foreign gods.

It is not the fault of modern scholars that essential aspects of this matter remain unknown, and much depends on mere conjecture. In the first place it must be remarked that participation in such secret worship, qualitatively as well as quantitatively, according to various regions, classes, and groups, remains largely a riddle. The number of initiates may have run into thousands, perhaps even into hundreds of thousands. It is possible that individual countries did not participate, by accident or because of some internal reason, and it is equally possible that relevant evidence — inscriptions and monuments — is still underground. But one general assumption may certainly be made: these mysteries were to be found in Rome early, partly even in the period of the Republic, but were humble and even despised. But with the third century participation in the mysteries mounts, in number as well as in the importance of the initiates. This involves a new and deeper content whose central point was the promise of immortality.

At the entrance of this labyrinth there stand the two handsome figures of Amor and Psyche, an allegory based upon Plato's concept of the human soul. It may be that these figures occur on earlier individual monuments, but it is a fact that none of the marble groups we know is earlier than the second century and that the two figures separately or in caressing union, in joy or in sorrow, are represented again and again from the second century to the end of the pagan period, especially on sarcophagi. The sole circumstantial literary treatment of the myth, in the pages of Apuleius in the age of the Antonines, is apt to lead the reader astray. Apuleius' account is a fairy story whose similarity with the allegory consists only in the fact that his lovers were made unhappy by a long separation due to the fault of one, and that a blessed reunion joined them forevermore. The author has made only partial and inconsistent use of the meaning of the allegory, the names of whose principal figures he used for his story, but he has not sufficiently adapted his poetic account to conform to the allegory. Contemporary ideas concerning the human soul persisted, untouched by Apuleius' story. Though of divine origin, the soul has fallen, and in its earthly passage is subject to error; through trials and purifications it must again be prepared for a life of blessedness. The heavenly

EROS who takes its part and leads it home as his bride is a revelation of deity which draws lost humanity back to itself and
unites it with itself.

We do not know whether special worship or rites were associated with this symbol in the Roman period. It is only a general
indication of a certain trend of thought. In the realm of art and
poetic allusion it is enlarged to take in various collateral images.
Psyche is represented as a butterfly in a series of scenes: Pallas
lowers her onto the head of man fashioned by Prometheus; she
soars up from his body at death and is led by Hermes to the
world below. Linked with this as a clear image is the final lib-
eration of Prometheus, who has been chained to the cliff and
whom Heracles frees from the eagle by a bolt from his bow;
thereafter he leads a divine life on Olympus.

From this general symbol of late Roman yearning for immortality we proceed to those mysteries in which some analogous
content is to be recognized.

The mysteries of BACCHUS which were still widely represented
in the Empire should perhaps be excluded. Their content at this
time cannot be determined; we only know that they still involved devouring the raw and bloody flesh of a kid and that the
initiates in their sacred madness wound serpents about themselves.

The mysteries of the three-formed goddess of the underworld,
HECATE (Luna, Diana, Proserpina), seem to be more closely related to belief in immortality. Writers give us no information
on the subject, but in the inscriptions this worship is placed on
a footing with that of the most important mysteries, those of
Mithras and of the Great Mother, and hence must have had
some importance. Upon an image of this *diva triformis* at Her-
mannstadt in Transylvania there are bands of relief which seem
to represent various scenes and grades of initiation. The resources devoted to this secret worship may be surmised from the
plan of the temple of Hecate built by Diocletian at Antioch —
365 steps underground, if our report is to be relied upon.

The latest form of the VENUS MYSTERIES, of which there are
scattered notices, is similarly unknown. But the most important
occult rites referred to certain foreign gods.

Two kinds of mysteries are connected with the PHRYGIAN CULT. The older form, occurring as early as Greece's period of bloom, is the secret worship of SABAZIUS. The ancient Thracians perhaps identified him with the sun-god, the Phrygians with Atys; but in Greece he was generally regarded as a personification of Dionysus and as such possessed a public cult. Its principal feature, after the Asiatic fashion, was noisy song with cymbal and tambourine and the wild *sikinnis* dance. Of the secret initiation as it was celebrated in the Greek period, we know only the external aspects of the ritual: draping with a fawn-skin (*nebris*), drinking or sprinkling out of mixing-bowls, purifications and the like, and finally the traditional cry of the initiates, "I fled the evil and found the good," as well as carrying a tub or a cradle around. Of the secret (according to Creuzer, cosmogonic) doctrine we know nothing and can scarcely be justified in assuming any lofty intention, for the conclusion, and for most of the participants probably the goal, of the initiation consisted in nocturnal excesses of the coarsest kind; these brought the entire worship of Sabazius into serious disfavor. Later these mysteries had considerable currency in the Roman Empire, perhaps with some new religious and philosophic content; they also entered into a kind of relationship with the Mithras cult which will be dealt with below. Now — if this was not done earlier — a golden serpent was lowered into the initiate's garment with symbolic versicles and then withdrawn below, presumably as a memorial of the love of Zeus and Demeter. Then the initiate was led into the innermost chamber of the sanctuary, pronouncing the words, "I have eaten out of the tambourine, I have drunk out of the cymbal, I am now an initiate" — to say nothing of other undecipherable formulae. We may also conjecture that at least in the third and fourth centuries these initiations of Sabazius, besides acquiring a new meaning, also achieved a more respectable attitude. The Christian writers who see in the golden serpent an obvious unmasking of Satan, who here finally calls himself by his true name, would certainly not have been silent if the ceremony were still closed by general license. Furthermore, persons of considerable standing must have participated in these mysteries; Firmicus (about 340) speaks of some of its adherents as clothed in purple, with gold and laurel in their hair.

Much more remarkable but unfortunately not much better known is the second, newer variety of Phrygian mysteries in the Roman Empire, the TAUROBOLIA. These were directly connected with the figures of the Great Mother and of Atys and included a direct promise of immortality.

From the age of the Antonines inscriptions are found which show that a *taurobolium* (sacrifice of a bull) and a *criobolium* (sacrifice of a ram) were offered to the Great Mother and to Atys. The sacrificer declares that he is IN AETERNVM RENATVS, that is reborn to eternity. We know nothing of the doctrine which conveyed this hope, and only little of the ceremonial which was involved. The classic locale for initiations at Rome was on the Vatican hill, whence constant communication with the provinces may have been maintained. The customary hour was midnight (*mesonyctium*). A deep pit was dug in the ground, and covered with boards perforated like a colander. The candidate for initiation, garbed in a symbolic dress with gold ornaments, took his place beneath. When the sacrificial animals, bull and ram and sometimes also a goat, were slaughtered above, he sought to intercept as much of the blood as possible with his face, hair, and dress. But this repulsive solemnity was not the end; the candidate was required permanently to wear the blood-stained garments in public, and to expose himself to mockery as well as to reverence. It appears that this purification by blood was valid only for a period of twenty years, and then had to be repeated, doubtless without prejudice to the eternity mentioned above. Nevertheless this was one of the commonest forms of initiation, and was undergone not only for the individual himself, but for others also, for the welfare of the imperial house, and even, at least in the second and third centuries, for whole cities. How the ceremony was modified when whole corporations participated in it is quite unknown. There were cases where such initiations were prescribed by the Great Mother, apparently in dreams. Difficult as it may be for us to associate loftier thoughts with

these crude practices, this exquisite age found comfort in the
vires aeternae, the eternal dedicatory blood of the bull. One initiate, Proconsul of Africa and City Prefect of Rome to boot,
earnestly thanks the gods for their care of his soul henceforward.

On dedicatory inscriptions, especially the later ones, Atys
is frequently called Menotyrannus; this shows his original identity or later identification with Men, the Asia Minor moon-god,
but is of no further service in explaining the mysteries.

More important and certainly more refined were the mysteries of Isis, which have left clearer traces in literature also.
Proselytes for these mysteries were solicited by books, which
appear to have been written mainly for this purpose. The
Metamorphoses of Apuleius is of this character, as is also
Xenophon of Ephesus' romance of *Anthia and Habrocomes,*
which dates to the second century. Here Isis is the divinity
who preserves and protects the lovers who are beset by countless adventures. Isis herself is much improved; she no longer
provides occasions for unchastity as she had previously done
in so many of her temples, but herself guards maidenly mod-
esty, whose triumph is the worthy theme of several of these
late romances.

We are dealing here not with the ancient and genuine Isis
festivals of Egypt, in which mangled Osiris was sought and
found, but with the universal occult worship of Isis of the imperial period. The meaning and content of this worship is difficult to determine with precision, because the Romans' popular belief in Isis was variable and changing in form. The only
consistent account is provided by Apuleius in the last book of
the *Metamorphoses,* to which we have already alluded, but we
are left uncertain whether his Lucius speaks rather as a speculative philosopher or as a devout initiate. But one thing is beyond doubt: these mysteries too, colorful as they were, promised a blessed immortality. "Queen Isis," who shows herself
to be Mother Nature and the basic principle of all divine
being, demands of the unlucky Lucius, as the price of his
transformation from an ass back to human form, that he must

never forget that his entire life henceforward to his last breath belongs to her. "But you will live happy, glorious in my protection; and when you have run the course of your time and go to the world below, you will find me there also as you see me here, illuminating the gloom of Acheron, ruling over the Stygian depths, and as dweller in the Elysian Fields you will pray for my grace without cease." In the same breath, indeed, Isis promises a long life on earth, if Lucius should please her by diligent service and penance; then the chief priest promises him direct protection and security against human destiny, which is normally controlled by the stars. It appears that there was still credulity for such illusions.

The sacred teaching which was imparted to candidates for initiation, presumably out of hieroglyphic books, was probably not profound. The external, spectacular ceremonial was made much too prominent for any loftier, spiritual element, any change of heart, even any lasting abstentions, to affect the spirit of the initiates. Was it really made clear to the initiate that Isis was Nature and at the same time the sum of all divine being, or was this merely the personal expression of Apuleius' own tendentious view? We only know, as has been indicated, that these mysteries were a favorite means of assuring oneself, by means of certain ceremonies and magic arts, against misfortunes in earthly life, against an unhappy existence in the beyond, or against total annihilation after death. The only aspect of these mysteries which suggests a systematic treatment of man's spiritual nature are the constant and surely not altogether involuntary dreams, in the course of which Isis' will on matters all and sundry was apprehended. Besides simple delusion from without — for dreams could be whispered into the ears of sleepers — there is the possibility of a persistent and artificially maintained nervous excitement. The external practices, on the other hand, were either taken over, half understood, from Egypt, or calculated to impress an easily aroused imagination. The preparations during the course of instruction were those customary in most of the mysteries: abstention from wine, meat, indulgence, for ten full days; a bath, sprinkling with sacred water, and the like; christening

gifts from friends and fellow candidates. The night of the
dedication, determined by a dream, was spent in the temple.
First one wore a rough linen robe, then clothing was changed
twelve times, until at last one received a flowered coat and
the Olympian stole decorated with painted figures of mystic
animals. Of the processions and spectacles exhibited to the
initiates Lucius can only hint that he had to undergo symbolic
death and then resurrection by the grace of Isis (*precaria
salus*). "I walked through the gates of death, I trod the threshold of Proserpina, and after I had traversed all elements I returned again. In the middle of the night I beheld the sun in
its brightest illumination. I approached the gods below and
above and supplicated them from near at hand." These are
things concerning which we shall never be certain. Are we to
assume the use for each initiation of optic and dioramatic arts
which would be necessary, by our standards, for even an outward illusion? There were sufficient means available, to be
sure, as we shall show in another connection, to make a contemporary believe in this or that conjuration or ghostly apparition; but the temper of the age was still sufficiently steeped
in the value of symbols to produce a deep impression upon
the imagination by the mere ritual display of effective sensual
images. Our modern world, in contrast, is so utterly alien to
the symbolic and so contemptuous of it that we can scarcely
understand a different point of view and grow impatient with
any formalities or ceremonies. We bring this same attitude to
bear on our judgment of the past. Rather than admit the profound effectiveness of symbol, we prefer to premise the costli-
est artifices of optical and mechanical illusion, that is to say,
actual deception.

But we return to the Isis temple at Corinth. The time is
toward dawn. Lucius, attired in his colorful garb, a burning
torch in his hand, a spiked crown of palm leaves upon his
head, stands upon a wooden platform before the image of
the goddess. Suddenly the curtain parts before his eyes, and
the crowd assembled without in the nave of the temple be-
holds him as the living image of the sun. Feast and revelry
conclude the ceremony.

But the true *sacrosancta civitas* of the Isis worshiper was Rome itself, where Lucius, too, subsequently fixed his abode at the temple of Isis Campensis. In the following year he is admonished in a dream to be mindful of Osiris also, and to make his way to a certain *pastophorus,* who for his part must naturally have dreamt of Lucius also. After numerous difficulties, partly of a pecuniary nature, the pious sufferer receives the initiation of Osiris also. This "all-greatest of all-highest gods" goes so far as to promise his express blessings for the legal career upon which Lucius has entered, and designates him, again in a dream vision, as member of the college of *pastophori.* The author gives no details of this initiation. According to his own statement, he had been initiated in most of the mysteries in Greece; but he clearly sets the greatest weight upon those of the Isiac circle of gods.

By far the mightiest of the secret religions was the worship of MITHRAS, which also claimed to assure redemption and immortality.

The most ancient Persian religion knew a sun-god called Mithras, and the later teaching of Zoroaster, since it could not banish him, assigned him the position of intermediary between Ormuzd and Ahriman, Light and Darkness. Mithras became the first of the heavenly *yazatas* and (with reference to the setting sun) also protector of the realm of the dead; he judged the souls upon the bridge Djinevat. But above all he was the protector of earth, of agriculture, of fertility, whose symbol — the bull — was associated with him from hoary antiquity. Numerous invocations to him are preserved in the Zend-Avesta.

But it is a mistake to expect that the characteristics of this ancient Mithras of the orthodox Persians are to be found unchanged in the Mithras of the declining Roman Empire. The later and powerful effect of Babylonian beliefs upon Persian had already made Mithras a sun-god and the head of the planetary world. Furthermore, the tradition which reached the Romans was heretical from the outset; that is, it proceeded from a religious faction in the Persian Kingdom which was hostile to the Magi. It was finally received at second hand and apparently much confused, specifically upon the occasion of the war of annihilation which Pompey the Great waged against the pirates who were mostly natives of Cilicia. These, we are told, celebrated various secret rituals and also introduced that of Mithras, which continued in being thereafter. Somehow or other, this fragment of Persian religion in half-Assyrian transformation took hold in Asia Minor. Mithras scholarship is overrich in curious hypotheses, and we must beware of adding to the number needlessly. Yet the experts may allow us one question: Was it among the Cilician pirates that Mithras-worship first took on that aspect of a martial religion of robbers which later made it so suitable as a Roman warrior religion? In any case, the Cilicians traveled widely as slave dealers, and they took their cult with them.

Numerous reliefs, some of very large scale, found in most of the collections of antiquities in Europe, present the enigmatic myth, but without explaining it. Their artistic merit is slight, and they are at best hardly older than the Antonines. A cave is to be seen, over which the ascending and descending chariot of the sun, or the sun and moon together, is indicated. In the cave a youth in Phrygian costume — Mithras himself — kneels upon a bull into whose throat he thrusts a dagger. From the bull's tail spring ears of grain; a dog leaps upon the bull, a serpent licks his blood, a scorpion gnaws at his genitals. At either side stands a torch-bearer, one with raised and the other with lowered torch. Over Mithras there appears a raven, customarily the bird of prophecy, perhaps also to be interpreted as the bird of battlefields. A lion's head, which is sometimes seen in the right-hand corner, may also be a symbol of light, of the sun. We pass over numerous other additions which occur on individual Mithras stones.

The original significance of these symbols has been demonstrated with fair certainty. In the first place it is the victory of the sun-hero over the bull, which represents the moon or the quick alternations of time in general, which must die that a new year may be born. The grain is the year's fertility, the dog indicates devouring Sirius, the scorpion the autumn (that is, the approaching death of nature). The torchbearers (sometimes explained as morning and evening star) represent the equinoxes. The reliefs on either side and above the cave, which occur on certain specially rich examples, are now explained in part as astral and elemental events; previously it was thought they represented individual stages in the secret initiations. But much is still unexplained. That all of these things retained a higher significance from the ancient Persian period is obvious.

The meaning which the late Roman period associated with these figures was a far cry from their original significance. Fortunately, inscriptions provide a plain hint; they read "To the unconquered god, Mithras," "To the unconquered sun, Mithras," "To the sun, the unconquered," and the like. The last form, incidentally, is one of the most frequent formulae on the coins of Constantine the Great, who throughout his life, perhaps, never completely detached himself from the externals of the Mithras-worship. The unconquered was doubtless at the same time the giver of victory, and thus peculiarly appropriate as a war-god; recent researches suggest that this was at least a secondary function of Mithras even in his ancient Persian form. Finally Mithras is the guide of souls which he leads from the earthly life into which they had fallen back up to the light from which they issued. This notion is taken up by the sentiment common in the later Roman world; it was not only from the religions and the wisdom of Orientals and Egyptians, even less from Christianity, that the notion that life on earth was merely a transition to a higher life was derived by the Romans. Their own anguish and the awareness of senescence made it plain enough that earthly existence was all hardship and bitterness. Mithras-worship became one, and perhaps the most significant, of the religions of redemption in declining paganism.

But ancient man experienced a feeling of misery without at the same time experiencing a sense of sin. Hence remission by words profited him little; he required redemption of a quite special character. To be able to attach himself to the savior-god, each individual must become his own redeemer through terrible voluntary suffering, which was a far more serious element here than in all other mysteries. And so the Mithraic initiations developed so-called trials, compared to which the *taurobolium* and the trials of Isis were mere child's play. What confronts us here was certainly not merely a device to discourage those not truly "called" and the masses generally; it was called "castigations," and must have cost many a candidate his life. These castigations involved eighty separate steps, such as fasting for fifty days, swimming a wide circle, touching fire, lying in snow up to twenty days, torments of all sorts, being scourged for two days, lying on a torture bench, enduring painful postures, another fast in the desert, and others. Seven various degrees of initiation are named, but their order is not certain; they include the degrees of raven, warrior, and lion, and the highest initiates were called Fathers. We do not know at which of these degrees the individual ceremonies were carried out which Christian contemporaries call simply sacraments. At the lion degree the celebrant washed his hands in honey and vowed to keep them pure of all misdeeds. Somewhere bread and a cup of water were used, and there was a bath which purified from sin. Then a garland tossed from a sword was aimed at the head of the "Mithras-warrior," which he was required to block with his hand and press down upon his shoulder, because Mithras himself was his garland and crown.

In view of the numerous Emperors, courtiers, and notable personages who participated in this cult, it has been persistently maintained that these imitations and castigations were not taken literally and that much of them had been reduced to symbolic gesture or even to mere verbal formula. Who could have bidden a Commodus, for example, to submit to those strange torments? Were not the hierophants of the various mysteries complaisant to important people generally? But our accounts of the actuality of the castigations are far too definite to be brushed aside with mere hypotheses. One thing may be freely admitted: since there was no common hierarchy to preserve and guide the cult, ritual usages may have taken on different forms in different parts of the Empire. So far as

M

they are known to the present writer, the Mithras stones which
contain a large number of pictures and reliefs at the sides and
over the cave have all been found on the Rhine, in Tyrol, and
in Transylvania; they come from Heddernheim not far from
Frankfurt, Neuenheim near Heidelberg, Osterburken between
Neckar and Tauber, Apuleum not far from Karlsburg, Sarmi-
zegethusa, also in Transylvania. There is a very important
specimen from Mauls in the Tyrol, now in Vienna; here two
registers of small pictures at the sides of the main relief contain scenes which were thought to represent the various initi-
atory tortures: standing in snow and in water, the bed of
torment, singeing by fire, and others. Different explanations
may now be offered, but it is enough for us to notice that in
these regions a circumstantial language of pictures was felt to
be necessary for reasons which are now completely unknown.
The many stones found in Italy, on the other hand, have nothing of this character. The individual lodges of the order (if
one remembers not to take the loose expression too precisely)
may have differed from one another substantially in admission, doctrine, and cult. The monuments enumerated above
mostly derive from the third century, a period of ferment for
paganism which, sensing its internal dissolution, sought, at
least partially, to restore and intensify itself and in places developed a sudden fanaticism. It may well be that beside local
differentiations, differences of time were also a factor.

The Mithras stones north of the Alps and the Danube which
have been mentioned derive in all probability, and partly demonstrably, from Roman soldiers. What part did the initiate
take in the daily life of the camp? How was this religious
service related to the military and political duties of higher
officers? Did it constitute an effectual bond among them? Did
the religion contribute morally to the spiritual regeneration of
Roman character in the second half of the third century? All
of these questions must remain unanswered as long as our
only sources of knowledge are the few passages in authors
who are mostly Christian. The site of the finds of Mithras
stones are caves, natural or artificial, and occasionally free-
standing buildings, often only a few feet square, whose rear

wall was occupied by the relief. The space could accommodate only a few people at most; if a crowd attended it must be thought of as standing outside. Even the large Mithreum at Heddernheim is less than forty feet long; its width of twenty-five feet is largely obstructed by adjacent cells, so that a passage of only eight feet is left. In the small Mithreum at Neuenheim, eight feet square, the interior was blocked by altars and statues of related deities, as for example Hercules, Jupiter, Victoria, and there were also implements, lamps, and other fragments. Structural additions such as richly decorated pillars and the like show that these sanctuaries did not need to keep hidden. Who would have dared desecrate them? The soldiers who performed their secret worship there were masters of the world.

The Mithras cave at Rome (which was on the declivity of the Capitoline hill) is to be thought of as much larger and more magnificent, as were doubtless those in the other great cities of the Empire. In Alexandria the sanctuary was deep underground. .When it was excavated in Christian times for the foundations of a church there were still current dark stories of many murders which had been perpetrated on the site, and in fact the "castigations" may have cost many an initiate his life. When actual skulls were found they were wrongly ascribed to victims who had been slaughtered for the sake of inspecting their entrails and for conjuring the dead. Mithras worship had nothing to do with such proceedings, but the Egyptian imagination, as we shall presently see, had always been filled with such cruelties.

About a hundred reliefs and inscriptions show that this worship had spread over the entire Empire. Thousands of others may yet lie underground, and it is to be hoped that their excavation will be as competent as those at Heddernheim, Neuenheim, and Osterburken. The content of a single well-preserved Mithras cave may well throw conclusive light upon this most remarkable of all ancient secret cults.

But in any case this cult was not unaffected by the great stream of other contemporary superstitions. In the first place, there were many who could not get enough of mysteries and therefore sought assurance of three-formed Diana, the *tauro-bolium* of the Great Mother, the Bacchic cults, Isis worship, and Mithras alike — a fusion of all pagan occult worship which became the rule in the course of the fourth century, but was surely not unusual in the earlier period. As the doctrine of the unity of all divine nature became a factor, men naturally grew indifferent to sharp distinctions among individual cults, so that one freely borrowed from the others. Neoplatonic philosophy entered into the Mithras religion as into all mysteries, and to Porphyry, one of its most distinguished devotees, we owe virtually our only treatment of the subject in a pagan source. But Porphyry's essay *On the Grotto of the Nymphs* deals not so much with the contemporary state of the worship as with its original significance, and that in a one-sided and capriciously symbolizing aspect in the interests of his school. We learn that the grotto is a symbol of the cosmos or universe; therefore Zoroaster had dedicated a flowery and well-watered cave in the mountains of Persia in honor of Mithras, creator and guide of the world. In this first cave the symbols of world elements and zones were employed; and from this cave all subsequent cave mysteries issued. On the other hand the entire essay is linked to the grotto in Ithaca described by Homer (*Odyssey* 13, 102–112, 346 ff.), and Porphyry had made that the focus of his symbolism. Porphyry follows the footless manner of seeking to find identity in myths and of always associating one echo with another. But isolated individual hints are of great value, as for example when he assigns the northern and southern gate of his world cave to the souls who descend to earth for birth and ascend to the gods at death, to genesis and apogenesis, and when he refers in general to the life and the purification of souls.

Finally there was a natural relationship with Mithras in the person of the Greco-Roman sun-god, whether he was thought of as Apollo, or as Sol or Helios apart from Apollo. We can probably never know how far Mithras was merged with this sun-god; perhaps Sol Invictus, who appears more frequently on coins and inscriptions after the middle of the third century, is everywhere to be taken as Mithras, even though he is openly represented only as the sun-god. The sun-worship of the early Emperors, as for example of Elagabalus, may have derived from a Semitic cult; in the case of Aurelian we are still completely in the dark as to the character of his religion. His mother was priestess of the sun at a place on the lower Danube, and it is not impossible that she was one of the female devotees of Mithras of whom there is scattered mention, perhaps a "lioness." On the other hand, when the Temple of the Sun at Palmyra was plundered, Aurelian commanded its restoration by one of his generals, and added, "I will write to the Senate and petition it to send a pontifex to reconsecrate the temple." This implies the customary Roman rite, though it is a sanctuary of a Semitic Baal which is involved. But in Rome itself Aurelian built a large and magnificent Temple of the Sun in which he deposited fifteen thousand pounds of gold (for surely it was to this temple and none other that the gift was made); and this building backed onto the Quirinal hill in such a fashion that the possibility of a Mithraic significance is not to be brushed aside. For Mithras was and remained "the god from the rock," and all his sacred sites must therefore have something of the character of a cave, even if the cave is not to be taken essentially as the symbol of the phenomenal world. We have already mentioned that the slaughter of the bull which appears in monuments takes place in a cave. Sol Invictus occurs on Aurelian's coin. The relationship of succeeding Emperors to the Mithras cult is a matter of uncertainty; we shall have to return to this point in our treatment of Constantine.

It may seem odd to follow our discussion of the Mithras cult with Manichaeism, which made its way into the Roman Empire from Persia, because Manichaeism does not belong with the mysteries. But Manichaeism is not to be regarded merely as a Christian sect, but rather as a special religion of redemption predominantly pagan. Whether it assumed more of a Roman-pagan character in Roman hands than it could have had in the Sassanid Kingdom is a matter for further investigation, as is its subsequent invasion of the Christian Church. Its dualism is specifically at variance with classical belief, in that it resolves everything into pure symbols through which the two great basic principles, light and darkness, God and matter, express themselves. The highest concept, the Christ of this system (with patent reference to Mithras), is world soul, son of eternal light, and redeemer, but hardly a person; his historic manifestation was thought of as a phantom. Consequently, redemption is not a single act, such as an immolation, but is continuous; out of the morally unfree state of struggle between spirit and matter (or between the good and the evil soul) Christ constantly helps the individual man upwards to the realm of light. It is difficult to determine how near these ideas approach to a strictly conceived personal immortality; the "basic epistle" of the sect, in any event, speaks of an "eternal and glorious life," and it was presumably this promise which impressed the Roman proselyte most. Further discussion of this remarkable system is not appropriate at this place.

Mani, the founder of Manichaeism, had himself sent forth apostles, and despite all persecution had left the beginnings of a hierarchy in his community. Barely ten or twenty years after his martyrdom (272–275) his doctrine was spread abroad in the Roman Empire. An imperial rescript (287 or 296) to Julian, Proconsul of Africa, shows that this was the case in Africa Proconsularis. Considerable disorders must have occurred there at the instigation of the new sect, and it was known that its attitude, like that of several Oriental religions, was not peaceful toward Rome but rather exclusive, and it was moreover doubly suspicious and despised because of its Persian origin. Diocletian's measures were drastic; he ordered that the founders together with their books be burned and that other participants should either be put to death, or (if they had the rank of *honorati* or held other positions of dignity) be sent to the mines and their property confiscated. The motive for this severity was essentially the hostility of the new religion to the old; the old felt that it possessed the most sacred right as a primordial establishment of gods and men. After this striking mention we lose sight of Manichaeism for several decades. It cannot have played any great part before the death of Constantine; at least it is not mentioned by name in the great edict of heretics. It is only in the fifth century that Manichaeism raises its head for a time as the most dangerous enemy to the Church.

The above discussion shows that the late pagans did not pray to the gods for fertility, wealth, and victory alone; gloomy anxiety concerning the beyond overpowered them and drove them to the most extraordinary doctrines and rites.

But this world, too, now appears in a different light. In connection with the Isis mysteries it was indicated how the laboriously achieved protection of a great divinity provided a hope of avoiding not only the destruction of the soul but also a troubled earthly destiny which depended upon the stars. We must now show how changed was the relationship of all supermundane elements to life on earth, how astrology, magic, and demonology obtained the upper hand over earlier sacrifices, oracles, and penances. These elements had always been present, and even Homer had depicted Circe as the archetype of all magic. Plato speaks of wandering miracle workers who claimed to bring blessings and curses by secret procedures; and we hear of magicians who claim to have control over weather and fertility, storm and calm. Thessaly was and continued until late in the Empire to be the classic land of love magic, by means of verbal spells as well as secret charms. Ancient Italy was hardly far behind Greece in this matter; the conjuring of the gods, for example, which worked such evil to Tullus Hostilius, had its place in the ancient Roman cult itself. The twenty-eighth and thirtieth books of Pliny are ample indication of the degree to which magic was involved in a mass of superstitious household remedies and the like. Especially well known was the magic of the Etruscans, Sabines, and Marsians, that is to say, of most of the inhabitants of central Italy. Aside from magic healing of every kind, the Romans believed that these arts could bewitch grain fields, control weather, arouse love and hate, transform persons into animals, and work other miracles. This belief is also reflected in very remarkable goblins, among others the blood-sucking lamias and Empusae.

Happy was he who protected himself adequately with salutary counter-magic! To this end amulets were hung over the body from head to foot, and there was even an entire system of magic defense, of which certain individual details may be cursorily presented.

A view of the great host of details of that magical practice which have been recorded might well lead to a conviction that the entire ancient world was wholly fettered by it and rendered continually fearful in all phases of daily life. And yet these earlier isolated superstitions were far less harmful to the ancient religion; they disturbed the naïve relationship of man to divinity far less than the later *systematic* superstition which grew predominant in the Empire.

We must speak first of astrology, which was regarded as an old prerogative of the Orient and whose adepts were regularly called Chaldeans, although very few of them actually derived from the country on the lower Euphrates. At least the better known among them, Tiberius' Thrasyllus and Otho's Seleucus and Ptolemy, bore Greek names. Besides the Babylonian wisdom, reference was also made to the Egyptian, associated with the names of Petosiris and Necepso, who were regarded as the authors of the most familiar astrological writings.

Aside from the fact that the astrologers were not content with astrology alone but turned their hands to other and more fearful ways of searching out the future, astrology itself provided a very strong impulse to atheism. The consistent devotee of astrology would scorn all moral consideration and all religion, for these could provide neither comfort nor aid against the fate which was made manifest in the stars. It was the practice of this secret science primarily which loaded the Emperors of the first century with the grimmest curses. The Chaldeans were continually being banished because their wisdom could not be made an imperial prerogative, as all the world clamored for their prophecies; and they were as often summoned to return because men could no longer do without them. If one returned to Rome with the welts of the fetters which he had worn on some Aegean island, he could be certain that people would compete for his attention. The content of this science was briefly that a list of destinies was correlated with every possible position of the planets with relation to the signs of the zodiac. Everything was determined by the hour; horoscopes could be cast for the most commonplace activities, as for example a pleasure excursion or a walk to the baths, as well as for a man's whole life — if one only knew the constellation at the moment of his birth. Those who kept their eyes open could see the futility of the delusion and palpably prove it worthless, as St. Hippolytus, for instance, did. How could the constellations have any definite and consistent significance for a man's destiny when their configuration at any given hour was quite different for an observer in Mesopotamia than it was for one on the Danube or the Nile? Why do people born at the same hour not have the same destiny? Why should the constellation have more significance at birth than at conception? Why should the greatest diversity in hours of birth not be a protection against some common destruction, as in earthquakes, the sacking of cities, storms at sea, and the like? Was the presumably sovereign fate of the stars to be extended to flies, worms, and other vermin? Might there not be — the question was put with some intimation of the true answer — more planets than were then known? And finally all reasonable people agreed that it was no blessing to know the future, and in any case the reverse of a blessing to have false notions concerning it.

But no reasonable grounds in the world could extirpate this alleged science among a people which even during the bloom of its culture was alien to the idea of a divine world order and an all-embracing system of moral purpose, and which now more than ever was confused by uncertainty and apprehension concerning the great questions of life. The need for superstition was grown the more desperate in the degree that the natural energy with which the individual confronts fate had disappeared. In the late Empire astrology sought to acquire an ethical content in the same remarkable way as did the secret cults referred to above. We have valid evidence for this transformation in the *Eight Books of Mathesis* of the pagan Firmicus Maternus, who wrote shortly after the death of Constantine. At the end of the second book of this complete theory of the religion of the stars there is a long and solemn admonition to the astrologer, calculated to minimize the compromising, sinister, and dismal elements in its practice. The *mathematicus* (as the astrologer was called) must lead a godly life, because his converse was with the gods. He must show himself accessible, righteous, not avid. He must give his responses openly and inform the inquirer in advance that his answers would be plainly uttered in order to prevent inadmissible and immoral questions. He must have wife and children and respectable friends and acquaintances; he must have no secret associations but show himself among people. He must keep away from all quarrels and accept no inquiries which involve injury or destruction to anyone to satisfy hate or vengeance. He must always behave as a man of honor, and must not combine any usurious money transactions with his calling — which implies that many disreputable astrologers must have done so. He must neither give nor require oaths, especially in money matters. He must endeavor to exert a beneficial influence upon erring people in his environment, and in general to guide passionate people to the proper path not only by formal responses from the stars but also by friendly counsel. He should avoid nocturnal sacrifices and ceremonies, public as well as private. He should also avoid the games of the Circus, so that no one should think that the victory of the Greens or the Blues was connected with his presence. Questions concerning paternity, always troublesome, and inquiries concerning the horoscope of third parties, should be answered reluctantly and hesitatingly, so that it should not appear that fault is being found with a man for actions determined by evil stars. The word *"decretum,"* decree, is a constantly recurring technical term.

Far the most dangerous imposition on astrologers, which often caused the destruction of themselves and their clients during the first two centuries of the Empire, were inquiries concerning the fate of the Emperor. Alexander the Great had not taken inquiries concerning his fate amiss, but had praised them; now the matter was far more ominous. The throne of the Caesars, with no dynastic succession, was besieged by ambitious people who wished to know from the stars when and how the Emperor would die and who would succeed him. But astrologic theory had found a way to avoid this question. Firmicus Maternus explains that nothing could be known about the fate of the Emperor because that matter was not subject to the stars but directly guided by supreme divinity. As ruler of the world the Emperor held the rank of one of the many daimones who had been set over the world by deity as creating and preserving powers, and hence the stars, which represented a lower potency, could say nothing concerning the Emperor. The *haruspices* were in the same situation when it was a matter of determining imperial fate by inspection of entrails; they purposely disturbed veins and fibers in order not to be compelled to deliver a response. But in the fourth century these concessions were not of much help to astrology; bound up as it was with all other kinds of superstitions, it was opposed alike by the throne and by Christianity, and along with magic and other secret arts succumbed to general prohibitions and persecutions. Space does not permit an abstract of Firmicus' doctrinal system, nor would any modern take the pains to read it through unless he himself is a victim of the same delusion — or unless he means to produce a new edition of the author, which in view of the scarcity of older editions might be timely. The secrets proper, for whose preservation the author demands a solemn oath before the highest God of his addressee (Mavortius Lallianus, a high official), are contained in the last two books. These are indices of those constellations which determine whether a man is to be a murderer, commit incest, be a cripple, or become a gladiator, lawyer, slave, foundling, and so forth. A logical consequence of this odious delusion would be the disappearance of any moral considerations, and doubtless that was the intention of the earlier unscrupulous Chaldeans. But the newly aroused morality had become so far effective that the author of the Constantinian period must endeavor to find some moral reconciliation, which might indeed have been for him more than a mere manner of speech. He expresses the belief (Book I, Chapter 3) that even the most fearful decrees of the stars may be countered by much prayer and diligent worship of the gods; Socrates, for example, was doomed by the stars to endure all passions and bore his fate visibly in his countenance, yet by his virtues he mastered them all. "For that which we suffer and which pricks us with burning torches [that is, the passions], belongs to the stars; but our own powers of resistance belong to the godliness of the spirit." The misfortunes of the good and the good fortune of the evil are primarily the effect of the stars. But this solace still seems to be merely an external attachment to the system, of little force in comparison to the precisely systematized theory of nonsense presented in several hundred folio pages. The system begins by distributing individual temperaments and bodily members among the seven planets, and complexions, tastes, climates, regions, positions in life, and illnesses among the twelve heavenly signs. The Crab, for example, signifies sharp salty taste, light and whitish color, water animals and creeping things, the seventh zone, still or flowing water, mediocrity, and all diseases of the heart and the diaphragm. On the other hand, the astrologer is not concerned with races and national characters; it is enough for him that individuals are conditioned by the stars. The numerous other curiosities which occur here and there in the book need not detain us here.

At various points in this system there is mention of a supreme god to whom all other superhuman beings are subject as mere intermediary powers. Could not philosophy grasp the concept of this god once and for all and present a reasonable theism?

It is a humbling testimony to the human spirit's want of freedom in the face of great historical forces that, precisely here, contemporary philosophy, represented in part by truly noble personalities and equipped with all the science of the ancient world, lost itself in shadowy byways, and that we can find no other classification for it, at least at the beginning of the fourth century, than as an intermediate between two kinds of superstition, though it does mark an advance in questions of ethics.

Parallel to the spiritual transformation noticeable after the end of the second century is the dying out of the ancient philosophical schools. Epicureans, Cynics, Peripatetics, and the others disappear — even the Stoics, whose temper was so closely allied to the best aspects of Roman character. Along with a highly developed theoretical skepticism, the open mockery of a Lucian proclaimed the meaninglessness of sectarian distinction. At the same time, as a reaction, a new doctrine, more dogmatic than all earlier philosophies and hence in certain respects in harmony with the new religious movement, waited at the door. This was NEOPLATONISM. Neoplatonism was preceded by an extraordinary affection for Oriental superstitions and by diligent investigations of the records of the ancient school of Pythagoras, which had long fallen into desuetude and whose wisdom was likewise believed to be of Oriental origin; otherwise the essential elements for the new structure were borrowed from the Platonic system itself. Plotinus, the protagonist of the school in the middle period of the third century, stands forth as a significant thinker, and the system with its impulse to mysticism as a possible advance over the old skepticism which had previously held the field. There is something of truth and even more of poetry in the doctrine of the emergence of all things from God in determined descending degrees of being, according to greater or lesser admixture of the material. No system assigned a higher position to the human soul; it is an immediate emanation from Divine Being and may at times completely unite with Divine Being and thus become exalted above all commonplace life and thought. Here, however, we are not so much interested in the doctrine of the school as in the practical attitude, moral as well as specifically religious, which Neoplatonism conferred upon or permitted its disciples. We see repeated here a phenomenon old and new, in which a speculative system, contrary to opinion, becomes only the bond, the accidental cohesive force, but in no sense the dominant central point for tendencies and forces which would have been present even without its contribution.

This latest philosophic sect of antiquity, it must be noticed

at once, shows no advance whatever in the direction of monotheism, which was far more developed in many earlier
thinkers than in the "One," the "absolute One," or whatever
other novel designation was given to the supreme deity or
prime being which was conceived as having consciousness,
but in a pantheistic manner, as immanent in the world. All of
polytheism, furthermore, was included in the system in the
form of a belief in daimones who, as subordinate deities, held
dominion over individual countries, nature, and conditions of
life. Daimones had always been present in Greek religions,
but in varying form, more or less distinguished from the gods
at different periods, and early woven into a theological system, not without some violence, by philosophers. Later popular belief regularly attributed to them a sinister and ghostly
character and considered them at times as avengers of evil
and as protectors, but predominantly as senders of sickness.
Neoplatonic philosophy, as we shall see, conceived of them as
demiurgic intermediary beings.

The ancient gods thus became superfluous, unless they were
daimonized and included in the ranks of these lesser powers.
Of the popular mythology, naturally, no more use could be
made, and so the myths were interpreted as shells for physical, religious, and moral truths. Some of the explanations
were fantastically involved, as was the case with Euhemerism,
of which this tendency is the obverse. In its teaching concerning the human soul the system, though it places the soul high
as a divine emanation, does not go as far as eternal blessedness but only to migration of souls. In the case of the best
souls, however, this belief is modified to allocation to definite
stars; we have seen that survivors sometimes thought they
could determine the star appropriate to the departed. Indeed,
glimpses of blessedness were sometimes vouchsafed to the initiates, but only very rarely to the earlier and better among
them, who believed they had visions of God.

More essential than this theosophy, indeed a significant
sign of the century, is the confluence of Neoplatonism with
the tendency toward morality and asceticism characteristic of
the period. This is sometimes contrasted, as something spe-

cifically Christian, with the free morality of antiquity, just as Christian other-worldliness is contrasted with the ancient concern with this world; but there is little justification for such contrast when one examines the paganism of the third century. Here, too, we recognize a remarkable premonition or reflection of what the following century would bring.

Specifically Neoplatonism sets up pagan ideals, the biographies of favored friends of the gods who, practicing absolute abstinence, traveled about among all of the famous peoples of antiquity, studied their wisdom and their mysteries, and through their constant intercourse with the deity developed into miracle workers and superhuman beings. The career of the divine Plato was too well and precisely known for such treatment to be given him, though the school always regarded him with the veneration due a daimon; a certain Nicagoras of Athens, for example, who visited the wonders of Egypt in the age of Constantine, wrote his name in the crypts at Thebes with the prayer, "Be gracious to me here also, Plato!" But Pythagoras was remote enough in the mythical distance to invite a reworking of his career. Such a reworking was undertaken by Iamblichus (in the age of Constantine), after his immediate predecessor Porphyry had described Pythagoras in a more reasonable historical manner. On the other hand, the life of the miracle worker Apollonius of Tyana, though it fell in the first century after Christ, was sufficiently mysterious and extraordinary to be worked into a tendentious romance; that task was undertaken by Philostratus in the reign of Septimius Severus. This is not the place to analyze this very remarkable book; we can only call attention to the peculiar compromise concluded between ancient Greek subjectivity and Oriental taste for miracles and abstinence. The same Apollonius who goes about barefoot in a linen garment, enjoys no animal food or wine, touches no woman, gives away his possessions, knows all and understands all — even the language of animals — appears in the midst of famine and insurrection like a god, works miracle upon miracle, exorcises demons, and raises the dead — this same Apollonius practices without restraint the Greek cult of personality and occasionally shows the self-conscious vanity of an affected sophist. He is of good family and handsome figure, speaks pure Attic, and had mastered all systems as a boy. He receives homage of all sorts with the greatest dignity. He realizes very early that he has reached the point where he need no longer investigate but only communicate the results of his investigations to others. There is as yet no trace of humility; on the contrary, the holy man endeavors to humble others, and anyone who laughs at his discourses is declared to be possessed and is accordingly exorcised. Many details of this picture were borrowed by Iamblichus a century later to enrich his ideal portrait of Pythagoras, which otherwise rests upon more or less genuine ancient tradition. In order to show himself as "a soul guided by Apollo" or even as Apollo incarnate in human form, Pythagoras is now made not only to lead an ascetic life but to perform miracles, to swoop down from Carmel to the seacoast, to conjure animals, to be in several places simultaneously, and much else of the same character.

The models for these personified ideals of conspicuous asceticism must obviously be sought in the penitents of various Oriental religions, from the Jewish Nazarites and Therapeutae to the abstaining Magi of Persia and the fakirs of India, who were quite well known to the Greeks as gymnosophists. But the doctrine of the fall of the human soul, which might theoretically lead to morality, of its being rendered impure by matter and of the necessity of its purification, is likewise Oriental and indeed most likely of Indian origin. However, neither penitence nor its speculative basis could have found entry from the East if the popular mood had not already been affected by a similar movement. Certain remarkable contacts of this system with Christianity, indeed reciprocal influence of one upon the other, were inevitable.

And now this school which called itself by Plato's name was drawn into the mustiest of all superstitions and at times completely reduced to actual magic and theurgy. In the great hierarchy of being emanating from God, spirit works upon spirit and spirit upon nature by ways of magic, and the initiate possessed the key to this magic. Works of this nature credited to half-mythical thaumaturgists, to a Pythagoras or an Apollonius, were henceforward believed to be within the scope of contemporary practitioners. Neoplatonists functioned as rhetors, sophists, educators, secretaries, as the philosophers had done in the early Empire; but in the midst of such activity they sometimes suddenly arose to conjure gods, daimones, and souls, to work miraculous cures, and to perpetrate occult impostures of various sorts.

In the Egyptian Plotinus (205–270), the noblest of the school, this aspect was not especially prominent. His impeccable morals and his asceticism, to which he also inspired others, including many distinguished Romans, of themselves vouchsafed him the gift of clairvoyance and prophecy; he proceeded to conjuring, as it appears, only under duress. He became the object of superhuman reverence, and as long as there were pagans "his altars never grew cold." In his disciple, the Phoenician Porphyry (born 233), there is to be noticed even an express disapproval of magic; he questioned the whole daimonology of his school, which regarded him with suspicion in consequence. His objections were followed by a reply, known under the inaccurate title *Of the Mysteries of the Egyptians*, perhaps equally inaccurately ascribed to the Coelesyrian Iamblichus, who was regarded as the head of the school under Constantine, or possibly the work of the Egyptian Abammon. In ancient India and also in the Germanic Middle Ages we encounter the frequently grandiose mysticism of a more or less conscious pantheism; here, on the contrary, we have a mysticism of polytheism, even though its gods have paled to daimones of various degrees without definite personality. How these spirits are to be worshiped, to be invoked, to be differentiated, how the whole life of god-beloved sages is to be devoted to the practices of cults of this nature, is in brief the content of the whole sorry concoction, and in the fourth century the general tendency of the school is all too clearly canted to such corruption; indeed it recognized in theurgy an essential weapon in the struggle against Christianity. Henceforward the Platonic elements in its doctrine and speculation are merely an appendage.

N

A cursory glance at the system of exorcism is not out of place here. The possibility of exorcism rests upon the transfiguration of the soul of the exorciser into an absolutely dispassionate state and its inward union with the relevant spiritual being raised to the point of identity. It is not so much that the spirit is summoned down by conjuration or compulsion as that the soul rises upward to it. Even external objects employed in the exorcism are not merely symbols but have a mystical relationship with the relevant divine element. There is mention, indeed, of the "One," the self-sufficing supreme God, but very few may achieve union with him, and the individual may attain such union only after he has worshiped the daimones and united with them. The rungs of spiritual beings, borrowed in part from Jewish theology, are in descending sequence: God, gods, archangels, angels, daimones, dominions, heroes, lords, and souls. Souls are completely individual; as the rungs ascend, the spirits approach even closer to unity or essence. All eight rungs are classified in a large table according to form, kind, changeability, aspect, beauty, speed, size, brilliance, and the like. More important are their capacities and gifts with reference to man. The gods purify souls completely and vouchsafe health, virtue, righteousness, and long life. Archangels do the same, but not so completely or permanently. Angels free souls from the bonds of matter and bestow similar gifts, but more in special senses. Daimones draw souls downwards to natural things, burden the body, send diseases, punishments, and the like. Heroes lead souls to preoccupation with sensually perceptible things and arouse them to great and noble deeds, but otherwise behave like daimones. Dominions hold the direction of worldly matters and bestow worldly goods and the necessities of life. Lords belong to the wholly material realm and bestow only earthly gifts. Souls, finally, when they appear, promote propagation, but their conduct varies greatly, according to their merit. Each spirit appears with a retinue of the next following rung, archangels with angels, and so on. Good daimones bring their benefactions along with them; avenging daimones exhibit likenesses of future torments; evil daimones come with raving animals. All of these spirits have their appropriate bodies, but are independent of them in the degree of their position on the ladder. If an error is committed in the ritual, evil spirits appear in the place of those summoned, assuming their form; the priest may recognize them by their proud ostentation. But a ritual correctly executed has its effect even if the conjurer is not an initiate, "for it is not knowledge that unites the sacrificer with the god, otherwise mere philosophers would obtain this honor exclusively." There is a striking inconsistency between the sacramental indifference concerning the celebrant and the requirement of freedom from passion and other preparations of the soul referred to above; but there are even greater inconsistencies elsewhere in this book.

Next we learn something of the external apparatus and the formulae required. In contrast to other Neoplatonic teaching, which admits only bloodless sacrifice, here, by an obviously Egyptian addition, each god is required to have the sacrifice of the animal over which he presides and with which he therefore has a magical relationship. Use is also made of stones, herbs, incense, and the like. The bad manners of certain Egyptian conjurers, their crude threats to the gods, are expressly discouraged; such behavior is effective only with certain slighter daimones, and was altogether avoided by the Chaldeans. Similarly, the magic script which some employed could at best produce only slight and blurred appearances, and furthermore demoralized the conjurer, who might then easily fall into the power of evil and deceptive daimones.

Let us step out of this cloud of delusion for a moment to ask how far objective actuality may have gone in these appearances; for we are not dealing with purely imaginary images. We know that exorcisms of the 18th century made great use of the magic lantern, whose images were reflected on heavy vapors which had a narcotic effect. Something similar took place in the incantations at the time of Porphyry. There is express mention of an art which permitted phantoms of the gods to appear in the air at favorable moments by means of certain vapors produced by fire. Iamblichus, or Abammon, admits no deception even in this slighter form of conjuration, although it is not without a genuine magic effect; but he states that phantoms of this sort which must vanish as soon as the vapor disperses were but little regarded by priests who had ever seen authentic divine figures; magic, then, could only touch an outward shell, a mere shadow of the deity. But there can be no doubt that deception was practiced over long periods and in great volume. We shall not unqualifiedly include as pure deception the use of a child for the interpretation of the appearance and for prophecy, for Apuleius, whom we do not regard as a deceiver, believed in it. Apuleius believed that the simple childish soul was peculiarly fit to be transformed to a semi-conscious state (*soporari*) by means of formulae and incense, and that it could thus approach its real — that is, divine — nature closely enough to foretell the future. He cites Varro for the revelation of the end of the Mithradatic war obtained by the inhabitants of Tralles by means of a boy who saw an image of Mercury in a vessel of water (a real image placed in the vessel or only a mirage? — *puerum in aqua simulacrum Mercurii contemplantem*) and then described the future in one hundred and sixty verses. But at the beginning of the third century St. Hippolytus in his *Refutation of the Heresies* unmasks a large number of hoaxes worked by prestidigitators. Here again we find the use of a boy as an unhappy victim, but lulled into a deep sleep, as was later done by Cagliostro at Mitau, and made to rave. But mainly, what was done to clients was pure mockery. Their inquiries to gods, written, as they thought, in invisible ink, could be read by the conjurers by chemical means and appropriate responses could be prepared. When it was a matter of the appearance of a desired daimon, the conjurers clearly reckoned on their clients' being well content, "swinging laurel and crying loud" in a dark chamber, if nothing appeared. It could not be expected, they were given to understand, that the divine should make itself visible; enough that it was present. The boy must then report what the daimones said, that is, what the conjurer whispered to him through a cleverly contrived tube. Balls of incense, in which explosive materials or materials which would produce a blood-red glow were included, and alum, which would make the embers on the altar seem to move when it liquefied, must have aided the illusion. Finally, some completely unintelligible oracle was kept in readiness for the curious. Much of what we are told has remained in the repertory not only of conjurers but of ordinary jugglers down to our own time: coloring eggs on the inside, or tricks with fire, either placing a hand in it, or walking upon it, or spitting it out of the mouth. More serious are recipes for leaving seals apparently unbroken on documents whose contents it is desired to know. Conjuring proper appears here and there among these tricks. Goats and rams drop dead by occult means; lambs even commit suicide. A house (treated with the juice of a certain sea creature) appears to be in flames. Thunder is produced artificially.* Writing appears on the liver of a sacrificial victim (because the cheat has written in reverse with strong ink on his left hand, on which the liver is placed). A skull lying on the ground speaks and then disappears — because it was made of a skin on modeled wax, which collapsed as near-by heated coals had their effect; the speaking was managed by a hidden accomplice through a tube fashioned out of a crane's esophagus. Moonlight could be kept ready unnoticed until all other lights were extinguished; a beam from a hidden light illuminated a water basin on the ground, and this was reflected in a mirror on the ceiling. At other times a hole in the ceiling was filled with a tambourine, and to this an accomplice in the upper chamber applied a light at a given signal after removing its cover. Even simpler was a lamp in a narrow vessel, which would throw a round beam upon the ceiling. The star-studded heaven could be simulated by fish scales pasted on the ceiling; these would gleam if the room were even dimly lighted. We come now to the actual appearances of the gods, which the conjurers took quite lightly, for they could count on the terror and obedience of their clients. In the dark of a moonless night, in the open, the conjurer would show Hecate flying through the air, when his accomplice, as soon as the formula was pronounced, would release an unlucky chicken hawk wrapped in

* Unfortunately, a recipe for an earthquake is incompletely preserved in the ms.

burning tow; the client had been bidden, the moment he saw a fiery object whirring through the air, to cover his face and fall silently to the ground. The appearances of a fiery Asclepius, for example, were more artfully contrived. A figure of Asclepius in high relief and perhaps life-size was modeled upon a wall and covered with highly inflammable material; at the instant the conjurer uttered his hexameter this was ignited and burned brightly for a few moments. To show animated gods moving about at will, finally, was more complicated and more expensive. The only solution for this problem was a cellar chamber in which costumed supers walked about. In the chamber above the believers looked through a large water basin fixed in the ground; the basin was of stone, but its bottom was glass.

Frequently, then, the appearances involved not ecstasies and hallucinations but objective actualities. Whether, besides simple charlatans, there were serious theurgists who employed delusions, but only as devout piety, remains a question; another is whether Iamblichus (or whoever wrote the treatise we have cited) intended his work for such devout practitioners.

Besides exorcisms, that author provides information on other problems in the realm of the supernatural also. In the matter of divinely sent dreams, for example, he tells us that they come not in sound sleep but that in a state of half or complete wakefulness a man will hear short whispered words, "Do this or that"; he will feel himself surrounded by a spiritual movement and sometimes see a pure and calm light. The prophetic significance of ordinary dreams, on the other hand, is reckoned very low. Individuals who are divinely inspired are said generally to live a divine, no longer animal, life, and hence feel neither fire nor pricks nor other tortures. Furthermore, the divine presence may affect only the soul or only individual members of the body, so that some dance and sing, others rise erect, hover in the air, even seem to be surrounded by fire; divine voices, sometimes clear and sometimes soft, are heard the while. Much lower stand the voluntary magic incitements induced by kinds of incense, potions, formulae, and the like, so that one perceives things hidden and things to be in water, in the clear night air, or on certain walls covered with sacred symbols. But so strong a current of premonition and prophecy runs through the entire visible world — that is, the system was so loath to forgo different popular superstitions — that it was possible to read the future in pebbles, reeds, wood, grain, even in the utterances of the insane. The flight of birds too is directed by divine powers to provide signs, so that even this proverbial freedom is rendered unfree. Ordinary astrology was looked down upon contemptuously as a futile by-way, even as error, for it was not the constellations and the elements which determined destiny but the attitude of the world-whole at the moment the soul descended to earthly life. But this did not prevent the astrologers from entering into contact with the system, as Firmicus Maternus, for example, demonstrates in many passages. One trait, it may be noticed in passing, clearly shows the un-Greek, thoroughly barbarian, origin of this theory of conjuration, and that is the undisguised pleasure it takes in the abracadabra of foreign and especially Oriental invocations. These we learn not from Iamblichus, indeed, but from other sources, and many of them have been bequeathed to the literature of magic which circulates to this day. Foreign names are preferred not merely because they are older or because they are untranslatable, but because they possess "great emphasis," that is, they sound impressive and meaningful. Newer complaints of the impotence of many incantations are based solely on the fact that the revered ancient ritual had been altered because of Greek eagerness for innovation. "The barbarians alone are serious in manner, consistent in the formulae of prayer, and therefore dear to the gods and heard by them."

This tasteless system, though it was taken literally by perhaps only a few, nevertheless more or less dominated all the philosophy of the fourth century, and no educated pagan was completely untainted by it. From the lives of the philosophers themselves, as Eunapius tells them, superstition rises to meet us like a gray fog. Iamblichus himself, for example, lets his disciples believe that in prayer he hovers ten cubits over the ground and assumes a golden-colored appearance. At the warm baths of Gadara in Syria he summons from the two springs the genii of Eros and Anteros. They appear as boys, the one with gold and the other with shining dark hair, to the great astonishment of the disciples and companions, and nestle up to Iamblichus, until he sends them back to their springs. His disciple Aedesius, who had forgotten the hexameter which a god had intoned for him in a vision, found it written in his left hand upon awakening, and therefore prayed to the hand. The woman philosopher Sosibia of Ephesus had been brought up from childhood by two daimones who had first hired themselves out to her father in the guise of field workers; her entire later life also was conditioned by magic and divination. Other stories, some very colorful, we pass over. It is obvious that the philosophers were by no means in agreement, in life as little as in doctrine. Within the Neoplatonic school itself there is a quite early example of evil magic, which the Alexandrian Olympius sought to work upon the great Plotinus. A conjurer summons Apollo in the presence of Iamblichus and several others, but Iamblichus proves that the apparition is nothing else than the phantom (εἴδωλον) of a newly fallen gladiator. What one produces the other regularly declares is a trifle. The philosopher Maximus was so far successful that he caused the image in the temple of Hecate at Ephesus to smile, in the presence of many persons, and the torches in its hands to ignite of themselves; but the Carian Eusebius finds that this is nothing remarkable. In the latest period, when sinking paganism mustered all its strength, such dissensions must have diminished. There was formed that great and confused conglomerate of philosophy, magic, and all the mysteries which gives the age of Julian its physiognomy. The more theurgy was compelled to retire into hiding under Constantine and his sons, the more spacious was its dominance for a short period when it enveloped with its delusions the young prince who was doomed to misfortune for all his merit. His teacher Aedesius had said to him: "If ever you participate in the mysteries you will be ashamed of even having been born human." It is to be wondered, indeed, that a man so preoccupied with the world of spirits should have developed into so competent a ruler and warrior. At this quite late period elegant Canopus on the coast of Egypt grew into a kind of teaching center for all magic, to be the "wellhead of daimonic activity." Attendance was extraordinary, especially when one of Sosipatra's sons, Antoninus, settled there; Antoninus himself did not practice theurgy but enjoyed superhuman regard as prophet and ascetic. All who came to Canopus by land or sea to perform their religious duties, regularly visited Antoninus and heard his prophecies. "These temples," he frequently lamented, "will soon become tombs" — and they did indeed, when they were transformed to monasteries and stocked with martyrs' relics.

A remarkable twofold effect issued from this activity. On the one hand the system demanded moral transformation and renunciation; on the other nothing was more calculated to destroy the remnants of true pagan morality and religiosity than this exclusive art of conjuration, aimed only at initiates and arrogantly oblivious of the great masses, whose belief in their old gods and heroes it only confounded. For while myth was denied or interpreted allegorically, the gods themselves are claimed as daimones, and even the heroes were fitted into the system at will. When a number of temples were searched under Constantine and the gold and silver portions of composite idols were removed for smelting, many pagans wondered that no daimon, no prophetic being, not even a shadowy and whispering apparition was to be found in the innermost parts of the temple or of the statues themselves. Men had learned to separate the beautiful artistic form of the god completely from its daimonic nature. The cult of Achilles in this daimonic sense, which was intensified after the third century, deserves special mention. Achilles appears to the inhabitants of the plain of Troy, significantly enough, no longer as the ideal of heroic beauty, but as a fearful apparition.

From what has been said we may deduce the fate of late pagan monotheism. Surely there continued to be pure souls and acute thinkers who clung to the oneness of God in the spirit of earlier and better times. But with the majority this belief was disturbed by daimonic additions. The paganism of an

Ammianus Marcellinus, for example, is not to be lightly esteemed, for he was one of the better spirits of the fourth century and saw through the philosophic sorcerers at the court of his hero Julian; but how qualified is his monotheism! The individual gods remain, if not directly as daimones, at least as virtually personified qualities. Nemesis is a sovereign right of the deity in action, but is called daughter of Justitia. Themis is eternal law, but was thought of personally as presiding over the auspices. Mercury is called *mundi velocior sensus,* that is, approximately, the moving principle of the universe. Finally, Fortuna still directs human destiny. Among these later pagans the supreme deity must have yielded his first quality, which is personality, to the subordinate gods and daimones, to whom the cult was then almost exclusively directed. Perhaps the supreme deity retained the greatest measure of personality among the worshipers of the sun, who referred all gods to the sun and worshiped it as the physical and spiritual principle of all existence. Constantine appears to have favored this religion, at least outwardly, although he conceived it in a Mithraic form; we shall consider this further presently. His father Constantius Chlorus is expressly credited with the worship of the one true God — unless Eusebius is again misrepresenting and idealizing ordinary Mithraism as pure monotheism. In this time of mixture of all religions, elements from Judaism may here and there have entered paganism and Parseeism, as for example among the Cappadocian Hypsistarii (that is, worshipers of the Highest God) at the beginning of the fourth century. These were true monotheists, but their influence was only provincial and so need not be considered here. Finally we find a quite worthless monotheism here and there among those who were eager to sail with every wind and to avoid all offense when Constantine's edict of toleration had moved all boundaries. Of this sort is the prayer of one of those panegyrists who have been characterized above: "We beseech thee, highest author of all things, whose names are as many as thou hast given tongues to peoples, without our knowing which name thine own will demands! Whether there be in thee a divine power and intelligence, through which, poured over the entire world, thou dost mingle with all elements and dost move thyself with no force from without; or whether thou be a power over all heavens and look down upon thine handiwork from a lofty tower; we beg and beseech thee that thou preserve this our prince forever." We see that the speaker leaves a free choice between an immanent and a transcendent god, and when he later ascribes to this indefinite supreme being omnipotence and beneficence, he straightway cancels these attributes by an impertinent closing formula: "If thou deny his merits their reward, then either thy power or thy goodness has ceased." This Gallic orator doubtless represented a large number of undecided and prudent persons who wished to see what success the edict would have.

Now that we have examined philosophic belief in daimones and its influence upon pagan monotheism, we shall have to bestow another glance upon the superstitions and magic wizardry of the transition period which belong rather to popular superstition. No sharp distinction, as we have indicated, is possible.

Many of these things are merely the continuation of earlier practices. Thus, for example, the Etruscan haruspices persisted, and indeed with increased splendor, after they had nearly died out in the first century. The haruspices were the official means for consulting the gods at the imperial court, and also enjoyed considerable private practice, at least in Italy. In the narrower sense the auspices denoted determination of the future from the entrails of animals and the flight of birds, divining of the will of heaven from lightning and even drawing lightning down, the regulation of foundations for cities, and much else of the same sort; but in the course of time they had coalesced with other superstitions, particularly with Chaldean astrology, and our authors do not always differentiate them properly from other branches of theurgy.

Neither were the oracles — that is, responses to inquiries concerning the future, issued at definite sacred sites — grown mute, although they had found formidable competitors in the itinerant conjurers. The various pagan religions throughout the Empire were at one in assuming that there were favored lo-

calities and sites where the will of the gods could be apprehended more clearly than elsewhere. In all provinces, therefore, there were oracular temples, oracular fountains, sacred
clefts in the earth, grottoes, and the like, some dating from
high, pre-Roman antiquity, which offered responses to every
possible kind of inquiry. Sleeping in the temples of Aesculapius and of Serapis for the purpose of inciting remedial
dreams belonged to this category; frequently the best society
foregathered on these occasions. In any case there were no
longer large, official, political consultations. Such inquirers
went about with great secrecy and preferred to turn to conjurers. But if no Croesus was longer counseled in hexameters
to cross the Halys, still the more reputable oracles continued
to be celebrated by pilgrims of various positions and interests
who brought their offerings. Pausanias visited all of those in
Greece, one after the other, out of motives of piety and curiosity. For Delphi we have a series of scanty notices, but never
wholly interrupted for a long period, reaching down to Constantine and then resuming. There are individual notices of
Hellenic and Asia Minor oracles at Abae, Delos, Miletus,
Colophon, and the like, down to a quite late period; we must
not be misled by Church writers, among whom it became virtually a dogma that the oracles were reduced to silence after
the birth of Christ. This is most likely to have happened in the
case of the very ancient oracle of Dodona. Rome retained and
still inquired from time to time of the Sibylline Books, which
were generally considered to be the highest authority for the
fate of the state. Nevertheless it appears that against the last
consultation of these books prior to Constantine, at the time
of the barbarian invasions under Aurelian, an enlightened or
heretical party arose in the Senate. The favorite private oracle
in the vicinity of Rome, consulted even by Emperors, was that
of the majestic Temple of Fortuna at Praeneste, which looked
down upon the surrounding regions from its high terraces. The
oracular temples at Antium and Tibur, which were highly
esteemed, were only of secondary rank as compared with the
"Praenestine lots." In upper Italy the warm spring of Aponus
near Padua enjoyed great credit not only for its curative

powers but also for its oracles, which were communicated, at least to Claudius Gothicus, in Vergilian hexameters. The spring of Clitumnus near Spoleto, with its surroundings so charming to this day, doubtless continued to be a sacred site of this sort, as it was at the time of the Younger Pliny. In early Christian times Christian emblems were introduced on the only one of the many temples and chapels that decorated this spot which has been preserved, apparently only to exorcise the prophetic daimones.

In Africa the Heavenly Goddess at Carthage continued to enjoy high esteem for its oracle down to the time of Diocletian. Even Gaul was not wholly devoid of oracles; at least the warm springs at the Temple of Apollo at Autun rendered decisions on oaths and perjury.

Of the oracles in the Eastern regions of the Empire, we have continual, individual reports concerning the Temple of Aesculapius at Aegae, the Apollo of Sarpedon at Seleucia, and the Temple of Mallos, all three in Cilicia, as well as concerning the Temple of the Paphian Venus on Cyprus, the oracle without temple on Mount Carmel, and several sanctuaries in Egypt. Of the great temples of the Asiatic interior, perhaps none was without claim to oracular authority. As late as the end of the fourth century the idol of the temple at Baalbek was periodically carried into the open, and (like the statue of Apollo at Hierapolis) indicated to its bearers the direction of the procession, which was given a prophetic interpretation. Other, ordinary, responses were issued in writing and by symbols. A remarkable feature is the diligent inquiry of the Palmyrenes, who turned to the Apollo of Sarpedon and to the Heavenly Aphrodite at Aphaka to obtain information concerning the duration of their realm.

For obvious reasons no reliable statistics concerning the extent of oracular practices in the age of Constantine can be offered. Parallel with the oracles there were constant daily inquiries concerning the future through observations of many quite external happenings which superstition had assigned to the realm of the ominous. The *sortes Vergilianae* (determined by opening a volume of Vergil at random) was one of the more intellectual devices of this kind. Bondage to more vulgar delusions has been noticed in the Introduction in Septimius Severus, who paid homage not only to omens but also to dreams, astrology, magic, the Attic mysteries, and others. With the ancient Roman superstitions there were mingled in the course of time those of the subject peoples and of the East. Men were frightened and their actions determined at every hour by omens and portents, and Chaldean or Egyptian almanacs were consulted for every step which was taken out of the house. Eusebius relates of Maximinus Daia that his fingers ventured to move nothing from its place without prophecy or oracle.

But this is not the sum of the aberration. Partly to discover the future, partly to affect it by magic means, the Roman of the early Empire often turned to repulsive methods, for which the same Chaldeans were employed who read the future out of the stars. Frequently the ends to be attained were criminal, and there were no scruples concerning the means. When Germanicus was assailed by deadly magic, and actually driven to his death by that means, no one was concerned that other murders must indubitably have been perpetrated to provide the magician with the necessary portions of the human anatomy. But even when it was not a matter of positive magic, of actual bewitching, but only of discovering the future or averting misfortune, the procedures were often of a frightful nature. Inspection of human entrails never wholly ceased as long as there was paganism. The desire for Emperor Hadrian's voluntary death cost his favorite Antinoüs his life. The fragmentation of cadavers for the sake of magic coercion, the conjuration of corpses to phantom life, and finally the invocation of souls continued to be a very familiar and by no means uncommon method of divination, to say nothing of lesser forms of sorcery, especially love potions. General terror of magicians must have been very widespread, at least to the extent that prominent and highly cultured people could be jeopardized by accusations of sorcery.

What was the relationship of these magic practices to the

new third-century tendencies of pagan religiosity and morality and to Neoplatonist philosophy?

Those elements in the occult sciences which were not directly criminal or repulsive persisted unhindered and were even officially supported, for the devout Alexander Severus assigned state pensions to the haruspices and astrologers and required them to lecture on their specialties. From graver practices and such as involved crime most of the Emperors abstained, especially when continuous warfare brought a more vigorous and healthier tone to the court and Decius made the restoration of the old religion a matter of state policy. Even the superstitious Diocletian appears blameless in this respect, so far as we know; but we shall find his colleagues sunk in desolate folly.

As regards the Neoplatonists, their doctrine of daimones is too closely parallel to certain aspects of ordinary magic for us not to presume a close complicity. Indeed, their exorcism in general derives in part from popular Oriental and Occidental beliefs in magic.

Thirdly, the Christians in their belief in daimones, partly of Judaizing and partly of popular origin, run parallel with the pagans. They have not the slightest doubt that there are numerous intermediate powers which exercise a potent effect upon the life of men and can by men be exorcised; these daimones are thought of as fallen angels or as giants, that is, as sons of angels and the daughters of men. But these spirits are all evil, hostile to the Kingdom of God and the salvation of man. Many were thought of as causing evil in nature, such as earthquakes and plagues, as well as in the moral world; indeed, they are the originators of the entire senseless and wicked paganism to which they have seduced the human species in order to retain it in their power beyond redemption. These notions are old and in part taken over from Judaism, but in course of time their outlines grew sharper. We may consult Lactantius as a witness from the period shortly after the great persecution of Diocletian: "These supermundane and earthly daimones know much of the future but not all; the genuine counsel of God they do not know. It is they who suffer themselves to be conjured by magicians, at whose invocation they deceive the mind of man with blinding jugglery so that he does not see what is but believes that he sees what is not. . . . They produce disease, dreams, madness, in order to fetter men more closely to themselves by terror. . . . But we need not revere them out of fear, for they are harmful only so long as they are feared; they must flee at the mention of the name of God, and a pious man can even force them to reveal their own names. . . . They have taught men to make images of deceased kings, heroes, inventors, and the like, and to worship them as divine; but beneath these names they themselves lie hidden as beneath a mask. The magicians indeed summon a daimon not by his alleged divine name, but by his true supermundane name. . . ." Further, Lactantius acknowledges that the daimones actually reside in temples and perform miracles, all to confirm unhappy men in their delusive belief. Therefore knowledge of the future, which they actually possess as being originally divine spirits, they employ for the purpose of occasionally announcing truth in oracles so that they may thereafter acquire the reputation of having themselves brought events to consummation. From the same period also come the statements of Arnobius, who acknowledges the complete objective actuality of magic in very broad scope and finds, for example, that the chief difference between Christ and the magicians consists in the fact that Christ performed his miracles through the power of his name, whereas the magicians performed theirs merely by the help of the daimones. The miracles of Simon Magus, particularly his fiery chariot, are referred to as something generally familiar. In all invocations and exorcisms, indeed, it is not certain whether only one and the same figure always appears — to wit, Satan.

These preliminary observations are essential to give an indication of the prevalence of belief in magic. Perhaps even the best men of the period were not entirely free of such belief. Details will appear in examples of the different kinds of magic.

The Neoplatonic conjurers, as has been remarked above, recognized the exorcism of human souls as a separate category.

Independently of their system and long anterior to it such exorcism is encountered frequently, because at all times much important information was expected of the dead, and in several ancient religious systems the deceased was regarded directly as a *genius*. In the first two centuries there is frequent mention of such evocations, carried out in part with fearful circumstance; we need only mention Nero and Horace's Canidia. The third century reveals Caracalla, who in a delirious fever believed that he was pursued by his father Severus and his murdered brother Geta, swords in hand, and who conjured a host of spirits to inquire for a means of relief. Commodus and Severus himself appeared at the summons, but the latter was accompanied by the uninvoked soul of Geta, and the horrified conjurer received no solace but only wild threats. Nothing similar, indeed, is reported of the later Emperors, but the conjuring of souls continued to be practiced, and the Christian writers often speak of it with horror as something present; accusations as well as prohibitions concerning conjuring reach far into the Christian period. But in later times they cannot always be distinguished from general charges and prohibitions concerning the crime of so-called *veneficium*, which embraced other illicit effects by external means as well as the compounding of poisons. Included, for example, were the magic means by which drivers in the Circus thought they could obtain victories. In Rome there continued to be "teachers of the evil arts," and if a man was unwilling to send his own son to school to them, he sought to compass the same end by sending a clever slave. As late as the middle of the fourth century we find a Sardinian slave who was expert in "evoking injurious little spirits and compelling ghosts to prophesy."

The true magician was able to restore life to a corpse for a short period and to cause it to speak. Greece had possessed necromantic oracles from ancient times, but in the later period which we are here dealing with the headquarters of this gruesome art was indisputably in Egypt, and even those who were not of Egyptian origin liked to assume the Egyptian tone in their incantations. In the second book of his *Metamorphoses* Apuleius places the scene of a necromancy in the forum of

o

Larissa in Thessaly, where there was an abundance of native wizards also; nevertheless it is an Egyptian, Zachlas, who is made to appear in white linen robe and shorn head and to consummate the miracle by thrice placing certain herbs upon the mouth and breast of the corpse and by a whispered prayer to the rising sun. Another story of the same kind, told without Apuleius' humor but with stark Egyptian detail, is to be found in Heliodorus. Here a mother conjures her son, who had been slain in battle, and the corpse utters truth, whereas in the former instance we are left in doubt whether the magician may not have evoked a false and deceptive life in the body. The author, in the person of the wise priest Calasiris, disapproves of this necromancy, indeed, and upon another occasion contrasts this inferior form of mantic with higher, genuine Egyptian wisdom, which looks toward heaven, converses with the gods, and so forth. But these are excuses of the fourth century, when the power of the state no longer regarded the affairs of magic as a jesting matter; possibly also they are aftereffects of the nobler doctrine of the Plotinian-Porphyrean school which consciously avoided operative magic. But what are we to think when we encounter individual examples of necromancy among pious Christian priests, and that not in the Middle Ages, but in the fourth and fifth centuries? St. Spyridon, Bishop of Trimithunt on Cyprus, who was later present at the Council of Nicaea, had a daughter named Irene, to whom an acquaintance had entrusted a valuable object. She died, and Spyridon, who wished to restore the treasure and did not know where it was hidden, called upon his daughter by name until she supplied the desired information out of the tomb. A later teller of the tale softens it with the words, "He besought God to show him the promised resurrection before its season for an example"; in fact, what we have is an obvious example of a remnant of pagan belief. From the last years of the Western Roman Empire we have the account of a necromancy with much more important motivation, very impressive in its context. St. Severin, at a time when his congregations on the Danube were in desperate need, evoked a deceased presbyter to momentary wakefulness and asked him to consent that God should again ask him for his life. But the dead man implored that he be left in his eternal rest and sank back to earth lifeless. Here the underlying psychologic view is quite different and indeed essentially Christian; but we shall not pursue this aspect further.

Finally, mention must be made of the misuse of individual portions of cadavers as means for magic purposes. To determine the primitive forms of this special delusion, we should have to descend deep to the source of all magic; suffice it that mention of human flesh and human bones occurs in the most diverse categories of magic, for the mere investigation of the future as well as for operative magic to affect others. Originally the design may have been to conjure the shade of the person from whose body the portions were taken, but this connection is not clear for the later period. The use of the means became general, and a long list of individual examples of it from the Greek period downward may be drawn up. But a single very significant instance may spare us disagreeable wandering through this realm of darkness. The story of the treasure of Rhampsinitus in Herodotus is familiar. Perhaps the hand of the thief which was cut off has magic implications; next to the skull, the right hand was always the most highly prized portion of the corpse. Now it happens that under Constantine, and indeed again in Egypt, the native heath of stark magic, an amputated hand was said to be employed for magic arts, and by no other than the great Athanasius of Alexandria, who is charged with having hewn off the hand of a bishop of the Meletian sect in Thebais, Arsenius by name, for magic purposes, and indeed to have had the man murdered. At the synod at Tyre, in the presence of the first bishop of the Empire, his opponents among the Egyptian clergy brought forward not only the charge but also the alleged *corpus delicti;* an actual hand — "whether of a man murdered for the purpose or of one who died otherwise God alone knows" — was placed before the eyes of the holy fathers. Athanasius annihilated the charge brilliantly by producing Arsenius alive and unmutilated in the midst of the council. But the fact that such a charge could be ventured and indeed in such a circle provides irrefutable testimony for the extent of the delusion and for the frequency of the practice.

Inspection of human entrails proceeds on another principle. This was practiced in antiquity and among various peoples, especially on captives of war. It is essentially of the character of divination, but inevitably operative magic becomes involved in it or is assumed without explanation by our sources, because popular belief in the magic value of portions of the corpse was too firmly rooted to be content with mere *extispicium*. For the persistence of this horror again a single example will provide sufficient proof. Among the rulers of this period, virtually all of whom were excessively superstitious, Maxentius, son of Maximianus Herculius, was particularly charged with dissecting pregnant women and also children for the purpose of inspecting their entrails, and of having evoked daimones by occult procedures. Although this story comes from Eusebius, whose notions of paganism in general are not always the most precise, and whose desire for truthfulness is not always compelling, nevertheless in view of the evil and savage nature of Maxentius there is no ground to doubt the tale. We do not find it incredible, consequently, when another source reports that he left his bloodstained palace two days before his end and moved to a private dwelling because the avenging daimones would no longer allow him sleep in the palace. Similar instances were doubtless of frequent occurrence throughout the third century. But these two categories by no means exhaust the magic use of human corpses. Sympathetic effects were achieved, for example, by the use of blood also, in which, according to prevalent beliefs, the essential life force was comprised. A story of this kind is even told of Marcus Aurelius, as melancholy as it is filthy, if we were compelled to regard it as true; even as a fable it casts an evil light upon a period whose educated men could believe in such things.

History's inquiries concerning the objective actualities in connection with this entire world of magic must always remain futile. Pagans, Jews, and Christians were equally convinced that spirits and the dead could be conjured up. Here we have to do not with evidence drawn by compulsion, as was the case with witchcraft in recent centuries, but with a hundred unconsidered, free, and consequently highly diverse statements given in part by writers who are very careful and of respectable morality. How much conscious deception, how much pious fraud, and how much self-deception and ecstatic exaltation was involved must remain a puzzle, as in the case of the Neoplatonic incantations. For each century has its own view of the hypersensual within and without man, and posterity can never fully enter into its beliefs.

Our account of paganism to this point was calculated to present merely the essential tendencies in contemporary belief. If all traces were to be cited individually, if all dissenting concepts of the world of gods in general could be recorded, if even all separate worship of amulets and of symbols could be enumerated, in a century when many an individual contented himself with the worship of a single little serpent as a good daimon and believed in nothing else, then it might be possible to prove at least theoretically the existence of the three hundred sects with which the philosopher Themistius was acquainted.

It was with this "polytheist madness" that Christianity was now again to enter into a decisive conflict. Fortunately, this conflict has a literary aspect also. The rational defenders of Christianity in this time of crisis, Arnobius and Lactantius, who have already been frequently cited, have an even higher value for us for their accounts of sinking paganism. To be sure, they stand upon the shoulders of their predecessors, especially Clement of Alexandria, but they contribute much that is new and that is truly significant for the decade of persecution and for contemporary attitudes. The highly respectable work of Lactantius is obviously the result of deep and many-sided studies. The writing of Arnobius, a quickly compiled outpouring of the gloomy and glowing wrath of a new convert, is the most immediate testimony of the moment. The modern reader is no longer disturbed by the constant and passionate misunderstanding of paganism with reference to its origins and development. He understands how to receive the

Euhemerism of these Church writers, and is eager for valuable revelations of all sorts which they offer along with error.

If we draw the final conclusions from what has been said, we find not only that the disintegration of paganism as such was generally favorable to Christianity, but that the individual symptoms of disintegration involved a presage of Christianity and an approach to it. The mixture of gods was in itself well calculated to prepare the ground for a new religion. It denationalized the divine and made it universal; it crushed Greek and Roman pride in their old native cults. Prejudice in favor of all things Oriental must inevitably, after long wandering in the realm of illusion, also work to the advantage of Christianity. Furthermore, the essential content of late pagan beliefs was directly analogous to Christianity. The aim of existence was no longer limited to life on earth and to its pleasures and destiny, but was extended to the beyond, even to union with deity. The one group hoped to secure immortality by occult rites; the other wished to force their way to deity by steeping themselves in profound matters or by magic compulsion. But all paid homage to the new notion of conscious morality, which went as far as castigations, and which obtained at least as a theoretical ideal even if it was not carried out in life. A reflection of this tendency is to be perceived in the relegation or reinterpretation by the philosophers of the Greek myths which were not in consonance with the new viewpoint. Monotheism was approached by declining paganism, at least upon occasion, in remarkable upsurges, even though these were soon entangled in the webs of daimonic beliefs. Whether the pagans went so far as to reach a sense of sin is very doubtful; but the prerequisites for such a sense are clearly present in the Neoplatonist teaching, which designates the soul's entry into earthly life as a fall, and its emergence from earthly life as a sort of redemption.

Christianity was bound to conquer in the end because it provided answers which were incomparably simpler, and which were articulated in an impressive and convincing whole, to all the questions for which that period of ferment was so deeply concerned to find solutions.

VII

SENESCENCE OF ANCIENT LIFE
AND ITS CULTURE

IF THE CRISIS in the life of the ancient world is anywhere clearly revealed, it is in the twilight of paganism which we have endeavored to present in its true colors. The question now arises whether Christianity might not have had the force to give new life to nationalities and new vigor to the state, whether it should not have refuted pagan complaint current as early as the third century that, after this new religion had begun to advance, the race of man was doomed. For the pagans were emphatic in their assertion that since Christianity the gods had forsaken the direction of human fate and that they had departed (*exterminatos*) out of the wretched world, where now only pestilence, war, famine, drought, locusts, hail, and so forth prevailed, while barbarians were attacking the Empire from all sides. Christian apologists were constrained to undertake the circumstantial refutation of these charges. "How little credit," they said, "does such childish petulance do your pagan gods! Why do they not bestow health and happiness upon you and chastise us Christians alone? Nature has not altered; sun and moon shine as before, the harvest grows green, trees bloom, oil and wine are pressed, and civic life proceeds as it always has. There have always been wars from the days of Ninus the Assyrian, and since Christ they have in fact diminished. The undeniable evils of the present are part of the necessary world process by which earthly things seek to renew themselves (*rerum innovatio*)."

But the hope of renewal, as this author understood it, was vain. Let us, for the moment, leave aside the one-sided direction taken by Christianity as soon as it became a state religion, a direction altogether unsuited for bringing new strength to the Empire. Indeed, the great advantage of the religion whose kingdom was not of this world was that it did not set itself the task of directing and guaranteeing any definite state and any definite culture, as the religions of paganism had done, and that it was rather in a position to reconcile with one another and mediate between diverse peoples and centuries, states and cultural stages. It was not Christianity, then, that could bestow a second youth upon the senescent Roman Empire; but it could so far prepare the Empire's Germanic conquerors that they did not wholly tread its culture underfoot. A century and a half later, when the decision was to be made on the Catalaunian Plains whether the Hun was to draw the death pall over Western life as later the Mongol did over Asiatic life, this preparation bore its fruit; Roman and Visigoth combined to ward off the attack.

For the senescence and corruption of conditions in the Empire, for which Christianity bears no responsibility, the entire history of this period bears eloquent testimony, and reference has been made to it on every page of the present work. But this is an appropriate place to bring together significant aspects of the old age of the ancient world. Such a collection will serve further to clarify the historic position of Christianity.

Complaints of evil times are to be found in all centuries which have left a literature behind them. But in the Roman Empire the decline is acknowledged in a manner which leaves no room for doubt. The feeling that anything in the present is trifling in comparison with a brilliantly conceived past is concomitant in growth to the colossal external expansion of the Empire and its interests; even those who depreciate the grandeur of early days do so only further to minimize the present. When Seneca in his philosophical polemic against history treats Philip and Alexander of Macedon as highwaymen, he adds, "But we regard these things as great because we ourselves are so small." More potent though silent testimony is implied in the fact that all philosophers and orators — and poets too, if not engaged in begging — in a word, all the free literature of the second, third, and fourth centuries never, except under compulsion, speaks of a man or an object posterior to the end of the Roman Republic. It would seem as if a pledge had been taken on the matter. For their school exercises the Greek sophists preferred to choose themes from the flowering period of Hellenism, from the Persian Wars, the Peloponnesian War, and sometimes from the life of Alexander the Great. They represent Xenophon as offering to die in Socrates' place, or Solon arguing against Pisistratus for rescinding the laws, or Demosthenes advising the Athenians to flee by sea, or other such topics. Dio Chrysostom (under Trajan) feels that he must make formal apology for having spoken in one of his discourses of events of the imperial period, "modern, inglorious things"; he believes his opponent would regard him as a babbler because he did not follow customary usage and speak of Cyrus or Alcibiades. The declamations ascribed to Quintilian treat either of subjects in the remote past or of imaginary cases at law which belong to no specific period. The easy explanation that the government took an unfavorable view of comment concerning the period of the Empire and may even have suppressed it is altogether mistaken. Surveillance of this sort over literature and the schools was not in the character of the Roman Empire, which was in general not concerned with regulating cultural tendencies and supervising them. In fact, the favorite subject for oratorical practice would seem, by our scale, objectionable and dangerous. In the Rome of Domitian, Juvenal complains of the deadly tedium of an orator who must for the hundredth time hear "his numerous class slay the cruel tyrant." Stories of Brutus and of Harmodius and Aristogiton were a proverbially favorite theme, whereas the most notable subjects of the imperial period, which could even be dealt with in panegyric, as for example the Jewish War, the deeds of Trajan, the rule of the Antonines, were never willingly touched upon and thus were left exclusively to the official eulogists.

And not only the orators but the peculiar category of Latin and Greek compilers who are sometimes together labeled grammarians do not readily go beyond the period of the Republic.

Aulus Gellius, for example, does so only when he speaks of the education of his time and of his own studies. Aelian's *Historiae Variae* has virtually nothing of the Empire. Alciphron places his *Letters* in the earliest Macedonian period. Athenaeus in his great encyclopedia of ancient enjoyment intentionally avoids the imperial period. Even two hundred years later Macrobius in his *Saturnalia*, aside from a short incidental mention of Trajan, makes a collection of anecdotes and witty remarks of Augustus the most modern element in his work. Professional philologists who are more intimately acquainted with the relevant literature than the present author can probably confirm these observations in a much broader scope.

This age, then, which contemporaries denied and ignored and from which they constantly turned back to earlier centuries, suddenly acquired a new content by means of Christianity. A Christian literature which had long been in preparation now broke like a flood into the empty channel of the century and in a short space surpassed in volume all that has survived from the world of pagan writers.

Yet Rome as the seat and ideal of world dominion was believed to be eternal; *Roma aeterna* is a common consolation upon monuments and coins, especially during the second half of the third century. To the Christians, as long as they saw and hated Rome as paganism personified, as the Babylon of the *Book of Revelation,* this notion was folly. They regarded Rome, as Arnobius plainly declares, as the "city created for the corruption of the human race, for the sake of whose rule the entire world has undeservedly been subjugated." Only an African, indeed, could utter such sentiments; even in pagan times the distinction was drawn between Rome and the Empire, and prayers were offered for the welfare of Rome as for the pagan Emperors and the armies. Later, under the Christian Emperors, the notion of Rome's world dominion became entirely acceptable. Prudentius finds it the highest historical effect of Providence: "Lo, the whole race of mortals has come under the rule of Romulus, the most diverse habits of life and thought have become amalgamated; thus has it been foreordained so that the dignity of the name of Christian might with a single bond embrace the whole world." But the most moving utterance on the subject is the poem of a late heathen, Claudius Rutilius Numatianus (about 417), who comforts Rome bowed down like a mother in deep grief and draws new hope for eternal survival out of Rome's historical grandeur.

How far such hopes could be justified by the institutions of the state and its external condition cannot be precisely determined by mere inferences. A government like the Roman may survive for a very long while, despite growing petrification, as the Byzantine Empire has shown. If the city of Rome had been so impregnable and so easy to defend as Constantinople later was, the Western Empire might have lasted much longer; and if the capital were saved it might time and again have reconquered lost provinces. A state is as able to survive nationality as a nationality a state. Thus the idea of senescence need not signify impossibility of survival but only the gradual failure of those sources of life which once gave the nation its nobler spiritual and physical stamp.

We may begin with the physical properties of the earth itself. To people in the Roman Empire it seemed as if rivers began to grow sluggish and mountains to lose height; Aetna could not be seen so far at sea as formerly, and the same phenomenon is reported of Parnassus and Olympus. Studious natural historians were of the opinion that the cosmos itself was going into general decline.

If we look at physical man, a degeneration of the race at this time, at least in the upper classes, is undeniable. Our judgment is not limited to statements of writers — who upon occasion made similar remarks in an earlier period — art also provides irrefutable demonstrations in countless monuments, and indeed in monuments whose evidence cannot be disregarded on the grounds of the artist's want of skill. Most of the figures of this period show in part a natural ugliness and in part something diseased, scrofulous, bloated, or sunken. Tombs, coins, mosaics, bases of drinking glasses — all are at one in giving this impression. Diocletian's colleagues and immediate successors with their repellant traits may not, being Illyrians, be considered average specimens. Constantine, whose outward appearance is definitely known from statues and coins, appears sound indeed and regularly formed, but there is something cunning in his expression; yet panegyrists and Church writers are at one in their exclamations of delight at his beauty. This is not mere flattery but evidence of a low standard of comparison. In the physiognomies of his sons we observe an essentially new species of expression which subsequently recurs frequently. The expression is what we call "priestly" in the pejorative sense. Constantine II also has the not altogether agreeable round head of his father; Constans' and Constantius' are rather longer drawn. Much clearer than these Illyriot visages, clearer perhaps than portraits in general, is the evidence of ideal figures of the period in which the artists sought to fix universals; these demonstrate the deterioration of the human type. The Arch of Constantine near the Colosseum is, to be sure, a hasty production, and this is a sufficient explanation for the great crudeness of the plastic execution, but not for the ugliness of the figures and the meanness of expression. There are of course periods in which art makes it an object to seek its effects in what is characteristic rather than in what is beautiful, and even exaggerates to the point of ugliness without the artist's environment being at fault. But here there can be no question of the artist's preference for character; rather it is his inability to preserve classic ideals of beauty even superficially when the world about him supplied no points of contact with such ideals. In the fifth century the mosaics provide a continuous scale for the same phenomenon. Here it must be noticed that art is not yet seeking to give expression to sanctity by ascetic emaciation and moroseness, as the Byzantine workers in mosaic later did; its figures are not yet definitely shrunken, but the visages are always ugly and irregular. Even excellent works in which all other features, drapery, motion, distribution in space, and the like are as good as can be expected in the Theodosian age — as, for example, the Twelve Apostles in the Orthodox Baptistry at Ravenna — are no exception in this particular.

The human physique had always been singularly varied in the Roman Empire, according to individual regions and according to their state of prosperity; some populations are to be imagined as robust and some as meager. But the average as presented in classic art at this time is in general that of Italy. When and through what circumstances did outward man here and perhaps in the entire Empire change for the worse?

The answer is ready at hand. Two fearful plagues, under Marcus Aurelius (167) and then again after Gallus (252), had shattered the population of the Empire beyond repair. The latter pestilence is said to have lasted for fifteen years, to have spared no area of the Empire, and to have desolated many cities completely. If we add the unceasing wars, internal wars of succession as well as external wars against barbarians, with their inevitable consequence of neglect of agriculture, we may deduce that famine continually added to the ravages of disease. The higher classes could no longer be spared anxiety and misery. Settlements of barbarians completed the task of transforming the human type in the Empire, and rather in the direction of improvement.

In such eras of misfortune an old race dies not only in the physical sense: old customs and usages, national viewpoints, spiritual goals of all sorts, also perish. But this does not inevitably involve the decline of morality; on the contrary, there is evidence of moral improvement in the second half of the third century. For the imperial throne itself improvement is undeniable (see Chapter I). The age of Caracalla and the Maximini was past, and Carinus falls because he is a belated anomaly in his decade. With the later so-called monsters, such as Maxentius, excesses and misdeeds are petty compared to those of the earlier Emperors. Police officers for the preservation of morals seem to have been increased, and outward conduct doubtless improved. Even Diocletian was much concerned to regulate matrimonial practices, which had grown rank, and to take measures against intermarriages in the same house and in forbidden degrees of consanguinity. Great and widespread scandals become noticeably reduced. That Constantine's own private life was virtually free of such abuses is a fair deduction from the silence of hostile historians. Government is more and more concerned with general humanitarian measures and recognizes its obligation to take full thought for its subjects; though at the same time it was compelled to exert heavy pressure, and frequently overreached itself even in its measures for improvement, as for example in fixing maximum prices for foodstuffs and in barbaric criminal punishment. We have already pointed to analogies for this heightened morality in late pagan religion and in the ascetic ideals of the philosophers, but the whole matter must be examined here afresh. For perhaps reform in the direction of sobriety and moderation was specifically a symptom of senescence, which is our concern here; so much the less would it be in a position to rejuvenate the tired old world.

Now that we have confirmed the decline in man's physical beauty, we proceed to treat his outward environment, and first of all his clothing. Here plastic art does not represent actual conditions, for it regularly retained the drapery of long-departed epochs of flourishing art, which themselves employed idealizations. Even the Panathenaic Procession on the Parthenon, for example, represents not the actual costumes of Athenians contemporary with Phidias, but only beautifully simplified elements of those costumes. When we find Roman statues of the age of Constantine garbed in toga and tunic, with the chlamys for nude figures, we must not conclude that these were the ordinary wear. Here literary monuments are a safer guide, and these tell us of elaborate and overburdened costume, which might well be called Roman rococo if we may use that profane expression.

Instead of transcribing a section from available histories of costume we shall content ourselves with a few indications. A poem of the first half of the fourth century addressed by Arborius, uncle of Ausonius, "to a nymph titivated to excess," supplies a description of a Gallic maid. Her hair is braided with ribbons and built up into a large spiral (*in multiplicem orbem*); and this was surmounted by a cap of golden material. Her neck-band appears to have been red, perhaps of coral. Her dress was high-necked, and was laced over the bust. Clinging dresses, and especially clinging sleeves, were becoming abundant. Such elaborate coiffures as are described had been fashionable for centuries, and in some marble busts are made detachable to accommodate changes in fashion. Before Arborius, Arnobius complains of the bands, apparently of gold brocade, with which many ladies covered their foreheads, and of their habit of curling their hair in masculine fashion. Facial make-up, which gave the face not only a new color but also a new shape, was particularly distasteful. Red as well as white applications were laid on so heavily that the women looked "like idols," and every tear that flowed over the cheek left a furrow behind it. Such, at least, is the ridicule of St. Jerome, who must have been well informed on the subject in his earlier days. A major change, perhaps to be ascribed precisely to this period, was the new use of patterned and flowered material instead of solid-colored, which is the only proper dress for human beings, for it alone permits an unhampered view of masses and folds and so indirectly of the form, attitude, and movement of the body. From foreign ambassadors Constantine received gifts of "barbaric garments worked with gold and flowers." Soon thereafter similar garments appear as the usual ceremonial dress in the mosaic designs of churches, and it was not long before priestly vestments and altar covers had whole stories embroidered upon them. Whatever was alien and barbaric enjoyed patent preference in late Roman fashion simply because it was dear and hard to obtain. Under Theodosius the Great the famous Symmachus found it necessary to refuse a magnificent foreign state coach with which the Emperor thought to make the journeys of the city prefect more majestic.

But barbarization extended much further than merely to clothing. The rise of German and especially of Gothic and Frankish officers in the army and at court, and the influence of Oriental etiquette and manners, must gradually have fixed an un-Roman stamp upon all external forms of life. The division of society according to position and rank, which was effected by the bestowal of titles, was a quite new departure; nothing was more contrary to the notion of citizenship upon which the classic world had been nurtured. Christianity also, which had consumed so many elements of ancient culture with its mighty flame, contributed indirectly to barbarization, as a glance at the art and the literature of the period will make clear.

Art in the highest sense of the word was once the breath of life to the Greek people. No other nation could have ventured to date its chronicles by the development of the beautiful through poets and artists, as is done, for example, in the chronicle of the Parian marble. In the train of Alexander's victorious arms and of his successors', Greek art marched through the Orient and suppressed, as far as might be, the ancient national forms, with the single exception of the buildings and statues of Egypt, from Alexandria upwards. The Romans also willingly adopted Greek art for their service, not merely as objects of luxury, but because it answered a need for the beautiful which was inherent in them but whose active development was hindered by the predominance of war and politics. Greek art contributed magnificently to give noble expression to Rome's majesty, religious and national, though not without sacrifice of its inner character. And finally from Rome the entire West accepted Romanized art as the law of the victor, and imitated it as it imitated the victor's language. Where colonies of Italian origin persisted in the West this art may have answered a real need.

The position which art held among the Greeks of the great period, to be sure, it never retained in this age of Roman domination. Denigration of the beautiful cannot now be spoken of as blasphemy as it was when the poet Stesichorus was blinded for having reproached Helen, the pattern of all beauty. Lucian, who spares neither gods nor men, can now mock at the ancient ideals of all beauty also, though in other connections his taste in matters of art is abundantly documented. The masterly series of *Dialogues of the Dead* in which he gives free rein to his mockery under the mask of the cynic Menippus contains a scene in which Hermes of the underworld exhibits to Menippus the skeletons of famous beauties of antiquity, Narcissus, Nereis, and others. "But I see nothing but skulls and bones; show me Helen." "This skull here is Helen." "Was it for this that a thousand ships sailed, that countless men died, that cities were destroyed?" "Ah, Menippus," Hermes answers, "you never saw the woman alive!" Nevertheless, though the early Empire is inculpated by contemporary aesthetes, by Petronius and the Elder Pliny, and with some justice, as an epoch of decline in art, in Italy at least the demand for artistic surroundings for life continued unbelievably strong. Pompeii alone, in Goethe's words, shows "an appetite for art and pictures on the part of a whole people of an extent that the most ardent *amateur* of today can have neither concept nor feeling nor need of." If we apply the scale of Pompeii to contemporary Rome the implications are dizzying.

But in the third century art encountered a formidable material enemy in the derangement of the Empire by plague, war, and poverty. The fact that the Emperors, especially after Aurelian, again engaged in large-scale building, and doubtless gave proportionate support to other arts also, might have restored the balance had not increasing pressure upon the wealthy and the prosperous brought with it permanent loss.

If we assume that nature always distributes a bountiful measure of talent — and this cannot be doubted even with the deterioration of all forms — the question arises, Whence came the false directions in which talents were lost? Why, further, the anonymity which covers practically all the art of the third and fourth centuries with so deathly a pall?

It is a fact that from approximately the middle of the second century the active production of works of art which had hitherto flourished ceases and degenerates to mere repetition, and that henceforward internal impoverishment and apparent over-elaboration of forms go hand in hand.

The deepest causes for this phenomenon can probably never be plumbed or comprehended in words. If the developed Greek system of forms could maintain itself for six centuries under all vicissitudes of history and always spring new shoots, why should it lose its power and its creative energy precisely from the age of the Antonines downward? Why could it not have lasted into the fourth century? Perhaps an *a priori* answer may emerge from a general philosophic consideration of the period, but it is more prudent not to seek to determine the life span of a spiritual force of such magnitude.

Collateral reasons for the phenomenon are clear enough: changes in the material and in the tasks and subjects of art, or indirectly, the changed viewpoint of the purchasers. Let us follow the fate of architecture first. Here the capital sounds the keynote for all devolution. In its travertine and peperino Rome

P

possessed a sober and powerful material for monumental building. But when, especially after Augustus, Romans insisted on marbles from Carrara and Africa because of their plasticity and their brilliant beauty, their feelings became habituated to the idea that the brick masonry of the structure and the marble facing which covered it were two disparate things. The latter must eventually come to be regarded as a veneer to be changed at will, as mere ornament. Still the white marble always compelled the artist to give his forms the utmost refinement. But when the most expensive and exotic materials came more and more to be the rage, when all the East and Africa were ransacked for precious building stone, porphyry, jasper, agate, and marbles of all colors, when the massive use of gilt grew out of all reason, then art and the artist could only retire. Material and color monopolized attention; profiles and decorative motifs were disregarded. The extraordinary hardness of many of these stones, moreover, limited the scope of the chisel. Under these conditions, those who supplied and dressed the stones were more important than the draftsman. And where white marble or other simple material was used, it now had to compete by heaping up members and multiplying ornament; taste for simplicity was now corrupted. Despite mass, the impression is often trivial and confusing, because external architectural richness, once conceived of as the guiding principle, soon exceeds all measure and is also applied to structural members whose function makes them incapable of receiving decorative treatment. We need not here enumerate the buildings of this style, for which the Palmyrene temple and the palace of Diocletian at Salonae have become proverbial. Except where their arrangement and proportion are reminiscent of a better period, they belong to the decline, and do not even compensate for the loss by exploiting the charm of perspective, such as the degenerate modern style has developed, for example, in the hands of a Bernini. Bernini understood how to focus the spectator's attention; but here everything is restless and scattered. Bernini ignores detail and strives for total effect; here the heaped-up individual forms pretend to significance in themselves.

If luxury in the sense here suggested necessarily promoted the decline of beautiful form in architecture, an innovating advance contributed no less to the final dissolution of the structural system inherited from the Greeks. We refer to the new requirement for large interiors, preferably arched. In the better periods of Empire architecture, for example in the construction of baths, the columns and their entablature were so joined to dome, barrel vaulting, and cross vaulting that they bypassed it, as it were, as a separate organism. But concern for such an effect could not long persist, especially after the Christian period brought a great increase in the demand for such structures and the concurrent tendency toward heightened magnificence silenced all other considerations. The Christian basilica, which is the first great model of interiors regarded solely from the viewpoint of perspective, carried arches and heavy, large clerestory walls upon its rows of columns. The domed church, with galleries above and below or accessory chapels round about, was a complete negation of the notion of the entablature, and employed columns virtually for their agreeable effect alone. It was late in the Middle Ages before Christian architecture finally exchanged ancient forms, repeated with increased misunderstanding until they were scarcely recognizable, for a new garb more appropriate to its principles.

Finally, Christian architecture from the beginning was constrained to share, to its disadvantage, in a tendency of the Church itself. That tendency was to make the entire structure and every stone in it a symbol of its power and its victory; hence the predominance of luxurious embellishment and of figured representation, in the interior as on the façades. The lavish use of mosaic, which covered every space and every surface with Biblical figures and stories, executed in the vivid and unshaded colors of glass paste, made genuine architectural articulation impossible; entablature and consoles consequently shrank to vestigial strips or were merely indicated in the mosaic ornament.

Nevertheless architecture retained a feeling for magnificently arranged and imaginatively constructed interiors and for great mechanical virtuosity. It is to the latter that we owe our knowledge of several artists of the Byzantine period, who were able to emerge from the anonymity spoken of above.

The decline of plastic art and painting resulted from the same or similar causes which determined the decline of architecture, and was aggravated by special considerations. Here too, in the first place, luxury in material surely had a corrupting effect. When it became customary to compose statues of three or even four different kinds of frequently very hard stone — to say nothing of many that were fashioned of gold and silver — the effect on style must in the long run have been adverse, for style demands primacy if it is to survive. Very mediocre style is characteristic, for example, of the colossal porphyry sarcophagi of Helena and Constantia (mother and daughter of Constantine), in the Vatican, the one with trains of horsemen, the other with genii preparing the vintage. The mere restoration of the first of these sarcophagi under Pius IV is said to have claimed the toil of twenty-five men for nine years, from which we can calculate the labor involved in the original production. There can be no question of any direct touch of artistic genius in this incredibly hard and unyielding stone; what is involved is slave labor after a given pattern. Painting must have been corrupted by mosaic in quite the same way. As long as mosaic was used only for pavement, it might be regarded as an expression of an overflowing love of art which was unwilling to leave any spot upon which the eye might fall without decoration — though there is something barbaric in treading on such a composition as the so-called Battle of Alexander at Pompeii. But after Pliny, mosaic ascended to walls and ceiling. In the baths, where ordinary painting might be damaged by dampness, there was much to be said for this change; but in other structures it needlessly deprived the artist of direct manual participation in his creation, and it also discouraged him, because the spectator would think first of a work's expense and elegance, then of its subject, and finally or not at all of the representation. With the introduction of Christianity, mosaic became the principal decoration, wherever means sufficed, for all walls and ceilings in churches.

But the decline is more decisively revealed in other symptoms, which rest upon other grounds. The small number of significant statues of gods which can be dated with certainty after the time of Alexander Severus is striking; on the other hand statues of

Mithras, of the execrable Aeons, of Dei Panthei, of Ephesian Dianas, and the like increase greatly. Here clearly religion was at work. Nothing was more calculated to distract the artist completely from the ancient god-types than the admixture of amorphous alien deities and the daimonization of native deities, which deprived them of their handsome anthropomorphic personalities. In any case it was difficult for the artist to steep himself in the ancient piety even if such works were requested. Instead, his task now was to produce thousands of sarcophagi, which were the principal occupation of the sculptors of the third century. Their reliefs, to be sure, present purely Greek myths and are hence free of the monstrosities of the alien religions; but other and weightier reasons prevented the production of significant works of art. Amalgamation of plastic and dramatic laws into a pure and perfect style of relief could be achieved only in an epoch of high artistic competence; so soon as luxuriant striving for effect got the upper hand — that is, in the late Greek period, which could still produce wonderful works in other departments — relief work was also bound to lose balance. Hence even the most beautiful work of the better Roman period, which rests directly on the late Greek tradition, as for example the reliefs on the Arch of Titus, are of qualified merit. But later, when richness took the place of beauty altogether, when men had grown used to every sort of plastic extravagance by the spiral reliefs of the Column of Trajan and its imitators and by the overcrowded triumphal arches, it was inevitable that the number and confusion of the figures should crowd out any large and true effect, just as multiplication of members had done in architecture. Sarcophagus decoration was further demoralized by the fact that work was seldom done on special order, but produced for the trade, and hence had to follow the vulgar and florid taste of the average purchaser. Finally, the subject matter grew dominant in a tendentious sense, to the disadvantage of art. The relevant myths were represented as symbolic husks of general ideas, and the separation between kernel and shell could in the long run be only injurious to art. Beneath the representations of the myths of Meleager, Bacchus and Ariadne, Amor and Psyche, Luna and Endymion, Pluto and Proserpina, beneath the battles of centaurs or of Amazons, the bacchanalia, the trains of Nereids, and the like, there lie hidden abstract thoughts concerning fate, death, and immortality. Such symbolism does indeed evoke the historical and poetical participation of the spectator, but art fails in another of its obligations, and that is, to recall in each of its figures what is abiding and eternal through nobility of form alone.

In the place of the pagan figures mentioned, Christianity introduced upon the sarcophagi Christ and the Apostles or certain scenes from the Old and New Testaments, presented as parallels or singly. No advance in style can be expected here; again the "message" dominates, again symbolic expression is paramount. As skill in continuous narrative, which is essential to relief, diminished, the sarcophagus came to be divided by little columns and arches into as many fields as there were persons or stories involved. Because of its multiplicity, representation grew altogether impoverished and childish.

Another function that still remained to sculpture was the portrait, as statue or bust, and particularly as half-figure in relief. On monuments and sarcophagi we not infrequently find those comfortable representations of man and wife, hand in hand, set into a niche; it is apparently a rule, as in the coins of the second half of the third century, that the entire upper body be included. Busts properly speaking are very rare, so that we know the great Illyrian Emperors, for example, virtually only from coins. There are many references to portrait statues, but with the exception of several erected in honor of Constantine, scarcely any are preserved, and of these the ponderous and distorted forms make the losses from this period easy to bear.

Along with the material, hugeness was in many cases the object of admiration. The effect of great monoliths in themselves was considerably exaggerated. People had long been used to having Egyptian obelisks dragged to Rome; Elagabalus had dreamt of a block of stone to be brought from Thebes, and to receive a winding staircase and serve his chief idol as a pedestal; but now Diocletian had granite pillars fifteen feet in girth brought from the Orient for his baths, and Constantine transported the largest of all obelisks from Heliopolis to Alexandria, whence Constantius later brought it to Rome. The largest piece of porphyry known, a pillar of a hundred feet, was made to bear the statue of the founder of the new city of Constantinople. Sculpture too came to be gauged by sheer mass in the third and fourth centuries. Alexander Severus had a crowd of gigantic statues set up in Rome, and conscripted artists from the ends of the earth for this enterprise. Gallienus had himself represented as a sun-god, reportedly of a height of two hundred feet; the lance in his hand was to be stout enough for a child to be able to climb up its interior, chariot and horses were to be fashioned on the same scale, and the whole, erected upon a lofty podium, was to crown Rome's highest point, the Esquiline. But the work, as might be expected, was not completed. More moderate were the two marble statues of the Emperor Tacitus and his brother Florianus at Terni, each of thirty feet, which were both completely destroyed by lightning soon after they were erected. After Phidias' statues of giants, after the hundred colossi of the sun at Rhodes, gods and men had often been represented in a scale far surpassing human without injury to art; but at a time of decline, when draftsmanship and modeling were no longer adequate to smaller tasks, art on a large scale became wholly distorted and corrupted the taste of entire generations because the spectator was everywhere overwhelmed by its gigantic figures. Extravagance in portrait statues, moreover, had a special significance which involved the fate of painting also.

Painting exhibits an internal law or at least an experience according to which periods of idealizing representation are followed by periods of realism, either because idealism had not treated the forms of nature with sufficient thoroughness, but had been content with the general, or because it had traversed the circle of its legitimate creation and hoped to discover new effects in coarse naturalism. Related collateral categories of painting, above all genre painting, develop this tendency into an independent existence. Something of the same sort happened in ancient art. Even in the period of flowering there were plenty of genre statues and genre paintings; whole schools were characized by close adherence to reality. But their efforts were wholly directed toward acquiring new aspects of the beautiful from reality, and thus interest in individual appearances was always kept at a high level. Should we not expect the third century to be a period of genuine naturalism, carefully executed shading, study of illusions of actuality? Analogies for such a movement are not wholly wanting — in literature, for example, as we shall see.

But the prerequisite for perfected genre painting, exquisite and acute perception, was in process not of growth but of rapid decline. Luxury in material and passion for decoration had largely deprived acute perception of the place of honor which is its due. The few wall paintings of mythologic content which have been preserved show crude repetition of older motifs and a stunting and ossification of the system of arabesques which was once so decorative. The paintings in the Christian catacombs are appealing by reason of the simplicity and the unpretentiousness of their representations. They are very remarkable, moreover, as the earliest documents for the types of sacred persons; but in composition and execution of details they exhibit great want of skill or else reminiscence of earlier work. The new Christian subjects spread a sunset glow over ancient art, but new content did not bring fresh quality. Mosaic was quickly claimed for the mighty programs of the victorious faith. It spread sacred figures and stories over all available space in the church, disregarding alike the laws of architecture as of painting. We can only wonder that so many relatively excellent works make their appearance as late as the sixth century. Ecclesiastical merit and completeness of the subject, along with magnificence of execution, were the only relevant considerations. For the artist's own joy in his work there is no room. Art had become serviceable to a symbol which lay outside itself, which had not grown up with it and through it; and the artist, even where his talent was considerable, was the nameless executor of something universally applicable, as had once been the case in Egypt. In the miniatures of manuscripts, as far as they are known directly or through late copies, we are not infrequently surprised by successful allegories and ingenious conceits, which proves that nonofficial art at least still possessed subjective vitality. Indeed, the pictures on a pagan calendar of the second half of the fourth century preserve several genuine genre figures with their baroque costume and surroundings. But the general tendency was irrevocably set in a quite different direction.

If we are to speak of a victory of realism in any aspect, we may find it in the vigorous growth of portrait painting after the third century. We have already seen how the colossal portrait statue had become a principal task of sculpture; and on sarcophagi the chief figure in the myth was regularly given the lineaments of the deceased. In painting, however, the tendency of the time was much less in the direction of lifelike representation of characters, but rather toward the so-called ceremonial picture, intended to celebrate an individual or a whole family with exact official vestments and solemn posture, frequently with symbolic accessories. Such treatment was obviously indicated in the case of rulers, and private persons followed their example. How essential costume was in such pictures is clear from the tablet in the palace of the Quintilii, which showed the Emperor Tacitus five times in different dress, with toga, chlamys, armor, pallium, and hunting garb. It is no wonder that even coins and tombstones no longer present the head alone but the entire upper body, whose dress now expresses rank and dignity. The two Tetrici had a mosaic picture made in their palace on the Caelian hill, showing Aurelian standing between them and receiving from them tokens of homage, scepter and oak wreath. On the wall of a dining hall in the palace at Aquileia there was a family portrait which celebrated the relationship of the houses of Maximian Herculius and Constantius Chlorus. Among others, the young Constantine appeared receiving a golden helmet with peacock feathers from little Fausta, who was later to be his wife. Similar family portraits can be imagined in the houses and country estates of prominent private citizens also. An echo of this category of art, which has otherwise perished, is extant in the pictures of the ivory diptychs, which usually surround the realistically conceived Emperor or official, in precisely observed official dress, with symbolic accessories.

When there were no printing presses it often became the duty of painting to make the power of the ruler known to the people, a function performed in modern times by manifestoes and proclamations. The first thing done at each accession was that the likeness of the new Emperor was sent about and everywhere received with great ceremony. Portable likenesses were carried in the field and set up at headquarters; we even find portrait figures (often of metal) used in battle standards. Victorious battles were painted upon large cloth surfaces or panels and publicly exhibited. Trains of foreign embassies, whole festivals and theatrical spectacles, triumphal processions, and solemnities of every sort received permanent monumental record as friezes in palaces. Constantine celebrated his victory over Licinius in a large encaustic picture of symbolic content which was set up before the gates of the imperial residence. He and his sons appeared, with the defeated general at their feet in the guise of a dragon, with arrows in his body and the abyss underneath; over the whole floated the sign of the cross. Later the Emperor had himself painted in the pediment of a palace gate in an attitude of prayer. And after his death a great painting was set up in his honor in Rome; this represented an allegory of heaven, with the transfigured Emperor enthroned.

Improvisations of this sort no longer had much to do with true art. But they do illustrate one aspect of the fate of art as a whole, for even in pagan times art had largely become the handmaid of propaganda, and with the victory of Christianity it could change only its master, not its position. Dominated by subject for many centuries on end, it could fulfill its internal laws not at all or only imperfectly. Actually this constitutes one of the most patent denials of the ancient outlook.

It was domination of subject over form that gave painting preference over sculpture in the realm of Christian art. Plastic expression of sacred figures, even if executed with the art of a Phidias, would have seemed a kind of idolatry; dressed in the forms of the period of decline, they were mere caricature as compared with the great works of antiquity. If it was to make any impression by means of art, therefore, Christianity required a narrative or a symbolically interrelated art, an art rich in figures; hence it must use painting primarily, or the intermediate form of relief. There is no need to speak of the prejudice against sculptors personally, who were despised as having been servants to idols.

Neither could poetry at this period supply what the fine arts were incapable of providing. Cut off from any living association with drama, surfeited to exhaustion with epic treatment of mythological material, rejecting historical subject matter along with everything modern, poetry could only withdraw to lyric and romance. Poetry continued to be composed in most categories, to be sure, in a consciously academic manner; but ever paler reminiscences of a better age, as is displayed for example in the bucolic and didactic poets of the third century, in Calpurnius Siculus, Nemesianus, Serenus, Sammoniacus, and others, cannot suffice to produce a living literature, however much talent may appear in individual cases. The lyric, on the other hand, is always capable of rejuvenation as is the human heart, and may produce individual lovely blooms even in periods of general wretchedness, though their form be imperfect. When epic and drama had lost their popular and living force, romance became the appropriate substitute form.

Unfortunately, this entire literature of the latest pagan age has reached us only in fragmentary form, and what we have lacks proper context; but romance does provide several attractive monuments. We have, for example, the *Shepherd's Tale* in Greek, ascribed to one Longus; but this name may well be the result of a misunderstanding, and in any case he cannot be dated to any definite period. But these charmingly told adventures of Daphnis and Chloë substantially determine a complete aesthetic judgment concerning the century — most likely the third — to which the doubtful author belongs. The descriptions, consistent in the naturalism of scenery and background and acute in their psychologic observation, go far beyond the bucolic characters and backgrounds inherited from Theocritus. The age capable of producing this book would appear to be not far removed from one amenable to genre and landscape painting. But *Daphnis and Chloë* stands completely isolated, and if we wish to compare it with other late Greek romances, we find that they and their authors likewise defy precise dating. Of Heliodorus (who has been several times cited), the author of the *Aethiopica*, it is doubtful whether he was the Bishop of Trikka in Thessaly of that name who flourished about 400, or whether it is not much more likely that the episcopal title was bestowed upon a pagan who lived at Emesa a century earlier (there is internal evidence for such authorship) in order to make his book eligible for preservation in Christian libraries. The author's aim, like that of Xenophon of Ephesus, is to present the greatest possible variety of adventures, and later romancers emulated this aim as well as they could. But there is no trace of the consistent and genuinely artistic character delineation of Longus or of his prudent limitations in costume and locale. Heliodorus offers diversion often not very agreeable.

Now and again (for example, at the opening of his book) Heliodorus purposely lingers over descriptions of landscapes, and similar efforts occur in Longus. I will not venture to offer a bad and abbreviated sketch of Humboldt's history of aesthetic feeling in regard to landscape; but at this point I can do no other than refer to that incomparable account which deals in masterly fashion with the subject itself and with its relations to other spiritual tendencies in late antiquity.

The true lyric of this period, if any was produced, is no longer extant. Echoes like the *Pervigilium Veneris* (about 252?) or like the *Prayer to Oceanus* can hardly date lower than the middle of the third century. Tolerable individual flights in elegiac and epigrammatic form, dating into the fifth century, are hardly adequate substitutes. These breathe too plainly of the air of the schools, especially in Ausonius, and are too consciously constructed as specimens of their respective categories to produce any living impression. The highly gifted improviser Claudian, with his panegyrics, mythical tales, and idylls (in a word, miscellaneous poetry), comes quite late. Claudian is an unworthy flatterer in a period of aesthetic decadence, and yet his brilliant colors are almost Ovidian in invention and execution. He serves as a warning to the history of literature not to fix limits between periods too rigidly. Rutilius Numatianus (about 417), who has been mentioned above, is also not without a nobler and more agreeable side, but his travel poem as a whole is quite formless.

The thing that was officially recognized as literature and admired in the age of Constantine was the most deplorable of all productions, grammatical tricks with words and verses. Great play was made with centos from Vergil, that is, partial use was made of Vergilian verses to construct new poems of quite different content. Whatever violence was done to the sense, at least these were the most melodious Roman verses in existence. Other artifices are more objectionable. Among these are epanalepsis, which repeats the beginning word of the hexameter at the end of the pentameter; figured poems, which when carefully written out take the form of an altar, a pan-pipe, an organ, or the like; the combination of all Roman meters in a single poem; enumeration of animal cries; anacylic verses, which could be read backwards or forwards; and other such aberrations. The impossible in these astonishingly laborious devices was achieved by a certain Publilius Optatianus Porphyrius. He had been banished into exile for some reason and now sought to regain Constantine's favor by quite desperate poetic leaps and vaults, and actually succeeded in so doing. He wrote twenty-six poems, most of them of twenty to forty hexameters, each containing the same number of letters, so that each poem had the appearance of a square. Certain individual letters, written in red, produced some figure, a monogram, an XP, or a flourish, and when read continuously, spelled out separate apothegms. The toil which the reader experiences is an index to the toil which the poet devoted to the most trivial content, compliments to Constantine and Crispus. At the end there follow four hexameters whose words could be arranged in eighteen different ways, each of which produced a kind of sense and meter. In a very gracious letter to Optatianus Constantine, in the attitude of a patron of the arts, accepts the surmounting of these difficulties as a genuine advance in art: "He who writes and composes in my century is followed by my favoring attention as by a gentle zephyr." The artificer of verse had already been recalled from exile; perhaps the City Prefect of Rome of the same name who is mentioned in 329 and 333 is the same Optatianus. This whole incident might have been passed over if it did not reveal the taste of the Emperor.

The advent of Christianity into ancient poetry was not as great a gain for poetry as might be imagined. Poetic treatment of Biblical history was in quite a different case from that of ancient myth. Myth was capable of manifold forms and aspects, and so with poetry and through it could serve as a continuous revelation of the beautiful. But Biblical incidents were delivered to poetry in a fixed and completed form; epic or plastic decoration might be dangerous from the point of view of dogma. Hence the dryness of the versified harmonies of the Gospels, from that of the Spaniard Juvencus (329) onwards. The declamatory element was no adequate substitute, and only betrayed the rhetorical education of contemporary Christian poets. Prudentius (about 400), also a Spaniard, the most significant of these poets, has passages of this sort that are good and almost lyrical; and in his accounts of the martyrs (*Peristephanon*) he moves with much greater epic freedom than was possible in purely Biblical material. But the total impression of his poetry is disproportionately rhetorical. Several excellent hymns of his and of his contemporary Ambrose are justly regarded as the foundation for all Christian lyric. The dominance of stress accent over quantitative, which here makes its first frank and consistent appearance, marks a transition to the poetry of the Middle Ages, only external, to be sure, but remarkable nevertheless. Later a new, medieval spirit was to be breathed into the calcified Latin.

But rhetoric still ruled as queen. Education continued to be controlled by rhetoric. Of the so-called seven liberal arts — grammar, rhetoric, dialectic, arithmetic, music, geometry, and astronomy — which once constituted the "encyclopedic" education of young men of good position, the first three had continued as such, while increase of subject matter had made the other four separate disciplines of scholarship. During the Empire all that was left alive of philosophy was attached to the three former, and the schools of rhetoric were regarded as essential to education for the practice of law. It is difficult for us to get a proper notion of the extent and importance of rhetoric during this period. Easy and rich expression was regarded as indispensable in daily life, and successful public speaking as the highest triumph. Every important city of the Empire strove to acquire one or several worthy rhetors. At Rome Greeks and natives vied for pre-eminence. There were institutions for cultivating rhetoric in Gaul at Marseilles, Narbonne, Toulouse, Bordeaux, Autun, Treves, and Rheims, in Spain at Cordova, in Africa at Carthage, Sicca, Madaura, and elsewhere. In Greece and the Near East the "sophists" were often the most important personages in a city, for besides their pedagogical functions they appeared publicly on all occasions as adherents of a given philosophic sect, as advocates, as orators on public affairs. Not infrequently very wealthy and generous men devoted themselves to this pursuit, and then cut as grand a figure as was at all possible under such a government as the Roman. Finally the state itself, which had previously left higher education to the cities and to private individuals, resolved to regard it as a public concern, gave it support here and there, and itself paid the salaries of sophists for various cities, their number depending on the rank of the city. But arrangements of this sort, which are mentioned from the time of Hadrian and Antoninus Pius downwards, can hardly have long remained in full force. Constantine still confirmed the professors appointed by the state and the similarly highly privileged physicians together with their families, at least in their immunity from burdensome offices and contributions, specifically the much-feared decurionate, and from military service. He was himself, as will be shown below, a zealous amateur of oratory; a number of his predecessors down to Numerian are praised for the same interest. But Constantine's taste in oratory can hardly have been better than his taste in poetry. Everything that issued from the imperial bureau after Diocletian, letters, edicts, and laws, all bear the same curled and bombastic character. But the Emperors customarily selected their private secretaries and many other important court officials from the class of rhetors, and accordingly must for some time have looked to aptitudes other than literary style. Eumenius, secretary of Chlorus, is probably to be regarded as a notable exception.

Did not antiquity exaggerate the importance of education in discourse and writing? Would it not have done better to fill the heads of boys and young men with useful realities? The answer is that we have no right to make a decision as long as formlessness in discourse and writing persists among us everywhere, as long as perhaps barely one of a hundred of our educated men possesses any notion of the true art of periodic structure. To the ancients, rhetoric and its collateral sciences were the indispensable complement to their norm of beautiful and free existence, to their arts and their poetry. Modern life has higher principles and aims in some respects, but it is uneven and disharmonious. What is most beautiful and delicate in it is found alongside the crudest barbarism. And our multitudinous preoccupations do not leave us leisure to take offense at the contradictions.

A glance at the school books of later Roman rhetoric which have been preserved is sufficient to fill us with shame. These writings of Rutilius Lupus, Aquila, Rufinianus, Fortunatianus, Rufinus, and others are in part not genuine Roman productions, but perhaps jejune reworkings of Greek models from the ages of Gorgias and Aristotle and later; nevertheless they show the course in which men sought to guide oratory even in the latest period of the Empire. Not only does the system give a name and treatment to every sort of sentence structure, figure of speech, and artifice of construction, which we would not know how to name without the ancients and of which our modern treatises use scarcely a tithe, but there is also circumstantial treatment of the categories of oratorical style and of the structure and execution of orations. Of the infinite refinement of the ear in those days, we may get some notion from the fact that metrical differences in words or short groups of words, to us indistinguishable, are dealt with circumstantially (in Rufinus) and assigned to appropriate positions in the sentence, whether at its beginning, end, or elsewhere. It was important to determine in what cases a sentence should open with an anapaest or a spondee. The art of delivery and of the

orator's outward bearing generally (in Fortunatianus) com-
pletes this discipline, and shows us again that all our modern
speech is mere naturalism and attains beautiful form only
through accidental talent and unconsciously. Every gesture of
the hand, every dropping or folding of the garment had its
own law. The orator was no less aware than the sculptor of
such laws as that arm and leg must never be extended simultaneously on the same side. It was only thus that eloquence
could be raised to virtuosity of the whole spiritual and physical man.

But the obverse was that of all virtuosity — a growing indifference to content and a concomitant increase in personal
vanity. The Greek sophists of the early Empire, as they are
described by Philostratus, exhibited themselves in such themes
as those mentioned above in a peculiarly arrogant manner,
and offered themselves to public admiration quite like certain
representatives of modern music, whose claims are strikingly
similar to those of the rhetoricians. How political oratory subsequently dissolved into panegyric in the West, and forensic
oratory sank lower and lower, this is not the place to show.
From the ages of Diocletian and Constantine we possess perhaps the best of the kind in the eulogies on the Emperors and
Caesars which have been several times cited. These are coun-
terbalanced by the poor diction of contemporary edicts. Among
the Christians style had been an incidental matter; it was only
some decades later that the famous succession of pulpit orators began. These finally reconciled the new content with the
traditional but transmuted form. A curious cleavage had to be
bridged: reverence for the classical style and horror at its
pagan associations, acceptance of the language of the Bible
and consciousness of its impurity. St. Jerome had to be shaken
by a fearful vision, in which the Judge of all the World was
about to condemn him as a *Ciceronianus, non Christianus.*

Meanwhile, throughout the fourth century rhetoric remained
a life interest for the pagans and for countless Christians. Certain countries, like Gaul and Africa, continued to be conscious,
and not without pride, of certain peculiarities of their styles,
and in these countries rhetors were among the most highly

Q

respected persons in society. In the Greek regions of the Empire the sophists sought by every means possible to maintain the position they had enjoyed in the age of the Antonines. But since they functioned simultaneously as Neoplatonic philosophers and miracle workers also, their historian Eunapius pays far less attention to their rhetorical activity; at most he characterizes their outward bearing and admires their pretentions. Our final section will deal with the situation in Athens; here we need only point to the hopeless competition the pagan sophists offered the Christian preachers. Considered as a matter of public partisanship on one side or the other, the struggle was altogether too uneven. But not every rhetor could be content with the solace with which Themistius shielded himself: "The value of a philosopher's discourse is not diminished if it is delivered under a solitary plane tree with none but cicadas to hear."

If almost all productions of the fourth century betray decline by labored and tortured form, by heaping up of *sententiae*, by the misuse of metaphor for the simple and the commonplace, by modern turgidity and artificial archaic aridity, still a peculiar reflection of the classic period rests upon many of these writers. They still show the requirement of artistic style, which is normally alien to us; that the style emerges as something calculated and self-conscious is the fault of the sinking age, which felt quite clearly that it and its culture was something secondary and derivative, and imitated the great models painstakingly and unevenly. But it is impossible to dismiss lightly authors like Libanius and Symmachus, for example, whose every little letter was wrought into a minor work of art — even though they attached too great importance to their performance and clearly reckoned on a reading public besides the addressee — as Pliny and others had done before them. Symmachus at least knew that the Ciceronian period of epistolography was over and why it was over.

Does a formal decline in poetry and representational art always imply a people's national decline also? Are those arts not blossoms which must fall before fruit can mature? Cannot the true take the place of the beautiful, the useful of the agreeable?

The question may remain unsolved, and between such alternatives as the last there can be no solution. But anyone who has encountered classical antiquity, if only in its twilight, feels that with beauty and freedom there departed also the genuine antique life, the better part of the national genius, and that the rhetorizing orthodoxy which was left to the Greek world can only be regarded as a lifeless precipitate of a once wonderful totality of being.

VIII

THE PERSECUTION OF CHRISTIANS
CONSTANTINE AND THE SUCCESSION

FROM THE MIDST of conditions whose history is clearly and precisely known there sometimes emerges a fact of the first importance whose deeper causes stubbornly elude the eye of the student. Such an event is the great persecution of Christians under Diocletian, the last war of annihilation waged by paganism against Christianity. At first glance there is nothing strange in these persecutions; Diocletian had all too many predecessors upon the throne of the world who similarly wished to extirpate the Christians, and scarcely any other course was to be expected of so zealous and confirmed a pagan as he was. But the question takes on a quite different aspect when we consider the circumstances in detail. From the time of Gallienus — that is, for more than forty years — the Christians had remained unmolested, and to this period belong the first eighteen years of Diocletian's own reign. Even after he had ordered the Manichaeans to be burnt at the stake (296), he left the Christians in peace for seven years. His wife Prisca and his daughter Valeria are said to have been not unfavorably disposed to the Christians; Diocletian himself even tolerated about his sacred person Christian chamberlains and pages to whom he was devoted as a father. Courtiers and their wives and children might practice the Christian religion under his very eyes. Christians who were dispatched to the provinces as governors were graciously excused from the solemn sacrifices which their position entailed. Christian congregations felt perfectly secure and were so greatly strengthened that their old meeting places nowhere sufficed. New buildings were constructed everywhere; in the large cities very handsome churches arose, and there was no fear.

If the government had any thought of persecution in the future it should not have suffered the Christians to expand to such power in the state without resistance. It may be said that the state became aware gradually and late that Christianity, if completely tolerated, would strive for predominance; but Diocletian cannot have been so heedless. The persecution cannot possibly have resulted, as it seems to me, either from his original or from his gradually formed conviction without special occasion. Judgment in this case must be conditioned by the fact that we have to do with one of the greatest of the Roman Emperors, with the savior of the Empire and of civilization, with the shrewdest judge of his time, whose political memory would be quite different if he had died in 302. "He was an outstanding man, clever, zealous for the state, zealous for those under his protection, prepared for any task that might come to his hand, always unfathomable in his thoughts, sometimes foolhardy but otherwise prudent; the stirrings of his restless spirit he suppressed with inflexible perseverance." *
What we have to determine, then, is whether the thing which darkens this great memory was merely an outbreak of inherent cruelty and brutality, or a consequence of the superstition which has been described above, or an unfortunate concession to colleagues who were of much less stature, or finally whether the historian is not here confronted with an obligation to seek an explanation beyond that to be derived from the letter of the records. The Christians heaped the name of Diocletian with curses, and neither could pagans of Greek or Roman education favor him because he introduced Orientalism into political and social life. The only historians who might possibly present a true nexus of events — Ammianus and Zosimus — are mangled, and perhaps for the very reason that they treated Diocletian fairly. Under such circumstances

* *Historia Augusta Numerian.*, ch. 13.

it is quite futile to look to extant sources directly for what is essential and conclusive.

The account which is usually regarded as basic — namely, Lactantius' *Of the Deaths of the Persecutors* — begins straightway with a demonstrable untruth. An important inspection of entrails in the presence of the Emperor was disturbed by the fact that Christian courtiers who were present crossed themselves and so expelled the daimones; the sacrifice was several times repeated in vain, until the chief of the haruspices surmised and declared the cause. Thereupon Diocletian in a fury of rage is said to have demanded idolatrous sacrifice of all the courtiers and even to have extended this command to the army under threat of dismissal; and there, for a time, the matter rested. This story rests upon a belief, adequately refuted by Eusebius, that the Emperor did not know that the Christians at his court were such and would not have tolerated Christians. The probability is that Christian chamberlains and pages either were not required to be present at sacrifices at all or, if they happened to be present, that they conducted themselves in a manner the Emperor thought seemly. Such a scene as that described either must have taken place much earlier, at Diocletian's accession, or was altogether unthinkable. The Emperor's pagan convictions, which accommodated themselves to the existence and power of the Christians for eighteen years, cannot have been the decisive motive for the persecutions, earnest and zealous as those convictions were.

The second untruth in Lactantius' account is Diocletian's timorous yielding to Galerius, who had arrived at Nicomedia (apparently from the Danube) in order to win the Emperor over for the persecution; Galerius for his part is said to have been incited by his mother Romula. Romula was a zealous devotee of the great Magna Mater (who is here designated a mountain goddess), and took it very ill that the Christians in her place of residence refused to participate, as the pagans did, in her daily sacrificial feasts. All of this gossip, which places ultimate responsibility upon the whim of a fanatical woman, is reduced to nothing when we understand that Diocletian was not afraid of Galerius and that Lactantius is culpable of very serious error concerning the whole character of Diocletian. No weight is to be attached to the alleged conversations said to have taken place at Nicomedia in the winter of 302–303, for the author elsewhere reveals himself as an amateur of dramatic fictions. He seeks to characterize Diocletian as more reluctant and more reasonable in order to heap greater hatred upon the monster Galerius. "When they were taking counsel throughout the winter, and no one was admitted, and everyone believed that they were dealing with matters of state, the elder long opposed the fury of his colleague and represented to him how dangerous it was to disturb the world and to shed streams of blood. The Christians would die gladly. It would be enough if courtiers and soldiers were required to renounce this religion. But Galerius persisted in his intention stubbornly, and Diocletian thereupon convoked a secret council of jurists and officers to decide on the question of the persecution. For it was in his character to draw many persons into his counsel for hateful measures in order to be able to shift the blame for evil; good things, on the other hand, he did without counsel in order to obtain the credit for himself." Such dealing is unthinkable, in view of all our other information concerning Diocletian. The concept of the ruler by which he was inspired took no account of what the people might find welcome or hateful, and took full responsibility for whatever was carried out through others, whether good or bad. For any measure which was allowed without the ruler's authority would be tantamount to a breach in his power, which must be his first and last consideration. But let us hear further. Upon the affirmative decision of the secret council Diocletian made an altogether superfluous inquiry of the Milesian Apollo, and naturally received the same response. Even now he gave his consent with the condition that no blood must flow, while Galerius is said to have been very eager to burn the Christians alive. But we have just heard from the senior Emperor's own mouth that he foresaw numerous martyrdoms of Christians! He was in better posi-

tion than anyone to know that the Christians must either be
left in peace or combated with extreme measures, and that
the stipulation of a bloodless procedure was folly.

This is the nature of the only consecutive account of the
great catastrophe. And Lactantius was in Nicomedia at the
time, and might have recorded, not, to be sure, the secret negotiations, but the essential course of events, and perhaps
with great exactness. For many details his treatise is as indispensable as so partisan a document can well be.

Eusebius finds it convenient to say nothing at all of special
reasons for the persecution. Aurelius Victor, Rufus, Festus,
Eutropius, and the rest do not even mention the persecution.

Diocletian himself can offer no defense. His edicts have
perished, and his secret designs may have been the exact opposite of those imagined.

Hence the field is open to conjecture, so long as conjecture
does not soar in the air but follows the true tracks that survive and is in keeping with the character of the times and of
the persons involved.

The readiest conjecture is that the rulers, like many of their
predecessors, were compelled to yield to popular fury against
the Christians. But such yielding does not appear in the
course of the events, and the power of the state was fully
adequate to suppress such fury. It did indeed happen that the
crowds at the games in the Circus Maximus shouted in rhyth-
mic chant some ten or a dozen times: *"Christiani tollantur,
Christiani non sint"* — "Out with the Christians, let there be
no Christians" — but this apparently happened after the persecution had been in progress for some time, and in any case
cries of this sort meant little.

Or it might be assumed that the pagan priests demanded
the persecution suddenly and unconditionally, and the Emperors were convinced of the need of it on some grounds of
superstition. With all his acumen, Diocletian was sufficiently
steeped in superstition to make such conjectures plausible; at
least there is no proof to the contrary. But in that case we
should have had the names of such powerful priests recorded;
the mere mention of Hierocles, Governor of Bithynia (known

from other sources as a zealous Neoplatonist), among the supporters and instigators is not sufficient.

Could Diocletian's sense of private morality have been involved? He was not indifferent to morality; the female haruspex who was constantly employed to foretell the future and its fate had not carried him beyond moral considerations. If this involves a logical inconsistency, it is all to his credit; a similar disharmony, as we have seen, characterized the better men of the third century generally, in whom belief in immortality, if it did not reconcile fatalism and morality, at least enforced an accommodation between them. The private life of the Emperor afforded no grounds of criticism even to the most censorious Christian, and he therefore could justly stand forth as the guardian of general morality in the state. He did so, among other instances, in the marriage law of 295 (which has already been cited), in which he laid down high principles: "The immortal gods will be favorably and kindly disposed to the Roman name as they have been in the past if we take care that all our subjects lead a pious, calm, and pure life. . . . Rome's majesty has attained its great height, by grace of all the gods, only because a pious and chaste life constitutes the keystone of all legislation. . . ." Can it be that the Christians gave moral offense?

We know that in the first and second centuries the Romans bandied about rumors of horrible cruelties which were supposed to take place at the worship of the Christians. But these rumors are not relevant here; they had long been silenced, and Diocletian, who saw a great many Christians at his court daily, cannot have given the slightest credit to gossip of this sort.

The case is apparently different with Eusebius' complaints concerning the internal demoralization of the Christian communities immediately before the persecution. A host of unworthy persons had invaded the Church and even forced their way to the episcopal thrones. Among these evils Eusebius mentions in particular the bitter feuds between bishops and between individual congregations, the hypocrisy and deception, beliefs well-nigh atheistic, wicked deeds (κακίας), and again, quarrel, envy, hatred, and the violent rule of the clergy.

But these are not transgressions of a sort the state would feel bound to persecute for the sake of morality. Similar things occurred among the pagans, and in more abundant measure. But remarkably enough, one of the few official documents of the pagan side which have been preserved, Galerius' edict of revocation of 311, appears to designate the serious and multiform cleavages among the Christians themselves as the principal cause of the persecution. They had backslid from the faith of their fathers and had formed sects, they had been bidden to return to the institutions of their elders, and so on. Every word in this passage, indeed, is so oblique and equivocal that most interpreters could as well understand "fathers" and "elders" to mean pagans. Yet several expressions seem rather to charge the Christians with backsliding from their own principles. Further along we read: "We saw that they neither paid due worship to the gods, nor honored the God of the Christians." This is somewhat reminiscent of the principles of the Catholic party in the Thirty Years' War; they felt on equal legal ground with the Lutherans only, and abhorred the Calvinists as a by-sect.

But neither can this track well be the correct one. Disagreements and cleavages among the Christians can never have been so significant that the state would feel compelled to do away with the entire community for their sake. Zealous pagans, if they gave the matter any thought, could have wished for nothing more earnestly than that the process of decay should continue undisturbed, for it must eventually have delivered the Christians into their hands.

What explanation, then, is left us? I believe that some important personal occurrence is involved, and that its traces were subsequently most carefully obliterated. An inscription in honor of Diocletian accuses the Christians of wishing to overthrow the state — *rem publicam evertebant;* in this form the statement is without value, but it may conceal a nucleus of truth. Could it be that the Christians, sensible of their growth and expansion, sought to gain control of the imperial office?

This could have been achieved quite peaceably, by convert-
ing Diocletian. That something of the sort was at least intended can be virtually demonstrated. There is extant a letter
of a Bishop Theonas to a Christian chief chamberlain named
Lucianus, containing instructions for conduct at the court of
a pagan Emperor; it is generally agreed that the Emperor can
only have been Diocletian. Lucianus had already been working as effectively as he could among his associates and had
converted many who had entered court service as pagans. The
superintendents of the imperial privy purse, the treasure, and
the wardrobe had already gone over to Christianity. Now
Theonas finds that it would be highly useful if a Christian
chamberlain, for example, would receive charge of the imperial library and on the occasion of literary conversations
could prudently and gradually convince the Emperor of the
truth of the Christian religion. Probably the Christians were
impressed by the seriousness and moral bent of the great
ruler and realized that his conversion would be more important and decisive than ever, now that the imperial authority
had been raised to unprecedented heights by victories over
barbarians and usurpers and by the reform of the whole internal machinery of state. It hardly needs to be said that all
attempts of this sort were bound to be futile with a pagan like
Diocletian.

We must notice carefully how the persecution began. Eusebius and Lactantius are agreed that some time before the
large general measures the Christians had been expelled from
the army. Perhaps as early as 298 or even earlier a muster took
place at which the Christian soldiers were given the choice of
becoming pagans and retaining their service or losing it. The
majority unhesitatingly preferred the latter alternative, and it
is said that a few lost their lives on that account. It is patent
that such a step would be taken only reluctantly and perforce,
for good soldiers and officers were the Empire's most valuable
resource at the time. We may venture the further conclusion
that this purge of the army was based not on religious but on
political reasons, for otherwise it might have begun with any
other class, for example, with the sudden arrest of all bishops,

a step that was actually taken later. Either the Emperors no
longer felt personally secure among Christian troops or they
believed they could not rely on their obedience, in war as in
peace. Refusal to participate in pagan sacrifice, if that were
alleged as reason for discharge, could only have been a pretext, for the military service of Christians had been looked
upon as a matter of course for a decade and a half. It might
indeed be said that the Emperors purged the army out of di-
abolic wickedness, so that it might be employed in the imminent persecution without objection on the part of Christians.
The contrary cannot be proved, for we do not know what
period elapsed between the purge and the persecution. If the
intervening period ran to several years, the probability of this
explanation vanishes utterly. Great deeds of blood may be
planned and prepared far in advance, but so striking a preparation as this, if the persecution were the sole object of the
purge, would be expected to be exhibited only a moment before the actual execution. The transitions are hard to distinguish. If Diocletian desired a purely pagan army, he desired
it for the sake of obedience generally, without calculating how
he might eventually employ it in extreme cases. Remarkably
enough, Diocletian kept his entire Christian court about him
until after the persecution had started, perhaps because he
wished to retain the personal trust to which he had grown
used as long as possible.

In connection with all of this we recall what Eusebius half
admits and half conceals, that at the beginning of the persecution insurrections broke out at two places, in the Cappadocian region of Melitene and in Syria. Eusebius is not entirely reliable for the chronology of events, but we have no
other resource here. He tells of the publication of the edict
first, and then the beginning of the persecution in Nicomedia
and indeed in the royal palace, and he describes the heroic
deaths of the Christian pages and chamberlains. Then he
speaks of the conflagrations in the palace and of the Christians
put to death on that occasion, and also of the exhumation of
the executed pages. Then he proceeds: "Forasmuch as not
long thereafter some in the region called Melitene and again

others in Syria sought to seize the rule for themselves, an imperial command was issued that the heads of congregations everywhere should be arrested and thrown into chains." Rightly or wrongly, then, the attempt at usurpation was ascribed to Christians, and in consequence the bishops were seized. But the immediate agents must have been in part soldiers, for at this time no usurpation was conceivable without soldiers, and if they were Christians they must have been retired soldiers. It may be objected that these usurpations arose out of despair at the persecution which had already been ordered, but it is equally probable that the Emperors had already had notice of unrest among the retired soldiers. If Eusebius' statements on chronology and incidents are correct, and we were indifferent to the implications and concerned only for the scientific interest, criticism would acknowledge without difficulty that the Emperors found an opposition ready armed against them and suppressed it.

Finally, the content of the edict itself, so far as it is known, is calculated not to annihilate the Christians directly but to degrade them consistently, as a means toward effecting their conversion. Their gatherings for worship were to be forbidden, their churches to be pulled down, their sacred scriptures burned. Those who possessed offices of honor and other dignities were to lose them. In judicial investigations torture might be employed against Christians of every class. The benefits of ordinary law were to be withdrawn from them; Christian slaves might never be manumitted as long as they remained Christian. Such, approximately, were the prescriptions which were published abroad 24 February 303 first in Nicomedia, at the time the residence of Diocletian and Galerius, and then throughout the Empire.

In Nicomedia itself the persecution began on the preceding day, on which the festival of the Terminalia fell, when a Prefect of the Guard accompanied by officers and officials had the great church plundered and demolished by his Praetorians.

After the edict was posted its first victim was a respected Christian who pulled it down and tore it into bits, with the scornful remark that victories over Goths and Sarmatae had again been posted up. The man was burned to death. Defiance such as this would be quite inexplicable unless we assume that even at that critical moment there was some secret hope for general resistance.

Next we are told of the cruel torture and execution of a number of palace officials and pages, of whom Peter, Dorotheus, and Gorgonius are mentioned by name. Eusebius, to be sure, informs us quite briefly only that they suffered for the sake of their piety; but if only piety were involved the law would have been content with their degradation. Why such cruelty against those who had previously been treated by the Emperors as "children of the household" despite their known Christianity? Clearly the Emperors believed they were on the track of a plot.

In the meanwhile fire twice broke out in the palace at Nicomedia. According to Lactantius, Galerius caused the fires to be set, in order to place the blame on the Christians, who were said to have agreed on the crime with the court eunuchs; and Diocletian, who always thought himself so clever, failed to realize the true situation but immediately fell into a boundless fury against the Christians. On this point it is impossible to plead with a partisan writer; but anyone who has studied the history of Diocletian will grant him sufficient intelligence to see through so clumsy a trick as that posited by Lactantius. The fire broke out in the portion of the palace inhabited by Diocletian himself. But Galerius would have been the last man to set his house afire over his head. The highest probability suggests that Christian courtiers whose safety was imperiled were the guilty parties; their intention may have been to intimidate the Emperor through superstition, not to cause his death. On a later ceremonial occasion Constantine, who had been present at Nicomedia at the time, sought to exculpate all and sundry by maintaining that the palace had been fired by a bolt of lightning, as if it were not easy to distinguish lightning from other causes of fire. Both Emperors, indeed, were convinced that the Christians were guilty, and the criminal investigation in the palace took a bloody course. "Even the mightiest eunuchs, who once ruled palace and Emperor, were put to death." It is not to be wondered that under the impress of this bitterness the general edict was carried out with drastic severity and supplemented by further orders.

Soon there followed the Christian uprisings in the East, which have been mentioned above, and these provoked the second edict, which ordered the arrest of all heads of communities.

Perhaps the reader will take exception to this investigation. Is it not altogether unjust to make the persecution a cause for incrimination? So had the fanatic party done in France in 1572, and so in Valtelline in 1620; to justify their frightful shedding of blood they subsequently charged that their subdued opponents had engineered a bloody plot, which they were compelled to forestall.

In the first place, no one can here speak of a general Christian conspiracy against the rulers or against pagans generally. Our more limited concept of the outline of the incident is somewhat as follows: Certain Christian courtiers, perhaps very few in number, and certain Christian commanders in the provinces thought they could put the Empire into Christian hands or hands favorable to Christians by a hasty *coup*, perhaps intending to spare the persons of the Emperors. It is possible that Galerius actually discovered traces of the affair before Diocletian, and that the latter could only with difficulty be persuaded.

In the second place no one will deny that among the Christians of the time there were persons whose conscience would not scruple at such a *coup*. Eusebius' characterization is sufficiently explicit. On the other hand, earthly power has never shown itself lenient when its existence has been threatened.

The great misfortune was comprised in the fact that the rulers generalized what had taken place and proceeded against all Christians as being implicated in the guilt, and in the fact that contemporary law was so quick with torture and with gruesome death penalties. But to be in a position to judge individual cases correctly we must have better sources than the *Acts of the Martyrs* usually are. In any case a very great majority accommodated themselves to participation in sacrifice

in the course of time, and Diocletian's last edicts, of which we
shall speak below, perhaps rest on the premise that success
had been achieved, by and large, and that only a remnant of
opposition was left to be overcome. The surrender of their
sacred scriptures was further calculated to deprive the community permanently of a spiritual support.

But there was more than enough of struggle left to maintain a state of high tension. It is not the task of this book to
follow the frightful course of events in detail. Of Diocletian's
colleagues, the Augustus Maximian proceeded to the persecution with zeal, whereas the gentle and monotheistic Caesar,
Constantius Chlorus, is said to have contented himself, in his
area of Gaul and Britain, with merely pulling down the
churches. In any case he retained Christians at his court at
Treves or York, and even for military employment. But in
other parts of the Empire the persecution was all the harder.
From the many cases of torture and martyrdom it appears that
the investigation had fallen in part into the worst hands; but
we must also consider the possibility that the judges thought
they were dealing with a political investigation, in which the
extortion of confessions is important. The attitudes of officials
varied greatly. In Africa, where political suspicions were perhaps wholly out of the question and where substantially all
that was involved was surrender of the sacred scriptures, the
Christians were frequently given to understand that even that
requirement would not be too rigidly enforced. But many purposely declared that they had sacred scriptures in their keeping which they would not surrender, and suffered death for
their defiance. Others immediately heeded the general order
and delivered all that they had; these were later branded
with the name *traditores,* "surrenderers." In general a varied
range of tempers was revealed, from the most cowardly weakness to fanatic provocation, and in between there were not
wanting splendid examples of calm and reasonable fortitude.
Here we learn something about the lower strata of the Christian community also. There were people who wished to ex-
piate some crime of which they were guilty by a Christian
martyr's death, quite like the thousands of robbers and mur-

derers who joined in the First Crusade. Others were indebted
to the state for taxes they could never pay or were burdened
by private indebtedness, and sought to escape their troubles
by death, or hoped to move rich Christians to help them by
their endurance under torture and in imprisonment. Finally,
there were destitute people who enjoyed a better life in prison
than outside, because Christians fearlessly supplied their captive brethren with more than bare necessities. In the face of
such abuses Bishop Mensurius of Carthage had the courage
and consistency to demand that those who had needlessly invited martyrdom must not be revered as martyrs.

Meanwhile, in the course of little more than a year, the investigation had sharpened into an actual, general persecution
of Christians. The second edict, which ordered the arrest of
the clergy, was followed by a third, according to which the
prisoners were to be released if they offered sacrifice, otherwise they were to be forced to do so by any means. In 304 a
fourth decree extended the latter provision to all Christians
generally, and by construction implied the death penalty. In
the East the persecution continued at this pitch of rigor for
some four years, and then with certain deviations for five
more; in the West they came to an end earlier.

Church history has long regarded it a sacred duty to preserve the memory of the noblest and most edifying of the
martyrdoms of this period. We must be content to refer to
Eusebius and the collections of legends for details. Despite
the exceptions which historical criticism may justly take to individual circumstances and especially to the miracles which
have become attached to them, the sight of this new society
with its new religion and philosophy struggling against the
most powerful of all states with its paganism and its millen-
nium-old culture, and eventually prevailing by its very suppression, is nevertheless a historical spectacle of the greatest
magnitude.

Apparently the persecutors became thoroughly demoralized
when Diocletian and his colleagues laid down their dignities
(305), Galerius and Constantius advanced to the rank of Augustus, and Severus and Maximinus Daia took their place as

R

Caesars. Henceforth the campaign degenerated, especially in the latter's realm — the southeastern portion of the Empire — to a true war of extermination; the reader may be spared the gruesome scenes of horror.

We now return to political history, which underwent highly important developments at this same time.

Soon after the beginning of the persecution, as early as the spring of 303, Diocletian journeyed to the West, and in the autumn arrived at Rome, there to celebrate, jointly with Maximian, the triumph for so many victories which had been saved up, and at the same time the vicennalia of his reign. In comparison with the luxury of a Carinus, the expense of the triumph and the duration of the festival were very moderate; and when the Romans murmured the Emperor replied jestingly that in the presence of the censors the games could not be so extravagant. He revealed his opinion of Roman gossip by leaving the city on 20 December, without awaiting the new year and the ceremonies incident to the change of consuls. This had been his first visit to Rome since his accession. That he had built (after 298) the most colossal of all baths appears to have earned him no gratitude; that he had even now presented the Romans with a greater gift in money (a congiary of 310 million denarii, equivalent to some sixty-two million talers) than had any of his predecessors did not improve the popular temper: the people had expected more sumptuous games, and they had been disappointed.

Diocletian greeted the new year (304) at Ravenna. He fell gravely ill on the wintry journey to Nicomedia, and from then till his abdication (1 May 305) he was scarcely seen in public. Of the great ceremony of abdication itself Lactantius gives a circumstantial description, vitiated only by Lactantius' essential unreliability. The hill three thousand paces from Nicomedia, the column with the statue of Jupiter, the tears of the old Emperor at his address to the soldiers, the traveling-carriage which stood ready for him — all this is doubtless true. But that everyone expected that Constantine, who was present, would be raised instead of Severus or Maximinus, that the

sudden advance of the hitherto unknown Maximinus aroused
the greatest astonishment, and that the procedure had been
expressly designed to take the soldiers by surprise — this we
may venture to doubt. What did the populace of Nicomedia
know of the senior Emperor's system of adoptions, or even of
his intention to proclaim new adoptions on the spot? But there
may well have been persons who wished to see the rise of
Constantine; whether there were such in the army is questionable, for as a mere tribune of the first rank he can hardly
have acquired wide popularity. What Diocletian thought of
him at this time we do not know; earlier he had been favorably
disposed to him, from the period of the campaigns — and Constantine subsequently repaid him by depreciatory remarks and
cunning plots.

The motives for the abdication we have endeavored to present in their true light in an earlier context. Unless our conclusions are wrong, the imperial office was to be limited to a
fixed period of twenty years, in order to regularize, as far as
possible, the wonderful dynasty which had no hereditary
rights, and to make a calm and undisturbed succession of
adoptions possible. It is not unlikely that superstition had its
word in this business also, at least in the matter of Diocletian's firm reliance on the obedience of his co-rulers. Here we
can only suppose that Diocletian had secret fatalistic grounds
for hoping to convince all his successors of the necessity of
his measures.

However that may be, Diocletian was content and happy,
at least for some time, in his camp-palace at Salonae. It is high
testimony in his favor that after long years of war and a dream
of rule that lasted for twenty years he sought out the sites and
the occupations of his youth and delved and planted his
vegetable garden with his own hands. May we not conclude
that he had always inwardly risen above the Oriental court
ceremonies which he introduced and that at Nicomedia he
had often longed for his Dalmatian home? In the case of this
remarkable man it will always remain impossible to distinguish what belongs to ordinary ambition, to a belief in destiny, and to the force of political genius. He understood how

to give the Roman Empire what it needed for its preservation, namely, permanence of rule; and he must have been driven to the throne inexorably in order to give his thoughts realization. Now his task was absolved, and he could retire to silence.

Maximian, who was obliged to carry out the same official act in Italy, but much against his will, retired to a beautifully situated estate in Lucania, while his son Maxentius chose despised Rome or its vicinity for his seat. Himself despised and reckoned unworthy to rule, he had a correct appreciation of the situation, and it is hard to believe that Galerius willingly allowed him to reside in this region. Perhaps objection was made at once, but he was not to be moved by fair means. One consequence of Diocletian's system, as has been noted above, was not provided for: sons of Emperors had either to be promoted or executed. But for reasons which we have sought to determine above, a hereditary dynasty was avoided, and of pure sultanism, as it appears, Diocletian would have no part, as previously, after the fall of Carinus, he would have no part of proscriptions. Furthermore, Maxentius had married Galerius' daughter, possibly against his own and Galerius' will and only for the sake of following an arrangement of the aged senior Emperor.

For several months the entire succession seemed to follow its prescribed course. But at the beginning of the year following (306), a new character appears in this remarkable drama. Constantine, whom history justly styles the Great, spirited himself away from the court at Nicomedia and suddenly appeared with his father Constantius Chlorus as the latter was on the point of sailing from the harbor of Gessoriacum (Boulogne) for Britain.

Constantine's historical memory has suffered the greatest misfortune conceivable. That pagan writers must be hostile to him is obvious and would do him no damage in the eyes of posterity. But he has fallen into the hands of the most objectionable of all eulogists, who has utterly falsified his likeness. The man is Eusebius of Caesarea and the book his *Life of Constantine*. The man who with all his faults was always significant and always powerful is here presented in the guise of a sanctimonious devotee; in point of fact his numerous misdeeds are amply documented in a number of passages. Eusebius' equivocal praise is basically insincere. He speaks of the man but really means a cause, and that cause is the hierarchy, so strongly and richly established by Constantine. Furthermore, to say nothing of the contemptible style, there is a consciously furtive mode of expression, so that the reader finds himself treading concealed traps and bogs at the most vital passages. The reader who notices these hazards in time may be easily misled into putting the worst possible construction upon what has been withheld from him.

The introduction of this biography is ecstatic enough: "When I gaze in spirit upon this thrice-blessed soul, united with God, free of all mortal dross, in robes gleaming like lightning and in ever radiant diadem, speech and reason stand mute, and I would willingly leave it to a better man to devise a worthy hymn of praise." Would that had been the case! If we only possessed instead the description of a reasonable pagan like Ammianus, we should come infinitely closer to the great historical phenomenon which was the man Constantine, even though his moral character might not have emerged unsullied. Then we could perhaps see clearly what we can now only surmise, namely, that virtually throughout his life Constantine never assumed the guise of or gave himself out as a Christian but kept his free personal convictions quite unconcealed to his very last days. That Eusebius is fully capable of ignoring and concealing such a fact he himself reveals by his earlier characterization of Licinius, whom he claims straightway as a Christian Emperor beloved of God as long as the war against Maximinus Daia is involved, though he must have known that Licinius was nothing else than a tolerant pagan. It is highly probable that his treatment of Constantine is of a similar character. Then at least the odious hypocrisy which disfigures his character would disappear, and we should have instead a calculating politician who shrewdly employed all available physical resources and spiritual powers to the one end of maintaining himself and his rule without surrendering himself wholly to any party. It is true that the picture of such an egoist is not

very edifying either, but history has had ample opportunity to
grow accustomed to his like. Moreover, with a little latitude
we can easily be persuaded that from his first political appearance Constantine consistently acted according to the principle
which energetic ambition, as long as the world has endured,
has called "necessity." It is that remarkable concatenation of
deeds and destiny to which ambitious men who are highly
gifted are drawn as by some mysterious power. In vain does
the sense of righteousness enter its protest, in vain do millions
of prayers of the oppressed rise to Nemesis; the great man,
frequently unconsciously, consummates higher decrees, and an
epoch is expressed in his person, while he believes that he
himself is ruling his age and determining its character.

With Constantine our judgment of his very first step is decisive. Galerius, it is said, planned his certain destruction in
the war against the Sarmatae and then in a "gymnastic" contest with wild beasts, but the fearless hero prevailed over
barbarians and lions alike, and laid them at the feet of the
new senior Emperor. Then, despite frequent requests of Constantius Chlorus to send him his son, Galerius in a quite hostile
spirit retained Constantine near his person like a prisoner, and
only yielded when it was no longer possible for him to refuse.
Provided then with permission, Constantine departed in greatest secrecy before the time fixed, and at the first stage lamed
the horses of the imperial post so that no one could pursue
him. From all of this we may probably accept so much — that
he seriously thought he was threatened. Galerius must have
hated him, as a rejected and yet ambitiously striving son of an
Emperor, but he *did* release him, though it is highly probable
that Constantine was deeply involved in court intrigues after
the persecution. In any case Constantius had the right to summon his son to himself.

After he joined his father, he participated in his father's victorious campaign against the Picts in Scotland. Chlorus was
by no means at the point of death, as Eusebius and Lactantius
say to make their account more moving, and had not summoned his son for that reason. But shortly after his return from
the war he did die (at York, 25 July 306). According to the

arrangements of Diocletian, to whom all concerned owed their positions, Galerius was now to nominate a new Augustus and to provide him with a new Caesar. But if the law of heredity were to be held a factor along with this imperial law, then the sons of Constantius by his marriage with Flavia Maximiana Theodora, the stepdaughter of the old Maximian — to wit, Dalmatius, Hannibalianus, and Julius Constantius — would have unquestioned precedence. They were all very young, however, the eldest being barely thirteen.

Instead, Constantine succeeded. It may be too much to spring to the defense of the wonderfully contrived Diocletianic ordinances for the succession; but by their strict letter Constantine was a usurper. He was born to Constantius of his concubine Helena at Nissa in Serbia in 274, and thus, strictly speaking, was ineligible even according to the laws of inheritance. The panegyrist Eumenius, to be sure, makes him out to be legitimate and thinks he would have willingly asked permission of the retired Emperors, but these are mere words. Aside from this, the panegyric in question is not without interest, because the sanctity of the right of inheritance is there defended with genuine warmth. With reference to his descent from the house of the great Claudius Gothicus, Constantine is thus addressed: "So exalted is the nobility of thy origin that the Empire can bestow no higher dignity upon thee. . . . It was no accidental agreement on the part of others, no sudden favor that made thee emperor; by thy birth didst thou merit rule, as a gift of the gods."

But the agreement and favor of others was not so trifling a matter for Constantine's accession to the throne. Whether his father directly empowered him to become his successor we cannot determine, because of the partisan nature of our sources. Perhaps the father summoned his thirty-two-year-old son, who was vigorous and experienced in war, only to protect his helpless family. Later authors, as for example Zonaras, have a convenient explanation: "Constantius Chlorus lay sick, and was troubled by the thought that his other children had turned out so badly. Thereupon an angel appeared to him and bade him leave the rule to Constantine."

Others, like Eusebius, Lactantius, and Orosius, do not take the trouble to find a motivation, but write as if Constantine's succession was altogether self-evident. The fact is that the soldiers of his father raised him to be Imperator Augustus. The principal voice was that of a chieftain of the Alemanni named Crocus (or Erocus) whom Constantius had recruited, together with his followers, for service in the war against the Picts. Hope for a rich donative was naturally a contributory motive. The panegyrist cited above provides a sentimental account of the transaction: "Upon your first riding forth the warriors cast the purple over you as you wept. . . . You wished to flee this demonstration of zealous devotion, and put spurs to your horse; but that, to speak plainly, was a youthful error. What steed could have proven fleet enough to withdraw you from the rule which pursued you?" To divine the details of the intrigue here enacted is futile.

When Galerius learned what had happened he did what he could; since Constantine could be disposed of only by a very dangerous internal war, he accorded him recognition, but only as second Caesar; he named Severus as Augustus, and Maximinus Daia as first Caesar. His true consecration as ruler Constantine procured in his campaigns against the Germans over a period of several years, which have been treated above. Gaul could be ruled at the time only by the man who was its defender and savior, and upon that field the father had left the son at least gleanings.

The immediate and inevitable consequence of Constantine's usurpation was the usurpation of Maxentius. What one Emperor's son had been permitted to do could hardly be denied to another's. Out of regard for Diocletian's prescriptions, Maxentius' father Maximian long opposed the usurpation, but he eventually proved unable to resist his own temptations and acceded to it. Although Maxentius was perhaps already known as profligate and vicious, he found natural allies in the ill will of the Romans, who had been deserted by the Emperors, and in the Praetorians, whose prestige had been so greatly reduced. It is also possible that Diocletian's last angry departure from Rome in 303 was somehow connected with the first beginnings of a plot of this character. Galerius had finally transgressed all limits by making the ancient world metropolis equally liable for his new imposts. Maxentius won over a few officers, a large contractor, and the Praetorians, who straightway proclaimed him Emperor. The city prefect, who was minded to oppose them, had already been put to death. It appears that all Italy quickly fell into the power of the usurper.

Now Galerius could no longer merely look on. He dispatched his colleague Severus (307), who as heir to the dominions of Maximian was presumably master of Italy. But Severus' army, consisting largely of Maximian's veterans, could not be used against Maxentius. There followed treason, retreat, and personal surrender in or near Ravenna; but this did not protect the lamentable Severus from a treacherous murder subsequently. Galerius marched to avenge his death, but his army proved no more reliable and he was compelled to turn back in haste.

In the meanwhile old Maximian, as has been stated, joined his son — if indeed Maxentius was born of him and the Syrian Eutropia and was not a changeling, as was maintained by certain pagans and Christians, whose evidence of the value which was again suddenly placed upon the law of inheritance must here be noticed. The relations between father and son, indeed, were so lacking in filial piety that such rumors must inevitably have arisen. Neither were the soldiers pleased with the old man, probably because they feared his discipline; at least he met with no response when he shortly thereafter sought to win them over against his son. They replied with defiant scorn, whereupon he is said to have declared that he was only testing their temper. Zonaras, who gives this account, even has him visit the Senate beforehand and there declare his son unfit for rule. In any event this is a remarkable decline from Diocletianic principles of rule, particularly so in view of Maximian's hostility to the senators (as mentioned in Chapter 2, above).

When the restless old man saw that his hopes for supreme rule were deceived, he proceeded to Gaul to endeavor to obtain of Constantine what he had failed to obtain of Maxentius.

He still had one pledge of rule with him, his younger daughter Fausta; her he married to Constantine, and in addition bestowed upon him the title of Augustus. It was his intention to wait until Maxentius was involved in war with Galerius, who was again ready for conflict, and then to intervene with superior force. But Constantine accepted the daughter and the title, and refused Maximian any further participation, whereupon nothing was left to Maximian but to return to Rome and procure some tolerable footing with his son.

We still possess a festive oration delivered on the occasion of the marriage. Perhaps no occasional orator has ever had a worse assignment than the unnamed Gallic rhetor who was to veil everything in silence and yet to declare everything; and we must acknowledge that he discharged his duty with talent and with tact. Of particular interest to us are the felicitations for the final establishment of a dynasty: "May the world dominion of Rome and the posterity of the Emperors alike be eternal and deathless!" Remarkably enough, the existence of Constantine's son Crispus by a previous marriage with Minervina was ignored, while the marriage itself was expressly mentioned and cited in praise of Constantine's high moral standards. In compensation the speaker praises Constantine's good fortune in acquiring Herculians, that is, sons of Fausta, for his house.

While Galerius was making his preparations against Italy, Maximian again fell to quarreling with Maxentius. Things came to a public scene in which the father sought to tear the purple robe from his son. Again he had to leave Rome.

In this general confusion Galerius resorted to the sagacity of the aged Diocletian, who upon his request (307) came to a meeting at Carnuntum (St. Petronell, not far from Haimburg). Lactantius has the senior Emperor go mad some years previously, but his colleagues appear not to have lost their faith in the energy of his mind when they met together on the Danube. Here, first of all, a tried old military comrade and friend of Galerius, the Illyrian Licinius, was named Augustus in place of the murdered Severus. Old Maximian also appeared but, instead of obtaining encouragement and help, was again persuaded to abdicate. Licinius was to be sole legal Emperor for the West. But Maximian could no longer endure rest or repose, and as soon as he was out of sight of his former colleagues and again with Constantine in Gaul, he could not resist the temptation to practice at the expense of his son-in-law what he had twice failed to do at the expense of his son. While Constantine was on a campaign against the Franks, Maximian assumed the purple for the third time, got possession of the treasury and the arsenal, and threw himself into the stronghold of Arelatum (Arles), whence he fled to Massilia when Constantine hastily turned in pursuit. Here, it appears, his men delivered him to his son-in-law, who is again said to have granted him life and liberty. But Maximian employed them only for new and dangerous intrigues, of which Constantine was informed by Fausta herself. There was nothing left but to remove the sinister old man from the world. He was permitted to choose the manner of his death, and chose to be strangled (310). At the beginning of the eleventh century his grave was discovered at Marseilles. The well-preserved body, richly embalmed and decked, was found in a lead coffin inserted in a marble sarcophagus. Archbishop Raimbald of Arles had the enemy of God and of Constantine with all his appurtenances thrown into the sea, which was said to seethe violently at that spot, night and day.

How these events must have embittered Diocletian's last years! Ambition, supported by the law of inheritance, had already overthrown half his system, and he was destined to experience the grief of seeing usurpation again raise its head outside the imperial families in the style of the third century, when an Aelianus and an Amandus, a Carausius and an Allectus, an Achilleus and a Julian, and their followers, paid for their presumptions to rule by streams of blood. A Governor of Africa, the Phrygian Alexander, whose homage had been foolishly solicited by Maxentius, suffered himself to be clothed with the purple by his soldiers half reluctantly (308). We cannot blame the aged gardener of Salonae, trying to fathom the future, for believing that he saw the most frightful calamities, the fall of the Empire itself, before his very eyes. Naturally, all of these civil wars were constantly reflected in the progress of the persecutions; the recurrences of frightful severity which took place from 308 to 313, in the intervals of relative calm, are intimately connected with questions of the succession. Of Maxentius, Eusebius tells us that he spared the Christians over a considerable period out of hostility to Galerius, and that he even posed as a Christian himself. Maximinus Daia was also alternately gentle or cruel to the Christians, according as he wished to defy or flatter Galerius.

Meanwhile the question of succession began to be simplified. Galerius died in 311, allegedly of a loathsome disease, at Sardica in Moesia. We shall allow Lactantius to revel in descriptions of the lower body, devoured by worms, to his heart's content, and affirm, in turn, that that prince, who was certainly savage and inhuman to Christians, was called by the pagans "a brave man and a mighty warrior." We must also remember to his credit that he possessed sufficient strength of character to forgo the throne for his own family in order to turn the imperial office to his friend Licinius, whom he regarded as the most worthy. Shortly before his death Galerius acknowledged the failure of the power of the state in its campaign against the Christians in a sullen edict of toleration, at the end of which he asks that those who had previously been persecuted intercede on his behalf before their God. His colleagues also subscribed to the edict; Constantine, Licinius, and even Maximinus Daia indirectly, in so far as a decree of his highest functionary could perform this office. The Christians returning home from prisons and mines were joyfully welcomed even by the pagan population, so weary had men grown of horrors. Details of regulations which followed the edict are no longer extant, and can only be surmised from a later ordinance. They appear to have been severe and to have been couched in the same surly tone as the edict itself.

A complication which threatened the succession was quite unexpectedly resolved, quickly and peacefully. Maximinus Daia, Galerius' former Caesar who had already assumed the title of Augustus on another occasion, thought he had grounds to fear that his Eastern realm would be curtailed by Licinius,

who had been designated Augustus of the West. Each marched
his army against the other, but they were reconciled at a conference aboard ship in the midst of the Hellespont (311), and
made it and the archipelago the boundary of their dominions,
so that Licinius retained the entire peninsula between that sea
and the Adriatic. What Diocletian thought of such a division
is not known.

At the same time Maxentius' generals subdued the revolt in
Africa. The usurper Alexander was defeated, overtaken in
flight, and strangled, and the unhappy province was chastised
with great severity. The city of Cirta suffered such drastic
punishment that it later had to be built anew under Constantine. When he celebrated his triumph in Rome, Maxentius
alluded to the enmity of ancient Carthage for Rome.

And now there were again two Western and two Eastern
rulers, Constantine and Maxentius, Licinius and Maximinus
Daia. But their relationship was far different from that of the
harmonious "tetrachord" which had once bound Diocletian to
his colleagues. No subordination and no mutual obligation was
recognized; each was Augustus on his own account, and measured the others with distrustful glance. Their dominions were
sharply delimited; none would venture to share the rule in the
realm of another, but neither would any come to the assistance
of another before he had exacted selfish terms in separate
treaties. The Empire lay divided in four portions, and Constantine, who had first broken the peace, now had the task of
instituting some new bond to replace the earlier.

We shall now follow the course of his life with reference
to the manner and means by which he fulfilled this task.

Among his three colleagues he sought out the most competent and at the same time the most legitimate, and allied
himself with him: Licinius was betrothed to Constantia, Constantine's sister. Thereupon war began against Maxentius (312).
Maxentius had meanwhile allied himself with Maximinus,
primarily against Licinius, from whom he designed to wrest
the Illyrian country. Constantine's overtures to him were in
vain; Maxentius rejected "the murderer of his father" and
armed himself against him. Which of the two was responsible

for the overt breach remains questionable. Eusebius claims this merit for Constantine, expressly praises him for it, and speaks of his great sympathy for poor and oppressed Rome: "He could no longer take pleasure in life if he should be compelled to see the sufferings of the metropolis continue." This is hardly a correct indication of Constantine's motive, but it is a correct indication of Eusebius' approach. Now Maxentius had assembled huge military forces, which did not betray him at the critical moment and would certainly have helped him to victory if he had not been so incompetent strategically and had not been sunk in cowardly indolence. Constantine's military strength, on the other hand, was comprised not in the heavenly legions under the leadership of the deceased Constantius Chlorus, with which writers of both religions honor him, nor yet in the sympathy of the Christians, perhaps not even in the despair of Italy, which had been trodden to earth, for the voice of the people is hardly to be heard in this conflict — but rather in the warlike energy of his some one hundred thousand men (Britons, Gauls, and barbarians) and in his own personality. If praise of this war did not derive from so suspicious a source we should perhaps find it as admirable as the Italian campaign of the youthful Napoleon, with which it has more than one battlefield in common. The storming of Susa, the battle at Turin where the enemy's heavy cavalry — men and horses alike armored — was struck down by iron clubs, the entry into Milan, the cavalry engagement at Brescia, all correspond to the opening of the campaign of 1796, and then we might balance Constantine's frightful battle for Verona with the forcing of Mantua. The enemy too is not unworthy of comparison with Napoleon's enemies. They fought with courage and perseverance and did not go over to Constantine's side, so that he was compelled, for example, to throw the entire captive garrison of Verona into chains to prevent them from making their way back to Maxentius. To put them to death was not in accord with the advanced ideas of humanity nor with the well-understood interests of the state, and their parole, it appears, was not to be relied upon; their swords therefore had to be forged into fetters. Verona yielded, how-

ever, only after another part of Constantine's army had taken
Aquileia and Modena by storm.

Thus a solid base was won for the conquest of all Italy.
Maxentius and his generals were taken by surprise. What they
might have achieved at slight cost by timely occupation of the
Alpine passes, even streams of blood could not compass at the
foot of the Alps and in the plain. Strategists may determine
whether Maxentius may not have had reasons for allowing the
enemy to advance almost to Rome. Our authors describe him
now as a cowardly stay-at-home and now as a superstitious
conjurer, and both descriptions may have elements of truth.
That the inhabitants of Rome hated the tyrant there can be
no doubt. In a dispute with his soldiers six thousand persons
were slain, and his dissolute life and his exactions could only
win him enemies. But all this was not a decisive factor. He
still had a large army on his side, and Rome itself was provided with enormous supplies for the event of a siege and had
been newly fortified with trenches, so that the enemy might
have been halted and perhaps suddenly enveloped. But if the
famous battle which began at Saxa Rubra nine miles from
Rome and ended at the Milvian Bridge was actually fought as
our authors say, there can be no question of strategic justification. Maxentius' army, to wit, was arranged in a long line, in
such a manner that it had the Tiber at its back. But this tor-
rential stream seems to have had no bridge other than the
Milvian and a bridge of boats near by. The first reverse must
prove irremediable. All who escaped the sword drowned. The
Praetorians resisted longest about the person of Maxentius,
who was their creature. But he too fled and sank in the river,
while the Praetorians suffered themselves to be cut down, as
Catiline's Troop had once done at Pistoia, on the spot where
they had stood at the beginning of the battle. Their destruction was of great advantage to the victor, for otherwise he
would still have had to reckon with them one day. Now it was
easy for him to destroy the Praetorian camp.

With this battle the entire West found its master; Africa
and the islands also fell to the conqueror. Between two il-
legitimate claimants, greater talent and determination, as

was fitting, decided the victory. Constantine, who had previously been known only through border wars, suddenly stood forth in the public eye with the radiance of a hero's glory. Now the problem was to base his new power, wherever possible, on foundations other than mere military strength.

If we listen only to the ceremonial orators, Constantine made it his first business, after removing the worst Maxentian abuses and persections, to pay honor to the Senate and raise its prestige by additions from the provinces. But it wants no special acuteness to perceive that after the events of the last three years there was no possibility of senatorial participation in rule. To please the Romans Constantine might well restore its external honors to that body, but he could hope for no substantial support from it, and he must therefore have remained indifferent to it. Indeed, he may already have cherished plans which would involve a cleavage between himself and the Senate. Nine years later a panegyrist who can call the Senate a blossom of the whole world and Rome the citadel of all peoples and queen of all lands, nevertheless allows the truth to appear between the lines: "This honored soul of the Roman people [i.e., the Senate], restored as it was of old, shows neither bold frowardness nor sorrowful humility. The constant admonition of the divine prince has brought it into such a path that, following his every gesture, it willingly heeds not his awefulness but his kindliness." In other words, the Senate, largely composed of pagans and with no influence upon the government, finds itself in an exposed position with regard to the Emperor. It still met regularly, and its sessions are even marked in the calendar—senatus legitimus, "lawful meeting of the Senate" — but with the exception of January these occur at most once a month.

In the meanwhile the Emperor had proclaimed himself protector of Christianity. The question of his personal beliefs may be disregarded for the moment; let us ask what political grounds might have moved a Roman Emperor to such a step. The Christians were still only a small minority, which did not require to be spared; how could toleration of them now seem a means of power to an ambitious man, or at least a profitable thing?

The puzzle is resolved if we assume that the majority of pagans whose opinion was to be considered disapproved of further persecution, that they looked with dissatisfaction upon the interruption of civic life and with anxiety upon the blood-thirstiness aroused in the mob, that in recent years ominous comparisons had been drawn between Gaul, which was not flourishing, to be sure, but nevertheless peaceful, and the disgraceful police methods of the east and south. Every terrorism falls lame when the mass of average persons has stilled its passion and itself begins to realize the untoward consequences. Fanatics who wish to perpetuate it are either destroyed by their own logic or are thrust aside. Even the persecuting Emperors had upon occasion allowed periods of toleration, either as a political device or only to annoy Galerius, and in his last terrible illness (311) Galerius himself had issued a very remarkable edict of toleration. With his two edicts of toleration at Rome and Milan (312 and 313) Constantine introduced nothing altogether new, nor did he use the question of toleration as a weapon against the other Emperors, but rather persuaded Licinius, who had in the meanwhile married into his family, to participate in the decrees at Milan (winter of 312–313), and both together negotiated with Maximinus Daia to join in the obligation and obtained his qualified consent. The toleration of the Christians would then be simply a matter of necessity, and require no further explanation. The edict of Milan which Licinius joined in signing went very far indeed. It granted unqualified freedom to all cults, including, in effect, the numerous Christian sects. As regards recognition by the state, Christianity was made fully equal to belief in the old gods; it received the character of a corporation, and recovered churches and other corporate property which had passed over to the imperial treasury or to private ownership.

But there was one occasion upon which the new master of the Occident indicated that his actual attitude to the Roman state religion was one of indifference. After the battle at the Milvian Bridge, in addition to other tokens of honor, Senate

s

and people awarded him a triumphal arch. The arch was put together hastily, in part out of handsome fragments from an arch of Trajan. Perhaps it was known that Constantine habitually referred to Trajan as "the weed on the walls" because of the many inscriptions which perpetuated his memory; all the less need for scruples, then, in using Trajan's stones. The inscription which is to be read on the arch states that Flavius Constantinus Maximus had prevailed over the tyrant and his entire party "by the impulse of the divine" (*instinctu divinitatis*); but underneath these words an earlier reading is to be distinguished, "by the nod of Jupiter Optimus Maximus" (*nutu I.O.M.*).° Probably the change was introduced for the occasion of the Emperor's first inspection of the inscription (which had been composed without his previous knowledge), that is, at his visit to Rome in 315, when his religious position had been more definitely determined. The original reading can only show that immediately after the victory nothing else was known than that the Emperor was a Roman pagan. The correction does not deny this, and even less does it represent the Emperor as a Christian; it only separates him from any direct profession of faith, and in any case leaves him free for monotheism. Some of the sculptures on the arch, as is well known, show pagan sacrifices, to Apollo, Diana, Mars, and Sylvanus, and also the combined sacrifices called *suovetaurilia.*

Not Eusebius alone, then, but the highest official quarters called Maxentius "tyrant," that is, according to contemporary usage, "unlawful ruler," "usurper." The term was equally applicable to Constantine, but men persuaded themselves that Maxentius was only a suppositious child and that his mother had admitted the fact. So soon as men can choose and are no longer compelled to content themselves with evil princes of the blood, they long for hereditary succession and yearn for a dynasty. Henceforth panegyric makes it a rule to speak of Constantine as the sole lawful ruler and of all others as tyrants.

In the face of such great ambition Diocletian's system of adoptions, which depended on so large a measure of renuncia-

° This "earlier reading" is in fact erroneous. — Translator.

tion, proved wrong. He procured his own death at this time (313), either through starvation or through poison. Constantine and the inexplicably blinded Licinius had intended to set a pitfall for him and had invited him to Constantia's marriage at Milan — which he would doubtless never have left a free man or a live one. He did not give them the satisfaction, but excused himself on the ground of his sixty-eight years. Thereupon they sent him threatening letters in which they charged that he sided with Maximinus Daia and had sided with Maxentius before his death. Diocletian was too weary of life or too convinced that his destiny had run out actually to throw himself into the arms of Daia, and he relished being strangled by the others as little. Although he died as a private citizen, the honor of apotheosis was granted him (probably by the Senate), for the last time in the ancient pagan sense. The decorative little temple in the palace at Salonae which previously passed for a sanctuary of Aesculapius is probably nothing other than the tomb of the great Emperor erected during his lifetime, and the sarcophagus bearing the reliefs of the Caledonian hunt which still lies near by once contained his corpse. But the Meleager who here confronts the boar is Diocletian himself at a decisive moment of his life (see above, page 41). Not everyone could see the sculpture; as late as a generation afterwards a purple pall covered the coffin.

What would the rulers of the period have been without him? At most, generals with more or less distant prospects for the imperial throne — and for assassination at the hands of soldiers or conspirators. Only through the constancy which he introduced into the imperial office, through the decisive period which he put to unbounded Caesarism, had it again become possible to speak of a right of succession and soon also of a hereditary right even if, in specific cases, such claims were of rather doubtful worth. Without Diocletian there could have been no Constantine, that is, no power strong enough to carry the Empire unshattered out of its old condition into the new and to remove the center of gravity of imperial power to new locations in accordance with the requirements of the new century.

The next victim bound to fall was Maximinus Daia. Debauched and uncommonly superstitious, he still possessed that bold decisiveness which is so essential an ornament to a ruler and which had probably moved Galerius to adopt him. Otherwise his reign, as appears from his conduct toward the Christians, seems to have been heartless and malicious; but he can hardly be judged from individual instances because, like Julian after him, he had in effect accepted priests and Magi as co-rulers. He had indeed yielded to the solicitations of the two other Emperors in the matter of participating in the measures of toleration, but obviously only under duress, so that the Christians, mindful of his earlier equivocations, were unwilling to venture into the light.

For years he had had a premonition that he would one day have to struggle for his existence, and for that reason he had once entered into secret alliance with the usurper Maxentius, as Licinius had done with the usurper Constantine. But Maxentius was of no help to him in his hour of peril, perhaps because he knew that Daia was beyond help; instead, he saved his strength for a new and sudden attack upon Licinius (313). With lightning speed he moved out of Syria through Asia Minor to Europe, and seized the stronghold of Byzantium as well as Heraclea, in the territory of his opponent. A battle with his surprised adversary took place between Heraclea and Adrianople. Contrary to the wishes of the two leaders, what was involved was patently a struggle between Christianity and paganism, for men knew that a victorious Maximinus would renew the persecution of Christians in the most frightful fashion. But it is very questionable whether the fighting armies were in any sense aware of this, although Lactantius has the Licinian army learn by heart a whole prayer which an angel is said to have communicated to the Emperor in a dream. Maximinus succumbed probably to the greater military skill or the warlike reputation of his opponent, to whom a portion of his own army went over. On his flight he mustered his forces again in Cappadocia and sought to bar the passes of the Taurus by fortifications, but he died, apparently of natural causes, at Tarsus in Cilicia. Licinius, who had already taken

Nicomedia and had there issued a new edict of toleration, now entered without further opposition into the inheritance of Asia and Egypt.

Constantine doubtless took great pleasure in the spectacle of the two legitimate rulers fighting among themselves and in their number being reduced by one. Licinius obliged him, moreover, by doing away with the families of Galerius, Severus, and Maximinus Daia, including their innocent children; even Prisca and Valeria, the widow and daughter of Diocletian, were later seized at Thessalonica and beheaded. Cruelties of this sort would have been rendered useless — nay, impossible — under the Diocletianic system. But as soon as men again began to think of a sort of hereditary right, such princes and princesses might become dangerous. The new master of the Orient found a natural solution in ordinary sultanism, which continues to murder until no possible pretender remains. As ruler, Licinius is said to have done meritorious service on behalf of the peasantry, from whom he himself derived, and also on behalf of the prosperity of the cities; if he speaks of literary education as a poison and plague to the state, he might rightly have wished, in that period of the Empire's need, that there were fewer orators (to wit, lawyers) and more industrious and vigorous hands. The most gruesome deed told of him — he is said to have had two thousand Antiochenes shot down in their circus because they mocked him — has been recognized by modern criticism as a fable; but he never hesitated at deeds of blood that might be useful, and among these may be reckoned the executions of wealthy men of which we hear. Besides their property, their women too are said to have fallen into the hands of the elderly libertine.

Meanwhile it was recalled from the age of Diocletian that designated successors or Caesars might still contribute to the security of the throne. Constantine made the first venture, and designated a certain Bassianus, who had one of his sisters, Anastasia, to wife. But his brother Senecio, a relative of Licinius, incited Bassianus against Constantine himself. Constantine found it necessary to put his own brother-in-law out of the way, and to demand of Licinius, his other brother-in-law, the surrender of Senecio. Licinius boldly denied the request; indeed, in one of the western border cities in the Licinian domain, at Aemona (Ljubljana), the statues of Constantine had already been pulled down. Upon these events, which presume some irreconcilable family intrigue, there blazed out a mighty war, in which Constantine must have been the aggressor. At least he marched into the realm of his brother-in-law, defeated him (8 October 314) at Cibalis on the Sava (modern Sevlievo), and pursued him to Thrace, where a second, apparently less decisive battle took place on the Mardian plain. Licinius for his own part had nominated a border commander named Valens to be Caesar. The first condition of the peace now negotiated was Valens' retirement to a private station, so that no third dynasty should arise. Besides, Licinius was forced to cede all his European holdings, that is the land south of the Danube, together with all Greece except Thrace and the coast of the Pontus.

Thus far had the legitimate Emperor been brought by his earlier alliance with the usurper who was so far his superior in spirit, and against whom, after the death of Galerius, all of the others would have had to unite if they hoped to maintain themselves. The less certain a power is of the legitimacy of its origin, the more inevitably is it forced to do away with everything legitimate in its orbit. To destroy Licinius utterly still appeared too difficult, but Constantine now clearly had the upper hand. As far as appearances went, complete equality subsisted between the two rulers. After some time (317), both nominated their sons as Caesars, Constantine naming Crispus and the younger Constantine, and Licinius naming Licinianus. But a glance at the ages of these Caesars betrays the unequal position of the Emperors; Crispus was a vigorous youth, soon to be able to command an army, whereas Licinianus was an infant of twenty months, and furthermore the only son of an elderly father, at whose death he would surely be helpless and easy to dispose of. It was for that reason that the legitimate Emperor, in keeping with the Diocletianic system, was eager to adopt comrades-in-arms, such as Valens and later Martinian, as Caesars; but Constantine would not allow it. Himself he permitted a second nomination; in addition to Crispus, his elder son by his first marriage, he placed in reserve his very young son by Fausta, who was his namesake.

Then Constantine waited patiently until 323 before he incorporated the domain of Licinius under his rule. He allowed the fruit to ripen until it fell into his hands virtually of its own accord.

These were the decisive years during which Constantine attentively observed how Christianity might contribute and be useful to a clever ruler. When he became convinced by the significant growth of the community, by the clearly developed character of its hierarchy, by the peculiar form of its synodic organization, and by the entire character of contemporary Christianity that a support for the throne might be contrived out of this enormous power — and that he must assure himself of it betimes because this power had already begun to assure itself of the Emperor — he realized that he had found an infallible lever against Licinius. Licinius during this same period had been so foolish as to divert his righteous anger against Constantine to the Christians (after 319), as if they were to blame for his opponent's ruthless lust for power. If he had still possessed or wished to use the means for a renewal of the persecution, he would at least have made an ally of terrorism, and the conflict of principles would then have had to be fought out on a grand scale. But he limited himself to dismissing Christians from his court, and to petty vexations, which then in any case grew to a sort of half-persecution by reason of the refractoriness of the greatly augmented numbers of Christians. Christians of every rank, from bishops down to the lowliest, now formed a natural propaganda against Licinius and in favor of Constantine, who furthered the tendency by patent provocations. The incomparably greater favor which he had always shown Christians in his domains must have embittered the Christians of the Licinian realm. Every synod, every meeting of bishops, was now grown actually dangerous, and Licinius forbade them. Every service was suspect as a gathering of subversives, and Licinius caused men and women to assemble separately, and then banished the entire cult from the cities to the open fields, on the ground that the open air was more salubrious than that of the prayer-houses. The clergy sought to influence the men through the women, and Licinius ordered that women should henceforth receive religious instruction only from women teachers. He degraded Christian officers; certain apparently especially suspicious bishops were put to death, certain churches were pulled down or closed. "He did not know," Eusebius sighs, "that prayers used to be offered for him in these churches. He believed that we prayed only for Constantine." Licinius indeed issued no general order which might have contravened the edict of toleration of his earlier period, and Arians like Bishop Eusebius of Nicomedia could remain in his favor and on his side to the end, but he did go as far as confiscations, exile to desolate islands, condemnation to the mines, deprivation of various civic privileges, sales into slavery, and all this in the case of highly respected and highly educated persons. The prince who was once tolerant, who once found it advantageous to keep his subjects in some doubt about his personal faith, finally turned altogether pagan and surrounded himself with Egyptian magicians, thaumaturgists, and sacrificers. He consulted interpreters of dreams and oracles, among others the Milesian Apollo, who replied in two threatening hexameters. Finally Eusebius represents him as assembling his most faithful friends and bodyguards in a sacred grove studded with statues of the gods. After solemn sacrifice he delivered a discourse of which the substance in brief was that the struggle which impended would constitute a decision between the old gods and the new alien God.

What could have moved Licinius to these desperate and foolish steps? The simplest reflection must have suggested that he vie with Constantine in favoring the Christians. Apparently his patience and his reason were exhausted when he became aware of his opponent's fearful malignancy, and he cursed his earlier yielding to the Christians who were represented by such a merciless leader. An attack upon Constantine's dominions was as much out of the question as it had been in 314. Eusebius thinks that he is again doing his hero great honor by having him take up arms purely out of sympathy for the unhappy subjects of

Licinius, that is, without Licinius having given him the slightest political occasion.

Of a sudden, Goths swarmed across the Danube into the territory of Licinius. Without being asked, Constantine marched against them, thrust them back, and forced them to give up the captives they had carried off. But Licinius complained of this intervention in his own domain — so far the notice of a monosyllabic and late but nevertheless important excerptor, the so-called Anonymus Valesianus. In this connection we must notice what Jornandes, the well-known historian of the Goths, has to say: "It often happened that the Goths were invited (by the Roman Emperors), as they were summoned by Constantine to immigration and bore arms against his brother-in-law Licinius, and when he was shut up in Thessalonica and robbed of his realm, murdered him with the sword of the conqueror." Anyone who has observed Constantine attentively knows or surmises how these bits are to be fitted together. At least the alleged invasion of the Goths was one of the immediate harbingers of war.

We pass over the individual events of this last struggle for world dominion, this second war of Actium. With Thessalonica and the other harbors of Greece, Constantine acquired, after 314, significant additions to his sea power and assembled two hundred warships; Licinius, who controlled the shores of the East, had three hundred and fifty. The same scale obtained in other arms of service, so that Constantine had one hundred and thirty thousand men altogether, and Licinius one hundred and sixty-five thousand. Such enormous forces had never been put into the field for a civil war since the time of Septimius Severus. But Constantine had a great advantage in the fact that the men of the Illyrian provinces were under his standards. At Adrianople, where Constantine won the first victory, thirty-four thousand men fell. Then his fleet under Crispus defeated Licinius' under Abantus (Amandus) not far from the entrance to the Hellespont, and a storm then destroyed Licinius' fleet utterly. Licinius could no longer remain in Europe and crossed over from Byzantium to Chalcedon, where he named Martinianus, one of his court officials, Caesar. At the beginning of the campaign this step might have had decisive value. By timely adoptions in the Diocletianic pattern, disregarding the protests of the usurper, the legitimate Emperor might have secured the three or four most reliable generals of his realm for his cause. But now, in the midst of discouragement and treason, it was too late.

After a pause the struggle was renewed. Martinianus, who was stationed at Lampsacus to prevent a landing of the enemy at the Hellespont, was hastily recalled by Licinius to the principal army at the Bosporus, where Constantine had succeeded in effecting a crossing. Finally a great and decisive land battle took place at Chrysopolis near Chalcedon, from which barely thirty thousand of Licinius' one hundred and thirty thousand soldiers (Goths among them) are said to have survived. The unhappy Emperor himself fled to Nicomedia, where he was promptly besieged, while Byzantium and Chalcedon opened their gates to the victor. Constantia, wife of Licinius and sister of Constantine, who came to the camp to negotiate, received assurances under oath that her husband's life would be spared. Thereupon the old comrade-in-arms of a Probus and a Diocletian strode forth out of the city, bent his knee to the conqueror, and laid his purple aside. He was sent to Thessalonica, and Martinian to Cappadocia. But in the following year (324) Constantine found it more expedient to put them to death; "he was instructed by the example of his father-in-law Maximianus Herculius and feared that Licinius might resume the purple to the discomfiture of the Empire." With this motive of undeniable expediency posterity should be content in the case of a character like Constantine's, but instead a fable was later spun of a military conspiracy in Thessalonica in favor of the deposed King — of which Eusebius would certainly have had something to say if it were true. But in his magisterial way he passes over Constantine's perjury and all the other circumstances with the bald remark that the enemy of God and his evil counselors were condemned and punished according to military law. So much is certain, that the old Emperor was throttled and the Caesar cut down by bodyguards. Of the equally dismal fate of Licinianus we shall speak shortly.

Eusebius idealizes this war as the purest contest of principles. Licinius is the enemy of God and wars against God. Constantine, on the other hand, wages war under the most direct divine protection, which takes on visible form in the *semeion*, the familiar ornamental fetish which was carried into battle. There is no lack of heavenly apparitions and of hosts of spirits, which move through Licinius' cities and perform other wonders. Eusebius is no fanatic; he understands Constantine's secular spirit and his cold and terrible lust for power well enough and doubtless knows the true causes of the war quite precisely. But he is the first thoroughly dishonest historian of antiquity. His tactic, which enjoyed a brilliant success in his own day and throughout the Middle Ages, consisted in making the first great protector of the Church at all costs an ideal of humanity according to his lights, and above all an ideal for future rulers. Hence we have lost the picture of a genius in stature who knew no moral scruple in politics and regarded the religious question exclusively from the point of view of political expediency. We shall see that he found it advisable to attach himself more closely to the Christians after this war, and that the elevation of Christianity to the position of state religion was thus consummated. But Constantine was a more honorable man than Eusebius; he rather allowed these events to transpire than intervened actively on their behalf, and as regards his own personal conviction, he enjoined definite beliefs upon his subjects as little as did Napoleon in his concordat.

To pass for a Christian would, indeed, have been a great presumption on his part. Not long after the Council of Nicaea he suddenly had Crispus, his excellent son by his first marriage and a pupil of Lactantius, put to death at Pola in Istria (326), and soon thereafter he had his wife Fausta, daughter of Maximian, drowned in her bath. The eleven-year-old Licinianus was also murdered, apparently at the same time as Crispus. Whether Fausta played Phaedra to her stepson, or by what device she maligned him to his father, or whether she was merely concerned for the elevation of her own sons, or whether it were the representations of the aged Helena who bewailed her grandson, that moved Constantine to murder his wife — all these questions may be mooted. But that the horror was not merely a family affair but possessed political implications can be deduced from the fact that Licinianus was included among the victims. In connection with this tale mention is often made of Philip II and of Peter the Great; but the true parallel is offered by Suleiman the Magnificent and his noble son Mustafa, who succumbed to the plots of Roxalana. With hereditary rule it was inevitable that sultanism should enter in as its complement, that is, that rulers should never for an instant feel safe in the midst of brothers, sons, uncles, nephews, and cousins who might one day be in line of succession, unless they were at any moment ready to resort to convenient throttlings and the like. Here Constantine took the lead; we shall see how his sons followed.

These sons, Constantine II, Constantius II, and Constans had meanwhile been advanced to the dignity of Caesar. The breed of the Herculians was multiplying claimants for the throne after the father had done away with the mother, the maternal grandfather, the uncle Maxentius, and the stepbrother. The seed of so abundant a curse was destined to grow rank.

For the moment we pass over the elevation of Byzantium to be Constantine's city and the capital of the world. Logically, Constantine required a residence and a populace that should be without previous commitments, that should owe everything to him and depend upon him for everything, and that should serve as center and instrument for so much that was new in state and society. Without these definite requirements he might have remained quietly in Nicomedia. The removal is the most conscious and purposeful act of his entire reign.

It is incomparably more difficult to explain Constantine's last great political decision, namely, his division of the Empire.

Of Constantine's brothers, Dalmatius had two sons, Dalmatius and Hannibalian, and Julius Constantius also had two, then still in their infancy, Gallus and Julian, whom posterity later called the Apostate. Of these four nephews Constantine, two years before his death, elevated Dalmatius, who had already held the consulship (333), to be Caesar (335). Previously Constantine had conferred distinction upon Dalmatius' father, the elder Dalmatius, and had relegated him, under the ambiguous

title of censor, to the important and perhaps dangerous post of
Antioch (332), as a generation later Constantius was to station
Gallus in the same post, to watch as well as pacify the old and
supplanted capital of the East. Later the elder Dalmatius was
even entrusted with a kind of kingship over Cappadocia. The
occasion for his like-named son being made Caesar in the same
year may have been the successful suppression of an insurrection
on Cyprus, where Calocerus, superintendent of the imperial
dromedaries, came forward as usurper. The younger Dalmatius
laid hands upon him and had him burned alive at Tarsus "as
a slave and thief."

Soon afterwards, still in 335 and so two years before Constantine's death, there followed a regular division of the Empire,
by which Constantine II received the lands of his grandfather
Chlorus, namely, Britain and Gaul together with Spain; Constantius II received Asia, Syria, and Egypt; and Constans Italy
and Africa. On the other hand the entire land mass between the
Black, Aegean, and Adriatic Seas, that is, Thrace, Macedonia,
Illyricum, and Achaia (with Greece), fell to Constantine's
nephew Dalmatius. Even Dalmatius' brother Hannibalian, who
is otherwise known for no special achievement or merit, received rule — we do not know whether unqualified or under
the authority of Constantius II — over Roman Armenia, Pontus,
and the surrounding territory, and was married, then or previously, to Constantia, daughter of Constantine and sister of his
co-heirs. This testament of empire was doubtless public and
generally known. But its contents are correctly given only in
the second Aurelius Victor, while other writers distort it or, like
Eusebius, have good reason to pass over it in silence.

The first question which cries out for answer is this: Why
did Constantine divide the Empire at all, after hundreds of
thousands had shed their blood for its unification? Next, it is
a matter for astonishment that the central area, including the
new capital, was given to his nephew and not to his sons. The
answer probably lies in the character of the sons. Eusebius has
a moving chapter on their education in the fear of God and in
all the virtues of rulers, of which we shall speak again presently.
Actually they were an abandoned lot, with neither scruple nor

faith. If their father named one of them sole heir, then as soon as his eyes were shut the murder of the other brothers and kinsmen would inevitably follow; and what would happen to the Empire if there were suddenly no more Herculians or Constantinians? Constantine was compelled to divide, in order to preserve the dynasty. Without doubt he foresaw the imperial wars of his sons, but he could still hope that out of three to five princely houses one heir of his race would survive, if only they would have time to multiply by begetting new princes. It was not for nothing that he dispersed his sons to their assigned provinces far and wide while he was still alive.

His bestowing the entire Illyrian-Greek peninsula together with Constantinople upon his nephew is perhaps to be explained by the fact that this pearl of the Empire must inevitably become the object of intense jealousy if it were placed in the hands of one of the three sons — as indeed happened in the sequel. It may be objected that Dalmatius was now thrust into a very difficult and dangerous position. But resources for defense were proportionate to the danger. Whoever held the Illyrian country with its generals and soldiers could defy all the rest of the Empire.

The endowment of Hannibalian, finally, seems to be a simple consequence of that of his brother. We cannot judge his special assignment at the northern border of Asia Minor more precisely.

This attempted explanation and motivation of the darkest point in Constantine's history may well not find acceptance, because it assumes such unnatural enmities in the imperial house. But I believe that I have not gone beyond probabilities.

Perhaps the only decent relationship in the circle of this great Constantine, "who persecuted what was nearest him and slew first his son and nephew, then his wife, then a crowd of friends," was that with his mother Helena. Whatever her position with reference to Chlorus may have been, in the Oriental view she was sufficiently legitimized by having given birth to the ruler. He is said to have been accessible to her counsel always. Purposely clothed with official honors, she spent her last years in charitable works, pious pilgrimages, and Church foundations. She died at an age past eighty, apparently not long before her son. Drepanum in Bithyniá was named Helenopolis for her.

Constantine himself was smitten by a fatal illness while making preparations for a defensive war against Shapur II of Persia. It was now that he had himself enrolled among the catechumens of the martyr-church of Helenopolis, and then taken to the Villa Achyrona near Nicomedia, where he received baptism and died on the last day of the Whitsun holiday, 337.

About his corpse, which the soldiers brought to Constantinople and laid out in a hall of the palace with great ceremony, the most curious events took place, and continued on into the year following.

The story begins with violent wailing on the part of the soldiers. Privates tore their garments and wept, officers lamented that they had been orphaned. This sorrow was surely deep and genuine, especially among the Germans of the bodyguard, who regarded their relationship to the Emperor as one of personal loyalty. The deceased had been a great general and had cared for his soldiers like a father: what else mattered to them? But these grieving soldiers were also, in the absence of the heirs, the authorities responsible for immediate arrangements; for example, it was they who determined that the burial of the Emperor must await the arrival of one of his sons. "In the meanwhile the officers (and in especial the taxiarchs or tribunes) dispatched trustworthy and devoted men out of the number to the Caesars with the sorrowful news. And as if by inspiration from above all the army was of a single mind, namely, to recognize none other than his sons as heirs. Thereupon they considered it right that these should no longer be called Caesars but Augusti. The armies sent one another their opinions in writing, and everywhere the harmony of the armies was made known at the same time." That is all Eusebius finds it necessary to say.

But where was Dalmatius? It was in his portion of the Empire and in his capital that the corpse lay and the soldiers ruled; why is he not even named when the soldiers deny him the Empire? Instead, Constantius hastens to the city and then leads the solemn military cortege from the palace to the Church of the Apostles. Had Constantine credited his nephew with greater determination than he actually possessed? Or were the intrigues set on foot against him too powerful? We do not know. Perhaps he was arrested straightway, perhaps he was cajoled for some time with a shadow of participation in government. But after a few months the coup was struck (338), from which certain authors vainly seek to absolve Constantius on the grounds that he rather condoned than commanded it. The soldiers or other assassins first disposed of Julius Constantius, brother of the great Constantine; his children Gallus and Julian were spared, the former because he was dangerously sick, the latter because of his extreme youth. Next, Dalmatius and Patricius Optatus were murdered, then Ablavius, formerly an all-powerful Prefect of the Guard, and finally Hannibalian also. It is a mere quibble to assert that the soldiers would recognize none other than the sons; to be sure, direct inheritance would be most comprehensible to them, especially to the Germans, but they would never have gone to such extremes without considerable instigation. For the credulous a story was contrived that the great Constantine was actually poisoned by the agency of his brothers but had become aware of the misdeed and in his last will called upon that one of his sons who should first appear on the scene to exact vengeance. Nothing simpler could be imagined.

To deal with the further destiny and the divisions of the supreme imperial power in greater detail lies outside our present purview. Constantine had strengthened that power greatly by his new organization of state and Church, and his sons could therefore use great license until they had entirely consumed the capital which they inherited, just as the sons of Louis the Pious, of whose history so much here is reminiscent, could carry on their fraternal wars for more than a generation until Charlemagne's shadow had quite lost its magic. The occasion for the first quarrel was naturally the legacy of Dalmatius, and particularly the possession of Thrace and Constantinople. The questions of compensation connected with the disposition of that legacy, specifically Constans' demand for a share in the rule of Africa and Italy, then led to war (340), in which Constantine II perished without leaving a dynasty. The victorious Constans would now have had to share with Constantius, if the latter were not detained in the East by his Persian war. But this was also evident to Constans' retinue, mostly hireling Germans, among whom because of his misdeeds he felt more secure than among Romans. In the presumption that the Emperor of the East could not lift a sword for intervention in the West and in Africa, whatever happened, the Frank Magnentius, at the time commander of the Jovians and Herculians, ventured to appear suddenly at a banquet in Autun clad in imperial purple (350). Constans was to be seized while hunting, but received word in time. Nevertheless he found himself suddenly deserted by soldiers and populace, so that nothing was left him but flight. Assassins, the Frank Gaiso at their head, overtook him in the Pyrenees.

While the entire West was now falling into the hands of Magnentius, the garrisons on the Danube thought they had the same right of usurpation, and elevated Vetranio, an old general. To give the story its element of comedy, a nephew of the great Constantine by his sister Eutropia, Nepotianus by name, proclaimed himself Emperor in Rome; but this unhappy collateral prince, who wished to re-enact the role of Maxentius, no longer had a Praetorian camp on his side, as Maxentius had had, but only the gladiators' barracks at Rome, and so the army dispatched by Magnentius disposed of him easily. But about Constantius, men had been wrong; he interrupted the Persian War and bent every effort toward suppressing opposition within the Empire. There is a remarkable report in Zosimus, according to which Constantius was able to inspire his soldiers for the dynasty as such, so that they shouted out that the false Emperors must be erased from the earth. In any event, Constantius showed skill and determination at this period. After he had held Vetranio off for some time, he subdued him with great presence of mind in the sight of his own army. Then he overcame Magnentius in a war which is among the most frightful in these internal struggles for the Empire. In consequence of this war a despicable horde of spies and informers was let loose over the entire West to persecute the adherents of the usurper.

T

But despite all his success, the victor must have been inwardly tormented by the most disconsolate reflections concerning the future of the Empire. While the army would no longer have any "false" ruler, Constantius suspected his genuine kinsmen, as many as he had not yet put out of the way, or hated them with a deadly hatred. His marriage with Eusebia was barren, and so in the end the son of Constantine the Great, in consequence of the unbounded sultanism of two generations, had arrived at the point from which Diocletian had departed — he was forced to resort to adoption. He had a sister worthy of himself, Constantia (or Constantina), widow of the murdered Hannibalian, who had subsequently allowed herself to be used to win Vetranio's confidence by giving him her hand. Then when it was a question of destroying the last surviving branch of the family, the sons of Julius Constantius, who was murdered in 338, Constantia married Gallus, the elder of these sons, and although she died before he was murdered we need have no doubt that she was somehow responsible for his destruction immediately thereafter. Now only Julian, Gallus' younger brother, survived, and when the Empire looked to him with respect as the savior of Gaul and victor over the Germans, his shameful cousin left him no choice but death or usurpation of the imperial throne. But Constantius died as the civil war was on the point of breaking out, whereupon Julian was generally recognized. With his memorable two-year reign the line of Constantine comes to an end, for Julian's marriage was childless.

The next successions, those of Jovian and Valentinian, were the concern of the armies, as most of those in the third century had been. But the principle of heredity had impressed the minds of men so strongly that it was henceforward reverted to and maintained at all costs. There followed the Valentinian dynasty and the Theodosian, which was related to it by marriage, both free at least of sultanic family murders. From the middle of the fourth to the middle of the fifth century the possession of the throne was indeed many times contested by pretenders and pressure of all sorts, but never for a moment was the succession doubtful from the point of view of law. The conviction of the generals, who were mostly German, and the view of the

Christians, based on the Old Testament, combined to give the right of heredity this late triumph. It retained its value throughout the Byzantine period, and despite interruptions due to sultanism and praetorianism, ever and again produced new and sometimes enduring dynasties.

IX

CONSTANTINE AND THE CHURCH

Attempts have often been made to penetrate into the religious consciousness of Constantine and to construct a hypothetical picture of changes in his religious convictions. Such efforts are futile. In a genius driven without surcease by ambition and lust for power there can be no question of Christianity and paganism, of conscious religiosity or irreligiosity; such a man is essentially unreligious, even if he pictures himself standing in the midst of a churchly community. Holiness he understands only as a reminiscence or as a superstitious vagary. Moments of inward reflection, which for a religious man are in the nature of worship, he consumes in a different sort of fire. World-embracing plans and mighty dreams lead him by an easy road to the streams of blood of slaughtered armies. He thinks that he will be at peace when he has achieved this or the other goal, whatever it may be that is wanting to make his possessions complete. But in the meantime all of his energies, spiritual as well as physical, are devoted to the great goal of dominion, and if he ever pauses to think of his convictions, he finds they are pure fatalism. In the present instance men find it hard to believe that an important theologian, a scholar weak in criticism, to be sure, but of great industry, a contemporary as close as was Eusebius of Caesarea, should through four books repeat one and the same untruth a hundred times. Men argue from Constantine's zealous Christian edicts, even from an address of the Emperor "to the assembly of the saints," an expression impossible on the lips of a non-Christian. But this address, it may be remarked in passing, was neither composed by Constantine nor ever delivered; and in writing the edicts Constantine often gave the priests a free hand. And Eusebius, though all historians have followed him, has been proven guilty of so many distortions, dissimulations, and inventions that he has forfeited all claim to figure as a decisive source. It is a melancholy but very understandable fact that none of the other spokesmen of the Church, as far as we know, revealed Constantine's true position, that they uttered no word of displeasure against the murderous egoist who possessed the great merit of having conceived of Christianity as a world power and of having acted accordingly. We can easily imagine the joy of the Christians in having finally obtained a firm guarantee against persecution, but we are not obliged to share that elation after a millennium and a half.

Tolerant monotheism Constantine appears to have derived as a memory from the house of Chlorus, who was devoted to it. The first definite notice of a religious act on the part of Constantine is his visit to the temple of Apollo at Autun (308) before his renewed attack upon the Franks. He appears to have consulted the oracle and to have made rich offerings. But this worship of Apollo does not necessarily contravene the monotheism of his parental home, for Chlorus conceived of the highest being as a sun-god. Constantine's nephew Julian speaks of Constantine's connection with a special cult of Helios. From a familiar obverse on coins of Constantine, representing the sun-god with the inscription SOLI. INVICTO. COMITI, we deduce that the personification of the sun as Mithras is here implied. Anyone who has dealt with ancient coins knows that out of five Constantinian pieces probably four will bear this obverse, so that there is high probability that this device was retained until the Emperor's death. Other devices which are frequent are Victories, the Genius Populi Romani, Mars and Jupiter with various epithets, and a number of female personifications. But the coins with unequivocal Christian emblems which he is said to have struck are yet to be found. In the period during which he ruled with Licinius the figure of the sun-god appears with the inscription

COMITI. AVGG. NN., that is, "To the comrade of our two Augusti";
and many coins of Crispus and of Licinius himself bear the
same obverse. On inscriptions and coins Constantine continually calls himself Pontifex Maximus, and has himself represented as such with head veiled. In the laws of 319 and 321 he
still recognizes the pagan cult as existing as of right; he forbids
only occult and dangerous practices of magicians and of haruspices, but he admits conjurers of rain and hail, and on the occasion of public buildings being struck by lightning he expressly
requests the responses of the haruspices. Zosimus, if we may
credit that fifth-century pagan, confirms Constantine's consultation of pagan priests and sacrificers in even larger scope, and
has them continue to the murder of Crispus (326), which, in
his view, is the correct period of Constantine's supposed conversion.

Opposed to all this is the fact that after the war with Maxentius (312) Constantine not only permitted the toleration of Christianity as a lawful religion, but spread abroad in the army an
emblem which every man could interpret as he pleased but
which the Christians would refer to themselves. The interlocked
letters X and P, which form the beginning of the word Christ
($XPI\Sigma TO\Sigma$), were introduced on the shields of the soldiers,
we are told, even before the war. At the same time or later the
same emblem, surrounded by gold and jewels, was attached to
a large battle standard, whereupon the sign received a special
and remarkable cult and the soldiers were inspired with the
greatest assurance of victory. Soon similar standards (*labarum,
semeion*) were prepared for all armies, and a special guard was
entrusted with the preservation of the emblem on the field of
battle. The emblem even had its own tent, into which the Emperor mysteriously retired before any important affair. Should
not all this signify an open profession?

First of all it is to be noticed that Constantine employed
this sign not among the populace but in the army. The army
knew him as a mighty and successful general from the time of
the Frankish wars; it had descended to him largely from his
father; and it was ready to accept any symbols or emblems he
chose. Among the Gauls and Britons in the army there were

certainly many Christians and indifferent pagans, and to the Germans the religion of their leader was a matter of no consequence. On his part it was an experiment that obliged him to nothing more than toleration, which was already in fact the rule in his previous domains and which he now extended to his conquests also. For him Christ may have rated as a god along with other gods, and the professors of Christ's religion along with the servants of the pagan deities. We shall not deny the possibility that Constantine developed a kind of superstition in favor of Christ, and that he may even have brought that name into some kind of confused relationship with the sun-god. But without doubt he was concerned exclusively with success; if he had met with a powerful resistance against *XP* in Italy, the symbol would quickly have disappeared from shields and standards. Instead, he could now apparently be fully convinced that the great mass of pagans was displeased with the persecution and that he incurred no danger in setting up his statue, *labarum* in hand, in the midst of Rome and inscribing underneath it that this saving sign was the true proof of all courage. If he had wished to make a proper profession of Christianity, surely a very different sort of declaration would have been in place. A glance at the year 312 would make everything clear if we were better informed concerning general conditions. Nothing is more difficult to prove, and yet nothing is more probable, than that the temper of the pagans was more yielding and milder at the critical moment at the end of the persecution than either before or after. They did not know, or they forgot, that Christianity, once tolerated, must inevitably become the predominant religion.

Neither, perhaps, did Constantine know it, but he allowed it to come about, and he kept his eyes open. As soon as his lucid, empiric logic informed him that the Christians were good subjects, that they were numerous, and that the persecution could no longer have meaning in a reasonably governed state, his decision was taken. From the political point of view, the practical execution of his decision is wholly admirable. In his victorious hands the *labarum* was a physical representation at once of rule, of warlike power, and of the new religion. The *esprit de corps* of his army, which had been victorious over one of the greatest armies of ancient history, hallowed the new symbol with the aura of the irresistible.

But the familiar miracle which Eusebius and those who copy him represent as taking place on the march against Maxentius must finally be eliminated from the pages of history. It has not even the value of a myth, indeed is not of popular origin, but was told to Eusebius by Constantine long afterwards, and by Eusebius written up with intentionally vague bombast. The Emperor indeed swore a great oath to the bishop that the thing was not imagined, but that he actually saw in heaven the cross with the inscription "In this sign thou shalt conquer," and that Christ actually appeared to him in a dream, and the rest; but history cannot take an oath of Constantine the Great too seriously, because, among other things, he had his brother-in-law murdered despite assurances given under oath. Nor is Eusebius beyond having himself invented two-thirds of the story.

A great inconsistency in Constantine's outward bearing persists; he accepts the monogram of Christ as the emblem of his army and has the name of Jupiter on his triumphal arch erased, but at the same time he retains the old gods on his coins, and especially the sun-god as his unconquerable companion, and on important occasions his outward conduct is entirely pagan. This cleavage rather increases than decreases in his latter years. But he wished to give direct guarantees to both religions, and he was powerful enough to maintain a twofold position.

His edicts of toleration, of which the second, issued at Milan (313) in common with Licinius, is extant, confer nothing more than freedom of conscience and of religion; the latter granted freedom of worship without limitation and qualification. The notion of a state religion was thus abolished, until Christianity clothed itself with the shell which paganism had discarded. One regulation soon followed upon the heels of another, especially when Maximinus Daia in hostility to Licinius and then Licinius himself in hostility to Constantine provoked the enmity of Christendom. The places of assembly and other landed property of the Christian communities which had been confiscated during the persecution were restored; the Christians were openly favored and their proselytization actively supported. A moment of anxiety because of the displeasure of the pagans is revealed in the laws of 319, cited above, in which the private practice of haruspices and home sacrifices are strictly forbidden, apparently because the secret consultation of haruspices and sacrificial feasts behind closed doors might be subversive politically. With the edict to the provincials of Palestine and with that to the peoples of the East after the last victory over Licinius (324), there follows an apparently quite unqualified personal devotion of the Emperor to Christianity, whose professors are freed of the consequences of the persecution with all possible indulgence, and are restored to their former position and property. These official decrees show a specifically polemic tone against polytheism; they speak of sanctuaries of falsehood, of darkness, and of miserable error which must still be suffered, and the like. But it is not Constantine's pen that wrote these things, though Eusebius maintains that he saw the autograph. The draftsman betrays himself at least in the second document, in which he has the Emperor say that he was "only a boy" at the beginning of the persecution, whereas in fact Constantine was almost thirty in 303. But indirectly the content is substantially the work of the Emperor, who, as is noticeable upon closer examination, does not once represent himself as a Christian. What personal tones are perceptible are those of the dreary deism of a conquerer who requires a god in order to justify his acts of violence by an appeal to something outside himself. "I, proceeding from the Britannic Sea and from the regions prescribed for the setting of the sun, dispersing and destroying through a higher power the evil which everywhere prevails, so that the race of men raised by my assistance might be recalled to the service of the loftiest law . . . I have arrived in the regions of the East which summoned me for help greater in the degree that their misery was more profound . . . you all see the quality of that power and grace which has caused an entire race of the most godless and troublesome men to disappear. . . ." These are things which a conquering caliph might as well have signed. Napoleon resorted to similar turns of expression in his Arabic proclamations in Egypt.

It is not impossible that in his deism, originally derived from the sun and Mithras, Constantine believed that he possessed a more general and hence presumably a loftier basic configuration of all religions. At times he tried to find basically neutral expressions for religious practices which Christians and pagans alike should observe. Of this character is the common Sunday and the common Pater Noster. "He taught all armies zealously to honor the Lord's Day, which is also called the day of light and of the sun. . . . The pagans too were required to go forth into an open field on Sunday, and together to raise their hands, and recite a prayer learned by heart to God as giver of all victory: 'Thee alone we acknowledge as God and King, Thee we invoke as our helper. From Thee have we obtained our victories, through Thee conquered our enemies. Thee we thank for past favors, of Thee we hope for future favors. Thee we all beseech, and we pray Thee that Thou long preserve to us unharmed and victorious our Emperor Constantine and his God-loving sons.' " Christians would be content with this formula, and the pagans who might have taken offense at such outspoken monotheism were before all else soldiers. That special thought was taken for believers in Mithras also Eusebius indicates quite clearly with his "day of light and of the sun." How significant is this so-called prayer! Emperor, army, victory — and nothing else; not a word for moral man, not a syllable for the Romans.

Before we proceed further we may briefly dispose of Eusebius' other reports of the alleged Christianity of his hero. After the war with Maxentius Christian priests always attended him, even on journeys, as "assessors" and "table companions." At the synods he took his seat in the midst of them. These facts are easily explained. It was essential for Constantine to have intelligence of the viewpoints of the contemporary Church; he had his own informants who delivered reports on the individual sects. With the eloquent reports of one of them,

Strategius by name, he was so pleased that he gave him the cognomen Musonianus. No clever and energetic ruler could let the praesidium of the synods out of his hands, for they were a new power in public life which it was unwise to ignore. One may deplore and contemn such egoism, but an intelligent power, whose origin is ambiguous, must of necessity act in this manner. When we are told further how frequently divine manifestations were vouchsafed the Emperor, how he secretly fasted and prayed in the tent of the *labarum,* how he daily shut himself in to converse with God on his knees, how he filled the watches of the night with thoughts on divine matters — on the lips of a Eusebius, who knew the truth, these things are contemptible inventions. In the later period Constantine was patently even more attentive to the bishops and gave them the first word at his court, apparently because he realized that it was to their greatest interest to support the throne in every way possible, and in the end because he could not do otherwise. In his encyclicals bishops are addressed as "beloved brother," and he himself affected to comport himself as one of them, "as a common bishop." He put the education of his sons, at least in part, in their hands, and in general so ordered matters that these sons should be regarded as unqualified Christians. Their personal environment, their court, consisted exclusively of Christians, whereas their father, by Eusebius' indirect admissions, did not hesitate to keep pagans in high positions about his person and as *praesides* in the provinces, along with the clergy, until the last period of his life. The prohibition of gladiatorial games was doubtless a concession to his clerical environment, although the relevant law speaks only of "peace in the land and domestic quiet" for which bloody spectacles were not appropriate. In any case this was one of those laws which were promulgated only to fall straightway into oblivion, for Constantine himself later paid no attention to it.

The sermons which Constantine delivered from time to time in the presence of the court and "many thousands of auditors" are a complete puzzle. He wished, it is said, to prevail over his subjects "by discourses with edifying purpose" and "to make the reign one of discourse." Assemblies were convoked for this purpose, and the master of the world nonchalantly stepped forward and spoke. If he touched upon religion his gestures and voice took on an expression of deep humility. Applause he deprecated with a gesture toward heaven. His themes were usually refutation of polytheism, monotheism, providence, redemption, and divine judgment. In this section (the court bishop continues) he scored his auditors most directly, for he spoke of robbers, and men of violence, and the avaricious; the scourge of his words smote certain of his confidants who stood in attendance, so that they cast their eyes to the ground. . . . His intention was righteous, but they remained deaf and stubborn. They clamored their approval, but their insatiability suffered no emotion to stir within them. Constantine wrote these discourses in Latin, and interpreters turned them into Greek.—What are we to think of this account? Would Constantine, who preserved the Diocletianic fashion of imperial appearance so zealously, and who set such great store by his personal majesty, condescend to show himself before the crowds in the capital? The criticism to which he would thus subject himself is the least of the problem, and perhaps his auditors would forgo criticism on very good grounds. But why speeches, when the Emperor possessed the fullest power to act? Perhaps one reason may be divined. In this period of religious crisis the spoken word, previously confined to rhetorical exercises and eulogies, now delivered from the preacher's pulpit, must have won so enormous an influence that Constantine could not entirely forgo it as an adjunct of power, just as the most powerful governments today must be represented in the periodical press. If it could occur to this unbaptized non-catechumen to give himself out as "a common bishop," he could equally well present himself as a Christian preacher. How he dealt with Christian dogma in these discourses we do not know; that he presented himself as an unqualified Christian is not even probable. Eusebius clearly indicates a collateral purpose of these discourses; they were a welcome occasion to express favor and disfavor, to inspire fear, and to present in an artfully ambiguous form things he could not well bring before people even in the most elaborate edicts. They were, in fact, the senatorial speeches of Tiberius in another form. We must not forget that among other things Constantine "put a great many of his friends to death," as the unsuspicious Eutropius says, and the more than suspicious Eusebius finds it well to pass over in silence.

A glimmer of edification still clings to Constantine because so many admirable Christians of all centuries have claimed him for their own. But this last glimmer must also vanish. The Christian Church has nothing to lose in this terrible though politically grandiose figure, just as paganism would have had nothing to gain by him. In any case the pagans fell into the same error of assuming that his conversion was genuine and not merely for outward show. Zosimus recounts the familiar hostile version. Because of the execution of Crispus and Fausta and the violation of his oath (to Licinius) the Emperor's conscience pricked him, and he turned to pagan priests (according to Sozomen, to the famous Neoplatonist Sopater) for absolution. When they told him that there was no expiation for such malefaction, an Egyptian (apparently Hosius) who had come to Rome from Spain succeeded in making his way to the Emperor through the ladies of the court and in convincing the Emperor that Christianity was able to wash every misdeed away. Thereupon he made his conversion known, first by his measures against pagan prognostications of the future, and then by building a new capital. It is possible that this account contains a kernel of truth, but the version before us is surely not authentic. Events so gruesome transpiring in his own house must have awakened whatever remained of Roman belief in the soul of Constantine, and despite his education in other respects he may have been crude enough to expect some alleviation, some washing away of the ugly impression, by means of powerful pagan exorcisms; but the causal nexus in the remainder of the account is demonstrably false.

It is precisely in the last decade of his life that Constantine gives certain very plain indications of un-Christian, even of directly pagan, sympathies. While he and his mother were

ornamenting Palestine and the large cities of the Empire with
magnificent churches, he was also building pagan temples in
the new Constantinople. Two of these, of the Mother of the
Gods and of the Dioscuri, may have been merely ornamental
structures to house the idols which were preserved in them
as works of art; but the temple and image of Tyche, the deified personification of the city, was intended to receive an
actual cult. At the consecration of the city certain occult pagan
practices were demonstrably celebrated; the solemnities involved superstitions of all sorts, which later writers vainly
seek to identify with Christian worship.

To others also Constantine granted permission to build
pagan temples. An inscription of the Umbrian village of Spello
(between Foligno and Assisi), which was long regarded as
spurious because of its strange content, a judgment seemingly
justified by its careless and barbaric script, is most probably
a perfectly genuine monument of this indulgence to the pagans,
and dates, indeed, from the last two years of the Emperor's
life. He permits the Hispellati to build a sumptuous temple to
his own family, which he calls the Gens Flavia, and his only
condition is that the temple should not be tainted "by the delusion of contagious superstition" — a prescription that every
man might interpret as he would. He issues binding decisions
also concerning the pagan priesthood of the place and concerning the removal of the games from Bolsena to Spello,
naming the gladiators expressly. During these same years he
releases certain priestly colleges of the pagans, the Sacerdotes
and the Flamines, who held life tenure, from burdensome
local offices, in which the Christians, especially in Africa,
wished to compel them to serve. It was indubitably with his
knowledge that the Senate procured the restoration of the
Temple of Concord as late as 331, to say nothing of the restoration of individual altars of the gods in the years immediately preceding.

Paganism approached the Emperor very closely during these
last years through personal contacts. The Neoplatonist Sopater,
a disciple of Iamblichus, appears with all the claims of a
proud Greek sophist. "For him other people were too insig-

nificant; he hastened to the imperial court in order to exert in the most direct manner a dominant influence over all of Constantine's deeds and thoughts. And the Emperor was in fact soon completely won over by him, and caused him to sit at his right hand, to the general envy and displeasure of the courtiers." So far Eunapius, who, however, deserves as little unqualified credit as Philostratus when he brags of the noble connections of the philosophers. But there is some truth at the bottom of this account; Sopater did stand in close relation to Constantine. That it was he who refused expiation for the execution of Crispus we may leave out of account; but he was undeniably employed at the ceremonial consecration of Constantinople. Later, in any case after 330, Ablavius, the Prefect of the Guard, caused his fall. During the famine in the new capital Ablavius is said to have imposed upon the Emperor the opinion that Sopater, by means of his extraordinary science, was holding bound the winds that were to move the Egyptian grain vessels over the sea. In any event Constantine had the sophist executed. That this was caused merely by an intrigue of Ablavius may however well be doubted, on the basis of a notice in Suidas. "Constantine put Sopater to death," says Suidas, "to show that he was no longer a pagan in religion. For previously he had been on terms of intimacy with him." We shall have to repeat in another connection (that of the story of Athanasius) the conjecture that the Christian priests had become somehow frightening to the aging Emperor and that he was unable, in his last years, to maintain consistently the personal freedom he had so long guarded. Many even feel justified in assuming that sometime toward the end of his life Constantine prohibited pagan sacrifices entirely, and if Eusebius merits consideration, that not only sacrifices, but also consultation of oracles, erection of idols, and celebration of mysteries were completely abolished. That a law against consulting oracles was issued some time after 326 is confirmed by Zosimus. But for all this, a blind eye must have been turned toward infractions. Even if the decree of Spello is spurious, there is still enough other evidence. Our chief source for the large-scale persistence of sacrifices and mysteries, the treatise of the Christian Firmicus, derives precisely from the years following the death of Constantine. His sons are admonished in the most vigorous language to do what their father is presumed already to have done: "Hew them down, hew them down with an ax, these temple ornaments! To the smeltry, to the mint, with these gods! All votive offerings are yours: take and use them!"

Even under Constantine, to be sure, temples were pulled down and destroyed and images melted down. A sanctuary like that of the Heavenly Goddess at Aphaka in the Lebanon deserved no better than that soldiers should be dispatched to raze it to the ground (about 330); the spot was in fact "unworthy that the sun shine upon it." More questionable was the razing of the famous Temple of Asclepius at Aegae in Cilicia, whither crowds of people had until that time resorted for the sake of curative dreams. Apparently the god ("the false guide of souls," Eusebius calls him) had become involved in political questions. At Heliopolis, whose cult was hardly less debauched than that of Aphaka, there was merely a prohibition and the enforced establishment of a bishopric, for which a congregation was then engaged for pay. Elsewhere it happened that converted populations pulled down local pagan sanctuaries of their own volition and then received official imperial approval. Probably as reward for such merits Majuma, the harbor city of Gaza, received the name of Constantia, and another Phoenician locality received the name of Constantina.

Constantine caused many temples to be plundered moreover, as it seems, out of desire for booty or need of pelf. Here too Eusebius dissembles the cause and the true extent of such spoliation, but he betrays himself unwittingly. For he does not speak of marble statues at all, but only of such whose interior consisted of some special material; Eusebius implies skulls, skeletons, old rags, hay, straw, and the like, but what is obviously intended are the wooden or other armatures that supported the hollow interiors of the so-called chryselephantine statues, that is, statues of gold and ivory, like that of the Zeus of Olympia. In his panegyric of Constantine this is fully avowed: "The valuable portions were melted down, and the

amorphous remainder was left to the pagans as a memorial of
their reproach." What and how many statues (perhaps the
finest in Greek art) met a fate inextricably involved in the
value of their material we cannot know. For the decoration of
his new capital, in any case, Constantine was very willing to
use images whose material was of no great value, as we shall
see. Of the brazen statues the same passage continues, "They
were haled forth like captives, these gods of antiquated myth,
they were dragged forth with ropes." Confiscation was in the
hands of trusted commissioners, who came directly from the
court. They encountered no resistance; priests were compelled
to open their most secret crypts to them. But it is conceivable
and not improbable that Constantine ventured such measures
only in thoroughly reliable, predominantly Christian cities in
the near vicinity of the imperial residence. He might have left
the statues of gold and silver untouched, but they were too
convenient and the temptation was too great in the face of
pressing financial need, which must take precedence over any
other consideration in rulers of this sort. In the same category,
doubtless, falls the removal of doors and beams, which is said
to have taken place in the case of several temples; these members were often of massive bronze, and well worth the trouble
of smelting. If this made a beginning of destruction and the
interior was then injured by partial collapse and inclement
weather, the inhabitants could hardly be prevented from
venturing on columns and other structural members, if only
for burning lime. We have official confirmation that such
things happened after 333, at least to pagan grave monuments.
Even earlier a law put'a period to the repair of dilapidated or
incompleted temples. How the temple properties fared is not
precisely known; in individual cases they were certainly confiscated, but it was only under Constantine's successors that
this was done in volume and systematically. It is out of the
question that Constantine could have issued a law enjoining
the general destruction of temples, as the *Chronicle* of Jerome
reports for the year 335. What Constantine did or suffered to
come about happened intermittently, out of frivolous desire
for plunder and through the influence of the clergy, and hence

U

his measures are not consistent. It is futile to seek for a logical system in a man who was intentionally illogical in this respect.

Of Constantine's profession of Christianity and his deathbed baptism, every man must judge according to his own criteria.

The great outward changes which the position and hence constitution of the Christian Church assumed through Constantine are sufficiently familiar and can be repeated here only briefly. Simultaneously with the first edict of toleration the clergy (*clerici*) were recognized as constituting a class or corporation; the effect of this recognition was of immeasurable importance for the whole development of the Church. The clergy had long been prepared for their new position; on the one hand they had isolated themselves from the laity, and on the other they had acquired the character of a corporation by community of official functions, especially in the institution of synods. But was it necessary for the state which had barely declared toleration to yield so fully on this point? Could it not have ignored the clergy as a class and addressed itself directly to the communities? Constantine found the clergy already so suitably organized for power and so elevated by the persecution that he must either rule through this corporation and its high credit or acquire its irreconcilable enmity. He therefore gave the clergy every possible guarantee of favor, even as far as a sort of participation in rule, and in return the clergy were the most devoted agents for spreading his power, and completely ignored the fact that he still stood with one foot in paganism and that his hands were over and again stained with blood.

The new position of the clergy involved a grave obverse. Out of the persecution, along with its noble moral consequences, there had arisen an evil spirit of strife. The party of enthusiastic devotion came to oppose fanatically not only those who had denied their faith during the persecution or had delivered up the sacred scriptures, but even those who had saved themselves by permissible means of Christian prudence. Hence there arose the Donatist schism in Africa and the Meletian in Egypt, almost while the persecution was still in progress. These were the first occasions for the Emperor, who had been merely tolerant, to intervene actively in Church quarrels, for of neutrality, once he had concerned himself with Church affairs, there could naturally be no question. Here, as later in the much more comprehensive Arian schism, Constantine usually showed great tact; he declared for one party, to be sure, but gave it no sort of power to penalize the other. Church unity would doubtless have been a desirable thing in his sight, for it seemed to be a parallel to unity of power, but he understood how to accommodate himself to a Church rent by strife and was far from compromising the imperial power itself by stubbornness or rigor on behalf of or against persons and things which could inspire no fanaticism in him. He had observed the Christian reaction to persecution of every sort thoroughly; just such schisms as the two named would inevitably have been exacerbated by nothing so much as new martyrdom. He must indeed have realized that not all of his successors would maintain similar independence; once called Christians, it was to be foreseen that their personal zeal must be involved for or against conflicting practices of the Church. But the sequel proved that the imperial power was strongly enough founded in other respects not to permit its course to be disrupted by even the most extreme trials, as for example the iconoclastic controversy of the eighth century.

As a corporation or class the clergy first received from Constantine release from all public obligations (*munera;* 313 and 319), which were comprised partly in burdensome offices and partly in imposts, or in the execrable decurionate which united both. (The immediate rush to clerical standing on the part of wealthy people eager for immunity had to be met in the year following [320] by a blunt general prohibition, which was then apparently not infrequently circumvented.) The next significant mark of corporate recognition accorded to the Church was permission to accept legacies (321), numbers of which it then received. Later, apparently after the victory over Licinius, the state accorded the Church regular revenues, chiefly in landed property and crop shares. An ample income and the foundation of great wealth was thus assured the

Church, and in addition the state relinquished also a portion of its prerogative of power. Previously the Christians had preferred to settle their quarrels through bishops as a sort of court of arbitration before they resorted to the worldly, pagan judges, to whom the sentence of the bishops could in any case be appealed; this right of appeal Constantine abolished and made the decisions of the bishops, once they were referred to, binding. Thus rivalry between the secular and clerical judges was obviated, as was also opportunity for strife between the two, which might now have been very dangerous whether the secular judge were still a pagan or already a Christian. This consideration alone is sufficient to explain the extraordinary concession, obviously dangerous to any vigorous state organization. Here, as in his handling of Church matters in general, Constantine did not introduce innovation of his own choice, but merely confirmed and regulated what had transpired without his agency. It is easy to reproach him, from the standpoint of modern theory, for not maintaining a sharper distinction between Church and state; but what was he to do when, by the general tendency of the age, the Church had turned into the state under his hands and the state into the Church, when every Christian official in his sphere of duty and every judge upon his tribunal might stray in his function by the confusion of religious and civic points of view, when the intercession of a bishop or of a sanctified eremite for or against any individual or any condition might throw everything into confusion? The theocracy which here developed was not the work of a single Emperor who favored the Church, and as little the conscious foundation of single especially clever bishops, but the large and necessary result of a process of world history. Considered from a higher point of view, it may well be deplored that the Gospel was made into law for those who did not believe in it, and specifically by a ruler who was not inwardly moved by the substance of the religion which he imposed upon others. "Christianity grows alien to its essence when it is made into law for those born instead of for those reborn" (Zahn, *Konstantin der Grosse und die Kirche.*) Constantine desired an imperial Church, and on political grounds;

but it is difficult to determine whether another in his place, pure in character and a convinced Christian, might not have been compelled to follow the same path.

Once the clergy was raised above society, its theoretical claims upon itself and others increased with remarkable rapidity. Celibacy had already been an issue; now the penalties which the state had previously imposed upon the unmarried had to be rescinded. And if a man who was himself an ascetic, a confessor, and an unrivaled exorciser, the old and blind Paphnutius, had not spoken against it at the Council of Nicaea, celibacy might even then have been decreed binding upon all clergy. Ordination or consecration was given an increasingly mystical value, and came to be regarded, in relation to men and things, as something magical, as a communication of supernatural powers. Within the priestly caste itself old distinctions were accentuated and new ones formed. Presbyter was separated from deacon, and bishop from presbyter; among the bishops themselves there were very diverse degrees of influence according to the rank of their cities. This influence came to be concentrated chiefly in the five (later) patriarchal seats—Rome, Alexandria, Antioch, Constantinople, and Jerusalem. To maintain the episcopal office as such in its higher prestige, the lowest grade of bishops, the so-called rural bishops (χωςεπίδκοποι), that is bishops of localities without the rank of city, were completely abolished not long after Constantine. According to the importance of the see, the ambition of the persons involved, and already existing partisanship, the election of a bishop was sometimes the subject of vigorous campaigns, which in individual cases might rock the entire Church. The candidate who thrust himself forward and succeeded was seldom the best man; rhetorical and political and especially financial talents, even personal influence of a most intimate nature, frequently bore off the victory over a man with a true vocation. The hierachy was extended downward not only, as previously, through the classes of doorkeepers and acolytes, but also through a large and sturdy company of servitors, the so-called *parabolani* and *fossores*, that is, sick nurses and gravediggers, of whom in Constantinople alone there were about a thousand, and in Alexandria about half that number.

This rich and mighty Church was not long wanting in brilliant outward show. The cult was made majestic by sumptuous church buildings and an imposing ritual; the life of the higher clergy, at least in the large cities, was princely. But these natural developments became clearly apparent only under the sons of Constantine and later. In one aspect in particular it is easy to perceive the means of power which the state had surrendered; the whole huge apparatus of public benefits with its influence upon the masses now devolved upon the clergy, who established shelters for the poor, hostels, almshouses, orphanages, hospitals, and other philanthropic foundations in many places, partly through gifts of the state, whereas the state came into contact with the individual only through its soldiers and its brutal tax collectors.

Who could prevent this clergy from constituting itself the state government after it had converted the pagan majority? What means were left to the ruler to remain master, or at least not servant or even pensioner of its priests? Emperor and local bishops alike now had their burial place in the Church of the Apostles at Constantinople, "forasmuch as the priesthood is the equal of the ruler in honor, and in holy sites even takes precedence."

Upon closer consideration we find that every care was nevertheless taken for the Emperor and his power. In the first place it was a piece of good fortune for the Emperor that the Old Testament, often as it depicts cleavage between the Kings and the high priests of Israel, still reports no theocratic revolution against the kingdom as such, but leaves the abolition of the kingdom to God and the King of Babylon. Appeal was made to the Old Testament theory of government at every turn as the only non-pagan precedent. As in the period of the English Puritans men overlooked the fact that the Old Testament referred to a particular and now vanished polity; the New Testament, however, to which men would surely have preferred to take recourse, concerns itself, as is well known, neither with forms of government nor with nationalities, because its compass is universal.

As long as the Emperor professed orthodoxy, he could not be impugned; what he might otherwise be as man and ruler did not enter into consideration. To the position of Constantine himself, who became the object of boundless flattery, history need no longer refer; but for subsequent Emperors there survived a theory of divine right which did not fall short of the deifications of pagan Emperors and in sincerity far surpassed them. "When the Emperor has received the name of Augustus," we read in Vegetius, at the end of the fourth century, "loyalty and obedience and ceaseless service are due him as to a present and incarnate deity. For in peace and in war it is a service to God to adhere loyally to him who rules at God's ordinance."

But materially also the imperial power with its military force, barbarized and in religious matters neutral, and its administrative system was far too well established to have to give way to a purely priestly government. And finally Constantine was clever or lucky enough to make himself head and center of the Church and to leave this position, in addition to his legacy of power, well established for his successors.

We have already noticed his claim to comport himself "as a common bishop." This was not merely a manner of speaking; actually the Church had no other central point. This appeared first of all in episcopal elections, in which, in all important cases, the court could exert paramount influence, for the bishops of the province in question who foregathered to choose a new shepherd for the orphaned community took the Emperor's wishes into consideration, because they themselves hoped to rise higher by imperial favor. To exploit its position fully the Church would, above all, have required higher principles. In the great imperial synods, furthermore, the Emperor was at an advantage, inasmuch as he determined time and place, and, more important, inasmuch as many sought to discover his desires so that they might vote accordingly. If he himself was not present he sent commissioners with plenipotentiary powers, and finally he reserved for himself the right of approval, without which no conciliar decree was valid, but with which it was raised to imperial law. In the end the synods with their equal right of voting proved an excellent means to counter the excessive power of the more important bishoprics when the court found them in any way troublesome.

The idea of a council, as it was developed in the early centuries of Christianity, was a lofty one, namely, that the spirit of God rested upon an assembly of the representatives of Christian communities when they had reverently prepared themselves to take counsel on important communal affairs. A feeling of this sort would pervade any assembly whose business concerned the highest matters and every one of whose members had perhaps ventured or would venture his life for the cause. But the period of the Church triumphant and grown worldly, whose councils became increasingly frequent and brilliant, quickly reveals a sad picture of essential devolution.

The first great occasion was the Council of Nicaea (325), whose chief purpose was to be the disposition of the Arian conflicts. It is one of the most intolerable spectacles of all history to see the Church, barely saved from persecution, particularly in the Eastern countries of the Empire, wholly consumed in strenuous conflict over the relations of the three Persons of the Trinity. Oriental rigidity and Greek sophistry, equally represented in the episcopal thrones, tormented themselves and the letter of Scripture to produce some symbol which would make the incomprehensible comprehensible and to give general validity to some expression of the idea. From *homoousios* and *homoiousios* ("equal" and "similar") the conflict proceeded through a hundred metamorphoses and several hundred years and split the Eastern Church into sects, of which one, in the form of the Greek Orthodox Church, remained to support the Byzantine Empire. A host of other interests, in part very worldly, attached themselves to the conflict and were concealed in it, so that it assumes the aspect of a merely hypocritical pretext. For the sake of this quarrel the Church made itself inwardly hollow; for the sake of orthodox dogma it suffered the inward man to be famished, and, itself demoralized, it completely forfeited its higher moral effect upon the individual. And yet this business, so distasteful in itself, was of supreme importance in world history. This Church with its collateral sects, grown rigid and cut off from all development, was for another millennium and a half to hold nationalities together against the pressure of alien barbarians, even to take the place of nationalities, for it was stronger than state or culture, and therefore survived them both. In it alone there persisted the quintessence of Byzantinism, which is not without its future; and of Byzantinism, the soul is orthodoxy.

It must be admitted, therefore, that strife over the Second Person of the Trinity had far-reaching historical justification. But we shall beware of pursuing the dogmatic aspects of the question further, and limit ourselves to a few notes concerning the relations of government and clergy as they appeared in the Council of Nicaea and in the events following.

When the Alexandrian Presbyter Arius stepped forward with his doctrine of the subordination of the Son to the Father, there arose against him the Alexandrian Deacon Athanasius and the Bishop himself, whose name was Alexander. As early as 321 Alexander had convoked a synod of the bishops of Egypt and Libya, who deposed Arius and excommunicated him. Thus his doctrine and position assumed an importance which they would not in themselves have had. Attention and partisanship on both sides grew immeasurably through preaching, solicitation, and correspondence. When Bishop Eusebius of Nicomedia took the part of the vain and peculiar but not impractical Arius, the struggle took on the aspect of a conflict between the sees of Alexandria and Nicomedia. In or near Nicomedia another synod was held, which declared in favor of Arius. At this time Eusebius of Caesarea was also inclined to this position; later, in his *Life of Constantine,* he presents an account of the conflict which is unique in its kind for dishonesty and intentional meagerness.

This was the state of affairs (323) when Constantine, in consequence of his last war against Licinius, assumed control of the East. He inherited the cleavage in its full bloom. His interest and inclination must certainly have tended to pacification, either by adjusting differences, or by a declaration for the stronger or more intelligent party, or by a shrewd balance between the two parties.

One of the most distinguished bishops of the Licinian realm, the same Eusebius of Nicomedia who had had such great influence over Constantia, sister of the Emperor and wife of Licinius, now half won Constantine over to the Arian side. But a court theologian of the West, Bishop Hosius of Cordova, who saw his own influence on Constantine imperiled, reached an understanding with the Bishop of Alexandria, and so confused matters that the Emperor saw that the only solution was the convocation of a general council. He must incidentally have welcomed an occasion to become personally acquainted with the clergy of his new realm and personally to impress them, and also to put an end to the dangerous abuse of provincial synods. Of the 318 bishops who assembled at Nicaea in June 325, barely a half dozen were Westerners. Bishop Sylvester of Rome did not appear in person but sent two presbyters, in accordance with a correct discretion which restrained his successors also from visiting Eastern synods. Moreover, of the perhaps thousand bishops of the East only those received invitations from the imperial secretariat whose opinions could be swayed or overborne.

And now when "the great priestly garland woven of colorful flowers," "the image of the apostolic roundelay," "the repetition of the first Whitsuntide," was assembled, when, beside the bishops, a numerous priestly retinue and a throng of "laymen expert in dialectic" had forgathered, Constantine in person opened the synod. He was stiff with purple, gold, and precious stones, and in this pomp Eusebius compares him to an angel of the Lord of Heaven. But an impressive personal appearance was not the sum. In the course of the proceedings it became evident that Hosius had influenced the Emperor against the Arians and that he and his party were using every means to persuade the great mass of those undecided to the same view, pointing especially to the fact that it enjoyed imperial favor. It was neither the speeches of Arius, then, nor the counter-arguments of Athanasius in honor of the eternity of the Son that determined the issue. A period was finally put to the debate by the exercise of imperial authority; Constantine insisted upon the questionable expression *homoousios* against the will of the majority, whereupon the majority patiently submitted. Only two bishops refused their signature, and so deserve to be mentioned, even if their action derived from irreligious stubbornness; they were Theonas of Marmarica and Secundus of Ptolemais. Their reward was deposition and excommunication. Eusebius of Nicomedia signed, but since his fall was predetermined, he and others were required to sign a supplementary article execrating his own former opinion. Upon his refusal to do so he was banished to Gaul, as was also Theognis, Bishop of Nicaea. Arius himself was dispatched to Illyria. Constantine had now learned to know, and largely to despise, his Eastern clergy. How these men, who could successfully have disjointed the Empire, had cringed before him! Many had secretly sent him letters incriminating their fellows; these libels he caused to be burned and he admonished them to harmony. Before the departure a great banquet was held at the court; "the gates of the palace were surrounded by bodyguards with bared swords, but the men of God strode fearlessly by and reached the inner chamber." The Emperor presented them with gifts and admonitions to peace for their journey. To the community of Alexandria he caused to be written, "What has pleased three hundred bishops is nothing other than the will of God."

But now the struggle began in real earnest. Three years later (328) Constantine, who had no real convictions on the theological question, found, allegedly upon the instigation of an Arian presbyter recommended to him by the dying Constantia, that a new turn was suitable or perhaps that it was just. Arius and the others who had been deposed were recalled from exile; Hosius was overthrown or at least vanished from his office for a very long time; the see of Antioch was taken, so to speak, by storm and occupied by an Arian — an affair which involved outrageous incidents and aroused the city's

populace, which was in any case menacing. Eusebius of Nicomedia, who played the principal role in these events, now
directed an attack against the hated see of Alexandria. But he
found it occupied by a formidable antagonist, Athanasius.
Athanasius is the first thoroughly consistent exponent of the
hierarchical personages of the medieval Church. He was
steeped from childhood in the dignity of the priestly office,
filled with large ideas and aims, as for example the conversion
of Abyssinia, had no fear of man or regard for circumstances
which might stand in the way of his principles, was ready for
any sacrifice the cause might demand, but as unyielding to
others as to himself and incapable of appreciating their viewpoint, and not always scrupulous in regard to means. The fate
of orthodoxy in the period immediately following, so far as
we can judge, unmistakably depended on Athanasius. Constantine demanded his rehabilitation of Arius; he refused, and
had his way. Thereupon his opponents adduced absurd political slanders, because Constantine could not be embittered on
the religious score; Athanasius hurried to the court and won
the Emperor over personally. Finally his opponents thought
they had found a proper device; they accused the bishop to
Constantine as being intolerant, as persecuting the Meletian
sect, which had received the peace of the Church at Nicaea.
Here Athanasius was actually not wholly guiltless, but the
Meletians had purposely been provoked against him. The
Emperor decided that the matter should be examined in a
synod, which was to meet at Caesarea in Palestine; Athanasius,
however, declared (334) that he would never stand before an
authority which consisted wholly of his deadly enemies. And
Constantine again yielded! But the incessant charges finally
prevailed, and in the following year (335) an assembly was
actually convoked, and in Tyre, whence the assembled fathers
were to go directly to Jerusalem to be present at the dedication of the Church of the Holy Sepulcher. The proceedings
were presided over by a high court official, named Dionysius.
The most serious charge (p. 211, above) Athanasius brilliantly
annihilated; for the lesser charges a partisan investigating
commission proceeded to Alexandria, and their report was

eventually followed by a decision. The Arians triumphed here, as the orthodox party had done at Nicaea. But at almost the same instant Athanasius was again at court. "As soon as I rode into Constantinople," the Emperor wrote, "he and his party suddenly met me; God is my witness that I did not even recognize him on the spot, and at the beginning would have nothing to do with him." The result of this encounter was that Constantine summoned the fathers of Tyre to the capital for a prompt justification of their conduct and their decisions. Here they ventured their first disobedience; instead of all the party, only its six chiefs appeared, and Constantine yielded, though not unconditionally. He banished Athanasius to Treves, but stipulated that the see of Alexandria should not be occupied, obviously with the intention that Athanasius should be restored at a suitable time. It is not easy to decide whether Constantine was frightened by the bishops' defiance, or what other considerations might have guided his decision. The plaintiffs charged that Athanasius had threatened to restrain the sailing of the Egyptian grain fleet, but probably the Emperor disbelieved this charge, even if he pretended to believe it. Thereupon he ordered Arius to Constantinople, apparently with the friendliest intentions. After a visit at the imperial palace Arius suddenly fell ill on the street, and died immediately (336) in a near-by public latrine, which was shown as a remarkable sight a century later. Whether he was given poison, and by whom, is doubtful; his death was of no advantage to Constantine.

Constantine would doubtless have been pleased to have a firm and harmonious Church, but now wide fluctuations had set in. In view of his own inward neutrality it was not difficult for him to keep the Church parties in suspense and not attach himself to any permanently. And so he allowed them to conquer in turn, and by energetic interventions provided only that he and his power should not be forgotten. He probably saw from the beginning that the conflict was waged largely for the sake of conflict, and that conciliation would be out of place. This attitude his successors failed to understand, because they were themselves seriously concerned with the theological questions involved, and they left the party which they supported free to use violence and vengeance against its opposition.

Living testimony of Constantine's impartiality is extant in the familiar edict on heresies, dating from the last years of his life. The clerical draftsman assails the heretics vigorously, Novatians, Valentinians, Marcionites, Cataphrygians, and all the rest; but after all the reproaches heaped upon them the conclusion is only that they are deprived of their places of assembly. Eusebius exults, "They were driven away, like animals were they driven out" — it is easy to see, however, that this far from satisfies Eusebius. Of the Novatians, it is specifically noted that Constantine only wished to frighten them a little. Persecution proper, it appears, was visited only upon the Montanists or Cataphrygians, who, as fanatics, might become dangerous, and even they were not molested in Phrygia, the home of the sect. In any case Constantine's regulations display certain remarkable inconsistencies. After the condemnation of Arius an order was issued to all the churches to burn Arius' writings, concluding with the words, "Whoso conceals a book shall be put to death. God preserve you!" — and Arius himself was allowed to live in exile in peace and subsequently restored to honor.

Immediately after Constantine's death his sons personally immersed themselves in Church partisanship. Their education was of that nature, and their disgraceful characters were no deterrents. Socrates Scholasticus tells how Constantius, for example, was won to Arianism. An unnamed presbyter, who is said to have delivered his father's will to Constantius and thus to have established himself at court, first brought the Grand Chamberlain Eusebius, a eunuch, over to the Arian side, and then the other eunuchs; these and the presbyter then won the Empress over, and finally Constantius himself made his decision. Thereupon the entire court staff, the military suite, and the city of Constantinople took sides. In the palace eunuchs and women disputed, and in the city every house became the scene of "dialectic battle." This situation spread over the whole East, while in the West Constantine II and then

Constans were convinced Athanasians. Frightful persecution, exile, murder, came in due course. All the tortures and hangman's arts of the Maximinian period were on occasion restored. Holy communion and baptism became objects of police enforcement, and strident factionalism beset the occupation of bishoprics.

These further crises are not part of our task. Along with the Church, rent by incurable obstinacy and ambition and by fantastic dialectic, there grew up the boy Julian, barely saved from the general murder which Constantine visited upon his own family. He and his brother Gallus were educated for the priesthood in the Villa Macellum in remote Cappadocia; their recreation consisted in building a chapel to the sainted martyr Mamas. It was under such impressions that the mind of the future pagan reactionary was formed.

We must not forget, however, that alongside a Church rapidly disintegrating in victory, there also was a religion. The lofty moral consequences of the introduction of Christianity disappear from view all too easily while dogmatic hierarchical quarrels wax huge. The great men of this and the following decades, Athanasius, Basil, Gregory Nazianzen, Jerome, Chrysostom, carried a more or less definite stamp of outward churchliness in addition to their religiosity, and hence seem more one-sided and less agreeable than the great, complete, and harmonious figures of antiquity; but their life principle is loftier, and indeed incommensurable.

The moral consequences of Christianity in profounder natures must not be measured according to the outlook of a Eusebius, who simply postulates earthly happiness and dominion as the divine reward for conversion to Christianity. What is involved is rather a new attitude to earthly matters, sometimes more consciously adopted and sometimes less consciously. The great mass sought as pleasurable a life in Christianity as could be managed and as the state's morals police permitted; but more serious people abstained from many pleasures entirely, and by the end of the third century even a Christian teacher found it necessary to express apprehension lest separation between man and wife might work injury to marriage. In respect to their worldly goods many felt themselves obliged to share with the poor and the churches, and some denied themselves use of their property altogether. The two great expressions of contemporary practical Christianity are charity and asceticism, if we may pass over a third, namely, the mission to the heathen peoples, as an almost exclusively clerical prerogative.

As for charity, the Christian, following the familiar proverb, could begin in his own home and with his slaves, partly by milder treatment, and partly by manumission. Slavery in itself was not regarded as wrong; even much later the very monasteries might possess slaves. But it was early recognized as a good work to manumit them, and under Diocletian Chromatius, the City Prefect of Rome, liberated fourteen hundred slaves. At the end of the fourth century much more extensive liberations took place in the devout circle of St. Jerome, but only among people who renounced the world entirely; even so, the contemporary Chrysostom demanded the unqualified abolition of slavery. As a soldier in his youth Martin of Tours retained his single slave, to be sure, tending him, however, with great humility, often drawing his shoes off and serving him at table. Constantine had already endeavored to abolish by law the right of the master over the life and death of the slave, although the legalistic distinction between the death of a slave *after* mistreatment and *in consequence of* mistreatment always provided the master an easy refuge. It is even posited that a slave might die a natural death under blows "through the necessity of fate." Theoretically the pagans abided by their old view of slavery; Themistius would grant the born slave no capacity for higher human rationality, and Macrobius deals seriously with the question whether slaves possess human standing and whether the gods concerned themselves with slaves. In point of fact the treatment of slaves by most pagans was not bad.

Charity in the narrower sense, which rested partly on the belief in worthlessness of earthly goods and partly on the obligation to alleviate poverty and misery, involved, in the manner of its expression, serious problems in national economy.

In the beginning, charity had been entrusted to a special office within the Church, that of the deacons; it had been abused by many unworthy of charity, but in the state of war of the *ecclesia pressa* there was something of the magnificent in not observing these things too narrowly. This was the result of a mood of exaltation, prepared for the very worst. The deacons, since the character of their task was local, were better able to test and become acquainted with individuals. But now alms were distributed lavishly under all forms and without restrictions. It is difficult for our own age, with its insistence upon work, to understand or approve; but it is questionable whether, apart from an agrarian law, any other solution was possible in an Empire which was almost exclusively agricultural and in which the distribution of landed property had been suffered to grow so unequal — in an Empire, moreover, whose cities were largely filled with propertyless proletariat and whose rural population had so diminished that it had everywhere to be supplemented by barbarian colonies. For centuries the urban population had received huge doles which were, however, not regarded as such; namely, the distribution of provisions, at first limited to the populace of Rome, who were presumed to be the masters of the Empire, and then extended, in the guise of imperial beneficence, to a large number of more important, and eventually to lesser, cities. The Empire, whose revenues were for the most part delivered in kind, fed the cities with the produce of the countryside. Certain grants of this sort were newly made in the age of Constantine.

When Christianity was introduced, the Church acquired very large means by gifts, in addition to the endowments of the state; henceforward it was more or less obliged to meet requirements for alms from these two sources. Above we have enumerated the institutions established by benevolent bishops and congregations out of these funds — *xenodochia* (hostels), *ptochotrophia* (poorhouses), *gerokomia* (homes for the aged), *nosokomia* (hospitals), and *orphanotrophia* (orphanages); the Basilias founded and built by Basil the Great at the end of the fourth century may be regarded as the ideal and model of

x

such institutions. For the larger part these were foundations for people actually helpless, and as such comprised a truly magnificent advance over the old pagan world, although the ancient world had long ago made a beginning of state activity in this direction.

The state itself, as has been remarked above, granted the Church these functions, and with them a means of influence. Constantine bestowed upon the church of Alexandria, for example, a special *annona* (grain supply) for distribution to the poor, besides which the general *annona*, confirmed to the city by Diocletian, doubtless continued in force. The Church *annona* was patently a not entirely immaculate means of proselytization, and Constantine's endowments generally have the aspect of conversionist treasuries. When he founded a bishopric at Heliopolis, for example, and the city nevertheless remained almost entirely pagan, he contributed generously to the support of the Christian poor, "so that so many the more might be converted to the Word." His personal benevolences and stipends were certainly of a predominantly political character, and only apparently planless; later he probably permitted himself to be guided by priests in this respect also. When he wished to make himself popular in Rome after his victory over Maxentius, he distributed to rich and poor alike large sums of money that he brought with him or found in Rome. People of social standing in reduced circumstances received money and dignities; girls of good family were given husbands from his retinue and provided with a dowry; and the ragged beggars of the Forum got alms, food, and decent clothing, the latter apparently because nakedness gave offense.

In later years Easter morning was the great occasion for gifts. If the court bishop gives way to bathos on such occasions, the incisive words of Ammianus may serve as a corrective: "As our sources have clearly shown, Constantine first opened the jaws of the people about him, and then Constantius stuffed them full with the marrow of the provinces." The gifts of an Emperor can never provide a criterion, for it can seldom be shown why he gives them or from what source he obtains them. There is something political and equivocal about even the charities of old Helena. When she traveled through the East she gave large sums to the inhabitants of individual cities, and additional amounts personally to those who approached her. She also distributed large sums to the soldiers; the poor, moreover, received money and clothing, and others were helped out of imprisonment for debt, exile, and oppression of every sort. Obviously Constantine regarded such an excursion by the only completely trustworthy member of his family as appropriate and as consonant with the spirit of the East. Of the financial system upon which this generosity was based we shall have to speak briefly in the sequel.

Let us now turn from the egoist robed in purple who measures and calculates all that he does or suffers to be done by the aggrandisement of his own power. Contrasted with this essentially frivolous authority of the state is the great and selfless devotion of many who gave away all of their possessions during their lifetime in order to "dedicate themselves to God"; here charity and asceticism merged completely. Men and women, in part of the upper classes which were used to all the pleasures of life, took Christ's command to the rich young man with strict literalness; they sold all their possessions and gave the proceeds to the poor, so that, in the midst of the world and surrounded by the clamor of great cities, they might live in voluntary poverty, free for the contemplation of the sublime. Even this did not content some; they fled out of the world and out of civilization as "men escaped," as anchorites.

History is wont to conceal the origins of great things, but it does provide a quite exact account of the rise of eremitism and its development into monachism. No other tendency or event characterizes the later third and the fourth century more sharply.

It is in the nature of man, when he feels lost in the large and busy external world, that he should seek to find his proper self in solitude. And the more deeply he has felt the inward

cleavage and rending, the more absolute is the solitude required. If religion adds to this a feeling of sin and a need for
abiding and uninterrupted union with God, then every earthly
consideration vanishes and the recluse becomes an ascetic,
partly to do penance, partly to owe the world without nothing
more than the barest existence, but partly also to keep the
soul capable of constant intercourse with the sublime. Quite
of his own accord the recluse sought to bind himself from a
return to his previous state by taking vows. If several inspired
by the same striving were met together in their retirement,
their vows and their general manner of life took on the character of a community, of a rule.

The anchorite way of life premises a not wholly healthy
state of society and the individual, but belongs rather to
periods of crisis, when many crushed spirits seek quiet, and at
the same time many strong hearts are puzzled by the whole
apparatus of life and must wage their struggle with God remote from the world. But if any man possessed by the modern
preoccupation with activity and its immoderately subjective
view of life would therefore wish to place the anchorites in
some institution for enforced labor, let him not regard himself as particularly healthy-minded; he is no more so than the
multitudes in the fourth century who were too weak or too
superficial to have any comprehension of the spiritual forces
which drove those towering personalities into the desert. Even
if we disregard the question of profit or loss which accrued to
the ascetic in the Thebaid or in the hills of Gaza, there remains an enormous effect upon history, which the student
must evaluate after his own manner. It was these anchorites
who communicated to the clerical order of succeeding centuries the higher ascetic attitude toward life, or at least the
claim to such an attitude; without their pattern the Church,
which was the sole pillar of all spiritual interests, would have
become entirely secularized and have necessarily succumbed
to crass material power. Our own age, in its enjoyment of free
work of the mind and free interchange of intellectual endeavor, too readily forgets that in this it still profits from the

halo of the supermundane which the medieval Church imparted to science.

The earliest Christian anchorites were Egyptians and Palestinians who led a solitary or at least a retired life in the vicinity of their homes and permitted younger men to join them in a kind of apprenticeship. But this half-eremite existence did not satisfy the natures of a Paul (235–341), an Anthony (252–357), or a Hilarion (292–373). To be entirely secure against the seductions of the world and to dedicate themselves wholly to God, they disappeared from the world and lived for sixty or eighty years in the literal desert. Some happened into solitude in their flight from the persecuting Romans; but more sought solitude for its own sake, and would never again leave it because it had become home to them, and because they could no longer think of life in the secular world and in corrupt society without horror. Furthermore, "when the world took on its Christian coloring, those were not the unworthiest members of Christian society who felt driven, for a time or permanently, into the desert, there to find the freedom which appeared to have vanished out of the victorious Church. This monachism in the first century of its existence bears venerable testimony against the lie of Constantine's creation" (Zahn, *Konstantin der Grosse und die Kirche*).

Paul the Hermit lived in a secluded mountain retreat where counterfeiters had plied their business in the days of Cleopatra. They had burrowed caves into the rockfaces, in which Paul still found rusty anvils, hammers, and mint blocks. An ancient palm shaded the secure spot, and a little spring watered it. Anthony first prepared for the anchorite life in the country not far from his home (at Heracleopolis in Middle Egypt), then he lived for a long while in a tomb, later in a deserted fort full of snakes, and finally escaped the devout in an oasis shielded by rocks, of which we shall speak below. Hilarion of Tabatha near Gaza sought out the worst robber-infested beat of his region, between the swamp and the sea, there to serve God at first with no shelter, then in a small reed hut, and then in a stone cell five feet high. The deprivations to which these men who had been

brought up in abundance subjected themselves are so drastic
that only an extraordinary constitution could face them. More
trying than the inadequacy of the food, in quantity and quality,
was, to our way of thinking, the repulsive filth and insects, to the
endurance of which these men believed they were obligated,
as did Friar Amandus (Suso) and others in the fourteenth century. A reaction of this sort was in any case quite natural, after
preceding generations had surrendered to every manner of carnal indulgence in the sumptuous baths. The greatest deprivation, that of human society, need not enter into the reckoning;
the only cultural resource of the eremites was that they knew
the Bible by heart. But this did not shield them from violent
inward trials, which manifested themselves in part by seemingly
external daimonic temptations. Here one might think of the personification of all spiritual forces which is peculiar to antiquity,
but no such explanation is required. Sometimes it is their own
sensuality, sometimes memories of their former life, sometimes
the reaction to the desert and its natural terrors, which inflict
these torturing visions upon the recluses. The appearance of
the hellish host in the tomb which served Anthony as a dwelling is world-famous, though it has been forever relegated to
the realm of the burlesque by Jacques Callot: "Then the walls
opened, and the daimones appeared as serpents, lions, bulls,
wolves, scorpions, leopards, and bears, all roaring and threatening"; at other times they appeared in human guise, clamoring,
whistling, and dancing, and they smote the saint half dead. Even
more colorful are the visions of Hilarion. Each night there arose
about him ghostly noises of every description, the wailing of
infants, the bleating of flocks, the bellowing of bulls, the tramp
of armies. In the clear moonlight a chariot drawn by wild horses
rushed upon him, but was swallowed up by the earth at his an-
guished cry of "Jesus." Naked women and richly laden tables
appeared, or wolves and foxes leapt by as the saint was at
prayer. Once a duel of gladiators rose before his eyes, and a
dying gladiator fell at his feet and with beseeching look begged
for burial. The evil spirit even takes on the harrowing character
which makes the ghost in Sindbad's voyages so unforgettable;
he leaps upon the kneeling but somewhat distracted Hilarion,

mounts his back like a rider, mockingly kicks his heels into his flanks, and refuses to be shaken off.

These eremites dispose most easily of certain daimones who appear honorably in their true shape as satyrs and centaurs and sometimes desire conversion and intercession. On the question of centaurs, the great Jerome refuses to decide whether they are merely disguises of the devil or whether the desert actually produces such creatures, but he insists on the genuineness of the satyr who showed Anthony on his journey the way to St.Paul and besought him for intercession. Under Constantius such a creature is said to have been found in the desert, brought to Alexandria alive, to have there straightway died, been salted, and sent to Antioch, so that the Emperor who resided there might have a look at him. St.Anthony's satyr, moreover, retained goat feet and horns, and thus was a Paniscus; he had also kept the crooked nose of the wanton old days.

After a period of such torments there followed in the life of the ascetic another stage, which he must have regarded with mixed feelings. The world which needed help discovered him, saw in him something lofty and unusual, and sought him out in the wilderness. He becomes a wonder worker, not through mysteries and phantasmagoria, but through sheer prayer. Did his soul profit thereby? Must spiritual pride not have been aroused? Admirers gathered about him and built cells near his; gradually he must recognize them as disciples, and in view of the volume of visitors he soon required assistants. Half against his will he soon became a "Father," a master. Anthony, who endured this new life for several decades, fled to the interior of the desert about 310 and discovered, parallel to Aphroditopolis, a rocky mountain whose rustling rills nourished a stand of palms. But here too the brethren searched him out, and he was compelled to allow two of them, Pelusian and the interpreter Isaac, to live with him. Again he was made the object of a large and uninterrupted pilgrimage; heretics and the orthodox, high Roman officials and pagan priests, the healthy and the sick, came in such numbers that it was found profitable to establish a regular camel post from Aphroditopolis through the desert to his dwelling. He had no choice but to build a quite inaccessible cell high upon a hill with a steep ascent, where he could withdraw at least periodically. The last concern of his life was that his burial place should be kept secret, for a rich property owner of the neighborhood was already lying in wait for his corpse, in order to install a *martyrium,* that is, a church containing the grave of the saint, at his country estate, perhaps for business reasons. The two disciples did in fact hold their counsel, apparently in the face of Hilarion himself.

For Hilarion had undertaken a journey to Egypt, which was also nothing other than a flight from the enormous concourse of visitors and from the growing care of the thousands of fellow eremites who had joined him in the desert of Gaza. His biography, one of the most interesting of Jerome's works, describes the origin and manner of this concourse quite vividly. It gradually became known in Gaza and its harbor city of Majuma that a holy anchorite was living in the desert. An important Roman lady, whose three children had fallen ill of fever on her travels, went on a pilgrimage to him with her maidservants and eunuchs, and by tears and lamentations moved him to come to Gaza, where he cured the children. Thereupon pilgrimages to him from Syria and Egypt went on incessantly, but in his immediate neighborhood paganism defended itself most vigorously. The great god Marnas in his temple at Gaza entered into direct competition with St. Hilarion, and in the pleasure-seeking commercial city there developed a cleavage, which requires some trouble to understand. The cleavage finds essential expression in the crowds of possessed persons who were constantly being dragged out to the saint in the desert, and who were for the most part surely nothing other than people morbidly divided and broken between two religions, both really daimonic. Theoretically, the victim was not conscious that he was possessed; according to the older, more generalizing view, the daimon might seek out its own people or its own animals at will, or it might be conjured into victims by the malice of magicians. Hilarion, for example, once had to cure a camel that was possessed. The daimon is always conceived of as a second person, distinct from the man possessed, and may for example speak Syrian or Greek when his victim understands only Latin or Frankish. He is a personification of the evil pagan gods, and in this case, of course, usually of Marnas. In his contest with the idol, the saint for once departed from his principle, and opposed the pagan magic with Christian magic. Of the Circus entrepreneurs at Gaza, one, a pagan city official, was a devotee of Marnas, and kept a magician who caused his patron's horses to win and slowed his opponent's horses. The latter, a Christian called Italicus, applied to Hilarion, who first ridiculed him and asked him why he did not sell his horses and give the proceeds to the poor. But Hilarion was softened by the man's conscientiousness in preferring to seek help of a servant of God rather than from magicians, and by the consideration that a triumph of Gaza's whole Christendom was involved. He gave Italicus a basin of water with which to sprinkle horses, chariot, stall, driver, and barriers. The spectators watched the beginning of the race with tense interest, the Christian's horses won easily, and even the pagans shouted, "Marnas is beaten by Christ," so that the day caused many to be converted. And yet on one occasion Hilarion cured a circus driver who was deathly sick only on condition that he give up his previous occupation entirely.

Just as the anchorite became a wonder worker half against his will, so he became a monk also. The cells of those who followed him into the desert gradually formed a monastery, which then submitted to his leadership with the greatest devotion.

In Egypt there was a precedent not only in the Jewish Therapeutae, who led a life of this sort by Lake Mareotis, but also in those who were walled into cells at the temples of Serapis (see p. 151, above); this was the hardest of all forms of asceticism, but it was to find followers, though few in number, throughout the Christian world. The climate, moreover, made great moderation not only possible but necessary, and, as we shall see, even the industrial character of the country rendered existence easy for an unmarried proletariat with little or no landed property. Innumerable fellow anchorites had gathered at the various stations of Anthony, and he enlightened them by prayer, example, and admonition; but he never considered it his goal in life to give them a fixed constitution and direct them according to a set plan. This was rather the function of Pachomius, whose life embraces approximately the first half of the fourth century. As a young man he had learned the value of a closed discipline in a short career as soldier, and he put his lesson into effect in the famous monachist district of Tabenna in Upper Egypt, between Tentyris and Thebes. Several thousand monks were gathered here even during his lifetime, and the rules which he set them obtained validity in other monastic colonies which arose at the same time or later. Of these the most important are: that at Arsinoë in the region of Lake Moeris (ten thousand strong in Valens' day); the great settlement in the Nitrian or Scetian Desert, west of the Delta; the so-called Eremica not far from Alexandria; and finally the scattered monasteries and cells along the entire coast of the Mediterranean and Lake Mareotis, including some on the Red Sea and the Sinai peninsula. But all these were surpassed by Tabenna, where in Jerome's day no fewer than fifty thousand monks were wont to celebrate Easter; not all of these lived in the central monastery (*monasterium maius*), but they came from all the monasteries belonging to the congregation of Tabenna. We can see that not all these colonies were situated in the desert; even before the end of the fourth century there were city monasteries, as part of the campaign against pagan remains and reminiscences. Thus, for example, the temple of Canopus in the city of that name was transformed into the monastery of Metanoia ("repentance"). According to organization the Egyptian institutions were partly cenobitic or partly monastic, that is, larger structures for many monks; and partly *lauras,* groups of cells which were at a specified distance from one another and thus were still in a manner hermitages. At the time mentioned there were at least one hundred thousand men in Egypt dedicated to this form of life. Along with these monasteries we begin to hear of nunneries also; of these one, under Pachomius' sister, counted four hundred nuns as early as 320.

A historical phenomenon of such magnitude has a profound basis in national history, and if it should cause a nation to perish, that would only be the necessary form of its fall. In Egypt it was natural for the question of religion to oscillate to extremes. Having emerged from fanatical paganism after a hard struggle, the Egyptian knew no bounds in his reaction, and believed that he must dedicate his life to the new religion in a manner analogous to his forebears' bondage to symbols. Thus there arose this remarkable fakir existence, the last product of the ancient Egyptian spirit to affect world history; for future centuries that spirit now falls passive.

The rule which Pachomius laid down for this host was a thing of the most urgent necessity, but at the same time it was the first step toward externalization and untruth; asceticism is now no longer the result of free individual inspiration but a common law to fetter many thousands of unequal persons permanently to an equal practice. And if one give truth its due he must confess that Pachomius assumed a low average and that his constitution presupposes a great number of persons without the proper vocation who must above all be kept in bounds. This was usefully done by means of work by which the monasteries lived. With the rise of monasticism a great change must have taken place in Egyptian industry. Now that the monasteries were very far from producing merely baskets and mats out of Nile sedge, but engaged in the important trade of weaving linen and tanning hides (to say nothing of their other products), many factories in the country found themselves at a disadvantage, for the monasteries could offer goods at much lower prices in the open market of Alexandria. The manager of a large monastery who distributed the tasks and arranged delivery was the equivalent of a great industrialist. Monks who lived alone could sell their work directly and sometimes accumulated a private fortune, the rule notwithstanding. Otherwise it was a guiding principle that the work of the monks was intended rather for the benefit of their souls than to supply necessities, and any excess must be distributed to the poor. Little is said of agriculture; on the other hand monasteries situated on the Nile maintained large boats, apparently also for the sake of profit.

Along with work, the monk was occupied with prayer, worship, and continuous castigations of every sort, which were the essential element in a life purposely contrived to be one-sided. In view of the origin and the tendency of the institution, literary occupation is not to be expected; what, indeed, had erudite Alexandria with all its Greek and Oriental scholarship

achieved? The monk pursued aims and ideals which were at
the opposite pole from pagan overeducation and immorality,
and if elsewhere there were points of accommodation, even of
rapprochement, between the two moral worlds called paganism and Christianity, here at least the essential and principal
relationship between them was one of permanent and basic
hostility. Every line that had come down from previous ages,
from hieroglyphs to Greek cursive, was tainted with paganism,
idolatry, or magic; all that was left to read, therefore (in so far
as reading was allowed), was devotional Christian literature
which had in part to be created by these very monks or translated into Egyptian from other languages. The relations to ancient art were the same as to ancient literature; Ammonius is
expressly praised, for example, because on his visit to Rome
he had looked at nothing more than the Basilicas of St. Peter
and St. Paul.

In its narrower sense, furthermore, the discipline was systematically calculated to cut the monk off from all his previous connections, especially from his family, and then to guard
him strictly and keep him at his work. By its predominantly
negative content the rule conveys a dreary, police-like impression, and is thus not remotely comparable to the Rule of St.
Benedict. The articles dealing with mockery and loose talk
from monastery to monastery, and with angry rivalries between them, clearly recall the character of the country in
which they flourished. Similarly, the rule of no Western order
required that the monks should sleep separately in locked
wooden stalls as in a sheath. Thoroughly Egyptian, moreover,
is the secret and mysterious language, which an angel is said
to have suggested to Pachomius and his disciples Cornelius
and Syrus, and which (to judge by extant examples) consisted
in nothing other than a conventional designation of individual
objects and persons by letters of the alphabet. Along with such
designations, Pachomius is said to have employed the device
of dividing his monks into twenty-four classes according to
their capacities and character and calling them *alpha, beta,
gamma,* and so forth. But it is hard to believe that a man so
practical in other respects was so at fault in his psychology.

Surely the ideal Christian life is not to be sought in the Egyptian monastic colonies. Along with these colonies, however, there persisted genuine anchorite practices, and to these, in view of conditions in the contemporary world, we must grant a high degree of justification. Most of the famous recluses of the fourth century spent part of their lives in the monasteries or at least in the *laura;* either previously or subsequently they retired to deeper solitude, to which the monastery sent them only bread and salt. Here too they were not always secure from spiritual pride, fearful temptations, and fantastic enthusiasms. Their penances were in part truly murderous in character; however, they not only usually regarded themselves as fortunate and their lives as worthily spent, but they left behind many a profound and beautiful saying which proves that their happiness was no mere delusion but derived from constant preoccupation with the sublime. The names of an Ammonius, an Arsenius, an Elias, the two Macarii, and a number of others will always belong among the memorable records of the Church.

A third form of Egyptian monachism were the somewhat disreputable Remoboth, who lived in twos or threes in cities and castles, and had no rule but followed their own inclinations, and hence frequently fell into bitter strife. They lived by trades, and were better paid than others because of their apparent sanctity. Their fasting is criticized as being vainglorious, and on festive days they are said to have indulged in gluttony.

The later development of Egyptian monachism, its sects, and its participation in the general dissensions of the Church do not belong in this place.

In Palestine monachism under St. Hilarion took on a different form in its economic relationships and hence received a physiognomy quite different from the Egyptian. Agriculture and viticulture predominated. Many monks even retained their personal property and are scarcely to be differentiated from unmarried farmers with paid servants. The founder himself continued to live in the uncultivated desert, and was greatly displeased that the desert had become populated on his account. But the "villas" of many of his comrades, where vines and grain flourished, must have been better situated. About Hilarion's cell a monastery proper seems to have developed in the course of time; otherwise the Palestinian monks constituted a large, widely dispersed, and loosely connected *laura*. In Egypt Pachomius was able to summon all the monks of his congregation to the Easter festival at Tabenna and all of its superiors and officials to the festival of forgiveness in the month of Mesore (August), whereas in Palestine Hilarion was forced to make periodic journeys over his entire domain in order to oversee his people. On these journeys he was accompanied by an army of two thousand monks, who at first carried their provisions with them but later were fed by landholders along the way. Since the saint did not wish to overlook the most remote and simplest cell, his travels often took him to Saracen villages, where he worked as a proselytizer.

Beyond Palestine through all of Roman Asia and into the kingdom of the Sassanids we have evidence of individual anchorites from the beginning of the fourth century, and not long thereafter also of monasteries as well as scattered institutions corresponding to the Egyptian *laura*. Of the latter sort was the monastic association at Mount Sigoron near Nisibis; these are called the grazing monks because at mealtime they went out with sickles to cut herbs, which were their only sustenance. Among these Syrian monks, those at Edessa early became famous, especially by reason of their great exorciser of daimones, Julian. For Armenia, Paphlagonia, and Pontus, Eustathius, the strict Bishop of Sebastia, was a principal founder of monachism; for Cappadocia and Galatia, somewhat later, Basil the Great, who was destined to give Eastern asceticism in general its permanent form. In these colder regions where life in scattered cells could not so easily be managed, the monks formed monasteries, mostly, indeed, in cities or villages.

In the more moderate countries of the West this tremendous example found imitators only gradually. It was not till the second half of the fourth century that monasteries arose in or near cities and that the little rocky islands of the Mediterranean which had previously served only as places of exile became filled with eremites. Enthusiastic Westerners traveled to the

East in order to learn the ascetic practice or even to stay there, for life. Even in the midst of the activity of cities men, virgins, and widows devoted themselves continuously to a life so rigorous and devout as could only be led in a cloister. This is the epoch of St. Martin of Tours, St. Ambrose, and St. Jerome, who knew and portrayed both the dark and the bright side of this entire movement. We shall have to refer to this briefly in our treatment of Rome and Palestine. Gaul soon had the victorious feeling of having equaled if not surpassed the East.

General discussion concerning the moral and religious value and the historical necessity of monachism and the entire ascetic movement is superfluous in this place. Views on the subject must always remain diametrically opposed. One frame of thought will always abhor these things in life as in history and oppose them, another will love and praise them. But if a man wish to dispute with those ancient heroes of the desert from a Christian standpoint, he must take care that his reasoning should not prove the less consistent. The doctrine of vicarious penitence is not yet present, and the ascetic therefore represents none but himself. Penitence was still regarded as giving him no more claim to salvation than any other good work; nevertheless he strove for absolute denial of everything sensual and everything worldly. Wherefore such rigor? Because there can be no connection with the outer world whatever if one takes certain words of the New Testament seriously and refuses to compromise their literal meaning. And as long as there is a Christianity there will be communities, sects, and individuals who will be unable to evade such strict interpretation.

X

COURT, ADMINISTRATION, AND ARMY
CONSTANTINOPLE, ROME, ATHENS,
AND JERUSALEM

CONSTANTINE used to say: "To become Emperor is a matter of destiny; but if the power of fate has imposed the necessity of rule upon a man, he must strive to appear worthy of the imperium."

All things considered, Constantine was in fact worthier of rule than all his contemporaries and colleagues, frightfully as he may at times have abused his power. None has contested his right to the title "Great," which despite all flatterers has adhered to so few men. The measureless praise of Christian writers has not been the decisive factor in this point; rather it was the powerful impression which Constantine made upon the Roman world. That world was first conquered by him, then reconciled to a new religion, and newly organized in highly important aspects. Such demonstrations of capacity justified the Romans in calling him "Great" even if all that he did would have proved injurious. In an age less unusual Constantine similarly endowed would hardly have attained such historical importance; he would have had to be content with the reputation of a Probus or of an Aurelian. But since "the power of fate," as he expresses it, placed him at the border of two world epochs and in addition granted him a long reign, it was possible for his qualities as ruler to manifest themselves in much greater variety.

But it is not our task to recount his biography; we shall also pass over the whole imaginary picture of the hero current in the Middle Ages, his alleged baptism by Pope Sylvester at Rome, his gift of Italy to the Pope, and the like. Just as our earlier pages have given only an indispensable sketch of his relation to throne and Church, so other aspects of his reign can be treated only briefly. Concerning most of the questions involved, historical judgment is in any case not uniform, and even the facts themselves are often in dispute.

This is the case, first of all, in the matter of the completed development of court ceremonial and court dignities. The so-called *Notitia Dignitatum,* a calendar of court and state deriving from the beginning of the fifth century, enumerates an elaborately graded hierarchy of officials of court and state which must have received its form largely through Constantine, even though the fact is not demonstrable. Many of the court dignities, however, must have existed under Diocletian and even far earlier, perhaps under Hadrian. As we have no detailed account of the procedures, one aspect of the list appears startling: the solemnity with which despotism surrounds its display of pomp. The adjective *sacer,* "sacred," occurs where we should expect simply "imperial"; several titles, for example, refer to the *sacrum cubiculum,* "the imperial chamber," and the like. But in order to reach a definite conclusion and to determine court procedure precisely we should have to know which of the many offices involved actual attendance and which were merely titular. Even today there are courts which are in fact moderately and economically organized but which distribute an inordinate number of honorary titles.

How accustomed the contemporary Roman world must have been to titles as symbols of rank we learn from the usual honorific epithets *illuster, spectabilis, honoratus, clarissimus, perfectissimus, egregius,* and the addresses *amplitudo, celsitudo, magnitudo, magnificentia, prudentia tua,* and the like, which were in part obligatory prerogatives of certain offices. The significance of these innovations has been briefly indicated in connection with Diocletian; here also we may conjecture that the rulers involved did not so much institute novelties out of

Y

caprice as confirm usages which had arisen out of the spirit of the age and reduce them to form and rule. Constantine indeed was perfectly aware of the character of the innovations; "he devised various titles of honor," says Eusebius, "in order to bestow distinctions upon as many as possible."

The prerogatives of the courtiers, consistently applied and extended, must moreover have gradually produced a new hereditary aristocracy. Not only were they raised above the entire oppressive tax structure and the distress of the municipalities into a loftier, transfigured sphere, but they were also protected against *calumnias,* the fate of ordinary mortals. Their privileges applied not only to themselves but also to their children and grandchildren, and continued in the case of retirement. There was already an aristocracy which rested upon hereditary immunity to taxation, namely, the senatorial families; now everything pointed toward the creation of a second aristocracy, comprising courtiers (*palatini*) and higher officials.

But as far as his own person was concerned, at least, Constantine was able to hold these things in proper balance. His court was very slippery ground, and anyone standing there must beware of a fall. In his immediate environment the Emperor had a crowd of "friends," "intimates," "confidants," and others, whatever their title might be; he was not one of the reserved, taciturn tyrants. Along with his constant "reading, writing, and reflection," he felt the needs of an expansive nature. But this does not exclude great inconsistency and duplicity. There are characters which are a peculiar mixture, in this respect, of loyalty and falseness, of gregariousness and cunning egoism; in an authoritarian ruler of Constantine's sort the latter is customarily swathed in the garb of "reasons of state." Thus we see how Constantine first raises his "friends" and makes them wealthy, even allowing them to wallow in the imperial treasury — abuses which extort profound sighs even from a Eusebius and which are recognized by Ammianus as a cancer in the Empire. But suddenly there followed catastrophes which must surely have frequently made the entire court tremble; the "friends" are executed and (we venture to assert) their possessions are confiscated. Perhaps those ser-

mons of the Emperor of which we have spoken above were
harbingers of warning, perhaps even immediate annunciations
of doom; a careful man could take warning. Even in his conversation Constantine was rather sneering than amiable, *irrisor
potius quam blandus.* The law of the year 325 was promulgated in an especially menacing mood: "Whoever, of whatever
place, condition, or rank he may be, is confident that he can
prove truthfully any impropriety or injustice against any of my
judges, higher officials, friends, or courtiers may come and
apply to me without fear; I shall hear and investigate his
claim in person and if its truth is demonstrated I shall myself
take vengeance . . . ; I shall avenge myself upon the man who
had previously deceived me with hypocritical innocence. But
the man who furnishes information and proof I shall reward
by dignities and by property. So may the Supreme Divinity
ever be gracious unto me and preserve me for the happiness
and prosperity of the state." Whether anyone heeded this ve-
hement invitation we do not know, for the entire internal history of the court lies in darkness. In any case there was no
improvement; even in the last decade of his life, Constantine
was mocked, because of his immoderate extravagances, as being a *pupillus,* that is, requiring a legal guardian. There is
something very puzzling about the entire situation. Here we
have a tirelessly energetic autocrat who is very far from allowing a professed regime of favorites to arise and yet tolerates and
provokes such a state of affairs, only suddenly to put a period
to it by terrible penalties — and then occasionally ruing his
haste and setting up statues to the men he had executed, as
was the case with the murdered Crispus. In this conduct we
may perceive either a calculated plan or an impulsive and in-
constant nature; we know too little of Constantine to decide
upon one or the other alternative, and, as has been indicated
above, prefer to assume a mixture of motives. With a certain
quantity of pragmatism and a certain quantity of imagination
one might easily construct a court romance out of the scattered
notices concerning Crispus, Helena, the Prefect Ablavius, the
usurper Calocerus, and the heir apparent Dalmatius; such a
romance might well be very interesting and at the same time

totally untrue from beginning to end. In any case there was a general conviction that in his last decade Constantine was no longer the ruler he had been in his vigorous years. Of the complete corruption of the court under his sons, Ammianus provides very adequate testimony.

The state of the finances, which must have been closely interrelated with the other court affairs, we here pass over, because essential data are wanting; we do not, for example, know whether the new taxes introduced by Constantine were on the whole a benefit or a burden. The true balance sheet of the Roman Empire, also for this time, remains an enigma. There was much amiss, as we have noted, in the system which Constantine inherited; of the elements probably added or expanded by Constantine, the monopoly on numerous branches of industry, which the state retained for itself and exploited through its serfs, was thoroughly bad, but we must not forget that modern economic theory has only recently rejected these and similar incubuses. The manner of collection, in particular the responsibility of the decurions for the taxes of their district (see p. 79), was perhaps worse than the greed of the state in itself. A series of laws of Constantine shows us by what desperate means men sought to evade the decurionate — marriage with slave women, escape into the army, promotion to the Senate, removal to cities less pressed, going into hiding and living incognito, later even flight to the barbarians. For a short period entry into the class of clergy provided safety; but this sudden rush produced as sudden a prohibition. The state was fully occupied in making evasions of tax responsibility impossible. Local distress became all the greater when local Christian churches were endowed by municipal property, as must have happened in at least certain instances.

Neither can the new division of the Empire be touched upon here with more than a word. Now the twelve dioceses and more than hundred provinces of Diocletian were grouped together in four large prefectures. Considered superficially, many reasons may be adduced both for and against this division. Whether these reasons actually correspond to Constantine's motives in individual cases is another question; surely he would not have introduced so great a change out of mere idle desire for innovation. It is to be assumed that the division involved a great increase in the number of officials; but we cannot easily discern how far the increase was useless and oppressive. Judgment on this matter can have no adequate basis as long as we are partly or wholly ignorant of the duties, activity, and pay of these officials, and as long as we have no notion of their number in relation to the population. Many and powerful officials were probably evil and corrupt in the days of Constantine, as they were in the days of his predecessors and successors.

Very clear, however, and of the highest importance, is the separation between civil and military powers. The former *Praefecti Praetorio*, who previously also had been prime ministers and frequently rulers of the Emperor, retained their title, it is true, but are henceforward only the highest administrative officials of the four great prefectures — Oriens, Illyricum, Italia, and Gallia; the significance of the name had wholly changed. For military affairs there were now two high generals, the *magister equitum* and the *magister peditum*. The fact that there were two and that their business was divided not according to regions but according to cavalry and infantry shows the deeper purpose which underlay the change; any thought of usurpation was rendered difficult or futile as long as the one could initiate nothing without the other. The general separation of civil and military administration was carried through consistently; those dangerous high provincial officials who as proconsuls, propraetors, rectors, and the like, had in the past held military command in their region, shared only with the legates who were subaltern to them, could now no longer render the throne anxious. The consequences of this separation for the fate of the Empire would be even more striking if the house of Constantine had not substituted domestic atrocities for the disused usurpation by generals.

In military matters considered in themselves, it is the general assumption that Constantine's reign marks rather a recession than an advance, in spite of the Emperor's military genius. The dissolution of the Praetorians which had been begun under Diocletian and consummated after the victory over Maxentius does not belong in this place; it was a matter of political necessity and the Empire suffered no great loss in that force, which was personally brave but politically evil. Naturally, a new bodyguard was formed, the *palatini*. The rest of the army, under the old names of legions, auxiliaries, and so forth, was divided, as it appears, according to their barracks into *comitatenses*, which were situated in the cities of the interior, and *pseudocomitatenses*, to which the troops on the frontier and in the frontier fortresses chiefly belonged. In the large reckoning of faults with which the pagan Zosimus concludes the biography of Constantine, the quartering of the *comitatenses* in large cities is sharply rebuked, on the grounds that the frontiers were half denuded and laid open to the barbarians and the cities needlessly subjected to distressing oppression, while the soldiers themselves learned the pleasures of the theater and of luxury. Under Diocletian, he continues, the Empire had been guarded very differently; all the troops were quartered on the frontier, so that any barbarian attack could be repulsed at once. The justice of this accusation can neither be assumed nor rejected without qualification. Perhaps the large cities also required guarding. Whether Constantine had actually grown so indolent toward the end of his life that he and his army took to flight before a few hundred Taifales, as the same author reports, is very doubtful. At least he made considerable preparations for a war against the Persians shortly before his death.

The increasing barbarization of the Roman army was a necessary consequence of depopulation in the interior and of the settlements of barbarians, which was undertaken as a remedy. Furthermore, the free peoples beyond the frontiers were safely stripped of their most warlike young men by recruiting them for hire. The Franks in particular must have occupied an important position in the army; at least later, under the dynasty of Constantine, Frankish officers made themselves heard at court. Preservation of the state took precedence over preservation of the Roman nationality; and even in regard to nationality it might still have been hoped that the incorporated barbaric elements would gradually be mastered and assimilated, as had been the case in the early conquests during the Republic and the first centuries of the Empire.

Whether Constantine actually showed preference for barbarians, and in what sense, cannot be determined. It is charged against him that he was the first Emperor to make consuls of barbarians, but there is no detailed evidence. The records of the consuls of his period show almost exclusively names of the native Roman nobility — except for the frequent recurrence of imperial personages. Other state dignities he did bestow upon barbarians, and these may well have been by no means his worst appointments. Captive barbarian soldiers of his opponents he ransomed on the field of battle from his own victorious soldiers, by the thousands. It is conceivable that he had in view the bold possibility of supplying the depleted Roman Empire with barbarians, even of making them a ruling caste, and still controlling the imperium from above; specific declarations on this point are naturally not to be expected. But the strongest negation of the essential Roman character is comprised not in this relationship to non-Romans but in the establishment of the New Rome on the Bosporus. Of this New Rome we must now speak.

What could have been the purpose of establishing a new capital under conditions then prevailing?

Much more than the mere change in the residence of the prince was involved. It was to be foreseen that the dwelling of the Emperor would be frequently changed, and for considerable periods, according to the state of peace or war on the several frontiers. Even though a remarkable truce prevailed under Constantine himself, his successors in the fourth century could in fact make little use of the new capital and its splendors. A mere change of residence, furthermore, would have had a quite different aspect; Constantine might have built a new palace in Byzantium as Diocletian had done in Nicomedia and have embellished the city, even have fortified it if circumstances required, and then have left it to his successors to do something similar elsewhere. In this case the greatest gain was the military security of the central government by reason of the incomparable situation of the city.

The entire question concerning the choice of place is made extremely difficult, however, by our uncertainty concerning Constantine's deepest political plans. He shed streams of blood to restore the unity of the Empire, and then himself mysteriously divided it. Had his decision already been taken when he founded the new capital? We shall never know. The ruler of the world was in no position to direct and secure the fate of his own dynasty, because they were an atrocious breed. He had to trust to chance regarding the heir to whom the Empire and Constantinople would ultimately fall.

Geographical considerations, which are usually regarded as paramount, must not be overrated. Byzantium, it is true, lay much nearer the threatened frontiers than Rome; the Goths of the Danube and the Pontus and the Persians could be far better observed here. But despite all victories over them, the affairs of the Franks and the Alemanni were not yet so settled that the remote Rhine frontier could be regarded as indubitably secure. It is a question, furthermore, whether the capital properly belonged in one of the most perilous regions of the Empire, where only a few decades before Gothic pirate fleets had plied their business. Now, it is true, the city was so fortified that for nine centuries the storms of invaders raged against its walls in vain.

But Byzantium has another geographic significance besides its impregnable military location. Let us recall the role which the so-called Illyrian triangle — that is, the land mass between the Black, Aegean, and Adriatic Seas — played in the third century. Its generals and soldiers, among them the family of Constantine himself, had saved and ruled the Empire. That triangle could now demand the imperial residence for itself, and so Constantinople is in the first instance the affirmation and the crowning honor of Illyricum. This interpretation is justified by a statement in Zonaras, who tells us that Constantine had originally thought of a city deep in the interior, namely, Sardica (modern Sofia, in Bulgaria); only consideration for a privileged people within the Empire could have suggested such a choice.

But Constantinople, wherever it was to be situated, was to

be not merely the imperial residence but the expression of new conditions in the state, in religion, and in life. Its founder was doubtless perfectly conscious of this fact; he must needs choose a neutral location, unhampered by traditions. Deservedly or not, history has endowed his deed with the stamp of greatness; in the City of Constantine history developed a peculiar spirit compounded of Church and politics, and a separate category of culture, to wit the Byzantine, which, whether a man love or hate it, must nevertheless be recognized as a world force. At its summit was despotism, infinitely strengthened by the union of churchly and secular dominion; in the place of morality it imposed orthodoxy; in the place of unbridled and demoralized expression of the natural instincts, hypocrisy and pretence; in the face of despotism there was developed greed masquerading as poverty, and deep cunning; in religious art and literature there was an incredible stubbornness in the constant repetition of obsolete motives — altogether its character had much that was reminiscent of the Egyptian, and with the Egyptian it shared one of its highest properties, namely, tenacity. But we have to do not with the later historical perspectives, but rather with their beginnings.

It has been assumed that Constantine conceived a decided dislike of Rome, and that the Romans had occasioned or requited this dislike by their objection to Constantine's neglect of pagan ceremonies. But there is no need for such an explanation. Since the time of Diocletian Rome's unfitness for the imperial residence had been clearly recognized, along with the necessity for the division of the Empire. The intermediate rule of a Maxentius had demonstrated, to the great injury of Rome, how dangerously the noble old name of the mistress of the world might be misused when the Emperors were far away in the East and the North; but after the dissolution of the Praetorians Constantine knew that nothing serious was to be apprehended from that quarter. No one longer seriously expected that he should reside in Rome. The center for highest imperial affairs had for a long while been situated in Diocletian's bureau, hence usually at Nicomedia. Later Constantine as ruler of the West, along with Licinius, visited Rome only periodically, but sojourned mostly in Gaul and in the army posts. But perhaps after the victory over Licinius he was in no position to deny the East (aside from the special claims of Illyricum) the privilege of harboring the capital, just as in other serious affairs also he appears to have let matters take their course. Perhaps the secret personal developments which accompanied the fall of Licinius might also have been a factor in the choice.

And finally the urge for building, one of the strongest in the natures of mighty princes, grew to a passion in Constantine. There can be no more solid external symbol of power than buildings of impressive character. Furthermore, building itself quickly executed with massive resources provides a similitude of the creative ruler, and in times of peace a substitute for other activity. For its founder a new city serves as image and pattern for a new world.

The new foundation was preceded by remarkable decisions and trials. Besides Sardica, the Emperor had his eye also upon Thessalonica, and then Chalcedon, on the Asiatic side of the Bosporus. But the first fixed decision involved a place no other than the region of ancient Troy, whence once through Aeneas the migration to Latium and hence the foundation of Rome issued. There is no more question of historic sentimentality in the case of Constantine than in the case of Caesar and Augustus, who cherished a similar plan. Certainly definite grounds of pagan superstition were a consideration, and we have seen that the Emperor was not above such considerations. Ilium was the sacred and ancient seat of the Romans; by some oracular utterance, of which we no longer have knowledge, they were instructed one day to remove the seat of their rule back to Ilium, whence their origin derived. Constantine in person proceeded to the famous fields where for a thousand years sacrifices had been offered at the sepulchral mounds of Homer's heroes; at the grave of Ajax, on the spot of the Greek encampment, Constantine himself began to mark the outlines of the future city. The gates had already been built when one night God appeared to him and admonished him to select another site; and thereupon he determined upon Byzantium. A century later voyagers passing Troy could see the structure which Constantine had left unfinished. If a reader wishes to see in this story a conflict between the pagan and Christian elements in the Emperor's suite, none can gainsay him. It is conceivable that the court clergy set every means of opposition in motion when Constantine occupied himself with essentially pagan ceremonies and oracles.

But neither did the foundation of Constantinople proceed without similar interventions. For the eagles which seized measuring tapes and building stones from Chalcedon and carried them across the Bosporus for the new building at Byzantium, Zonaras and Cedrenus may answer; several similar details express the need of contemporaries for some superhuman connotations for great events. Constantine was compelled to indulge in superstition for the sake of the pagan population of the Empire, and apparently he himself was not wholly free of it. His own utterance upon the event was monotheistic, but in an indefinite and enigmatic sense: "We have endowed the city with an eternal name at God's bidding." What is this eternal name? Apparently not Constantinople, perhaps not even New Rome, but Flora or Anthusa, "the Flourishing," which was the priestly occult name of Rome. But the god who prescribed this name was hardly the God of the Christians. Neither has the dream vision which later chronicles ascribe to the Emperor — a ragged woman asking him for clothing — any Christian character whatever.

The ceremonial foundation of the western wall took place on 4 November of the first year of the 276th Olympiad, that is, the year 326, when the sun was in the sign of Sagittarius but the Crab ruled the hour. Shortly before, the heir apparent and perhaps also the Empress had been executed. It was the period when Constantine had become intimate with the Neoplatonist Sopater (see p. 302), and we find Sopater present at the foundation, acting as *telestes;* that is, he carried out certain symbolic actions which were to secure the fate of the new city by magic means. Besides Sopater, the hierophant Praetextatus, apparently a Roman pontifex, is named. Later a legend was in circulation that under the porphyry pillar in the Forum of Constantinople which supported the statue of the new founder there lay the Palladium which he had secretly abstracted from Rome. This would be a true *telesma,* such as was frequently carried out in antiquity for averting plagues and conjuring fortune; Apollonius of Tyana, for example, had employed such means in Byzantium itself to avert floods of the river Lycus, pestilential fleas and gnats, the fright of horses, and other such evils.

Now the city of Byzas was no longer concerned with such trifles, but with the fate of the world, which was to be linked to this spot. The ancient history of the city, which was now regarded with heightened interest, the old myths and oracles which could be interpreted as referring to it, everything seemed full of presage of a great future nearing fulfillment. Byzantium had drawn the attention of the world to itself by its energetic recovery from the catastrophe it suffered under Septimius Severus and Gallienus, particularly by its heroic defense against the former; now it was appointed to be the world's mistress.

We shall not attempt to describe the ancient city or the new. Only such details of the great enterprise as are characteristic for Constantine himself may be briefly mentioned.

He himself, spear in hand, indicated the outlines of the encircling wall. A legend relating to this circumstance may have a kernel of truth. His attendants found that he was walking in too wide a sweep, and one ventured the question, "How much further, Sire?" Thereupon he replied, "Until he who walks before me stops walking," as if he saw some superhuman being moving before him. It is quite conceivable that he found such a reply useful, if the others believed or pretended to believe in such apparitions. We cannot determine whether the remaining ceremonies were actually nothing but a repetition of those that took place at the foundation of Rome, as they are described by Plutarch in the eleventh chapter of his *Life of Romulus.*

Almost four years later, on 11 May 330, there followed with renewed great solemnities and sumptuous circus games the dedication of the new foundation and its naming as Constan-

tinople. That Constantine dedicated the city to the Virgin
Mary is surely a later invention. In all reason, he dedicated it
above all to himself and his glory. It was not enough for him
that the name of the city and its every stone recalled his name
and that a number of magnificent monuments were expressly
dedicated to him; annually upon the day of dedication a large
gilded statue representing him with Tyche, that is, the tutelary
genius of the city, upon his outstretched right hand, was to be
carried in a solemn torch procession through the Circus, upon
which the current Caesar was required to arise from his place
and prostrate himself before the image of Constantine and of
Tyche. Who could prevent people from gradually bestowing
a kind of cult upon the porphyry pillar with its colossal statue
of Constantine, mentioned above, and from burning candles
and incense before it and making vows to it? The Arian Phil-
ostorgius blames the Christians for this development, and
despite all protests may well be right; for where the ruler of
the world points the way with such an example, Christians
and pagans alike need not hesitate to deify him, even while he
is still alive.

The same spirit finds expression in the manner in which the
new city received its population under compulsion and was
endowed with special privileges. Its equality with Rome was
conceived in a quite literal sense, and accordingly it received
the same institutions, officials, and prerogatives; it even possessed seven hills like the Rome on the Tiber. Above all, it had
to have a Senate, even if no one knew why; at most the court
required figurants for its processions. A small number of Roman
senators did settle in Constantinople, moved by material advantages such as mansions and estates; and if a later legend is
correct, this was done with a very delicate courtesy, for the
Emperor surprised them with facsimiles of their Roman villas
and palaces on the shore of the Bosporus. He also built them
a magnificent Senate House; but neither the statues of the
Muses, which had once stood upon the sacred hill of Helicon,
nor the statues of Zeus of Dodona and Pallas of Lindos, which
now decorated the doors of the building, could avail to make
the new body more than a cipher.

Besides courtiers, officers, officials, and senators, the new city also required a population worthy of itself. On the year of dedication St. Jerome notes: "Constantinople is dedicated, while almost all other cities are denuded." This refers primarily to population. Whether it was that Constantine used the collapse in the conquered East of Licinius to enforce migration, or that he assembled a populace for the imperial residence by enticements of another sort, in any case he achieved his wish. This wish, in the realistic and unfriendly language of the pagan Eunapius, is expressed as follows: "From the subjugated cities he brought a populace together at Byzantium, so that many drunkards might alternately applaud him in the theater and spew forth their wine. He was pleased with the acclamations of persons who were not in control of their senses, and he rejoiced to hear his name called by men who were mindful of no name at all had it not been thrust upon them by daily usage." The vanity of great men and their thirst for praise is always a matter difficult to judge if we do not have first-rate sources. In the case of Constantine the strikingly vain and pompous appearances which a number of writers notice may well have had a consciously political purpose. There can be no question that he inwardly despised the Constantinopolitans.

But Jerome's remarks have still another significance. The Empire must have been more or less oppressed to produce the charges for the new establishment. Constantine is said to have expended sixty millions of francs of our money — an estimate which is clearly too low rather than too high, if we consider the volume and expense of the new buildings. The distribution of grain, wine, and oil, which became regular after 332 and without which the large population could not have survived, constituted a heavy and continuous drain. Eunapius complains that all the grain fleets of Egypt, Asia Minor, and Syria could not suffice to satisfy the mob. In the fifth century, when Eunapius wrote, the city was already more populous than Rome.

Finally, many cities of the Empire were robbed of their art treasures, which was always a grievous experience for men of Greek education. We have already spoken of the plunder

and smelting of statues made of precious materials; in addition
the most disgraceful and extensive thefts of art in all history
were committed for the purpose of decorating the new capital.
Here Constantine is neither pagan nor Christian — for he af-
fronted both religions by carrying images of the gods off to
Byzantium — but a self-seeking plunderer for the sake of glorifying his own name. There is no sadder reading for the amateur of ancient art than the inventory of art works set up in
Byzantium by and after Constantine, especially if one remembers their eventual destruction on the occasion of the fourth
crusade. When Eusebius, for example, speaks of the Pythian
and the Sminthian Apollo and when we read elsewhere of the
Samian Hera, the Olympian Zeus, and the like, it is not necessarily the actual original of the statue in question that is
involved; but the loss of any Greek work of art is irreplaceable,
and the originals of the statues named have in any case vanished. The heaping up of incompatible works, for example the
427 statues in front of Saint Sophia, must have produced a
crude and repellent effect; in certain cases elements of the
statues were altered in quite barbaric fashion, as when Constantine set his own plump portrait-head upon a colossal statue
of Apollo, for display upon the great porphyry pillar of which
we have spoken. From Rome there was brought, among other
things, a number of statues of Emperors; it was perhaps accidental that one of Maxentius was included, and when the
pagans of the new capital paid it reverence, perhaps for political reasons, Constantine is said to have caused the image to
be removed and its worshipers to be put to death. But far the
greater number of works came from Greece and western Asia
Minor. Once Roman proconsuls and Emperors had plundered
the same regions, and they may be forgiven because Rome and
its culture historically depended upon Greek art for its completion and transfiguration; but Byzantium wished to swallow
up all that was beautiful only in order that the provinces might
not possess it. It knew no other means of paying honor to its
statues than by contriving superstitious explanations and anecdotes and lame imitations of ancient epigrams for them.

We can have no conception, despite relatively abundant

sources on the subject, of the buildings of Constantinople
which were similarly erected in part of plunder, specifically
of the columns of older buildings in the vicinity. At the time
architecture was in a period of crisis. Arched construction with
its relatively new static organism was engaged in its decisive
struggle with the vestigial and ineffective forms of earlier
Greek temple architecture. The prevailing character of Constantinian building must have been a colorful and odd sumptuousness. Cupolas, niches, round halls, precious incrustations,
gold plating, and mosaic are the essential elements of this rich
and restless complex. Constantine's own impatience was clearly
expressed in the hasty and structurally imperfect execution,
which brought its own punishment in the rapid ruin of several
buildings and in the need for extensive repairs.

In addition to many and magnificent churches, Constantine's building includes two undeniably pagan temples. The
one, belonging to the Circus, was dedicated to the Dioscuri,
Castor and Pollux; the other was the Tycheion, the sanctuary
of Tyche, or the tutelary divinity of the city. We have already
encountered the annual dedicatory procession in the Circus in
which the statue of Constantine with a small Tyche on its
outstretched right hand was carried. Several other statues of
this goddess are mentioned besides, of which one had been
brought from Rome. Obviously this theft of the goddess was
more than a mere symbol; it was intended to put a magic seal
upon the transfer of world dominion to its new site. The Emperor, indeed, made remarkable efforts to remove her purely
pagan significance from Tyche. For example, a cross was affixed
to her forehead, and indeed at the great dedicatory festival in
330 there is a curious intermingling of prayer to Tyche and
the *kyrie eleison;* but the basic pagan sentiment was and continued to be predominant. A fortune-amulet was even affixed
to a publicly displayed cross. Over the ornamental structure
of the Miliarium there were to be seen the statues of Constantine and Helena, together bearing a cross at the center
of which a chain was to be observed. This chain was said to
possess the magic virtue of assuring the New Rome victory
over all peoples and security from all hostile attacks; and it,

too, was called the Tyche of the city. It is possible that this whole ornament is of more recent origin and that the significance of the chain existed only in the imagination of the Byzantines, but Constantine had surely given occasion for the rise of such legends by his own magic procedures.

The reaction on the part of the Christian courtiers and clergy is to be recognized, as we have suggested, in the fall and execution of Sopater. From the period immediately preceding the dedication the fall of another pagan philosopher, Canonaris by name, is reported. Canonaris appeared in public and cried out to the Emperor: "Do not raise yourself above our ancestors, because you have made our ancestors [that is, their customs and religion] nought!" Constantine had the philosopher approach him and admonished him to desist from his pagan sermon, but Canonaris shouted that he would die for his ancestors, and was thereupon decapitated.

We now turn our glance from the proud new cosmopolis back to the old.

Rome had retained one advantage, which appeared perhaps not of particularly great weight at that moment, to wit, the acknowledged precedence of its bishop over all the clergy of the Empire. Men of the time could not yet surmise that at a distance from the imperial throne of Byzantium there would arise the throne of a Western high priest and that the hierarchy, overshadowed in Constantinople by worldly dominion, and weakened in Antioch, Jerusalem, and Alexandria by heresy and by the sword of Islam, would at Rome one day become the center of a new spiritual world. Constantine's personal relationships to the Roman community are very ambiguous. His alleged donation is a fiction; the fabulous sumptuousness of his church building and offerings as it is depicted by Anastasius Bibliothecarius is in fact to be reduced to relatively small compass, which induces some doubt concerning the Emperor's generosity in general. Finally his alleged baptism by Bishop Sylvester in the Baptistry of the Lateran is a mere legend, born of the wish to supplant the Arian Eusebius of Nicomedia by an orthodox baptizing priest. In the Arian conflict the

z

Roman bishopric was not able to avoid involvement and maintain the position of a mere observer and arbiter. Later also it found itself deeply implicated in the political storms of the Church, and only gradually did it rise to the position of a world power.

For the time being, the great pagan majority in Rome itself was a significant hindrance to the Church. All through the fourth century the physiognomy of the ancient cosmopolis continued to be predominantly pagan.

This was true even externally, as regards architecture. A long period of destruction and persistent rebuilding was subsequently required before Christian Rome with its basilicas, patriarchies, and monasteries arose out of the Rome of the Empire. Even the buildings of the third century were largely calculated to serve the glorification of paganism, its culture and its pleasures. The Baths of Caracalla, of Alexander Severus, of Decius, and of Philip, and later those of Diocletian and of Constantine, the elaborate decorations of the Forum of Trajan, the magnificent villa of the Gordians, the Temple of the Sun of Aurelian, the Basilica and the Circus of Maxentius, and finally the project cherished by the younger Gordian, enlarged by Gallienus, but never carried out, of erecting a sumptuous colonnade with terraces to traverse the entire Campus Martius and then flank the Via Flaminia as far as the Milvian Bridge — all of these things characterize the spirit of building in that epoch. From the second half of the fourth century we still possess the *Regionary Catalogues* (poorer in their genuine form, to be sure, than with the interpolations which were formerly regarded as authentic and which enumerated, among other structures, more than one hundred and fifty temples by name). But even conservative calculation on this basis leads to enormous figures. The *Regionary Catalogues* (the so-called *Curiosum Urbis* as well as the *Notitia*) present specifically not the structural content of the fourteen regions of the city but only their boundaries; even in defining the boundaries they name an extraordinarily large number of temples, forums, basilicas, baths, gardens, halls, buildings for games, statues, and the like, though no single church. This omission was probably intentional, for in the age of Constantius and of

Theodosius there must have been many very considerable churches which only a pagan would ignore. Though we may imagine these churches as magnificent and extensive as we will, in keeping with the wealth and power of Rome's Christian community, they could nevertheless not compare with the ancient pagan magnificence. The summary of important items at the end of the two books named is unreliable precisely in the matter of numbers, but we shall still perhaps fall short of the truth if to the twenty-eight libraries, the eleven forums, the ten large basilicas, the eleven colossal baths, we add only two amphitheaters, three theaters, two circuses, and the like, for these additions still fall short of extant remains. Besides these and other colossal and handsome buildings we must imagine — and it is not easy to do — an endless abundance of majestic monumental decoration, such as the thirty-four (or thirty-six) marble triumphal arches and countless public statues and groups; all of this picturesquely distributed over valley and hill, enlivened and interrupted by gardens and groves (*luci*), accompanied by the gay murmur of springing waters which descended to the city from the surrounding hills upon nineteen lofty arched aqueducts to keep man and beast, air and foliage in the mighty city fresh. Many peoples, ancient and modern, have known how to build upon a colossal scale; but the aspect of ancient Rome will remain unique in history, because never again will the delight in the beautiful aroused by Greek art be coupled with such resources for its outward execution and with such a desire for magnificent environment. One who came to Rome fresh from the impressions of Constantinople, as Constantius did, for example, in 356, when he celebrated his triumph over conquered Magnentius, could only fall mute with astonishment and believe, each time he saw something new, that he was looking upon the most beautiful of all. The Forum of Trajan with its Basilica Ulpia was regarded, as we learn on this occasion, as the apex of the marvelous.

And all of this magnificence was available to a population whose number is equaled or exceeded by several of our modern capitals. The queen of the world Empire, whose population under Vespasian can be estimated at 120 million souls, probably

never had more than a million and a half in population. Modern
research has receded from earlier estimates, some unconscion-
ably exaggerated, when calculations were made of the area of
Rome and its suburbs and the large extent of the uninhabited
area on the basis of the relationship between the density of
population in modern capitals and the space devoted only to
traffic and ornament. One may well ask whence in fact came
the people who were to use and enjoy all of these temples, theaters, circuses, baths, and parks. The Colosseum itself could
perhaps contain a fifteenth of the entire population, the Circus
Maximus more than a tenth. To fill such structures required a
people which had been educated by its rulers to such amusement for centuries, which lived on bounties, and knew and demanded nothing other than ceaseless and constantly accentuated
pleasure. The considerable numbers of unmarried persons with
little or no occupation, the migration of rich provincials, the
concentration of luxury and corruption, and finally the confluence of large governmental and financial affairs must have made
of the Roman a type whose like is not easily to be imagined
elsewhere.

In this colorful mixture and through all its classes there were
two separate societies, a pagan and a Christian. How the latter
developed and comported itself in the first three centuries of the
faith and during the age of persecution is not our present business. From the critical period of Constantine, when it certainly
increased and underwent internal change, we have no adequate
sources; but descriptions from the second half of the fourth century, specifically those of St. Jerome, show the community as degenerated. The world with its pleasures had thrust itself into the
upper as well as the lower classes of the Roman community; one
could be zealously devout and at the same time quite immoral.
At times the entire community was stirred by terrible crises;
from Ammianus we learn that upon the occasion of the conflict
of Damasus and Ursinus over the bishopric (366) one hundred
thirty-seven casualties lay in the Sicinian basilica. Jerome, who
became secretary to the victorious Bishop Damasus, came in
contact with high and low in his new position. He knew how general the practice of abortion was; he saw two persons of the pop-

ulace marry, of whom the man had already buried twenty wives
and the woman twenty-two husbands; nowhere does he make a
secret of the general corruption. The greatest detail he devotes
to his description of the upper classes and certain of the clergy,
and indeed on their reciprocal influences. The grand lady, the
rich widow, moves about royally with full cheeks brightly
rouged; her sedan chair is surrounded by eunuchs. With this
retinue she appears regularly in the churches, and strides ma-
jestically through a gantlet of beggars, dispensing alms. At
home she has Bibles written in gold upon purple parchment and
set with precious stones, but she will allow the needy to starve
if her vanity is not served. A crier makes the rounds of the city
when the lady deigns to entertain at an *agape* or love-feast. On
other occasions also she is free with her board; among other
flatterers the clergy appear, kiss their hostess, and make a gesture with their hands — for a blessing, one would think? — no,
but to receive a gift; nothing makes the lady so proud as the
dependence of the priests. The widow's freedom is much more
delicious than the rule of a husband, and moreover presents an
appearance of abstinence, for which many found compensation
in wine and gourmandizing. Others who go about in haircloth
cowls like night owls, sighing continuously, and secretly indulg-
ing in coarse voluptuousness are no better. The austere churchly
teacher is wholly suspicious of artificial relationships based on
so-called spiritual bonds, which were injurious to normal family life. There were men who deserted their wives and formed
alliances with others under some pious pretext; women who
adopted lads as their spiritual sons and eventually indulged in
carnal intercourse with them, and many similar abuses, particularly of certain Tartuffes who attached themselves to women
as a sort of confessor and then lived with them. The clergy
proper, as has been indicated, was not spared either. Jerome
condemns unqualifiedly their habit of living with spiritual sisters, the so-called *agapetes* (otherwise *syneisactes*), and even
more vigorously their haunting prominent houses for the sake
of procuring legacies, power, and luxury. Some masqueraded
as ascetics with long hair, goatees, black cloaks, and bare feet;
they deceived sinful women by apparent fasting, for which they

compensated by gluttony at night. Others — somewhat like the abbés of the last century — had themselves consecrated as presbyters and deacons only to be able to associate with women more freely. This sort was elegantly attired, with elaborate hairdress, breathing of perfumes, all their fingers glittering with stones; because of their chic footwear they tiptoed mincingly; their aspect was rather of a bridegroom than of a priest. Such, likely, was the bearing of Jovinian, "in silk robe of the fine stuff of Arras and Laodicea, red-cheeked, with shining skin, his hair falling partly over his shoulders and partly curled over his forehead." Some devoted themselves wholly to discovering names, addresses, and tempers of women. Jerome knows of one such cleric who had made himself dreaded by carrying wicked gossip about from one house to another. From morning to night he rode about the city with fast and handsome horses, so that he was generally called the city postillion (*veredarius urbis*). Frequently he surprised people while they were still in their bedchambers; whatever stuff or vessels took his fancy he praised in such a tone that anyone who was clever at once made him a present of it. We even have the portrait of a clerical wastrel of the interesting type. Jerome tells with ardent displeasure of the wolf who broke into the sheepfold; but we should not relate a secret love story to expand an episode which has already carried us down to the second generation after Constantine.

Clearly the institution of monasteries with a rule of confinement which would separate ascetics from the temptations of city life once and for all was a genuine contemporary need. Asceticism was an inevitable urge of the times, because of the number of those who were rent in two by the clash of the old religion and old habits with the new ones, and sought salvation in an extreme resolve; they could not, however, wholly protect themselves against backsliding. Jerome devoted all of his efforts, at least in the devout circle which hearkened to him, to raise complete abstinence to a life-principle. The precept and example of this one-sided but mighty man may have dominated the outlook and the thoughts of his Paula, Marcella, and Eustochium throughout their lives and made them insensitive to all earthly happiness. Celibacy seemed to him the indispen-

sable condition of all higher life; because of celibacy higher secrets were revealed to the virgin apostle John than to the others
who had been married.

The invasion of the Empire by German tribes, and the threatening collapse of all institutions — *orbis ruit!* — doubtless accentuated the mood of resignation in him and in others to an
enormous degree. There were already in Rome and in the entire
West many men and women who with a deep and abiding resolution had espoused asceticism. The rocky cliffs of the Mediterranean and the desolate shores of Italy began to be populated
with anchorites and soon with monasteries; certain islands were
visited as the burial places of martyrs, as, for example, one of
the Ponza islands. It was possible to live in complete seclusion
in the midst of Rome itself, as was done, for example, by the
wealthy Asella, who sold her jewels, lived in a narrow cell on
bread, salt, and water, addressed no man, and only went out to
visit the graves of the Apostles. She was completely separated
from her family and rejoiced that no one any longer knew her.
Jerome was confident of his rare ability to discern between the
genuine city nuns and those who simulated.

A thing which must certainly have existed but is not to be
found in the descriptions of the zealous Church Father is the
picture of simple and sound-thinking Christian families without
asceticism and without debauchery. He is more concerned to
present the extraordinary and the extreme.

Between this Christian society and the more educated and
nobler pagans of the fourth century we insert the description of
the great masses of Rome as it is presented to us, to be sure not
without artful illumination, by Ammianus Marcellinus.

Ammianus begins on the occasion of a commotion because of
a shortage of wine, and teaches us, incidentally, that the Roman
populace was very bibulous; even today there is somewhat more
drinking in Rome than in Florence or Naples. The distributions
of wine instituted in the time of Constantine did not suffice; anyone with money to spend passed whole nights in the taverns.
When it was rumored of the City Prefect Symmachus that he
would rather use wine to slake lime than reduce its price his

house was set afire. When Rome was mentioned anywhere, there was at once talk of riotous drinking-houses. Like *morra* today, dice was the pastime inside and outside the inn and filled all leisure; this was accompanied by jarring cries which penetrated the marrow of all within earshot. If games with *tesserae* were considered more respectable than those with *aleae,* Ammianus is of the opinion that the difference is no greater than that between a thief and a highwayman. Unfortunately, he says, gambling companionship was the only bond which still held people together. The ordinary Romans were moreover still a defiant people filled with conscious pride; despite accretions of half a millennium from all lands, there were still many ancient citizen families who prided themselves on such names as Cimessor, Statarius, Cicimbricus, Pordaca, Salsula, and the like, even if they went barefoot. From time to time, at least in the theater, the wild and menacing cry was heard, "Out with the foreigners!" — these foreigners, says Ammianus, who were their sole support and salvation. But the chief cry of Rome was still *panem et circenses.* As regards bread, there was no more anxious moment than when the corn fleets from Africa were held back by war or adverse winds. On one such occasion the City Prefect Tertullus (359) presented his children to the raging mob as a pledge, and thereby so far calmed them that it was possible to proceed to the ever-green Tiber Island near Ostia, fragrant with roses and adorned with the temple of the Dioscuri, where the Roman people were accustomed to celebrate a gay festival annually; there Tertullus offered sacrifice to Castor and Pollux, and the sea became calm and a gentle south wind wafted the corn-laden fleet to the shore. That part of the holiday crowd which was not content with the bread, wine, oil, and pork which had been distributed took places at the vents of cookshops and enjoyed at least the aroma of roasts and other food.

The Romans were altogether insatiable for anything that might be called a spectacle. In the fourth century state subsidies for the purpose were far from sufficient, and the want was supplied by the munificence of newly nominated higher officials and of senators. This obligation constituted a very heavy burden upon these persons, who were not necessarily wealthy, for every-

one must seek to outdo his predecessors, not merely out of ambition but even more because of the insatiability of the populace.
A great part of the correspondence of Symmachus is devoted to
the anxiety which the necessity of providing entertainment, at
the time of his own promotion and that of his relatives and
on other occasions, caused him. Since Diocletian there was no
longer such imperial extravagance in entertainment as had suggested to Carinus the notion of covering half a quarter in the
region of the Capitol with a wooden amphitheater, decorating
it most sumptuously with precious stones, gold, and ivory, and
then displaying, among other rarities, mountain goats and hippopotamuses, and presenting fights between bears and seals. The
Emperor still provided for the buildings, as for example when
Constantine carried out a magnificent restoration of the Circus
Maximus; but the spectacles themselves had become predominantly the affair of wealthy dignitaries who were required to
compensate the state in this fashion and to expend their incomes
in return for their immunity from taxation. It was of no avail to
leave Rome; the registrars of taxes, as it appears, presented the
games in the name of the absent donor in such cases. A man was
lucky if he could import the exotic beasts duty-free. The most
important item was always the choice of horses for the Circus;
it was in the horse races that the distinguished like the ordinary Roman satisfied his superstitious passion for wagering, and
where a jockey could acquire the greatest personal glory and
even a kind of inviolability. Roman taste in these matters had
grown so refined that breeds had to be constantly changed; commissioners traversed half the known world to find something
new and extraordinary and to transport it carefully to Rome.
Symmachus' letters to these agents could not be more obsequi-
ous. For the beast fights in the theaters and the Colosseum and
for the hunts (*sylvae*) in the Circus Maximus there were required
gladiators, "a band of fighters worse than those of Spartacus."
Captive barbarians, as for example Saxons, occasionally appeared, but by now, in keeping with the spirit of the time, fights
between animals probably predominated. Here we find the
givers of the games in constant embarrassment as to how the
requisite animals were to be provided — the bears, which some-

times arrived in an emaciated state and sometimes were exchanged in transit, the Libyan lions, the crowds of leopards, Scottish hounds, crocodiles, and even animals whose identity cannot now certainly be determined, such as *addaces, pygargi,* and the like. There is mention of the Emperor's helping out with a few elephants after a Persian victory, but this was an exception.

To this same category belongs the scenic decoration of the Circus or a specific theater, for which Symmachus once summoned artists from Sicily. Of Symmachus, we can assume that he did only what his office required and was himself above such interests; but there were as fanatic admirers of individual gladiators in his day as ever there had been in the earlier Empire. The very extensive but somewhat barbarized mosaics in the Villa Borghese representing gladiatorial games and beast fights probably derive from the fourth century; the persons who appear in these mosaics have their names inscribed by their figures. Art now had often to reconcile itself to perpetuating such displays and to decorating entire halls and façades with them. The theater proper still had its ardent admirers also, among them persons bearing great names, like that Junius Messala who, in the age of Constantine, bestowed upon the mimes his entire wealth, including the valuable clothing of his parents. "Comedy" at least still enjoyed a certain interest in Rome, but more among ordinary people, whose greatest pleasure was said to be in hissing the actors off the stage, a fate which the actors are said to have sought to avoid by bribery. We may presume that the "comedy" in question is the farce (*mimus*). Much more important was the pantomime, that is, the ballet, which, according to a perhaps hyperbolic statement, still employed three thousand dancing girls and a large number of musicians.

If our sources are adequate on the subject of bread and circuses, we are left wholly in the dark concerning a thousand other details which are necessary for a complete picture of contemporary Rome. For example, the prime question of the numerical relationship of slaves to freemen cannot be answered even approximately, and attempted estimates vary widely. Here and there a chasm opens before the eyes of the researcher and provides a glimpse into that cross between state factory and

slave galley where work was done for the public need. This is
the case with the great bakeries which provided for the general
distribution of bread. In the course of time the superintendent
of these bakeries (*mancipes*) built taverns and brothels near by,
from which many an imprudent man was suddenly shanghaied
into the factory to spend the rest of his life in slave labor; he
disappeared completely, and his family regarded him as dead.
The Romans must have known of the practice, and the victims
were usually foreigners. The officials were informed about it as
surely as certain modern governments are informed concerning
the impressing of sailors; and if Theodosius put an end to the
cruelty on a specific occasion, we may not therefore infer that
it was first discovered at that time.

Ammianus' account of the life and conduct of the upper classes
raises a strong suspicion that that proud and spirited man was
unduly irked by a feeling of offended pride. As an Antiochene
he had no special justification for depreciating the Romans; but
as a courtier of Constantius and Julian his reception in the great
Roman families was probably not very cordial. Many of his
complaints are directed against the vices which are ascribed to
rich and prominent people at all times and in all places; others
refer to his own age in general. Ammianus deplores the prodigious passion for gilded honorific statues on the part of a class
immersed in trivial novelties and complete effeminacy. He scores
the habit of refusing to know strangers who have been presented
after their first visit, and of making it plain that persons who are
seen again after a long absence have not been missed. He describes the unfortunate practice of giving dinner parties only
to discharge social obligations — dinner parties at which the
nomenclatores (a sort of master of ceremonies of the slave class)
sometimes provide substitutes from the common people for a
gratuity. Even in Juvenal's day vanity frequently found an outlet in riding at breakneck speed and in showing fanatical enthusiasm for one's own and for the circus horses; this fashion
also continued. Many would appear in public only if they were
surrounded by a whole procession of servants and domestics;
"under the command of the majordomos with their staves there
marched by the carriage first a company of slave weavers, then

the kitchen slaves in black dress, then the other servants of the household, mingled with idle folk from the neighborhood; the procession is closed by an army of eunuchs of every age, from old men to mere lads, all sickly and deformed." At home even in the better families, as presently among ourselves, music concealed numerous social gaps. Song and harp sounded continuously; "instead of the philosopher, the singer was employed; instead of the rhetor, the teacher of the arts of enjoyment; while the libraries were closed tight like a tomb, hydraulés were constructed and lyres as big as stagecoaches." Rage for the theater was characteristic of the higher classes also, and the coquetry of many a lady was comprised in imitating theatrical poses with slight variations. Gestures and bearing continued to be of studied artifice; Ammianus knew a city prefect named Lampadius who took it amiss when the sense of style he displayed in spitting was not properly appreciated. The practice of maintaining clients and parasites was probably not much changed since Juvenal's day; neither was legacy-hunting among the childless rich and many other similar abuses of the early Empire. But it must be emphasized that despite his sour mood Ammianus has almost nothing to say of the iniquities and enormities which Juvenal excoriates. Christianity contributed little to this improvement; the transformation which caused the new moral standard had already made its appearance in the third century.

This fashionable society is plainly pagan, as can be observed in the first instance by its superstitions. Whenever there was a question of wills and legacies, for example, the haruspices were summoned, to seek a decision in the entrails of animals. Even unbelievers would refuse to walk in the street, take their place at table, or go to the bath without consulting the *ephemeris*, or astrological calendar, for the position of the planets. We know from other sources that the majority of the Senate was pagan until the times of Theodosius. Everything possible was done to maintain the priesthoods and the ceremonies in their complete forms; this endeavor cost Symmachus enormous effort and anxiety. But along with the public *sacra*, the most respectable Romans of the fourth century addressed themselves with great enthusiasm to occult worship, and indeed, as we have observed above, in a peculiar amalgamation. By taking practically all available secret initiations, the individual sought to secure and strengthen himself against the inroads of Christianity.

All things considered, Rome's pagan Senate may still have been the Empire's most respectable assembly and society. Despite Ammianus' slanders, the Senate must still have contained many men — provincials as well as Romans — of the old stalwart Roman spirit, in whose families traditions were cherished which would be sought in vain in Alexandria and Antioch and certainly in Constantinople. Above all, the senators themselves revered the Senate, the *asylum mundi totius*. They still demanded a specific simple and serious style of eloquence, which should display nothing of the theatrical; always the effort was made to maintain at least the fiction that Rome was still its ancient self and that the Romans were still citizens. These are merely big words, to be sure, but there were men of stature among the senators and it was not their fault if big things did not issue from them. In Symmachus himself the courage of his advocacy for persons oppressed arouses high admiration and, like the patriotism of Eumenius (p. 76), balances the inevitable flatteries in which he elsewhere indulges. As a gentleman of large and independent stature he was personally above the titles of dignity which were the ambition of so many others.

The higher education which prevailed in these circles can no more be judged according to the literal words of Ammianus than can other matters. He allows the Romans no other reading than Juvenal and the imperial history of Marius Maximus, of which we know that the first half of the *Historia Augusta* is a jejune reworking. Of the literary rendezvous at the Temple of Peace (where one of the twenty-eight public libraries was located) there is not much to say, for even a Trebellius Pollio could display his wares there. But the circle of friends which Macrobius gathered about himself, the environment in which Symmachus himself moved, shows how much true education still survived in the upper classes. We must not be misled by the pedantry of the former (very useful to us) or by the Plinian preciosity of the latter. The literary age is indeed one of decline, more appropriate for collection and criticism than for creation. The epigone

betrays himself by his wavering between Plautine archaisms
and the most modern abstract substantives. We may even be
tempted to recognize in prefiguration the one-sidedness of the
Romance peoples, who would keep a literature alive by the use
of a dictionary; the dainty affectation of Symmachus' letters and
notes is certainly conscious artifice. But the reverence for the
ancient literature, to which indeed we may owe its preservation,
was of as great importance for contemporary cultural life as
is the cult of Ariosto and Tasso for modern Italy. The finest
gift which Symmachus can make to a friend is a copy of Livy.
Vergil was virtually worshiped; he was incessantly analyzed, ex-
pounded, learned by heart, worked into centos, and even consulted for fortune telling. It may well have been in this age that
the life of the great poet began to be transformed into something miraculous and magical.

And finally the rural life of these upper-class Romans deserves
a fleeting glance. The same man who accounts it a great praise
for his daughter that she is an industrious spinster or at least
supervises the maidservants engaged in spinning, possessed
dozens of villas whose enormous ménage required the services
of an army of superintendents, notaries, collectors, builders, car-
riers, and messengers, to say nothing of thousands of farm slaves
and share farmers. As many of the great families died out, the
latifundia, which had long been "the ruin of Italy," were concentrated in fewer and fewer hands. No one denies that this was
on the whole an evil, and Italy's dependence upon the African
grain fleets demonstrates the fact. The owners themselves were
not always happy; they were looked upon by the government
with suspicion, burdened with honorific obligations, annoyed
by billeting requirements, perhaps frequently pressed by a complicated financial economy, and could thus derive only qualified
satisfaction from their well-nigh princely position. But those who
could still take pleasure in their possessions enjoyed their so-
journs at their country estates, moving from one to the other
according to the season of the year; of these estates at least the
older might still have recalled the spacious elegance of Pliny's
villas. Symmachus' holdings included — to begin in the vicinity
of Rome — country houses on the Via Appia and on the Vatican,

at Ostia, Praeneste, Lavinium, and cool Tibur, then an estate at Formiae, a house at Capua, as well as estates in Samnium, Apulia, and even in Mauretania. The inventory includes as a matter of course properties on the heavenly coast of Naples as well. The Romans had always given the Gulf of Baiae a preference, unintelligible to us, over the Bay of Naples. To sail on gaily colored boats from Lake Avernus out to sea to Puteoli was still looked upon as a blissful excursion; over the quiet waters songs echoed from all the boats, from the villas built out over the sea there came the sounds of gay parties, and far from the shore the splashing of bold swimmers. Lucullan luxury was the paramount pattern, and the solitude which visitors pretended to seek was hardly to be found in the row of villas and palaces which extended for miles; genuine Roman country life flourished rather upon estates which were actually operated as farms. Here the Roman delighted to celebrate his harvest-home: "The new wine has been pressed and stowed in kegs; ladders reach to the tops of the fruit trees; now is the olive pressed; now the hunt takes us to the woodland, and keen-scented hounds follow the tracks of the boar." As regards the hunting, which we may conjecture to have been excellent, Ammianus is of opinion that the effeminacy of many made them content to be mere spectators; but for those whose limbs were vigorous the hunt, in the fullest sense of the word, was surely as important an activity as it is for the modern Italian. Even for this occupation a poem rather than a handbook divided into sections was required. Just as the *Georgics* provided artistic representation of country life in general, so the *Cynegetica* and *Halieutica,* some of which may go down to the fourth century, glorified hunting and fishing. A few verses of Rufus Festus Avienus, of the end of the fourth century, are our last reflection of the mood which inspired the country life of the Roman pagan. "At dawn I pray to the gods, then I go over my estate with the servants and show each his appropriate task. Then I read and I call upon Phoebus and the Muses, until it is time to anoint myself and to exercise in the sand-strewn palaestra. In happy mood, remote from money affairs, I eat, drink, sing, play, bathe, and rest after supper. While the small

lamp consumes its modest measure of oil these lines are indited
to the nocturnal Camenae."

The number of those who were able to enjoy life so fully
must, however, have grown scant, for the crisis of the Empire,
the belief in daimones, and anxiety concerning the beyond had
shattered the pagan spirits also. That peculiar view of the world
which combined nobler Epicureanism with Stoicism and made
the earthly life of better men into so admirable and amiable a
whole was dying out. A late echo of this spirit, from the age
of Constantine, is provided, among others, by Pentadius' little
poem, *On the Happy Life*. But his lines are mere reminiscences
of Horace and need not be repeated here, because one can
never know whether their author was in true earnest.

There was another city in the ancient world Empire, a city
which was perhaps never named under Constantine, but concerning whose life and survival our sympathetic curiosity may
well be aroused.

The position of ATHENS had been greatly diminished after
the Peloponnesian war, and after the conquest of Sulla it had
grown more and more deserted and was reduced to small compass. But the aura of glory which surrounded the city, its easy
and pleasant life, the majestic monuments, the reverence for
the Attic mysteries, and the awareness of the whole Hellenic
world of its debt to Athens — all of this drew a continual stream
of free and educated spirits to the city; philosophers and rhetors appeared, and numerous disciples followed. From the time
of Hadrian — the new founder of Athens, as gratitude styled
him — study burgeoned into a sort of university, which was in
a way made secure by imperial endowments and later became
the most important source of livelihood for the impoverished
city.

All who cherished antiquity in these late ages must needs
love the Athenians. Lucian has his Nigrinus utter beautiful and
moving words concerning this people, among whom philosophy
and poverty were equally at home, and who were not ashamed
of their poverty but regarded themselves rich and happy in
their freedom, the moderation of their life, and in their golden

leisure. "The climate there is altogether philosophical, the fairest for fair-thinking men; indeed, one who wishes luxury, power, flattery, lies, servitude, must live in Rome." But not only the Syrian of Samosata, who is otherwise so seldom serious, but also an Alciphron, a Maximus of Tyre, a Libanius of Antioch, and other even later figures burst into flame whenever the Athenians are mentioned; we can never be certain whether in a given case ancient Athens of the period of bloom is thought of or whether the virtues of ancient Athens are discovered or assumed in the contemporary population. Speaking of forgiveness for insults which might be avenged, Libanius says, for example, that such conduct is "worthy of the Greeks, the Athenians, and godlike men." Heliodorus of Emesa has an Athenian girl who has been captured by Egyptian robbers write: "Barbarian love is not of so much worth as Athenian hatred." These later pagans, who could not be at ease either in the organized life of Rome or in the Christian Church, adhered to the most sacred site of ancient Greek life with a genuine tenderness. Anyone who could spend his life in that environment counted himself happy.

But the studies for which sophists and their disciples assembled in Athens bore the stamp of their age all too plainly. Just as Philostratus and Gellius are copious sources for the school of Athens in the early Empire, so are Libanius and Eunapius for its condition in the fourth century, and it cannot be said that it had improved in the interval. The one-sided predominance of rhetorical education and the extravagance and mysterious airs of individual Neoplatonists, the vanity of the teachers and the partisanship of their devotees — all of this disrupted the calm of Athens with a peculiar kind of rivalry. The very arrival of the student was a perilous affair; at the Piraeus, if he had not already been encountered at the headland of Sunium, men stood ready to watch for new students in order to recruit them for one or another lecture hall (*didascaleion*), even employing threats to change a decision which the student might already have taken at home. Teachers suddenly appeared at the harbor to make sure of their prey. If a man got safely to Athens, perhaps under the protection of the ship's captain, he found himself exposed to actual vio-

AA

lence; not infrequently there were assault, murder, and consequent criminal investigations, and all because of the rivalry of teachers. The student's country of origin was a matter of great importance; when Eunapius was a student in Athens the Easterners mostly adhered to Epiphanius, the Arabs to Diophantus, the men of Pontus to their divine countryman Proaeresius, who also attracted many from Asia Minor, Egypt, .and Libya. But no student was bound to follow this practice, and moreover the incessant transfers from school to school kept enmities constantly aflame. The students were divided into armed "choruses" with *prostates* at their head; their bloody brawls appeared to them "of equal value with battles for the fatherland." If things went so far that two parties, comprised of teachers and auditors, were required to answer for their deeds before the proconsul of Achaia at Corinth, a regular ceremonious rhetorical contest was staged in the presence of the proconsul, especially when it was worth while, when the official was "quite well educated for a mere Roman." There was no sort of comradely feeling. It had long been imprudent to venture an appearance in public theaters and halls, which might immediately arouse bloody riots. The more prosperous sophists built themselves small theaters in their homes. Eunapius gives us a description of the house of Julianus, which was so equipped: "It was a small, modest house, but it breathed of Hermes and the Muses, so like was it to a sanctuary, with statues of its owner's friends; the theater was of stone masonry, an imitation of the public theater on a small scale." But a teacher who was as poor as Proaeresius, who at first shared only a robe, a cloak, and a few carpets with his friend Hephaestion, had to help himself as best he could.

In the "choruses" of the students there were great and deeply rooted abuses. At his first arrival the new student was pledged to a costly and elaborate initiation and permanent obligations under oath, and this not infrequently led to acquaintanceship with usurers. By day there was a great deal of ball playing; by night wanderings and visits to "the sweet-singing sirens." Crude and unscrupulous elements thought it a prank to attack unprotected houses in robberly fashion.

When Libanius finally disentangled himself from these "fraternities" — not without some difficulty — he took pleasure in peaceful excursions, especially to Corinth. Apparently many still journeyed, as they had done at the time of Philostratus, to the Olympian, Isthmian, and other national festivals, which were even then held in great esteem. But the greatest prize which a zealous pagan could take with him from Athens was the Eleusinian initiation.

All of this colorful activity took place among the most majestic monuments of the world, in which the noblest of forms and the most significant of historical reminiscences united to produce an inexpressible effect. We no longer know what these works meant to the sophist of the fourth century and his pupils. It was the period during which one mainspring after another of the Greek genius died, until only hair-splitting dialectic and lifeless compilation remained. The Parthenon of Pallas Athene and the Propylaea looked down upon the city in their ancient and virtually undisturbed majesty; despite the Gothic incursion under Decius and despite the plunder under Constantine, perhaps most of what Pausanias had seen and described in the second century still survived. But the pure harmony of architectural forms, the untrammeled grandeur of the images of the gods, uttered a language that was no longer wholly intelligible to the spirit of this age.

The century was eager to find a new home for its thoughts and aspirations. For zealous Christians their earthly-heavenly fatherland existed, and its name was Palestine.

We shall not here repeat what Eusebius, Socrates, Sozomen, and others relate of the official glorification of the country by Constantine and Helena, of the magnificent church buildings of Jerusalem, Bethlehem, Mamre, on Mount Olivet, and elsewhere. In the case of Constantine the motive which impelled him to such expenditures was quite superficial. The highest spiritual value which he could perceive in reverence for holy objects was a sort of belief in amulets; he had the nails of the True Cross worked into a bit for his horse and a helmet for use in battle.

But in countless numbers of the faithful there arose the natural and irresistible urge to visit in person the localities which they held sacred. It is true enough that a thoroughly spiritual man can forgo such pilgrimages, indeed that pilgrimages make what is essentially sacred superficial and dependent upon a given locality. Nevertheless a man who is not wholly unfeeling will visit at least once the sites which are for him hallowed by associations of love or of worship. In the course of time, when passion has become habit, the mood of the pilgrim will be reduced to a sort of superstitious "good works," but this by no means impugns its pure and beautiful origin.

From the apostolic age downward there must always have been visitors to the sites in Palestine which so strikingly combined memories of the ancient covenant between God and man with those of the new. Perhaps the earliest pilgrimage to remote parts was that of the Cappadocian Bishop Alexander, who visited Jerusalem — at the time called Aelia Capitolina — under Caracalla "for the sake of prayer and of the history of the spot." Origen also came "to seek out the paths of Christ, the disciples, and the prophets." But at the time of Constantine longing for Palestine was remarkably interwoven with the growing cult of the burial places of martyrs and of relics. Jerusalem itself was at once the greatest and holiest of all relics, and it was surrounded by a series of sacred sites of the first importance, involving journeys of many days. From the itinerary of a pilgrim of Bordeaux who visited the Holy Land in 333, we can see how pious legend, and perhaps profit interest also, had filled the whole country with classic sites, whose authenticity continued unquestioned in the Middle Ages. Visitors were shown the chamber in which Solomon wrote the Book of Proverbs, the bloodstains of the priest Zacharias on the floor of the former temple, the house of Caiaphas and that of Pilate, the sycamore of Zacchaeus, and many other objects which might afford historical criticism amusement. Some decades later, in his description of Paula's journey, Jerome enumerates the sacred sites from Dan to Beersheba in much greater detail. Though otherwise very level-headed in his views concerning relics, Jerome himself settled in Bethlehem for the remainder of his life, and drew after him all those who were devoted to him. Toward the end of the fourth century there lived in Jerusalem and its vicinity, with great self-denial, a large colony of devout persons from all quarters of the Empire; "there were almost as many chanting choirs as there are diverse peoples." Among them were Westerners of high rank and great wealth who had left everything behind them in order to live their lives out in purer contemplation than was possible elsewhere. Those whom circumstances prevented from so doing were deeply grieved; Jerome wrote more than one letter to pacify such persons and to assure them that eternal blessedness did not depend upon a visit to Jerusalem.

But this much envied existence was by no means ideal. Aside from external danger because of plundering Saracens whose raids reached the very gates of Jerusalem, paganism persisted with desperate stubbornness in the near vicinity, in Arabia Petraea and in Coele-Syria; furthermore, daimonic activity, which had so long been native to Palestine, was as vigorous as ever. We have already seen St. Hilarion as an exorciser of daimones (p. 328). Jerome himself takes us to the tombs of the prophets not far from Samaria, where a large number of possessed persons waited for relief; they could be heard at a distance, howling with the cries of various animals. These were the stray spirits who hovered over the battlefield of all religion, the land between the Jordan, the desert, and the sea.

A strange providence brought it about that even in what Constantine did for Palestine there was an effect upon world history which endured for many centuries. If it had not been for the splendor which he bestowed upon Jerusalem and its vicinity, the reverence of the Roman world and consequently that of the Middle Ages would not have been so ardently fixed upon these sites, and the land would not have been wrested back after half a millennium of bondage under Islam.

ADDENDA ET CORRIGENDA

(Under this heading Burckhardt appended a number of notes written in the light of later research, partly bibliographical and partly expanding certain points made in the text. Of the latter category two are especially noteworthy as revealing Burckhardt's mind more fully, and are included here.)

Page 297: In the *résumé* of the edict of 324 A.D. it should have been emphasised (as I now realize from Brieger's work °) that, despite all expressions of contempt, continued toleration of paganism is specifically enjoined. Constantine desiderates a kind of parity, which was in fact bound to work out in favor of Christianity. But he had no intention to make his calculations explicit, and it is difficult to reduce him to a hard and fast principle.

This affords occasion for an additional word on Constantine's historical achievement in general. He ventured one of the boldest strokes imaginable, a stroke before which perhaps more than one Emperor had doubtless retreated in dismay, to wit, the separation of the empire from the old religion, which, in its dilapidated condition, could be of no further help to the authority of the state, despite the cult of the Emperor which it imposed. This implies that even in his youth, even before the persecution, Constantine must have reached a decision concerning the Christian Church also: small as was the minority it comprised in the face of the entire pagan world, it was nevertheless the only organized force in the Empire — aside from the army — when all else was crumbling dust. His perspicacity in perceiving in this force a future support for the Empire and in acting accordingly constitutes Constantine's enduring claim to fame. Along with an intelligence as cold

° Brieger, *Konstantin d.Gr. als Religionspolitiker*, Brieger's Zeitschrift fuer Kirchengeschichte IV, 2. Gotha 1880.

and hard as it was lofty, along with complete inner inde-pendence of any Christian sentiment, this implies extraordinary determination and resourcefulness. Like Henry VIII of England, Constantine understood how to accommodate his individual measures to prevalent trends at every turn, and almost until the end he was fearless enough to offer paganism at once defiance and a degree of favor.

Page 323 ff.: The entire concept of the actual and chronological development of monachism has newly been considerably modified by Weingarten's work on "The Origin of Monachism in the Post-Constantinian Era" (*Der Ursprung des Mönchtums im nachkonstantinischen Zeitalter,* Jena, 1877). Here, to say nothing of numerous other critical conclusions, the *Life of Paul* is declared to be a romance by Jerome, and the *Life of Anthony* not of Athanasian authorship. If, these arguments notwithstanding, I fail to alter my previous account substantially, I may justify my course by the consideration that such pieces of fiction — if that is what they are — were nevertheless fashioned in the spirit of their time and place, and may hence claim truth from the viewpoint of cultural history. (In the case of Anthony I regard a combination of extreme asceticism and previously acquired theological and philosophical education as quite possible.) But I feel constrained to lay much greater weight than Weingarten does on the anchorite as preparation to the cenobite stage. Furthermore, the *argumentum ex silentio* as applied to Eusebius and other bishops seems to me somewhat questionable; perhaps they had little regard for monachism, and were preoccupied with matters which seemed to them very much more important. Finally, I regard asceticism generally, even in its fearful stages, as a quite possible consequence of rigorous Christian doctrine and Christian views. That the very remarkable recluses of the temple of Serapis survived in those of the Christian period I do not deny; but a recluse — however austere his life might be — and an eremite living in the open differ much more than our author assumes.

ON THE ANCIENT SOURCES

FOR HIS historical reconstructions Burckhardt made full use of ancient sources — numismatic and epigraphic as well as literary, and *belles lettres* as well as professed history — and of modern authorities. The latter are now largely antiquated, in a measure by Burckhardt's own work. Among the ancients the authors most frequently referred to, as is inevitable in any treatment of the subject, are Eusebius (mainly the *Life of Constantine*) and Lactantius (mainly the *On the Deaths of the Persecutors*) among the Christians, and among the pagans, the *Scriptures Historiae Augusta*, Ammianus Marcellinus, Aurelius Victor, and the *Panegyrici*. On the historical worth of all these sources widely differing opinions have been held, and it may serve the reader's convenience to have a brief statement concerning them.

Eusebius of Caesarea (*ca.* 265–340) was a prolific writer on Biblical exegesis, apologetics, and church history. His work on the Bible included, besides regular commentaries, such helps as an *Onomasticon* of Biblical place names; his principal 'apologetic' works are the *Preparation for the Gospel* in fifteen books and the *Demonstration of the Gospel* in twenty (of which more than half are extant); his *Church History* in ten books (aside from a briefer work on chronology) is a pioneer work in its field and was widely used by subsequent historians. All of his longer works are especially valuable for their copious extracts from earlier writers. Eusebius wrote after Christianity had become an established religion, and he is the first writer to apply to church scholarship generally the techniques of the objective secular researcher. Considered from the viewpoint of objective historiography the *Life of Constantine* is in fact clearly liable to the stricture Burckhardt pronounced upon it (see pp. 261 ff.). But it is not altogether just to regard it from that point of view, for it really belongs to the genus of panegyric, in which it was universally recognized that objective truth must yield to fulsome adulation. But if such exculpation saves the character of Eusebius, it does not establish the veracity of the *Life.*

Lactantius (born *ca.* 250) marks the same transition in Latin patristic writing as Eusebius does in Greek. His doctrinal works include *On the Creation, The Divine Institutes,* and *On the Wrath of God,* but it is *On the Deaths of the Persecutors* which contains historical data. This treatise relates the horrible deaths suffered by all earlier Emperors who persecuted Christians — the abdication of Diocletian and Maximian is interpreted as a divine chastisement — with a view to demonstrating God's care for His elect, possibly in order to deter Licinius from hostile measures against the Christians. After Burckhardt's day there was a tendency among scholars to deny the genuineness of this treatise, but latterly the pendulum has swung in the direction of regarding it as a work of Lactantius. The author, whoever he may have been, gives every indication of having been an eyewitness, however biased, of the persecutions in Nicomedia.

The *Historia Augusta* presents biographies of Emperors, Caesars, and usurpers from Hadrian to Numerian (117–284), with a lacuna for the period 244–253. It purports to be the work of six authors — Aelius Spartianus, Vulcacius Gallicanus, Aelius Lampridius, Julius Capitolinus, Trebellius Pollio, and Flavius Vopiscus — and to have been written between the reigns of Diocletian and Constantine, or about 330. Some scholars accept this genesis as true, but others hold that the work was written by a single hand almost a century later, and that the names of the six authors were attached to give it credit. As history the book rates low in any case, being chiefly concerned with petty gossip and sprinkled with palpable untruths.

Ammianus Marcellinus (born *ca.* 325) wrote a history of the period from Nerva to Valens in thirty-one books, of which the first thirteen are lost; what remains covers the years 353–378. Historians generally agree with Gibbon's judgment that Ammianus is "judicious and candid" and that his testimony is "unexceptionable." But such passing remarks as that "the enmity of the Christians towards each other surpassed the fury of savage beasts against man" (22.5) has been taken in some quarters to imply a general anti-Christian bias on the part of Ammianus.

Aurelius Victor was personally acquainted with Ammianus Marcellinus, was Prefect of Rome in 389, and assembled his tripartite history in 360. The first two parts, *Origin of the Roman Race* (on the Aeneas legend) and *On Illustrious Men* (on the early monarchy and the republic) are irrelevant here; the third part, called *Caesars,* deals with the Empire and has much the same merits as Ammianus' work. What Burckhardt refers to as the "Second Victor" is an epitome, ostensibly of Victor but really an independent work, attached to the *Caesars.*

The *Panegyrici* is a corpus of twelve cloyingly fulsome orations addressed to various emperors on special occasions. They are indubitably genuine and, cautiously used, a valuable historical source. Eight refer to our period: II, to Maximian, on 21 April (the birthday of Rome) 289, in some northerly city of the Empire; III, to Maximian, for his birthday; IV, a petition of Eumenius to rebuild the schools of Autun; V, to Constantius, 1 March 297, on the subjugation of Britain; VI, for the marriage of Constantine and Fausta, 307; VII, for Constantius, on the birthday of Treves, 310; VIII, gratitude to Constantine in the name of Treves, 311; IX, felicitation to Constantine for his victory over Maxentius, at Treves, 313; X, Nazarius' panegyric of Constantine for the fifth year of his accession, 321.

Among other writers frequently cited by Burckhardt mention may be made of the historians Dio Cassius, Zonaras, Eutropius, Herodian; the church historians Socrates, Sozomen, Moses of Chorene; the church writers Tertullian, Jerome, Athanasius, Arnobius; the biographers of the rhetoricians Philostratus and Eunapius; the novelists Apuleius, Heliodorus, Longus.

MOSES HADAS

CHRONOLOGY OF THE EMPERORS

98–117	Trajan	248–249	Philip the Arab and son
117–138	Hadrian		
138–161	Antoninus Pius	249–251	Decius
161–169	Marcus Aurelius Lucius Verus	251–253	Gallus and son
169–177	Marcus Aurelius	253	Aemilianus
177–180	Marcus Aurelius Commodus	253–260	Valerian Gallienus
180–193	Commodus	260–268	Gallienus
193	Pertinax	268–270	Claudius Gothicus
193	Didius Julianus	270	Quintillus
193–198	Septimius Severus	270–275	Aurelian
198–208	Septimius Severus Caracalla	275	Interregnum of about one month
208–211	Septimius Severus Caracalla Geta	275–276	Tacitus
		276	Florianus
211–212	Caracalla Geta	276–282	Probus
		282–283	Carus
212–217	Caracalla	283–284	Carinus Numerianus
217–218	Macrinus		
218	Macrinus Diadumenianus	284–286	Diocletian
		286–305	Diocletian Maximian
218–222	Elagabalus	305–306	Constantius Chlorus Galerius
222–235	Alexander Severus		
235–238	Maximinus	306–307	Galerius Severus
238	Balbinus Maximus	307–308	Galerius Constantine [Maximian Maxentius]
238–244	The Gordians		
244–248	Philip the Arab		

308–310	Galerius	324–337	Constantine
	Licinius	337–340	Constans
310–311	Galerius		Constantius II
	Licinius		Constantine II
	Maximinus Daia	340–350	Constans
	Constantine		Constantius II
311–313	Licinius	350–361	Constantius II
	Maximinus Daia	361–363	Julian
	Constantine		
313–324	Constantine		
	Licinius		

INDEX

Abae, oracle of, 204

Abammon, hypothetical author of *On the Mysteries of the Egyptians*, 193, 198

Abdication, of Diocletian (305), 258 f.; of Maximian (305), 260; Lactantius on, 258

Abdolkais, Arab tribe, 98

Ablavius, Prefect of Constantine, executes Sopater, 303, 339

Abraham, in shrine of Alexander Severus, 161

Acdestis, form of Great Mother Goddess, 146

Achaia, bequeathed to Dalmatius, 285

Achilles, cult of, 91, 201

Achilleus, usurper in Egypt, 120

Acts of the Martyrs, inadequate historical source, 255

Adoniazusae of Theocritus, 145

Adonis, cult of, 145 f.

Adrianople, victory of Licinius at, 276; Lactantius on same, 276; victory of Constantine at, 281

Aedesius, disciple of Iamblichus, 200

Aegae, oracular temple of Asclepius at, 205, 304

Aelian, *Historiae Variae*, 218

Aelianus, "Emperor" of Gaul, 73 f.

Aemilian, usurper on Danube (253), 31

Aemilianus, usurper in Egypt (262-265), 33, 117

Aethiopica of Heliodorus, 235 f.

Africa, Quinquegentiani in, 123; bequeathed to Constans, 285

Agathias, historian (536-582), on Persians, 102

agentes in rebus, political police, 69

Aglibol, Palmyrene deity, 140

agriculture, in Egypt, 112; in Rome, 366; in Gaul, 79

Ahriman, in Persian religion, 174

alchemy, Egyptian, 122

Alciphron, author (fl. 170), 218

Alemanni, German tribe, 36, 75; defeated by Constantius Chlorus at Windisch (274), 71

Alexander of Abonoteichos, religious charlatan, 149; Lucian on same, 149

Alexander, bishop of Cappadocia, in Palestine, 372

Alexander the Great, Caracalla's model, 23; mosaic of, 228

Alexander Phrygius, usurper at Carthage (308), 267

ALEXANDER SEVERUS (222-235), descent of, 24; equestrian class under, 25; murdered by soldiers, 26; religion of, 82, 130, 160 f.; literary interests, 161; sculpture, 231

Alexandria, greatness and corruption of, 110; Roman opin-